THEATRE
AND DRAMA
IN THE MAKING

Isabella Andreini, the famous amorosa of the Gelosi, and other members
of her troupe. Venice, late sixteenth century.

Theatre and *Drama*

IN THE MAKING

From Antiquity
to
The Renaissance

JOHN GASSNER
FORMERLY OF YALE UNIVERSITY

RALPH G. ALLEN
QUEENS COLLEGE OF THE CITY UNIVERSITY
OF NEW YORK

Enlarged and Revised
by Ralph Allen

APPLAUSE
🌷 **BOOKS** 🌷
211 WEST 71 STREET • NEW YORK NY • 10023

THEATRE & DRAMA IN THE MAKING: ANTIQUITY TO
THE RENAISSANCE

Library of Congress Cataloging-in-Publication Data
Theatre & drama in the making : the Greeks to the Elizabethans /
  edited by John Gassner, Ralph Allen. -- New & rev. / revised by
  Ralph Allen.
        p.   cm.
  Includes bibliographical references.
  ISBN 1-55783-073-8 (pbk.) : $14.95
  1. Drama. 2. Theater.   I. Gassner, John, 1903-1967. II. Allen,
  Ralph G. III. Title: Theatre and drama in the making.
  PN1621.G3 1992
  792' .09--dc20   92-24861
                                                              CIP

Applause Theatre Books
211 West 71st Street
New York, NY 10023
Phone: 212-595-4735 Fax: 212-721-2856

Photographs courtesy of The Queens College Theatre Collection

First Applause Edition: 1992

For

F. CURTIS CANFIELD
and

ALOIS M. NAGLER

CONTENTS

Part One

THE CLASSICAL THEATRE

Part Two

THE MEDIEVAL THEATRE

Part Three

THE RENAISSANCE THEATRE

A Note on the Revised Edition

The past doesn't change but perceptions of it do. When John Gassner and I first edited *Theatre and Drama in the Making* in 1964, we tried to represent the best of contemporary opinion about important matters of theatre history and dramatic literature.

Most of the selections have stood the test of time, but there is new information to be taken into account (notably, the discovery of the foundations of the Rose and Globe theatres) and new opinions to sample (for example, a changed attitude toward Calderón's religious plays). Also, my own sense of the subject, informed by twenty-six years of teaching, has altered with time.

I have added material to every section and revised many of the introductions. About a third of the book is entirely new.

In 1964 *Theatre and Drama in the Making* was published in two volumes. At the suggestion of Glenn Young of Applause, I have divided the material into three parts, of which this book is the first. I only wish the late John Gassner had been here to help me. But, alas, he was not, and I dedicate this revision to my mentor, collaborator, and friend.

Ralph Allen
1992

xi

INTRODUCTION
to the First Edition

This book is the first volume of a two-volume annotated anthology designed to provide the student with an introduction to the methods and materials of research in theatre history and dramatic criticism. We use the word "introduction" advisedly. We have not attempted to compile a comprehensive documentary history of the development of dramatic art from antiquity to the twentieth century. Our more modest intention has been to collect some major essays, documents, and critical accounts — many of them difficult of access — which illustrate the important position the theatre has held in human concerns for more than twenty-four hundred years.

The premise of this anthology differs in some respects from the premise of other collections of this general type. The editors of *Theatre and Drama in the Making* are not purists. Although we would not subscribe by any means to the notion that drama and theatrical productions should be viewed primarily as documents in the history of ideas, we nevertheless believe that theatre history should not be studied in a vacuum, that drama after all is about something, that a given theatrical style exists only as the product of a particular social, philosophical, and cultural environment which it reflects and to which it should be related in historical and critical studies. We recognize the importance of examining a work of art in its own terms. But we firmly believe also in the utility of research which attempts to show the ways in which the theatre of a particular epoch mirrors the emotional and intellectual assumptions of its audience.

Our anthology, though not the first of its kind, is probably unique in combining matter that relates to *both* theatre and drama, and in reprinting important secondary as well as primary source material. A book of this aim and scope will inevitably be as notable for its omissions as for its inclusions. The standards for selection must be somewhat arbitrary and subjective, geared to the tastes and current interests of the editors, who would be the first to admit that many documents which are not collected here have as much claim to significance and interest as those which are. We reluctantly decided.

for example, against attempting to include any materials on the Oriental theatre, on the ground that it would be impossible to do justice to this complex subject in the compass of these volumes without scanting the already abbreviated account of the Western theatre. Similar considerations dictated other editorial decisions; and rather than attempt the impossible task of summarizing in a few pages every important aspect of a major era in the history of dramatic art, we have concentrated in each period on a few key controversies and ideas. An effort has been made to combine necessary familiar selections with less familiar but equally interesting or revealing ones.

We hope, of course, that the reader will be sufficiently excited by the material presented here to conduct further investigations in related theatrical and dramatic subjects. Some topics for further study have been included at the end of the volume, together with brief selective bibliographies confined for the most part to English-language works. But the serious and imaginative student who judiciously supplements *Theatre and Drama in the Making* with additional reading will soon discover subjects for investigation which extend in breadth far beyond our lists of suggested topics. He may wish to study, for example, the history of middle-class drama from the Elizabethan period (*Arden of Feversham, The Yorkshire Tragedy*) to the present, with particular stress on the eighteenth-century Enlightenment, especially the plays and theoretical writings of Diderot, Beaumarchais, and Lessing. He may wish to examine the development of an offshoot of middle-class drama — the nineteenth-century problem play with reference to the works of Dumas *fils*, Ostrovsky, Ibsen, Sudermann, Brieux, and Augier. Twentieth-century developments in this genre might provide him with a further subject for research, as might also such related matters as the development of collective lower-class drama (*Fuente Ovejuna, The Weavers, The Plough and the Stars, The Lower Depths*), the sources of modern psychological drama, and the history of regional drama, both urban and rural, in America, Ireland, Spain, England, and elsewhere.

If the student wishes, he may use the material in this anthology as the starting point for a study of special types of pre-modern drama: the development of "New Comedy," for example, during the Hellenistic period and its influence on later writers as revealed through adaptations of Menander, Plautus, and Terence by William Stevenson, Nicholas Udall, George Gascoigne, and Shakespeare during the English Renaissance, by Molière during France's Golden Age, by

Goldoni in eighteenth-century Italy, and by Giraudoux and others in the twentieth century.

Perhaps the student's research will stress the relationship between the theatre and the major cultural and social forces which have shaped the world as we know it. A study of the drama of the Protestant Reformation, for example (John Bale's *The Treachery of Papists, The Three Laws of Christ,* and *King Johan,* R. Wever's *Lusty Juventus,* Sir David Lyndsay's *Satire of the Three Estates*), and of the Counter-Reformation (*Interlude of Hicke-Scorner,* the *Interlude of Youth,* the *autos* of Calderón) will add much to the student's knowledge of those movements. A brief look at English pantomimes and operettas during the second half of the eighteenth century will help illuminate the thirst for discovery and freedom which led to the wild excesses of the Romantic movement. A study of the great national theatres or theatres associated with a particular country (the Comédie-Française, the Hamburg National Theatre, the Park in New York) will help to document a history of national and cultural aspirations.

The theatre and its drama is a broad and fascinating area of study. From the beginning of recorded history it has been, and in the future it will continue to be, in Hamlet's words, the abstract and brief chronicle of its time. If our volumes can contribute to a more complete reading of that chronicle than is usual, we shall be satisfied.

ACKNOWLEDGMENT

The valuable editorial assistance of R. B. Allen, Professor Emeritus at Rutgers University, and Harriet Nichols, who also provided some of the translations, cannot be acknowledged too gratefully.

PART ONE

The Classical Theatre

I

The Origin of Tragedy

The origin of tragedy and comedy is a subject which has caused considerable scholarly debate. The most widely held theory traces the dramatic impulse to religious enthusiasm, specifically the dithyramb of the sixth century B.C.—a wild, improvised song in honor of Dionysus, the Greek god of revelry. The dithyramb was chanted or sung by a chorus of fifty satyrs, frenzied men dressed in animal skins, the traditional costume of the attendants of Dionysus. This chorus had a leader, the *exarchon*, whose function was to answer the grotesque questions of the disguised worshippers. Some time during the sixth century, the dithyramb acquired an elevated style. At the same time its structure was beginning to change. Gradually, the role of the *exarchon* was expanded until he assumed a position independent of the other celebrants. In time, perhaps, he ceased to function as a worshipper at all, and began instead to impersonate, in speech, in action, and in costume, the character of Dionysus himself. This innovation, credited by tradition to the poet Thespis, was the beginning of drama.

Our principal authority for the theory that tragedy developed from the dithyramb is the philosopher Aristotle, who in the second half of the fourth century B.C. included the following brief historical and theoretical note in his monumental book of dramatic criticism, the *Poetics*.

Aristotle

THE ORIGIN OF POETRY AND TRAGEDY

(from the *Poetics*, Chapter IV)*

*P*oetry in general seems to have sprung from two sources, each of them lying deep in our nature. First, the instinct of imitation is implanted in man from childhood, one difference between him and other animals being that he is the most imitative of living creatures, and through imitation learns his earliest lessons; and no less universal

---

* This translation, slightly revised by the editors, is by S. H. Butcher.

3

is the pleasure felt in things imitated. We have evidence of this in the facts of experience. Objects which in themselves we view with pain, we delight to contemplate when reproduced with minute fidelity: such as the forms of the basest animals and of dead bodies. The cause of this again is, that to learn gives the liveliest pleasure, not only to philosophers but to men in general, whose capacity, however, of learning is more limited. Thus the reason why men enjoy seeing a likeness is, that in contemplating it they find themselves learning or inferring, and saying perhaps, "Ah, that is he." For if you happen not to have seen the original, the pleasure will be due not to the imitation as such but to the execution, the coloring, or some such other cause.

Imitation, then, is one instinct of our nature. Next, there is the instinct for "harmony" and rhythm, metres being manifestly sections of rhythm. Persons, therefore, starting with this natural gift, developed by degrees their special aptitudes, till their rude improvisations gave birth to Poetry.

Poetry now diverged in two directions, according to the individual character of the writers. The graver spirits imitated noble actions and the actions of good men. The more trivial sort imitated the actions of meaner persons, at first composing satires, as the former did hymns to the gods and the praises of famous men. A poem of the satirical kind cannot indeed be put down to any author earlier than Homer; though there were probably many such writers. But from Homer onward, instances can be cited — his own *Margites*,[1] for example, and other similar compositions. The appropriate metre was also here introduced; hence the measure is still called the iambic or lampooning measure, being that in which people lampooned one another. Thus the older poets were distinguished as writers of heroic or of lampooning verse.

As, in the serious style, Homer is pre-eminent among poets, for he alone combined dramatic form with excellence of imitation, so he too first laid down the main lines of Comedy by dramatizing the ludicrous instead of writing personal satire. His *Margites* bears the same relation to Comedy that the *Iliad* and *Odyssey* do to Tragedy. But when Tragedy and Comedy came to light, the two classes of poets still followed their natural bent: the lampooners became writers of Comedy, and the Epic poets were succeeded by Tragedians, since the drama was a larger and higher form of art.

Whether Tragedy has as yet perfected its proper types or not; and whether it is to be judged in itself, or in relation also to the audience, — this raises another question. Be that as it may, Tragedy — as also Comedy — was at first mere improvisation. The one originated with the readers of the Dithyramb; the other with those of the phallic

[1] Aristotle was apparently mistaken in assigning this lost poem to Homer.

songs, which are still in use in many of our cities. Tragedy advanced by slow degrees; each new element that showed itself was in turn developed. Having passed through many changes, it found its natural form, and there it stopped.

Aeschylus first introduced a second actor; he diminished the importance of the Chorus and assigned the leading part to the dialogue. Sophocles raised the number of actors to three,[2] and added scene painting.[3] Moreover, it was not till late that the short plot was discarded for one of greater scope, and the grotesque diction of the earlier satyric form for the stately manner of Tragedy. The iambic measure then replaced the trochaic tetrameter, which was originally employed when the poetry was of the satyric order, and had greater affinities with dancing. Once dialogue had come in, Nature herself discovered the most appropriate measure. For the iambic is, of all measures, the most colloquial: we see it more frequently than any other kind of verse; rarely into hexameters, and only when we drop the colloquial intonation. The additions to the number of "episodes" or acts, and the other accessories of which tradition tells, must be taken as already described; for to discuss them in detail would, doubtless, be a large undertaking.[4]

A startling revaluation of the traditional theories concerning the origin of tragedy has been offered in recent years by Arthur Pickard-Cambridge and H. D. F. Kitto. In the following article Professor Kitto eloquently states his objections to the Aristotelian theory. This thought-provoking essay serves as an excellent illustration of the continued scrutiny of which ancient evidence is subjected by inquiring and original scholars.

---

[2] Exclusive of mutes there were never more than three actors (the protagonist, the deuteragonist, and the tritagonist) in any Greek tragedy. However, at no time were the plays limited to three characters. The actors, aided by a change of mask and costume, often played more than one part. The addition of the tritagonist, or third actor, ascribed here to Sophocles, was borrowed by Aeschylus for his last plays, notably the *Oresteia*, 458 B.C.

[3] Vitruvius, the author of a famous treatise on architecture (written in the first century A.D.), denies Sophocles the honor of having invented scene painting. Instead he tells us that Aeschylus employed a designer named Agatharcus to create perspective scenery for one of his plays.

[4] Aristotle has very little to say about the history of comedy. In Chapter V of the *Poetics*, he informs us that the successive changes through which comedy passed, and the inventors of those changes, are not known. Comedy, he adds, has no history, "because it was not at first treated seriously."

H. D. F. Kitto

GREEK TRAGEDY AND DIONYSUS*

*I*t has become a firm article of belief that tragic drama, in Greece, grew out of the worship of Dionysus; that is to say, out of ideas and rites connected with the circling year, the mysteries of death and rebirth, alternating joy and sorrow, the sufferings and the triumph of the god, and so on. No doubt this might have happened; it sounds plausible. But did it happen? I think there are good reasons for being very sceptical about the whole theory.

If it were only a matter of theory — of literary archaeology, so to speak — there would be little justification for discussing it in this journal; it might well be left to Classical scholars, historians of religion, and anthropologists. But the theory has affected, or infected, the criticism of Greek tragedy. Scholars of what we may call the anthropological school have not only convinced themselves that Greek tragedy was Dionysiac by origin, but also have found a Dionysiac spirit, even a ritual form, reflected or embedded in the plays which have come down to us; and this very much concerns our own understanding of the plays, and therefore our understanding of the minds both of the dramatists who created them and of the audiences for which they were composed. For surely, if the poets were following, more or less, an accepted ritual sequence, the audience in its turn would see, in the events of the play, the recreation of something familiar, if not even obligatory; but if ritual pattern is (as I believe) modern moonshine, then the dramatists will have started each time with a clean slate, and the audience with open minds, ready to accept anything; the structure of the plays will in no sense be something "given," but will be in every detail what was forged by the dramatist in the effort to say what he wanted to say; and this also will be the spirit in which the audience will have contemplated what the poet put before it. If on the other hand the argument is that ritual ideas, or anything else of the kind, exist in the plays, both for the dramatist and for his audience but on a subconscious level, then we, as students of dramatic literature and of the theatre are surely justified in declaring a total lack of interest; our primary interest is in the ideas which are in the play, not in the remoter question of how these ideas came into existence.

To illustrate the distorting effect of irrelevant anthropology I will take an imaginary case — at least, I *think* it is imaginary. By delving

* From *Theatre Survey*, 1960. Copyright 1960 by the American Society for Theatre Research.

into Greek religious practices it is possible to discover a lot of evidence that Greek communities, at sundry times and in divers places, used the religious device of the Scapegoat: at first a citizen, then perhaps a slave, then an animal, was deemed to have taken upon himself all the guilt of the community and was cast out, guilt and all. Armed with this information the critic advances boldly upon *Oedipus Rex* and says, "There you are! The archetypal scapegoat is recreated in Oedipus himself." The inconveniences would be two: first, that it would make nonsense of the structure of the play, since Oedipus in fact is *not* driven out; second, that the imported "ritual significance" would effectively obscure the fact that Sophocles is saying, through the play, something vastly more important and up-to-date. This is something of a parody, but a parody of things which have got into print.

Let us then consider Dionysus — and let it be made clear that in what follows there is not much that is new. I lean very heavily on the accumulation and sober appraisal of the evidence which is to be found in Pickard-Cambridge's *Dithyramb, Tragedy and Comedy,* a book which perhaps has not had as much influence as it might have had, since it did not occur to its author to offer any translation of the many Greek writers whom he quotes.

Suppose we had preserved to us, from Greek antiquity, nothing but the existing manuscripts of the tragic plays, together with the existing fragments and recorded titles of plays now lost: would anyone ever have deduced from these, or even suspected, that Tragedy had any connection with Dionysus? I think the only possible answer is "No." From the general tone and substance of the plays we should perhaps infer that they were performed not semi-privately, to some intelligent *coterie,* but, substantially, to the whole Athenian people, on some important recurring public occasion. That this was in fact a festival of Dionysus, and not for example of Athena, would certainly not become apparent. As it happens, of the surviving thirty-three plays only one — and that a late one, *The Bacchae* — handles a Dionysiac theme; but scrutiny of surviving titles makes it clear that at no period to which we have access were Dionysiac subjects more frequent than one would in any case expect, seeing how rich in dramatic situations the Dionysus cycle was.

How far can we go back? Suidas, an encyclopaedist of the tenth century A.D., records the titles of four plays by Thespis, who has more claim than anyone else to be regarded as the first tragic poet. The titles are: *Pentheus, The Trials of Pelias, The Priests,* and *The Youths.* Of these four, the first would certainly be Dionysiac in theme, the second certainly not; the other two might be anything. However, the genuineness of these titles is far from certain, so that effectively we cannot go further back than Phrynichus, who gained his first victory in 511 B.C., twenty-four years after the institution of the tragic contests. Eight plays of his are known by title; not one of them has anything to do with Dionysus. Two of them indeed, *The Capture of Miletus* and *The Phoenissae*, deal with events in contemporary history. Add to this that the earliest surviving play of Aeschylus, *The Persians* (for it now appears that his *Supplices* is a later play), also takes for its theme a contemporary event. Therefore, if we had only existing plays, fragments and titles, there would be a strong temptation to believe that Greek tragedy, from the beginning, handled mainly historical subjects, whether contemporary history or history as enshrined in myth.

This general indifference of the tragic poets towards Dionysus, or — to put it more carefully — this absence of any special interest in him, is the more interesting in that it contrasts so sharply with the prominence of the Dionysiac element in Comedy and in the Satyr-drama. Moreover, we know something about the Dithyramb in the fifth century. Here is a form of the choral lyric which was, to begin with, exclusively addressed to Dionysus. From being at first a more or less improvised revel-song it became more sober, was given an elaborate artistic form, and then began to use quite freely non-Dionysiac subjects; yet what we have of the fifth-century dithyramb makes it clear that the original connection with Dionysus was still maintained. We may contrast this with the mention of Dionysus in Sophocles' *Antigone*. In this play the first ode ends with an invocation to Dionysus, and the last ode is entirely concerned with him. Dionysus as the god of Nature, of death and rebirth? Not in the least. On each occasion he is appealed to, by this Theban chorus, as preeminently the god of Thebes, born of Zeus and Semele in this very city; though in the first of these two invocations there is a particular appropriateness: the chorus is summoning the citizens to celebrate the victory over Eteocles by nightlong dances, and Dionysus was particularly interested in dancing. Other deities loved poetry, singing, the lyre, athletics, but Dionysus was particularly a patron of the dance. But Dionysus the Suffering God or Nature God has nothing to do with these invocations.

Again, and to a similar effect: Sophocles contrives two impressive moments (in *Oedipus Rex* and *Electra*) when a frightened queen makes solemn sacrifice to the god, with prayers for deliverance. The god will obviously be Dionysus: the festival is dedicated to him, his altar stands in the middle of the orchestra, his statue is in the theatre, and his priest occupies the throne of honour in the middle of the front row. These two scenes will be the tragic counterpart of the lovely comic scene in *The Frogs*, where the stage-Dionysus, frightened out of his wits, runs to the front of the orchestra and implores the help of his Priest, sitting five yards away. But not at all: the sacrifices and prayers are offered to Apollo.

But this lack of any special contact between the plays and Dionysus exists on a much deeper and more significant level. The current doctrine about the origin of Greek Tragedy would lead the unwary beginner to expect a religious drama which dealt, above all, with such ideas as the mysterious forces of nature, communion with the divine, ecstasy and mystery, suffering and death, and victory over suffering and death. What we find is something utterly different. Such ideas as these are of course to be found in *The Bacchae* and no doubt existed in other plays which took a specifically Dionysiac theme, but in general we find a drama firmly based not on mystery or ecstasy but on reason and moral law; one which speaks not to the individual soul but to social and political man; one in which suffering is the result of error, and is not followed by triumph; one in which the major gods are such as Zeus, Apollo, Dike and her ministers the Erinyes, Aphrodite — not Dionysus in particular. The form of the plays is so flexible, so evidently moulded by the spirit and content of the individual play — ending for example "happily" or "unhappily," as the theme dictates — that it is quite impossible, without endless make-believe, to see any Dionysiac ritual-sequence behind it, even if we knew what a normal Dionysiac ritual-sequence was, which in sober truth we do not.

If all this is true — and it seems to me incontrovertible — the next question is obvious: why has the belief in a Dionysiac origin taken so firm a hold? The answer to the question is equally obvious. It is (1) that Tragedy, in Athens, as soon as it became a recognizable art-form, was incorporated by Peisistratus in an ancient Festival of Dionysus to which he was giving a more splendid form, and (2) that Aristotle asserts, without argument or any sign of hesitation, that Tragedy grew out of the Dithyramb, through the Satyr-drama — and about the essentially Dionysiac character of these there is no doubt. Does not this settle the matter? No.

Aristotle certainly had much more material at his disposal than we have, but it is very much open to question if he had any texts or records or first-hand evidence that antedated the institution of the Festival in 535. Further, it is fair to point out that he was interested primarily not in the history but in the ideal form of Tragedy, and that what he says about its growth has something of a perfunctory air. But the real difficulty in his account is that it is almost impossible to believe it, unless, like the medieval writer, we hold that the authority of Aristotle is second only to that of Holy Writ.

One difficulty has been discussed already, that whereas in the fifth-century dithyramb we find ample signs of its Dionysiac allegiance, nothing of the kind appears in Tragedy. But there are others.

Ancient testimony is unanimous that the decisive step of introducing an actor to share the performance with the chorus was taken by Thespis. We know, roughly, when he lived: he was awarded the first

prize in the new tragic contest in 535. (Aristotle does not say in the
Poetics that it was Thespis who did this, but Themistius quotes him as
saying it elsewhere.) In Aristotle's account the relevant points are
these. (1) Tragedy grew out of the *exarchon* of the dithyramb. (2) It
reached dignity little by little, as the poets added to it those features
which obviously belonged to it, as Aeschylus added a second actor and
Sophocles a third. (3) It went through many changes until it "achieved
its own nature," and then its development stopped. (4) Leaving behind insignificant (or "short"?) plots and ludicrous diction, "through
its passing out of the satyric stage" (or possibly "through its passing
out of its grotesque form"), it was late in attaining dignity. (5) First
it used the trochaic tetrameter because its style of composition was
satyric and dance-like, but when speech (or dialogue) was introduced
the use of the iambic trimeter naturally suggested itself.

All this is difficult. The early dithyramb had an *exarchon:* he was
the soloist who sang a lament (or something else) to a chorus which
came in with a refrain. But the early dithyramb was a tumultuous
revel, as unlike tragedy as anything well can be. By the late sixth
century the dithyramb had become serious and dignified, but in the
process it had shed the *exarchon*. It had a chorus-leader, as also had
fifth-century tragedy, but no *exarchon;* and this makes Thespis' action
look much more like deliberate innovation than the continuation and
enlargement of an existing functionary. But, as a matter of history,
when are these changes supposed to have happened? (2) and (3)
together give quite a clear picture — and remind us also that Aristotle
is thinking much more like a biologist than a historian. Tragedy can
hardly be said to have reached even its rudimentary form until Thespis
gave to it the first actor. We know very roughly when Aeschylus and
Sophocles must have introduced the second and third: say ca. 490 and
470 respectively. It had completed its growth, "achieved its own nature," clearly in those plays which Aristotle so much admired, *Oedipus
Rex* and *Iphigeneia in Tauris;* we may then say that it stopped growing 'round about the middle of the fifth century. (5) is agreeable with
this: it is the case, for example, that *The Persians* (472) makes considerable use of the trochaic tetrameter in its dialogue. (But for that
matter, so also do certain of the later plays of Euripides.) What Aristotle meant by "short" plots (if that is the correct rendering of his
adjective; it is certainly the literal one) is perhaps not clear. If he
meant not short *plays* but plays of which the actual *plot* is simple and
concise, not containing the admired complexities of peripeteia and
recognition-scenes, and the inevitable or natural transit from "happiness" to "unhappiness," then (5) falls within the same period of
growth, for the actual plots of certain Aeschylean plays — the *Seven
against Thebes, Prometheus,* even the *Agamemnon* — are distinctly

"short" compared with those of Sophocles. This, however, is not a point on which to lay stress. But if in general Aristotle is thinking of the period Thespis-Sophocles (as one would naturally suppose), then "ludicrous diction" becomes very hard to swallow; it would telescope the whole development to a most unlikely extent. If on the other hand we push back this part of the development, the "ludicrous diction," to the earlier part of the sixth century, we make it the more improbable that Aristotle had firm evidence from which to draw his conclusions.

Even so, the major difficulty remains. Why should so notably serious an art as Tragedy have "grown" out of a cheerfully grotesque art like that of the Satyr-drama? For one thing, the chorus of satyrs consisted of imaginary beings half-human, half-horse, relatives of the centaurs; the tragic chorus was utterly different — and not merely in the fact that it was not provided with tails. It was eminently a chorus of responsible men, or women; it was regularly the representative of mankind in his political, moral, social aspect. Between Tragedy and the Satyr-drama there undoubtedly is a connection: they resemble each other in structure, in metre, and to some extent in diction. In these respects the Satyr-drama is much closer to Tragedy than it is to Old Comedy. But if common sense and common experience are to be allowed any status in this debate, one would say that it is very much more likely that the lighthearted form of drama "grew" out of the serious and strenuous one by way of parody, than that the serious one should have grown out of the other by rejecting everything in it which made it what it was. In this instance common sense is in the enviable position of being able to adduce something like evidence. We know that Tragedy had been given a definite form by 535; there is a statement in Suidas that the first poet to "write" (i.e. to compose deliberately) satyr-plays was Pratinas, a Peloponnesian from Phlius. It would be wanton to set aside this explicit statement, especially as it is to some extent corroborated by Pausanias the Roman Baedeker, who says, writing of Phlius: "Here is also the tombstone of Aristias the son of Pratinas. Satyr-plays were written by this Aristias and by Pratinas his father, more famous than any except those of Aeschylus." Pratinas (who also wrote tragedies) competed in Athens with Aeschylus at some time between 499 and 496. That is to say, the satyr-drama first received a definite form about a generation later than tragedy, which clearly increases the probability that tragedy influenced the form of the satyr-drama, not vice versa.

Pickard-Cambridge, after a close analysis of the evidence, arrives at the conclusion that Aristotle was merely theorising, and it seems difficult not to agree with this. But although Aristotle found it more natural to think in biological than historical terms, and although his brief historical excursus is no integral part of the *Poetics,* he was not a silly man, and we should have more confidence in disbelieving what he says if we could see good reason why he should have said it. That is not difficult. Aristotle, writing at about the middle of the fourth century or a little later, was familiar with a form of the dithyramb which had become semi-dramatic, antiphonal. The purely dramatic forms, tragedy, comedy, and the satyr-drama, were all grouped together, with the dithyramb, in the festivals of Dionysus. The last two, like the dithyramb, were unquestionably Dionysiac by origin; and the satyr-drama, in its outward form, had a distinct resemblance to tragedy. Therefore, especially if one was thinking of Art-forms in the abstract, it was natural to suppose that all of them developed out of some Dionysiac archetype, and that would naturally be the dithyramb, for that was structurally the simplest of all the four forms.

It seems therefore that the crux of the whole affair is the association of Tragedy with the Festival of Dionysus. Even if we have the hardihood to reject the authority of Aristotle — and of certain later theorists, on the grounds that they were probably only repeating and amplifying what Aristotle said, or speculating on the derivation and true significance of words like "tragedy" itself (= "goat-song") — we yet have this firm and unshakeable link between Tragedy and Dionysus. Is not this enough? No.

Since discussion of the origin of Tragedy has always been, of necessity, speculative, we might for a change speculate on rather different lines, not thinking, in abstract and quasi-biological terms about the growth of art-forms, but thinking rather about men who were once alive — and, being Greeks, very much alive. Two of them concern us in particular: Peisistratus who remodelled the Festival, and Thespis who was writing this very modern stuff which attracted the notice of Peisistratus. (I will speak of Thespis for brevity, though I do not overlook the possibility that he may have been only one of several Attic poets of the time who were all moving in the same direction.)

We know a lot about Peisistratus; it is not difficult, nor very hazardous, to infer some of his problems and motives. He was one of those "tyrants" who were always cropping up in Greece, especially in the seventh and sixth centuries: aristocrats for the most part, who, with popular support, seized power from the aristocratic oligarchy in times of political and economic stress, with a program of reform. Authoritarian rulers follow a general pattern: they have to conciliate the populace, and they like to glorify their regime. As these Greek tyrants were usually civilized men, it is a fairly constant feature of their policy that they encourage the arts and try to attract to their courts artists from other Greek states, as for example Polycrates of Samos patronised sculptors and gem-workers, as well as first-rate civil engineers, or as

Hiero of Syracuse gave lavish commissions to Pindar and Bacchylides, and apparently to Aeschylus also; and perhaps there is no need to be cynical when we notice that some of them also paid attention to religious matters. Herodotus tells a delicious story about Peisistratus (I, 60) which proves that at least he was no simple pietist; but, from whatever motives, he did pay great attention to public religion in Athens. He began the erection of a temple to Zeus Olympios on so majestic a scale that it was left incomplete until, more than six hundred years later, a still more powerful autocrat, Hadrian, finished it. He purified the island of Delos, sacred to Apollo. There was in Athens an ancient festival to Athena — religious, artistic, and athletic, in the Greek manner; Peisistratus instituted a more splendid form of the Panatheneia to be held every fourth year, in the third year of the Olympic festival — an obvious attempt to emulate, in Athens, the other great international festivals at Olympia and Delphi. Public recitals of Homer were a feature of this festival; the tradition, first recorded in Cicero, that Peisistratus "edited" the texts of the *Iliad* and *Odyssey* may have some remote foundation on fact.

This is the background against which we may consider his refounding, on a more splendid scale, the old festival to Dionysus. What he did for Athena explains itself, but why Dionysus? Dionysus, though by now his worship had spread far and wide in Greece, was particularly associated with Thebes. Yet there is one aspect of Dionysus which may well have commended it to an astute ruler who was anxious to dignify and perpetuate his regime in Athens and to increase the prestige of Athens among the Greeks at large. Certain other deities had their specific associations — as, obviously, Athena had with Athens; certain of their cults were associated with particular groups or clans; Dionysus, as preeminently a nature-god, was universal; his appeal cut across all divisions, social or national. Athens already had her ancient Eleusinian Mysteries, a form of nature-worship, and Dionysus, in his more mystical aspect, was now firmly associated with them. These mysteries had a universal appeal also; initiation into them was open to all, Greek or barbarian, bond or free, and they were everywhere held in the highest honour. It is natural to suppose that Peisistratus saw his glorified Greater Dionysia as a counterpart of the renowned Mysteries: in the Festival the emphasis would be thrown on the human aspect of Dionysus (if the phrase may pass) rather than on his mystical aspect.

There is a further point. Thespis was creating something new, something that was exciting and seemed full of promise. Assuming that for reasons of cultural policy Peisistratus wished to give it what we today should call official patronage, how was he to set about it? We should reflect that among the Greeks there was no such thing as a purely

secular festival of the arts, or of athletics either: the Olympian Games
were a festival of Zeus, the Pythian Games (which now included contests in music) of Apollo. The question, therefore, would be simply
which god to choose, so to speak, as the patron of the new art. The
answer was obvious, in the circumstances. Two deities seem particularly to have rejoiced in music and the dance: Apollo and Dionysus —
Dionysus, specifically, as a god of inspiration and release. Therefore,
when we find Peisistratus dedicating this nascent art of tragedy to
Dionysus, we are by no means obliged to infer that it already had a
peculiarly Dionysiac character, or Dionysiac ancestry. Nor, contrari-
wise, are we obliged to think that Dionysus must have been irritated
when the tragic poets took their themes not from the Dionysiac cycle
but from the epic tradition or even from contemporary history. Dionysus was himself something of an artist and he enjoyed especially the
more dramatic arts.

As it happens, not corroborative but "similar-case" evidence is afforded us by Herodotus' pleasing story (V, 67) of an action taken by
another tyrant, Cleisthenes of Sicyon, perhaps fifty years earlier, *in re*
Adrastus. Here also we are in that area where state policy and public
religion meet. Sicyon was at war with the nearby city of Argos. In
Sicyon there was a festival in honour of Adrastus, and Adrastus was
an Argive hero who, in his lifetime, had been king of Argos. Cleisthenes therefore determined to rid Sicyon of Adrastus and his cult.
Consulting the oracle, he got little encouragement; therefore (as
Herodotus puts it) he devised a plan for making the unwanted Argive
hero withdraw of his own accord. He sent to Thebes and brought into
Sicyon the hero Melanippus, who, when they had both been alive, had
been Adrastus' worst enemy. "Cleisthenes dedicated the sacred enclosure," says Herodotus, "to the Theban hero Melanippus, and gave
the sacrifices and the subsequent feasts to him, taking them away from
Adrastus. The Sicyonians had been accustomed to honour Adrastus
very highly indeed, in particular by celebrating his sufferings with
tragic dances, honouring not Dionysus but Adrastus. But Cleisthenes
dedicated the dances to Dionysus, and the rest of the celebration to
Melanippus." So says Herodotus, and we may suppose that Adrastus
took the plain hint and removed himself from Sicyon.

Herodotus knew Athens, and was in fact well acquainted with
Sophocles; when therefore he speaks of "tragic dances," we should
naturally infer that they were, in his opinion, of the kind which he
had seen in Athenian tragedy. But in Sicyon they had had nothing
to do with Dionysus, until Cleisthenes deliberately made them part of
a Dionysiac celebration. Further, we should naturally infer that there
had been no public cult of Dionysus in Sicyon until Cleisthenes instituted this one. It is certainly interesting to find two sixth-century

tyrants promoting the worship of Dionysus, and the fact that the dances dedicated to him in Sicyon had previously been quite unDionysiac (and presumably remained so, in character) strengthens our surmise that the same may well have been true of the "tragic dances" in Athens. Dionysus was a natural patron of dancing; *c'était son métier*. That was enough.

So much for Peisistratus and what he did. But Thespis also was once a living man, and this simple fact gives an air of unreality to some of the arguments that have been used to substantiate the Dionysiac origin of Greek tragedy.

In the well known passage in the *Ars Poetica* (275–277) Horace records the tradition that Thespis, the inventor of tragedy, transported his plays on waggons, and that "they" (his chorus) stained their faces with wine-lees. This clearly points to an autumn vintage-revel. Pickard-Cambridge (*op. cit.* 121) is sceptical about much of the ancient Thespis-lore, on the grounds that it is "either definitely based on Aristotle, or may be supposed with great probability to be an interpretation of his statements." But let it all be true; let us believe without reserve that Thespis made a name for himself in Attica by raising the traditional vintage-revels to an altogether new artistic level, with the help of a picked and trained chorus: does this prove that the choral art of his which Peisistratus took up and transferred to his remodelled city festival was a Dionysiac vintage-revel made polite? One has only to ask a very simple question to see how unsafe the assumption is: What was this rural genius doing during the other nine or ten months of the year? To put the point in different terms: Aeschylus, to us, is a tragic poet, yet in antiquity he had a great reputation as a comic-poet — as a composer of satyr-dramas; why then must we suppose that Thespis never used his talents and his choruses for serious purposes? One cannot assert that he did, but it does not seem sensible to assume, silently, that he did not. Yet if we do not assume this, the argument that his contribution to the new festival was Dionysiac loses its cogency, especially since Peisistratus' festival was not held during the time of the vintage.

At this point it may not be a mistake to ask another question. In sixth-century Greece there were dozens of city-states which had at least as much claim as Athens to be considered civilized and cultured; why did it happen that Tragedy came to birth only in Athens, and for long remained a purely Athenian art? This is a question which, I think, should be asked, even though it is not possible to construct more than a very tentative answer. The answer that will be offered here will take us back to Thespis.

Aristotle records that the Dorian Greeks claimed the credit for both comedy and tragedy, and supported the claim by etymological arguments — which in fact are ridiculous. Nevertheless it can be allowed that there is one fact which would partially support the Dorians. The form of early tragedy shows, even upon casual inspection, that it is the result of the grafting of something for actors upon a choral-lyric stem. There is no doubt which was stem and which was graft: what we can see for ourselves in the early plays of Aeschylus, reinforced by what we are told about Phrynichus, renowned for the sweetness of his lyrics, proves that the choral lyric was already a mature art-form. It was also preeminently, though of course not exclusively, an art-form which had flourished among the Dorians of the Peloponnesus. We have met already the "tragic choruses" which honoured Adrastus in Sicyon. There is also a fairly solid tradition about the earlier Arion, who was indeed born on the island of Lesbos (at about 664 B.C.) but settled in Corinth, composed songs, hymns, and dithyrambs, "and is said to have been the inventor of the tragic mode" — viz. the *musical* mode (Suidas). He is said also to have been the pupil of Alcman, one of the great poet-composers of Sparta — Terpander being another. Perhaps the greatest in this kind was Pindar of Thebes, the contemporary of Aeschylus: he claimed to be Dorian by descent, and was proud of it; he received most of his commissions from Dorian cities, and his massive conservatism and his firm faith in the aristocratic tradition are typically Dorian in spirit. The distinguished names of Simonides and Bacchylides, contemporary composers of the choral lyric among the Ionian Greeks, warn us not to press this argument too far; nevertheless, it was in the main a Dorian art. It was essentially communal not only in form but also in spirit, and more individual forms of poetry seem not to have flourished among the Dorians.

Among the Ionian Greeks, on the other hand, they did — in the thriving commercial and bourgeois cities of the Aegean islands and the Asian coast. The Ionians too had their choral performances, but they also had their many poets, men like Archilochus and Anacreon who were singing with a very individual voice about their own pleasures and vexations, reflecting political and personal quarrels, mercilessly lampooning men whom they hated.

Such, in very broad outline, was the literary scene in which Thespis grew up in Attica. Still trying to think of him as a man who was once alive, and assuming, as we surely may, that he was no uncultivated genius but would know something of what was going on elsewhere, we can reflect that the Athenians stood half-way between the Dorian and the Ionian traditions, Ionians by descent and very largely in sympathy too, but wide open to Peloponnesian influences, and still, like most Peloponnesian cities, a society based on agriculture rather than on commerce. It may not be irrelevant to observe that when, in the fifth century, Attic architecture and sculpture reached their zenith, they did this by achieving a fusion of Dorian strength and seriousness with Ionian lightness and grace. So, in the sixth century, also in Attica, the long tradition of the choral lyric, predominantly Dorian, received an infusion of something quite different — the individual actor. This is not a matter of form only; it goes much deeper. For certainly in its early maturity, perhaps therefore in its inception also, the new art of tragedy combines, in a perfect harmony, the vivid presentation of the character, motives, fate, of the individual hero with the steady and conscious presentation, through the chorus, of that universal aspect of human experience which, because it is universal and does not change, the Greeks thought of as Divine Law. It is the clarity of this combination of the universal with the particular that is the outstanding feature of Attic Tragedy. As for this new idea of expressing universal truth partly in terms of an individual hero, which is not in the Dorian tradition, it would be reckless and unnecessary to ascribe it to direct Ionian influence; nevertheless, if a Hellenist were bluntly asked why Greek Tragedy arose in Athens and not elsewhere, he might well reply, "Where else in Greece *could* it have arisen?"

Now, the central question has always been: what was Tragedy derived from?, and the orthodox answer is, "From Dionysiac rites." I suggest that we should ask it in a different form: whence did Thespis derive the idea of combining, in one performance, an actor who should impersonate a hero, and the traditional chorus? Put in this way, it becomes a biographical question — and of course we have no biography at our disposal. My own tentative answer to the question would be "From Thespis."

As for the choral part of it, unless we are to accept Aristotle without question, it seems gratuitous to suppose that Thespis had trained himself solely in composing dithyrambs, knew of nothing but dithyrambs, and thought of his chorus as a dithyrambic one. That he *did* produce Dionysiac performances, having his choruses stain their faces with wine-lees, is asserted by ancient writers, and it may well be true. That he neither knew of nor composed other forms of the choral art is an assumption that may well be called foolish — particularly as it is so hard to find any proof that his new art was at all Dionysiac in character.

As for the mimetic half of his new art we are equally in the dark, and can only speculate, but our speculations may as well be reasonable ones. Ridgeway asserted that the whole idea of impersonation had descended from rites performed at the tombs of heroes, in which some exploit or suffering of the hero would be enacted; but he was unable to produce any evidence that there ever had been such a mimetic rite. The rival theory has been that Thespis got the idea from ritual performances of the agôn and sufferings of Dionysus — though the ritual in question has to be hypothetically constructed in order to support the hypothesis. There is indeed record that in the Attic village of Eleutherae, from which the worship of Dionysus Eleuthereus was transferred to Athens, there was a ritual and mimetic fight in which Dionysus Melanaegis ("of the black goat-skin") aids Melanthus ("black man") to kill Xanthus ("fair man"), and it is likely enough that this represents the triumph of a winter-spirit over the summer-spirit — but here there is no chorus, so that tragedy cannot have "developed" out of this — unless indeed it makes us happier to suppose that the originality of Thespis consisted not in his adding something histrionic to a chorus, but a chorus to something histrionic.

But in framing theories of this kind are we not trying to strangle ourselves in ropes of sand? If the persistence in tragedy of an agôn, struggle, conflict, is an argument for Dionysiac origin, must we not then assert a Dionysiac origin also for the Socratic dialogue? Is no one ever to be allowed to have thought of something for himself? Is it not really a biographical question? The idea of dramatic impersonation is surely not a very recondite one. Not long after this, Pratinas, in Phlius, was combining, for amusement only, dramatic impersonators with the riotous and Dionysiac satyr-chorus. What we are told about Pratinas is not that he invented this entertainment, but that he was the first to give it literary form. The differences between what Pratinas did and what Thespis did are that the one was comic, the other serious, and that while the developed satyr-drama always maintained its Dionysiac character, tragedy cannot be shown ever to have had any. Here, certainly, is one form of impersonation, and it is Dionysiac, but are we really to suppose that the idea of dramatic impersonation was one which the jealous gods withheld from mankind until it was revealed by Dionysus? It seems to have dawned upon Epichermus in Sicily, and on the satirical mimers, *phlyakes*, of southern Italy.

Suidas found, and recorded, one factual statement about Thespis which does not have the air of being based on hypothesis or sheer invention. It concerns his use of masks. A lot has been written, and doubtless with the utmost accuracy, about the religious significance of masks in South America, Mexico, and other places. Masks were used also in the Athenian theatre. What Suidas says of this is that Thespis first "overshadowed" his face with purslane, then used white lead, and finally made a mask of plain linen. Does this suggest that Thespis had magical or religious preoccupations, or that he was an intelligent man of the primitive theatre who was grappling with a quite familiar theatrical problem?

To sum up. We may, on the one hand, deferentially accept as conclusive all that Aristotle says, and so to bed — but hardly to sleep, because what Aristotle says will raise too many doubts. If on the other hand we conclude that Aristotle was only theorising, we can see, in the first place, how natural it was that he should have formed this particular theory; and, in the second place, both the evidence and general probability leave it open to us to form a different theory, one which is free from the improbabilities inherent in Aristotle's. His theory, quite congenial to his normal habit of thought, would easily have been evolved from the conjunction of tragedy, satyr-drama, comedy, the dithyramb, and festivals of Dionysus; but there is no sign that he, or any other writer of antiquity, had at his disposal the kind of evidence that would make the theory convincing, namely a series of works in which the supposed development could be traced. (It is perhaps significant, certainly characteristic, that the anonymous "Dorians," whom Aristotle cites as claiming both tragedy and comedy, base their claim to tragedy on nothing more than doubtful etymology, and if they themselves used better evidence, Aristotle shows no interest in it. The Greek mind, including that of Aristotle himself in some of his scientific writings, was always liable to be deflected from the patient scrutiny of facts by the superior attractions of a general theory.) Of these four arts, the other three continue to show their Dionysiac origins even in their maturity; in tragedy, it is impossible to find at any stage signs of a Dionysiac affiliation. Admittedly, the evidence we have is not much, but at least of the eight plays of Phrynichus whose titles have come down to us, not one can have dealt with a Dionysiac subject. The outward resemblances between tragedy and satyr-drama are most easily explained by the hypothesis that tragedy influenced the satyr-drama, not vice versa. Finally, the fact that Peisistratus incorporated tragedy in his reconstructed Dionysiac festival does not in the least prove that it was Dionysiac either in origin or in spirit: to assert that it does prove this is merely to overestimate the extent to which the Greeks, in "religious" matters, were dominated by religious cults, and to underestimate the extent to which they naturally made artistic, and indeed athletic, activities a part of their "religion." In any Greek context our word "religious" can be treacherous.

The Greeks have often — and too superficially — been reproached with creating gods who had many of the regrettable shortcomings of humanity, but at least most of the gods they created took pleasure also in the noblest of human activities. The dedication of tragedy to Dionysus does not *prove* any more than this: that here was an art worthy of being offered to Dionysus, and one in which this god would take a natural interest and pleasure — and no less pleasure if, from the beginning, its inspiration came from heroic myth and the epic tradition rather than from the religion of Dionysus himself.

Therefore I suggest that the influence of Dionysiac forms on the origin of tragedy may have been none at all; more probably perhaps

— when we think of the dithyramb as a form of choral lyric — one influence among many; that any influence of Dionysiac *ideas* appears to
be much less likely; and that the connection between Dionysus and
tragedy, once tragedy had got under way, was simply that this eminently humane god (now that Hellenism had worked upon him!) was
happy to preside over so noble an achievement, in art, of the human
mind.

II

Theory and Criticism of Tragedy

❧ The most important and influential ancient document on the history and theory of tragedy is, of course, Aristotle's *Poetics,* a small part of which has already appeared at the beginning of this book. The *Poetics* is empirical in its approach. The observations of the philosopher are based almost entirely on his examination of the plays which he himself had seen and read. His intention is rather analytic than philosophic. He presents us for the most part not with generalizations on the nature of poetry, but rather with a systematic catalogue of the varieties of poetic experience known to him.

The text of the *Poetics* is often elliptical; it contains in its present incomplete form many corrupt passages, and, as a consequence, it is very difficult to translate. The version which survives has all the earmarks of a transcription of notes by an enthusiastic but imperfect student or admirer. The obscurities of the text are further complicated by the fact that many of the plays cited by the critic have been totally lost or exist only in fragments.

Despite these difficulties, the *Poetics* has endured until the present day as an extremely significant contribution to the understanding of drama and poetry. Indeed, it has left its mark on nearly every subsequent period in the history of the theatre.

The strengths of the book will be readily apparent, as will, indeed, its weaknesses. Most of the latter can be explained, if not excused, by placing Aristotle in the proper historical perspective. The *Poetics* was written a hundred years after the great period of Greek tragedy. Between the fifth and fourth centuries, an enormous change had taken place in the practice of playwriting. The tragic form had become debased. The ethical and moral content of the plays of Aeschylus, Sophocles, and Euripides had been superseded by more melodramatic themes. Ingenuity in plotting was now considered the greatest of all dramatic virtues, and, as a result, the tragedies of the fourth century were for the most part empty and mechanical.

These fourth-century plays made up the bulk of the program at the Great City Dionysia when Aristotle was composing his book of criticism. There were revivals of the older poets, yes, but even these revivals were corrupted and distorted to suit the talents of virtuoso actors. Aristotle's overemphasis on the mechanics of playwriting (including his tortuous analysis, for example, of the technicalities of the recognition scene) can be attributed in large part to the kind of play he was forced to watch.

Not so easy to justify is Aristotle's insistence on a simple moral code for drama — his belief that a tragedy must never show a guiltless man destroyed by circumstances beyond his ordering. Nowhere, for example, in the *Poetics* is there any indication that the philosopher really understood the satanic fury of *Oedipus the King*, one of the plays he cites most frequently in his study. The spectacle of a man wilfully destroyed by an intelligent malicious universe, punished far in excess of any of his trifling crimes — this kind of cosmic terror was never recorded by Aristotle, although his admiration for Sophocles makes us suspect that, in the theatre, at least, he was not a stranger to this absolute tragic experience.

Aristotle

THE NATURE OF TRAGEDY

(from the *Poetics*)*

IV

*E*pic poetry agrees with Tragedy insofar as it is an imitation in verse of characters of a higher type. They differ, in that Epic poetry admits but one kind of metre, and is narrative in form. They differ, again, in their length: for Tragedy endeavours, as far as possible, to confine-itself to a single revolution of the sun, or but slightly to exceed this limit; whereas the Epic action has no limits of time.[1] This, then, is a second point of difference; though at first the same freedom was admitted in Tragedy as in Epic poetry. . . .

VI

Of the poetry which imitates in hexameter verse, and of Comedy, we will speak hereafter.[2] Let us now discuss Tragedy, resuming its formal definition, as resulting from what has been already said.

Tragedy, then, is an imitation of an action that is serious, complete, and of a certain length and scope; in language pleasurably embellished with each kind of artistic ornament, the several kinds being found in

---

* The translation by S. H. Butcher has been shortened and slightly altered by the editors. The notes, unless otherwise indicated, are by the editors.

[1] This mildly worded distinction between tragic and epic action becomes the basis for the neoclassical insistence on "unity of time" as one of the rules for drama. Nowhere in the *Poetics* does Aristotle mention "unity of place."

[2] The book on comedy is lost, if indeed it was ever written.

separate parts of the play; in the form of action, not of narrative; through pity and fear effecting the proper purgation (catharsis) of these emotions.[3] By "language pleasurably embellished," I mean language into which rhythm, "harmony," and song enter. By "the several kinds in separate parts," I mean, that some parts are rendered through the medium of verse alone, others again with the aid of song.

Now as tragic imitation implies persons acting, it necessarily follows, in the first place, that Spectacular ornament will be a part of Tragedy. Next, Song and Diction, for these are the media of imitation. By "Diction" I mean the mere metrical arrangement of the words: as for "Song," it is a term whose sense every one understands.

Again, Tragedy is the imitation of an action; and an action implies personal agents, who necessarily possess certain distinctive qualities both of character and intellect; for it is by these that we judge the quality of actions, and these — intellect and character — are the two natural causes from which actions spring, and on actions again all success or failure depends. Hence, the Plot is the imitation of the action: — for by plot I here mean the arrangement of the incidents. By Character I mean that which allows us to ascribe certain qualities to the agents. Intellect is required wherever a statement is proved, or, a general truth enunciated. Every Tragedy, therefore, must have six parts, which parts determine its quality — namely, Plot, Characters, Diction, Intellect, Spectacle, Song. Two of the parts constitute the medium of imitation, one the manner, and three the objects of imitation. And these complete the list. These elements have been employed, we may say, by the poets to a man; in fact, every play contains Spectacular elements as well as Character, Plot, Diction, Song, and Intellect.

But most important of all is the structure of the incidents. For Tragedy is an imitation, not of men, but of an action and of life, and life consists in action, and its end is a mode of action, not a quality. Now character determines men's qualities, but it is by their actions that they are happy or the reverse. Dramatic action, therefore, is not

[3] Aristotle's theory of catharsis has caused considerable debate. Each age has reinterpreted the doctrine in its own image. In the Renaissance, for example, it was felt that catharsis was the process of reducing excessive pity and fear, of bringing those emotions under proper control. In the eighteenth century, when pity was considered a great virtue, catharsis was interpreted as a cleansing of pity, a purifying and intensifying process which prepared man for sympathetic and charitable action. Some writers have even suggested that pity and fear were nothing more than the cleansing agents and that the end result was the purifying of whatever *other* emotions were dramatized on the stage. The French dramatist, Corneille, for example, goes so far as to suggest that in *Oedipus the King* the spectator is purged through pity and fear of the emotion of curiosity.

Most modern scholars now agree that Aristotle is attributing a curative effect to tragedy. To him pity and fear are painful, not desirable. Tragedy empties man of pity and fear, and thereby gives him relief and pleasure.

intended as a representation of character: character comes in as subsidiary to the actions. Hence the incidents and the plot are the end of a tragedy; and the end is the chief thing of all. Again, without action there cannot be a tragedy; there may be without character. The tragedies of most of our modern poets fail in the rendering of character;[4] and of poets in general this is often true. It is the same in painting; and here lies the difference between Zeuxis and Polygnotus. Polygnotus delineates character well; the style of Zeuxis is devoid of ethical quality.[5] Again, if you string together a set of speeches expressive of character, and well finished in point of diction and intellect, you will not produce the essential tragic effect nearly so well as with a play which, however deficient in these respects, yet has a plot and artistically constructed incidents. Besides which, the most powerful elements of emotional interest in Tragedy — *peripeteia* or Reversal of the Situation, and Recognition scenes — are parts of the plot. A further proof is, that novices in the art attain to finish of diction and precision of portraiture before they can construct the plot. It is the same with almost all the early poets.

The Plot, then, is the first principle, and, as it were, the soul of a tragedy; Character holds the second place. A similar fact is seen in painting. The most beautiful colors, laid on in a disorganized fashion, will not give as much pleasure as the bare outline of a portrait. Thus Tragedy is the imitation of an action and of the agents mainly with a view to the action.

Third in order is Intellect,[6] — that is, the faculty of saying what is possible and pertinent in given circumstances. In the case of oratory, this is the function of the political art and of the art of rhetoric; and so indeed the older poets make their characters speak the language of civic life; the poets of our time, the language of the rhetoricians. Character is that which reveals moral purpose, showing what kind of things a man chooses or avoids. Speeches, therefore, which do not make this manifest, or in which the speaker does not choose or avoid anything whatever, are not expressive of character. Intellect, on the other hand, is found where something is proved to be or not to be, or a general maxim is enunciated.

Fourth among the elements enumerated comes Diction, by which I

---

[4] By "modern poets" Aristotle means the writers of the fourth century, whom he compares unfavorably with the great dramatic writers who preceded them by a hundred years.

[5] When Aristotle remarks that the paintings of Zeuxis are devoid of ethical quality, he is suggesting that the painter is unable to delineate "character." To Aristotle character is always a moral and ethical concept.

[6] The Greek here is difficult to translate. Intellect is an emendation of the editors. Butcher uses the word "thought," and other translators have suggested "understanding," "sentiment" (in the sense of belief or opinion), and "the faculty of thinking."

mean, as has been already said, the expression of the meaning in words; and its essence is the same both in verse and prose.

Of the remaining elements Song holds the chief place among the embellishments.

The Spectacle has, indeed, an emotional attraction of its own, but, of all the parts, it is the least artistic, and connected least with the art of poetry. For the power of Tragedy, we may be sure, is felt even apart from representation and actors. Besides, the production of spectacular effects depends more on the art of the stage machinist than on that of the poet.

VII

These principles being established, let us now discuss the proper structure of the Plot, since this is the first and most important thing in Tragedy.

Now, according to our definition, Tragedy is an imitation of an action that is complete, and whole, and of a certain length and scope; for there may be a whole that is wanting in length and scope. A whole is that which has a beginning, a middle, and an end. A beginning is that which does not itself follow anything by causal necessity, but after which something naturally is or comes to be. An end, on the contrary, is that which itself naturally follows some other thing, either by necessity, or as a rule, but has nothing following it. A middle is that which follows something as some other thing follows it.[7] A well-constructed plot, therefore, must neither begin nor end at haphazard, but conform to these principles.

Again, a beautiful object, whether it be a living organism or any whole composed of parts, must not only have an orderly arrangement of parts, but must also be of a certain magnitude; for beauty depends on magnitude and order. Hence a very small animal organism cannot be beautiful; for the view of it is confused, the object being seen in an almost imperceptible moment of time. Nor, again, can one of vast size be beautiful; for as the eye cannot take it all in at once, the unity and sense of the whole is lost for the spectator; as for instance if there were one a thousand miles long. As, therefore, in the case of animate bodies and organisms a certain magnitude is necessary, and a magnitude which may be easily embraced in one view; so in the plot, a certain length is necessary, and a length which can be easily embraced by the memory. The limit of length in relation to dramatic competition and sensuous presentment is no part of artistic theory.

---

[7] Aristotle clearly means that a middle is something which follows logically, or as an inevitable consequence. He does not mean a series of events which follow merely chronologically.

For had it been the rule for a hundred tragedies to compete together,[8] the performance would have been regulated by the water-clock, — as indeed we are told was formerly done. But the limit as fixed by the nature of the drama itself is this: — the greater the length, the more beautiful will the piece be by reason of its size, provided that the whole be perspicuous. And to define the matter roughly, we may say that the proper magnitude is comprised within such limits that the sequence of events, according to the law of probability or necessity, will admit of a change from bad fortune to good, or from good fortune to bad.

VIII

Unity of plot does not, as some persons think, consist in the unity of the hero. For infinitely various are the incidents in one man's life which cannot be reduced to unity; and so, too, there are many actions of one man out of which we cannot make one action. Hence the error, as it appears, of all poets who have composed a Heracleid, a Theseid, or other poems of the kind. They imagine that as Heracles was one man, the story of Heracles must also be a unity. But Homer, as in all else he is of surpassing merit, here too — whether from art or natural genius — seems to have happily discerned the truth. In composing the *Odyssey* he did not include all the adventures of Odysseus — such as his wound on Parnassus, or his feigned madness at the mustering of the host — incidents between which there was no necessary or probable connexion; but he made the *Odyssey*, and likewise the *Iliad*, to center round an action that in our sense of the word is one. As therefore, in the other imitative arts, the imitation is one when the object imitated is one, so the plot, being an imitation of an action, must imitate one action and that a whole, the structural union of the parts being such that, if any one of them is displaced or removed, the whole will be disjointed and disturbed. For a thing whose presence or absence makes no visible difference is not an organic part of the whole.

IX

It is, moreover, evident from what has been said, that it is not the function of the poet to relate what has happened, but what may happen, — what is possible according to the law of probability or necessity. The poet and the historian differ not by writing in verse or

[8] During the fifth and fourth centuries at the Great City Dionysia, three tragic poets competed in every contest. Each poet exhibited four plays—three tragedies and a satyr play. This last, invented by the poet Pratinas in the late sixth century, was a burleque of tragic themes, similar no doubt to the grotesque "tragedies" of the earliest period. See, Kitto, above pp. 6-20.

in prose. The work of Herodotus might be put into verse, and it would still be a species of history, with metre no less than without it. The true difference is that one relates what has happened, the other what may happen. Poetry, therefore, is a more philosophical and a higher thing than history; for poetry tends to express the universal, history the particular. By the "universal" I mean how a person of a certain type will on occasion speak or act, according to the law of probability or necessity; and it is this universality at which poetry aims in the names she attaches to the personages. The particular is — for example — what Alcibiades did or suffered. In Comedy this is already apparent, for here the poet first constructs the plot on the lines of probability, and then inserts characteristic names — unlike the lampooners who write about particular individuals. But tragedians still keep to real names, the reason being that what is possible is credible; what has not happened we do not at once feel sure to be possible, but what has happened is manifestly possible, or otherwise it would not have happened. Still there are even some tragedies in which there are only one or two well known names, the rest being fictitious. In others, none are well known — as in Agathon's *Antheus,* where incidents and names alike are fictitious, and yet they give none the less pleasure.[9] We must not, therefore, at all costs keep to the received legends, which are the usual subjects of Tragedy. Indeed, it would be absurd to attempt it; for even subjects that are known are known only to a few, and yet give pleasure to all. It clearly follows that the poet or "maker" should be the maker of plots rather than of verses, since he is a poet because he imitates, and what he imitates are actions. And even if he chances to take an historical subject, he is none the less poet; for there is no reason why some events that have actually happened should not conform to the law of the probable and possible, and in virtue of that quality in them he is their poet or maker.

Of all plots and actions the "episodic" are the worst, for the acts succeed one another without probable or necessary sequence. Bad poets compose such pieces by their own fault, good poets, to please the players; for, as they write show pieces for competition, they stretch the plot beyond its capacity, and are often forced to break the natural continuity.

But again, Tragedy is an imitation not only of a complete action, but of events inspiring fear or pity. Such an effect is best produced when the events come on us by surprise; and the effect is heightened when, at the same time, they follow as cause and effect. The tragic wonder will then be greater than if they happened of themselves or by accident; for even coincidences are most striking when they have an air of design. We may instance the statue of Mitys at Argos, which fell upon his murderer while he was a spectator at a festival, and killed

---

[9] Agathon's plays are lost.

him. Such events seem not to be due to mere chance. Plots, therefore, constructed on these principles are necessarily the best.

X

Plots are either Simple or Complex, for the actions in real life, of
which the plots are an imitation, obviously show a similar distinction.
An action which is one and continuous in the sense above defined, I
call Simple, when the change of fortune takes place without Reversal
of the Situation[10] and without Recognition.

A Complex action is one in which the change is accompanied by such
Reversal, or by Recognition, or by both. These last should arise from
the internal structure of the plot, so that what follows should be the
necessary or probable result of the preceding action. It makes all the
difference whether any given event follows as the result of what went
before, or simply follows after.

XI

Reversal of the Situation is a change by which the action veers
round to its opposite, subject always to our rule of probability or
necessity. Thus in the *Oedipus*, the messenger comes to cheer Oedipus and free him from his alarms about his mother, but by revealing
who he is, he produces the opposite effect. Again in the *Lynceus*,
Lynceus is being led away to his death, and Danaus goes with him,
meaning to slay him; but the outcome of the preceding incidents is
that Danaus is killed and Lynceus saved.[11]

Recognition, as the name indicates, is a change from ignorance to
knowledge, producing love or hate between the persons destined by
the poet for good or bad fortune.[12] The best form of recognition is
coincident with a Reversal of the Situation, as in the *Oedipus*. There
are indeed other forms. Even inanimate things of the most trivial
kind may in a sense be objects of recognition. Again, we may recognize or discover whether a person has done a thing or not. But the

[10] The word translated by Butcher as "reversal of situation" is *peripeteia*.
Aristotle's explanation of this word in Chapter XI suggests that the "reversal"
must be sudden and distinctively ironic in its effect.

[11] A lost play.

[12] Aristotle's conception of recognition is a mechanical one. It refers entirely
to the sudden discovery by one person of the identity of someone else, the realization reached by Electra, for example (in Euripides' play), that the stranger
standing before her is Orestes, her lost brother. Aristotle never means, as Racine
and other commentators have assumed, the recognition by one character of the
true nature of his deed, the discovery by Orestes (in the same play) that his
matricide was a bloody impure crime, rather than a holy, impersonal act of
vengeance. Aristotle's failure to discuss this second more subtle kind of recognition is one of the major weaknesses of the *Poetics*.

recognition which is most intimately connected with the plot and action is, as we have said, the recognition of persons. This recognition, combined with Reversal, will produce either pity or fear; and actions producing these effects are those which, by our definition, Tragedy represents. Moreover, it is upon such situations that the issues of good or bad fortune will depend. Recognition, then, being between persons, it may happen that one person only is recognized by the other — when the latter is already known — or it may be necessary that the recognition should be on both sides. Thus Iphigenia is revealed to Orestes by the sending of the letter; but another act of recognition is required to make Orestes known to Iphigenia.

Two parts, then, of the Plot — Reversal of the Situation and Recognition — turn upon surprises. A third part is the Scene of Suffering. The Scene of Suffering is a destructive or painful action, such as death on the stage, bodily agony, wounds, and the like.

X I I [13]

[The parts of Tragedy which must be treated as elements of the whole have been already mentioned. We now come to the quantitative parts — the separate parts into which Tragedy is divided — namely, Prologue, Episode, Exode, [14] Choric song, this last being divided into Parode [15] and Stasimon. These are common to all plays; peculiar to some are the songs of actors from the stage and the Commoi.

The Prologue is that entire part of a tragedy which precedes the Parode of the Chorus. The Episode is that entire part of a tragedy which is between complete choric songs. The Exode is that entire part of a tragedy which has no choric song after it. Of the Choric part the Parode is the first undivided utterance of the Chorus; the Stasimon is a Choric ode without anapaests or trochaic tetrameters; the Commos is a joint lamentation of Chorus and actors. The parts of Tragedy which must be treated as elements of the whole have been already mentioned. The quantitative parts — the separate parts into which it is divided — are here enumerated.]

XIII

As the sequel to what has already been said, we must proceed to consider what the poet should aim at, and what he should avoid, in constructing his plots; and by what means the specific effect of Tragedy will be produced.

A perfect tragedy should, as we have seen, be arranged not on the

---

[13] This passage may well be an interpolation.
[14] Also called the *exodos*.   [15] Also called the *parados*.

simple but on the complex plan. It should, moreover, imitate actions which excite pity and fear, this being the distinctive mark of tragic imitation. It follows plainly, in the first place, that the change of fortune presented must not be the spectacle of a virtuous man brought from prosperity to adversity: for this moves neither pity nor fear; it merely shocks us. Nor, again, that of a bad man passing from adversity to prosperity: for nothing can be more alien to the spirit of Tragedy; it possesses no single tragic quality; it neither satisfies the moral sense nor calls forth pity or fear. Nor again, should the downfall of the utter villain be exhibited. A plot of this kind would, doubtless, satisfy the moral sense, but it would inspire neither pity nor fear; for pity is aroused by unmerited misfortune, fear by the misfortune of a man like ourselves. Such an event, therefore, will be neither pitiful nor terrible. There remains, then, the character between these two extremes — that of a man who is not eminently good and just, yet whose misfortune is brought about not by vice or depravity, but by some error or frailty.[16] He must be one who is highly renowned and prosperous — a personage like Oedipus, Thystes, or other illustrious men of such families.

A well-constructed plot should, therefore, be single in its issue, rather than double as some maintain. The change of fortune should be not from bad to good, but, reversely, from good to bad. It should come about as the result not of vice, but of some great error or frailty, in a character either such as we have described, or better rather than worse. The practice of the stage bears out our view. At first the poets recounted any legend that came in their way. Now, the best tragedies are founded on the story of a few houses — on the fortunes of Alcmaeon, Oedipus, Orestes, Meleager, Thyestes, Telephus, and those others who have done or suffered something terrible. A tragedy, then, to be perfect according to the rules of art should be of this construction. Hence they are in error who censure Euripides just because he follows this principle in his plays, many of which end unhappily. It is, as we have said, the right ending. The best proof is that on the stage and in dramatic competition, such plays, if well worked out, are the most tragic in effect; and Euripides, faulty though he may be in

16 The Greek word translated by Butcher as "error or frailty" is *hamartia*. Some commentators have felt that Aristotle was referring here simply to intellectual error or to a mistake in judgment. The majority, however, would define *hamartia* as a moral flaw. The editors side reluctantly with the majority. It is impossible to read this passage without concluding that Aristotle's theory of tragedy was intensely moral. The great fourth-century critic must, therefore, be held partly responsible with Horace for the naïve doctrine of poetic justice which pervaded critical thinking for many years after the Renaissance. The concept of *hamartia* is, of course, wholly inadequate as an explanation for the suffering of any of the great tragic heroes. It does not begin to account for the discrepancy between the "crime" of Oedipus (his only wilful "transgression" was a laudable intellectual curiosity) and his terrible punishment.

the general management of his subject, yet is felt to be the most tragic of the poets.

In the second rank comes the kind of tragedy which some place first. Like the *Odyssey*, it has a double thread of plot, and also an opposite catastrophe for the good and for the bad. It is accounted the best because of the weakness of the spectators; for the poet is guided in what he writes by the wishes of his audience. The pleasure, however, thence derived is not the true tragic pleasure. It is proper rather to Comedy, where those who, in the piece, are the deadliest enemies — like Orestes and Aegisthus — quit the stage as friends at the close, and no one slays or is slain.

XIV

Fear and pity may be aroused by spectacular means; but they may also result from the inner structure of the piece, which is the better way, and indicates a superior poet. For the plot ought to be so constructed that, even without the aid of the eye, he who hears the tale told will thrill with horror and melt to pity at what takes place. This is the impression we should receive from hearing the story of the *Oedipus*. But to produce this effect by the mere spectacle is a less artistic method, and dependent on extraneous aids. Those who employ spectacular means to create a sense not of the terrible but only of the monstrous, are strangers to the purpose of Tragedy; for we must not demand of Tragedy any and every kind of pleasure, but only that which is proper to it. And since the pleasure which the poet should afford is that which comes from pity and fear through imitation, it is evident that this quality must be impressed upon the incidents.

Let us then determine what are the circumstances which strike us as terrible or pitiful.

Actions capable of this effect must happen between persons who are either friends or enemies or indifferent to one another. If an enemy kills an enemy, there is nothing to excite pity either in the act or the intention — except so far as the suffering in itself is pitiful. So again with indifferent persons. But when the tragic incident occurs between those who are near and dear to one another — if, for example, a brother kills, or intends to kill, a brother, a son his father, a mother her son, a son his mother, or any other deed of the kind is done — these are the situations to be looked for by the poet. He may not indeed destroy the framework of the received legends — the fact, for instance, that Clytemnestra was slain by Orestes and Eriphyle by Alcmaeon — but he ought to show invention of his own, and skilfully handle the traditional material. Let us explain more clearly what is meant by skilful handling.

The action may be done consciously and with knowledge of the

persons, in the manner of the older poets. It is thus too that Euripides
makes Medea slay her children. Or, again, the deed of horror may be
done, but done in ignorance, and the tie of kinship or friendship be
discovered afterwards. The *Oedipus* of Sophocles is an example.
Here, indeed, the incident is outside the drama proper; but cases
occur where it falls within the action of the play: one may cite the
Alcmaeon of Astydamas, or Telegonus in the *Wounded Odysseus.* [17]
Again, there is a third case — [to be about to act with knowledge of
the persons and then not to act. The fourth case is] when some one
is about to do an irreparable deed through ignorance, and makes the
discovery before it is done. These are the only possible ways. For
the deed must either be done or not done — and that wittingly or
unwittingly. But of all these ways, to be about to act knowing the
persons, and then not to act, is the worst. It is shocking without being
tragic, for no disaster follows. It is, therefore, never or very rarely
found in poetry. One instance, however, is in the *Antigone,* where
Haemon threatens to kill Creon. The next and better way is that the
deed should be perpetrated. Still better, that it should be perpetrated
in ignorance, and the discovery made afterwards. There is then
nothing to shock us, while the discovery produces a startling effect.
The last case is the best, as when in the *Cresphontes* Merope is about
to slay her son, but, recognizing who he is, spares his life. [17] So in the
Iphigenia, the sister recognizes the brother just in time. [18] Again in the
Helle, the son recognizes the mother when on the point of giving her
up. [19] This, then, is why a few families only, as has been already
observed, furnish the subjects of tragedy. It was not art, but happy
chance, that led the poets in search of subjects to impress the tragic
quality upon their plots. They are compelled, therefore, to have recourse to those houses whose history contains moving incidents like
these.

Enough has now been said concerning the structure of the incidents
and the right kind of plot.

X V

In respect of Character there are four things to be aimed at. First,
and most important, it must be good. Now any speech or action that
manifests moral purpose of any kind will be expressive of character:

[17] Lost plays.
[18] In Euripides' *Iphigenia in Tauris.* It is difficult to see why Aristotle considered this last kind of action the best. Certainly, his remarks here are inconsistent with his earlier statement (in Chapter XIII) that "the change of fortune [in a tragedy] should be not from bad to good, but, reversely, from good
to bad."
[19] A lost play.

the character will be good if the purpose is good. This rule is relative to each class. Even a woman may be good, and also a slave, though the woman may be said to be an inferior being, and the slave quite worthless. The second thing to aim at is propriety. There is a type of manly valor; but valor in a woman, or unscrupulous cleverness, is inappropriate. Thirdly, character must be true to life: for this is a distinct thing from goodness and propriety, as here described. The fourth point is consistency: for though the subject of the imitation, who suggested the type, be inconsistent, still he must be consistently inconsistent. [20] As an example of motiveless degradation of character, we have Menelaus in the *Orestes;* [21] of character indecorous and inappropriate, the lament of Odysseus in the *Scylla* and the speech of Melanippe; [22] of inconsistency the *Iphigenia at Aulis* — for Iphigenia the suppliant in no way resembles her later self.

As in the structure of the plot, so too in the portraiture of character, the poet should always aim either at the necessary or the probable. Thus a person of a given character should speak or act in a given way, by the rule either of necessity or of probability; just as this event should follow that by necessary or probable sequence. It is therefore evident that the unravelling of the plot, no less than the complication, must arise out of the plot itself; it must not be brought about by the *Deus ex Machina* — as in the *Medea,* or in the Return of the Greeks in the *Iliad.*[23] The *Deus ex Machina* should be employed only for events external to the drama — for antecedent or subsequent events, which lie beyond the range of human knowledge, and which require to be reported or foretold; for to the gods we ascribe the power of seeing all things. Within the action there must be nothing irrational. If the irrational cannot be excluded, it should be outside the scope of the tragedy. Such is the irrational element in the *Oedipus* of Sophocles.

Again, since Tragedy is an imitation of persons who are above the

[20] By "consistent," Aristotle apparently means "true to a mythological prototype." Hercules, for example, must be shown as a man of great endurance and courage. A cowardly portrait would be inconsistent with his legendary character and hence disturbing to the Athenian audience.

[21] In Euripides' play of that name.

[22] The *Scylla* is lost. *Melanippe* is a play by Euripides, only fragments of which survive.

[23] "Deus ex machina" is a Latin translation of a Greek phrase meaning "god from the mechané." The mechané was a kind of crane, a primitive flying machine used for the appearance of supernatural beings. Euripides, in particular, was fond of rescuing his characters from difficulty by the fortuitous arrival of a heavenly messenger. The phrase *deus ex machina* has passed into the vocabulary of dramatic criticism. It now stands for any solution to a plot which is extrinsic in nature and not a logical development of the previous action. The rich uncle who suddenly arrives in the last act of a 19th-century melodrama to save an unlucky family from bankruptcy and despair is an example of a modern *deus ex machina*.

common level, the example of good portrait-painters should be followed. They, while reproducing the distinctive form of the original,
make a likeness which is true to life and yet more beautiful. So too
the poet, in representing men who are irascible or indolent, or have
other defects of character, should preserve the type and yet ennoble
it. In this way Achilles is portrayed by Agathon and Homer.

These then are rules the poet should observe. Nor should he neglect
those appeals to the senses, which, though not among the essentials,
are the concomitants of poetry; for here too there is much room for
error. But of this enough has been said in our published treatises.

XVI

What Recognition is has been already explained. We will now
enumerate its kinds.

First, the least artistic form, which, from poverty of wit, is most
commonly employed — recognition by signs. Of these some are congenital — such as "the spear which the earth-born race bear on
their bodies," or the stars introduced by Carcinus in his *Thyestes*.[24]
Others are acquired after birth; and of these some are bodily marks, as
scars; some external tokens, as necklaces, or the little ark in the *Tyro*[24]
by which the discovery is effected. Even these admit of more or less
skilful treatment. Thus in the recognition of Odysseus by his scar, the
discovery is made in one way by the nurse, in another by the swine-
herd. The use of tokens for the express purpose of proof — and indeed, any formal proof with or without tokens — is a less artistic mode
of recognition. A better kind is that which comes about by a turn
of incident, as in the Bath Scene in the *Odyssey*.[25]

Next come the recognitions invented at will by the poet, and on
that account wanting in art. For example, Orestes in the *Iphigenia*
reveals the fact that he is Orestes. She, indeed, makes herself known
by the letter; but he, by speaking himself, and saying what the poet,
not what the plot, requires. This, therefore, is nearly allied to the
fault above mentioned — for Orestes might as well have brought
tokens with him. Another similar instance is the "voice of the shuttle"
in the *Tereus* of Sophocles.[26]

The third kind depends on memory when the sight of some object
awakens a feeling: as in the *Cyprians* of Dicaeogenes,[26] where the
hero breaks into tears on seeing the picture; or again in the *Lay of
Alcinous*, where Odysseus, hearing the minstrel play the lyre, recalls
the past and weeps; and hence the recognition.[27]

The fourth kind is by process of reasoning. Thus in the *Choëphori:*

[24] Lost plays.   [25] Book XIX.   [26] Lost plays.
[27] *Odyssey*, Book VIII.

— "Some one resembling me has come; no one resembles me but Orestes: therefore Orestes has come." Such too is the discovery made by Iphigenia in the play of Polyidus the Sophist.[28] It was a natural reflexion for Orestes to make, "So I too must die at the altar like my sister." So, again, in the *Tydeus* of Theodectes,[28] the father says, "I came to find my son, and I lose my own life." So too in the *Phineidae*[28] the women, on seeing the place, inferred their fate: — "Here we are doomed to die, for here we were cast forth." Again, there is a composite kind of recognition involving false inference on the part of one of the characters, as in the *Odysseus Disguised as a Messenger.*[28] A said [that no one else was able to bend the bow; . . . hence B (the disguised Odysseus) imagined that A would] recognize the bow which, in fact, he had not seen; and to bring about a recognition by this means — the expectation that A would recognize the bow — is false inference.

But, of all recognitions, the best is that which arises from the incidents themselves, where the startling discovery is made by natural means. Such is that in the *Oedipus* of Sophocles, and in the *Iphigenia;* for it was natural that Iphigenia should wish to dispatch a letter. These recognitions alone dispense with the artificial aid of tokens or amulets. Next come the recognitions by process of reasoning.

XVII

In constructing the plot and working it out with the proper diction, the poet should place the scene, as far as possible, before his eyes. In this way, seeing everything with the utmost vividness, as if he were a spectator of the action, he will discover what is in keeping with it, and be most unlikely to overlook inconsistencies. The need of such a rule is shown by the fault found in Carcinus. Amphiaraus was on his way from the temple. This fact escaped the observation of one who did not see the situation. On the stage, however, the piece failed, the audience being offended at the oversight.

Again, the poet should work out his play, to the best of his power, with appropriate gestures; for those who feel emotion are most convincing through natural sympathy with the characters they represent; and one who is agitated storms, one who is angry rages, with the most life-like reality. Hence poetry implies either a happy gift of nature or a strain of madness. In the one case a man can take the mould of any character; in the other, he is lifted out of his proper self.

As for the story, whether the poet takes it ready made or constructs it for himself, he should first sketch its general outline, and then fill in the episodes and amplify in detail. The general plan may

[28] Lost plays.

be illustrated by the *Iphigenia*. A young girl is sacrificed; she disappears mysteriously from the eyes of those who sacrificed her; she is transported to another country, where the custom is to offer up all strangers to the goddess. To this ministry she is appointed. Some time later her own brother chances to arrive. The fact that the oracle for some reason ordered him to go there is outside the general plan of the play. The purpose, again, of his coming is outside the action proper. However, he comes, he is seized, and, when on the point of being sacrificed, reveals who he is. The mode of recognition may be either that of Euripides or of Polyidus, in whose play he exclaims very naturally: — "So it was not my sister only, but I too, who was doomed to be sacrificed"; and by that remark he is saved. [29]

After this, the names being once given, it remains to fill in the episodes. We must see that they are relevant to the action. In the case of Orestes, for example, there is the madness which led to his capture, and his deliverance by means of the purificatory rite. In the drama, the episodes are short, but it is these that give extension to Epic poetry. Thus the story of the *Odyssey* can be stated briefly. A certain man is absent from home for many years; he is jealously watched by Poseidon, and left desolate. Meanwhile his home is in a wretched plight — suitors are wasting his substance and plotting against his son. At length, tempest-tossed, he himself arrives; he makes certain persons acquainted with him; he attacks the suitors with his own hand, and is himself preserved while he destroys them. This is the essence of the plot; the rest is episode.

XVIII

Every tragedy falls into two parts, — Complication and Unravelling, or *Dénouement*. Incidents extraneous to the action are frequently combined with a portion of the action proper, to form the Complication; the rest is the Unravelling. By the Complication I mean all that extends from the beginning of the action to the part which marks the turning-point to good or bad fortune. The unravelling is that which extends from the beginning of the change to the end. . . .

There are four kinds of Tragedy, the Complex, depending entirely on Reversal of the Situation and Recognition; the Pathetic (where the motive is passion) — such as the tragedies on Ajax and Ixion; [30] the Ethical (where the motives are ethical) — such as the *Phthiotides* and the *Peleus*. [31] The fourth kind is the Simple. We here exclude the

---

[29] Again *Iphigenia in Tauris* by Euripides. Apparently, Polyidus also wrote a play on the same subject from which the phrase quoted by Aristotle is taken.

[30] Sophocles' *Ajax* is the only one of the many plays written about that character which has survived. No play about Ixion has come down to us.

[31] Lost plays.

purely spectacular element, exemplified by the *Phorcides,* the *Prometheus,* and scenes laid in Hades.[32] The poet should endeavour, if possible, to combine all poetic elements; or failing that, the greatest number and those the most important; the more so, in face of the cavilling criticism of the day. For whereas there have hitherto been good poets, each in his own branch, the critics now expect one man to surpass all others in their several lines of excellence.

In speaking of a tragedy as the same or different, the best test to take is the plot. Identity exists where the Complication and Unravelling are the same. Many poets tie the knot well, but unravel it ill. Both arts, however, should always be mastered.

Again, the poet should remember what has been often said, and not make an Epic structure into a Tragedy — by an Epic structure I mean one with a multiplicity of plots — as if, for instance, you were to make a tragedy out of the entire story of the *Iliad.* In the Epic poem, owing to its length, each part assumes its proper magnitude. In the drama the result is far from answering to the poet's expectation. The proof is that the poets who have dramatised the whole story of the Fall of Troy, instead of selecting portions, like Euripides;[33] or who have taken the whole tale of Niobe, and not a part of her story, like Aeschylus,[34] either fail utterly or meet with poor success on the stage. Even Agathon has been known to fail from this one defect.[35] In his Reversals of the Situation, however, he shows a marvellous skill in the effort to hit the popular taste — to produce a tragic effect that satisfies the moral sense. This effect is produced when the clever rogue, like Sisyphus, is outwitted, or the brave villain defeated. Such an event is probable in Agathon's sense of the word: "it is probable," he says, "that many things should happen contrary to probability."

The Chorus too should be regarded as one of the actors; it should be an integral part of the whole, and share in the action, in the manner not of Euripides but of Sophocles. As for the later poets,[36] their choral songs pertain as little to the subject of the piece as to that of any other tragedy. They are, therefore, sung as mere interludes — a practice first begun by Agathon. Yet what difference is there between introducing such choral interludes, and transferring a speech, or even a whole act, from one play to another?

.   .   .   .

[32] *Phorcides* is a lost play written by Aeschylus, who also wrote the extant drama *Prometheus Bound.*

[33] As, for example, in *The Trojan Women.*

[34] Aeschylus' tragedy *Niobe* is lost.

[35] Agathon was a younger rival of Euripides. His plays are all lost.

[36] Aristotle is referring to the poets of the fourth century, from whom only fragments survive.

XXVI

The question may be raised whether the Epic or Tragic mode of imitation is the higher. If the more refined art is the higher, and the more refined in every case is that which appeals to the better sort of audience, the art which imitates anything and everything is manifestly most unrefined. The audience is supposed to be too dull to comprehend unless something of their own is thrown in by the performers, who therefore indulge in restless movements. Bad flute-players twist and twirl, if they have to represent "the quoit throw," or hustle the coryphaeus when they perform the *Scylla*. Tragedy, it is said, has this same defect. We may compare the opinion that the older actors entertained of their successors. Mynniscus used to call Callippides "ape" on account of the extravagance of his action, and the same view was held of Pindarus. Tragic art, then, as a whole, stands to Epic in the same relation as the younger to the elder actors. So we are told that Epic poetry is addressed to a cultivated audience, who do not need gesture; Tragedy, to an inferior public. Being then unrefined, it is evidently the lower of the two.

Now, in the first place, this censure attaches not to the poetic but to the histrionic art; for gesticulation may be equally overdone in epic recitation, as by Sosistratus, or in lyrical competition, as by Mnasitheus the Opuntian. Next, all action is not to be condemned — any more than all dancing — but only that of bad performers. Such was the fault found in Callippides, as also in others of our own day, who are censured for representing degraded women. Again, Tragedy like Epic poetry produces its effect even without action; it reveals its power by mere reading. If, then, in all other respects it is superior, this fault, we say, is not inherent in it.

And superior it is, because it has all the epic elements — it may even use the epic metre — with the music and spectacular effects as important accessories; and these produce the most vivid of pleasures. Further, it has vividness of impression in reading as well as in representation. Moreover, the art attains its end within narrower limits; for the concentrated effect is more pleasurable than one which is spread over a long time and so diluted. What, for example, would be the effect of the *Oedipus* of Sophocles, if it were cast into a form as long as the *Iliad*? Once more, the Epic imitation has less unity, as is shown by this, that any Epic poem will furnish subjects for several tragedies. Thus if the story adopted by the poet has a strict unity, it must either be concisely told and appear truncated; or, if it conform to the Epic canon of length, it must seem weak and watery. Such length implies some loss of unity, if, I mean, the poem is constructed out of several actions, like the *Iliad* and the *Odyssey*, which have many such parts, each with a certain magnitude of its own. Yet these poems are as perfect as possible in structure; each is, in the highest degree attainable, an imitation of a single action.

If, then, Tragedy is superior to Epic poetry in all these respects, and, moreover, fulfils its specific function better as an art — for each art ought to produce not any chance pleasure but the pleasure proper to it, as already stated — it plainly follows that Tragedy is the higher art, as attaining its end more perfectly. . . .

With the exception of Aristotle's *Poetics*, no book of dramatic theory and criticism survives from the ancient Greek theatre. We have to content ourselves instead with fragments. The following brief remarks are attributed to Antiphanes and Timocles, two fourth-century comic poets. Our source is *The Deipnosophists* (*The Banqueting Scholars*), a compendium of miscellaneous information (most of it concerned with cookery), compiled by Athenaeus in the third century B.C.

Athenaeus

Antiphanes and Timocles on Tragedy

(from *The Deipnosophists*)*

Since you ask me every time that you meet me, my friend Timocrates,[1] what was said by the Deipnosophists, thinking that we are making some discoveries, we will remind you of what is said by Antiphanes, in his *Poetics*,[2] in this manner —

> In every way, my friends, is Tragedy
> A happy poem. For the argument
> Is, in the first place, known to the spectators,
> Before one single actor says a word.

* From *The Deipnosophists or Banquet of the Learned of Athenaeus*, translated by C. D. Yonge (London: G. Bell & Sons, Ltd., 1909), Vol. I, b. 6, pp. 353–354; reprinted by permission of the publisher. The English version is slightly revised by the editors.

1 *The Deipnosophists* is for the most part a monologue delivered by the author to his friend Timocrates.

2 The rest of the *Poetics* of Antiphanes has been lost.

So that the poet need do little more
Than just remind his hearers what they know.
For should I speak of Oedipus, at once
They recollect his story — how his father
Was Laius, and Jocasta too his mother;
What were his sons', and what his daughters' names,
And what he did and suffer'd. So again
If a man names Alcmaeon, the very children
Can tell you how he in his madness slew
His mother; and Adrastus furious,
Will come in haste, and then depart again;
And then at last, when they can say no more,
And when the subject is almost exhausted,
They lift an engine easily as a finger,
And that is quite enough to please the theatre.
But our case is harder. We are forced
T'invent the whole of what we write; new names,
Things done before, done now, new plots, new openings,
And new catastrophes. . . .

But Timocles the comic writer, asserting that tragedy is useful
in many respects to human life, says in his *Women Celebrating the
Festival of Bacchus*[3] —

My friend, just hear what I'm about to say.
Man is an animal by nature miserable;
And life has many grievous things in it.
Therefore he has invented these reliefs
To ease his cares; for oft the mind forgets
Its own discomforts while it soothes itself
In contemplation of another's woes,
And e'en derives some pleasure and instruction.[4]
For first, I'd have you notice the tragedians;
What good they do to every one. The poor man
Sees Telephus was poorer still than he,
And bears his own distress more easily.
The madman thinks upon Alcmaeon's case.
Has a man weak sore eyes? The sons of Phineus
Are blind as bats. Has a man lost his child?
Let him remember childless Niobe.

---

3 A lost play.
4 This is one of the earliest explicit suggestions in dramatic criticism that a
tragedy should serve a useful purpose. Timocles, although he speaks somewhat
facetiously, is nonetheless anticipating the theories of the Roman writer Horace,
who tells us that a great play should combine "the useful and the sweet."

He's hurt his leg; and so had Philoctetes.
Is he unfortunate in his old age?
Oeneus was more so. So that every one,
Seeing that others have been more unfortunate,
Learns his own griefs to bear with more content.

⊱ Even more influential than Aristotle's *Poetics* in determining the dramatic taste of the Renaissance was *The Art of Poetry* (An Epistle to the Pisos) by the Roman poet Quintus Horatius Flaccus, or Horace (65 B.C.–8 B.C.). This short compendium of dramatic rules was based on the critical works (now lost) of Neoptolemus of Parium. The precepts advanced by Horace—particularly his insistence on pleasure and instruction in tragedy (ll. 194ff. in this abridgement)—were accepted without question by most playwrights of the Italian Renaissance and by the great English comic writer, Ben Jonson. Indeed, Horace's observations continued to exert a considerable influence on dramatic theory until the nineteenth century.

Horace

from THE ART OF POETRY*

A comic subject needs a humble verse,
Thyestes' banquet[1] scorns a comic style.
Let every theme have its appropriate place.
Yet sometimes comedy may raise her voice,
And Chremes[2] be allow'd to foam and rail.
Tragedians, too, lay by their rant to grieve;

---

* From the translation by the Earl of Roscommon, 1860. Abridged and revised, with additional notes, by the editors.

[1] Thyestes, the son of Pelops in Greek legend, seduced the wife of his brother, Atreus. To avenge himself, Atreus invited Thyestes to a banquet and served the latter's children to their unsuspecting father. Later, Aegisthus, a surviving child of Thyestes, helped Clytemnestra to murder Agamemnon, the son of Atreus. The banquet of Thyestes is the subject of a tragedy by Seneca (d. A.D. 65).

[2] Chremes is a character in *The Ecclesiazusae*, a comedy by Aristophanes. The name was borrowed by fourth-century comic writers and applied to important secondary characters.

Peleus and Telephus[3] exil'd and poor
Forget their swelling and gigantic words
To move their auditors with simple grief.
A poem must be more than beautiful;
It must be tender and affecting too,
If it will bear the souls of men away.
We weep and laugh, as we see others do:
He only makes me sad who shows the way,
And first is sad himself; then, Telephus,
I feel the weight of your calamities,
And fancy all your miseries my own.
But if you act them ill, I sleep or laugh:
Your speech must alter, as your subject does,
From kind to fierce, from wanton to severe:
For Nature forms, and softens us within,
And writes our fortune's changes in our voice.
Pleasure enchants, impetuous rage transports,
And grief dejects, and wrings the tortur'd soul,
And these are all interpreted by speech;
But he whose words and fortunes disagree,
Absurd, unpity'd, raises public laughter.
Observe the characters of those that speak,
Whether an honest servant, or a cheat,
Or one whose blood boils in his youthful veins,
Or a grave matron, or a busy nurse,
Extorting merchants, careful husbandmen,
Argives, or Thebans, Asians, or Greeks.

Follow tradition or invent a tale
That is at least consistent to itself.[4]
Describe Achilles, as report has made him,
Impatient, rash, inexorable, proud,
Scorning all judges, and all law but arms;
Medea must be unyielding in revenge,

---

3 Peleus, the legendary king of Phthia and father of Achilles, was exiled from his native land for committing an infamous murder. Telephus, the son-in-law of Priam of Troy, was wounded by Achilles. Informed by an oracle that the wound would heal only if cured by the man who inflicted it, Telephus left his native state, Myola, and sought out Achilles. In return for restoring his health, Achilles demanded that Telephus help him besiege the Trojans.

4 Horace is referring to consistency of character here. If you do invent a new story, he is saying, let the persons of the drama exhibit the same characteristics at the end of the play that they revealed on their first appearance. Thus, a wise man must not suddenly appear foolish, nor a brave man exhibit cowardly inclinations.

Ino all tears, Ixion all deceit,
Io must wander, and Orestes mourn.[5]

If your bold muse dare tread unbeaten paths,
And bring new characters upon the stage,
Be sure you keep them up to their first height.
New subjects are not easily explain'd,
And you had better choose a well-known theme,
Than trust to an invention of your own;

   ·   ·   ·   ·   ·   ·   ·   ·   ·

But then you must not copy trivial things,
Nor put entire legends on the stage,
Nor word for word too faithfully translate,
Nor (as some servile imitators do)
Prescribe at first such strict uneasy rules,
As they must ever slavishly observe,
Or all the laws of decency renounce.

   ·   ·   ·   ·   ·   ·   ·   ·   ·

Now hear what ev'ry auditor expects,
If you intend that he should stay to hear
The epilogue, and see the curtain rise.[6]
Mind how our tempers alter with our years,
And by those rules form all your characters.
One that hath newly learn'd to speak and go,
Loves childish plays, is soon provok'd and pleased,
And changes ev'ry hour his wav'ring mind.
A youth that first casts off his tutor's yoke,
Loves horses, hounds, and sports and exercise,
Prone to all vice, impatient of reproof,
Proud, careless, fond, inconstant, and profuse.
Gain and ambition rule our riper years,

[5] Ino was the daughter of Cadmus and the beloved of Athamas. Athamas, persecuted by the goddess Hera, went mad, killing one of his and Ino's children. In sorrow and desperation Ino threw herself and her surviving son into the ocean where they were transformed into sea deities. Ixion, a king of the Lapithae, was a legendary figure renowned for his evil cunning. Once to avoid a marriage payment, he cunningly arranged a trap for his bride's father, causing the old man to fall into a pit containing burning coals. Avoided by mankind because of this terrible deed, Ixion was befriended by Zeus, but soon betrayed the confidence of his benefactor by attempting to seduce Hera. For this final act of treachery, he was condemned to the unerworld where he was placed for all eternity on a burning wheel. Io, a daughter of the king of Argos, was loved by Zeus and jealously persecuted by Hera, who forced her to wander the face of the earth, pricked on and tormented by a gadfly. Orestes was the son of Agamemnon, who avenged his father's death by killing his mother and her lover.

[6] Roman theatres of Horace's day had an *auleum* or curtain in a trough at the front of the stage which rose to hide the action when the fifth act of the play concluded.

And make us slaves to interest and pow'r.
Old men are only walking hospitals,
Where all defects, and all diseases, crowd
With restless pain, and more tormenting fear,
Lazy, morose, full of delays and hopes,
Oppress'd with riches, which they dare not use;
Ill-natur'd censors of the present age,
And fond of all the follies of the past.
Thus all the treasure of our flowing years,
Our ebb of life for ever takes away.
Boys must not have th' ambitious care of men,
Nor men the weak anxieties of age.

Some stage events are acted, some reported,[7]
And what we hear moves less than what we see;
Spectators only have their eyes to trust,
But auditors must trust their ears and you;
Yet there are things improper for a scene,
Which men of judgment only will relate.
Medea must not draw her murd'ring knife,
And spill her children's blood upon the stage,
Nor Atreus there his horrid feast prepare.
Cadmus' and Procne's metamorphoses,[8]
(She to a swallow turn'd, he to a snake)
And whatsoever contradicts my sense,
I hate to see, and never can believe.

Five acts are the just measure of a play.
Never presume to make a god appear,
But for a business worthy of a god;
And in one scene a fourth should seldom speak.[9]
A chorus should supply what action wants,
And hath a generous and manly part;
Bridles wild rage, loves rigid honesty,
And strict observance of impartial laws,
Sobriety, security, and peace,
And begs the gods to turn blind fortune's wheel,

---

[7] "Reported"; i.e., by a messenger or other bearer of off-stage tidings.

[8] Cadmus, the legendary founder of Thebes, was turned into a serpent by the gods to relieve him of the afflictions and sorrows of human life. Procne, the daughter of Pandion, killed her son to avenge herself against her husband, Tereus, who had betrayed her with her sister, Philomena. Procne was transformed into a nightingale by the gods.

[9] Quite obviously, Horace derives this rule from the stage practice of Greek tragedy, in which three actors performed all the speaking parts.

To raise the wretched, and pull down the proud.
But nothing must be sung between the acts
But what some way conduces to the plot.[10]

First the shrill sound of a small rural pipe
(Not loud like trumpets, nor adorn'd as now)
Was entertainment for the infant stage,
And pleas'd the thin and sober audience
Of our well-meaning, frugal ancestors.
But when Rome's walls and limits were enlarg'd,
And men (grown wanton by prosperity)
Study'd new arts of luxury and ease,
The verse, the music, and the scenes improv'd;
For how should ignorance be judge of wit,
Or men of sense applaud the jests of fools?
Then came rich clothes and graceful action in,
Then instruments were taught more moving notes,
And eloquence with all her pomp and charms
Foretold us useful and sententious truths,
As those delivered by the Delphic god.

The first tragedians found that serious style
Too grave for their uncultivated age,
And so brought wild and naked satyrs in,
Whose motion, words, and shape were all a farce,
(As oft as decency would give them leave)
Because the mad ungovernable rout,
Full of confusion, and the fumes of wine,
Lov'd such variety and antic tricks.
But then they did not wrong themselves so much
To make a god, a hero, or a king,
(Stripped of his golden crown and purple robe)
Descend to a mechanic dialect,
Nor (to avoid such meanness) soaring high
With empty sound, and airy notions fly;
For, tragedy should blush as much to stoop
To the low mimic follies of a farce,
As a grave matron would, to dance with girls:
You must not think that a satiric style
Allows of scandalous and brutish words,

---

[10] The chorus, an integral part of ancient Greek drama, had been reduced by the time of Horace to an intermission feature, an interlude designed to entertain the audience between the acts of a comedy or tragedy. Horace pleads for a slightly more integrated dramatic structure in which the odes of the chorus will at least be germane to the issues at hand.

Or the confounding of your characters.
Begin with truth, then give invention scope,
And if your style be natural and smooth,
All men will try, and hope to write as well;
And (not without much pains) be undeceiv'd.
So much good method and connection may
Improve the common and plainest things.
A satyr that comes staring from the woods
Must not at first speak like an orator;
But, tho' his language should not be refin'd,
It must not be obscene and impudent;
The better sort abhors scurrility,
And often censures what the rabble likes.

.   .   .   .

Consider well the Greek originals,
Read them by day, and think of them by night.
But Plautus was admir'd in former time
With too much patience and complacency.
His harsh, unequal verse, was music then,
And rudeness had the privilege of wit.

When Thespis first expos'd the tragic muse,
Rude were the actors, and a cart the scene,[11]
Where ghastly faces strain'd with lees of wine
Frighted the children, and amus'd the crowd;
This Aeschylus (with indignation) saw,
And built a stage of tolerable size,
Invented masks, found out a decent dress,
And taught men stately tones and graceful movement.
Next comedy appeared with great applause,
Till her licentious and abusive tongue
Waken'd the magistrates coercive pow'r,
And forc'd it to suppress her insolence.

.   .   .   .

Sound judgment is the ground of writing well:
And when philosophy directs your choice
To proper subjects rightly understood,
Words from your pen will naturally flow;
He only gives the proper characters,

---

[11] From this passage derives the unsupported tradition that Thespis toured his rudimentary tragedies from town to town on a primitive cart, performing wherever he could find an audience.

Who knows the duty of all ranks of men,
And what we owe to country, parents, friends,
How judges, and how senators should act,
And what becomes a general to do;
Those are the likest copies, which are drawn
By the original of human life.
Sometimes in rough and undigested plays
We meet with such a lucky character,
As being humour'd right, and well pursu'd,
Succeeds much better than the shallow verse
And chiming trifles of more studious pens.

   •   •   •   •   •   •   •   •   •   •   •   •

A poet should instruct, or please, or both;
Let all your precepts be succinct and clear,
That ready wits may comprehend them soon,
And faithful memories retain them long;
For superfluities are soon forgot.
Never be so conceited of your parts,
To think you may persuade us what you please,
Or venture to bring in a child alive,
That cannibals have murder'd and devour'd.
Old age explodes all but morality;
Austerity offends aspiring youths;
But he that joins instructions with delight,
Profit with pleasure, carries all the votes:
These are the volumes that enrich the shops,
These pass with admiration through the world,
And bring their author an eternal fame.

III

Playwrights and Their Sources

THE HOUSE OF ATREUS

Antiphanes in his rather simple-minded way has pinpointed an important fact about Greek tragedy. The plot of the play was generally known to the audience in advance.

Most of the complex tragic ironies of Aeschylus, Sophocles, and Euripides depended on this foreknowledge. By employing familiar heroic legends these writers were able to place their audience at some distance from the events of the plot — in an almost god-like position with respect to the actors on the stage.

As a result, a tension was created in the spectator between his knowledge of the outcome and his sympathy for the sufferings of the hero — a tension which was resolved only when the hero learned what the audience had known from the first — when the action, in an Aristotelian sense, was complete.

It has always been believed that in the earliest days of drama, during the time of Thespis, the plots of tragedy were centered almost wholly on the traditional adventures of Dionysus and his followers. Professors Pickard-Cambridge and Kitto have cast some doubt on this belief, as we have seen. In any case, the legend of Dionysus was soon exhausted, and Aeschylus and his contemporaries turned for inspiration to the stories of other gods and heroes.

One of the most popular dramatic subjects was the legendary curse on the house of Atreus. All told, eight of the surviving Greek tragedies deal with some portion of this grim tale. The story in brief outline is this:

The King of Argos, or Mycenae in some versions, Pelops, has two sons, Atreus and Thyestes. Thyestes seduces Atreus' wife, and in revenge Atreus murders all of his brother's children except one, the prince Aegisthus. Not content with simple murder, Atreus feeds the dead children to their unwitting father at a banquet, and as a result of this terrible crime, a curse is visited on his house.

The curse is inherited by Atreus' two sons, Agamemnon and Menelaus. These two brothers marry two sisters, Clytemnestra and Helen. Helen, judged the most beautiful woman in the world, is abducted by Paris, prince of Troy, and the Greeks begin to raise a war party to bring her back. Under the command of Agamemnon, the Greek kings assemble their forces at Aulis to embark. However, the goddess Artemis refuses to allow them a favorable wind until Agamemnon agrees to offer his daughter, Iphigenia, as a holy sacrifice. After some soul-searching, Agamemnon permits the sacrifice to take place, and the troops set sail. The war with Troy lasts ten years, after which the victorious Greeks set sail for home.

In Agamemnon's absence, however, Clytemnestra has taken a lover, Aegisthus, surviving son of Thyestes, and the deadly enemy of her husband. The two lovers intend to murder Agamemnon as soon as he arrives home.

Agamemnon returns a hero, bringing with him the princess Cassandra, his captured Trojan concubine. Clytemnestra and Aegisthus slaughter both of them. In the years following the double murder, Electra, Agamemnon's daughter, grows to hate her mother. She lives for the day when her exiled brother, Orestes, will return to Argos and revenge their father's death. Orestes returns, and with his sister he successfully carries out the act of vengeance against Clytemnestra and Aegisthus.

Orestes is now pursued by the Furies, the terrifying earthspirits whose task it is to punish the crime of matricide. Eventually, these Furies are placated through the intervention of Athene, and the family curse is laid forever.

This story served as the plot for Asechylus' great trilogy—the *Oresteia*—first produced at the Great City Dionysia in 458 B.C. In addition, both Sophocles and Euripides wrote Electra plays based on that part of the story leading up to the murder of Clytemnestra and her lover. A comparison of these three very dissimilar works will indicate to the student the ways in which each of the great poets took traditional material and shaped it to conform to his own particular moral and theological point of view.

Equally instructive is a comparison of the *Agamemnon* of Aeschylus (the first play in the Oresteian trilogy) with the story of the doomed general as it appears in the ninth-century (?) epic, the *Odyssey*. In that work, the history of the King of Argos serves as a brief but impressive counterpoint to the story of another unhappy return from Troy, the voyage of Odysseus.

Homer

THE STORY OF AGAMEMNON

(from the *Odyssey*)*

From Book I[1]

*T*hen among them the father of gods and men began to speak, for
he bethought him in his heart of noble Aegisthus, whom the son of
Agamemnon, far-famed Orestes, slew. Thinking upon him he spake
out among the Immortals:

"Lo you now, how vainly mortal men do blame the gods! For of
us they say comes evil, whereas they even of themselves, through the
blindness of their own hearts, have sorrows beyond that which is ordained. Even as of late Aegisthus, beyond that which was ordained,
took to him the wedded wife of the son of Atreus and killed her lord
on his return, and that with sheer doom before his eyes, since we had
warned him by the embassy of Hermes the keen-sighted, the slayer
of Argos, that he should neither kill the man, nor woo his wife. For
the son of Atreus shall be avenged at the hand of Orestes, so soon
as he shall come to man's estate and long for his own country. So
spake Hermes, yet he prevailed not on the heart of Aegisthus, for all
his good will; but now hath he paid one price for all."

From Book III[2]

"Nestor, son of Neleus, now tell me true: how died the son of
Atreus, Agamemnon of the wide domain? Where was Menelaus?
What death did crafty Aegisthus plan for him, in that he killed a man
more valiant far than he? Or was Menelaus not in Argos of Achaia[3]
but wandering elsewhere among men, and that other took heart and
slew Agamemnon?"

* Translated by S. H. Butcher and A. Lang.

1 The scene in Book I is a gathering of the gods at Mt. Olympus to discuss a
plea by Athene that Odysseus, now restrained by the goddess Calypso, be permitted to return to his kingdom in Ithaca. Zeus opens the discussion by complaining that the gods are blamed for many evils which are created by man
alone. His example is Aegisthus, who had sealed his own doom by murdering
Agamemnon.

2 In Book III, Telemachus, the son of Odysseus, is searching for his father.
He visits the sage, Nestor, at Pylos. During the course of their conversation, the
younger man inquires about the murder of Agamemnon.

3 Agamemnon was King of Mycenae. Homer and Aeschylus make him ruler of all of
Argos.

Then Nestor of Gerenia, lord of chariots, answered him: "Yea now, my child, I will tell thee the whole truth. Verily thou guessest aright even of thyself how things would have fallen out, if Menelaus of the fair hair, the son of Atreus, when he came back from Troy, had found Aegisthus yet alive in the halls. Then even in his death would they not have heaped the piled earth over him, but dogs and fowls of the air would have devoured him as he lay on the plain far from the town. Nor would any of the Achaean women have bewailed him; so dread was the deed he contrived. Now we sat in leaguer there, achieving many adventures; but he the while in peace in the heart of Argos, the pastureland of horses, spake ofttimes, tempting her, to the wife of Agamemnon. Verily at the first she would none of the foul deed, the fair Clytemnestra, for she had a good understanding. Moreover there was with her a minstrel, whom the son of Atreus straitly charged as he went to Troy to have a care of his wife. But when at last the doom of the gods bound her to her ruin, then did Aegisthus carry the minstrel to a lonely isle, and left him there to be the prey and spoil of birds; while as for her, he led her to his house, a willing lover with a willing lady. And he burnt many thigh slices upon the holy altars of the gods, and hung up many offerings, woven-work and gold, seeing that he had accomplished a great deed, beyond all hope. Now we, I say, were sailing together on our way from Troy, the son of Atreus and I, as loving friends. But when he had reached holy Sunium, the headland of Athens, there Phoebus Apollo slew the pilot of Menelaus with the visitation of his gentle shafts, as he held between his hands the rudder of the running ship, even Phrontis, son of Onetor, who excelled the tribes of men in piloting a ship, whenso the storm-winds were hurrying by. Thus was Menelaus holden there, though eager for the way, till he might bury his friend and pay the last rites over him. But when he in his turn, faring over the wine-dark sea in hollow ships, reached in swift course the steep mount of Malea, then it was that Zeus of the far-borne voice devised a hateful path, and shed upon them the breath of the shrill winds, and great swelling waves arose like unto mountains. There sundered he the fleet in twain, and part thereof he brought nigh to Crete, where the Cydonians dwelt about the streams of Iardanus. Now there is a certain cliff, smooth and sheer towards the sea, on the border of Gortyn, in the misty deep, where the South-West Wind drives a great wave against the left headland, towards Phaestus, and a little rock keeps back the mighty water. Thither came one part of the fleet, and the men scarce escaped destruction, but the ships were broken by the waves against the rock; while those other five dark-prowed ships the wind and the water bare and brought nigh to Egypt. Thus Menelaus, gathering much livelihood and gold, was wandering there with his ships among men of

strange speech, and even then Aegisthus planned that pitiful work at
home. And for seven years he ruled over Mycenae, rich in gold,
after he slew the son of Atreus, and the people were subdued unto
him. But in the eighth year came upon him goodly Orestes back
from Athens to be his bane, and slew the slayer of his father, guileful
Aegisthus, who killed his famous sire. Now when he had slain him,
he made a funeral feast to the Argives over his hateful mother, and
over the craven Aegisthus. And on the selfsame day there came to
him Menelaus of the loud war-cry, bringing much treasure, even all
the freight of his ships. So thou, my friend, wander not long far
away from home, leaving thy substance behind thee and men in thy
house so wanton, lest they divide and utterly devour all thy wealth,
and thou shalt have gone on a vain journey."

From Book IV [4]

"But now when he [Agamemnon] was like soon to reach the steep
mount of Malea, lo, the storm wind snatched him away and bore him
over the teeming deep, making great moan, to the border of the country where of old Thyestes dwelt, but now Aegisthus abode there, the
son of Thyestes. But when thence too there showed a good prospect
of safe returning, and the gods changed the wind to a fair gale, and
they had reached home, then verily did Agamemnon set foot with
joy upon his country's soil, and as he touched his own land he kissed
it, and many were the hot tears he let fall, for he saw his land and
was glad. And it was so that the watchman spied him from his tower,
the watchman whom crafty Aegisthus had led and posted there,
promising him for a reward two talents of gold.[5] Now he kept watch
for the space of a year, lest Agamemnon should pass by him when
he looked not, and mind him of his wild prowess. So he went to the
house to bear the tidings to the shepherd of the people. And straightway Aegisthus contrived a cunning treason. He chose out twenty of
the best men in the township, and set an ambush, and on the further
side of the hall he commanded to prepare a feast. Then with chariot
and horses he went to bid to the feast Agamemnon, shepherd of the
people; but caitiff thoughts were in his heart. He brought him up to
his house, all unwitting of his doom, and when he had feasted him

---

[4] Next, Telemachus visits Menelaus in Sparta. Menelaus recounts how Proteus,
the thrall of Poseidon, told him the story of the two Greek leaders who had
perished on their return from Troy. The first was Aias, destroyed by Poseidon
for his rash pride. The second was Agamemnon, saved by Hera from shipwreck,
only to suffer a more terrible fate.

[5] In the *Agamemnon* of Aeschylus, there is no suggestion that the watchman
is in the pay of Aegisthus.

slew him, as one slayeth an ox at the stall. And none of the company of Atreides that were of his following were left, nor any of the men of Aegisthus, but they were all killed in the halls." 6

From Book XI 7

"Now when holy Persephone had scattered this way and that the spirits of the women folk, thereafter came the soul of Agamemnon, son of Atreus, sorrowing; and round him others were gathered, the ghosts of them who had died with him in the house of Aegisthus and met their doom. And he knew me straightway when he had drunk the dark blood, yea, and he wept aloud, and shed big tears as he stretched forth his hands in his longing to reach me. But it might not be, for he had now no steadfast strength nor power at all to move, such as was aforetime in his supple limbs.

"At the sight of him I wept and was moved with compassion, and uttering my voice, spake to him winged words: 'Most renowned son of Atreus, Agamemnon, king of men, say what doom overcame thee of death that lays men at their length? Did Poseidon smite thee in thy ships, raising the dolorous blast of contrary winds, or did unfriendly men do thee hurt upon the land, whilst thou wert cutting off their oxen and fair flocks of sheep, or fighting to win a city and the women thereof?'

"So spake I, and straightway he answered, and said unto me: 'Son of Laertes, of the seed of Zeus, Odysseus of many devices, it was not Poseidon that smote me in my ships, and raised the dolorous blast of contrary winds, nor did unfriendly men do me hurt upon the land, but Aegisthus it was that wrought me death and doom and slew me, with the aid of my accursed wife, as one slays an ox at the stall, after he had bidden me to his house, and entertained me at a feast. Even so I died by a death most pitiful, and round me my company likewise were slain without ceasing, like swine with glittering tusks which are slaughtered in the house of a rich and mighty man, whether at a wedding banquet or a joint-feast or a rich clan-drinking. Ere now hast thou been at the slaying of many a man, killed in single fight or in strong battle, yet thou wouldst have sorrowed the most at this sight, how we lay in the hall round the mixing-bowl and the laden

---

6 This version of Agamemnon's death differs in some details from the version used by Aeschylus. According to the first part of the *Oresteia*, Agamemnon was murdered in his bath immediately upon his return home. The story of the feast recounted by Homer is reminiscent of Euripides' *Electra*, where Orestes slaughters Aegisthus like an ox at a holy sacrifice.

7 In Book XI, we read about the descent of Odysseus into Hades. In the abode of the dead, the great wanderer meets the shade of Agamemnon and talks with him.

boards, and the floor all ran with blood. And most pitiful of all that
I heard was the voice of the daughter of Priam, of Cassandra, whom
hard by me the crafty Clytemnestra slew. Then I strove to raise my
hands as I was dying upon the sword, but to earth they fell. And
that shameless one turned her back upon me, and had not the heart
to draw down my eyelids with her fingers nor to close my mouth. So
surely is there nought more terrible and shameless than a woman who
imagines such evil in her heart, even as she too planned a foul deed,
fashioning death for her gentle lord. Verily I had thought to come
home most welcome to my children and my thralls; but she, out of the
depth of her evil knowledge, hath shed shame on herself and on
all womankind, which shall be for ever, even on the upright.' "

THE TROJAN WOMEN

In general it was not the custom for Greek tragic poets to
deal directly with a contemporary or near-contemporary situation. Only one of the thirty-two surviving tragedies describes an
event which had occurred within the recent memory of its audience. That play is *The Persians* by Aeschylus (first produced in
472 B.C.), a lyrical description of the grief in the Persian camp
following the defeat of Xerxes at the battle of Salamis eight
years before.

The Persians was acceptable to the Athenian audience because
it was set in a remote country and because it described a great
national victory. Not so acceptable were plays dealing with the
recent distress of a friendly people. In approximately 492 B.C.,
the tragic poet Phrynichus had written a play (now lost) about
the recent Persian destruction of a Greek city, Miletus. The audience was so moved by the sufferings of their allies that they
angrily fined Phrynichus a thousand drachmae for dramatizing
the unhappy event.

Since recent history could be represented without disguise on
the Athenian stage only at some risk to the author, Euripides, the
great iconoclast of Greek tragedy, was fond of taking a recent
occurrence and shaping it into one of the traditional, and hence
acceptable, tragic plots. Thus, in the case of his passionate
anti-war play, *The Trojan Women* (first performed in 415 B.C.),
the poet undoubtedly drew his inspiration from a barbaric event
which had taken place only the year before. Locked in a life-
and-death struggle with Sparta, the Athenian forces had ruthlessly slaughtered all the male inhabitants of a neutral state,
the island of Melos. This outrage Euripides blended with the

pathetic story of Hecuba, Andromache, Cassandra, and the other
royal captives who figured so importantly in the last book of the
Iliad.

The following excerpts from Homer and Thucydides illustrate
Euripides' dual source. Thucydides' account considerably post-
dates *The Trojan Women*, of course, but it contains the same
kind of bitter emotion which the poet must have felt when he
first attacked the chauvinistic leaders of Athens.

Homer

THE DIRGE FOR HECTOR

(from the *Iliad*, Book XXIV)*

*A*nd they with wail and moan drave the horses to the city, and the
mules drew the dead. Nor marked them any man or fair-girdled
woman until Kassandra, peer of golden Aphrodite, having gone up
upon Pergamos, was aware of her dear father as he stood in the car,
and the herald that was crier to the town. Then beheld she him that
lay upon the bier behind the mules, and thereat she wailed and cried
aloud throughout all the town: "O men and women of Troy, come
ye hither and look upon Hector, if ever while he was alive ye rejoiced when he came back from battle, since great joy was he to the
city and all the folk."

Thus spake she, nor was man or woman left within the city, for
upon all came unendurable grief. And near the gates they met Priam
bringing home the dead.[1] First bewailed him his dear wife and lady
mother, as they cast them on the fair-wheeled wain and touched his
head; and around them stood the throng and wept. So all day long
unto the setting of the sun they had lamented Hector in tears without the gate, had not the old man spoken from the car among the
folk: "Give me place for the mules to pass through; hereafter ye shall
have your fill of wailing, when I have brought him unto his home."

Thus spake he, and they parted asunder and gave place to the
wain. And the others when they had brought him to the famous
house, laid him on a fretted bed, and set beside him minstrels, leaders
of the dirge, who wailed a mournful lay, while the women made moan
with them. And among the women white-armed Andromache led
the lamentation, while in her hands she held the head of Hector slayer
of men: "Husband, thou art gone young from life, and leavest me a

* Translated by Ernest Myers.
[1] In Euripides' play, the action begins after the death of Priam and considerably after the dirge for Hector.

widow in thy halls. And the child is yet but a little one, child of ill-fated parents, thee and me; nor methinks shall he grow up to manhood, for ere then shall this city be utterly destroyed. For thou art verily perished who didst watch over it, who guardedst it and keptest safe its noble wives and infant little ones. These soon shall be voyaging in the hollow ships, yea and I too with them, and thou, my child, shalt either go with me unto a place where thou shalt toil at unseemly tasks, labouring before the face of some harsh lord, or else some Achaian will take thee by the arm and hurl thee from the battlement,[2] a grievous death, for that he is wroth because Hector slew his brother or father or son, since full many of the Achaians at Hector's hands have bitten the firm earth. For no light hand had thy father in the grievous fray. Therefore the folk lament him throughout the city, and woe unspeakable and mourning hast thou left to thy parents, Hector, but with me chiefliest shall grievous pain abide. For neither didst thou stretch thy hands to me from a bed in thy death, neither didst speak to me some memorable word that I might have thought on evermore as my tears fall night and day."

Thus spake she wailing, and the women joined their moan. And among them Hecuba again led the loud lament: "Hector, of all my children far dearest to my heart, verily while thou wert alive dear wert thou to the gods, and even in thy doom of death have they had care for thee. For other sons of mine whom he took captive would fleet Achilles sell beyond the unvintaged sea unto Samos and Imbros and smoking Lemnos, but when with keen-edged bronze he had bereft thee of thy life he was fain to drag thee oft around the tomb of his comrade, even Patroklos whom thou slewest, yet might he not raise him up thereby. But now all dewy and fresh thou liest in our halls, like one on whom Apollo, lord of the silver bow, hath descended and slain him with his gentle darts."

Thus spake she wailing, and stirred unending moan. Then thirdly Helen led their sore lament: "Hector, of all my brethren of Troy far dearest to my heart! Truly my lord is godlike Alexandros[3] who brought me to Troy-land — would I had died ere then. For this is now the twentieth year since I went thence and am gone from my own native land, but never yet heard I evil or despiteful word from thee; nay, if any other haply upbraided me in the palace-halls, whether brother or sister of thine or brother's fair-robed wife, or thy mother — but thy father is ever kind to me as he were my own — then wouldst thou soothe such with words and refrain them, by the gentleness of thy spirit and by thy gentle words. Therefore bewail I thee with pain at heart, and my hapless self with thee, for no more is any

---

[2] In Euripides' play, Andromache's son is murdered in just this manner.
[3] Another name for Paris.

left in wide Troy-land to be my friend and kind to me, but all men shudder at me."[4]

Thucydides

THE MELIAN CONFERENCE AND THE FATE OF MELOS

(from *The Peloponnesian War*, Bk. V, Chap. XVII)*

*T*he next summer Alcibiades sailed with twenty ships to Argos and seized the suspected persons still left of the Lacedaemonian faction to the number of three hundred, whom the Athenians forthwith lodged in the neighbouring islands of their empire. The Athenians also made an expedition against the isle of Melos with thirty ships of their own, six Chian, and two Lesbian vessels, sixteen hundred heavy infantry, three hundred archers, and twenty mounted archers from Athens, and about fifteen hundred heavy infantry from the allies and the islanders. The Melians are a colony of Lacedaemon that would not submit to the Athenians like the other islanders, and at first remained neutral and took no part in the struggle, but afterwards upon the Athenians using violence and plundering their territory, assumed an attitude of open hostility. Cleomedes, son of Lycomedes, and Tisias, son of Tisimachus, the generals, encamping in their territory with the above armament, before doing any harm to their land, sent envoys to negotiate. These the Melians did not bring before the people, but bade them state the object of their mission to the magistrates and the few; upon which the Athenian envoys spoke as follows: —

Athenians. — "Since the negotiations are not to go on before the people, in order that we may not be able to speak straight on without interruption, and deceive the ears of the multitude by seductive arguments which would pass without refutation (for we know that this is the meaning of our being brought before the few), what if you who sit there were to pursue a method more cautious still! Make no set speech yourselves, but take us up at whatever you do not like, and settle that before going any farther. And first tell us if this proposition of ours suits you."

The Melian commissioners answered: —

Melians. — "To the fairness of quietly instructing each other as you propose there is nothing to object; but your military preparations are too far advanced to agree with what you say, as we see you are

---

[4] This is, of course, a much more sympathetic portrait of Helen than Euripides gives us.

* Translated by Richard Crawley.

come to be judges in your own cause, and that all we can reasonably expect from this negotiation is war, if we prove to have right on our side and refuse to submit, and in the contrary case, slavery."

Athenians. — "If you have met to reason about presentiments of the future, or for anything else than to consult for the safety of your state upon the facts that you see before you, we will give over; otherwise we will go on."

Melians. — "It is natural and excusable for men in our position to turn more ways than one both in thought and utterance. However, the question in this conference is, as you say, the safety of our country; and the discussion, if you please, can proceed in the way which you propose."

Athenians. — "For ourselves, we shall not trouble you with specious pretences — either of how we have a right to our empire because we overthrew the Mede, or are now attacking you because of wrong that you have done us — and make a long speech which would not be believed; and in return we hope that you, instead of thinking to influence us by saying that you did not join the Lacedaemonians, although their colonists, or that you have done us no wrong, will aim at what is feasible, holding in view the real sentiments of us both; since you know as well as we do that right, as the world goes, is only in question between equals in power, while the strong do what they can and the weak suffer what they must."

Melians. — "As we think, at any rate, it is expedient — we speak as we are obliged, since you enjoin us to let right alone and talk only of interest — that you should not destroy what is our common protection, the privilege of being allowed in danger to invoke what is fair and right, and even to profit by arguments not strictly valid if they can be got to pass current. And you are as much interested in this as any, as your fall would be a signal for the heaviest vengeance and an example for the world to meditate upon."

Athenians. — "The end of our empire, if end it should, does not frighten us: a rival empire like Lacedaemon, even if Lacedaemon was our real antagonist, is not so terrible to the vanquished as subjects who by themselves attack and overpower their rulers. This, however, is a risk that we are content to take. We will now proceed to show you that we are come here in the interest of our empire, and that we shall say what we are now going to say, for the preservation of your country; as we would fain exercise that empire over you without trouble, and see you preserved for the good of us both."

Melians. — "And how, pray, could it turn out as good for us to serve as for you to rule?"

Athenians. — "Because you would have the advantage of submitting before suffering the worst, and we should gain by not destroying you."

Melians. — "So that you would not consent to our being neutral, friends instead of enemies, but allies of neither side."

Athenians. — "No; for your hostility cannot so much hurt us as your friendship will be an argument to our subjects of our weakness, and your enmity of our power."

Melians. — "Is that your subjects' idea of equity, to put those who have nothing to do with you in the same category with peoples that are most of them your own colonists, and some conquered rebels?"

Athenians. — "As far as right goes they think one has as much of it as the other, and that if any maintain their independence it is because they are strong, and that if we do not molest them it is because we are afraid; so that besides extending our empire we should gain in security by your subjection; the fact that you are islanders and weaker than others rendering it all the more important that you should not succeed in baffling the masters of the sea."

Melians. — "But do you consider that there is no security in the policy which we indicate? For here again if you debar us from talking about justice and invite us to obey your interest, we also must explain ours, and try to persuade you, if the two happen to coincide. How can you avoid making enemies of all existing neutrals who shall look at our case and conclude from it that one day or another you will attack them? And what is this but to make greater the enemies that you have already, and to force others to become so who would otherwise have never thought of it?"

Athenians. — "Why, the fact is that continentals generally give us but little alarm; the liberty which they enjoy will long prevent their taking precautions against us; it is rather islanders like yourselves, outside our empire, and subjects smarting under the yoke, who would be the most likely to take a rash step and lead themselves and us into obvious danger."

Melians. — "Well then, if you risk so much to retain your empire, and your subjects to get rid of it, it were surely great baseness and cowardice in us who are still free not to try everything that can be tried, before submitting to your yoke."

Athenians. — "Not if you are well advised, the contest not being an equal one, with honour as the prize and shame as the penalty, but a question of self-preservation and of not resisting those who are far stronger than you are."

Melians. — "But we know that the fortune of war is sometimes more impartial than the disproportion of numbers might lead one to suppose; to submit is to give ourselves over to despair, while action still preserves for us a hope that we may stand erect."

Athenians. — "Hope, danger's comforter, may be indulged in by those who have abundant resources, if not without loss at all events without ruin; but its nature is to be extravagant, and those who go

so far as to put their all upon the venture see it in its true colours
only when they are ruined; but so long as the discovery would enable
them to guard against it, it is never found wanting. Let not this be
the case with you, who are weak and hang on a single turn of the
scale; nor be like the vulgar, who, abandoning such security as human
means may still afford, when visible hopes fail them in extremity, turn
to invisible, to prophecies and oracles, and other such inventions that
delude men with hopes to their destruction."

Melians. — "You may be sure that we are as well aware as you of
the difficulty of contending against your power and fortune, unless
the terms be equal. But we trust that the gods may grant us fortune
as good as yours, since we are just men fighting against unjust, and
that what we want in power will be made up by the alliance of the
Lacedaemonians, who are bound, if only for very shame, to come to
the aid of their kindred. Our confidence, therefore, after all is not so
utterly irrational."

Athenians. — "When you speak of the favour of the gods, we may
as fairly hope for that as yourselves; neither our pretensions nor our
conduct being in any way contrary to what men believe of the gods,
or practise among themselves. Of the gods we believe, and of men
we know, that by a necessary law of their nature they rule wherever
they can. And it is not as if we were the first to make this law, or to
act upon it when made: we found it existing before us, and shall
leave it to exist for ever after us; all we do is to make use of it, knowing that you and everybody else, having the same power as we have,
would do the same as we do. Thus, as far as the gods are concerned,
we have no fear and no reason to fear that we shall be at a disad-
vantage. But when we come to your notion about the Lacedaemonians,
which leads you to believe that shame will make them help you, here
we bless your simplicity but do not envy your folly. The Lacedaemonians, when their own interests or their country's laws are in question, are the worthiest men alive; of their conduct towards others
much might be said, but no clearer idea of it could be given than by
shortly saying that of all the men we know they are most conspicuous in considering what is agreeable honourable, and what is
expedient just. Such a way of thinking does not promise much for
the safety which you now unreasonably count upon."

Melians. — "But it is for this very reason that we now trust to
their respect for expediency to prevent them from betraying the
Melians, their colonists, and thereby losing the confidence of their
friends in Hellas and helping their enemies."

Athenians. — "Then you do not adopt the view that expediency
goes with security, while justice and honour cannot be followed without danger; and danger the Lacedaemonians generally court as little
as possible."

Melians. — "But we believe that they would be more likely to face even danger for our sake, and with more confidence than for others, as our nearness to Peloponnese makes it easier for them to act, and our common blood insures our fidelity."

Athenians. — "Yes, but what an intending ally trusts to, is not the goodwill of those who ask his aid, but a decided superiority of power for action; and the Lacedaemonians look to this even more than others. At least, such is their distrust of their home resources that it is only with numerous allies that they attack a neighbour; now is it likely that while we are masters of the sea they will cross over to an island?"

Melians. — "But they would have others to send. The Cretan sea is a wide one, and it is more difficult for those who command it to intercept others, than for those who wish to elude them to do so safely. And should the Lacedaemonians miscarry in this, they would fall upon your land, and upon those left of your allies whom Brasidas did not reach; and instead of places which are not yours, you will have to fight for your own country and your own confederacy."

Athenians. — "Some diversion of the kind you speak of you may one day experience, only to learn, as others have done, that the Athenians never once yet withdrew from a siege for fear of any. But we are struck by the fact, that after saying you would consult for the safety of your country, in all this discussion you have mentioned nothing which men might trust in and think to be saved by. Your strongest arguments depend upon hope and the future, and your actual resources are too scanty, as compared with those arrayed against you, for you to come out victorious. You will therefore show great blindness of judgment, unless, after allowing us to retire, you can find some counsel more prudent than this. You will surely not be caught by the idea of disgrace, which in dangers that are disgraceful, and at the same time too plain to be mistaken, proves so fatal to mankind; since in too many cases the very men that have their eyes perfectly open to what they are rushing into, let the thing called disgrace, by the mere influence of a seductive name, lead them on to a point at which they become so enslaved by the phrase as in fact to fall wilfully into hopeless disaster, and incur disgrace more disgraceful as the companion of error, than when it comes as the result of misfortune. This, if you are well advised, you will guard against; and you will not think it dishonourable to submit to the greatest city in Hellas, when it makes you the moderate offer of becoming its tributary ally, without ceasing to enjoy the country that belongs to you; nor when you have the choice given you between war and security, will you be so blinded as to choose the worse. And it is certain that those who do not yield to their equals, who keep terms with their superiors, and are moderate towards their inferiors, on the whole succeed best. Think over the matter, therefore, after our withdrawal, and reflect once and again that it is for your country that you are consulting, that you have not more than one, and that upon this one deliberation depends its prosperity or ruin."

The Athenians now withdrew from the conference; and the Melians, left to themselves, came to a decision corresponding with what they had maintained in the discussion, and answered, "Our resolution, Athenians, is the same as it was at first. We will not in a moment deprive of freedom a city that has been inhabited these seven hundred years; but we put our trust in the fortune by which the gods have preserved it until now, and in the help of men, that is, of the Lacedaemonians; and so we will try and save ourselves. Meanwhile we invite you to allow us to be friends to you and foes to neither party, and to retire from our country after making such a treaty as shall seem fit to us both."

Such was the answer of the Melians. The Athenians now departing from the conference said, "Well, you alone, as it seems to us, judging from these resolutions, regard what is future as more certain than what is before your eyes, and what is out of sight, in your eagerness, as already coming to pass; and as you have staked most on, and trusted most in, the Lacedaemonians, your fortune, and your hopes, so will you be most completely deceived."

The Athenian envoys now returned to the army; and the Melians showing no signs of yielding, the generals at once betook themselves to hostilities, and drew a line of circumvallation round the Melians, dividing the work among the different states. Subsequently the Athenians returned with most of their army, leaving behind them a certain number of their own citizens and of the allies to keep guard by land and sea. The force thus left stayed on and besieged the place.

About the same time the Argives invaded the territory of Phlius and lost eighty men cut off in an ambush by the Phliasians and Argive exiles. Meanwhile the Athenians at Pylos took so much plunder from the Lacedaemonians that the latter, although they still refrained from breaking off the treaty and going to war with Athens, yet proclaimed that any of their people that chose might plunder the Athenians. The Corinthians also commenced hostilities with the Athenians for private quarrels of their own; but the rest of the Peloponnesians stayed quiet. Meanwhile the Melians attacked by night and took the part of the Athenian lines over against the market, and killed some of the men, and brought in corn and all else that they could find useful to them, and so returned and kept quiet, while the Athenians took measures to keep better guard in future.

Summer was now over. The next winter the Lacedaemonians intended to invade the Argive territory, but arriving at the frontier found the sacrifices for crossing unfavourable, and went back again. This intention of theirs gave the Argives suspicions of certain of their fellow-citizens, some of whom they arrested; others, however, escaped them. About the same time the Melians again took another part of the Athenian lines which were but feebly garrisoned. Reinforcements afterwards arriving from Athens in consequence, under the command of Philocrates, son of Demeas, the siege was now pressed vigorously; and some treachery taking place inside, the Melians surrender at discretion to the Athenians, who put to death all the grown men whom they took, and sold the women and children for slaves, and subsequently sent out five hundred colonists and inhabited the place themselves.

IV

The Greek Chorus

⊠ One of the most distinctive features of Ancient Greek drama.
was the chorus. Indeed, as we have seen, tragedy may have
developed from a choral song, the dithyramb.

In the sixth century, at the time of Thespis, the number of
chorus members in tragedy was apparently fifty. This number
was altered to twelve by Aeschylus, then raised to fifteen by
Sophocles. Aeschylus followed the precedent set by his younger
rival in the Oresteian trilogy (458 B.C.). From that date until
the Hellenistic period, fifteen became the standard number in
the tragic chorus.

The structure of a typical Greek tragedy, as outlined by Aristotle
(see p. 22) and others, can be described as follows: after an expository
prologue, the chorus sang its entering or processional ode (*the
parados*)* as they danced into the orchestra from the west gateway.
After the *parados* came a scene between the characters of the drama
(*episode*), followed by the first choral interlude (*stasimon*). *Episodes*
(in which occasionally the leader of the chorus took part as well as the
actors) and *stasima* alternated until the action of the play was
complete, whereupon the chorus sang its recessional ode (*exodos*).

Not very much is known about the *emmeleia*, the dance executed by the chorus members during the *stasima*, except that,
in the fifth century at least, the movements were elegant and
graceful. Each *stasimon* is divided into three parts: the *strophe*,
the *antistrophe*, and the *epode*. Without considering technical
questions of metre, we might describe the *strophe* as a stanza
containing a complete unit of thought. The *antistrophe* is another stanza, metrically identical with the *strophe*, containing
still another unit of complementary thought. After a series of
alternating *strophes* and *antistrophes*, the *epode* or short concluding stanza is sung. The meaning of the words, *strophe*
(turn) and *antistrophe* (counter-turn), have led some scholars
to assume that during the *strophe* the chorus dancing in block
formation executed a number of figures while moving in one direction, then for the *antistrophe* turned abruptly around and performed the mirror image of those movements until it had arrived
at its initial position.

Professor Roy C. Flickinger has calculated that in all but one of
the extant plays of Aeschylus the chorus occupies from one-half to

---

* Sometimes spelled *parodus*.

three-fifths of the elapsed stage time. The percentage in the plays of Sophocles and Euripides is somewhat smaller, but in the works of both these younger dramatists the choral function remains extremely important.

Just what dramatic purposes does the chorus serve? First of all, the chorus provides a sense of community involvement in the issue of the action. This function, it might be noted, is one of the distinctive features of ancient drama. In most modern plays, the fate of the hero has little significance for anyone but himself and his family or friends. In *Oedipus Rex*, however, the unwitting crime of Oedipus is reflected in the misfortunes of a whole community, and the chorus is our constant reminder of that fact. The chorus serves also on occasions as the spokesman for compromise, for the everyday point of view as opposed to the heroic, unbending attitude of the hour. It provides, in other words, the necessary background for the heroic act. Without a reminder of how ordinary people think and behave, it might be impossible to recognize how extraordinary is the behavior of Oedipus or Electra or Hecuba.

At times, however, the chorus ceases to behave as the representative of the fears and small selfish concerns of typical humanity and serves instead as a kind of lyrical commentator on the action, as a spokesman for the right point of view. Some modern critics have argued that this last use of the chorus is inconsistent with its other uses. But to see inconsistency in the chorus is to view ancient drama from the somewhat limited point of view of the modern realist. The Greek theatre was not a realistic theatre, and consistency of characterization was not considered by Sophocles or Euripides a necessary dramatic virtue. The chorus is a flexible instrument, which can sometimes operate as a part of the time scheme of the play and sometimes stand back from the action to deliver a timeless comment.

No one has written more perceptively about the use of the chorus in tragedy than the German playwright Friedrich von Schiller (1759–1805), who in 1803 attempted, not entirely successfully, to restore the chorus to its ancient dignity in his drama *The Bride of Messina*. The preface to that play, reprinted here, remains an important critical document. Its observations appear as applicable to the theatre of fifth-century Athens as they are to the theatre of nineteenth-century Germany.

Friedrich von Schiller

ON THE USE OF THE CHORUS IN TRAGEDY*

A poetical work must vindicate itself: — if the execution be defective, little aid can be derived from commentaries.

On these grounds, I might safely leave the Chorus to be its own advocate, if we had ever seen it presented in an appropriate manner. But it must be remembered that a dramatic composition first assumes the character of a whole by means of representation on the stage. The Poet supplies only the words, to which, in a lyrical tragedy, music and rhythmical motion are essential accessories. It follows, then, that if the Chorus is deprived of accompaniments appealing so powerfully to the senses, it will appear a superfluity in the economy of the drama — a mere hindrance to the development of the plot — destructive to the illusion of the scene, and wearisome to the spectators.

To do justice to the Chorus, more especially if our aims in Poetry be of a grand and elevated character, we must transport ourselves from the actual to a possible stage. It is the privilege of Art to furnish for itself whatever is requisite, and the accidental deficiency of auxiliaries ought not to confine the plastic imagination of the Poet. He aspires to whatever is most dignified, he labours to realize the ideal in his own mind — though in the execution of his purpose he must needs accommodate himself to circumstances.

The assertion so commonly made, that the Public degrades Art, is not well founded. It is the artist that brings the Public to the level of his own conceptions; and, in every age in which Art has gone to decay, it has fallen through its professors. The People need feeling alone, and feeling they possess. They take their station before the curtain with an unvoiced longing, with a multifarious capacity. They bring with them an aptitude for what is highest — they derive the greatest pleasure from what is judicious and true; and if, with these powers of appreciation, they begin to be satisfied with inferior productions, still, if they have once tasted what is excellent, they will, in the end, insist on having it supplied to them.

It is sometimes objected that the Poet may labour according to an Ideal — that the critic may judge from ideas, but that mere executive art is subject to contingencies, and depends for effect on the occasion. Managers will be obstinate; actors are bent on display — the audience is inattentive and unruly. Their object is relaxation, and they are

* From *The Works of Frederick Schiller*, translated from the German (London, 1872), III, 439–444. The English version of this essay is by A. Lodge.

disappointed if mental exertion be required, when they expected only amusement. But if the Theatre be made instrumental towards higher objects, the pleasure of the spectator will not be increased, but ennobled. It will be a diversion, but a poetical one. All Art is dedicated to pleasure, and there can be no higher and worthier end than to make men happy. The true Art is that which provides the highest degree of pleasure; and this consists in the abandonment of the spirit to the free play of all its faculties.

Every one expects from the imaginative arts a certain emancipation from the bounds of reality: we are willing to give a scope to Fancy, and recreate ourselves with the possible. The man who expects it the least will nevertheless forget his ordinary pursuits, his every-day existence and individuality, and experience delight from uncommon incidents: — if he be of a serious turn of mind, he will acknowledge on the stage that moral government of the world which he fails to discover in real life. But he is, at the same time, perfectly aware that all is an empty show, and that, in a true sense, he is feeding only on dreams. When he returns from the theatre to the world of realities, he is again compressed within its narrow bounds; he is its denizen as before — for it remains what it was, and in him nothing has been changed. What, then, has he gained beyond a momentary illusive pleasure which vanished with the occasion?

It is because a passing recreation is alone desired, that a mere show of truth is thought sufficient. I mean that probability or vraisemblance which is so highly esteemed, but which the commonest workers are able to substitute for the true.

Art has for its object not merely to afford a transient pleasure, to excite to a momentary dream of liberty; its aim is to make us absolutely free; and this it accomplishes by awakening, exercising, and perfecting in us a power to remove to an objective distance the sensible world (which otherwise only burdens us as rugged matter, and presses us down with a brute influence), to transform it into the free working of our spirit, and thus acquire a dominion over the material by means of ideas. For the very reason also that true Art requires somewhat of the objective and real, it is not satisfied with a show of truth. It rears its ideal edifice on Truth itself — on the solid and deep foundations of Nature.

But how Art can be at once altogether ideal, yet in the strictest sense real; — how it can entirely leave the actual, and yet harmonize with Nature, is a problem to the multitude: — and hence the distorted views which prevail in regard to poetical and plastic works; for to ordinary judgments these two requisites seem to counteract each other.

It is commonly supposed that one may be attained by the sacrifice of the other: — the result is a failure to arrive at either. One to whom nature has given a true sensibility, but denied the plastic imaginative power, will be a faithful painter of the real; he will adapt casual appearances, but never catch the spirit of Nature. He will only reproduce to us the matter of the world, which, not being our own work, the product of our creative spirit, can never have the beneficent operation of Art, of which the essence is freedom. Serious, indeed, but unpleasing, is the cast of thought with which such an artist and poet dismisses us; — we feel ourselves painfully thrust back into the narrow sphere of reality by means of the very art which ought to have emancipated us. On the other hand, a writer, endowed with a lively fancy, but destitute of warmth and individuality of feeling, will not concern himself in the least about truth; he will sport with the stuff of the world, and endeavour to surprise by whimsical combinations; and as his whole performance is nothing but foam and glitter, he will, it is true, engage the attention for a time, but build up and confirm nothing in the understanding. His playfulness is, like the gravity of the other, thoroughly unpoetical. To string together at will fantastical images, is not to travel into the realm of the ideal; and the imitative reproduction of the actual cannot be called the representation of nature. Both requisites stand so little in contradiction to each other that they are rather one and the same thing; that Art is only true insomuch as it altogether forsakes the actual, and becomes purely ideal. Nature herself is an idea of the mind, and is never presented to the senses. She lies under the veil of appearances, but is herself never apparent. To the art of the ideal alone is lent, or rather, absolutely given, the privilege to grasp the spirit of the All, and bind it in a corporeal form.

Yet, in truth, even Art cannot present it to the senses, but by means of her creative power to the imaginative faculty alone; and it is thus that she becomes more true than all reality, and more real than all experience. It follows from these premises that the artist can use no single element taken from reality as he finds it — that his work must be ideal in all its parts, if it be designed to have, as it were, an intrinsic reality, and to harmonize with nature.

What is true of Art and Poetry, in the abstract, holds good as to their various kinds; and we may apply what has been advanced to the subject of tragedy. In this department, it is still necessary to controvert the ordinary notion of the natural, with which poetry is altogether incompatible. A certain ideality has been allowed in painting, though I fear, rather for conventional reasons, than on grounds of conviction; but in dramatic works what is desired is illusion, which, if it could be accomplished by means of the actual, would be, at best, a paltry deception. All the externals of a theatrical representation are opposed to this notion; all is merely a symbol of the real. The day itself in a theatre is an artificial one; the metrical dialogue is itself ideal; yet the conduct of the play must forsooth be real, and the general effect sacrificed to a part. Thus the French, who have utterly misconceived the spirit of the ancients, adopted on their stage the unities of time and place in the most common and empirical sense; as though there were any place but the bare ideal one, or any other time than the mere sequence of the incidents.

By the introduction of a metrical dialogue an important progress has been made towards the poetical Tragedy. A few lyrical dramas have been successful on the stage, and Poetry, by its own living energy, has triumphed over prevailing prejudices. But so long as these erroneous views are entertained little has been done — for it is not enough barely to tolerate as a poetic license that which, is in truth, the essence of all poetry. The introduction of the Chorus would be the last and decisive step; and if it only served this end, namely, to declare open and honourable warfare against naturalism in art, it would be for us a living wall which Tragedy had drawn around herself, to guard her from contact with the world of reality, and maintain her own ideal soil, her poetical freedom.

It is well known that the Greek tragedy had its origin in the Chorus; and though, in process of time, it became independent, still it may be said that poetically, and in spirit, the Chorus was the source of its existence, and that without these persevering supporters and witnesses of the incident a totally different order of poetry would have grown out of the drama. The abolition of the Chorus, and the debasement of this sensibly powerful organ into the characterless substitute of a confidant, is, by no means, such an improvement in tragedy as the French, and their imitators, would have it supposed to be.

The old Tragedy, which at first only concerned itself with gods, heroes and kings, introduced the Chorus as an essential accompaniment. The poets found it in nature, and for that reason employed it. It grew out of the poetical aspect of real life. In the new Tragedy it becomes an organ of art which aids in making the poetry prominent. The modern poet no longer finds the Chorus in nature; he must needs create and introduce it poetically; that is, he must resolve on such an adaptation of his story as will admit of its retrocession to those primitive times, and to that simple form of life.

The Chorus thus renders more substantial service to the modern dramatist than to the old poet — and for this reason, that it transforms the commonplace actual world into the old poetical one; that it enables him to dispense with all that is repugnant to poetry, and conducts him back to the most simple, original, and genuine motives of action. The palaces of kings are in these days closed — courts of

justice have been transferred from the gates of cities to the interior
of buildings; writing has narrowed the province of speech; the people
itself — the sensibly living mass — when it does not operate as brute
force, has become a part of the civil polity, and thereby an
abstract idea in our minds; the deities have returned within the
bosoms of mankind. The poet must reopen the palaces — he must
place courts of justice beneath the canopy of heaven — restore the
gods, reproduce every extreme which the artificial frame of actual
life has abolished — throw aside every factitious influence on the
mind or condition of man which impedes the manifestation of his inward nature and primitive character, as the statuary rejects modern
costume: — and of all external circumstances adopts nothing but
what is palpable in the highest of forms — that of humanity.

But precisely as the painter throws around his figures draperies
of ample volume, to fill up the space of his picture richly and gracefully, to arrange its several parts in harmonious masses, to give due
play to colour, which charms and refreshes the eye — and at once to
envelop human forms in a spiritual veil, and make them visible —
so the tragic poet inlays and entwines his rigidly contracted plot and
the strong outlines of his characters with a tissue of lyrical magnifi-
cence, in which, as in flowing robes of purple, they move freely and
nobly, with a sustained dignity and exalted repose.

In a higher organization, the material, or the elementary, need
not be visible; the chemical colour vanishes in the finer tints of
the imaginative one. The material, however, has its peculiar effect,
and may be included in an artistical composition. But it must deserve its place by animation, fulness and harmony, and give value to
the ideal forms which it surrounds, instead of stifling them by its
weight.

In respect of the pictorial art, this is obvious to ordinary apprehension, yet in poetry likewise, and in the tragical kind, which is our
immediate subject, the same doctrine holds good. Whatever fascinates
the senses alone, is mere matter, and the rude element of a work of
art: — if it take the lead it will inevitably destroy the poetical —
which lies at the exact medium between the ideal and the sensible.
But man is so constituted that he is ever impatient to pass from what
is fanciful to what is common; and reflection must, therefore, have its
place even in tragedy. But to merit this place it must, by means of
delivery, recover what it wants in actual life; for if the two elements
of poetry, the ideal and the sensible, do not operate with an inward
mutuality, they must at least act as allies — or poetry is out of the
question. If the balance be not intrinsically perfect, the equipoise
can only be maintained by an agitation of both scales.

This is what the Chorus effects in tragedy. It is, in itself, not an individual but a general conception, yet it is represented by a palpable body which appeals to the senses with an imposing grandeur. It forsakes the contracted sphere of the incidents to dilate itself over the past and the future, over distant times and nations, and general humanity, to deduce the grand results of life, and pronounce the lessons of wisdom. But all this it does with the full power of fancy — with a bold lyrical freedom which ascends, as with godlike step, to the topmost height of worldly things; and it effects it in conjunction with the whole sensible influences of melody and rhythm, in tones and movements.

The Chorus thus exercises a purifying influence on tragic poetry, insomuch as it keeps reflection apart from the incidents, and by this separation arms it with a poetical vigour; as the painter, by means of a rich drapery, changes the ordinary poverty of costume into a charm and an ornament.

But as the painter finds himself obliged to strengthen the tone of colour of the living subject, in order to counterbalance the material influences — so the lyrical effusions of the Chorus impose upon the poet the necessity of a proportionate elevation of his general diction. It is the Chorus alone which entitles the poet to employ this fulness of tone, which at once charms the senses, pervades the spirit and expands the mind. This one giant form on his canvas obliges him to mount all his figures on the cothurnus, and thus impart a tragical grandeur to his picture. If the Chorus be taken away, the diction of the tragedy must generally be lowered, or what is now great and majestic will appear forced and overstrained. The old Chorus introduced into the French tragedy would present it in all its poverty, and reduce it to nothing; yet, without doubt, the same accompaniment would impart to Shakespeare's tragedy its true significance.

As the Chorus gives life to the language — so also it gives repose to the action; but it is that beautiful and lofty repose which is the characteristic of a true work of art. For the mind of the spectator ought to maintain its freedom through the most impassioned scenes; it should not be the mere prey of impressions, but calmly and severely detach itself from the emotions which it suffers. The commonplace objection made to the Chorus, that it disturbs the illusion, and blunts the edge of the feelings, is what constitutes its highest recommendation; for it is this blind force of the affections which the true artist deprecates — this illusion is what he disdains to excite. If the strokes which Tragedy inflicts on our bosoms followed without respite — the passion would overpower the action. We should mix ourselves up with the subject matter, and no longer stand above it. It is by holding asunder the different parts, and stepping between the passions with its composing views, that the Chorus restores to us our freedom, which would else be lost in the tempest. The characters of the drama need this intermission in order to collect themselves; for they are no real beings who obey the impulse of the moment, and merely represent individuals — but ideal persons and representatives of their species, who enunciate the deep things of Humanity.

Thus much on my attempt to revive the old Chorus on the tragic stage. It is true that choruses are not unknown to modern tragedy; but the Chorus of the Greek drama, as I have employed it — the Chorus, as a single ideal person, furthering and accompanying the whole plot — is of an entirely distinct character; and when, in discussion on the Greek tragedy, I hear mention made of choruses, I generally suspect the speaker's ignorance of his subject. In my view the Chorus has never been reproduced since the decline of the old tragedy.

I have divided it into two parts, and represented it in contest with itself; but this occurs where it acts as a real person, and as an unthinking multitude. As Chorus and an ideal person it is always one and entire. I have also several times dispensed with its presence on the stage. For this liberty I have the example of Aeschylus, the creator of tragedy, and Sophocles, the greatest master of his art. . . .

V
Old Comedy and New

Critical pronouncements on ancient comedy are scarce. Aristotle's book on the subject has been lost, and even his observations on the origin of the highly popular art are tantalizingly brief. The word "comedy" in his view, is derived from the Greek *komos* (or *comus*), which was apparently the name for a primitive sixth-century processional entertainment combining extemporal wit (much of it based on personal invective), boisterous drunken dancing, and frenzied choral chant. The steps by which this phallic and loosely structured entertainment developed into the elaborate satires of Aristophanes (c. 448-380 B.C.) and the other fifth-century writers (referred to as Old Comedy) are not known. However, it is clear that Old Comedy retained many of the features of the improvised revels from which it had sprung.

A typical Aristophanic play begins with a prologue in which a character presents a fantastic idea. Following the prologue a chorus of twenty-four, hostile to the idea, enters. The idea is then debated during the *agon* with the chorus eventually convinced. Then comes a choral ode called the *parabasis*, a direct address to the audience by the playwright, usually unrelated to the action of the drama. Following the *parabasis* comes a series of episodes and odes showing the results of the fantastic idea, and the play concludes with a final song during which the *kordax*, a drunken dance, is performed by the chorus and the principal actors. The humor of the play is typically broad and coarse; frequently real persons are burlesqued. (Socrates himself, for example, is the target of a savage lampoon in *The Clouds*. Euripides is also a frequent butt of Aristophanic jokes, as is the tyrant Cleon.)

By contrast, Hellenistic or New Comedy, of which Menander (342-291 B.C.) is the chief representative, is tame indeed. Intended for the members of the new leisure class, who composed most of the typical audience after the defeat of Athens by Alexander (338 B.C.), New Comedy is the first comedy of manners. Gone is the chorus except as a kind of intermission entertainment between episodes. Gone too are the parabasis, the phallic atmosphere, the fantastic setting and the satirical tone. The comedy is built around a series of intrigues involving the upper-class citizens of Athens and their immediate circle of acquaintances. Stock characters (many of them based on types described by the philosopher Theophrastus, in his treatise *Ethical Characters*) recur in play after play, and Menander and his colleagues prided themselves on their ability to make nice distinctions between apparently similar

73

types.

Menander's humor is certainly more sophisticated than Aristophanes', and instead of a loose arrangement of satirical incidents, the fourth-century playwright offered his audiences a carefully constructed intrigue plot. The inspiration for that kind of plot comes not from any comic writer, but from Euripides whose "tragedy" *Ion* anticipates many features of Hellenistic comedy.

The modern taste prefers Aristophanes and misses in Menander the great profusion and vitality of the older poet. Still the latter remained the more popular with ancient commentators as this abstract from Plutarch (written in the first century A.D.) clearly indicates.

The felicities of Menander's style and his neatly turned moral epigrams recommended him to an audience that would have found the wild fantastic world of Aristophanes excessively coarse and strange.

And, as we know, the future belonged to the comedy of manners.

Plutarch

AN ABSTRACT OF A COMPARISON BETWIXT ARISTOPHANES AND MENANDER*

To speak in sum and in general, he prefers Menander by far; and as to particulars, he adds what here ensues. Aristophanes, he saith, is importune, theatric, and sordid in his expression; but Menander not so at all. For the rude and vulgar person is taken with the things the former speaketh; but the well-bred man will be quite out of humor with them. I mean, his opposed terms, his words of one cadence, and his derivatives. For the one makes use of these with due observance and but seldom, and bestows care upon them; but the other frequently, unseasonably, and frigidly. "For he is much commended," said he, "for ducking the chamberlains, they being indeed not chamberlains but bugbears." And again,—"This rascal breathes out nothing but roguery and affidavitry;" and "Beat him well in his belly with the entrails and the guts;" and, "I shall laugh till I go to Laughington;" and, "Thou poor sharded ostracized pot, what shall I do with thee?" and, "To you women surely he is a mad plague, for he grew up himself among these mad worts;"—and, "Look here, how the moths have eaten away my crest;" and, "Bring me hither the gorgon-backed circle of my shield;"—and much more of such like stuff. There is then in

*From *Plutarch's Essays and Miscellanies* (Boston: Little, Brown and Co., 1909), III, 11-14; translated by William Baxter, Gent.

the structure of his words something tragic and something comic, something blustering and something prosaic, an obscurity, a vulgarness, a turgidness, and a strutting, with a nauseous prattling and fooling. And as his style has so great varieties and dissonances in it, so neither doth he give to his persons what is fitting and proper to each, — as state (for instance) to a prince, force to an orator, innocence to a woman, meanness of language to a poor man, and sauciness to a tradesman, — but he deals out to every person, as it were by lot, such words as come next to his hand, and you would scarce discern whether he that is talking be a son, a father, a peasant, a God, an old woman, or a hero.

2. But now Menander's phrase is so well turned and contempered with itself, and so everywhere conspiring, that, while it traverses many passions and humors and is accommodated to all sorts of persons, it still shows the same, and even retains its semblance in trite, familiar, and everyday expressions. And if his master do now and then require something of rant and noise, he doth but (like a skilful flutist) set open all the holes of his pipe, and then presently stop them again with good decorum and restore the tune to its natural state. And though there be a great number of excellent artists of all professions, yet never did any shoemaker make the same sort of shoe, or tireman the same sort of visor, or tailor the same sort of garment, to fit a man, a woman, a child, an old man, and a slave. But Menander hath so addressed his style, as to proportion it to every sex, condition, and age; and this, though he took the business in hand when he was very young, and died in the vigor of his composition and action, when, as Aristotle tells us, authors receive most and greatest improvement in their styles. If a man shall then compare the middle and the last with the first of Menander's plays, he will by them easily conceive what others he would have added to them, had he had but longer life.

3. He adds further that of dramatic exhibitors, some address themselves to the crowd and populace, and others again to a few; but it is a hard matter to say which of them all knew what was befitting in both the kinds. But Aristophanes is neither grateful to the vulgar, nor tolerable to the wise; but it fares with his poesy as it doth with a courtesan who, when she finds she is now stricken and past her prime, counterfeits a sober matron, and then the vulgar cannot endure her affectation, and the better sort abominate her lewdness and wicked nature. But Menander hath with his charms shown himself every way sufficient for satisfaction, being the sole lecture, argument, and dispute at theatres, schools, and at tables; hereby rendering his poesy the most universal ornament that was ever produced by Greece, and showing what and how extraordinary his ability in language was, while he passes every way with an irresistible persuasion, and wins

every man's ear and understanding who has knowledge of the Greek tongue. And for what other reason in truth should a man of parts and erudition be at pains to frequent the theatre, but for the sake of Menander only? And when are the play-houses better filled with men of letters, than when his comic mask is exhibited? And at private entertainments among friends, for whom doth the table more justly make room or Bacchus give place than for Menander? To philosophers also and hard students (as painters are wont, when they have tired out their eyes at their work, to divert them to certain florid and green colors) Menander is a repose from their auditors and intense thinkings, and entertains their minds with gay shady meadows refreshed with cool and gentle breezes.

4. He adds, moreover, that though this city breeds at this time very many and excellent representers of comedy, Menander's plays participate of a plenteous and divine salt, as if they were made of the very sea out of which Venus herself sprang. But that of Aristophanes is harsh and coarse and hath in it an angry and biting sharpness. And for my part I cannot tell where his so much boasted ability lies, whether in his style or persons. The parts he acts I am sure are quite over-acted and depraved. His knave (for instance) is not fine, but dirty; his peasant is not assured, but stupid; his droll is not jocose, but ridiculous; and his lover is not gay, but lewd. So that to me the man seems not to have written his poesy for any temperate person, but to have intended his smut and obscenity for the debauched and lewd, his invective and satire for the malicious and ill-humored.

Only one complete play and several lengthy fragments by Menander have survived to the present day. And we have nothing at all by Diphilus, Philemon and the sixty-plus other authors of Greek New Comedy.

In fact we know the form mostly through the plays of Titus Maxxius Plautus (254-184 B.C.) and Publius Terentius Afer, "Terence" (185?-159 B.C.), the two great dramatists of Republican Rome. Plautus and Terence wrote *fabula palliata*, that is to say, stories in Greek dress,[1] or, to put the matter more plainly, adaptations from Greek New Comedy.

How free were these adaptations? In matters of plot and characterization, not very free at all. But both authors were masters of colloquial Latin, and although forced by custom to masquerade as translators, they were writers of great humor and originality.

[1] *Pallium* was the Latin name for a Greek cloak.

Their work is the link between antiquity and the Renaissance. It was not the Greek writers who were rediscovered in the fifteenth century, but the Romans, and it would be impossible to overestimate Roman influence on subsequent drama.

Plautus and Terence were produced during the sixteenth century in Spain, Italy, France and England, both in Latin and vernacular translations. The stock situations and characters of New Comedy inspired many later authors. The parasites, cunning slaves, braggart warriors, lecherous old men and scolding wives of the Republican stage found new life in the plays of Shakespeare, Lope de Vega, Jonson, Molière, Machiavelli and many of their contemporaries. Falstaff, Polonius, Volpone, Mosca, Orgon, Dorine and Lope's Tristan, all have their progenitors in Roman comedy.[2]

Although Plautus and Terence both wrote *palliata*, and although both had a lasting influence on subsequent drama, their differences are as striking as their similarities. Plautus has often been described as a writer of raucous low comedies with a broad popular appeal. Terence, who needed to please a reading public as well as a viewing one, is considered the more sophisticated of the two and the possessor of the more refined wit.

Generalizations can be misleading, but Edith Hamilton in *The Roman Way* allows this one a certain validity. Clearly, she prefers the broad-chested fun of Plautus to the polite laughter of Terence but, of course, finds that both of them lack the fire of Aristophanes, that genius who founded no school and had no followers.

Edith Hamilton
THE ROMAN COMEDIES*

*I*f the Greek tragedians had been lost and we had only Aristophanes left, we should have a very fair idea of the private citizen in Periclean Athens. How little resemblance he had to the theatre-going man elsewhere, what a completely different sort of amusement he wanted, may be seen in every one of Aristophanes' plays. Aristophanes has his own receipt for comedy, unlike, so he himself tells us, all that went before him and certainly never followed by any dramatist since. In choruses of the

---

[2] Many important plays by later writers were based directly on Plautus and Terence. From Plautus comes Udal's *Ralph Roister Doister* (1553, *The Braggart Warrior*), Shakespeare's *Comedy of Errors* (ca. 1594, *The Menaechmi*), Jonson's *Epicene* (1609, *Casina*), Moliere's *The Miser* (1665, *The Pot of Gold*). Adaptations of Terence include Moliere's *School for Husbands* (1661, *The Brothers*) and *The Tricks of Scapin* (1611, *Phormio*), Wycherly's *The Country Wife* (1675, *The Eunuch*), Steele's *The Conscious Lovers* (1722, *The Girl from Andros*). The list is by no means comprehensive.

*From Edith Hamilton, *The Roman Way* (New York & London; W.W. Norton & Co., 1932), pp. 16 ff., abridged by the editor.

Wasps and the *Peace*, the methods are described which were used by the most popular playwright in Athens to draw his public:

> Your poet in all of his plays has scorned to show you upon the stage
> A few paltry men and their mean little ways. A great theme he gave
>   you—the age.
> He has stripped bare the monster with eyes flaming red, foul vice
>   with his vile perjured band.
> He has battled with spectral shapes, the pains and pangs that are
>   racking our land.[1]
> It was he that indignantly swept from the stage the rabble that
>   cluttered its boards,
> Greedy gods, vagabonds, swindling scamps, whining slaves, sturdy
>   beggars, despicable hordes.
> Such vulgar, contemptible lumber at once he bade from the theatre
>   depart,
> And then like an edifice stately and grand he raised and ennobled
>   the art.
> High thoughts and high language he brought to the stage, a humor
>   exalted and rare,
> Nor stooped with a scurrilous jest to assail some small-man-and-
>   woman affair.[2]

Here is clearly written what Aristophanes and his audience wanted from the Comic Muse. In their eyes she was great Comedy, fit to stand beside Tragedy, of equal dignity and with essentially the same deep seriousness. The Old Comedy of Athens stands alone. It is as unlike the comedy of all other countries and periods as the age of Pericles is unlike all others. No small-man-and-woman affair for Aristophanes. Great themes, a grandiose conception of the world, belonged to Comedy, as he saw her, just as much as they did to Tragedy, as Aeschylus saw her. That rabble he swept from the stage, those stock characters, each with his fixed form of antics, his thread-bare joke—"a few paltry men and their mean little way"—gave place to marvelous figures: birds building a city in the sky that put all earthly cities to shame; a band of tight-waisted buzzing wasps to show up the law-courts; radiant Peace in all her beauty; the inexorable world of the dead where art receives its final award. This was Aristophanes' idea of Comedy's province. It died with him and was never found again within the theatre.

The old kind of fun-making came to the fore when he and his audience were gone. That edict of banishment he had proclaimed in great Comedy's name did not hold beyond his lifetime. Back came the exiles, the tricky servant, the braggart, the quack, the drunkard, the cunning

---

[1] *Wasps*, v. 1027.
[2] *Peace*, v. 739.

thief, familiar stock characters, so his words tell us, four hundred years and more before Christ. The depth of our ignorance about the past is not often so vividly brought to mind. None of that crowded, busy theatre is known to us, nothing of what must often have been brilliant entertainment made by brilliant minds. A marvelous sense for the absurd and a very genius for observing and characterizing human nature put first upon the stage the personages which have held their place there ever since, with the brief exception of Aristophanes' lifetime. Latin comedy and through it all modern comedy have drawn upon the figures of fun unknown Greek playwrights made in the dim past. The small-man-and-woman affair, too, disdained by the great Athenian and his age, took lasting possession not only of the stage, but of literature as well. Aristophanes stands alone indeed. The men who fought at Salamis and planned the Acropolis and carved the Parthenon sculptures gave the laws to the Athenian drama, and when they died there was no audience any more for great Tragedy and great Comedy.

•••

The [fifth-century] theatre audiences ... were people of highly cultivated tastes who could not be amused with the commonplace. But fourth century Athens was another matter. The aristocrats were gone and democracy was in secure possession. There was no need of fighting and suffering in its behalf. Athens was comfortable and undistinguished; life was lived on an easy middle-class level. The New Comedy, one ancient writer after another assures us, reflected the age, in especial the chief ornament and exponent of the innovation, Menander. An enthusiastic Alexandrian exclaims: "O Life, O Menander, which of you two was the plagiarist?"

Of all his fellow artists he alone has survived, but only in small part. No complete play has come down to us.[3] Indeed, up to a few years ago he was directly known through short extracts merely, lines cited to illustrate some point, and the like. Indirectly, however, much was deduced from the unqualified praise and devoted imitation of him by ancient critics and writers. But the discovery of nearly the whole of one play and considerable portions of several others has made it dubious how far that great reputation was deserved. They are pleasantly written, these plays, the characters not infrequently drawn with skillful and delicate touches, the dialogue occasionally entertaining, the plot contrived with

[3] Since Hamilton wrote this essay, a complete play by Menander has been discovered. It has been translated variously under the titles *The Curmudgeon* and *The Testy Old Man*.

some ingenuity; but more than that cannot be said of them at their best and at their worst they are very dull indeed. They are not funny. They are little dramas of little folk; a miniature art done in very quiet tones; subdued pictures of a well-to-do, completely commonplace society, showing the bad punished and the good rewarded, but moderately as the vices and virtues are moderate, and always a happy marriage to bring down the curtain. What would Aristophanes have made of them, one wonders. There is not the faintest reminiscence of his soaring imagination, not the most distant echo of his roaring laughter. The difference between the two playwrights illuminates as nothing could better the change that had come over the Athenians in the space of hardly fifty years.

•••

...Comfort, prosperity, safety, was the order of the new day that produced the New Comedy. Under their soothing influence the Athenians changed so swiftly they were themselves surprised, and seeking for a cause laid it to Sparta's account. The world ever since has echoed them, but to read Menander is to understand perfectly how inevitable was the passing of the Periclean age, to perceive other far more potent causes than the victory of Sparta in the Peloponnesian War.

In Rome, comedy has an even greater significance for us. The two Roman comedians are immensely important, beyond the Greek even from one point of view, in that they made the actual models upon which European comedy formed itself. With them we enter the great sphere of Latin influence, mighty in moulding our civilization, direct and all-penetrating as never was that of Greece. Aristophanes founded no school. He had no followers, ancient or modern. Menander has lived only as a shadow in Roman plays. Plautus and Terence were the founders of the drama as we know it today. Their influence has been incalculable. The two main divisions of comedy under which all comic plays except Aristophanes' can be grouped, go back to the two Roman playwrights. Plautus is the source for one, Terence for the other. The fact is another and a vivid illustration of how little the material of literature matters, and how much the way the material is treated. Both dramatists deal with exactly the same sort of life and exactly the same sort of people. The characters in the plays of the one are duplicated in the plays of the other, and in both the background is the family life of the day, and yet Plautus' world of comedy is another place from Terence's world.

The two men were completely unlike, so much so that it is difficult to conceive of either viewing a play of the other with any complacency. Plautus would have been bored by Terence, Terence offended by Plautus. Precisely the same material, but a totally different point of view, and the result, two distinct types of comedy.

Plautus was the older by a generation. His life fell during a restless period when Rome was fighting even more than usual. He could have taken part in the Second Punic War and the wars in the east which followed it, but whether he did or not is pure conjecture. All that is actually known about him is that he was the son of a poor Umbrian farmer, that he worked once in a mill and wrote three of his plays there, and that he was an old man when he died in 184 B.C. But it is impossible to read him without getting a vivid impression of the man himself. A picture emerges, done in bold strokes and unshaded colors, of a jovial, devil-may-care vagabond, a Latin Villon; a soldier of fortune who had roamed the world hobnobbing with all manner of men, and had no illusions about any of them; a man of careless good humor, keen to see and delighting to laugh at folly, but with a large and indulgent tolerance for every kind of fool.

Terence was a man of quite another order. He was born a slave in one of Rome's African colonies and brought up in a great Roman house where they recognized his talents, educated and freed him. These talents, too, found him a place in a circle of young men who were the intelligentsia and the gilded youth of Rome combined. The leader was the young Scipio, but the elegant Laelius, no mean poet, and the brilliant Lucilius, the inventor of satire, were close seconds, and it was an astonishing truth that the former slave, once admitted, proved inferior to none of them. It requires no imagination to realize his pride and happiness at being made one of their number. When envious people declared that his grand friends wrote his plays for him, he answered proudly that he boasted of their help.

It was a very youthful company. Terence is said to have died before he was twenty-six and they were all much of an age. The plays show nothing more clearly than that the audience they were primarily written for was this little band of close friends and not the vulgar crowd. Every one is laid in the Utopia of a young man about town in Republican Rome. Undoubtedly the members of the group in their bringing up had had a great deal required of them in the way of the antique Roman virtues. The father and mother of the day, as Plautus shows them, were

not given to overindulgence, and Scipio Africanus Maior, the young
Scipio's grandfather by adoption, must have been a man very much to be
reckoned with in the family circle, while the ladies of the Scipio
household were notable for their practice of the domestic virtues. The
redoubtable Cornelia herself was his aunt and her jewels were his
cousins. No doubt at all he and his friends had had to walk a narrow path
with watchful guardians on either side.

But under Terence's guidance, art, the liberator, set them free. He took
them away to an enchanted world where fathers were what they ought to
be and young men had their proper position in the world. Plautus' fathers
were hard on their sons—more intolerable still—the young fellows were
held up to ridicule. Terence altered all this delightfully. For the most part
his fathers are of an amiability not to be surpassed. "Does my darling son
want that pretty flute girl? The dear boy — I'll buy her for him at once."
"Extravagant do you call him? Well, all young men are like that. I was
myself. I'll gladly pay his debts." There is never any joking at that sort
of thing. Such sentiments are the part of the right-minded man. Indeed,
there are no jokes at all where the young men are concerned. They are all
wonderfully serious and completely noble and accorded the deepest
respect. Plautus' young lover on his knees before the door that shuts in
his lady-love, undoubtedly moved the audience to laughter when he
declaimed:

> Hear me ye bolts, ye bolts. Gladly I greet you, I love you.
> Humbly I pray you, beseech you, kneel here before you to beg you,
> Grant to a lover his longing, sweetest bolts, fairest and kindest.
> Spring now like ballet-girls dancing, lift yourselves up from the
>   door-post.
> Open, oh open and send her, send her to me ere my life blood
> Drains from me wasting and waiting.

But who would laugh at Terence's estimable young man, so admirably
concerned for his love:

> I treat her so? And she through me wronged, made wretched,
> She who has trusted love and life, her all, to me?
> So will I never do.

They are all like that. Whatever the audience thought of them, they were
certainly not amused. But whereas Plautus was out to get a laugh by any

and every means possible, Terence had an entirely different object in view. Plautus talked directly to the spectators when the action failed to get a response, calling out to the man in the back row not to be so slow to see a joke, or to the woman in front to stop chattering and let their husbands listen, or making an actor warn another,

> Softly now, speak softly.
> Don't disturb the pleasant slumbers of the audience
> I beg.

His object was to amuse. But Terence's mind was bent upon the approval of what he thought the most fastidious, polished people that ever there had been, and he worshipped where they did, at the shrine ever dearest to youth, good taste, as laid down by the canons of each youthful circle, "the thing," which is and isn't "done." Plautus makes fun of everyone, gods included. Terence has few comic characters, and they are in general confined to the lower classes. One catches a glimpse of an English public-school feeling for good form in that little circle of serious young men of which he was so proud to be a member. Making gentlemen ridiculous was simply not "done." Fortunately, in the circumstances, Terence's sense of humor was such that it could be perfectly controlled. No doubt to him Plautus was a horrible bounder—Plautus, the comedian pure and simple, who when he is not funny, is nothing at all. Terence is a serious dramatist, able to write an amusing scene; but seldom choosing to do so. His interest is in his nice people. above all his nice young men, and in their very well-bred-man-of-the-world doings. It is not to be presumed that Plautus knew anything about well-bred men, and no one ever had less concern for good taste. His quality is Rabelaisian—diluted—and certainly he would have been as much disconcerted by Terence's fine friends as they would have been uncomfortable with him.

With dissimilarities so marked it is not surprising that they disagreed about the whole business of drama-making. The fundamental question of how to secure dramatic interest each solved in his own way, completely unlike the other's. They constructed their plays differently and two forms of comedy, widely divergent from each other, was the result.

There are only two main sources for dramatic interest in a comedy. The first is the method of suspense and surprise, depending upon plot or upon the reaction of character to character, or to situation. But the second method is precisely the reverse: it acts by eliminating suspense and making surprise impossible. The dramatic interest depends upon the spectators knowing everything beforehand. They know what the actor does not. It is a method found in both tragedy and comedy; it is common ground to the sublime and the ridiculous. The Greeks who made great use of it, called it irony. Nothing in tragedy is more tragic. Oedipus invokes an awful curse upon the murderer of his wife's first husband:

> I charge you all: Let no one of this land
> Give shelter to him. Bar him from your homes,
> A thing defiled, companioned by pollution.
> And solemnly I pray, may he who killed,
> Wear out his life in evil, being evil.

And we know it is he himself he is cursing, he is the murderer; he killed his father, he married his mother. This is tragic irony. It lies at the very foundation of Greek tragedy. The audience knew beforehand what the action of each play would be. They sat as beings from another world, foreseeing all the dire results of every deed as it took place, but perceiving also that thus it must be and not otherwise. The feeling of the inevitability of what is being done and suffered upon the stage, of men's helplessness to avert their destiny, which is the peculiar power of Greek tragedy, depends in the last analysis upon irony, upon the spectators' awareness and the actors' unconsciousness of what is really happening. The darkness that envelops mortal life, our utter ignorance of what confronts us and our blinded eyes that cannot see the ruin we are bringing down upon ourselves, is driven home so dramatically and with such intensity as is possible to no other method.

The use of it may be as comic as it is tragic. We, the audience, are in the secret that there are two men who look exactly alike. The poor, stupid actors do not dream that it is so. How absurdly unable they are to escape their ridiculous mishaps, and what a delightfully superior position our omniscience assures to us.

We cannot trace back the use of the suspense method. Plot is as old as the very first story-teller and the interest of what the effect will be of a situation or of one character upon another is at least as old as Homer and the Bible. But irony begins with Greek tragedy, and, as far as our evidence goes, comic irony begins with Roman comedy. Among the fragments we have of Menander there are two in which irony is evident, but in neither passage is it used humorously. It is found so used for the first time in Plautus. If he was indeed the originator of it, if it was he who perceived to what comic uses tragic irony could be turned, he deserves a place in literature far higher than that now given him. Irony is his chief source of dramatic interest and he is a master of it. It follows, of course, that he offers nothing notable in plots. Suspense is automatically shut out when irony is used. Plautus' plots, when he has one, are extremely poor, and there is a distressing similarity between them. But no one will ever put irony to better comic use. His usual way is to explain the action of the piece in a very long and exceedingly tiresome prologue, but the result of the detailed explanation is that the spectators are free to give their entire attention to the absurdities they are now in a position to see through.

In the *Amphitryon*, it will be remembered, Jupiter is in love with Amphitryon's wife, Alcumena. When Amphitryon is away at war Jupiter assumes his form to gain access to Alcumena. Mercury, who guards the house whenever Jupiter is in it, under the form of Amphitryon's slave Sosia, absent with his master, speaks the prologue, and explains in minutest detail all that is going to take place throughout the play. Jupiter and Amphitryon will look exactly alike, he warns the audience, and so will he and Sosia, but in order that they may have no bother as to which is which, Jupiter will have a bright gold tassel hanging from his hat and

> I shall wear this little plume on mine,
> Note well: the other two are unadorned.

With this the play begins. The scene is a street at night before Amphitryon's house where Mercury stands on guard. To him enters his duplicate, Sosia, sent ahead by Amphitryon to prepare his wife for his unexpected return. It is too dark for Sosia to see how Mercury looks. As he goes up to the door the latter stops him.

MERCURY:
May I know where you come from, who you are, and why you're here? Just you tell me.

SOSIA:
Well, I'm going in there. I'm the master's slave. Do you know it all now? Just you tell me.

MERCURY:
Is that your house?

SOSIA:
Haven't I said so?

MERCURY:
Then who is the man that owns you?

SOSIA:
Amphitryon. General commanding the troops. He's got a wife —
name Alcumena.

MERCURY:
What stuff are you giving me? What's your name?

SOSIA:
It's Sosia. My father was Davus.

MERCURY:
Well, you've got your cheek. You're Sosia? You? What's your
game? Didn't you know I was he? Eh? *(Strikes him)*

SOSIA:
Oh, you'll kill me!

MERCURY:
You'll find if you keep this up there are things
a whole lot worse than dying.
Now, Say who you are.

SOSIA:
I'm Sosia, please —

MERCURY:
He's mad.

SOSIA:
I'm not. Why, you rascal.
Didn't a ship bring me in from the battlefields this very night? Didn't
my master send me here to our house? And you say I'm not—Well, I'll
go straight to my mistress.

MERCURY:
Every word a lie—I'm Amphitryon's slave. We stormed the
enemy's city, killed the king—cut his head off, Amphitryon did.

SOSIA:
(awestruck)
He knows it all.

(pause, then recovering)

Just you tell me,
if you are me, when the fight was on, where were you?
What were you doing?

MERCURY:

A cask full of wine in the tent and my own pocket flask.
What d'you think I'd be doing?

SOSIA:

(overwhelmed)

It's the truth. Wretched man that I am.

(shakes head, then suddenly holds lantern up so that the light falls on MERCURY)

Well, well. He's as like me as I myself was. Oh, immortal gods!
When was I changed? Did I die?

Have I lost my memory?

Did they leave me behind in foreign parts? I'm going straight back
to my master.

(Runs off, and re-enters following AMPHITRYON who is completely nonplussed at the report of what has happened)

AMPHITRYON:

(angrily)

The boy's drunk. You, speak up. Tell the truth, where
you got the stuff.

SOSIA:

But I didn't.

AMPHITRYON:

(uneasiness getting the better of his anger)

Who's that man you saw?

SOSIA:

I've told you ten times. I'm there at the house and I'm here, too.
That's the straight truth.

AMPHITRYON:

(trying to persuade himself it's all nonsense, but uncomfortable)

Get out. Take yourself off. You're sick.

SOSIA:

I'm just as well as you are.

AMPHITRYON:

Ah, I'll see that you aren't. If you're not mad, you're bad.

SOSIA:
(tearfully)
I tell the truth. You won't hear me.
I was standing in front of the house before I got there.

AMPHITRYON:
                                    You're dreaming.
That's the cause of this nonsense. Wake up.

SOSIA:
No, no. I don't sleep when you give me an order.
I was wide awake then—I'm wide awake now. I was wide awake
when he beat me.
He was wide awake, too. I'll tell you that.

AMPHITRYON:
(gruffly)
It'll bear looking into. Come on then.

This is the way Plautus handles comic irony. Molière follows him closely. In his *Amphitryon* the dialogue between Mercure and Sosie is essentially a reproduction of the Latin and no one can say that the great master of comedy used the device at any point more skillfully than the Latin poet.

Playwright after playwright took it over from him. Shakespeare's ironical play, *The Comedy of Errors*, is not as close a parallel to Plautus' *Menaechmi* as Molière's is to the *Amphitryon*, but the entire play is only a variation on Plautus' theme. Scenes in Shakespeare and Molière where the comedy depends upon irony are so many, to run through them would mean making a resume of a large part of their comedies. The basis of the fun in *Much Ado About Nothing* is the spectator's knowledge of the plot against Beatrice and Benedict. The great scene in *L'Avare* is funny because we know the miser is talking about his money box and the young man about his lady-love, while each supposes the other has the same object in mind. Here, too, Molière drew directly from Plautus. Whether the latter first employed the method or whether he got it from the Greek New Comedy, it is certain that its use upon our own stage goes directly back to him.

Terence never used it. It seems strange at first sight that he did not, but upon consideration reasons appear. A plot intricate enough to supply a full measure of suspense and surprise can be enjoyed only by an intelligent and attentive audience, especially when programs, outlines, synopses of scenes, all the sources of printed information, have to be dispensed with. Plautus' audience was not up to that level; Terence's was—the real audience he wrote for, his little circle of superior people. Plautus had to hold the attention of a holiday crowd, and hold it too, as he says in many a prologue, against such competitors as chattering women and crying babies. No method of playwriting requires so little effort on the part of the spectator as comic irony. Comedies based upon it are merely a succession of funny scenes strung on the thread of a familiar story. There was sound sense in Plautus' preference for it, and equally good reason for Terence's rejection. His audience enjoyed using their minds on an ingenious plot. He could dispense with the obviously comic and follow his own strong bent toward character and situation. The germ of the novel lies within his plays. His plots are never poor. Perhaps the best of them is that of the *Mother-in-Law*, where the suspense is excellently sustained to the very end. Indeed, as the curtain falls the two chief characters pledge each other to keep the solution of the mystery to their own selves. "Don't let's have it like the comedies where everyone knows everything," one of them says.

It is a good story throughout and the characters are well drawn. Nevertheless when the play was presented to the public it failed. The prologue, spoken at a second presentation, declares the reason was that

> A rope-dancer had caught the gaping people's mind.

Yet another prologue—for still another presentation, presumably—says that the entire theatre was thrown into an uproar by the announcement of a gladiatorial show, and the play could not proceed. Clearly the road of the early dramatist in Rome was not an easy one, but there is never a hint that Plautus found it hard. Perhaps he had the happy faculty of not taking himself too seriously, and merely went along with the crowd when such occasions worked havoc with his play. One feels sure that even so he would have enjoyed the rope-dancer. But the young playwright, hardly more than a boy, felt poignantly the hurt to his feelings and the wrong to his genius. Every one of his prologues contains an attack upon the critics or his public. They are fearfully serious productions, warranted to make any audience restless and any other show irresistibly attractive, but to his own inner circle, those very somber and cultured young men, no doubt they appeared admirably distinguished from the well-worn, old-fashioned method of appeal to the vulgar.

The marked difference between the two writers is another proof of the Roman character of Roman comedy. Plautus and Terence owed something, no doubt, much perhaps, to their Greek originals, but much more to their own selves. They were Roman writers, not Greek copyists, and the drama they bequeathed to the world which still holds the stage today, is a witness to the extent of our legacy from Rome.

VI

Roman Tragedy

The only surviving Roman tragedies, indeed the only plays of any kind from the Roman Empire, are ten dramas—nine of them *palliata*—attributed to Lucius Annaeus Seneca (4 B.C.-65 A.D.), the Corduba-born Stoic philosopher and tutor of Nero.

Nearly everything about these plays is problematical. Two of them may not have been by Seneca at all, and scholars have suggested that, from several of the others, the philosopher had collaborators.

Moreover, it is not known whether the tragedies were performed during the author's lifetime. Perhaps they were designed to be read privately, or to be recited as chamber pieces to a small audience. Most scholars favor the latter view, although Dana Ferrin Sutton,[1] among others, has argued persuasively that Seneca's dramas are conceived theatrically and were intended for full production in a public theatre.

Sutton notwithstanding, it's easy to see why T.S. Eliot[2] and others have held the opposing view, that these plays do not have the shape of a practically planned stage performance.

The scene of action is never clearly defined. We seldom know where we are—whether inside a temple, say, or outside a palace. Entrances and exits are not managed precisely. Is a character who has finished speaking present or absent? If present, why doesn't he seem to notice that his wife just killed herself? Also, speeches tend to great length; a hundred lines or more is not uncommon. A Senecan act often seems to be a succession of long rhetorical monologues rather than a fully-realized dramatic sequence.

Some squeamish readers have argued that the plays are too horrible to be produced. And, certainly, in this respect Seneca lacks the reticence of Attic tragedy. In his version of *Phaedra*, for example, the dismembered pieces of Hippolytus' body are brought on stage, and Theseus, the distraught father, attempts to put them together again. In *Thyestes*, the grisly banquet is shown, in which Atreus feeds his brother the flesh of his own children. Whenever possible Seneca chose Greek myths that contained horrific elements and then exploited them in a sensational and sometimes unintentionally amusing way.

[1] In *Seneca on the Stage* (Leiden: E.J. Brill, 1986).
[2] In *Selected Essays* (New York: Harcourt Brace, 1932).

But the horror of the action is no reason to suppose that Seneca's tragedies were not staged—not in Imperial Rome where the competing entertainments included gladiatorial fights to the death and the spectacle of men being torn to pieces by wild beasts.

And, regardless of their fate in Seneca's lifetime, his plays definitely were produced in revival during the Renaissance. Indeed, in the sixteenth century when Terence and Plautus were the paradigms of comedy, Seneca was the model writer of tragedy. His reputation was especially high in England, where his influence was felt not only in the developing popular theatre, but in intellectual circles as well.[3]

What was his appeal to the Tudor and Jacobean dramatists? To the less finicky, his bloody spectacles, his ghosts, his mystic rites were liberating. Fed by his example, revenge plays multiplied in the public and private theatres, crude ones like *Gorboduc* at the Middle Temple and sublime ones like *Hamlet* and *The Duchess of Malfi* at the Globe.

Indeed, as Lucas puts it, "In the realm of letters it has been Seneca's destiny, like Banquo's, to beget in his posterity a greatness denied himself ... [F]rom ... the decadent silver Latinist ..., by a seeming freak of fortune can be traced the direct descent of the lordliest names in the dramatic literature of Western Europe."[4]

Can a playwright with such progeny be wholly slipshod and depraved? Clearly not. And recently there has been some effort to restore his flagging reputation. Eliot's piece is cautiously flattering. Also influential is an essay by C. D. N. Costa, in which Seneca's rhetoric, that persuasive discourse so admired by the Elizabethans, is analyzed in its own historical context and given more than modest praise.

---

[3] For a more extended treatment of this subject, see F.L. Lucas, *Seneca and Elizabethan Tragedy* (Cambridge: Cambridge University Press, 1922).
[4] *Ibid.*, p. 1.

C. D. N. Costa*
The Tragedies of Seneca

Senecam nullo Graecorum maiestate inferiorem existimo,
cultu vero ac nitore etiam Euripise maiorem. (J.C. Scaliger, 1561)[1]

[Seneca's whole writings] penned with a peerless sublimity
and loftinesse of style are so far from countenauncing vice,
that I doubt whether there bee any among all the Catalogue of
Heathen wryters, that with more grauity of Philosophical
sentences, more waightynes of sappy words, or greater authority
of sound matter beateth down sinne, loose lyfe, dissolute dealinge,
and unbrydled sensuality: or that more sensibly, pithily, and
bytingly layeth doune the guerdon of filthy lust, cloaked
dissimulation and odious trachery: which is the dryft, whereunto
he leueleth the whole yssue of ech one of his Tragedies.
(Thomas Newton, 1581)

In the plays of Seneca, the drama is all in the word, and the
word has no further reality behind it. His characters all seem
to speak with the same voice, and at the top of it; they recite
in turn. (T.S. Eliot, 1927)

The tragedies ... suggest the clever immaturity of a youngish
man. Though false standards of taste and their peculiar
survival-position gave them an undue influence on the early
moulding of modern tragedy in England and elsewhere, it is
now less by their own merits than as a clue to the author's
character that they interest us. (E.P. Barker. 1949)

*T*hese criticisms give some idea of the change of attitude towards
Seneca's tragedies during the last four hundred years. The
veneration in which they were held by translators and imitators in
the sixteenth and seventeenth centuries was succeeded by dislike,
contempt and neglect, and it is only in comparatively recent years
that the plays are being evaluated on their own terms, and judged in
relation to the educational training which produced them. Aspects of
their influence on English literature are examined elsewhere in this
volume: this essay will confine itself to the tragedies themselves,
and try to arrive at some conclusion on Seneca's purpose in writing
them, by considering first some dominant literary influences which
gave them birth and then their characteristic stylistic features.

So far as we know the plays attributed to Seneca—the only surviving

---

*From C.D.N. Costa, ed., *Seneca* (London & Boston: Routledge & Kegan Paul, 1974), pp.
96-125. Slightly abridged by the editors.

[1] "I think that Seneca in his majesty is inferior to none of the Greeks; truly in refinement
and brilliance, he is greater than Euripides."

complete Latin tragedies—represent virtually his whole poetic output, for most of the epigrams that passed under his name are very probably spurious. The titles are: *Hercules Furens, Troades, Phoenissae, Medea, Phaedra* (or *Hippolytus*), *Oedipus, Agamemnon, Thyestes, Hercules Oetaeus, Octavia*.[2] The Octavia has a scarcity interest only as the only extant Latin historical play, a fabula praetexta, but on good grounds (partly of metre) it is nowadays usually held to be not of Seneca. Of the others, *Hercules Oetaeus* is in all likelihood not entirely his, and the *Phoenissae* is fragmentary.

It is worth mentioning that earlier scholars postulated multiple authorship of the plays: in the introductions to their editions Lipsius (1588) and Daniel Heinsius (1611) argued seriously for four or five different authors of the corpus. Furthermore, many early editions of the *opera omnia* of 'Seneca the philosopher' exclude the tragedies, a practice which survived at least until the Didot edition of 1844. This can nowadays be regarded as a curious quirk of scholarship; there is no good reason to doubt that most of the plays were written by the Younger Seneca. They cannot be dated with any certainty,[3] but it is not improbable that their composition diverted many an empty hour during the long years of Seneca's exile in Corsica, 41-9.

Greek tragedy supplied the themes of these plays, as the titles indicate, though the treatment and approach are vastly different, and often little but the framework of the legend survives its metamorphosis in Seneca's hands. Euripides lurks dimly behind the *Hercules Furens, Troades, Medea* and *Phaedra*; Sophocles behind *Phoenissae, Oedipus* and *Hercules Oetaeus*; Aeschylus's play is a notional exemplar for the *Agamemnon*. No Greek *Thyestes* survives, but Sophocles and Euripides wrote plays with that title, as did earlier Latin tragedians. Formal comparisons between Seneca and the Greek writers are to a large extent misconceived and unrewarding. He was engaged in a quite different exercise, and while we can show that he has used a speech in the original here, or adapted a scene there, we have to be cautious about generalizing and putting forward a theory about Seneca's use of his sources.

Even more uncertain is Seneca's relation to earlier Latin tragedy. Only fragments survive of the large output of the old tragedians, and we have, therefore, to be cautious in drawing inferences, but it seems that in its heyday in the third and second centuries B.C. Latin tragedy, however freely it used its sources, was comparable in treatment, as it was in

---

[2] The best edition of the tragedies to date is that of G.C. Giardina, Bologna, 1966. An edition by O. Zwierlein is in preparation for the Oxford Classical Text series. This note and others are Costa's.

[3] Though many attempts have been made, using various criteria, e.g., O. Herzog in *Revue des Etudes Latines*, 77 (1928) p. 51 ff.

theme, with Greek tragedy.[4] If so, Seneca was, apart from the language he wrote in, as distant in the essentials of his art from Ennius, Pacuvius and Accius, as he was from Aeschylus, Sophocles and Euripides. He retained the chorus, as his Latin predecessors apparently did,[5] and therewith the framework of episodes divided by moralizing choral lyrics. He used the stock figures of the messenger and the nurse, and gave them characteristic functions. The messenger reports horrific news of events off-stage, like the death of Hippolytus in the *Phaedra*, and the destruction of Creusa and Creon in the *Medea*;the nurse is the conventional loyal confidante to Medea, Phaedra and Deianira, and Seneca thus helped to steer her onwards into French and English literature. But apart from these and a few other formal elements, like the use of the iambic trimeter in dialogue, Seneca's plays stand on their own. He took from the Greeks what he needed in plot-outline and the basis of the leading characters, and he may have taken something too from earlier Latin plays; but the distinctive stamp and features of his plays derive from his own time.

Few people nowadays deny that at least one accurate descriptive label for the tragedies is 'rhetorical' or 'declamatory', but behind this apparent unanimity lies a wide range of reactions to them, from the favorable through the bored to the frankly hostile. Let us for the moment avoid value judgements and try to assess objectively what is meant by this description. Rhetoric, the technique of persuasion, had to a greater or lesser degree been a characteristic of Latin literature from its beginnings, and as a formal educational training it dated at least from Cicero's boyhood.

Attendance at a school of rhetoric was the third stage in a boy's education after successively passing through the hands of a *litterator* and a *grammaticus*. The point to grasp is that this phase of training under a professional declaimer, *rhetor*, had by the time of Seneca's youth become extremely important and influential, and the young man's performance at a rhetorical school could make or mar his professional life, whether forensic or literary. In fact, as the political conditions of the early Empire discouraged the development of real forensic talents, it was literature which mainly benefitted, and suffered, from the education in rhetoric.

The teaching techniques and exercises of the disclaimers are fortunately well documented for us, largely through the labours of Seneca's own father. His interest in rhetoric, his industry, and his astonishing memory have left us collections of school exercises,

---

[4] But for important differences between Latin and Greek tragedy, see H.D. Jocelyn, *The Tragedies of Ennius* (Cambridge, 1967), pp. 23 ff.
[5] See ibid., pp. 18ff., 30ff.

Suasoriae and *Controversiae*, which tell us in the clearest terms what went on. This is invaluable to us, for even a brief look at the schools helps to explain the nature of Seneca's tragedies. To put it shortly, *suasoriae* were speeches composed to be put into the mouths of historical characters facing a crisis and deliberating what to do, e.g. 'Cicero deliberates whether he should beg Antony to spare his life'(*Suas.* vi); *controversiae* were debating speeches concerning a legal or moral issue. An invented situation was offered to the students of rhetoric, often of a quite extraordinary contrived and far-fetched nature, and the object of the exercise was to arrive at a conclusion through a maze of arguments and counter-arguments which matched in their intricacy the situation under discussion. Typical examples of the problems offered are:

> A girl is captured by pirates and sold to a pander, who makes her
> a prostitute. She asks for money from those who come to her,
> and when a soldier refuses to pay and offers her violence she
> kills him. She is tried and acquitted, and returns to her own
> people, where she seeks the priesthood (for which chastity
> is a necessary qualification). (*Contr.* i.2)

> The penalty for rape is either death or marriage to the wronged
> girl. In one night, a man rapes two girls: one demands his death,
> the other, marriage. (*Contr.* i.5)

> A father refuses to ransom his son who has been captured by
> pirates. As a condition of freedom, the son is forced to swear
> to marry the chief's daughter. He returns home and marries her,
> and when he subsequently refuses to divorce her and marry
> another woman on his father's orders, his father disinherits
> him. (*Contr,* i.6)

It is not hard to imagine the kind of talents fostered by such dialectical brain-teasers. Skill and inventiveness in language were mainly evoked, and the subtlety of the argument mattered more than the rights or wrongs of the case. There was a premium on all the tricks and flourishes of rhetoric for which the Latin language is in any case a highly suitable vehicle: elaborately structured antithesis, epigram, every kind of striking linguistic effect, and, more than all, that favorite handmaiden of persuasion, the *sententia*, a terse thought crisply expressed. Almost every page of the Elder Seneca's collection reveals examples of this dialectic ingenuity, and almost every page of his son's prose works and tragedies shows the fashionable rhetorical tricks informing a literary style. It is in any case unreal to distinguish the rhetorical from the literary in much first-century Latin literature; but in Seneca, as in his nephew Lucan, the symbiosis is nearly complete.[6]

Thus Seneca had, as it were, a domestic interest in rhetoric inherited from his father, in addition to the routine training he underwent himself; and his natural and very considerable gifts as a writer found a congenial outlet in the current declamatory style. When he turned to the writing of tragedies, the results formed one of the most curious and interesting byways of Latin literature. It should not be necessary nowadays to labor the point that they were not written for performance, if by that we mean a full-dress stage production. With a few notable exceptions, the writing of tragedy had declined steeply by the Neronian age, and the evidence we have suggests that the production of complete plays was giving place to the presentation of single scenes as the material for a solo recital. So, in Tacitus's *Dialogus* (referring to A.D. 74-5) we are told that Curiatius Maternus had recently recited (*recitaverat*) his tragedy *Cato*, and under Nero he won fame *recitatione tragoediarum*.[7] The picture is uncertain, but at any rate, the characteristic features of Seneca's tragedies are best explained on the assumption that they were not meant for production.

We need not take seriously the old arguments that the horror and bloodshed were unactable (e.g. Thyestes's feast in the *Thyestes*, the mutilated body of Hippolytus in the *Phaedra*): the Elizabethans successfully managed a great deal in that line, and the public were used to such sights in the arena of Neronian Rome. More cogent reasons can be found in the structure of the plays: the fragmentation of the dramatic action and the dominance of the individual scene; uncertainty about entrances and exits, so that we often do not know exactly who is present during a scene; and, perhaps most important, the careful and circumstantial descriptions by characters of the actions or personal appearances of others which would obviously be visible to the audience of a staged play. Examples of this are: the murder by Hercules of his wife and children (*Hercules Furens* 1001ff.)—one can cheat by supposing that he goes offstage to do it, but there is no indication of this in the text; the sacrifice in Oedipus 302ff. (there is some excuse here in that Manto is reporting to the blind Tiresias); the frenzied Medea rushing about, flushed, shouting, weeping—the nurse details all the signs of strong emotion (*Med.* 380ff.); Thyestes eating his horrible meal (*Thy.*

---

[6]For the whole subject of rhetoric in Roman education and its influence on Seneca see the excellent book of S.F. Bonner, *Roman Declamation* (Liverpool, 1949). He remarks (p. 167): 'There is scarcely an aspect of declamatory rhetoric which could not be illustrated from his plays.'

[7] Tacitus *Dial.* 2 and 11. See too the sensible remarks of E.F. Watling in the introduction to his *Seneca: Four Tragedies and Octavia* (Harmondsworth, 1966), p. 21, on the unreal distinction between 'performance' and 'recitation' by two or more persons.

909ff.).

If we accept, then, that we are dealing with a special kind of declamatory drama, we can make sense of and appreciate features of these plays which have offended critics who expected of them what they were never intended to offer. Their style, founded as we have seen on the training of the schools, is epigrammatic, 'pointed', and crisply antithetic. The plots usually advance, if they can be said to advance, through a succession of debating scenes or set-piece monologues. In the arguments between characters, the techniques of stichomýthia (dialogue in alternating lines) and antilabe (division of a line between two speakers) are often used, where one speaker caps a point made by another, often by repeating or varying the phraseology of the other. So Medea and the nurse argue (*Med.* 159-63):

> M. fortuna fortes metuit, ignavos premit.
> N. tunc est probanda, si locum virtus habet.
> M. numquam potest non esse virtuti locus.
> N. spes nulla rebus monstrat afflicis viam.
> M. qui nil potest sperare, desperet nihil.

> (M. Fortune fears the brave and crushes the cowardly.
> N. Only then should courage be proved if there is a place for it.
> M. Never can there be no place for courage.
> N. No hope points out a course for our shattered fortunes.
> M. Let him despair of nothing who can hope for nothing.)

Pyrrhus and Agamemnon debate whether to slay Polyxena (*Tro.* 327-36):

> P. est regis alti spiritum regi dare.
> A. cur destra regi spiritum eripuit tua?
> P. mortem misericors saepe pro dabit.
> A. et nunc misericors virginem busto petis?
> P. iamne immolari virgines credis nefas?
> A. praeferre patriam liberis regem decet.
> P. lex nulla capto parcit aut poenam impedit.
> A. quod non vetat lex, hoc vetat fieri pudor.
> P. quodcumque libuit facere victori licet.
> A. minimum decet libere cui multum licet.

> (P. It is the act of a great king to grant life to a king.
> A. Why did your hand take life from a king?
> P. Often will one in pity give death instead of life.
> A. And now in pity you seek a maiden for the tomb?
> P. What? Now you think it wrong that maidens be sacrificed?

A. It is right for a king to put his country before his Children.
P. No law spares a captive or prevents punishment.
A. What the law does not forbid, shame forbids.
P. A victor can do whatever he likes.
A. Who can do much should like to do least.)

This kind of cut-and-thrust dialectic was very dear to Seneca, and loses much in the English translation, with its lack of inflection and its more inflexible word-order.

The set speeches are of various kinds, the most characteristic being the 'To be or not to be' variety, or dramatized *suasoria* (Hamlet's soliloquy, incidentally, is a lineal descendant of the Roman *suasoria*), as in *Medea* 893ff. (should she kill her children?); and the speech of self-defense: *Hercules Furens* 399ff. (Lycus defends his usurping of Thebes, raising and demolishing imaginary objections); *Medea* 236ff. (Medea recalls the moral dilemma she had faced at Colchis between obeying her father and rescuing the Argonauts). The importance of the set speech, whether a soliloquy or in dialogue, leads in turn to the dominance of the single scene as a virtually self-contained unit in the play. This point can be well illustrated from the *Medea*, where the plot consists essentially of a progression of debates between Medea and, successively, the nurse, Creon and Jason. One can very similarly analyze other plays, e.g. the *Troades* and *Phaedra*, where the major scenes explore a tension between a harshly contrasted pair of attitudes, and the reader forgets the wider aspects of the total play in concentrating on the polarity before him. This would be a structural fault in an acted play, where one expects a homogeneous whole with, in Aristotelian terms, a beginning, a middle and an end. But this is not what Seneca is doing.

It must also be admitted that many soliloquies and dialogues are marred by an obvious reliance on contrived rhetorical techniques, which take command over the natural sentiments of the speaker. There is a cold intellectuality in Andromache's soliloquy which reflects the debating schools rather than the anguished decision she has to make, whether to give up her son to death or allow her husband's tomb to be desecrated (*Tro.* 642ff.):

quid agimus? animum distruit geminus timor:
hinc natus, illinc coniugis sacri cinis.
pars utra vincet? testor immites deos,
deosque veros coniugis manes mei:
non aliud, Hector, in meo nato mihi
placere quam te. vivat, ut possit tuos
referre vultus. — prorutus tumulo cinis
mergetur? ossa fluctibus spargi sinam

> disiecti vastis? potius hic mortem oppetat. —
> poteris nefandae deditum mater neci
> videre? Poteris celsa per fastigia
> missum rotari? potero, perpetiar, feram,
> dum non meus post fata victoris manu
> iactetur Hector. — hic suam poenam potest
> sentire, at illum fata iam in tuto locant. —
> quid fluctaris? statue, quem poenae extrahas.
> ingrata, dubitas? Hector est illinc tuus —
> erras: utrimque est Hector, hic sensus potens,
> forsan futuris ultor extincti patris —
> utrique pasci non potest: quidnam facis?
> serva e duobus, anime, quem Danai timent.

(What am I to do? A double fear tears my soul apart: on this side my son, on that my sacred husband's ashes. Which side will conquer? I swear by the pitiless gods, and that true god, my husband's ghost: nothing else, Hector, is dear to me in my son than yourself. Let him live, to recall your features.—Are your ashes to be cast from their tomb and sunk in the sea? Shall I allow your bones to be scattered wide over the mighty waves? Rather let Astyanax meet his death.— Can you his mother watch him handed over to an unholy death? Can you see him thrown hurtling over the lofty roof-tops? I can, I will steel myself to do it, endure it, so long as my Hector is not scattered after his death by the conqueror's hand.—But Astyanax can feel punishment, while Hector is now in the haven of death.—Why hesitate? Decide whom you are to save from vengeance. Ungrateful one, can you still doubt? Your Hector is on that side—no, Hector is on both sides; but his son can still feel pain, and may one day avenge his dead father. I cannot save both: what to do? Of the two, my soul, save the one whom the Greeks fear.)

To even the most casual reader, the most memorable literary feature of the tragedies must be the ubiquitous *sententiae*. These pithy, balanced epigrams had in the inflections and flexible word-order of Latin a most admirable vehicle, and the 'Silver' writers enjoyed them enormously. No one showed a more refined skill than Seneca in composing them in both prose and verse, and (like Juvenal) he owes his popularity as a source of adages to the neatness of his *sententiae*.

In these epigrams the flavor of declamation tends to distance the thoughts from reality and human feeling, and Seneca seems to abandon the exploration of mankind's behavior in favor of formulating its more unoriginal thoughts. But as expressions of the axiomatic they are unbeatable, and it is fair to Seneca to see this as a conscious part of his purpose.

The tragedies have not many passages of great lyrical charm, but Seneca does occasionally evoke a scene of natural beauty, as at *Phaedra*

9ff.:

> hac, hac alii qua nemus alta
> texitur alno, qua prata iacent,
> qua rorifera mulcens aura
> Zephyrus vernas evocat herbas ...

> (Here, here let others go, where the grove is interwoven with
> tall alders, where lie the meadows, where the West Wind,
> soothing with his dewy breeze, brings forth the
> springtime growth...)

So, too from the attractive *aubade* in the *Hercules Furens* (139ff.):

> pastor gelida cana pruina
> grege dimisso pabula carpit;
> ludit prato liber aperto
> nondum rupta fronte iuvencus,
> vacuae reparant ubera matres;
> errat cursu levis incerto
> molli patulans haedus in herba.
> pendet summo stridula ramo
> pinnasque novo tradere soli
> gestit querulos inter nidos
> Thracia paelex, turbaque circa
> confusa sonat murmure mixto
> testata diem.
> carbasa ventis credit dubius
> navita vitae, laxos aura
> complente sinus. hic exesis
> pendens scopulis aut deceptos
> instruit hamos aut suspensus
> spectat pressa praemia dextra:
> sentit tremulum linea piscem.

(The shepherd, putting out his flock, pastures them on the ground
white with hoar frost. The bullock still with hornless brow
sports freely in the open meadow, while the cows at leisure
fill again their udders. On the soft grass the saucy kid
wanders, skipping aimlessly about. The shrill nightingale perches
on the top of a tree among her plaintive nestlings, longing to
spread her wings to the early morning sun, and all around
confused sounds of the bird-throngs' mingled voices announce
the dawn. The sailor hazarding his life entrusts his sails to
the winds, as the breeze swells the loose canvas folds. A fisherman
perching on weather-beaten rocks prepares again his cheated hooks,
or, gripping tightly, excitedly watches for his prize, as the line feels

the quivering fish.)

The chorus in Seneca fulfills much the same function as the Euripidean chorus. It moralizes in more or less general terms on a theme drawn from the action (e.g., the irresistible anger of a wronged wife, *Medea* 579ff.; the beauty of Hippolytus, suggesting the theme of beauty as an ambiguous blessing, *Phaedra* 741ff.), and in this way puts the characters and their world perspective against a wider background of history or mythology. Thus, the chorus gives Seneca scope for his absorbing interest in geography (often muddled) and mythology; and one of the more tiresome features of the lyrics is his fondness for extensive catalogues of people and places. In addition, the chorus serves the practical purpose of filling up time in the action while something happens off-stage, and it sometimes enters the action, for example in order to interrogate a new arrival (*Med.* 881ff.). At least once it plays a much more organic role, when it forms the wedding procession and sings the epithalamium for Jason's marriage to Creusa at *Medea* 56ff. This lyric in the *Medea*, as well as being an interesting example of a minor literary genre, shows that Seneca in retaining the dramatic chorus is not simply paying lip-service to an outworn convention; though elsewhere in the plays the chorus is generally the 'ideal' listener and commentator familiar to us from Euripides.

In one important respect, however, Seneca's choruses depart from the Greek practice: though the metres (mainly anapaestic, sapphic, glyconic, and asclepiadic) are Greek, there is no attempt at responsion, and in fact only one strophic chorus (*Med.* 579ff.). Partly for this reason it is a fair charge against Seneca that in many places his lyrics are metrically boring, as the same unvaried metre is hammered out for too long; and to our ears there does seem to be an insensitivity here which is hard to explain. However, at least in the *Medea*—which is, in general, one of the more carefully written plays—he has made a real attempt at metrical variety. The *Medea* also illustrates clearly a point which has long been noticed: Seneca's strong debt to Horace in many of his lyrics: e.g. *Medea* 301ff. and Horace C. i.3, on the folly of the first navigator.[8]

Another interesting chorus is the long dithyramb to Bacchus in the *Oedipus* (403ff.), in which the learned Senecan treatment of myth is given a successful buoyancy for a hundred lines by the vigorous metrical variety. The closing lines, describing the wedding of Bacchus and Adriadne, are (488-508):

[8] For the influence of Horace, see I. Spika, *De imitatione Horatiana in Senecae canticis choris* (Jahresb. 1889-90, Staatsgymn. Wien II, Vienna, 1890), pp. 3ff.

Naxos Aegaeo redimita ponto
tradidit thalamis virginem relictam,
meliore pensans damnum marito.
Pumice ex sicco fluxit
Nyctelius latex;
garruli gramen secuere rivi,
conbibit humus alta sucos
niveique lactis candidos fontes
et mixta adoro Lesbia cum thymo.
ducitur magno nova nupta caelo:
sollomne Phoebus carmen
infusus humero capillis
cantat et germinus Cupido
concutit taedas;
telum deposuit Iuppiter igneum
oditque Baccho veniente fulmen.

lucida dum current annosi sidera mundi,
Oceanus clausum dum fluctibus ambiet orbem
Lunaque dimisso dum plena recolliget ignes,
dum matutinos praedicet Lucifer ortus
altaque caeruleum dum Nerea nesciet Arctos,
candida formosi venerabimur ora Lyaei.

(Naxos, surrounded by the Aegean Sea, gave him to wed the
deserted maiden, requiting her loss with a better husband. Wine
flowed from the dry rock; babbling streams criss-crossed the
meadows; the earth drank deeply of sweet juices—both springs of
snow-white milk and wine mingled with fragrant thyme. The new
bride was brought to the high heavens; with his hair flowing over
his shoulders Phoebus sang a festive song, and twin Cupids
flourished the bridal torches; Jupiter put aside his fiery weapon,
hating the thunderbolt when Bacchus came. As long as the bright
stars run their courses; as long as the ocean flows round the earth
and bounds it with his waters; as long as the full moon regains the
brightness she lost at waning; as long as the morning star foretells
the rise of day and the lofty Bear shall never know the blue sea; so
long shall we worship the radiant face of fair Bacchus.)

The *Hercules Oetaeus* is an oddity in that it has two choruses, but its
authorship is suspected on many grounds, and Seneca may have been
only partly responsible for this shapeless play of nearly two thousand
lines, the longest surviving classical drama.

If we look for an answer to the question why Seneca wrote these rather
unusual plays, we may first clear the ground of unlikely suggestions. The
tragedies were not written as spectacles for reasons outlined above. It is

most likely that they were written, as Miss B. Marti once suggested, to
be a formal program of Stoic teaching. This theory supposed that the
order of the plays in the Etruscus manuscript was canonical, and that
they were intended to give in dramatic verse form a kind of teaching
comparable to that of the prose Letters.[9] There are certainly many
passages reflecting Stoic doctrine (as there are also Epicurean
sentiments), and the leading Stoic writer of his day would have a
predictable interest in Hercules, the great Stoic hero-savior. (He is the
central figure in one genuine and one questionable play, and there are
several other references to him, e.g. the extended list of his deeds at
Agamemnon 808-66.) But it needs a good deal of special pleading to
infer Stoic teaching from all the plays, though it may well have been a
conscious, if minor, ingredient in some.

One mistake is to look for a uniform purpose behind the plays, and to
regard them as a planned collection. Another possible mistake is to
assume too august a motive in Seneca's mind. It is less forced and more
straightforward to see in the tragedies an attempt at a new form of
literary drama. Seneca was perhaps the greatest stylist of his generation,
and whereas the Letters and the treatises were written with the
philosopher's pen, the plays were the *tour de force* of an experimenting
litterateur. He was steeped in Greek drama, and chose the old tales as his
framework. Contemporary conditions discouraged staged plays, and his
training in rhetoric steered him towards arguments embroidered in
language rather than characters evolving in action. The declaimers
moved in a world of type-figures (the tyrant, the loyal, the
misunderstood son, the wronged wife), and a feature of the tragedies is
the metamorphosis of some leading figures of legend into these types.
So, for example, Lycus in the *Hurcules Furens* and Creon in the *Medea*
are clearly stock *tyranni*. By generalizing and exaggerating characters
Seneca could set up starker contrasts and intensify the clash of wills and
arguments.

Perhaps from the same motive he sometimes simplifies a received
plot, as in the Medea. In this play he is largely indebted to Euripides's
version (though Ovid's *Medea* was no doubt a contributing influence),
but he has cut out the Aegeus scene altogether and reduced the number
of confrontations between Medea and Jason. The nurse has a bigger role
than in Euripides, so that she can play a more equal part in her verbal
tussles with Medea. Furthermore, as Medea dominates the play with her

[9] See B. Marti in *Transactions of the American Philological Association*, 76 (1945) pp.
216ff. and *Revue des Etudes Latines*, 27 (1949), pp.189ff. The theory is criticised by N.T. Pratt
in *Transactions of the American Philological Association*, 79 (1948) pp. 1ff.

own statements of her claims and rights, a further balance is ensured by making the chorus hostile to her, whereas in Euripides it was sympathetic to her.

The *Medea* is a particularly good example of Seneca's treatment of a traditional plot, but similar points could be made about the other plays where parallels are possible with an exemplar. The conclusion seems to be that Seneca the dramatist wanted most of all to explore the tensions and struggles of human beings, usually in hopeless or nearly hopeless situations, as typified and highlighted by the characters of legend. Of course most playwrights are doing something like this, but Seneca concentrates on the formulation of the arguments by which passionate individuals in conflict justify themselves, particularly ringing the changes on the anguish of hatred, love or despair. It was with some justification that Regenbogen saw the words from the *Hercules Oetaeus* 252-3 *et formas dolor/errat per omnes* as a Senecan motto.[10] In doing this, as a child of his time he used all the resources of declamation of which he was undisputed master. This approach tends, of course, to superficiality: the psychology of the plays is generally unsubtle, and the well-springs of human conduct are scarcely revealed. But even a self-conscious debating speech or a reflective monologue can tell us something about men and women, however they may be tricked out with endless rhetorical questions and self-apostrophes. Seneca's characters, like Chekhov's, spend much of their time exposing their souls to us; but in Seneca it is not the revelation but the technique of exposure which is paramount.

It would be a very biased apologist who denied that there is much in these works that is banal, unlovely and boring. No one defends the piling up of horror at the climaxes of the *Thyestes* and *Phaedra*. It is hard not to take as a grotesquely sick joke lines like Atreus' remark to Thyestes, who has just knowingly eaten his sons, *hic esse natos crede in amplexu patris* (*Thy.* 976);[11] or the words of the blinded Oedipus, feeling his way over the stage on which Jocasta lies dead, *i prouge vade — siste, ne matrem incidas* (*Oed.* 1051).[12] But the plays should not be remembered only for lines like these, and I appended some passages which give an idea of the range of descriptive and reflective poetry (mainly in the choruses) which Seneca was capable of writing. (See also the passages quoted on pp. 197ff.)

---

[10] O. Regenbogen, *Schermz und Tod in den Tragidien Senecas* (Vortr. Bibl. Warburg, 1927-8, Leipzig-Berlin, 1930), p. 193. [The phrase can be translated literally as follows: "And sorrow wanders through all shapes." Figuratively Seneca means "Sorrow wanders about and takes many forms" or perhaps "Sorrow wanders (at random?) and afflicts all degrees"—Eds.]

[11] "Here believe the children are in the embrace of their father," Thyestes has just eaten his children.

[12] "Go exile, hasten—stop, lest you strike against your mother" Eds.

It is fair to claim for the plays a judgment which regards what they aim to be and not what the critic thinks they should have been. As exercises in declamatory drama they are not simply the only surviving Latin tragedies but unique in European literature. Seneca is often accused of having an unoriginal mind: his plays, at least, are an original creation.

The grove where Atreus sacrificed Thyestes's sons (Thy. 650-6, 665-79):

> arcana in imo regio secessu iacet,
> alta vetustum valle compescens nemus,
> penetrale regni, nulla qua laetos solet
> praebere ramos arbor aut ferro coli,
> sed taxus et cupressus et nigra ilice
> obscura nutat silva, quam supra eminens
> despectat alte quercus et vincit nemus . . .
> fons stat sub umbra tristis et nigra piger
> haeret palude: talis est dirae Stygis
> deformis unda quae facit caelo fidem.
> hinc nocte caeca gemere ferales deos
> fama est, catenis lucus excussis sonat
> ululantque manes. quidquid audire est metus
> illic videtur: errat antiquis vetus
> emissa bustis turba et insultant loco
> mairora ntis monstra; quin tota solet
> micare silva flamma, et excelsae trabes
> ardent sine igne. saepe latratu nemus
> trino remugit, saepe simulacris domus
> attonita magnis. nec dies sedat metum:
> nox propria luco est, et superstitio inferum
> in luce media regnat.

(In a remote retreat there lies a secret place, enclosing in a deep vale an ancient grove, the inner sanctum of the kingdom, where no tree extends cheerful branches or suffers the pruning-knife. Only the yew, cypress and woods of dark ilex wave their gloomy leaves, and above them all, tallest in the grove, a lofty oak looks down ... In the gloom a melancholy spring emerges, oozing along its black and miry course, like the ugly stream of fearful Styx by which the gods swear their oaths. They say that late at night the gods of death groan in this place; the grove echoes with the clanking of chains, and there is a shrieking of ghosts. All that is fearful simply to hear of is there actually seen: a crowd of the ancient dead leave their old tombs and prowl around, while monstrous forms, greater than any known before, leap about the place. More than that, through the wood there is always the gleam of fire, and lofty trees glow though no flames are seen. Often the grove echoes with a triple barking; often the dwelling is terrified by great phantom shapes. Nor does daylight soothe the fear: night is the grove's natural condition, and a dread awe of the underworld reigns even at midday.)

In praise of a quiet life (*Thy.* 391-403):

> stet quicumque volet potens
> aulae culmine lubrico:
> me dulcis saturet quies;
> obscuro positus loco
> leni perfruar otio,
> nullis nota Quiritibus
> aesta per tacitum fluat.
> sic cum transierint mei
> nullo cum strepitu dies,
> plebius moriar senex.
> illi mors gravis incubat
> qui, notus nimis omnibus,
> ignotus moritur sibi.

(Let whoever wishes stand on the slippery height of royal power; let me have my fill of sweet repose. In a humble place let me enjoy untroubled calm, while unknown to my fellow-townsmen let my life's course go quietly on. So, when my days without uproar have passed by, let me die, an old man of lowly rank. On him death lies heavy who, too well known to all others, dies unknown to himself.)

The captive Trojan women reflect on death (Tro. 371-408):

> verum est timidos fabula decipit
> umbras corporibus vivere conditis,
> cum coniunx imposuit manum
> supremusque dies solibus obstitit
> et tristis cineres urna coercuit?
> non prodest animam tradere funeri,
> sed restat misieris vivere longius?
> an toti morimur nullaque pars manet
> nostri, cum profugo spiritus halitu
> immixtus nebulis cessit in aera
> et nudum tetiget subdita fax latus?
> quidquid sol oriens, quidquid et occidens
> novit, caeruleis Oceanus fretis
> quidquid bis veniens et fugiens lavat,
> aetas Pegaseo corripiet gradu.
> quo bis sena volant sidera turbine,
> quo cursu properat volvere saecula

astrorum dominus, quo proerat modo
obliquis Hecate currere flexibus:
hoc omnes petimus fata nec amplius,
iuratos superis qui tetigit lacus,
usquam est. ut calidis fumus ab ignibus
vanescit, spatium per breve sordidus,
ut nubes, gravidas quas modo vidimus,
arctoi Boreae dissicit impetus:
sic hic, quo regimur, spiritus effluet.
post mortem nihil est ipsaque mors nihil,
velocis spatii meta novissima.
spem ponant avidi, solliciti metum:
temups nos avidum devorat et chaos.
mors individua est, noxia corpori
nec parcens animae: Taenara et aspero
regnum sub domino limen et obsidens
custos non facili Cerberus ostio
rumores vacui verbaque inania
et par sollicito fabula somnio.
quaeris quo iaceas post obitum loco?
quo non nata iacent.

(Is it true, or does a myth cheat our timid hearts, that souls live on
though bodies have been buried, when the wife has closed her
husband's eyes, the last day has shut out the sun, and our ashes fill
the mournful urn? Is there no good in giving up the soul to death,
but some wretched existence then still remains? Or do we wholly
die and nothing of us remains, when with the last breath the spirit
has passed into the air and mingled with the clouds, and the funeral
torch has touched the naked corpse? Everything the rising sun,
everything the setting sun knows, everything the ocean washes with
his blue waters and his double ebb and flow, time will consume
with the swiftness of Pegasus. Swiftly as the whirling rush of the
Zodiac signs, swiftly as the lord of the stars sends the ages rolling
onward, swiftly as the moon hastens on her slanting curve, so do we
all make for our dooms, and he no more exists who has once
reached the waters which give the gods their oath. As smoke from
blazing fires passes away and is foul for but a moment, as clouds
which just now seem heavy are scattered by the onset of northern
Boreas, so this breath of life which rules us will waft away. There is
nothing after death and death itself is nothing—the final goal of a
swift life's course. Let the greedy abandon their hopes and the
anxious their fears: greedy time and chaos swallows us up. Death is
indivisible: it cannot spare the soul while it destroys the body.
Taenarus and the harsh lord's realm and Cerberus, guarding the
threshold not easy to pass, are idle stories and empty words, a tale

worthless as a feverish dream. Do you ask where you will lie after
death? Where lie all those unborn.)

On immutable fate (Oed. 980-94):

fatis agimur: cedite fatis.
non sollicitae possunt curae
mutare rati stamina fusi.
quidquid patimur mortale genus,
quidquid facimus venit ex alto,
sevatque suae decreta colus
Lachesis nulla revoluta manu.
omnia secto tramite vadunt
primusque dies dedit extremum:
non illa deo vertisse licet
quae nexa suis currunt causis.
it cuique ratus prece non ulla
mobilis ordo: multis ipsum
metuisse nocet, multi fatum
venere suum dum fata timent.

(We are driven by fate: yield to fate. Anxious cares cannot change
the threads on the unalterable spindle. Whatever we mortals endure,
whatever we do, comes from above, and Lachesis keeps firm the
decrees of her distaff which no hand can reverse. All things travel
on an established path, and our first day has determined our last.
God cannot alter those things which, linked to their causes, move
swiftly onward. For each man the fixed pattern of his life goes on
and no prayer can change it. To be afraid is in itself harmful to
many, for many have come to their doom through their fear of it.)

VII

Greek and Roman Stage Production

To conclude this section on the drama and stagecraft of Antiquity, here are selections from the works of two important classical scholars and theatre historians, Roy Caston Flickinger and W. Beare.

Professor Flickinger's book, *The Greek Theatre and Its Drama*, first published in 1918, remains to this day a significant contribution to our knowledge of the Attic theatre. Professor Flickinger's concern is not the collecting of information for its own sake, but the reconstruction of theatrical conditions for the purpose of gauging their effect on the conventions of the written drama. His chapter on theatre architecture, for example, is an excellent introduction to this extremely important subject. The great outdoor Theatre of Dionysus with its rising tiers of seats, its circular *orchestra* (or dancing place), and its modest scene house was the original setting for the great fifth-century tragedies, and a beginning student is advised to become familiar with this setting if he wishes to read the plays with any understanding. In many ways, Professor Flickinger's account of the physical theatre is superior to some of the more technical studies, if only by virtue of its close concentration on the relationships between architecture and literature. Reprinted below is Professor Flickinger's examination of the effect of acting conventions, particularly the so-called "three-actor system," on the structure of the plays.

Some of his observations are based on the Aristotelian theory concerning the origin of drama that Professor Kitto (see pp. 6-20) attacks. But the general sense of his account of the relationship of staging to meaning in Greek drama survives some of its questionable assumptions.

Professor Beare's account of the conventions of the Roman theatre is likewise very useful. Much space has been devoted in theatre histories to the elaborate permanent theatres that were erected in the Latin world after the time of Pompey. Professor Beare examines instead the simpler temporary arrangements that served as a background for the first performances of Plautus and Terence. Professor Beare's account, like Flickinger's, is based to a large extent on a meticulous examination of the plays and is moreover intended as an illumination of those plays.

111

Roy Caston Flickinger

THE INFLUENCE OF ACTORS ON GREEK DRAMA*

The dithyramb and the comus, together with their derivatives, early tragedy and early comedy, were entirely choral. Actors were first developed in tragedy. . . . Inasmuch as the early dithyramb and early tragedy were devoted to the worship of Dionysus and since their choreutae[1] were his attendant sprites (satyrs or sileni), it followed that their songs would mostly take the form of prayers addressed to him, hymns in his honor, or odes descriptive of his adventures, sufferings, etc. A lyric duet between the coryphaeus[2] and the other choreutae was also possible. Such performances bore much the same relationship to later tragedy that the modern oratorio bears to a sacred opera. That is to say, the choreutae were not differentiated in character, and there was no dramatic impersonation . . . ; despite their costumes the chorus sang as human worshipers of Dionysus, not in accordance with their character as sileni. From the duet between the coryphaeus and the other choreutae it was only a step, but a highly important one, no longer to think of the coryphaeus as one silenus among his fellows but as Dionysus himself in the midst of his followers, and then to set him off by himself as an actor in contradistinction to the choreutae and their (new) coryphaeus. This innovation was the work of Thespis, and however long the name "tragedy" may already have been applied to the previous performances this step marked the first beginning of tragedy in the modern sense. . . . Now that the new actor had to impersonate Dionysus, the necessity rested likewise upon the sileni in the chorus to live up to their own, previously neglected, character. It was not long until by a change of mask and costume the actor was enabled to represent other personages as well as Dionysus himself. This practice made possible a much more involved type of drama than the limited resources would at first glance seem to permit.

Aeschylus' earliest extant play, the *Suppliants*, belongs to the two-actor period, but employs the second actor so sparingly as to afford a very good idea of the possibilities of the one-actor play.[3] Omitting the

* From Roy C. Flickinger, *The Greek Theater and Its Drama* (Chicago: University of Chicago Press, 1918), pp. 162–195 abridged by the editors. Copyright 1918, 1922, and 1926 by the University of Chicago.
    [1] Chorus members.   [2] Leader of the chorus.
    [3] It is now believed that *The Suppliants* is not the earliest of Aeschylus' surviving plays — that honor belonging to *The Persians*. Without question, however, *The Suppliants* is the most primitive of the extant Greek tragedies, the closest in spirit and technique to the earliest experiments in dramatic writing. — Eds.

choral odes, the action runs as follows: The fifty daughters of Danaus (the chorus) seek sanctuary near Argos to escape the unwelcome suit of their cousins. At vs. 176 Danaus begins to admonish his daughters and a dialogue (vss. 204–33) ensues between them. At vs. 234 the king of Argos enters and engages with the chorus in a dialogue and a lyric duet (vss. 234–417). During this scene Danaus is present, silent, inactive, and all but unnoticed; cf. vs. 318. Of course in a one-actor play this character must have been removed so that the single actor might reappear as the king. But that could easily have been managed and would affect the present piece in no essential way. After an ode the dialogue between the king and the chorus is resumed (vss. 438–523), broken in upon only by a brief conversation between the king and Danaus (vss. 480–503). The former instructs Danaus how to supplicate the citizens in the town and, upon the latter's request for protection, orders attendants to accompany him. Here for the first time are the two actors simultaneously employed, but their words serve no more important purpose than to motivate the exit of one of them. At vs. 523 the king likewise withdraws. At vs. 600 Danaus reappears and with but a slight interruption on the part of his daughters (vss. 602–4) informs them that the Argives have decided to shield them (vss. 600 f., 605–24). At vs. 710 Danaus descries the suitors' fleet in the distance and declares, "I will return with helpers and defenders" (vs. 726). Nevertheless, the scene is continued until vs. 775, when Danaus departs to spread the alarm, incidentally releasing this actor to play the part of the suitors' herald. At vs. 836 the herald enters and to the accompaniment of a lyric duet between himself and the chorus tries to drag the Danaids away. At vs. 907 this attempt at violence is brought to a standstill by the king's return. The following altercation between the herald and the king (vss. 907–53) provides the only bit of genuine dramatic conflict, visually represented, in the play and the only instance of both actors being fully made use of together. In a one-actor play such a passage would have been impossible but could have been presented indirectly by means of a messenger's narrative. At vs. 953 the herald withdraws, discomforted, and the king turns to the chorus (vss. 954–65). In reply the chorus ask that their father be returned to them (vss. 966 ff.). The interval having been sufficient to enable the actor to shift from the mask and costume of the herald to those of Danaus, the latter re-enters at vs. 980 and converses with his daughters until the final ode. Of all the extant plays of Aeschylus the *Suppliants* probably makes the slightest appeal to the modern student. Its principal value for us lies in the fact that it could readily be revamped for presentation by one actor and in the light which it thus sheds upon the character of one-actor drama.

Several times in this play, as appears from the foregoing outline, an

actor participates in a dialogue with the chorus. It was not the practice for the choral part in such dialogues to be spoken by all the
choreutae in unison, but by the chorus leader alone. Thus, though a
sharp distinction was drawn between actors and chorus, the former
being furnished by the state and the latter by private means . . . , yet
the coryphaeus served as a bond of connection between the two. We
have seen how the first actor was developed from the chorus leader;
doubtless the successive additions to the number of actors were suggested in each case by the advantages arising from this quasi-
histrionic function of the coryphaeus. Thus in addition to the regular
actors, at each stage of development the tragic poet always had at
his disposal also one quasi-actor for carrying on his dialogues. . . .
In the one-actor period this quasi-histrionic function of the coryphaeus
resulted in a convention which continued long after the necessity for
it had passed away. It is obvious that at that juncture the single actor
could converse with no one but the chorus. This practice became so
stereotyped that in the two-actor period whenever a character came
into the presence of the chorus and another actor he directed his remarks to the chorus before turning to the other character. Of course
oftentimes this was the natural thing to do. But the force of tradition
is seen in the fact that the principle was sometimes observed under
unfavorable conditions. . . . [I]n the *Persians* a messenger from Greece
ignores his queen (vss. 249 ff.) and reports the Persian disaster to
the chorus of elders. Not until vs. 290 does Atossa address him, and
in typical Greek fashion Aeschylus strives to make her words gloss
over the unreality of his characters' compliance with convention. "For
a long time have I kept silence," she begins, "dumbfounded by catastrophe. This ill exceeds my power to tell or ask our woes." The same
convention persisted even into the three-actor period. Clytemnestra's
husband has been gone ten years or more, yet she must excuse herself
to the chorus (Aeschylus' *Agamemnon*, vss. 855–78) before greeting
her lord. . . . Moreover the coryphaeus sometimes exercises an important influence upon the plot. For example, in Aeschylus' *Libation-
Bearers*, vss. 766 ff., it is the coryphaeus who induces the servant to
alter the wording of the summons with which she is sent to Aegisthus.
By this device he comes unescorted and falls an easy victim to the
conspirators.

In view of the normal employment of the coryphaeus as a quasi-
actor, Aeschylus took an easy and obvious step, or rather half-step, in
advance when he introduced the second actor. We have seen that the
deuteragonist was already made use of, though sparingly, in the *Suppliants*. Also the *Persians*, the *Seven against Thebes* . . . , and the
Prometheus Bound require but two actors for presentation. The great
advantage accruing from the second actor is manifest. Instead of

being compelled to resort to a messenger's report of an altercation or dialogue between two personages, the playwright was now enabled to bring the characters face to face in person upon his stage. On the other hand, so limited a number of actors often seriously embarrassed the dramatist in the economy of his play. Perhaps the best example of this is afforded by Aeschylus' *Prometheus.* In the opening scene Cratos and Bia (Strength and Force) drag Prometheus to a remote spot in Scythia and Hephaestus nails him to a crag. How can these four characters be presented by two actors? In the first place Bia has no speaking part, and mutes were freely employed in addition to the regular actors. In the second place Prometheus was represented by a wooden figure. This explains how it was possible for a nail to be driven right through his breast (vss. 64 f.). It explains also why so great emphasis is laid upon the fastening process; first the hands are pinned down (vs. 55), then the arms (vs. 60), the breast (vs. 65) and sides (vs. 71), and finally the legs (vs. 74). Thus the immobility and lifelessness of the supposed Prometheus are accounted for. Neither Hephaestus' sympathy nor Cratos' insults elicit a single word of reply from his lips. Although this silence arises naturally from the Titan's unyielding disposition, yet the real reason lies in the use of a dummy. At vs. 81 Hephaestus retires, and after six lines of further insults Cratos follows him. A slight pause would naturally ensue, so that Prometheus might be sure that his enemy had passed beyond the sound of his voice. These intervals enabled the former actor to take his place at some crack or opening behind the lay figure and break Prometheus' speechlessness (vs. 88). The other actor reappears in a succession of rôles throughout the play, as Oceanus (vs. 284), Io (vs. 561), and Hermes (vs. 944); but these shifts were easily managed.

Soon after Sophocles' first appearance (468 B.C. or possibly 471 B.C.) he introduced the third actor. First of all this innovation permitted a larger number of characters to be presented. In Aeschylus' two-actor plays the characters number three in the *Suppliants* in addition to the chorus and coryphaeus, four in the *Persians,* six in the *Prometheus,* and five in *Seven against Thebes.* In the three-actor plays Aeschylus' characters range from five to seven, Sophocles' from five to nine, and Euripides' from seven to eleven, except that Euripides' satyr-play, the *Cyclops,* has but three characters. Secondly, a third actor allowed greater flexibility in handling entrances and exits. An artificial pause, more or less improbably motivated, to enable an actor to change his mask and costume before appearing in another rôle would now be less frequently required. . . . Thirdly, it allowed three personages to appear side by side in the same scene, whereby in turn a certain aesthetic effect became possible. I refer to the varied emotions which one actor's statements or conduct sometimes produce in two other characters. An excellent illustration is afforded by the scene with the Corinthian messenger in Sophocles' *Oedipus the King*, vss. 924 ff. As the awful conviction is brought home to Jocaste that Oedipus is her son as well as her husband, she rushes from the stage to hang herself; but Oedipus, on the contrary, still lacking the fatal clue, becomes elated at the prospect of discovering his parents' identity. Similarly in the same playwright's *Electra*, vss. 660 ff., the false report of Orestes' death cheers his mother with the assurance that her murder of Agamemnon must now remain unavenged, but plunges Electra into the desperation of despair. Such situations would have been impossible in the two-actor drama. Finally, the introduction of a third actor contributed to the decay of the chorus. . . . In the prehistoric period the chorus and its coryphaeus, from the nature of the case, monopolized every line. After Thespis had brought in the first actor the chorus yielded but a small place to its rival. Even in the two-actor period in our earliest extant play, the *Suppliants*, the chorus sang five hundred and sixty-five verses out of a total of a thousand and seventy-four, and in addition to this the coryphaeus spoke ninety verses. In six of Aeschylus' seven extant pieces the choral element varies from three-fifths to about one-half of the whole play. The *Prometheus*, for special reasons, is exceptional, the fraction being only one-sixth. The effect of the third actor is seen in the fact that in Sophocles the proportion varies from one-fourth to one-seventh and in Euripides from one-fourth to one-eighth.

The question naturally arises, Why were the Greek dramatists so slow in increasing the number of actors? This was due partly to a paucity of histrionic talent and partly to difficulty in mastering the dramatic technique of the dialogue.

In the dithyramb and the prehistrionic drama the poet was his own coryphaeus. Accordingly when Thespis introduced the first actor he served in that capacity himself, appointing another as coryphaeus. So did Phrynichus, Aeschylus, and the other dramatists of that period. Since there were then no retired actors and no opportunity to serve an apprenticeship, it is obvious that these early poets had to teach themselves how to act. At this stage it was not possible for anyone except a playwright to become an actor, and actors must have been correspondingly scarce. The situation improved somewhat after Aeschylus introduced the second actor, for though the poets still carried the major rôles it now became possible for men with natural histrionic ability to develop it and gain experience in minor parts. By the time of Sophocles, actors had become so plentiful, relatively speaking, that he could increase the number employed by each poet from two to three and could retire from personal participation in the public presentation of his works. His weak voice is said to have been responsible for this second innovation; but he occasionally appeared in scenes where this weakness was no great hindrance, e.g., as a harp player in *Thamyris* and as an expert ball player in *Nausicaa*. By 449 B.C. the profession was so large and its standing so well recognized that a contest of tragic actors was made an annual event in the program of the City Dionysia.[4] This course of development reveals one reason for the long duration of the one- and two-actor stages in Greek drama.

We shall now pass to the second reason. In the prehistrionic period a series of lyric questions and answers between chorus and coryphaeus was the nearest approach to a dialogue that was possible . . . . With the invention of the first actor this interplay of question and answer, still lyrical in form, could be carried on by the actor and the chorus (including the coryphaeus). Such a duet, which came to be known as a *commus,* continued in use, especially for dirges, as long as the chorus lasted. Side by side with this, however, there quickly developed a non-lyric interchange of spoken lines between actor and coryphaeus. But not until the second actor was added did true dialogue in the modern sense become possible. Yet the poets could not at once make full use of even these simple resources. Our analysis of Aeschylus' *Suppliants* . . . shows that in two instances Danaus stood silent and unaddressed during a conversation between the other actor and the coryphaeus. Moreover, priority of usage constrained the playwrights to give the actor-coryphaeus dialogue precedence over actor-actor dialogue. . . . They seemed unable to weld the two types together with a technique which would employ all three persons at once. In the three-actor period the embarrassment of riches made their helplessness the more striking. "A" might engage in a dialogue with "B" while "C" remained inactive; then with "C" while "B" was silent; and finally "B" and "C" might converse, with "A" remaining passive. Often the transitions are marked or the longer speeches set off by a few more or less perfunctory verses (usually two) spoken by the coryphaeus. The type is not frequently worked out as completely as I have just indicated, but the principle is illustrated on a lesser scale in almost every play. Compare, for example, Euripides' *Helen,* vss. 1186–1300, and *Andromache,* vss. 547–766. Such an arrangement, needless to say, falls far short of a genuine trialogue or tetralogue. Yet we must not be unfair in condemning this practice. The Greek poets were feeling their way and could not immediately attain to every refinement. Even in Shakespeare and the modern drama, despite centuries of continuous experimentation and the numerous examples of superior technique, the tandem arrangement of dialogue is still not uncommon.

[4] A spring festival dedicated to Dionysus and including in its program the performance of tragedies and comedies. — Eds.

A half-step in advance consisted in the silent actor interrupting the dialogue with some electrifying utterance. For example, in Aeschylus' *Libation-Bearers* (458 B.C.), Clytemnestra's appeal to Orestes on the score of her motherhood stays his hand in the very act of murdering her, and he weakly turns to his trusted friend, Pylades, for guidance. The latter's ringing response,

> Wilt thou abjure half Loxias' behest,
> The word of Pytho, and thy sacred troth?
> Hold all the world thy foe rather than Heaven
> [vss. 900–903, Warr's translation],

is as effective as if uttered by the god in person, and urges Orestes on to the deadly deed. These are the only words that Pylades utters in the whole tragedy. In another play belonging to the same trilogy, the *Eumenides*, Aeschylus rose to the full possibilities of his histrionic resources — Orestes, the coryphaeus, Apollo, and Athena all participating in the conversation between vss. 746 and 753. Similarly, in Sophocles' *Oedipus at Colonus*, Antigone, Oedipus, Ismene, and the coryphaeus all speak between vss. 494 and 506, and in Euripides' *Suppliants* the herald, the coryphaeus, Adrastus, and Theseus divide four lines among them (vss. 510–13). But after all, such instances are comparatively rare and seldom extend over a very long passage.

In contradistinction to tragic practice Aristophanes in the last quarter of the fifth century employed not merely three but occasionally even four comic actors in ensemble scenes. For example, in the *Lysistrata*, vss. 78–246, Calonice, Myrrhina, Lysistrata, and Lampito engage in a running fire of conversation quite in the modern manner. Again, in the *Frogs*, vss. 1411 ff., Dionysus, Aeschylus, Euripides, and Pluto all have speaking parts, although the last two do not address one another. In the same play (vs. 555) Dionysus utters three words while three other participants in the dialogue are present. Under similar circumstances Pseudartabus interposes two verses (100 and 104) in the *Acharnians*, and Triballus parts of five verses (1615, 1628 f., and 1678 f.) in the *Birds*. In these passages the comic coryphaei have no speaking parts. Trialogues are not so rare in Old Comedy as to justify an enumeration of the instances, and they are sometimes embellished by the participation of the coryphaei. Nevertheless, the old tandem arrangement is still the more common one when three characters are present.

We thus pass from one problem to another: Why this disparity between the technique of tragedy and comedy? Must we suppose that the comic dramatists were more clever artists than their tragic confrères? By no means. Comedy was more mobile and reacted more quickly to the actual conditions of contemporaneous life; tragedy was more conventional, never could free itself entirely from the power of tradition, and could only slowly modify that tradition. . . .

But were the resources of the tragic writers as great as those of the comedians? We have seen how the first, second, and third actors were added to Greek tragedy. Is there reason to believe that the tragedians of Athens ever followed the comedians in employing a larger number? . . .

It can be said at once that if we are willing to grant that the Greeks made use of certain desperate expedients it is physically possible to stage all the extant tragedies with three actors. But these expedients are so offensive to modern feeling as to be tolerable only as a last resort. It will be best to begin at a point where comparative agreement is possible, viz., with Aeschylus' earlier plays, which nearly everyone would admit were intended for two actors alone. Do they reveal any indication of this limitation?

In the analysis of Aeschylus' *Suppliants* . . . , the reader will remember that Danaus, having declared "I will return with helpers and defenders," took his departure at vs. 775; after an ode, the suitors' herald arrived on the scene (vs. 836) but was balked by the entrance of the Argive king (vs. 907). One would surely expect Danaus to accompany the king, but as a matter of fact he does not reappear until vs. 980. The reason for this is plain — Danaus and the herald are played by the same actor, and consequently the former can return only after the latter's departure at vs. 953. Moreover, Aeschylus sought to gloss over the blemish by having Danaus refer in advance to the possibility of his being slow in spreading the alarm (vs. 730) and by having the chorus request the king to send their father back to them (vss. 968 ff.), as if his absence had been perfectly natural. This incident teaches us four things: (1) A single actor could carry several rôles; the simplicity and sameness of ancient costumes and the ease of slipping them off and on, together with the use of masks by the actors, made this practice more feasible than it is with us. Overzealous classicists have not merely asked us to tolerate this practice but even to admire its results. Thus, when one character returns to report the death of another the spectators are supposed to have been doubly moved if they could penetrate the messenger's disguise and from the identity of stature, build, and voice recognize the ghost, as it were, of the departed visibly before them(!). (2) This practice oftentimes necessitated the arbitrary withdrawal of a character from the scene of action and his enforced absence when he would naturally be present. (3) By inventing an inner reason for this the poet strove to conceal or gloss over his yielding to external need. (4) The intervals between the withdrawal of Danaus and the entrance of the herald (vss. 776– 836) and vice versa (vss. 953–80) afford an inkling as to the length of time required for such shifts in rôles.

Further information is derived from Aeschylus' *Prometheus Bound.*
. . . (5) Supernumeraries may be employed for silent parts, e.g., that
of Bia. (6) A part may be divided between a lay figure and an
actor, as in the case of Prometheus himself. From the nature of things,
this expedient would not be frequently employed; but an analogous
device (6a) is common, viz., to give the silent portions of a rôle to a
mute and the speaking portions to an actor. (7) The stubborn silence
of the mutes and supernumeraries employed according to principles
(5) and (6a) is sometimes extremely embarrassing and difficult to
motivate. (4a) The interval required for a "lightning" change from
one character to another was much shorter than the *Suppliants* led us
to suppose. Six verses and a slight pause in the action enabled the
actor impersonating Hephaestus to withdraw by the side entrance after
vs. 81 and to get in position to speak from behind the wooden figure
of Prometheus at vs. 88. This conclusion is confirmed by certain evidence in Plautus' translation of Greek comedies, which indicates that
about thirteen lines would suffice.

Still other principles are derivable from Aeschylus' *Persians.* The
ghost of Darius having requested his widow to meet their son Xerxes
with a change of raiment, Atossa replies (vss. 849 ff.): "I shall en-
deavor to meet my son . . . . and," turning to the chorus, "if he comes
hither before me, do you comfort him and escort him to his palace."
These words are clearly intended to prepare us for her failure to appear in the dénouement, and in fact she does not appear. But since
one of the two actors is disengaged in the final scene, at first glance
there seems to be no external reason for her absence. It is evident that
Aeschylus valued the parts of Atossa and Xerxes so highly that he
wanted them both played by the better of his two actors, the *protagonist.* If Atossa had appeared with her son, she must have been
impersonated by a different actor than in the opening scenes. The
poet preferred to sacrifice verisimilitude somewhat rather than to
"split" Atossa's rôle in this fashion. Hence, we must conclude (8) that
at any cost star parts were reserved for the leading actor, (9) that
split rôles were to be avoided, and (10) that sometimes for purely
technical reasons the dramatist would unnaturally keep a character
off the stage entirely in certain scenes.

If we could be sure that the final scene of Aeschylus' *Seven against
Thebes* is genuine, it would be possible to deduce a final principle.
The main support for the charge of interpolation is that this scene in
a two-actor play apparently requires three actors. From vs. 961 to vs.
1004 Antigone and Ismene engage in a lyric duet; at vs. 1005 a herald
enters and converses with Antigone. From this scene, which I am
inclined to accept as genuine . . . , we must concede either that a
supernumerary could occasionally bear a brief singing (or speaking)

part or preferably that the herald, standing in the side entrance concealed from the spectators and already dressed for his own rôle, sang Ismene's share of the duet while a mute went through the dumb show of her part before the audience; at the conclusion of the duet he promptly appeared in *propria persona*. Though the latter alternative is offensive to present-day taste, it is not unparalleled in the annals of the modern stage. In any case one of these alternatives is the last principle (11) to be drawn from the two-actor drama.

Now these eleven principles are so manifestly operative in the other Greek tragedies as to raise an irresistible presumption that some restriction (to three or at most to four actors) applied also to them. It would obviously be out of place to pass every play in review here; I must content myself with a few typical illustrations and then consider the crucial cases.

In order to avenge his daughter, Menelaus is on the point of murdering her rival (Andromache) and the latter's son when he is interrupted by the arrival of Peleus, Hermione's father-in-law. There is no reason why Menelaus should fear the old man's blusterings; nevertheless he suddenly leaves Hermione in the lurch and takes his departure with the words:

> Now, seeing that my leisure serveth not,
> Home will I go; for not from Sparta far
> Some certain town there is, our friend, time was,
> But now our foe: against her will I march,
> Leading mine host, and bow her 'neath my sway.
> Soon as things there be ordered to my mind,
> I will return, etc.
> [Euripides *Andromache*, vss. 732 ff., Way's translation]

Surely no excuse was ever less convincing than this! No wonder Professor Verrall's ingenuity has built up a whole reinterpretation of the play around it. The real reason for the sudden leaving is only too apparent — Orestes is presently to make his appearance (vs. 881) and Menelaus' actor is required for his rôle. This exemplifies (1), (2), and (3).

Again, in Sophocles' *Maidens of Trachis*, Lichas, Deianira, and a messenger are on the scene when Deianira spies Iole in a throng of captives and questions her (vss. 307 ff.). Iole makes no reply whatsoever. Lichas explains her refusal to answer by stating that from grief and weeping she has not uttered a word since leaving her fatherland (vss. 322 ff.). Since three actors are already occupied in this scene it is evident that Iole is played by a mute and cannot speak. This illustrates principles (5) and (7).

Still again, up to vs. 1245 of Euripides' *Orestes*, when he enters the palace, Pylades speaks freely. At vs. 1554 Menelaus, Orestes, Her-

mione, and Pylades enter the scene. The last two are now played by
mutes, the third actor appearing as Apollo at vs. 1625. Orestes threatens to kill Hermione; and after vainly striving to deter him Menelaus
turns to Pylades with the query (vs. 1591): "Do you, also, share in
this murder, Pylades?" What is a mute to do under such circumstances? Orestes relieved the situation by saying: "His silence gives
consent; my word will suffice." There can be no doubt that the playwright intended Menelaus' question to create the illusion that Pylades
could have spoken had he so desired, principles (6a) and (7). . . .

Finally, for the presentation of his *Phoenician Maids,* Euripides
must have had a leading actor of great musical attainments. For such
a performer the rôles of Jocaste and Antigone were especially adapted,
and he seems to have played them both, principle (8). The piece
opens with a soliloquy by Jocaste, who withdraws at vs. 87. Immediately a servant appears on the palace roof and tells Antigone to tarry
upon the stairs until he can assure himself that there is no one near to
see her and to spread scandalous reports of her indiscretion. Thus,
Antigone's appearance is delayed for fifteen verses (vss. 88–102),
which is sufficient to enable Jocaste's actor to shift to the new rôle,
principle (4a). The protagonist continues to play both parts without
difficulty, except at vss. 1270–82, the latter speaking some six verses.
Obviously Antigone's lines in this brief scene must have been delivered
by one of the subordinate players, though such splitting of a rôle
violates Aeschylean practice, see principle (9). Perhaps the procedure in this case was condoned by the fact that Antigone's part
previously and (for the most part) subsequently was entirely lyric,
while her few words here are in plain iambics. The difference between the singing and the speaking voice would help to conceal the
temporary substitution of another actor. It is true that by assigning
Jocaste's and Antigone's rôles to different actors throughout it is possible to distribute the parts in this play among three actors without
any difficulty whatever. But this would require us to ignore the peculiar technique of the opening scenes, the true inwardness of which
was recognized by ancient commentators.

These examples are by no means exhaustive, but it is high time
that we turn to the passages which are of crucial importance to the
three-actor theory. In Aeschylus' *Libation-Bearers* a servant has just
informed Clytemnestra that her paramour is slain, and she cries out:
"Let some one quickly give me an ax to slay a man withal" (vs. 889).
We are to suppose that the slave at once makes his exit to comply with
her command. She speaks two lines more and Orestes enters. They
divide seven more lines between them, and Orestes' purpose is beginning to waver when he catches sight of Pylades entering and
asks: "Pylades, what shall I do? Shrink from **killing my mother?**"

Pylades' electrifying response has already been quoted. . . . Here we have four speaking characters between vss. 886 and 900 and consequently four actors, unless the servant can be transformed into Pylades within the space of nine lines, vss. 891–99. This would be a "lightning" change indeed (4*a*), and it is not surprising that it has been challenged. Yet the ancient scholiast accepts it and I do not believe we are warranted in pronouncing it impossible, especially since the shift is merely from one male character to another.

Another sort of difficulty is presented by Euripides' *Andromache*. Melenaus, Andromache, and her son, Molossus, all have speaking (or singing) parts just before the entrance of Peleus at vs. 547. Since none of the earlier speakers has withdrawn and since Peleus at once begins to talk, it would seem at first glance that we had four actors indisputably before us. Not so, answer the defenders of the traditional view, for it is significant that Molossus becomes utterly dumb after Peleus enters. Therefore we are asked to believe that Molossus was played by a mute throughout, and the actor who is presently to appear as Peleus delivered from behind the scenes the words which belong to Molossus, the mute furnishing only the gestures. We have already found support for this kind of thing in a suspected scene of Aeschylus' *Seven against Thebes*, principle (11), second alternative. . . . But we are asked to go further and believe that this was always the practice when children seemed to sing or speak upon the Greek stage; and in confirmation of this it is pointed out that whenever children have a part, as in Euripides' *Alcestis*, vss. 393 ff. and *Medea*, vss. 1271 ff., one of the actors is always off the scene and available for this purpose. The most difficult example of this problem has recently come to light in the fragments of Euripides' *Hypsipyle*, vss. 1579 ff. The heroine and Amphiaraus converse from the beginning of the fragment to vs. 1589, where the latter makes his exit. Two lines of farewell (vss. 1590 f.) are addressed to him and are assigned by the papyrus to "the children of Hypsipyle." Moreover, they are of such a nature that one line must have been spoken by each of the two youths. Next, *one* of them converses with his mother until Thoas, who also has a speaking part, appears at vs. 1632. Here, then, if the children's parts are taken by actors we have four actors required in two successive scenes. The only alternative lies in supposing that mutes impersonated the boys and that Thoas' actor, already dressed for his introit at vs. 1632, spoke their lines from behind the scenes. This would include twelve lines for one youth and one line, *in a different voice*, for the other.

But the most intractable play of all is Sophocles' *Oedipus at Colonus*. Antigone and Oedipus are on the stage continuously for the first eight hundred and forty-seven verses (the latter until vs. 1555), while the

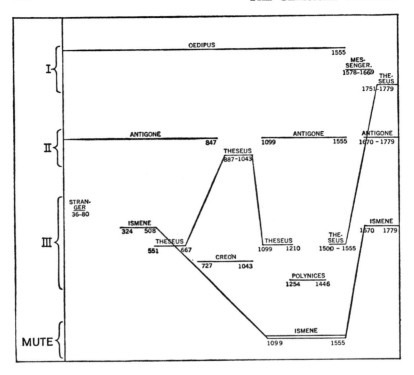

Distribution of Rôles to Actors in
Sophocles' *Oedipus at Colonus*

third actor appears successively as a stranger, Ismene, Theseus, and Creon. . . . So far there is no difficulty; but at this point Creon hopes to bring Oedipus to time by announcing that his guards have already seized Ismene (off-scene) and by having them now drag Antigone away. Creon threatens to carry off Oedipus as well, but at vs. 887 Theseus reappears and prevents further outrage. Note, however, that if only three actors were available Theseus must now be impersonated by Antigone's actor, whereas previously he was represented by the actor who is now playing Creon's part. Such splitting of a rôle is directly contrary to Aeschylean practice, principle (9), and has not in this instance the justification which Euripides had for splitting Antigone's part in the *Phoenician Maids*. . . . For Theseus' second actor participates in the dialogue more extensively than did hers and his lines are prose throughout, while hers were entirely prose for one actor and (almost) entirely lyric for the other. But there are still other obstacles ahead. At vs. 1043 Creon and Theseus withdraw; after a choral ode Antigone, Theseus, and Ismene rejoin Oedipus (vs. 1099). Inasmuch as Ismene now has no speaking part she is evidently played by a mute, principle (6a). Presumably the other two are represented by the same actors as at the beginning, although this second transfer in Theseus rôle doubles the chances of the audience noticing the shift. The only alternative, however, is to split also Antigone's rôle at this point. Theseus retires at vs. 1210 and reappears at vs. 1500, his actor having impersonated Polynices in the interval (vss. 1254–1446). At vs. 1555 all the characters exeunt. In the final act a messenger is on the stage from vs. 1578 to vs. 1669. Since Antigone and Ismene enter immediately thereafter (vs. 1670), it is necessary to suppose that they are played by the same actors as at the beginning and that Oedipus has become the messenger. At vs. 1751 Theseus makes his final entrance, represented this time by Oedipus' actor, so that this important rôle is played in turn by each of the three actors! This means splitting Theseus' rôle twice. It is also possible to split his rôle and Ismene's (or Antigone's) once each, or to split his rôle once and to have the final actor in this part sing from behind the scenes the few words which fall to Ismene just before Theseus' last entrance, principle (11). On the other hand, though a fourth actor would obviate all these difficulties we should then have no explanation for the complicated system of entrances and exits and for the strange silence of Ismene during vss. 1099–1555, especially during vss. 1457–99. . . .

I do not consider it warrantable to draw a categorical conclusion from the data considered in the last fifteen paragraphs. But in my opinion the technique of almost every tragedy is explicable only on the assumption that the regular actors were restricted to three; and, as I stated at the beginning, it is physically possible to stage every play with that number. In the case of a few pieces, however, this limitation imposes practices which so outrage the modern aesthetic sense that we instinctively long for some manner of escape. According to late and unreliable evidence an extra performer was called a *parachoregema*. This name would indicate that he was an extra expense to the man who financed each poet's plays (the choregus . . .), and consequently that his employment would be determined by the wealth or liberality of the latter. But whether it was in fact possible for the tragic playwrights occasionally to have the services of such an extra, and, if so, under what conditions and how, are questions which in the present state of our knowledge can receive only hypothetical answers. It must be recognized, however, that the paucity of actors in the early days resulted, as we have just seen, in conventions of staging which perhaps were afterward accepted as part of the tradition, however unnecessary they may in the meanwhile have become. The technique of composition also makes it clear in my opinion that extra performers, if such were in fact engaged, were not on a par with the other three nor employed freely throughout the whole play but merely recited or sang a very few lines at those crises in the dramatic economy which were occasioned by the limitation in the number of regular actors. . . .

For about a century, beginning with 449 B.C., the state annually engaged three tragic protagonists to be assigned by lot to the three poets who were about to compete with plays. Each protagonist seems to have hired his own subordinate actors (deuteragonist and tritagonist) and with their assistance presented all the plays (at the City Dionysia three tragedies and one satyric drama) which his poet had composed for the occasion. The victorious actor in each year's contest was automatically entitled to appear the following year. The other two protagonists were perhaps selected by means of a preliminary contest. . . . These regulations applied, *mutatis mutandis*, also to the contest of comic actors and to the tragic and comic contests at the Lenaea. Thus at the Lenaea of 418 B.C. Callippides acted in the two tragedies of Callistratus, and Lysicrates in the other dramatist's two plays. And it should be noted that, whereas Callippides won the prize for acting, Callistratus was defeated in the competition of tragedies. This must have been a point of considerable difficulty, for an actor's chances must have been greatly hampered by his being required to present a poor series of plays; and a poet, likewise, must have suffered by reason of an inferior presentation of his dramas. But sometime in the fourth century, when the playwrights were no longer required to write satyr-plays . . . , a more equitable system was introduced. Each of the protagonists in turn now acted one of the three tragedies of each poet, the histrionic talent at the disposal of each dramatist being thus made exactly the same. For example, at the City Dionysia of 341 B.C. . . . Astydamas was the victorious playwright; his *Achilles* was played by Thettalus, his *Athamas* by Neoptolemus, and his *Antigone* by Athenodorus. The same actors likewise presented the three tragedies of Evaretus and those of the third dramatist. On this occasion Neoptolemus won; a year later, under similar conditions, he was defeated by Thettalus.

We have seen how slow was the rise of actors into a profession distinct from the poets. At a later time, however, they were strongly organized into guilds under the name of "Dionysiac artists" (οἱ ἀμφὶ τὸν Διόνυσον τεχνῖται). Their strongest "union" (κοινόν or σύνοδος) was centered at Athens and it was also the earliest (fourth century B.C.). Others were situated at Thebes, Argos, Teos, Ptolemais,

Cyprus, and in all parts of the Greek-speaking world. Now already in the fifth century traveling troupes had presented at the country festivals plays which had won popular acclaim in Athens. For economic reasons it was to the advantage both of the players who had to divide their emoluments and of the communities which hired them to make these traveling companies as small as possible and consequently to restrict their repertoire to plays capable of being performed by a minimum of actors. With the organization of guilds the presentation of dramas "in the provinces" or even at important festivals would be taken over by them; and the same economic causes as before would operate to restrict the number of players in a company. There is reason to believe that a normal troupe in the time of the *technitae* consisted of three actors. Inscriptions for the Soteric festival at Delphi for the years 272–269 B.C. inclusive contain the names of ten companies of tragic actors and twelve of comic actors. These performers belonged to the Athenian guild and in every case there are three names to a company. There is no reason to doubt that this number was customary also in the wandering troupes of the pre-technitae period. . . . [I]f the officials of a city contracted with the union for one or more troupes for a dramatic festival they would be provided with three-actor companies; but if they desired to witness some four-actor play or to avoid the infelicities arising from the splitting or ill-assorted doubling of rôles . . . they might *at extra expense* secure a parachoregema [or supplementary performer] in the form of a fourth actor and so gratify their wishes. . . .

The fact that women's parts in Elizabethan drama were played by boys has been used to explain the fondness of Elizabethan heroines for masquerading in masculine attire. Now the Greek theater, likewise, knew no actresses — all parts, regardless of sex, were presented by men. Can any effect of this practice be traced in the extant plays? In the first place Greek drama also was not unacquainted with the spectacle of masculine performers impersonating women who were disguised as men; cf. the rôle of Mnesilochus in Aristophanes' *Women at the Thesmophoria,* and the chorus and several characters in the same author's *Women in Council.* But in the Greek theater this occurrence was too rare to be significant. Secondly, it has frequently been observed that the heroines of Greek tragedy are as a rule lacking in feminine tenderness and diffidence and are prone to such masculine traits as boldness, initiative, and self-reliance. On the other hand the women who have speaking parts in comedy are usually either impaired in reputation or disagreeable in character — courtesans, ravished maidens, shrews, scolds, jealous wives, intriguing mothers-in-law, etc. Now these facts are doubtless the resultant of many factors. For example, tragedy has little direct use for the modest violet type

of woman, and the sharp demarcation between dramatic genres . . .
tended to prevent their indirect employment in scenes meant merely
to relieve the tragic intensity of the main plot. Likewise, social conditions must have had a great deal to do with the exclusion of women
of unblemished reputation and attractive years from the comic stage.
. . . Nevertheless when all is said I consider it quite possible that the
representation of women by men actors was partially responsible for
such a choice and for the delineation of female rôles. At least male
performers must have found such types of women much easier to
impersonate. Finally, if children were represented only in pantomine
and their words spoken by a grown actor from behind the scenes . . .
we can understand why girls never have a speaking part and one
reason why the words put in boys' mouths are often too old for them.
A competent critic has declared: "Euripides' children do not sing what
is appropriate to children in the circumstances supposed but what the
poet felt for the children and for the situations. In particular the song
of the boy over the dead body of his mother in the *Alcestis* is one of
his grossest errors in delineation." This situation, also, is capable of
several explanations, but who will deny that the practice of having
children's parts declaimed by adults belongs among them?

In France the court compelled actors to furnish amusement and the
church damned them for complying. In Rome the actors were slaves
or freedmen and belonged to the dregs of society. Only in Greece did
no stigma rest upon the histrionic profession. . . . [T]he actors were
active participants in a religous service and during the festival performances their persons were quasi-sacrosanct. As such, they were
entitled to and received the highest respect, and their occupation was
considered an honorable one. Consequently, they were often the con-
fidants and associates of royalty and wielded no mean influence in the
politics of their native lands. In particular as they traveled from court
to court they often acted as intermediaries in diplomatic negotiations.
Thus Aeschines, an ex-actor, was almost as influential in the Athenian
faction which favored the Macedonians as was Demosthenes in that
which opposed them. And though the latter in his speeches indulged
in frequent sneers at Aeschines' theatrical career, this was not on
account of his profession per se but because Demosthenes claimed
he had been a failure at it. Aeschines and Aristodemus, another actor,
twice went as ambassadors from Athens to Philip, king of Macedonia,
with whom the latter was *persona gratissima*. Thettalus was an especial favorite of Alexander the Great, who sent him as an emissary to
arrange his marriage with a Carian satrap's daughter. When Thettalus was defeated by Athenodorus at Tyre in 332 B.C. Alexander
said that he would rather have lost a part of his kingdom than to have
seen Thettalus defeated. These men were contemporaries of Aristotle,
who declared in his *Rhetoric* that in his day actors counted for more

in the dramatic contests than the poets. The huge fees that they received are often mentioned. In view of all this it is not surprising that
they arrogated to themselves many liberties. Aristotle states that
Theodorus always insisted upon being the first actor to appear in a
play, doubtless on a principle analogous to that which Mr. William
Archer mentions: "Where it is desired to give to one character a
special prominence and predominance, it ought, if possible, to be the
first figure on which the eye of the audience falls. . . . The solitary
entrance of Richard III throws his figure into a relief which could by
no other means have been attained." This anecdote may mean merely
that Theodorus assumed the rôle of the first character, however insignificant, in order to appear first upon the scene. But some have
thought that he actually had the plays modified so that the character
which he was to enact might appear first. Even upon the first hypothesis, however, slight alterations might sometimes have been necessary.
For example, if he wished to impersonate Antigone in such a play as
Euripides' *Phoenician Maids* and if no passage were provided like vss.
88–102 to enable the actor to shift from Jocaste, who opens the tragedy, to Antigone . . . , then perhaps the simplest solution would have
been to interpolate a few such lines for this purpose. But however
this may have been in Theodorus' case there can be little doubt that
the actors did sometimes take such liberties with their dramatic
vehicles. To correct this abuse Lycurgus, who was finance minister
of Athens in the last third of the fourth century B.C. and "completed" the theater . . . , is said to have had state copies of old plays
provided from which the actors were not allowed to deviate; and
Lycon was fined ten talents, which Alexander paid, for having interpolated one line in a comedy.

Naturally most actors were peculiarly adapted to certain types of
characters. Thus Nicostratus was most successful as a messenger,
Theodorus in female rôles, etc. The interesting significance of the
parts borne by Apollogenes, an actor of the third century, has only
recently been recognized. At Argos he impersonated Heracles and
Alexander, at Delphi, Heracles and Antaeus, at Dodona, Achilles, etc.,
in addition to winning a victory in boxing at Alexandria. Evidently
this actor was a pugilist for whom rôles and plays were carefully
chosen which would display his physique and strength to the best
advantage. Now these special predilections and accomplishments of
the actors, as well as their physical qualities, must often have run
afoul of the constant doubling and the occasional splitting of rôles as
required by the restricted number of players. Professor Rees makes
good use of such points in arguing against the three-actor limitation
in fifth-century tragedy. But in such matters custom is all-important;
we cannot be sure to what extent the Greeks were offended by infelicities of this nature. In my opinion such considerations are not strong

enough to break down the arguments drawn from dramatic technique. . . .

I ought not to conclude this chapter without a few words concerning the manner in which act divisions arose from the alternation of choral odes and histrionic passages in ancient drama. The earliest tragedies, such as Aeschylus' *Suppliants* and *Persians,* began with the entrance song of the chorus, which is called the *parodus.* In later plays it was customary for one or more actors to appear before the choral parodus in a so-called *prologue.* The first instance of this which is known to us occurred in Phrynichus' *Phoenician Women* (476 B.C.). After the parodus came an alternation of histrionic scenes (*episodes*) and choral odes (*stasima*), concluding with a histrionic *exodus.* These are nontechnical definitions and do not cover every variation from type, but they will suffice for present purposes. Thus Aeschylus' *Prometheus Bound* falls into the following divisions: prologue, vss. 1–127; parodus, vss. 128–92; first episode, vss. 193–396; first stasimon, vss. 397–435; second episode, vss. 436–525; second stasimon, vss. 526–60; third episode, vss. 561–886; third stasimon, vss. 887–906; exodus, vss. 907–1093. Though the number of stasima (and of episodes) was more usually three, as in this case, there was originally no hard-and-fast rule on the subject. In several plays there were four stasima and four episodes, and in Sophocles' *Antigone* five of each. Therefore in a normal tragedy like the *Prometheus* the number of histrionic divisions would be five — prologue, three episodes, and exodus. In the early plays which had no prologue the histrionic divisions fell to four — three episodes and an exodus. In several of the later plays, on the other hand, they rose to six, and in the *Antigone* to seven. As the lack of connection between chorus and plot increased and the size and importance of choral odes diminished . . . there was the more excuse for ignoring the choral elements and for concentrating attention upon the histrionic divisions. . . .

W. Beare

THE ROMAN STAGE AND THE ACTORS' HOUSE*

Our notions of the appearance of the Plautine stage are derived to some extent from the still visible remains of the imperial theatres, the extant illustrations dating from imperial times, and the description written by Vitruvius in the time of Augustus. Such information may be misleading. There is nothing more certain than that the imperial

* From W. Beare, *The Roman Stage* (London: Methuen & Co. Ltd., 1950), pp. 168–175; reprinted by permission of the publisher. The footnotes are Beare's.

theatre was ornate; there is nothing more likely than that the Plautine theatre was simple. From the evidence of the plays I will endeavour to describe the simplest arrangement which would permit these plays to be staged.

The essential feature of the Roman theatre from the earliest times was the wooden stage; Plautus calls it *scaena* or *proscaenium*,[1] and the Latin for "dramatic festival" is *ludi scaenici*. It was probably not more than five feet high, but may even in the days of Plautus have been of considerable length and some depth.[2] Between the stage and the foremost tier of seats lay a flat space, corresponding roughly to the Greek orchestra or "dancing-place" and called orchestra by later generations of Romans, but not normally used by Roman performers; here some movable seats were sometimes set for distinguished spectators. From the orchestra a short flight of steps led up to the stage; this flight of steps would have been convenient for any member of the public who wished to appear on the stage (like the prostitutes who are forbidden to do so in *Poen.* 17–8), but it does not seem to have been used by the actors in the performance of a play.

Behind the stage stood the actors' house or dressing-room, the front wall of which formed the permanent back-scene. At either end the stage was enclosed by the projecting wings of the actors' house. The front wall of the house was pierced by three doorways containing folding-doors (normally kept closed). At either end of the stage an cpen passage or side-entrance led into the projecting wing (Vitruvius calls it *uersura*) of the house. Thus actors had five means of communication between the stage and the dressing-room: the three doorways in the back-scene and the two side-entrances.

The doors must have been solidly constructed, for they had to stand a good deal of hard knocking. Apart from the doors, the back-scene seems to have been a blank wooden wall. The house was of modest height, and had a practicable roof. (There was as yet no roof over the stage.) In *Amph.* 1008 Mercury announces his intention of climbing on to the roof from inside the house in order to drive Amphitruo from the door by emptying pots on his head.

The only object permanently to be seen on the stage was the altar, which figures in so many plays. There was probably as yet no scenery and no attempt to adapt the setting for any particular play or scene of a play. There was no drop-curtain; the back-scene, such as it was, lay permanently open to view.[3]

[1] *Scaena* can mean (1) scene-building, (2) stage, (3) a picture, whether on the stage (e.g., one of the panels displayed on the *periacti*) or not.

[2] This is the usual view, but in considering the evidence of the plays we should remember that actors can make surprising use of even a small stage.

[3] Vitruvius remarks that musicians would turn towards the stage-doors when they wished to obtain *superior tonus*. Evidently the doors were still of wood in his day, though the rest of the scene-building was now built of stone.

Our only evidence on these matters is the text of the plays — that is, the words which the dramatists put into the mouths of their characters. We have no direct evidence as to how these plays were actually staged. The responsibility for the staging and production belonged not to the dramatist but to the actor-manager. The dramatist was acquainted with the general conditions of the contemporary stage; but we have no evidence that he instructed the actor-manager as to how particular plays, or scenes in plays, were to be shown. It seems to me fallacious to argue from a particular reference in a play that there was something unusual in the way in which that play was actually staged — whether at the first production or at a revival performance. The actor-manager no doubt had his own ideas — which may not have been those of the dramatist, or of other managers. All that we can hope to establish is the general conditions necessary for the production of our Latin plays — which do not contain (and perhaps never did contain) any stage-directions other than what is implied by the words put into the mouths of the characters.

The Conventions and Practices of Roman Stagecraft

Roman drama owed what success it achieved not to the craft of the scene-painter but to the art of the dramatist and actor. That art was exercised according to the conventions of the ancient theatre, conventions accepted almost unconsciously by the contemporary audience, yet puzzling and surprising to the reader of another age and country. All drama rests upon convention of some kind. It is absurd that people should discuss their most intimate concerns within hearing of the public; yet without this convention drama would be impossible. Convention enables the imagination to redeem material deficiencies; yet a certain amount of realism in dress, scenery and properties has often been found helpful. When we attempt to use the Latin plays as evidence for the way in which they were staged, we have frequently to ask ourselves whether the passage we are considering is an instance of convention or of realism. The fact that an actor mentions some object as present may sometimes be evidence that that object was actually shown on the stage; at other times we know that the object was not and could not be shown to the eye, and therefore had to be suggested to the imagination by words and gestures. The entry of an actor carrying a lamp may serve to indicate that it is early morning; the lamp is real, the darkness is indicated by the actor's actions and words.

The modern convention which enables our theatre-going audience to see into the interior of a house would have startled the Greeks and Romans. Their basic convention was quite different. The stage represented for them an open street, or some other open place; they were the general public assembled on the other side of the street or in the open country, and looking at the buildings which fronted on the street or open space. Every scene, in order to be shown on the stage, had to be thought of as taking place in the open air. In Mediterranean countries much does take place in the open which in our latitudes would occur indoors; but the real and sufficient reason for staging a banquet, a toilet-scene or a confidential conversation on the street was that otherwise such a scene could not be staged at all.

The expedients to which the dramatists are forced to resort by this convention are evidence of the validity of the convention itself. If it is necessary to disclose what is supposed to be taking place within the house, a character on the stage may be asked to peep inside the door and report what he sees (*Bacch.* 833 ff.). The spectators can never look through those doors with their own eyes. The test case is the banquet in the *Asinaria*. The party begins indoors (ll. 745, 809–10), but at 828 the revellers appear; are we to understand that, as the Loeb editor would have it, the doors are opened and they are shown just inside? Admittedly this would make it easier to understand why Artemona, who comes out of her own house at line 851, does not see them till the Parasite points them out to her at line 880. But this solution raises more difficulties than it removes, and the evidence of the text is against it. Lines 828–9 (omitted by the Loeb editor, following Leo) show the party coming out and the slaves setting tables for them. Artemona's failure to see them at first is to be explained not by the presence of any physical obstacle but by the convention that the actor does not see what the dramatist does not want him to see; in other words, she takes care not to look in their direction. Her dramatic irruption on the party would lose its effect if we supposed it to take place within the actors' house; the wrangle between husband and wife must have occurred on the open stage. At line 940–1 Artemona carries her husband off, and the two remaining members of the party go into Philaenium's house.

Our modern stage convention enables us to look for a while into the interior of a house, which at the end of the scene will be hidden from us by the drop curtain. The ancient stage, which represented the open street, lay, like the street, permanently open to view. The plays of Plautus are so constructed as to make it clear that no drop curtain was used or known. Each play begins with an empty stage; characters come from their houses or from one of the side-entrances, usually explaining in their opening words who they are, whence they have come and whither they are going. At the end of the play some pretext is made for getting the characters off the stage, but before they go one of them informs the audience that the play is over and asks for their applause. There is no such thing as an opening or final tableau; and at the end of the play the stage is empty and set for the beginning of the next play. If in the course of the play some object has to be brought on the stage for a particular scene, we presently see it being taken away again when it has served its purpose. Of this we have a striking example in the *Mercator:* When the cook has set down his dishes at the door and walked off in high annoyance, the unhappy husband has to ask his wife to have the now detested dishes taken inside, lamely remarking that they will improve the family meal (ll. 800–2).

The absence of a curtain implies the absence of special scenery for any one play or scene in a play. The opening scenes of the *Rudens* present us with a picture of a wild landscape, covered with rocks, full of caves, overgrown with rushes. If we suppose that these features were actually depicted on the stage, then we have to face the dilemma that either they remained on the stage throughout the rest of the play (in which they are entirely ignored) or that they were bodily removed under the eyes of the spectators during the course of the play. It is much more likely that the references to the natural surroundings were addressed to the imagination, and that the efforts of the two girls to find each other (220–243) are frustrated for so long by nothing but the fact that they take care not to look in the right direction. It would, no doubt, as Dr. Pickard-Cambridge has suggested to me (cf. his *Theatre of Dionysus*, p. 68), have been a simple matter for the stage-carpenter to contrive a suitable setting for a particular occasion; but such a setting would have been a positive embarrassment when the occasion for it was over. Yet how could it be removed? The same considerations seem to apply to the setting of a play as a whole. That play succeeded play with the same permanent background seems to be indicated by *Pseud.* I, 2, and *Men.* 72–6. Such as it was, therefore, the scenery probably remained unchanged from play to play.

Reduced to the barest terms, the permanent scenery consisted of the plain wall at the back with its three doors, the two projecting wings with the side-entrances, the flat roof of the actors' house, and on the stage itself an altar. The roof is actually used in the *Amphitruo* (1008 and frag. iv–vi) and would seem to be mentioned in *M.G.* 156 ff. and *Rud.* 85 ff.; the five entrances were in constant use. The three doors at the back could represent one, two, or three separate houses;[4] perhaps the side-entrance on the right of the spectators was supposed to lead to the near distance, that on the left to the more remote

---

[4] That unwanted doors were temporarily concealed by a curtain is conceivable, but unproved. In the *H.T.* the third door is used once, and only once, in the play. That the Greek dramatists sometimes used a two-door setting which the Latin dramatists have altered to a three-door setting is alogether unlikely.

distance. Thus if the action were laid in town the right-hand side-entrance might lead to the town centre, that on the left to the country and harbour. In the *Rudens* the setting is a lonely spot near the African sea-shore; in the background are the cottage of Daemones and the temple of Venus, represented by two of the three doors; the side-entrance on the right would lead to the beach near by, that on the left to the town and harbour of Cyrene. In *Amph.* 333, set in the city of Thebes, Sosia is speaking as he enters from the harbour, i.e. from the spectators' left; Mercury, facing the audience, says "some one is speaking on my right." Other relevant passages are *Men.* 555, *Rud.* 156, *And.* 734. The significance of the stage-doors and the side-entrances in any particular play is usually made clear in the prologue and in the remarks of the characters.

In the normal way any one entering or leaving any of the "houses" or making his way between the town centre on one side and the harbour or country on the other must appear on the stage. When for some reason the dramatist wishes to move a character from one of these places to another without bringing him on to the stage he falls back on another convention, the use of the *angiportus* (or *angiportum*).

The word *angiportus* means "street," and can be used even of the street represented by the stage. Its special significance in drama is to denote the back-street supposed to run behind the houses which face on to the stage, connecting them by means of their back-doors and gardens with each other and also with the town, harbour and country. The angiportus is not shown and could not be shown to the eye; its use is exceptional, and requires express mention; it is a device which enables the dramatist to escape at times from the general rule that a character who leaves the stage by a particular door or wing must return by the same door or wing.

In order to make the plot easily intelligible to the spectators (and incidentally to help the actors when rehearsing the play) it is usual for each entrance on the stage to be announced beforehand. These announcements, which are part of the dialogue, serve as stage-directions, and were probably meant to give a waiting actor his cue. The general custom that a character already on the stage shall warn the audience that some one else is about to appear leads to some interesting results. That a character standing on the stage, which represents a street, should be able to see farther up and down the street than the spectators can see, and so should be able to perceive some one approaching from the town-centre or harbour before they can do so, is quite natural; but it would not seem so natural for him to announce that some one is coming out of one of the house-doors, which faces the audience and is behind his back. This difficulty is got over by

The ancient theatre at Epidaurus in Greece as it appears today. This stone theatre dates from the fourth century and was constructed within a few years of the first stone theatre in Athens built by the legislator, Lycurgos. During the great period of Greek Drama (fifth century, B.C.), the theatre of Dionysus in Athens had wooden *ikyria* (i.e. stands or seats), a circular *orchestra* (or dancing place), where most of the dramatic action took place, and a very simple one-story *skene* (scene building). There was no raised stage. This elegant later building at Epidaurus is still used for theatrical performances.

Two Imperial Roman theatres at Sabratha, Libya (top) and Orange, France (bottom). The plays of Republican Rome, including those of Terence and Plautus, were first performed on temporary stages erected in athletic arenas. The first permanent theatre building in Rome was built by Pompey in 55 B.C.

making the opening door creak and so draw the actor's attention. Like the whole of the actor's technique, this device is of Greek origin. Sometimes the Greek dramatist describes the person coming out from the house as "striking" the door (i.e., in the act of opening it). This phrase, misunderstood in late antiquity, gave rise to the absurd notion that the early Greeks knocked on doors not only when they wanted to go in but also when they were coming out.

A grand principle of the stage was that a character saw and heard only what the dramatist meant him to see and hear. We are familiar with the situation in which one character spies on another and over-hears his words while himself remaining (at least temporarily) un-observed. Both actors are on the stage, in full view of the spectators. There is no physical object on the stage behind which the eaves-dropper can take shelter. He usually secures his temporary invisibility merely by standing at the back of the stage, and he is always liable to be detected as soon as the other actor allows himself to look in the right direction. This is absurd, perhaps, but no more absurd than that other convention of the ancient stage, the "aside," audible to thou-sands of spectators, yet inaudible, or only partly audible, to a character standing only a few yards from the speaker.

When we reflect on the fact that all the actors[5] wore masks and that a very large part of their lines was not spoken but declaimed to the accompaniment of the flute-player, we realize that the Roman style of acting must have differed widely from the naturalistic, conversa-tional style of our own day. Our actors talk to each other; the Roman actors declaimed to the audience. They stood, where possible, well to the front of the stage; they faced the audience, they kept their eyes on the audience, they aimed above all things at making their words carry even to the farthest seats.[6] If an actor entered from a house-door he usually walked to the front of the stage, looking neither to his left nor to his right. This made it easy for others already on the stage to step back and observe him. A character coming in from a side-entrance would also address himself to the audience and turn as best he could towards them while making his way to the middle of the stage. It is thus not surprising if for some time he fails to notice the presence of other characters on the stage. To face the audience was very necessary if one's words were to carry to the back of the large, open-air theatre. The art of the actor lay not in naturalism or in mimicry but in clear utterance conveying the appropriate emotion and supported by appropriate gesture. It seems probable that the

[5] Excluding, perhaps, the speaker of the prologue when appearing in his own person.

[6] Vitruvius points out how important it is that the *case-endings* of words should be audible even in the "gods." Of course I do not mean that an actor was *never* allowed to turn away from the spectators.

actor made no attempt to alter his voice according to whether he was taking the part of a gentleman or a slave, a man or a woman. In the same way the dramatist makes all his characters talk the same kind of Latin. The art of gesture, on the other hand, was carried in ancient times to a height which we can scarcely comprehend. When we try to imagine a scene from a Roman play, we must picture to ourselves the masked actors, their gestures, their carefully plotted movements on the stage, their voices raised in rhythmical declamation, while the flute-player stepped up now to one, now to another, playing the accompaniment for each actor in turn. When we consider how widely the style of Roman acting must have differed from our own and how misleading Roman writers often are on this subject, we realize how dangerous it is to use our own notions of fitness as a guide to the practice of the Roman stage.

PART TWO

The Medieval Theatre

I

Origins

RELIGIOUS DRAMA

Medieval Europe created new forms of drama instead of continuing the dramatic traditions of the ancient world. A classic influence appears only in the academic, if occasionally lively, exercises of the tenth-century Saxon nun, Hrotsvitha, who patterned her saint plays after the comedies of Terence.

In fact, except for the survival of an acting tradition in the performances of wandering minstrels and mimes, and in some enactments by amateurs of pre-Christian folk rituals, the theatre died with the Roman empire and had to be reborn. Whatever we may think of the ritual origin of ancient drama, this second birth certainly had its beginnings in religious ceremony.

Indeed, early in the Middle Ages, the church itself served as a kind of theatre, and short plays were actually performed in connection with the ritual of the mass. These short plays were a development of liturgical poems called tropes—chanted additions to the authorized service of the church, sung responsively by the choir and a leader or leaders, frequently the celebrant himself.

The most important of the tropes—for our purposes—was an Easter trope added to the Introit of the mass.

AN EARLY EASTER TROPE*
(The *Quem Quaeritis* Trope)

Question:[1]
> Whom do you seek in the sepulchre, O Christian women?

Response:[2]
> Jesus of Nazareth who was crucified, O celestial ones.

The Angels:
> He is not here; he is risen, just as foretold. Go, announce that
> he is risen from the sepulchre.

The *Quem Quaeritis* Trope quickly developed into a liturgical
play based on the visit of the three Marys to the empty tomb of
the risen Jesus (Matthew 28: 1-7). Directions for performing this
play are included in the *Regularis Concordia*, a rule-book for
Benedictine monasteries in England, written between 965 and 975
by St. Ethelwold, Bishop of Winchester, at the request of King
Edgar.

* From a manuscript (9th century) in the Abbey of St. Gall in Switzerland, as printed and
translated in *Chief Pre-Shakespearean Dramas*, ed. Joseph Quincy Adams (Boston: Houghton
Mifflin, 1924), p. 3. The original, in Latin, starts *"Quem quaeritis in sepulchro."*
   [1] The question of the angels, i.e., choir boys or priests dressed as angels.
   [2] Response of the Marys, i.e., choir boys or priests impersonating the three New Testament
Marys.

Ethelwold

from the REGULARIS CONCORDIA*

While the third lesson is being chanted, let four brethren vest themselves; of whom let one, vested in an alb, enter as if to take part in the service, and let him without being observed approach the place of the sepulchre, and there, holding a palm in his hand, let him sit down quietly. While the third responsory is being sung, let the remaining three follow, all of them vested in copes, and carrying in their hands censers filled with incense; and slowly, in the manner of seeking something, let them come before the place of the sepulchre. These things are done in imitation of the angel seated in the monument, and of the women coming with spices to anoint the body of Jesus. When therefore that one seated shall see the three, as if straying about and seeking something, approach him, let him begin in a dulcet voice of medium pitch to sing:

Whom seek ye in the sepulchre, O followers of Christ?

When he has sung this to the end, let the three respond in unison:

Jesus of Nazareth, which was crucified, O celestial one.

To whom that one:

He is not here; he is risen, just as he foretold.
Go, announce that he is risen from the dead.

At the word of this command let those three turn themselves to the choir, saying:

Alleluia! The Lord is risen to-day,
The strong lion, the Christ, the Son of God.
Give thanks to God, huzza!

This said, let the former, again seating himself, as if recalling them, sing the anthem:

Come, and see the place where the Lord was laid.
Alleluia! Alleluia!

And saying this, let him rise, and let him lift the veil and show them the place bare of the cross, but only the cloths laid there with which

---

* From the version given in *Chief Pre-Shakespearean Dramas*, ed. Joseph Quincy Adams (Boston: Houghton Mifflin, 1924), pp. 9–10.

the cross was wrapped. Seeing which, let them set down the censers which they carried into the same sepulchre, and let them take up the cloth and spread it out before the eyes of the clergy; and, as if making known that the Lord had risen and was not now therein wrapped, let them sing this anthem:

The Lord is risen from the sepulchre,
Who for us hung upon the cross.

And let them place the cloth upon the altar. The anthem being ended, let the Prior, rejoicing with them at the triumph of our King, in that, having conquered death, he arose, begin the hymn:

We praise thee, O God.

This begun, all the bells chime out together.

NON-BIBLICAL FOLK DRAMA

In addition to the plays which developed from the tropes, there was another kind of folk drama in medieval England — a drama which presumably had its origin in pre-Christian ritual. The theme of this drama was death and resurrection, the anticipated return of spring during a cold and barren season. One form of this folk ritual was the "sword dance" — a primitive pantomime which was performed every year almost without alteration from the early Middle Ages until well into the nineteenth century. The Sword Dance took many forms. Here follows a description of one such dance, performed in Yorkshire on St. Stephen's Night (December 26), 1811. The performance then was not very different from entertainments that country folk might have witnessed eight hundred years before:

"On the Feast of St. Stephen, six youths (called *sword dancers* from their dancing with swords), clad in white and bedecked with ribbons, attended by a fiddler and another youth curiously dressed, who generally has the name of 'Bessy,' and also by one who personates a 'Doctor,' begin to travel from village to village, performing a rude dance called the *sword dance.* One of the six acts the part of 'King' in a kind of farce, which consists of singing and dancing. 'The Bessy' interferes while they are making a hexagon with their swords and is killed. — These frolics they continue till New Year's Day, when they spend their gains at the ale-house. . . ."

(*The Gentleman's Magazine,* 1811)

The Sword Dances began as pantomimes, but in some parts of England they soon acquired dialogue. From the county of Durham comes the following survival.

An English Sword Dance Play*

*E*nter dancers, decorated with swords and ribbons, the Captain of the band of players wearing a cocked hat, and the Clown or "Bessy," who acts as treasurer [he collects the money for the performance], being decorated with a hairy cap and a fox's brush dependent [hanging]. The Captain forms with his sword a circle, around which he walks. The Bessy opens the proceedings by singing:

> Good gentlemen all, to our Captain take heed,
>   And hear what he's got for to sing;
> He's lived among music these forty long years
>   And drunk of the elegant spring.[1]
>
> My mother was burnt for a witch,
>   My father was hanged on a tree,
> And it's because I'm a fool
>   That nobody meddled wi' me.

The dance now commences. It is an ingenious performance, and the swords of the actors are placed in a variety of graceful positions, so as to form stars, hearts, squares, and circles, etc., etc. The dance is so elaborate that it requires frequent rehearsals, a quick eye, and strict adherence to time and tune. Before it concludes, grace and elegance have given place to disorder, and at last all the actors are seen fighting. The Parish Clergyman rushes in to prevent bloodshed, and receives a death-blow. While on the ground, the actors walk round the body, and sing as follows, to a slow psalm-like tune:

> Alas! our parson's dead,
>   And on the ground is laid;
> Some of us will suffer for't,
>   Young men, I'm sore afraid.
>
> I'm sure 'twas none of me,
>   I'm clear of *that* crime;

* From Bell's *English Poets*, 1857, as reprinted in *Earlier English Drama*, ed. Thomas Whitfield Baldwin (New York: Thomas Nelson and Sons, 1929), pp. 25–28.
1 The spring of Helicon; poetic inspiration.

'Twas him that follows me
That drew his sword so fine.

I'm sure it was *not* me,
I'm clear of that fact;
'Twas him that follows me
That did this dreadful act.

I'm sure 'twas none of me,
Who say't be villains all;
For both my eyes were closed
When our good priest did fall.

The Bessy sings:

Cheer up, cheer up, my bonny lads,
And be of courage brave,
We'll take him to his church,
And bury him in the grave.

The Captain speaks:

O, for a Doctor,
A ten pound doctor, oh.

Enter a Doctor, who says:

Here I am, I.
Captain. Doctor, what's your fee?
Doctor. Ten pounds is my fee!
But nine pounds, nineteen shillings, eleven pence, three farthings, I
will take from thee.
Bessy. There's ge-ne-ro-si-ty!
The Doctor sings:

I am a doctor, a doctor rare,
Who travels much at home;
My famous pills they cure all ills,
Past, present, and to come.

My famous pills, who'd be without,
They cure the plague, the sickness and gout,
Anything but a love-sick maid;
If *you're* one, my dear, you're beyond my aid.

*Here the Doctor occasionally salutes one of the fair spectators; he
then takes out his snuff-box, which is always of very capacious dimen-*

sions (*a sort of miniature warming-pan*), *and empties the contents*
(*flour or meal*) *on the Clergyman's face, singing at the time:*

> Take a little of my nif-naf,
> Put it on your tif-taf;
> Parson rise and preach again,
> The doctor says you are not slain.

*The Clergyman here sneezes several times, and gradually recovers,
and all shake him by the hand.*
The ceremony terminates with the Captain singing:

> Our play is at an end,
>   And now we'll taste your cheer;
> We wish you a merry Christmas
>   And a happy new year.

The Bessy:

> And your pockets full of brass,
> And your cellars full of beer.

(*A general dance concludes the play.*)

The Sword Dance was a Christmas season performance. It
is closely related to another species of folk drama, the St. George
Play, an interlude centered on the patron saint of England.
There were many versions of the St. George Play, and like the
Sword Dance it stubbornly survived in England for almost a
thousand years. The version which follows is from the West
Country.

THE PLAY OF ST. GEORGE*

Enter Father Christmas.

Here come I, old Father Christmas,

> Welcome, or welcome not,
> I hope old Father Christmas
> Will never be forgot.

* From *Earlier English Drama*, ed. Thomas Whitfield Baldwin (New York:
Thomas Nelson and Sons, 1929), pp. 29–32.

I am not come here for to laugh or to jeer,
But for a pocketful of money and a skinful of beer;
To show some sport and pastime,
Gentlemen and Ladies in the Christmas-time.
If you will not believe what I do say,
Come in the Turkish Knight — clear the way.

Enter the Turkish Knight.

Open your doors and let me in,
I hope your favours I shall win;
Whether I rise, or whether I fall,
I'll do my best to please you all.
St. George is here, and swears he will come in,
And if he does, I know he'll pierce my skin.
If you will not believe what I do say,
Come in the King of Egypt — clear the way.

Enter the King of Egypt.

Here I, the King of Egypt, boldly do appear.
St. George, St. George, walk in, my son and heir.
Walk in, my son, St. George, and boldly act thy part,
That all the people here may see thy wondrous art.

Enter St. George.

Here come I, St. George, from Britain did I spring,
I'll fight the Dragon bold, my wonders to begin.
I'll clip his wings, he shall not fly;
I'll cut him down, or else I die.

Enter the Dragon.

Who's he that seeks the Dragon's blood,
And calls so angry, and so loud?
That English dog, will he before me stand?
I'll cut him down with my courageous hand.
With my long teeth, and scurvy jaw,
Of such I'd break up half a score,
And stay my stomach till I'd more.

St. George and the Dragon fight; the latter is killed.

Father Christmas. Is there a doctor to be found
   All ready, near at hand,
To cure a deep and deadly wound,
   And make the champion stand?

Enter the Doctor.

Ah! yes, there is a doctor to be found,
　All ready, near at hand,
To cure a deep and deadly wound,
　And make the champion stand.

Father Christmas. What can you cure?

Doctor. All sorts of diseases,
Whatever you pleases,
The phthisic, the palsy, and the gout;
Whatever disorder, I'll soon pull him out.

Father Christmas. What is your fee?

Doctor. Fifteen pounds, it is my fee,
　The money to lay down;
But as 'tis such a rogue as he,
　I'll cure him for ten pound.
I have a little bottle of Elicumpane,
　Here Jack, take a little of my flip-flop,
　Pour it down thy tip-top,
Rise up and fight again.

The Doctor gives his medicine. The Dragon comes to life again, and fights with St. George, and again is killed.

St. George. Here I am, St. George, that worthy champion bold,
And with my sword and spear I've won three crowns of gold:
I've found the fiery Dragon, and brought him to the slaughter;
By that I've won fair Sabra, the King of Egypt's daughter.

The Turkish Knight advances.

Here come I, the Turkish Knight,
Come from the Turkish land to fight.
I'll fight St. George, who is my foe,
I'll make him yield before I go;
He brags to such a high degree,
He thinks there's none can do the like of he.

St. George. Where is that Turk that will before me stand?
I'll cut him down with my courageous hand.

They fight; the Turkish Knight is overcome, and falls on one knee, saying:

Oh! pardon me, St. George, pardon of thee I crave.
Oh! pardon me this night, and I will be thy slave.

St. George. I'll never pardon a Turkish Knight;
So rise thee up again, and try thy might.

They fight again. The Knight is killed, and a scene with Father Christmas occurs as before, and the Knight is cured. The Doctor has a basin of girdy grout[1] given him, and a kick, and is driven out. Fair Sabra now comes forward to St. George.

Father Christmas. Now, ladies and gentlemen, your sport is just ended;

So prepare for the box[2] which is highly commended.
The box it would speak, if it had but a tongue;
Come throw in your money and think it no wrong.

Christmas was not the only season when medieval folk plays were performed. In England, the May-Day celebration (like the Sword Dance, a survival of pagan ritual) was another long-lasting source of popular theatre. The focal point of this spring festival was the Maypole itself, decorated with flowers and surrounded by gaily-costumed dancers. During the fifteenth century, a reveler dressed as the colorful English outlaw, Robin Hood, presided over the games as Lord of the May. In the evening this same figure became the hero of some primitive plays based on popular ballads.

One of the few Robin Hood plays extant is this fragment concerning an encounter between Robin Hood and a Potter.

A ROBIN HOOD FOLK PLAY*

Enter Robin Hood and his men.

Robin. Listen to me, my merry men all,
And hark what I shall say;
Of an adventure I shall you tell,
That befell the other day.
With a proud potter I met,

---

1 Coarse meal.
2 The box in which voluntary contributions were collected from the spectators.
* From F. J. Child, ed., *English and Scottish Popular Ballads* (Boston: Houghton Mifflin, 1882–98), V, 114–115, as given in *Earlier English Drama*, ed. Thomas Whitfield Baldwin (New York: Thomas Nelson and Sons, 1929), pp. 20–23.

And a rose garland on his head,
The flowers of it shone marvellous fresh;
This seven year and more he hath used this way,
Yet was he never so courteous a potter
As one penny passage to pay.
Is there any of my merry men all
That dare be so bold
To make the potter pay passage
Either silver or gold.
    Little John. Not I, master, for twenty pound ready told;
For there is not among us all, one
That dares meddle with that potter, man for man.
I felt his hands not long agone,
But I had rather have been here by thee;
Therefore I know what he is.
Meet him when ye will, or meet him when ye shall,
He is as proper a man as ever you meddled withal.
    Robin. I will lay with thee, Little John, twenty pound so red,
If I with that potter meet,
I will make him pay passage, at risk of his head.
    Little John. I consent thereto, so eat I bread;
If he pay passage, at risk of his head,
Twenty pound shall you have of me.

    Robin and his men hide. The Potter's boy, Jack, enters and says:

Out alas, that ever I saw this day!
For I am clean out of my way
From Nottingham town.
If I hie me not the faster
Ere I come there the market will be done.
    Robin (as he comes forward). Let me see, are the pots whole and
      sound?
    Jack. Yea, master, but they will not break the ground.
    Robin. I will them break, for the rogue thy master's sake;
And if they will break the ground,
Thou shalt have three pence for a pound.
                                (Robin smashes the pots.)
    Jack. Out, alas! what have you done?
If my master come he will break your crown.

    The Potter enters, and says to Jack:

Why, thou rascal, art thou here yet?
Thou shouldst have been at market.

Jack. I met with Robin Hood, a good yeoman;
He hath broken my pots
And called you a rogue by your name.

    The Potter (to Robin). Thou mayst be a gentleman, so God me
        save,
But thou seemest a naughty knave.
But if thou be a good fellow,
I will sell my horse, my harness, pots and panniers too;
Thou shalt have the one half, and I will have the other.
If thou be not so content,
Thou shalt have stripes, if thou wert my brother.

    Robin. Hark, Potter, what I shall say;
This seven year and more thou hast used this way,
Yet wert thou never so courteous to me
As one penny passage to pay.

    Potter. Why should I pay passage to thee?

    Robin. For I am Robin Hood, chief governor,
Under the greenwood tree.

    Potter. This seven year have I used this way up and down,
Yet paid I passage to no man,
Nor now will I not begin; so do the worst thou can.

    Robin. Passage shalt thou pay here under the greenwood tree.

    Potter. If thou be a good fellow, as men do thee call,
Lay aside thy bow,
And take thy sword and buckler in thy hand
And see what shall befall.

    *They fight, and the Potter uses his quarter-staff with such goodwill
that Robin is forced to call his band.*

    Robin. Little John, where art thou?

    Little John. Here, master, I make God avow.
I told you, master, so God me save,
That you should find the potter a knave.
Hold your buckler fast in your hand,
And I will stiffly by you stand,
Ready for to fight;
Be the knave never so stout,
I shall rap him on the snout,
And put him to flight.[1]

---

1 The rest of the play is lost, but we know from the ballad of *Robin Hood
and the Potter* that Robin borrowed the Potter's wares and dressed himself in
the Potter's clothes, then went to the Nottingham market.

II

Playwrights and Their Sources

The mainstream of medieval drama flowed from the liturgy of the church. Two types of plays evolved—moralities and miracles.

Moralities (the term is a modern one) are didactic, non-Biblical dramas designed to illustrate some point of doctrinal truth. Often, as in *The Castle of Perseverance* (ca. 1425), the longest and most ambitious piece of this type, moralities dramatize a battle of life allegory in which good and evil forces are shown to be at war for the soul of man.

The hero of a morality play is often a character representative of the whole human race—called variously Everyman or Mankynd or Humanus Genus. He has allies—Shrift, Truth, Knowledge, Good Deeds and the like; he is beset by vices—among them Folly, Gluttony, Luxury, Lecherie, Covetyse and World. These vices are comic as well as threatening. We see in them the beginnings of a native farce tradition that culminates in characters like Parolles, Toby Belch, Sir Epicure Mammon, Caliban and Volpone.

Glynne Wickham and A.P. Rossiter trace the origins of the morality play to the medieval sermon, "the one vernacular element in the church service...the place for topical comment...[and] the direct application of doctrine to human conduct."[1]

The central conceit in both sermon and play is the *exemplum*, an expanded metaphor not unlike one of the parables of Christ. An initial figure is elaborated into a full-fledged anagogue with the action being carried by abstract characters.

There are more than sixty extant medieval moralities in English. They range in tone from amusing and scatological (*Mankynd*, ca. 1465) to the somber (*Everyman*, ca. 1495). The last named, closely related to a Dutch play called *Elckerlijk*, is the masterpiece of the style. Unlike the other seven, it contains no comic vices. Its theme is the Christian preparation for death, and the play is distinguished by its economy (921 lines) and the elegant, moving simplicity of its language.

---

[1] From Glynne Wickham, *Early English Stages 1300 to 1660* (London & New York: Routledge and Kegan Paul, 1959), Vol. 1, pp. 231-32.

Miracles are a different matter altogether. Sometimes called mysteries after the French fashion, the miracles have a biblical source. According to the orthodox account of their history, they are derived from liturgical plays and therefore ultimately from tropes like the *Quem Quaeritis*.[2]

In this view, the elaboration of thematic material, the translation from Latin into the vernacular, were factors which led to the creation of cycles of plays. These plays collectively comprised a religious drama of tremendous scope, a drama that embraced Heaven and Hell and presented a sacred history of the world from Creation to the Last Judgement.

According to the same theory, the history of the medieval theatre is one of literal and figurative emergence from the church building. The productions soon grew too ambitious and spectacular for the altar area or the nave. At first the plays moved only to the church steps. (A transitional work, like the Anglo-Norman *Adam*, appears to have been performed in front of a cathedral.) Next, the acting space was shifted to the market place and other parts of the medieval city, as control of proceedings passed at least partly into the hands of the burghers, who no doubt influenced the dramatic treatment.

In the fourteenth century this growth of theatrical activity led to a great open-air drama festival throughout Europe. In some countries, notably England and Spain, this festival became the principal event of the Corpus Christi holiday, a processional Church celebration honoring the Eucharist and designed to demonstrate the relevance of the central sacraments to the daily life of the people.

No effort or expense was spared to insure the success of these cyclic productions by communities that prided themselves on their ingenuity and ostentation. In the fifteenth and sixteenth centuries major performances were held in Lucerne, Alsfeld, Valenciennes, Eger, Donnaueschingen, Frankfort, Bourges, Paris and at other continental centers. In England recurring festivals took place in Coventry, York, Wakefield, Chester, Beverley, various places in Cornwall and, we may assume, in many other

---

[2] But see Rosemary Woolfe, *The English Mystery Plays* (Berkeley & Los Angeles: University of California, 1972), pp. 3-24. Woolfe calls the influence of Latin liturgical drama on the mystery plays both "important and negligible": important, because the vernacular cycles could not have existed without the liturgical dramas, and negligible since the instances of direct borrowing concern trivial matters. She challenges the traditional view that the cycles were simply church plays that outgrew their indoor space.

cities.[3]

On the continent local conditions determined the most appropriate place for the cyclic performance. A ducal courtyard (Valenciennes), a market square (Lucerne) and the remains of a Roman amphitheater (Bourges) were among the choices.

In many of the English cities, each craft guild assumed or shared responsibility for the production of one of the plays in the cycle. (See Salter, "A Day's Labour," p. 215 below.) Of the four surviving English compilations, one, the problematic N-towne plays, was given a stationary performance, similar to those in France and Germany. There seems to be evidence that the other three were staged as part of a procession on pageant wagons, each containing the mansions (or scenic units) necessary for the performance of one of the short constituent plays.

The evidence for processional staging seems persuasive, but not conclusive. As many problems are raised by the theory as solved, and, lacking further evidence, the last word may be A.M. Nagler's observations on the subject. "An open question. An attempt to answer it will only lead us into a thickset underbrush of revocable surmises."[4]

What can we say about the literary quality of these English miracle plays? For years critics refused to take them seriously. Even their anthologists thought them crude and naive.

But the naiveté was in the beholder, not the object. The plays vary in quality, of course, but the best of them compare favorably to the masterpieces of medieval literature — to the folk ballads and Chaucer. Their rude strength and natural humor make them stageworthy even today, and their ambitiousness commands respect.

Collectively these plays are folk art of the highest order, the efforts of anonymous redactors, who may have based their work

[3] In addition to Chester (25 or 26 plays), York (48 plays), Wakefield (32 plays) and N-towne (43 plays), there are two longish plays (out of 10 or 12) remaining from the Coventry cycle. The "N-towne plays" are so called because a notation in their surviving banns lists their place of performance as "N-towne" (for *nomen*, as in the marriage service?). Perhaps these plays were performed in several cities, Lincoln among them. Other names for the N-towne cycle are the Hegge plays and the Ludus Coventriae. The latter name comes from a misattribution by a seventeenth-century scholar who thought he had found the lost Coventry plays. The Wakefield cycle is sometimes called the "Townley plays" from the surname of the Lancashire family that for many years owned the manuscript. The Beverley plays have not survived, but we still have five scriptural plays in the Cornish language and several non-cyclic English plays, notably an *Abraham and Isaac from Suffolk*.

[4] In *The Medieval Religious Stage, Shapes and Phantoms* (New Haven & London: Yale University Press, 1976), p. 55.

on Latin originals but who enriched their borrowed stories with lively images from the ordinary life of their audiences. Thus Lucifer becomes a recognizable village braggart, Noah's wife a common North-country scold.

In some of the plays, notably those of the Shepherds, there is great comic zest. Of the more solemn pieces, one of the best is the Abraham and Isaac play, preserved in a fifteenth-century manuscript from Brome Manor, Suffolk. A modernized version of the play follows, preceded by a translation from the Latin vulgate of the biblical source.

ABRAHAM AND ISAAC

ABRAHAM'S DEVOTION

*A*fter these things, God tempted Abraham, and said to him: Abraham, Abraham. And he answered: Here I am.

2 He said to him: Take thy only begotten son Isaac, whom thou lovest, and go into the land of vision: and there thou shalt offer him for an holocaust upon one of the mountains which I will shew thee.

3 So Abraham raising up in the night, saddled his ass: and took with him two young men, and Isaac his son: and when he had cut wood for the holocaust, he went his way to the place which God had commanded him.

4 And on the third day, lifting up his eyes, he saw the place afar off.

5 And he said to his young men: Stay you here with the ass: I and the boy will go with speed as far as yonder, and after we have worshipped, will return to you.

6 And he took the wood for the holocaust, and laid it upon Isaac his son: and he himself carried in his hands fire and a sword. And as they two went on together,

7 Isaac said to his father: My father. And he answered: what wilt thou, son? Behold, saith he, fire and wood: where is the victim for the holocaust?

8 And Abraham said: God will provide himself a victim for an holocaust, my son. So they went on together.

9 And they came to the place which God had shown him, where he built an altar, and laid the wood in order upon it: and when he had bound Isaac his son, he laid him on the altar upon the pile of wood.

10 And he put forth his hand, and took the sword to sacrifice his son.

11 And behold an angel of the Lord from heaven called to him, saying: Abraham, Abraham. And he answered: Here I am.

12 And he said to him: Lay not thy hand upon the boy, neither do thou any thing to him: now I know that thou fearest God, and hast not spared thy only begotten son for my sake.

13 Abraham lifted up his eyes, and saw behind his back a ram amongst the briers sticking fast by the horns, which he took and offered for a holocaust instead of his son.

14 And he called the name of that place, The Lord seeth. Whereupon even to this day it is said: In the mountain the Lord will see.

---

* In the Douai translation.

15   And the Angel of the Lord called to Abraham a second time from heaven, saying:

16   By my own self have I sworn, saith the Lord: because thou hast done this thing, and hast not spared thy only begotten son for my sake:

17   I will bless thee, and I will multiply thy seed as the stars of heaven, and as the sand that is by the sea shore: thy seed shall possess the gates of their enemies.

18   And in thy seed shall all the nations of the earth be blessed, because thou hast obeyed my voice.

19   Abraham returned to his young men, and they went to Bersabee together, and he dwelt there.

THE BROME
ABRAHAM AND ISAAC*

[A *hilly landscape. Abraham and Isaac are kneeling on a level piece of ground.*]

> *Abraham:* Father of Heaven, omnipotent
> With all my heart to thee I call.
> Thou hast given me both land and rent,
> And my livelihood thou hast me sent.
> I thank thee highly evermore for all.
>
> First of the earth thou madest Adam,
> And Eve also to be his wife;
> All other creatures from these two came.
> And now thou hast granted to me, Abraham,
> Here in this land to lead my life.
>
> In my age thou hast granted me this
> That this young child with me shall dwell.
> I love nothing so much in this,
> Except thine own self, dear Father of Bliss,
> As Isaac here, my own sweet son.
>
> I who have many children mo'
> Love them not as half so well.[1]
> This fair sweet child he cheers me so
> In every place wherever I do go,
> That of no affliction may I tell.

* Modernized version by John Gassner. Brackets indicate interpolated stage directions; parenthesis indicate stage directions found in the original text.

[1] In *Genesis* 22:2 (see above) Isaac is Abraham's "only begotten son."

And therefore, Father of Heaven, I thee pray
  For his health and also for his grace.
Now, Lord, keep him both night and day
That never discomfort nor dismay
  Come to my child in any place.
    [*Rising*]
Now come on, Isaac, my own sweet child,
  Go we home and take our rest.

Isaac: Abraham, mine own father so mild,
To follow you I am full pleased,
  Both early and late.

Abraham: Come on, sweet child. I love thee best
  Of all the children that ever I begot.

    [*Abraham and Isaac start on their homeward journey.
    God and an Angel appear*]

God: Mine angel, fast hie thee thy way,
  And unto middle-earth anon thou go —
Abram's heart now will I assay,
  Whether that he be steadfast or no.

Say I commanded him for to take
  Isaac, his young son that he loves so well,
And with his blood sacrifice he make,
  If any of my friendship he would feel.

Show him the way unto the hill
  Where that his sacrifice shall be.
I shall assay now his good will,
  Whether he loveth better his child or me.
All men shall take example by him
  My commandments how they shall keep.

    [*As the Angel descends, Abraham, moved in spirit,
    kneels again*]

Abraham: Now, Father of Heaven, that formed everything,
  My prayers I make to thee again,
For this day a tender offering
  Here must I give to thee certain.
Ah, Lord God, almighty King,
  What manner of beast would'st thou fain?
If I had thereof true knowing,

It should be done with all my main
    Full soon by me.
To do thy pleasure on a hill,
Verily, it is my will,
    Dear Father, God in Trinity!

[*The Angel reaches Abraham, while Isaac has wandered off*]

The Angel: Abraham, Abraham, be at rest!
    Our Lord commandeth thee to take
Isaac, thy young son whom thou lovest best,
    And with his blood that sacrifice thou make.

Into the Land of Vision do thou go,
    And offer thy child unto thy Lord;
I shall thee lead and show also.
    To God's behest, Abraham, accord,
And follow me upon this green!

Abraham: Welcome to me be by Lord's command!
    And his word I will not withstand.
    Yet Isaac, my young son in land,
A full dear child to me has been.

I had rather, if God had been pleased,
    To have forborne all the goods that I have,
Than Isaac, my son, should be deceased, —
    So God in heaven my soul may save!

I have loved never a thing so much on earth,
    And now I must the child go kill!
Ah, Lord God, my conscience lacketh mirth!
And yet, my dear Lord, I am sore afeared
    To grudge anything against thy will.

I love my child as my life,
    But yet I love my God much more
For though my heart should make any strife,
Yet will I not spare for child or wife,
    But do after my dread Lord's lore.

Though I love my son never so well,
    Yet smite off his head soon I shall.
Ah, Father of Heaven! to thee I kneel —

A hard death my son shall feel,
  For to honor thee, Lord, withal!

The Angel: Abraham, Abraham, this is well said,
  And all these commandments look that thou keep, —
But in thy heart be nothing dismayed.

Abraham: Nay, nay forsooth, I hold me well repaid
  To please my God to the best that I may.
For though my heart be heavily set
  To see the blood of my own dear son,
Yet for all that I will not let,
But Isaac, my son, I will go get,
  And come as fast as ever we can.

[*The Angel departs and Abraham looks for his son*]

Abraham: Now, Isaac, my own son, dear
  Where art thou, child? Speak to me.

Isaac: My father, sweet father, I am here,
  And make my prayers to the Trinity.

Abraham: Rise up, my child, and fast come hither,
  My gentle bairn that art so wise,
For we, too, child, must go together,
  And unto my Lord make sacrifice.

[*Isaac rises and goes to him*]

Isaac: I am full ready, my father, lo!
  Given to your hands, I stand right here;
And whatsoever ye bid me do, even so
  It shall be done with glad cheer,
    Full well and fine.

Abraham: Ah, Isaac, my own son so dear,
  God's blessing I give thee, and mine.

Hold this faggot upon thy back,
  And I myself fire shall bring.

Isaac: Father, all this here will I pack;
  I am full fain to do your bidding.

Abraham: Ah, Lord of Heaven!
 [*Abraham looks up to heaven, and wrings his hands*]
This child's words all do wound my heart!
 [*Controlling himself and turning to Isaac*]
   Now, Isaac, son, go we on our way
   Unto yon mount with all our main.

Isaac: Go we, my dear father, as fast as I may;
   To follow you I am full fain,
     Although I be slender.

 [*Abraham stops as they arrive at the mountain, his
 eyes fixed on heaven*]

Abraham: Ah, Lord, my heart breaketh in twain
   This child's words, they be so tender!
     [*Again controlling himself*]
Ah, Isaac son, anon lay it down,
   No longer upon thy back it hold,
For I must make ready prayer soon
   To honor my Lord God as I was told.

   [*Isaac drops the faggots*]

Isaac: Lo, my dear father, here it is.
     [*Moving close to him tenderly*]
   To cheer you always I draw me near.
But, father, I marvel sore at this,
   Why ye make this heavy cheer,

And also, father, even more dread I —
   Where is your quick beast that ye should kill?
Both fire and wood we have ready nigh,
   But quick beast have we none on this hill.
     [*Anxiously*]
A quick beast, I wot well, must be slain,
   Your sacrifice to make.

Abraham: Dread thee nought, my child, I would fain;
Our Lord will send me unto this place
   Some manner of beast for to take
     Through his command.

Isaac: Yea, father, but my heart beginneth to quake
   To see that sharp sword in your hand.

Why bear ye your sword drawn so?
   Of your countenance I have much wonder.

Abraham: [*Aside*] Ah, Father of Heaven! such is my woe,
   This child here breaks my heart in sunder.

Isaac: Tell me, my dear father, ere that ye cease —
   Bear ye your sword drawn for me?

Abraham: Ah, Isaac! sweet son, peace, peace!
   For in truth thou break'st my heart in three!

Isaac: Now truly, on something, father, ye think,
   That ye mourn thus more and more.

Abraham: Ah, Lord of Heaven, let thy grace sink,
   For my heart was never half so sore!

Isaac: I pray ye, father, that ye me know will let
   Whether I shall have any harm or no.

Abraham: Alas, sweet son, I may not tell thee yet,
   My heart is now so full of woe.

Isaac: Dear father, I pray you, hide it not from me,
   But some of your thought, I pray tell me.

Abraham: Ah, Isaac, Isaac, I must kill thee!

Isaac: Kill me, father? Alas, what have I done?
If I have trespassed against you aught,
   With a rod ye may make me full mild;
And with your sharp sword kill me naught,
   For in truth, father, I am but a child.

Abraham: I am full sorry, son, thy blood for to spill,
But truly, child, I may not as I please.

Isaac: Now I would to God my mother were here on this hill.
She would kneel for me on both her knees
      To save my life.
And since that my mother is not here,
I pray you, father, change your cheer,
      And kill me not with your knife.

Abraham: Forsooth, my son, save I thee kill,
  I should grieve God right sore, I dread,
It is his commandment and also his will
  That I should do this same deed.

He commanded me, son, for certain,
  To make my sacrifice with thy blood.

Isaac: And is it God's will that I should be slain?

Abraham: Yea, truly, Isaac, my son so good;
  And therefore my hands I wring!

Isaac: Now father, against my Lord's will,
  I will never grouch, loud or still.
He might a-sent me a better destiny,
  If it had been his pleasure.

Abraham: Forsooth, son, if not this deed I did,
  Grievously displeased our Lord would be.

Isaac: Nay, nay, father, God forbid
  That ever ye should grieve him for me!

Ye have other children, one or two,
  Which ye should love well in natural kind.
I pray you, father, make you no woe;
For, be I once dead and from you go,
  I shall be soon out of your mind.

Therefore do our Lord's bidding,
  And when I am dead, then pray for me.
But, good father, tell ye my mother nothing,
Say that I am in another country dwelling.

Abraham: Ah, Isaac, Isaac, blessed mayest thou be!
My heart beginneth wildly to rise
  To see the blood of thy blessed body!

Isaac: Father, since it may be no other wise,
  Let it pass over as well as I.

But, father, ere I go unto my death,
  I pray you bless me with your hand.

[*Isaac kneels; Abraham places his hand on the lad's head*]

Abraham: Now Isaac, with all my breath
  My blessing I give thee upon this land,
  And God also thereto add his.
Isaac, Isaac, son, up thou stand,
  Thy fair sweet mouth that I may kiss.

Isaac: Now farewell, my own father so fine,
  And greet well my mother on earth.
But I pray you, father, to hide my eyne
  That I see not the stroke of your sharp sword
  That my flesh shall defile.

Abraham: Son, thy words make me to weep full sore;
Now, my dear son Isaac, speak no more.

Isaac: Ah, my own dear father! wherefore?
  We shall speak together here but a while.

And since that I must needs be dead,
  Yet, my dear father, to you I pray,
Smite then but few strokes at my head
  And make an end as soon as ye may,
  And tarry not too long.

Abraham: Thy meek words, child, do me dismay;
  So "wellaway" must be my song,

Except alone for God's good will.
  Ah! Isaac, my own sweet child,
Kiss me yet again upon this hill;
  In all the world is none so mild!

Isaac: Now, truly, father, all this tarrying,
  It doth my heart but harm —
I pray you, father, make an ending.

Abraham: Come up, sweet son, unto my arm.
  [*He binds him*]
I must bind thy hands too
  Although thou be never so mild.

Isaac: Ah, mercy, father! Why should ye so do?

Abraham: That thou should'st not stay me, my child.

Isaac: Indeed nay, father, I will not stay you.
   Do on, for me, your will;
And on the purpose that ye have set you,
   For God's love, keep it steadfast still.

I am full sorry this day to die,
   But yet I will not cause my God to grieve.
Do your desire for me hardily;
   My fair sweet father, I do give you leave.

But, father, I pray you evermore,
   Nothing to my mother tell,
If she wist it, she would weep full sore;
   Indeed she loves me, father, well,
     God's good blessing may she have!

Now farewell, my mother so sweet,
We two are like no more to meet.

Abraham: Ah! Isaac, Isaac, son, thou makest me grieve,
   And with thy words thou so distemperest me.

Isaac: Indeed, sweet father, I am sorry to grieve you;
   I cry you mercy for what I have done,
And for all trespass ever I did do.
Now, dear father, forgive all I have done. —
   God of Heaven be with me!

Abraham: Ah! dear child, leave off thy moans!
In all thy life thou grieved me never once.
Now blessed be thou, body and bones,
   That ever thou were bred and born;
Thou has been to me child full good.
   But in truth, child, though I mourn never so fast,
   Yet must I needs here at the last
In this place shed all thy blood;

Therefore, my dear son, here shalt thou lie, —
   [He places him on the altar]

Unto my work I must proceed.
In truth, I had as lief myself to die
    If God were pleased with the deed
        That I my own body should offer.

Isaac: Ah, mercy, father, mourn ye no more;
Your weeping maketh my heart sore
    That mine own death I am to suffer.
Your kerchief, father, about my eyes wind.

Abraham: So I shall, my sweetest child on earth.

Isaac: Now yet, good father, have this in mind,
    And smite me not often with your sharp sword,
        But hastily that it be sped.

(*"Here Abraham laid a cloth on Isaac's face, thus saying:"*)

Abraham: Now farewell, my child so full of grace.

Isaac: Ah, father, father, turn downward my face,
    For of your sharp sword I am ever adread!

[*Abraham looks up to Heaven resignedly*]

Abraham: To do this deed I am full sorry,
    But, Lord, thine behest I will not withstand.

Isaac: Ah! Father of Heaven, to thee I cry;
    Lord, receive me thou into thy hand!

[*Abraham falters and pleads again*]

Abraham: Lo, now is the time come for certain,
    That my sword in his neck shall bite.
Ah, Lord! my heart riseth there again,
    I may not find it in my heart to smite.
        My heart will not now thereto!
Ah, fain I would work my Lord's will,
But this young innocent lies so still,
I may not find it in my heart him to kill.
        Oh, Father of Heaven! what shall I do?

Isaac: Ah, mercy, father, why tarry ye so,
    And let me lie there so long on this heath?
Now I would God the stroke were done also;

Father, heartily I pray you, shorten my woe,
   And let me not wait thus for my death.

Abraham: Now, heart, why would'st thou not break in three?
   Yet shalt thou not make me to my God unmild.
I will no longer stay for thee,
For that my God aggrieved would be.
   Now have thy stroke, my own dear child.

    ("*Here Abraham drew his stroke, and the Angel took
    the sword in his hand suddenly.*")

The Angel: I am an angel, thou mayest see blithe,
   That from heaven to thee is sent.
Our Lord thanketh thee a hundred time
   For the keeping of his commandment.

He knoweth thy will, and also thy heart,
   That thou dreadst him above all thing;
And some of thy heaviness for to depart
   A fair ram yonder I did bring;

He standeth, lo, among the briars tied.
   Now, Abraham, amend thy mood,
For Isaac, thy young son, here by thy side
   This day shall not shed his blood.

Go, make thy sacrifice with yon ram.
Now farewell, blessed Abraham,
For unto heaven I go now home, —
   The way is full straight. . . .
    Take up thy son now free!

   [*Exit*]

Abraham: Ah, Lord! I thank thee for thy great grace,
   Now am I eased in diverse wise.
   Arise up, Isaac, my dear son, arise,
Arise up, sweet child, and come to me!

Isaac: Ah, mercy, father, why smite ye naught?
Ah, smite on, father, once with your knife.

Abraham: Peace, my sweet son, and take no thought,
   For our Lord of Heaven hath granted life
   By his angel now,
That thou shalt not die this day, son, truly.

Isaac: Ah, father, full glad then were I;
   In truth, father — I say, I — wis,
     That this tale were true!

Abraham: A hundred times, my son fair of hue,
   For joy thy mouth now will I kiss.

Isaac: Ah, my dear father Abraham,
   Will not God be wroth that we do thus?

Abraham: No, no! hardly, my sweet son!
   For yon same ram he hath now sent
   Hither down to us.
Yon beast shall die here in thy stead,
   In the worship of our Lord, alone.
Go fetch him hither, my child, indeed.

Isaac: Father I will go seize him by the head,
   And bring yon beast with me anon.
    [Isaac gets the ram]
Ah, sheep, sheep, blessed may thou be,
   That ever thou wert sent down hither!
Thou shalt this day die for me,
   In worship of the Holy Trinity.
    Now come fast and go we together,
     To my father of Heaven.
Though thou be never so gentle and good,
Yet I had liefer thou shed thy blood
    In truth, sheep, than I!
    [He leads it to Abraham]
Lo, father, I have brought here, full smart,
   This gentle sheep, and him to you I give.
    [With a sigh of relief]
But, Lord God, I thank thee with all my heart!
   For I am glad that I shall live,
    And kiss once more my dear mother!

Abraham: Now be right merry, my sweet child,
For this quick beast, that is so mild,
    Here I shall offer before all other.

Isaac: And I will fast begin to blow;
   This fire shall burn a full good speed.
    [Hesitating, however]
But, father, if I stoop down low,
Ye will not kill me with your sword, I trow?

Abraham: No, hardly, sweet son; have no dread.
    My mourning is past!
Isaac: Yea, but would that sword were sped —
    For, father, it doth make me yet full ill aghast.

(*"Here Abraham made his offering, kneeling and saying thus:"*)

Abraham: Now, Lord God of Heaven in Trinity,
    Almighty God omnipotent,
My offering I make in the worship of thee,
    And with this quick beast I thee present.
    Lord, receive thou mine intent,
As thou art God and ground of our grace.

God: Abraham, Abraham, well mayest thou speed,
    And Isaac, thy young son, thee by!
Truly, Abraham, for this deed,
    I shall multiply both your seed
    As thick as stars be in the sky,
      Both of bigger and less.
And as thick as gravel in the sea,
So thick multiplied your seed shall be;
    This grant I you for your goodness.

Of you shall come fruit unknown,
    And ever be in bliss without end,
For ye dread me as God alone
And keep my commandments, every one.
    My blessing I give wheresoever ye wend!

Abraham: Lo, Isaac my son, how think ye
    Of this work that we have wrought?
Full glad and blithe may we be
    That 'gainst the will of God we muttered nought
      On this fair heath.

Isaac: Ah, father, I thank our Lord every deal
That my wit served me so weel
    For God to fear more than my death.

Abraham: Why, dear-worthy son, wert thou afraid?
    Boldly, child, tell me thy lore.

Isaac: Yea! by my faith, father, be it said,
    I was never so afraid before,

As I have been on yon hill!
Ah, by my faith, father, I swear
I will nevermore come there,
    Except it be against my will!

Abraham: Yea, come on with me, my own sweet son,
    And homeward fast let us be gone.
Isaac: By my faith, father, thereto I agree!
I had never such good will to go home,
And to speak with my dear mother!

Abraham: Ah, Lord of Heaven, I thank thee,
    For now I may lead home with me
    Isaac, my young son so free,
The gentlest child above all other, —
    This may avowed be.
Now, go we forth, my blessed son.

Isaac: I grant, father, let us be gone,
For, by my troth, were I home then,
I would never go out as thus again.
I pray God give us grace evermore true,
And all those that we be beholden to!

[*Abraham and Isaac go out. The Doctor enters*]

Doctor: Lo, now sovereigns and sirs, thus did we show
    This solemn story to great and small.
It is a good lesson for both learned and low,
    And even for the wisest of us all,
        Without any barring.
For this story showeth you deep
How to our best power we should keep
    God's commandments without doubting.

Think ye, sirs, if God sent an angel,
    And commanded you your child to slay,
By your truth, is there any of you
    That would balk or gainsay?
How think ye now, sirs, thereby?

There be three or four or more, I trow,
And those women that weep so sorrowfully
    When that their children from them die
        As nature takes of our kind.
It is folly, as I may well avow,

Against God to grudge or to grieve so low;
For ye shall never see them mischiefed, well I know,
    By land or water, — have this in mind!

And grudge not against our Lord God,
    In wealth or woe whatever he you send,
Though ye be never so hard bestead;
    For when he willeth, he may it amend,
His commandments truly if ye keep with good soul,
    As this story hath now showed you before,
And faithfully serve him, while ye be whole,
    That ye may please God both even and morn.
Now Jesu, that wore the crown of thorn,
    Bring us all to heaven's bliss!

FINIS

THE ADORATION OF THE SHEPHERDS

❧ The English miracle plays were performed for more than two hundred years. Their period of greatest glory coincided with the reign of Henry VII and the first half of the reign of Henry VIII during the long peace which followed the War of the Roses.

But they were still extremely popular at the end of the sixteenth century when they died not of degeneration as some have supposed, but because the new Church of England wished to suppress anything that reminded people of Rome and Roman doctrine.

During the long history of the plays, they must have been frequently altered and adapted to suit new generations and circumstances. The manuscripts that we now possess represent the plays at a specific time and tell us little about their earlier or later versions.

Since we can assume a continuous process of revision, sometimes extemporally by the actors, sometimes more deliberately by a volunteer or hired adapter, we can deduce that most of the surviving plays had a collective authorship. Only in the case of the Townley plays do we find a body of work which shows such originality and individual strength that we can confidently assign it to a single author of genius.

That anonymous playwright is usually called the Wakefield Master. He can be identified by his characteristic nine-line stanza—a form that appears nowhere else in medieval drama. His work displays a rich sense of humor, a social conscience and an unsentimental but reverent approach to the central mysteries of the Church. He is brutal and tender

by turns, tough-minded but gentle in spirit. He is a master of all moods
of verse and an innovator in matters of dramatic structure.

He wrote five of the pieces in the Townley cycle—*Noah, The First
Shepherds' Play, The Second Shepherds' Play, Herod* and *The Buffeting*.
He is also responsible for most of *The Killing of Abel*, and his hand can
be detected in several of the other plays.

His masterpiece is *The Second Shepherds' Play*. Included below is the
brief biblical reference which formed the core of the drama. To this the
Wakefield Master grafted the amusing invented scene of the sheep-
stealing. But his was no simple farcical addition. Consider the complex
cross-references between the two parts of the story: the remarks about
Gil's miraculous birth, the reminder that Christ is "the Lamb of God,"
the offer by Mak to eat Gil's child. Is this a burlesque of the central
mysteries of Christianity? If so, the burlesque in no way diminishes or
belittles the true miracle which concludes the play.

In *The Second Shepherds' Play* we see the beginning of a
characteristically English way of writing plays, one that anticipates the
dark comedy of the gravedigger in *Hamlet*, the clown in *The Winter's
Tale* and the whole madhouse plot in *The Changeling*.

The Shepherds at the Crib (Luke 2:8-20)*

> 8. And there were shepherds in the same district living in the fields
> and keeping watch over their flock by night. 9. And behold, an angel
> of the Lord stood by them and the glory of God shone round about
> them, and they feared exceedingly.
>
> 10. And the angel said to them, "Do not be afraid, for behold, I
> bring you good news of great joy which shall be to all the people; 11.
> for today in the town of David a Savior has been born to you, who is
> Christ the Lord. 12. And this shall be a sign to you: you will find an
> infant wrapped in swaddling clothes and lying in a manger." 13. And
> suddenly there was with the angel a multitude of the heavenly host
> praising God and saying, 14. "Glory to God in the highest, and on
> earth peace among men of good will."
>
> 15. And it came to pass, when the angels had departed from them
> into heaven, that the shepherds were saying to one another, "Let us go
> over to Bethlehem and see this thing that has come to pass, which the
> Lord has made known to us."
>
> 16. So they went with haste, and they found Mary and Joseph, and
> the babe lying in the manger. 17. And when they had seen, they
> understood what had been told them concerning this child. 18. And all
> who heard marvelled at the things told them by the shepherds. 19. But
> Mary kept in mind all these things, pondering them in her heart. 20.
> And the shepherds returned, glorifying and praising God for all that
> they had heard and seen, even as it was spoken to them.

*In the Dovai translation.

The Second Shepherds' Play*

1ST SHEPHERD	MAK	ANGEL
2ND SHEPHERD	GIL, HIS WIFE	MARY
3RD SHEPHERD		JESUS

1ST SHEPHERD Lord, but this weather is cold, and I am ill wrapped,
      My hands in frost's hold, so long have I napped;
      My legs they fold, my fingers are chapped,
      It is not as of old, for I am lapped
        In sorrow.
      In storms and tempest,
      Now in the east, now in the west,
      Woe to him who has no rest
      Now or tomorrow.

      But we simple shepherds that walk on the moor,
      Are soon by richer hands thrust out of door;
      No wonder as it stands, if we be poor,
      For the tilth of our lands lies as fallow as the floor,
        As you know
      We are so lamed,
      Overtaxed and maimed,
      And cruelly tamed,
        By our gentleman foe.

      Thus they rob us of our rest, may ill luck them harry!
      These proud men are our pest they make the plough
                    [tarry.
      What men say is for the best, we find it contrary:
      Thus are ploughmen oppressed, no hope now to carry
        Alive.

* Modernized by Martial Rose in *The Wakefield Mystery Plays* (New York: W.W. Norton, Inc., 1961), pp. 207-234.

Thus hold they us under,
Thus bring us into blunder;
It were a great wonder,
   If ever we should thrive.

If one gets a modish sleeve or a brooch nowadays,
Take care if you grieve or once cross his ways!
Dares no man bid him leave the power that he sways,
And yet may not believe one word that he says
   The better
He grasps for his gain
In his bragging vein,
And boasts men maintain
   Him, who are far greater.

There shall come a swain, a proud peacock you know,
He must borrow my wain, my plough also,
This for my gain I must grant ere he go.
Thus we live in pain, anger and woe;
   By night and day.
He craves what comes to his head,
And I give in great dread;
I were better be dead,
   Than once say him nay.

It does me good as I walk thus on my own,
Of this world for to talk, and so make my moan.
To my sheep will I stalk and listen anon;
There abide on a balk or sit on a stone
   Full soon.
For believe you me,
True men, if they be,
We get more company
   Ere it be noon.

                            [2ND SHEPHERD *enters.*

2ND SHEPHERD *Benedicite dominus!* What may this mean?
         The world faring thus, how oft have we seen?
         Lord, this weather works through us and the wind is
                                    [so keen
         And frost will undo us, fast blind I have been,
           No lie.

Now in dry, now in wet,
Now in snow, now in sleet,
When my shoes freeze to my feet,
    It's not at all easy.

But as far as I ken or yet as I go,
We poor wedded men suffer much woe;
We have sorrow ever again, it falls often so;
Old Capel, our hen, both to and fro
    She cackles;
But begin she to croak
To prod or to poke,
For our cock it is no joke
    For he is in shackles.

These men that are wed have not their own will,
When full bitter they have sped their tongue they keep
                                       [still:
God knows they are led in a grim dance full ill;
In bower and in bed, but speak not their fill
    Nor chide.
My part I have found,
Learnt my lesson sound.
Woe to him who is bound
    For he must abide.

But now late in our lives a marvel to me
That I think my heart rives such wonders to see.
Where that destiny drives it should so be;
Some men will have two wives, and some men three
    In store.
Some are woe without any,
But so far as I see,
Woe is him that has many,
    For he rues it sore.

But young men a-wooing, on God be your thought,
Be well warned of wedding, and think ere you're
                                      [caught,
"Had I known" is a thing too lately you're taught;
Much bitter mourning has wedding home brought:
    You achieve

With many a sharp shower,
What you catch in an hour,
Which shall savour full sour,
    A life-time to grieve.

As I've read Paul's Epistle, my helpmate is here,
As sharp as a thistle, as tough as a spear;
She is browed like a bristle, with a sour looking cheer;
If she once wets her whistle she can sing full clear
    Her paternoster.
As great as a whale withal,
She has a gallon of gall,
By him that died for us all
    I would I had lost her.

1ST SHEPHERD   Look over the hedgerow, are you deaf as you stand?

2ND SHEPHERD   The devil take you for so long have I scanned.
    Where saw you Daw go?

1ST SHEPHERD   Here on the lea land.
    I heard his pipe blow: he comes near at hand
        Hereby;
    Stand still.

2ND SHEPHERD   Why?

1ST SHEPHERD   For he comes, say I

2ND SHEPHERD   He will beguile us with a lie
        Unless we be spry.

                      [*Enter* 3RD SHEPHERD.

3RD SHEPHERD   Christ's cross me speed and Saint Nicholas!
    Thereof have I need; it is worse than it was.
    Who knows should take heed, and let the world pass;
    It is doomed as decreed and brittle as glass
        And slithers.
    The world fared never so:
    As great marvels grow,
    Move us from weal to woe,
        The whole world withers.

    Was never since Noah's flood such floodings seen;
    Winds and rains so rude and storms so keen;

Some stumbled, some in doubt, as I ween;
Now God turn all to good, I say as I mean,
   And ponder.
These floods they so drown,
Both in fields and in town,
And bear all things down,
   And that is a wonder.

We walk in the nights our cattle to keep,
We see fearful sights when other men sleep.
Now I think my eye lights on some rascals that peep;
And to put all to rights I must give my sheep
   A turn.
But full ill I have meant,
And amend my intent,
I may lightly repent,
   My toes if I spurn.

Ah, sir, God you save, and master mine!
A deep drink would I have and somewhat to dine.

1ST SHEPHERD	Christ's curse, you slave, you are a sluggish swine!
2ND SHEPHERD	What! Let the boy rave; sit down and dine.

   We have had our fill
Ill luck be thy fate
Though the lad come late,
Yet he is in a state
   To sup if he will.

Such servants as I who work till we sweat
Eat our bread quite dry and that makes me fret;
We are often weak and weary when our masters sleep
                                    [yet;
Late home and dreary, in food and drink we get
   Less than our due.
Both our dame and our sire,
When we run in the mire
They dock us of our hire
   And pay us late too.

But hear the truth master, for what I am paid

I shall work no faster than a stubborn jade;
I shall be slacker and sport like a maid,
For never has my supper my stomach dismayed
    In fields,
Why should I weep?
With my staff I can leap;
Men say a bargain cheap
    Poorly yields.

1ST SHEPHERD   You were an ill lad to go a-wooing
With a master that had but little for spending.

2ND SHEPHERD   Peace, I say, lad, no more of jangling,
Or you will rue it sad, by heaven's king!
    Hold your tongue!
Where are our sheep, boy, we've shorn?

3RD SHEPHERD   Sir, this same day at morn
I left them in the corn,
    When matins were rung.
They have pasture good they cannot go wrong.

1ST SHEPHERD   That is right, by the rood! These nights are long,
Yet ere we went I would someone gave us a song.

2ND SHEPHERD   So I thought as I stood, our mirth to prolong.

3RD SHEPHERD   I grant.

1ST SHEPHERD   Let me sing the tenor free.

2ND SHEPHERD   And I shall sing the trebel key.

3RD SHEPHERD   Then the alto falls to me.
    Let's see how we chant.

    [SHEPHERDS *sing. Then* MAK *enters. He wears a short
    mantle over his gown.*

MAK   Now Lord, in thy names seven that made both moon
        [and stars,
More than I can count in heaven, thy will from bliss
        [me bars;
My life is uneven with jingles and jars;
Now would God I were in heaven where no bairn's
        [tear mars
    The still.

1ST SHEPHERD	Who is it that pipes so poorly?
MAK	Would God ye knew of me, surely! Footing the moors so sorely, Drudging against my will.
2ND SHEPHERD	Mak, where hast thou been? Tell us thy tidings.
3RD SHEPHERD	If Mak come on the scene, look well to your things.

[3RD SHEPHERD *takes away* MAK's *mantle.*

MAK	What! I be a yeoman true and one the king's;
	One who from no mean lord a mighty message
	                                [brings.
	    No lie.
	Fie on you go hence
	Out of my presence!
	I must have reverence;
	    Why? Who am I?

1ST SHEPHERD	Why are your quirks so quaint? Mak, you do wrong.
2ND SHEPHERD	Would you rather be a saint, Mak? Your wish is so [strong.
3RD SHEPHERD	If the knave can paint to the devil might he belong.
MAK	I shall make complaint; beaten you'll be ere long, At a word, And wracked without ruth.
1ST SHEPHERD	But, Mak, is that truth? Now take out that southern tooth, And set in a turd.
2ND SHEPHERD	Mak, the devil's in thee, a blow you'll be getting.
3RD SHEPHERD	Mak, know ye not me? Your blood I'll be letting.
MAK	God save you all three, now why are you fretting? You are a fair company.
1ST SHEPHERD	What snare are you setting?
2ND SHEPHERD	Why creep You so late on your toes, What will men suppose? And thou hast an ill nose For stealing of sheep.

MAK   That I am true as steel no men debate,
                 But a sickness that I feel has brought me to this state,
                 My belly lacks a meal and suffers ill fate.

3RD SHEPHERD   Seldom lies the devil dead by the gate.

MAK   Therefore
                 Full sore am I and ill,
                 If I stand stone still
                 I've ate not a needle
                        This month and more.

1ST SHEPHERD   How fares thy wife, by my hood, how fares she?

MAK   Rolls around by the rood; by the fire she'll be,
                 And a house full of brood, with the bottle she's free,
                 Cares not for any good, whatever she may see;
                        But so
                 Eats as fast as she can,
                 And each year that comes to a man
                 Adds another to our clan;
                        And some years two.

                 Now were I richer than the Pope of Rome
                 I would be eaten out of house and home.
                 So foul a wench, if close you come
                 You'll scarce believe; no worser one
                        A man's peace stole
                 Would you see what I would proffer;
                 I'd give all within my coffer
                 If tomorrow I might offer
                        A prayer for her soul.

2ND SHEPHERD   I have watched without nodding as none in this shire;
                 I must sleep though it means taking less for my hire.

3RD SHEPHERD   I am cold and ill-clad and long for a fire.

1ST SHEPHERD   I am worn out with walking and covered in mire.
                        Look to!

2ND SHEPHERD   Nay, down I shall lie
                 For I must sleep soundly.

3RD SHEPHERD   As good a man's son I
                        As any of you.
                 But, Mak, come hither, and with us lie down.

MAK   Then your whisperings between you with snores I
                                                [would drown.

                     Pay heed;
From my top to my toe,
Manus tuas commendo,
Pontio Pilato,
                     Christ's cross me speed!

[*When the* SHEPHERDS *are asleep* MAK *rises.*

MAK   It is now time to strike ere the iron grows cold,
And craftily creep then into the fold,
And nimbly to work, but not be too bold,
For bitter the bargain, if all were told
                     At the ending;
My doubts may dispel,
But he needs good counsel
That would gladly fare well
                     With but little for spending.

Put about you a circle as round as the moon,
Till I have done what I will, until it be noon.
Lie you stone still as though in a swoon,
While I summon my skill some magic to croon
                     Over you.
Above your heads I raise my hand.
Your sight is lost on sea and land!
But I must gain much more command
                     To get my due.
Lord, but they sleep hard, as you may well hear;
Never yet was I shepherd, but of that I've no fear,
If the flock be scared, then I shall nip near
Till one I've ensnared. Then will soon disappear
                     Our sorrow.

                                  [MAK *seizes a sheep.*

A fat sheep I dare say,
A good fleece I dare lay,
I'll requite when I may,
                     But this will I borrow.

                                 [MAK *goes home.*

How Gil, are you in? Get us some light!

MAK'S WIFE	Who makes such a din, this time of the night?
	I've sat down to spin; I hope now I might
	Not rise for a pin. I'll curse in my spite
	With no pause;
	A housewife that has been
	Fretted betwixt and between,
	Has no work to be seen
	For such small chores.
MAK	Good wife, open this hatch; see you not what I bring?
MAK'S WIFE	I will let you draw the latch. Come in, my sweeting.
MAK	You care not a scratch for my long standing.
MAK'S WIFE	Now your neck may catch a rope at a hanging.
MAK	Away!
	I earn what I eat,
	For in a fix I can get
	More than they that toil and sweat
	All the long day.
	Thus it fell to my lot, Gil, you cannot gainsay.
MAK'S WIFE	It were a foul blot to be hanged, as you may.
MAK	I have escaped scot-free a far fiercer fray.
MAK'S WIFE	But so long goes the pot to the water, men say,
	At last
	Comes it home broken.
MAK	Well know I the token,
	But let it never be spoken,
	But come and help fast.
	I would he were slain, I want so to eat.
	For more than a year I've dreamt of this treat.
MAK'S WIFE	They'll come ere he's slain, and hear the sheep bleat.
MAK	Then might I be ta'en; that gives me cold feet!
	Go bar
	The outer door.
MAK'S WIFE	Yes, Mak,
	For if they pounce on your back . . .

MAK   Then might I get from the whole pack
                 A jolt and a jar.

MAK'S WIFE   A fine jest have I spied, since you think of none;
               Here shall we hide him until they are gone,
               In my cradle to abide, but let me alone,
               And I shall lie beside in childbed, and groan.

MAK   Them warn
               I shall that in the night
               Was born a boy for our delight.

MAK'S WIFE   Now bless I that day bright
                 That ever I was born!

               This is a cunning play and well cast;
               What a woman may say can help at the last.
               None will gainsay; but get you back fast.

MAK   If when they wake I'm away, there'll blow a cold
                                                          [blast.
                 I will go sleep.

           [MAK *returns to the* SHEPHERDS *and resumes his place.*

               Yet sleeps the whole company
               So I must tread carefully,
               As though it had never been I
                 That stole their sheep.

1ST SHEPHERD   *Resurrex a mortruis!* Hold hard my hand!
               Judas carnas dominus! I scarcely can stand.
               My foot sleeps, by Jesus, my belly's a brand;
               My dream seemed to bring us quite near to England.

2ND SHEPHERD   Say ye!
               Lord, but I slept well;
               As fresh as an eel.
               As light I do feel
                 As leaf on a tree.

3RD SHEPHERD   Blessed all be within! My heart so quakes
               To leap out of its skin such noise it makes.
               Who makes all this din? My head sorely aches.
               I must stir from within for my fellows' sakes.
                 We were four.
               Saw you ought of Mak now?

1ST SHEPHERD	We were up ere thou.
2ND SHEPHERD	Man, I give God a vow,
	He's still in the straw.
3RD SHEPHERD	I dreamt he was wrapped in a wolf's skin.
1ST SHEPHERD	Many such have entrapped now our poor kin.
2ND SHEPHERD	When long had we napped I dreamt of Mak's sin,
	A fat sheep he had trapped by stealth with no din.
3RD SHEPHERD	Be still!
	Your dream proves you mad;
	Your fancy's a fad.
1ST SHEPHERD	God keep us from bad
	If it be his will.
2ND SHEPHERD	Rise, Mak, for shame! Thou liest right long.
MAK	Now Christ's holy name be us among!
	What is this? By Saint James, I can't get along!
	I trust I be the same. Ah! My neck has lain all wrong
	In this hole.

[*They help him.*

Many thanks! since yester-even,
Now by Saint Stephen,
A dream sent from heaven
    Struck fear in my soul.

I dreamt Gil in her smock cried out full sad,
Gave birth at the first cock to a young lad,
To add to our flock; then be I never glad.
Of cares I've a stock more than ever I had.
    Ah, my head!
Those moans of hunger pains,
The devil knock out their brains!
Woe to him whose brood complains
    Of too little bread.

I must go home, by your leave, to Gil, as I thought.
First look up my sleeve that I've stolen naught:
I am loth you to grieve, or from you take ought.

[MAK *goes home.*

3RD SHEPHERD	Go forth, ill-luck achieve! Now would I we sought
	This morn
	For the sheep in our care.
1ST SHEPHERD	First I shall fare.
	Let us meet.
2ND SHEPHERD	Where?
3RD SHEPHERD	At the crooked thorn.

                                       [*The* SHEPHERDS *part.*

MAK	Undo this door! Who is here? How long shall I stand?
MAK'S WIFE	Who roars then out there? Be ye one or a band?
MAK	Ah, Gil, what cheer? It is I, Mak, your husband.
MAK'S WIFE	Ah, then never fear, the devil is at hand
	With guile.
	Lo, he strikes a harsh note,
	As though held by the throat,
	And cares never a groat
	My work to beguile.
MAK	Oh, the fuss that she makes when I stir her repose.
	She feigns all her aches and picks at her toes.
MAK'S WIFE	Why, who works, and who wakes, who comes and
	[who goes?
	Who brews and who bakes? Who darns all your hose?
	And then
	It is sad to behold,
	Or e'er to be told,
	How woeful the household
	That wants a woman.
	But how have you sped with the shepherds, Mak?
MAK	The last word that they said when I turned my back'
	They would count each head of the sheep in their
	[pack.
	Now have we no dread when they their sheep lack,
	Pardy;
	But howe'er the game goes,
	They'll be here, I suppose,

        Our theft to disclose,
           And cry out upon me.
        Now do as you promised.

MAK'S WIFE   To that I agree,
        I'll swaddle him now, in his crib he will be;
        A fine trick to twist on our poor shepherds three.
        To bed! Come assist. Tuck up!

MAK   Let me.

MAK'S WIFE   Behind.
        Come Coll and his mate
        To pry and to prate,
        For help I'll cry straight
           The sheep if they find.

        Hark now for their call; on the breeze be it blown.
        Come make ready all and sing on thine own;
        Sing lullay you shall, for loud I must groan,
        And cry out by the wall on Mary and Joan
           Full sore.
        Sing lullay quite fast
        When you hear them at last
        If my part is miscast,
           Trust me no more.

3RD SHEPHERD Ah, Coll, good morn, why sleepest thou not?

1ST SHEPHERD Alas that ever I was born! A sad grief we have got.
        Lost! A fat wether unshorn.

3RD SHEPHERD   By God, a foul blot.

2ND SHEPHERD Who should give us this scorn? It won't be forgot.

1ST SHEPHERD   This he shall rue.
        I have searched with my dogs
        All Horbury shrogs,
        And of fifteen hogs,
           Found I but one ewe.

3RD SHEPHERD Now trust me, if ye will, by St. Thomas of Kent,
        Either Mak or Gil, had a hand in this event.

1ST SHEPHERD Peace, man, be still! I saw when he went.

You slander him ill, you ought to repent
With good speed.

2ND SHEPHERD   Now as ever I might thrive,
As I hope to keep alive,
Only Mak could contrive
To do that same deed.

3RD SHEPHERD   Then off to his homestead, be brisk on our feet.
I shall never eat bread till we've proved this deceit.

1ST SHEPHERD   Nor have drink in my head till with him I meet.

2ND SHEPHERD   I will rest in no stead till him I may greet,
My brother.
My promise I plight
Till I have him in sight,
Shall I ne'er sleep one night.
May I do no other.

      [*They go to* MAK'S *house — singing within.*

3RD SHEPHERD   Do ye hear how they croak? My lord will now croon.

1ST SHEPHERD   Ne'er heard I sing folk so clean out of tune;
Call him.

2ND SHEPHERD   Mak, may you choke! Undo your door soon!

MAK   Who is it that spoke, as if it were noon?
Who scoffed?
Who is that I say?

3RD SHEPHERD   Good fellows, were it day!

MAK   As far as ye may,
Speak soft,
Over a sick woman's head, who is not at her ease,
I had rather be dead than she had a disease.

      [*The* SHEPHERDS *enter* MAK'S *home.*

MAK'S WIFE   Be off from the bed, let me breathe, if you please!
Each step that you tread from my nose to my knees
Goes through me.

1ST SHEPHERD   Tell us, Mak, if ye may,
How fare ye, say?

MAK	But are ye in town today? Now how fare ye?

	Ye have run in the mire, and now are all wet.
	I shall make you a fire now we are met.
	A nurse I would hire. Think ye on yet
	My dream which entire has fulfilled its threat
	    In due season.
	I have bairns if ye knew,
	Far more than a few,
	But we must drink as we brew,
	    And that is but reason.

	Would ye dined ere ye went? Ye sweat, as I think.
2ND SHEPHERD	Our feelings be vent not for meat nor for drink.
MAK	Is ought then ill meant?
3RD SHEPHERD	Yea, in a wink, A sheep lost we lament, borne off ere we blink.
MAK	Drink sirs. Had I been there Some had suffered full dear.
1ST SHEPHERD	In that is our fear; None of us errs.
2ND SHEPHERD	Against you goes the grouse, Mak, thief that ye be, Either you or your spouse, and so say we.

MAK	Nay, knit not your brows against my Gil or me.
	Come comb through our house, and then ye may see
	    Who had her.
	If any sheep I've got,
	Alive or in the pot —
	And Gil, my wife, rose not
	    Here since she laid her.

	As I am true as steel, to God here I pray, That this be the first meal that I shall eat this day.
1ST SHEPHERD	Mak, is such thy zeal! Then be advised, I say: He learns in time to steal that never could say nay.
MAK'S WIFE	I faint!

	Out thieves from my home,
	Ere I claw with my comb!
MAK	If you marked but her foam,
	You'd show some restraint.
MAK'S WIFE	Out thieves from my cot, step you soft on the floor.
MAK	If ye knew her harsh lot, your hearts would be sore.
	Your behaviour's a blot, here to rant and to roar:
	Gil's plight ye've forgot. But I say no more.
MAK'S WIFE	Ah, my middle!
	I pray to God so mild,
	If ere I you beguiled,
	That I should eat this child
	That lies in this cradle.
MAK	Peace, woman, for God's pain, and cry not so:
	Thou'lt burst thy brain and make me full of woe.
2ND SHEPHERD	I believe our sheep be slain, and that ye know.
3RD SHEPHERD	Our search has been in vain, now let us go.
	He chatters
	His way through our mesh.
	Here's to be found no flesh,
	Soft nor hard, salt nor flesh,
	But two empty platters.
	No creature but this, tame or wild,
	As hope I for bliss, smelt so defiled.
MAK'S WIFE	No, so God bless me, and give me joy of my child!
1ST SHEPHERD	We have aimed amiss; we be but beguiled.
2ND SHEPHERD	Have done!
	Sir, our Lady him save!
	Be this a boy brave?
MAK'S WIFE	Any lord might him have.
	This child for his son.
	When he wakes he smiles that joy is to see.
3RD SHEPHERD	May now the world's wiles this bairn leave be.
	Who stood at the font that so soon were ready?

MAK	The first folk of these isles.
1ST SHEPHERD	A lie now, hark ye!
MAK	God give them thanks. Parkin and Gibbon Waller, I say, And gentle John Horn in grey. He made such a droll display With his long shanks.
2ND SHEPHERD	Mak, friends will we be, for we are all one.
MAK	We? count not on me, for amends I get none. Farewell all three! And gladly begone.

[They leave the cottage.

3RD SHEPHERD	Fair words there may be, but love there is none This year.
1ST SHEPHERD	Gave ye the child anything?
2ND SHEPHERD	Not I, ne'er a farthing.
3RD SHEPHERD	I shall find an offering. Wait for me here.

[He returns to the cottage.

3RD SHEPHERD	Mak, by your leave, your son may I see?
MAK	A mere mock I believe; his sleep you may mar.
3RD SHEPHERD	This child will not grieve, that little day star. Mak, by your leave, thy bairn never bar From sixpence.
MAK	Nay, go away, he sleeps.
3RD SHEPHERD	I think he peeps.
MAK	When he wakes he weeps; I pray you go hence.

[The other SHEPHERDS *come back.*

3RD SHEPHERD	Give me leave him to kiss, and once lift him out. What the devil is this? He has a long snout!
1ST SHEPHERD	He is marked amiss. Come, best meddle nowt.
2ND SHEPHERD	The ill-spun weft is ever foully turned out. Quit talk! He is like to our sheep.

3RD SHEPHERD How, Gib! May I peep?

1ST SHEPHERD Aye, cunning will creep
              Where it may not walk.

2ND SHEPHERD A ruse to record, and craftily cast.
              It was a fine fraud.

3RD SHEPHERD And prettily passed.
              Let's burn this bawd and bind her fast.
              This shrew with a cord will be hanged at last.
                  So shalt thou.
              Will you see how they swaddle
              His four feet in the middle.
              Saw I never in a cradle
                  A horned lad ere now.

MAK   Peace, I say, what! Let be your blare!
              I am he that him got, and yon woman him bare.

1ST SHEPHERD Have you named him not, nor made him your heir?

2ND SHEPHERD Now leave him to rot, and God give him care,
                  I say.

MAK'S WIFE   A pretty child is he
              As sits on a woman's knee;
              A dillydown dilly,
                  To make a man gay

3RD SHEPHERD I know him by the ear mark; that is a good token.

MAK   I tell you sirs, hark! His nose here was broken.
              Warned was I by a clerk what such spells did betoken

1ST SHEPHERD Do you hear the dog bark? Would fists first had
                                                    [spoken!
              Let be

MAK'S WIFE   He was witched by an elf;
              I saw it myself:
              When the clock struck twelve,
                  Misshapen was he.

2ND SHEPHERD Both be of ill-spun weft of twisted thread.
              Since they uphold their theft, let's strike them dead.

MAK   If more I thieve, bereft may I be of my head.

                          [MAK *kneels to the* SHEPHERDS.

              At your mercy I am left.

1ST SHEPHERD   Sirs, hear what's said.
       For this trespass
      We will neither curse nor chide,
      No more deride,
      Nor longer bide,
        But toss him in a canvas.

    [*They toss* MAK *in a canvas, after which* MAK *and his* WIFE
    return home.

1ST SHEPHERD Lord, but I am sore; to leave now were best.
              In faith I may no more, therefore must I rest.

2ND SHEPHERD As a sheep of seven score pound he weighed on my
                                      [chest,
              Now to sleep out of door I'd count myself blest.

3RD SHEPHERD   Then, I pray,
              Lie down on this green,

1ST SHEPHERD Brisk have these thieves been.

3RD SHEPHERD Never split your spleen
              For them, I say.

    [*They sleep. The* ANGEL *sings "Gloria in Excelsis" then speaks.*

ANGEL   Rise, shepherds, attend! For now he is born
              Who shall fetch from the fiend what from Adam was
                                      [torn.
              That warlock to end, this night is he born.
              God made your friend; now at this morn —
                Leave your flocks:
              To Bethlehem go see
              Where he lies so free,
              A child in a crib poorly,
                Between ass and ox.

1ST SHEPHERD This was a sweet sound as ever yet I heard;
              To tell would astound where we this averred.

2ND SHEPHERD That God's son be unbound from heaven, spoke he
                                      [word;
              And lightning then crowned the woods as they stirred
              In there fear.

3RD SHEPHERD He came us to warn,

| | In Bethlehem will be born |
| | A babe. |

1ST SHEPHERD   Be we drawn
By yon star there.

2ND SHEPHERD   Say, what was his song? Heard ye not how it went?
Three shorts and a long.

3RD SHEPHERD   The very accent.
With no crochet wrong, and no breath misspent.

1ST SHEPHERD   For to sing us among as he merciful meant,
I can.

2ND SHEPHERD   Let's see how ye croon.
Can ye bark at the moon?

3RD SHEPHERD   Hold your tongues full soon!

1ST SHEPHERD   Or sing after, man.

                                                    [*He sings.*

2ND SHEPHERD   To Bethlehem he bad that we should go:
And sure we be mad to tarry so.

3RD SHEPHERD   Be merry and not sad, our mirth may overflow:
To be forever glad is the reward we shall know
And choose.

1ST SHEPHERD   Then let us hither hie,
Though we be wet and weary,
To that child and that lady;
We have no time to lose.

2ND SHEPHERD   We find by the prophecy — let be your din —
Of Isaiah and David, and more of their kin,
They prophesied by clergy that in a virgin
Should God come to lie, to atone for our sin,
And abate it.
Our folk freed from woe,
Isaiah said so.
For a maid comes to show
A child that is naked.

3RD SHEPHERD   Full glad may we be and abide that day,
That sweet sight to see who all power may sway.

Lord so bless me, for now and for ay,
Might I kneel on my knee some word for to say
   To that child.
But the angel said
In a crib was he laid;
He was poorly arrayed,
   Both meek and mild.

1ST SHEPHERD Patriarchs have been, and prophets have sworn,
They desired to have seen this child that is born,
Past hope now to glean the gold of this corn.
To see him we mean now ere it be morn,
   As a token.
When I see him and feel,
Then know I full well
It is as true as steel
   What prophets have spoken.

To so poor as we are that he would appear
First, and to us declare by his messenger.

2ND SHEPHERD Go we now, let us fare, the place is us near.

3RD SHEPHERD I am glad to go there; set off in good cheer
   To that mite mild.
Lord, if thy will be,
We are unlearned, all three,
Grant us thy gracious glee
   To comfort thy child.

1ST SHEPHERD Hail, comely and clean! Hail, young child!
Hail, maker, I mean, of maiden so mild!
Thou hast crushed in his spleen, the warlock so wild;
That false traitor has been beyond doubt beguiled.
   Lo, he merry is.
Lo, he laughs, my sweeting,
A welcome meeting:
   Have a bob of cherries.

2ND SHEPHERD Hail, sovereign saviour, for thou hast us sought!
Hail, joyous food and flower, that all things hast
                                          [wrought!
Hail, full of favour, that made all of nought.

Hail, I kneel and I cover. A bird have I brought,
    Bairn that ye are.
Hail, little tiny mop,
Of our creed thou art top,
At your mass I shall stop,
    Little day star.

3RD SHEPHERD Hail, darling dear, full of godhead!
I pray thee be near when that I have need.
Hail, sweet is thy cheer! My heart would bleed
To see thee sit here in so poor a stead
    With no pennies.
Hail, hold forth thy hand small;
I bring thee but a ball:
Have thou and play withall,
    And go to the tennis.

MARY   The father of heaven, God omnipotent,
Made all in days seven, his son has he sent.
My name has he given, his light has me lent.
Conceived I him even though his might as he meant,
And now he is born.
May he keep you from woe!
I shall pray him do so.
Tell of him as you go;
    Have mind on this morn.

1ST SHEPHERD Farewell, lady, so fair to behold,
With child on thy knee!

2ND SHEPHERD But he lies full cold.
Lord, well is me, now back to our fold.

3RD SHEPHERD In truth already it seems to be told
    Full oft.

1ST SHEPHERD What grace we have found.

2ND SHEPHERD Come, now are we unbound.

3RD SHEPHERD Let's make a glad sound,
And sing it not soft.

[*The* SHEPHERDS *leave singing.*

THE MIRACLE CYCLES

⤳To early twentieth-century critics, the homely comedy of the miracle cycles seemed inappropriate to a sacred subject. The sexual and scatological allusions also caused problems. Joseph Quincy Adams, one of the first modern editors of these plays, felt obliged to publish expurgated texts for fear of offending his readers' sensibilities.

But surely the audiences of the middle ages saw no irreverence in humor. Moreover, our generation, taught by Ionesco, Beckett, Arrabal and the other comedians of despair, will find nothing offensive in the jokes of the Wakefield Master.

Indeed, the material excised by Adams is the very element that makes the cycles so startling and original. A new generation of critics have been more appreciative of the tone and style of medieval sacred comedy. Arnold Williams' essay is representative of the latest opinions.

Arnold Williams
THE COMIC IN THE CYCLES*

I

*I*f all drama must be either comedy or tragedy, it is obvious that the cycle plays must be comedy, for they cannot be tragedy. To the Middle Ages tragedy meant chiefly a story with an unhappy ending, one whose main character, as Chaucer's monk phrased it, "is yfallen out of heigh degree / Into miserie, and endeth wrecchedly." More sophisticated critics added that it had to concern magnates and kings and be written in high style.[1] The scriptural drama of the cycle plays fits none of these criteria. If the cycle ended with the fall of Adam and Eve, or the punishment of the wicked in the Last Judgement, perhaps the requirement of going from joy to misery would be met. No cycle is so arranged. Those episodes which in themselves have the possibility of tragedy, the Crucifixion, for example, are followed or accompanied by other episodes which reverse the movement. The Fall is a fortunate fall, for it opens the way for the great manifestations of love in the redemption. The horrors

*From *Medieval Drama*, ed. Neville Denny (London: Edward Arnold, 1973), pp. 109-123.
[1] Paul Strohm, 'Storie, Spelle, Geste, Romaunce, Tragedie', *Speculum* XLVI (1971), pp. 356-9. The footnotes are the author's.

of the Crucifixion are really prologue to the joys of the Resurrection. The condemnation of the wicked is preceded and nullified by the rewarding of the just.

This holds true for the other criteria. The history of the human race, which is the subject of the cycle plays, involves kings and magnates, but not exclusively. In fact the emphasis is rather more on the humble. The Shepherds worship the infant Jesus before the Kings. Common people like the man born blind or the woman taken in adultery play quite as large a role as those in absolute authority like Pharaoh, Caesar Augustus, the two Herods, Pilate, Annas and Caiaphas, all of whom are tyrants and villains. Some of the playwrights attempted to differentiate between high and low characters by assigning the high characters mixtures of French and English, as in the Cornish and Chester cycles, or macaronic Latin-English, as in the Towneley Pilate, or 'aureate' English, as in the two Coventry plays. The results, however, do not appeal, at least to the modern reader, as 'high style' in the sense that Shakespeare or Milton achieved it.

If, as a common medieval belief voiced by Vincent of Beauvais and Dante held,[2] the main requirement of comedy is a happy ending, the cycle plays are comedy. However, we are accustomed to expect other things of comedy. One of these is a unity, which in the ancient drama of Greece and Rome is achieved in either or both of two ways. The Old Comedy of Aristophanes is unified by the target of its satire, often a specific person or an identifiable group. *The Clouds* is aimed directly at Socrates, whom Aristophanes saw as a perverter of morals. The target of *Lysistrata* is more diffuse, the war party concreted in the chorus of old men, who continued the wasteful and hopeless war with Sparta.

In the New Comedy of Menander and his Roman followers, Terence and Plautus, plot is the unifying element, and in its basic elements the plot is almost invariable: a man, nearly always young, desires a woman and overcomes obstacles to attain her finally. The devices by which this standard plot is worked out include intrigue, mistaken identity, disguise, misunderstanding, surprise, discovery. Classical comedy also created certain stereotyped characters, for instance the braggart, the parasite, the

---

[2] 'Comedy is poetry reversing a sad beginning by a glad end'—Vencent of Beauvais quoted in C.S. Baldwin, *Medieval Rhetoric* (originally published in 1928, reprinted Gloucester, Mass., 1959), p. 176. 'Comedy begins with sundry adverse conditions but ends happily'—Dante, letter to Can Grande, in Paget Toynbee, *Epistolae* (2nd edn., Oxford, 1966), pp. 200-01. It is perhaps significant that Dante calls his great work both a comedy (*Inferno* XVI, 128) and a tragedy (*Inferno* XX, 113). We shall see a similar ambivalence in the cycle plays.

foolish old man, the shrew.

Some of the stereotypes have parallels in the cycle plays. The soldiers sent out by Herod to massacre the infants easily fall into the mold of the 'miles gloriosus' or braggart, as do those sent by Pilate to guard the sepulchre. The discomfiture of Herod's soldiers by the women produces farce in some of the plays, especially in the Digby play of the *Killing of the Children*, which develops a boasting coward named Watkyn. In both York and Towneley Cain is given a comic servant, Brewbarret and Pikeharness respectively. The greatest development is of the *senex*, the foolish old man. Two characters lend themselves to this role; Noah, who is five hundred years old when commanded to build the ark, and St. Joseph, who is not only the grumbling and self-pitying old man called on for tasks beyond his strength (catching doves for the presentation in the temple in the Coventry *Weaver's Pageant*, 461-520) but also convinced that he is cuckolded. In all treatments he addresses the men in the audience, warning them not to take young wives. York and Towneley are especially notable for the rapid changes in tone, as Joseph first perceives Mary's pregnancy and breaks forth into denunciation; then is enlightened by the angel in a dream, and becomes solicitous for his wife's welfare and reverently adores the infant; then begins grumbling again when he has to pack the family off to Egypt.

In other respects, the cycle plays resemble neither the Old nor the New Comedy. Since they tell the story of mankind from creation to doomsday, they cannot have unity of plot in any conventional sense. They do not have a single cast of personages for the whole of the cycle. Adam and Eve are succeeded by Cain and Abel and they by Noah and his family, and so on. It would be hard to imagine a plot structure that would accommodate all the episodes shown in even the most abbreviated cycles, such as the one at Coventry, which was limited to New Testament scenes alone. To my knowledge the only post-medieval play having a different cast for each of its episodes is Gerhard Hauptmann's *The Weavers*, which like the cycle plays is unclassifiable as comedy or tragedy.

If the cycle as a whole can be neither comedy nor tragedy, can a single episode? Generally not, because the action of the episodes is an element uncontrollable by the dramatist. The material of the cycles is history, which has often provided characters and actions to the tragic writer, seldom to the comic. When, partly in reaction to the theology of the medieval Scriptural drama and partly in deference to the new respect for the classics, sixteenth-century authors tried to write regular plays on Scriptural subjects, they chose the tragic form but had, for theological reasons, to give their plays a happy ending. The results were generally feeble, as in Beza's *Abraham Sacrifiant.* Only Milton's *Samson Agonistes* commands respect from the modern reader, and then principally as a closet drama. So far as I know no Renaissance, Reformation or Counter-Reformation playwright attempted a comic treatment of a Scriptural subject. Probably it would have appeared indecorous.

Fortunately, the authors of the cycle plays were little troubled with decorum in the restricted sense in which critical theorists use the word. That opened a channel into the comic, and the incorporation of non-Scriptural materials furnished an opportunity for a freer development that might approach formal comedy. Only one play in the entire corpus of cycle plays has something like a formal plot. This is the *Second Shepherds' Play* of the Towneley Cycle, a dramatization of the adoration of the shepherds. Scripture says nothing except that while the shepherds were watching their flocks, an angel appeared to them announcing the birth of the Messiah, they went to see the infant, and subsequently spread the news abroad. Several of the authors of the cycle plays expand the characterization of the shepherds; only the Wakefield Master (and then apparently only in his second attempt) introduces the element of plot in the episode in which the scoundrelly Mak, despite the precautions of the shepherds, succeeds in stealing one of their sheep and almost succeeds in concealing it. This is the nearest approach to a comic plot in the whole of medieval Scriptural drama. It is not, of course, the standard boy-meets-girl plot, but it does incorporate some of the standard devices: disguise (Mak trying to pass himself off as a stranger from the south, the sheep disguised as a baby), mistaken identity (the sheep as a babe in the cradle), discovery (when Third Shepherd lifts the coverlet and finds a sheep) and, most important, burlesque, for the whole scene of the visit of the shepherds to Mak's cottage is a parody of the later visit to the Christ child in the stable.

One other element needs a bit of explanation. Comedy has its villains or antagonists as well as tragedy. The difference is that the comic antagonist is punished, but never mortally. Slaves are beaten, Malvolio is gulled, Harpagon becomes ridiculous, but nobody is killed, or even imprisoned. Mak suffers just this kind of punishment. Legally he could be executed for sheep-stealing—but the shepherds content themselves with tossing him in a blanket.

If the *Second Shepherds' Play* is the nearest approach to formal plotted comedy, comic elements appear elsewhere in the cycles. Some of the stereotyped characters occur—the shrew in several of the Noah plays, the foolish old man with a young wife in the characterization of Joseph, the braggart in soldiers who guard the tomb of Jesus. In all such instances it is safer to suppose that they are independent inventions rather than imitations of the classics. Generally speaking, the comic comes in quite different forms and from quite different sources.

Comedy's requirements are more basic than agreement with the classic tradition. Comedy should be fantastic, festive, and above all funny. Comedy deals mainly with the impossible or the illogical. The sudden multiplication of Falstaff's assailants is a sample of the fantastic, as is Socrates in his basket between heaven and earth in *The Clouds*. These can be matched by the scene in the Towneley *First Shepherds' Play* in which two shepherds almost come to blows over the pasturing of some non-existent sheep.[3]

Greek comedy takes its name from the revels accompanying the festival of Dionysius. The drama of the Middle Ages arose from the celebration of the two great Christian festivals, Easter and Christmas. Just as the festival elements are still prominent in Shakespeare's 'romantic' comedies, two of which, *A Midsummer Night's Dream* and *Twelfth Night*, are named from holidays,[4] so are they in the cycle plays, most of which were given on the feasts of Whitsuntide or Corpus Christi. They incorporate elements derived from folk festivals, which in turn contain the remnants of pagan rituals, for example the wrestling contests in the Chester Nativity and Cornish Passion plays,[5] and the meal in both the Chester Nativity and the Towneley First Shepherds'.[6]

We should probably not be too far wrong in seeing many of the great farce situations in the cycles as primarily festive high spirits. Such are the fight between Noah and his wife in the dramatizations of the deluge;

---

[3] *cf.* Lope de Rueda's amusing *Los Olivos* (included in *Medieval Interludes*), where a similar brawl erupts over an as yet non-existent achievement.

[4] Barber, *Shakespeare's Festive Comedy*, esp. pp. 3-57.]

[5] Norris, CC: *Passio*, 2509. The wrestling was enacted in full view of the audience in the Piran Round revival of the Cycle, as the in-the-round staging situation would seem to demand. (See Neville Denny's discussion of multiple-action staging below, pp. 136ff.)

[6] For samples of these elements from folk festivals see Speirs, 'The Mystery Cycle: Some of the Towneley Cycle Plays', pp. 86-117, 246-65.

the debates of the shepherds over the words of the angels' song, whether
it was 'gle, glo, glas glum' or 'glorum, glarum with a glo / and much of
celsis', or what not (Chester VII, 387; Ludus XVI, 85; Coventry
Shearmen and Tailor's Pageant, 272-7—the incident, evidently made
familiar by dramatic representations and a favorite with audiences, is
depicted in the Holkham Bible Picture Book); and the knockabout
business that was evidently included as an accompaniment to those great
set-pieces, the Ark and Temple-building sequences.

II

The important last requirement, that comedy be funny, furnishes the
opportunities, but also the problems. Philosophers and critics display a
striking lack of unanimity in their definitions of what is funny, what
makes us laugh or even smile. The probable source of the difficulty is
that the laughable always involves some violation of the decorous, and
the decorous differs widely from one society to another. Comedy is
notoriously subject to the accidents of time and space. Undergraduates
rarely need any convincing to accept Oedipus the King as tragic. It
requires a great deal of labor to get them to see The Clouds as funny.
(The best example from my own experience was seeing a Japanese
kabuki tragedy, *Kanjincho*, followed by a comedy, the *Zen Substitute*.
Despite my complete ignorance of the conventions of Japanese drama,
even of the essential attitudes of Japanese society, *Kanjincho* produced
in me, as in most of the Western audience, much the same response as
Oedipus or Lear. The *Zen Substitute* elicited no response at all.)

The society of fifteenth-century England is perhaps closer to our own
than is that of eighteenth-century Japan; but the question of what is
comic is no less puzzling. How, for instance, are we to take the
numerous situations in which an evil personage goes into a rage that
seems to us comic? Herod is the stock example. After learning that the
three kings have gone home another way and so evaded the trap he has
set for them, the Coventry Herod breaks forth into this ridiculous speech:

> I stampe! I stare! I loke all abowtt!
> Myght I them take, I shuld them bren at a glede!   *fire*
> I rent! I rawe! and now run I wode!   *mad*
> A! thatt these velen trayturs hath mard this my mode!
> The schalbe hangid yf I ma cum them to!

and the stage-directions read, 'Here Erode ragis in the pagond an in the strete also' (*Shearmen and Tailors' Pageant*, 779-83). The whole corpus of English Scriptural drama must contain more than a score of such scenes, in which Cain, Pharaoh, the two Herods, Pilate, and even Satan himself go into such apparently comic rages. Were they comic to the spectators?

It is quite possible that what we see as funny was utterly serious, in fact terrifying to the audience. The nineteenth-century tear-jerker melodramas like *Thorns and Orange Blossoms* are invariably played nowadays as comedy, but we know that the audiences for whom they were written took them seriously, weeping at the heroine's tribulations and hissing the villain.

Beyond this ambiguity is still another: laughter is a possible response to something threatening. This can be the so-called nervous laughter. Under certain circumstances the downright terrifying can produce laughter. When either the supposedly terrifying is shown to be harmless (the noise is being made by the wind, not by a ghost) or when the terror is not actual but only make-believe, the recognition of that fact may produce laughter. Film-makers have capitalized on this close association of terror and laughter in horror pictures of the 'Abbott and Costello Meet Frankenstein' sort. The conditions for this comic resolution of terror are met over and over again in the cycle plays in the threatening speeches of the tyrant figures, Pharaoh, Caesar Augustus, both Herods, Pilate, the devils that burst onto the stage singly or in troops. It is hard for a sophisticated modern reader to see how the medieval actors could have played these scenes straight or the audience taken them seriously. But we cannot be sure.

Even less knowable is the attitude of the medieval audience towards two other effects that are enormously amusing to us. These are the constant anachronisms and the proneness of the style to become burlesque. Both flow from the essential purpose of the craft cycles, to reach the sensibility of the common man by representing the great events of Christian history as strictly contemporary happenings. The authors seemed to have bent every effort towards portraying the Crucifixion as an execution that might have happened in York the week before. Thus evil personages like Cain, Pharaoh, the two Herods, Pilate, even the Jewish high priests swear by Mahound. Annas and Caiaphas are 'bishops'. St. Joseph becomes the foolish old man wed to a young wife—the January-May motif of folk humor—in constant fear of being cuckolded.

It is a great temptation to the critic to explain these anachronisms in terms of the naivete of the audience, perhaps of the playwrights also, for instance the numerous vows and greetings of a Christian nature peppering the Old Testament sequences. In the Towneley *Second Shepherds' Play*, Second Shepherd salutes First Shepherd thus:

> He saue you and me / ouerthwart and endlong   *across along*
> that hang on a tre / I say you no wrang
> Cryst saue vs.   (48-50)

The fact that Christ is not yet born is of no significance. If you want your audience to accept the Judean shepherds who watched their flocks near Bethlehem as exactly like the Yorkshire ones who watch theirs near Wakefield, you cannot have them greet each other with the historically appropriate 'sholom aleichem' or its English translation, 'peace be unto you'. The operative principle, as in costuming and portraiture, is contemporaneity of reference. Invocations of Christ, Our Lady, or one of the saints establish the virtue and religion of the character, just as the oaths by Mahound establish the opposite—it is the only oath an audience will recognize as non-Christian, as heathen, and hence indicative of utter villainy.

But this is not the whole story. Later in the same play First Shepherd awakens and, after another anachronistic oath partly in mangled Latin, 'Iudas carnas dominus', proceeds to describe his experiences while sleeping:

> My foytt slepis, by ihesus / and I water fastand
> I thought that we layd us / full nere yngland.   (351-3)

This is an obvious double-take, much like the lines which Shaw gives Britannus in *Caesar and Cleopatra*. Assuring Rufio that the enormous lighthouse crane is operated by an old man and a boy, he admits he does not understand its mechanics: 'They have counterweights, and a machine with boiling water in it which I do not understand: it is not of British design.' Shaw was pulling someone's leg, and so was the Wakefield Master. This comic use of anachronism, though rare in the cycle plays, surfaces often enough to warn the critic to be wary. Its most common form is the inclusion of a local place-name in an evocative catalogue of far-away places like Syria and India. Thus Nuntius in the Towneley Herod the Great enumerates Herod's dominions:

> Tuskane and turky
> All Inde and Italy
> Cecyll and surry

which are sufficiently confused and anachronistic, but then he caps the list with

> ffrom Egypt to mantua vnto kemp towne.[7] (xvi, 42-50)

This, of course, is the work of the Wakefield Master, but the use of local place-names to draw a laugh is common in the cycles. One of the Chester shepherds has led his sheep from 'comlie conway unto clyde', and the magnates in the plays of the Cornish Cycle customarily reward their followers with gifts of local estates, as when King David bestows on his Herald 'charter rights to Carnsew and Trehembis' for organizing the work on the temple (*Origo Mundi*, 2311-12).The total effect of such passages, whether or not indicated by the author, is one of disparity, a chief producer of the comic. In fact, disparity lies at the root of all burlesque, and there is much of that in the cycle plays. We have already noted that the visit to Mak's cottage is an anticipatory parody of the visit to the manger. All the treatments of the adoration of the shepherds except that of the Hegge ('N-town') Cycle anticipate the gifts of the magi with the gifts of the shepherds—a bob of cherries, a pair of old hose, a pipe, a spoon that holds forty or a hundred peas. Authors seem to vie with one another to see who can invent the most outrageous gifts.

Nearly all the burlesque in the cycles is of the same sort, sometimes called diminishing burlesque or travesty. As against mock heroic, represented by Pope's *Rape of the Lock*, in which trivial matter is augmented by being expressed in high style, travesty creates a disparity by expressing high matter in low style. The vehicle of the cycles is rhymed stanzaic verse, too often of the jog-trot variety parodied by Chaucer in *Sir Thopas*. Imagery, too, is often derived from every-day life, as when the Chester St. Joseph, worshipping the newborn Christ, uses the imagery of brewing:

> for thou art come mans blisse to brewe
> to all that thy law will shewe.   (vi, 525-6)

Even the Hegge plays, which have the least comic content of any of the

[7] Clarence Steinberg, '*Kemp Town* in the Towneley *Herod* Play', *Neuphilologische Mitteilungen* LXXI (1970), pp. 253-60, considers it likely that this was a local place-name.

cycles, occasionally show this disparity between matter and expression.
Speaking to the soldiers returning from their unsuccessful watch over the
tomb of the dead Christ, Pilate says more in sorrow than in anger:

> Now all zour wurchep is lorn
> And euery man may zow wel scorn
> And bidde zow go sytten in (pe)corn
> And chare a-way (pe) ravyn.   *scare*   (xxxiv, 1548-51)

The image diminishes one of the great failures of all time to the
dimensions of a scarecrow.

A common quality emerges from all these comic rages, anachronisms,
parodies and travesties: an essential ambiguity which adds the dimension
of irony characteristic to all great comedy. The ambiguity of the cycles is
multiple. We cannot be sure that what we perceive as funny was so
perceived in the fifteenth century. We can partly solve this puzzle by
abandoning all historical perspective and agreeing that whatever we find
funny is in fact funny. But even then much of the ambiguity remains.
Are the comic gifts of the shepherds really comic? When we have
finished laughing it may finally strike us that the significance goes
deeper. These are poor men. They have no gold, frankincense or myrrh
to give, but what they have they give joyously, even if it is only a pair of
old hose. If we choose we can pursue this line of feeling into
sentimentality. Or we can pursue Pilate's figure into dizzying heights of
theological speculation: compared to the power of God, the uttermost
efforts of evil men have only the terror of a scarecrow put in a field to
frighten birds. Perhaps St. Joseph is not comparing the divine gift of
salvation to a mash of malted barley; perhaps his brew is medicinal (the
more likely interpretation perhaps) and Christ the healer. On the other
hand 'brewe' may be of much humbler derivation, from domestic
cooking, used simply to suggest 'preparation' or 'accomplishment'. Or
the choice of image may merely reflect the playwright's lack of
expertise; 'brewe' is the only word he can think of that rhymes with
'Ihesu', 'knewe', 'trewe', 'new', and 'shewe'.

                                        III

We have noted that the cycle plays slightly resemble the New Comedy
in the treatment of certain comic stereotypes, but differ in their lack of
plot. They also resemble the Old Comedy in their satire, but differ in

their lack of specificity. The cycle plays contain a good bit of topical satire, little of it directed at specific individuals. The best known sample is the complaints of the shepherds in the Towneley *Second Shepherds' Play*. One grumbles about the gentry who oppress the peasantry by taxation and confiscation; another is bitter about women, particularly his wife; and the third vents his spleen on the weather. This rather broad spectrum of targets is thoroughly representative of the satire of the cycles.

In the Towneley *Judgement* the devil Titivillus, created by the same hand as the shepherds, recites a long and miscellaneous roll of sinners: false swearers, extortioners, simonists, women who wear horned headdresses. Cheats and corrupters are a common target. The Chester Harrowing of Hell contains a confession of a 'tavernere, a gentill gossippe and a tapster', who adulterated the beer, watered the wine, and gave short measure (XVII, 261-308).[8]

Perhaps the most pointed of such satires is the character Den (probably 'dean') in the Hegge *Trial of Joseph and Mary*. The episode opens with a monologue in which he warns all evil-doers.

Two 'detractors' have reported Mary to the 'bishop' Abijachar for adultery. Den is sent to summon them. Like Chaucer's Summoner he uses his office for extortion:

> But zit sum mede and ze me take
> I wyl withdrawe my gret toth
> gold or sylvyr I wol not forsake.

and the author is then careful to universalize the characterization: 'evyn as all sumnorys doth' (XIV, prologue by Den and 113-36).

The root cause of the satire in the cycles is the point of view. This is particularly apparent in the treatment of kings and ecclesiastical dignitaries. With the exception of the Three Kings, who are, after all, away from home and without authority, all kings and 'bishops' are villains. Somewhere in every cycle we have a situation in which some humble person has to confront established authority, and always he hates or fears it, often with good reason. In the common York and Towneley *Doctors*, when Joseph and Mary discover Jesus in the temple teaching the doctors of the law, Joseph hesitates to enter. 'With men of myght can I not mell,' he says, 'they are so gay in furry fyne.' And Mary has to lead

---

[8] This piece, not found in all manuscripts, looks as though it originally belonged to the Judgment play.

the way and reprove the young Jesus (York xx, 229-32; Towneley xviii, 217-20).

Perhaps Joseph's reluctance is more awe than fear, but in the healing of the man born blind, Chester definitely makes fear the motivation. The parents of Chelidonius, as the blind man is called, find themselves summoned to testify before the Pharisees. In fact, they are in a crossfire, for the two Pharisees disagree among themselves about the validity of the miracle, and both are anxious to convict Jesus of fraud or blasphemy. The mother says bitterly, 'a vengeaunce on them . . . / the neuer did poore man good.' The father, however, points out that they must go, 'or ells they would without delay / cursse us and take our good' (XIII, 162-9).

A similar theme, but with a different emphasis, appears in the N-town (Hegge) dramatization of the woman taken in adultery (Play XXIV). Again the attempt of the Pharisees to score a point against Jesus furnishes the motivation, but the Pharisees appear not only vindictive but also cowardly. The play opens with Jesus preaching repentance and forgiveness of sins. Accusator suddenly appears to tell the Pharisees that he knows where they can catch a pair of adulterers, which one of the Pharisees sees as an opportunity for tripping up Jesus. The three break in on the sinners. The young man flees, dressed in a doublet with the points untied and carrying his breeches in his hand, as the very explicit directions tell us. When the three try to stop him, he pulls a knife and threatens that if anyone tries to stop him, 'I xal pis daggare put in his crop'. The reaction of one of the Pharisees reminds us of Dogberry's instructions to the watch: 'With such a shrew wyll I not melle.' The poor woman is, of course, left to bear the entire burden of guilt. When the Pharisees call on Jesus for judgement he underlines their cowardice by writing their sins in the earth, whereupon they sneak off.

The exploitation of this worm's-eye view of established authority produces as its ultimate extension something like the 'dark comedy' or 'sick humor' of contemporary literature.[9] This tragic-comic mood breaks through when the Towneley Cain, the smoke from his rejected sacrifice still blinding him, invites his virtuous brother 'com kys the dwill right in the ars', a prelude to murder, and then, when God summons him, blasphemously calls God 'that hob-ouer-the-wall' (II, 287-97). The attitude is even more evident in the responses of the soldiers Herod sends out to kill the Innocents. In one cycle they enjoy the task, in another they

---

[9] See Styan, *The Dark Comedy*, for a thorough analysis of this phenomenon. Most of what follows is theoretically based on Styan's discussion.

feel it beneath them to kill babies and fight women, in still another they fear that Herod's actions will precipitate a revolt, which of course they will have to suppress. It seems likely that the attack of the women was sometimes played for laughs, and one play, the Digby *Killing of the Children*, creates a comic braggart-coward Watkin, who fears the mothers.

This sort of grim humor reaches its apogee in the Passion sequences, particularly in the York and Towneley cycles. The behavior of the soldiers detailed to nail Christ on the cross might have been written as an illustration of Bergson's theory that comedy results when human beings act as though they were mechanical automatons.[10] To the York soldiers the Crucifixion is simply a job. As good craftsmen they would like to do it well, but everything goes wrong. The hole into which they should drive the nail for the feet is bored in the wrong place — 'it failis a foote and more' — so that they have to pull on the body with ropes to stretch it into a fit. The hole in the ground into which the cross must slot has been dug too wide, and they have to drive in wedges to keep the cross from wobbling (XXXV, 107-248). The Towneley Torturers are a little less professional, and a little more personal. They take the old motif of Jesus the Jouster, familiar to us from *Piers Plowman* (B, XVIII, 10-28) and up end it. As Jesus is king he must join in a tournament. They have just the horse for him, the cross, and he will not fall off. They would be 'full lothe on any wyse that ye fell downe' and so on and on, squeezing every drop of oafish raillery from the occasion (XXIII, esp. 89-118).

The triumph of dark comedy is the Towneley *Talents*. Much about this play is puzzling. It duplicates material already presented in the preceding play. It seems to have been borrowed from some area further to the south than Wakefield.[11] The title 'Processus Talentorum' is manifestly a scribal error; it should be *talorum*, 'bones', for it deals with the dicing for the clothes of the crucified Christ. This Scriptural incident (*Matthew* 27, 35) is briefly treated in all the cycles, but only Towneley devotes a whole play to it.

Positioned between the Crucifixion and the Harrowing of Hell, the *Talents* also falls between comedy and tragedy. It begins with the usual boasting and threatening speech by Pilate. Then the three Torturers enter one after the other, each in a hurry. They have brought with them Jesus's

---

[10] *Laughter*, tr. Cloudesley Brereton and Frd Rothwell (New York, 1937), esp. pp. 86-8.
[11] Martin Stevens, 'The Composition of the Towneley Talents Play: A Linguistic Examination', *Journal of English and German Philology* LVIII (1959), pp. 423-33.

clothes, which each is anxious to possess, or at least get a fair share of. The question is how to keep Pilate from taking all for himself. Pilate is somewhat grumpy on being awakened. The Torturers are right in fearing that Pilate will want everything for himself. When they grumble, Pilate suggests dividing up the garments. They cannot find a seam on which to divide the gown and Pilate will not have the garment cut up. Finally, Third torturer remembers he has three dice, and all agree that high throw will win all. Pilate is, of course, first and when two of the Torturers fail to beat his thirteen, it looks as if he will get the clothes after all. However, Third Torturer throws fifteen, which ought to win. But Pilate is determined to have the clothes and suggests, as only one in absolute authority can 'suggest', that the winner give them to him as a favor. Reluctantly Third Torturer gives up the garments—after all Pilate is his commanding general. The play closes with the three Torturers moralizing, somewhat in the vein of Chaucer's Pardoner, on the evils of gambling.[12]

On the more serious level, the play is an apt summation of the forces of greed and selfishness that have killed Christ. This is their highest moment, for the next play begins the ascent into light and love with the Harrowing of Hell, to be followed by the triumph of truth in the Resurrection, after which even Pilate and the high priests have to admit that their 'law is lorn'. It is a remarkable achievement that Pilate in his moment of triumph is not heroic evil but meanness, a Roman procurator who cheats a common soldier out of his winnings in a game of chance. The subtlety of this play has escaped many critics. For instance, anyone who finds the moralizations or the Torturers naive is reading his own naivete into the play. What has actually happened is that the modulation from the tragic mood of the Crucifixion to the comic one of the Resurrection has resulted in a thorough mixture of the two kinds, grim humor, jesting seriousness.

Though the cycle plays because of their very nature never achieved formal comedy, the comic still bulks large in their total effect. With a few exceptions—the Mak episode of the Towneley *Second Shepherds' Play* is the most notable—the comic is always intrinsic to the dramatic structure of the piece. We find no examples of the sort of thing represented by the episode of the quack-doctor in the Croxton *Play of the Sacrament* (525-652), an episode not at all necessarily connected with

---

12 The robe is magic, and hence of immense value. In the Cornish Death of Pilate sequence it preserves Pilate from the punishment he deserves as long as he wears it.

the purpose of the piece, but apparently written only to provide an opportunity for a pair of comics. In the cycle plays the comic always flows directly from the method of the cycles, which is the attempt to make Scriptural story human and contemporary. We see everything through the eyes of the common citizen, and the disparity between that point of view and the one we are accustomed to in 'religious' literature produces a comic irony that is never absent for long in any of the cycles. It is probably this effect more than any other that has produced the great popularity of the cycles in their modern revivals. In fact, they are consonant with the modern temper in their frequent transition to dark comedy. Certainly the constant undertone of comic irony preserves them from the sanctimoniousness which mars most post-medieval dramatic treatments of Scriptural themes.

Pictorial evidence concerning the English mystery cycles is scant. We must turn to the Continent to get a graphic view of polyscenic production during the middle ages. Here is Jean Fouquet's miniature of *The Martyrdom of St. Appolonia* (ca. 1455). Notice the six mansions arranged in a semi-circle; the "director," wand in hand, prompting the actors; the extreme realism in the depiction of the torture of the Saint. In the productions of this period, violent actions were dramatized very directly and without reticence.

A drawing by Hubert Cailleau of a passion play in the garden of
a ducal residence in Valenciennes (1547). The performance in
question took place over 25 days. The drawing does not represent
the arrangement of the mansions at any given moment. Instead,
we see a selection of some of the many pieces employed
throughout the extended run. Notice the mixture of the three-
dimensional and painted elements. Hell, in these plays, was often
represented as a monster's mouth. One such mouth is at the right
of the picture, balanced by a circular (spherical?) heaven-disk at
the left.

213

III

Medieval Stage Production

In recent years a great many of the standard theories about medieval production have been subject to reexamination. No longer is it believed, for example, that liturgical plays were forced out of the cathedrals and monasteries because they had become "secularized"—because the clegy were unable to approve the realism of some of the comic scenes.[1] It is now recognized that the Church retained control of the plays long after the responsibility for production had been assumed by the craft guilds. The guilds, moreover, were not, as some commentators have pictured them, primitive equivalents of a trade union or manufacturer's association. They were quasi-religious organizations dedicated both to the glory of their craft and to the glory of God. In England, the mystery plays survived until the late sixteenth century when they perished not because they had offended the Catholic hierarchy, but because they were actively opposed by the reformed church.

Major credit for this new perspective on medieval drama belongs to two scholars: F.M. Salter of Canada, whose slim volume of lectures, *Medieval Drama in Chester* (1955) successfully attacks a number of weighty but troublesome assumptions about the early religious plays; and Glynne Wickham of Bristol, whose *Early English Stages 1300-1600,* continues the Salter attack, with some notable and telling additions.

Both scholars devote considerable space to details of staging, and both are unhappy with the conventional picture of an English pageant wagon: a two-story top-heavy carriage with an acting area above and a dressing room below, minimal scenery and quaint primitive equipment.

Salter takes issue with this notion in one of his lectures, "A Day's Labour." His attack on the early theories is irrefutable, but some scholars think that his substitute conjectures may also be open to question.[2] For now, however, we will let him have the last word.

---

[1] The notion of "secularization" was first proposed by E.K. Chambers in his monumental but flawed account of the plays, *The Medieval Stage*, 1903.

[2] See Alois Nagler, *The Medieval Religious Stage* (New Haven & London: Yale, 1976), pp. 55-58, 67-68.

F. M. Salter

A Day's Labour*

The earliest attempt to describe the production and staging of the Chester Mysteries is to be found in the *Breviarye* of Chester history, ascribed to Archdeacon Robert Rogers, but actually compiled by his son, David Rogers, in the seventeenth century, at least one generation after the last performance of the Plays — and probably two. The earliest copies of this *Breviarye* are Harley MSS. 1944 and 1948. These vary slightly in form and wording, but they are the onlie begetters of a great many, if not all, of the later accounts of the Chester Plays. Associated with the great name of Robert Rogers, the *Breviarye* has been granted the authority of an eye-witness account, although there is hardly an accurate statement about the Plays in it, and although the author was by no means in sympathy with his subject.

Archdeacon Rogers died in 1595 or earlier.[1] Morris therefore dates the *Breviarye* 1590.[2] But Harley 1944 contains the Banns of the Plays as they were revised for a projected revival in 1600. These are signed D. R., apparently the initials of David Rogers. Harley 1948 says on fol. 18r that the materials "were collected by the Reverend mr Robert Rogers . . . and written by his sonne David"; but it has an account of the St. George's Day Race on the Roodee, starting, "In anno Dom. 1609, Mr. William Lester, etc.," and ending, "This was the first beginninge of St. George's race, etc." It seems unlikely that Archdeacon Rogers, who was certainly dead by 1595, collected this item after 1609. Further, this statement surely cannot have been written in the very year when the St. George's Race was first organized. Indeed, there is a later reference to a change made in the Race in 1623. Nevertheless, Chambers dates both Harley MS. 1944 and Harley 1948, 1609.[3] Doing so, he sails very near the wind.

---

* From F. M. Salter, *Medieval Drama in Chester* (Toronto: University of Toronto Press, 1955), pp. 54–80; reprinted by permission of the publisher. The footnotes are Salter's.

[1] George Ormerod, *The History of the County Palatine and City of Chester*, 2nd ed., by T. Helsby, London, 1882, III, 443, says, "Archdeacon Rogers, as appears from the list of rectors of Gawsworth, died 1595." The Ven. R. V. H. Burne, "Chester Cathedral in the Reigns of Mary and Elizabeth" (*Journal of the Chester and N. Wales A., A. & H. Society*, XXXVIII (1951), pp. 49–94), says (p. 75), with reference to *Sheaf*, 3rd ser. XXIX, 1, which I have not been able to check, that Rogers died in 1587. A copy of his will, dated June 17, 1580, may be seen in Harley MS. 2037, fol. 207r.

[2] *Chester in the Plantagenet and Tudor Reigns*, Chester: G. R. Griffith, (?) 1893, p. 315.

[3] *The Mediaeval Stage* (Oxford University Press, 1903), II, 348.

Even if the *Breviarye* had been written in 1609, that date is thirty-four years later than the last performance of the Chester Mysteries; and a boy who was sixteen in 1575 would be fifty in 1609, sixty-four in 1623. It could fairly be questioned whether David Rogers ever saw the Plays at all.

Nevertheless, for what it is worth, here is the account of the Chester Plays from Harley MS. 1944, fol. 21ᵛ:

Now of the playes of Chester called the whitson playes when they weare played & what occupationes bringe forthe at theire charges the playes & pagiantes.

Heare note that these playes of Chester called the whitson playes weare the woorke of one Rondall a moncke of the abbaye of St. Warburge in Chester, who redused the whole history of the byble into Englishe storyes in metter, in the englishe tounge, and then the firste mayor of Chester, namely Sir Iohn Arneway knighte he caused the same to be played, the manner of which playes was thus: They weare deuided into 24 pagiantes or partes, and euery Company brought forthe their pagiente which was the cariage or place which they played in: And yarlye before these were played there was a man fitted for the purpose [fol. 22ʳ] which did ride as I take it upon St. Georges daye throughe the Citie and there published the tyme and the matter of the playes in breefe which was called the readinge of the banes. They weare played upon monday, tuseday and wenseday in witson weeke. And they first beganne at the Abbaye gates & when the firste pagiente was played at the Abbaye gates then it was wheeled from thence to the pentice at the high crosse before the Mayor, and before that was donne the seconde came, and the firste wente into the watergate streete & from thence unto the Bridgestreete, and soe all one after an other tell all the pagientes weare played appoynted for the firste daye, and so likewise for the seconde & the thirde day: these pagiantes or cariage was a highe place made like ahowse with ij rowmes beinge open on the tope the lower rowme they apparrelled & dressed them selues, and in the higher rowme they played, and they stoode upon 6 wheeles And when they had done with one cariage in one place they wheeled the same from one streete to an other. first from the Abbaye gate to the pentise then to the watergate streete, then to the bridge streete throughe the lanes & so to the estgate streete. And thus they came from one streete to an other keapeinge a direct order in euery streete, for before the first cariage was gone the seconde came, and so the thirde, and so orderly till the laste was donne all in order without any stayeinge in any place for worde beinge broughte how euery place was neere done they came and made no place to tarye tell the last was played.

These playes are now abolished

the description of the pagintes they played in:

At this point in Harley MS. 1944, the Banns follow. These do not appear in Harley MS. 1948. In the latter manuscript also the carriages have four wheels rather than six. The attitude of David Rogers may be seen in the following statement which appears next after the Banns in Harley MS. 1944:

> And thus much of the Banes or Breife of the whitson playes in Chester for if I shoulde heare resite the whole storye of the whitson playes it woulde be too tediouse for to resite in this breauarye as alsoe they beinge nothinge proffitable to any use, excepte it be to shewe the Ignorance of oure forefatheres, and to make us theire ofspringe unexcusable before God that haue the true and synceare worde of the gospell, of our lord & sauioure Iesus Christe, if we apprehende not the same in oure life & practise to the eternall glorie of our god and the salutation & comforte of oure owne soles:
> Heare followeth all the Companyes as they weare played upon theire seuerall dayes, which was Monday: Tuesday: & wenseday in the whitson weeke And how manye pagiantes weare played upon euery day at the Charge of euery Companye.[4]

At this point Rogers lists twenty-five plays, although he has just told us there were twenty-four. It is difficult to believe that so hostile a witness ever actually saw the Plays. One thing he certainly did not see was the riding of the Banns, for the Banns were not *read* by one person as he says, but *ridden:* every company sent out its representatives for the occasion in the costumes in which they played on the great day itself. No doubt it is from this *Breviarye* that Randle Holme gets the idea that the City Crier rode the Banns, for in the accounts of the Smiths in Harley MS. 2054 . . . , he had tacked on "the citty Crier ridd" to the item, "for ridinge the banes xiij^d." If every one of the twenty-four or twenty-five gilds in Chester paid the Crier 13^d for riding the Banns, that gentleman, as I shall presently explain, must have had one of the best grafts in history. David Rogers, also, has given us in his account other statements which I have shown in previous lectures to be untrue. We would do better to base our ideas of the production of the Chester Plays upon other evidence.[5]

Let us start with the Pageant Houses. These were simply large sheds in which the wagons or carriages which served as stages for the mystery plays were stored. Unfortunately, our ancestors did not know that we might be curious about such things, and the records which they kept for their own purposes are not very illuminating.

---

[4] These materials from Harley MSS. 1944, 1948 are quoted in Morris, *Chester*, pp. 303–10; in F. J. Furnivall, *The Digby Plays* (Early English Text Society, Extra Series, LXX), p. xviii ff.; and in Chambers, *Med. St.*, II, 354–5.

[5] C. F. Tucker Brooke, however, in *The Tudor Drama* (New York: Houghton Mifflin, 1911), p. 12, accepts Rogers literally. So does Allardyce Nicoll, who in *British Drama* (London: Harrap, 1925), p. 25, speaks of Rogers as contemporary with the Plays. And, not to cite further examples, A. P. Rossiter, the latest in the tradition that stems from Chambers, is equally explicit (see *English Drama from Early Times to the Elizabethans*, Hutchinson's University Library, 1950, p. 63).

The earliest records about the pageant houses are to be found in Harley MS. 2158 in which Randle Holme copied as well as he could a number of the Murengers and Treasurers of Chester. He seems to have been most careful in copying, but the rolls had suffered seriously before he got hold of them. He explains the fragmentary nature of his copy by frequent remarks such as, "Roll 9. A bundle of Rentalls both broke & obscure but by the hand & names should be in Ed. 4 tyme & part of H7"; "Roll 11. This Roule much decayd but abstracted what may be legable"; "Roll 34. a broken peece of a Treasurers Roll temp. Jo Southworth maior 18 E 4." The rolls from which he copied ran from 1435–6 to 1482–3. I have already drawn upon them for information regarding the possessors of plays; and need only repeat here that the Drapers, the Fishmongers, the Mercers, the Saddlers, the Shearmen, and the Tailors rented from the City places where they maintained pageant houses.[6] The rental paid by the Fishmongers was 4ᵈ a year. The Mercers paid 6ᵈ.

The next record in time is an agreement made in 1531 between the Stewards of the Vintners and those of the Dyers on one hand and the Stewards of the Goldsmiths and Masons on the other that the Goldsmiths and Masons may have free use of the carriage of the Vintners and the Dyers providing they pay a yearly rental and sustain "the thrid parte of all & euery reparacon" and "the thrid part of all the rents due or to be due for the house wher [the] said Carriage now standeth or hereafter shall stand."[7] Unfortunately, this record is fragmentary, and time has carried away the very thing we should like most to learn: i.e., the amount of money involved. But the language, "the thrid parte," etc. suggests that the carriage was already shared in 1531 between the Vintners and the Dyers who had separate plays; and that it was now to be shared by a third gild, the Goldsmiths and Masons. By means of this document, we can nail down one inaccuracy in David Rogers' account of the plays. He says, "euery Company brought forthe their pagiente which was the cariage or place which they played in." Actually, there were fewer carriages than plays; and the Vintners, the Dyers, and the Goldsmiths shared a single stage. How could they do so?

As the cycle comes to us, the Vintners had the play of the Magi, no. VIII, performed toward the close of the first day. The Goldsmiths had Play X of the Slaughter of the Innocents, the first performance of the second day. And the Dyers had Antichrist, no. XXIII, played toward the end of the third day. One carriage could readily be adapted to all their needs.

---

6 See *ante*, Lecture II, p. 46. [In Salter's book. — Eds.]

7 "Book Containing Fragments of Assembly Orders," Chester Town Hall; Morris, *Chester*, p. 317 n.

The next document is a record of City rents in the time of Henry Gee, Mayor, 1539–40. It is to be found in handwriting of that date within Harley MS. 2150; and it lists rents received by the City from the Shearmen, the Smiths, the Tailors, the Saddlers, the Drapers, and the Mercers. The Shearmen, Smiths, Tailors, and Saddlers each pay 4ᵈ; the Mercers 6ᵈ; and the Drapers 8ᵈ. Some of these gilds occupy the same places as they had occupied a century earlier. Here is the record itself:

The Northgate strete
The occupacion of Shermen for A place to sett theire carriage iiijᵈ.
The occupacion of the Smythes for A place to sett theire cariage adionyng to the Shermen under the walles negh unto a Towre called the Dilles towre   iiijᵈ.

. . . .
. . . .
. . . .
Lovelane

. . . .
. . . .
. . . .
The occupacion of the tailleours for A cariage house by yere iiijᵈ.

. . . .
. . . .
. . . .
The occupacion of the Sadlers for a place called truantes hole by yere   iiijᵈ.

. . . .
. . . .
. . . .
Gray ffrere Lane
The occupacion of the drapers for A certeyn place to byld on whiche thei putt theire carriage in nigh to the yate of the ffreres mynors be yere   viijᵈ.
The occupacion of the mercers for a certeyn place to byld A house on in the whiche thei putt theire cariage   vjᵈ.

We may be puzzled by the statement that the Drapers and the Mercers are to build; both have been paying the same rentals for a hundred years. Perhaps it was necessary to rebuild.[8]

Whatever the number of the Plays — and I have tried to show that

---

[8] Morris, *Chester*, p. 306 n., referring to Harley MS. 2150, says: "Thus the Drapers paid viiijᵈ rent for their 'caredge house nere to yᵉ Greve frere lane ende'; the Tailors ijˢ vjᵈ for theirs in Fleshmonger lane near Wolf's gate; the Shermen, in Northgate Street, iiijᵈ; the Smyths for a place to sett their carriage adjoining to the Shermen under the Walles nigh unto a towre called the 'Dilles Towre,' paid the Weavers the comparatively large sum of iiijˢ yearly." Four shillings would indeed have been a "comparatively large sum" if it had ever been paid; but it was not. The Smiths paid the City, not the Weavers, 4ᵈ. The Tailors paid the same amount, not 2/6.

there were twenty-six in 1540[9] — we know that during the fifteenth century the Drapers, Mercers, Saddlers, Shearmen, and Tailors had pageant wagons, as they still had in 1540. We know that the Fishmongers also had had a wagon in 1435, but it is not recorded in 1540; and we know that in 1540 the Smiths had a wagon. We know, further, that nine years earlier, in 1531, the Vintners, Dyers, and Goldsmiths agreed to share a carriage; and the rental paid by those gilds which paid ground rent to the City was between 4[d] and 8[d] a year.

The next carriage of which record exists is that of the Coopers. In 1572, the Coopers "reseuyd of the paynters and of the skynners for the caryge x[s]viij[d]." In 1574, they "receaved of the stuardes of the paynters for our cariadge, v[s] iiij[d]" and "of the stuardes of the hatmakers & skynners v[s] iiij[d]."[10] This also was a convenient arrangement, for the Painters had the Play of the Shepherds on the first day; the Coopers had the Trial and Flagellation of Christ, performed on the second day; and the Skinners had the Resurrection on the third day. It would seem unlikely that there ever were as many carriages as plays; half as many would be a fair guess.

Five shillings and fourpence is an enormous rental to pay for a carriage. We have seen that the pageant houses which sheltered the wagons rented at from fourpence to eightpence a year. If we think of a modern garage as renting for $90 a year — as it does in Edmonton — and equate that sum with sixpence, then 5/4 would be worth on the same scale eleven times as much, or roughly $1000. For a thousand dollars we could build a quite elaborate "float" for a modern parade. These carriages were not built for that sum; they rented for it for one day's use.

Obviously, so large a figure for one day's rental cannot be correct. Another record will enlighten us. In 1574, Richard Dutton, Mayor, leased the Tailors' carriage house to Robert Hill.[11] The Tailors had paid a rental of 4[d], but Hill was to pay 2/6. The rentals paid by the

[9] "The Banns of the Chester Plays" (*Review of English Studies*, XV (1939), 432–57; 1–17; 137–48), at XVI, 16.

[10] See *post*, pp. 72, 74. [In Salter's Book. — Eds.]

[11] Harley MS. 2009, fol. 41v: "Sciant etc. R. Dutton Armiger maior etc. concessimus ad feodi firmam Roberti Hill totam illam edificium siue domum vocatam the Taylers Carriage howse jacentem in parte Austriale cuiusdam venelle vocatae flesshmongers lane adiacentem terram vocatam wolffes gate aut newgate modo in tenuro Aldermannorum et seneschallorum Artis sutarium vestiarium infra dictam cuitatem continentem in longitudine 5 virgatas regias et in latitudine 3 virgatas et dimidium habendum in perpetuum Reddendi inde annuatim vt supra ij[s] vj[d] ad festum St. Michielis et Annuncionis beate Marie etc. Atturnasse etc. Tho Thropp serviens ad Claudes etc. Dat. Cestr. 10 Aug. 16 Q. E." See also Harley MS. 1996, fol. 263; and Morris, *Chester*, p. 306. Perhaps this document gives rise to the Morris's error (see note 8 above) regarding the rental paid by the Tailors.

craft gilds, therefore, must have been nominal; and if the ratio of 4 to 30 represents the ratio between the nominal and the actual value, we could simply divide the end-figure of the calculations above ($1000) by seven. In that event, we should find a day's rental of the Coopers' carriage worth about $135. Even this figure is startling.

The value of money, it need hardly be said, is difficult to work out. We all know that at the time when the King James Bible was translated, a penny was a fair wage for a day's work. That is what the workers in the Vineyard received. In Harley MS. 2093, fol. 33, rates of pay are listed for all the trades in Chester for an earlier year, 1592–3, when, because of near-famine, all prices had gone up. The highest pay for a day's work, "with meat and drink" is 4^d for master carpenters. Millwrights receive 3^d; smiths, wheelwrights, and plowwrights, 2^d; rough masons and bricklayers, 2½^d; plasterers, sawyers, lime-makers, brick-men, tilers, tile-makers, 2^d; the remainder, 1^d.[12] If we equate the penny with the eight or nine dollars a day that rough labour now receives in Edmonton, then a carriage renting at 5/4 brought in something over $500 for one day's use. It must have been a most elaborate and expensive vehicle. Let us say that this attempt at equating values is completely wild; but even if we divided $500 by five, we must still be dealing with a carriage that is a great deal better than makeshift. Indeed, the very fact that it was stored from year to year suggests a vehicle worth storing.

Robert Hill's lease might have been more useful to us than it actually is. The Tailors' carriage house is described in it as being 5 royal virgates long, and 3 virgates wide. The trouble is that we don't know the length of a virgate! According to the *Oxford Dictionary*, it was equal in the eighteenth century to a rod or pole, i.e., 16½ feet; but a carriage house more than 80 feet long and 55 feet wide is surely unlikely. Before the standardization of weights and measures, these varied greatly all over England. The virgate may have been only a yard. Randle Holme so translates it in the seventeenth century.[13]

---

12 J. E. T. Rogers in *Six Centuries of Work and Wages* (14th ed., London: T. Fisher Unwin, 1919) says (p. 327) that in "the fifteenth century and the first quarter of the sixteenth," "the wages of the artizan . . . were generally, and through the year, about 6^d a day. Those of the agricultural labourer were about 4^d." Rogers estimates that a payment of 4^d plus meat and drink would be worth about 6^d.

13 Harley MS. 2172, fol. 17^r: "16 Q. E. Rich dutton maior, etc. grant in fee farme to Robt hill Tayler the whole buildinge or howse called the Taylers Carriage howse lyinge on the south pt to a lane called ffleshmonger lane nere to the land called wolfes gate or New gate now in tenure of the Aldermen & stewards cetus sutar' vestiarium infra dictum Ciuitatem contayninge in length v yards in bredth 3 yards & halph paying ij^s vj^d at feasts St. Mich. & lady day prouffe as before dated Aug. 16 Q. Eliz. Tho Thropp sergant ad lawes attorney to deliuer possession. Red lib. 8 in latyn." The last statement is of course added by Holme.

But if his yard was the same as our yard, a building 15 feet long by 10½ feet wide would seem too small to accommodate a carriage which could rent at certainly more than $100 for one day's use.

Our difficulties in interpreting records regarding the carriage houses are not solved by records of the carriages themselves. We have accounts of the expenses of the Coopers' gild for the production of their play in 1572 and 1574.[14] This gild did not rent a carriage house, but took their wagon apart each year and stored it in John Joanson's cellar. In putting it together, getting it and their gear painted, using it, with 2/4 paid to the "putters" on the day of the plays, and breaking it down again for storage, they spent in 1572, 27/10. That is, they spent 334[d], more than the equivalent of a man's wage at rough labour for a full year. In modern terms, the day's use of their own carriage came to more than $2500.

In case our ideas of the size and equipment of the mediaeval stage should become too inflated, however, it should be pointed out that seven men could place the stage and haul it around the town. Only, those seven men received 2/4 for their day's work — that is to say, 4[d] each, which, as we have seen, was the highest wage any craftsman could receive for a day's labour during the inflation of 1593. The money paid to the "putters" suggests that they had horses, but there is no actual mention of horses in the Chester records.[15]

The accounts of the Smiths exist for the years 1554–78.[16] This company made a special assessment of its members in the years when they produced their play; and the normal individual contribution of the thirty-one gild members was 2/4. Perhaps I should point out again that gild members were *not* the "simple craftsmen" continually spoken of by modern scholars as the producers of mystery plays. They were *employers*. Can you believe that an ordinary craftsman would be able to give a full month's wages for the production of plays? The records show that while the gildsmen of the Smiths paid 2/4 each, the whole body of journeymen altogether gave 5[s], perhaps a penny or halfpenny each.

In 1561 the Smiths built a new carriage, and in 1562 they paid the Weavers 4[s] presumably as rental for a place in which it had been stored. This item continues to appear in their annual accounts. The total cost of building and preparing and using the carriage in 1561

---

14 See *post*, pp. 72–6. [In Salter's Book. — Eds.]

15 Horses were used at Coventry. Hardin Craig, in *Two Coventry Corpus Christi Plays* (Early English Text Society, Extra Series, LXXXVII), p. 85, lists payments for "horssing of the padgeant" and "for ij cords for the draught of the paygaunt." In the pages following he prints many references to "driving" the pageant. At Chester seven or eight men would have had great difficulty getting even a light wagon up the hill from the Roodee.

16 Copies of these accounts appear in Harley MS. 2054, fols. 13v–21r.

is 38/4¼, and we cannot be sure that some further costs may not be disguised in the accounts, or omitted. Even so, 38/4 was a goodly sum of money in days when it could buy a man's labour for a full year and a half. Or, said otherwise, a decent man could support his wife and family for a year and a half on the sum of money which the Smiths paid for building a carriage in 1561. If they had parts of an older vehicle which could be used again, even 38/4 would not represent the full value of the new one.

Of course the cost and comfort of living, or the living standard, has risen greatly in the Western world since the sixteenth century. It is hardly correct to say that a peasant in the Far East today gets the same reward for his day's rough labour as a workman in Canada. Nevertheless, making all allowances, 38/4 was a large sum of money in the sixteenth century. The carriage of the Smiths, however, must have been smaller or less cumbersome than that of the Coopers, for they paid only 18ᵈ to the putters of it, while the Coopers paid 28ᵈ.

The point I am leading up to so tediously is this: that the mystery plays must have had stages that were sizable, with ample floor space for quite elaborate spectacles. We may turn now to the plays involved — those of the Smiths, Skinners, Coopers, and Painters — and ask what these plays demanded of the stage in the way of properties, space, and equipment.

Play VII, the Painters' Play of the Shepherds, seems to require a mound or hill. When the Third Shepherd comes in, he says to the First:

> Hankin, hold up thy hand and haue me
> That I were on height there by thee.

Of course, these lines might mean that the Third Shepherd comes on to the open space before the carriage, and asks for help to get on to the stage itself. But in l. 217, there is a further reference to "this hill." It is a sizable hill since the Three Shepherds and the Boy Trowe are able to move about on it, and even to engage in wrestling matches. At l. 310, there is a stage direction (in Latin), "Then they will sit down, or walk about, and the star will appear." Where does this star appear? We have seen that it was possible to rig up a moving star within the church at an earlier date; a less satisfactory mechanism would hardly be acceptable at a later time when the plays had developed further. At l. 368, a stage direction reads, "Then the Angel will sing 'Gloria in excelsis.'" In one manuscript the music is provided for this hymn. Where is the Angel while singing? He is not seen. At l. 474 we are told, "And the Angel will appear." Later he disappears. How are these appearances and disappearances managed? The Angel could hardly clump on to the stage with the same sort of entrance that other characters have. At l. 470, the Shepherds travel toward Bethlehem; and at l. 492 the First Shepherd exclaims:

> Here I see Mary
> And Ihesu Christ fast by,
> Lapped in hay.

There is no other reference to the stable or to the ox and ass, but these would be obligatory — and, in fact, the Painters' accounts for 1568 have the following item: "payd to tho beryg for payntyng of our ox & asse & our pyg in the common hall   iiij^d." Whether the ox, ass, and pig were fabricated animals or paintings on a backdrop, it is evident that the Painters did try to represent a stable.[17]

The Shepherds Play, then, requires a mound at one side of the stage, a stable at the other, a moving star, and an appearing and dis-appearing angel. No doubt there is a "discovery" of the stable with Mary, Joseph, and the Babe; that is to say, at the appropriate moment curtains are drawn disclosing them. The Painters' accounts for 1561 have a payment of 3^d "for 3 Curten cowerds." Sir E. K. Chambers says that the scenery of the mysteries "must have been rather sketchy, to allow of a view from all sides."[18] But I do not know how a stable can be viewed from all sides, especially if it has a backdrop and dis-covery.

The Coopers had the same carriage the next day for the Flagellation of Christ. At the beginning of the play Christ is led before Annas and Caiaphas, the high priests. One would expect them to appear high, placed on raised seats of some sort. At l. 72, a direction reads, "Then the Jews place Jesus in the cathedra." In classical Latin, *cathedra* is only a chair; but we are not dealing with classical Latin; in mediaeval Latin, according to DuCange, a *cathedra* was a church. Later in the play, Jesus is despoiled of His garments and bound to a column. Further, the Coopers in 1574 paid Richard Doby 2^d, for what service we are not told. Richard Doby was a glasier.[19] I suggest that the *cathedra* of the Flagellation play is represented by a window, perhaps even a stained-glass one, at the mid-rear of the stage.

In addition to the *sedes* for Annas and Caiaphas, this play requires *sedes* for Pilate and Herod; but it is noticeable that the stage direction says that *two* of the Jews lead Jesus to Herod, while the whole crowd appears before Annas and Caiaphas and before Pilate. It would seem that the pageant wagon has now been pushed to the limits of its

17 The Painters' accounts for the latter part of the sixteenth century are in the possession of the modern Painters' gild of Chester.
18 *English Literature at the Close of the Middle Ages* (Oxford: Clarendon Press, 1947), p. 19.
19 It is true that the Painters in 1575 paid "rychard dobye for goynge one the styltes at the barres rydenge vj^d," and for the same service on Midsummer Eve; but there would be no "goynge one the styltes" at the Whitsun plays.

space; if we are to have *sedes* for three separate officials, and a representation of a church with columns and altar window, something has to be scamped — and Herod *is* scamped.

The general lay-out of the stage, however, is similar to that needed by the Painters who used the same carriage with a hill on one side, the Holy Stable on the other, and an open space between. Now in 1572, the Coopers paid "for the payntyng of our gere iij^s viij^d." This is an enormous amount of money when we realize that it would secure the services of an unskilled workman for forty-four days, and of a workman of the highest skill for eleven days. What was there about a pageant wagon that required so much painting? The account for 1574 has a similar item: "Ite paied for the payntynge the playars clothes, ij^s viij^d." But surely the players' costumes could not have been painted, for these were largely ecclesiastical garments. I take it that what was really painted were *cloths:* curtains, backdrops, and scenery; and that the Painters trimmed up for the Coopers a simulated church with columns in the foreground, to one of which Christ was bound.

The Skinners also used the Coopers' carriage for the Resurrection. This play needs a *sedes* for Pilate, and it needs a Tomb large enough for a man to enter; indeed, large enough for two angels to be seen within, for there is a stage direction, "Then two angels, after Christ has risen, will seat themselves in the Sepulchre, of whom one will sit at the head and the other at the foot." Further, the three Mary's enter the Tomb and look around. This Tomb, with a different exterior appearance, could be the same structure that serves for a mount or hill in the Shepherds Play. Just how Christ *rises* in this play must be left for the moment, to speculation. The stage direction reads: "Then two angels will sing, 'Christ arising from the dead, etc.,' and Christ will then rise, and, the song having been finished, will speak as follows." But how Christ leaves the stage after His speech, we are not told. It would hardly seem likely that He merely walks off.

The Smiths had a different carriage; and we do not know whether they shared it with any other gild. Their play combines two incidents that seem difficult because of the time element: the first is that of Simeon receiving the infant Jesus; the second is that of the boy Jesus among the Doctors. Both parts need a representation of the inside of a temple, and there is, again, an appearing and disappearing angel. At the beginning, Simeon reads in the prophecies, "Behold a Virgin shall conceive and give birth to a child." In doubt and bewilderment, he erases the word Virgin and writes in, "A good woman." He places the book on the altar, and the angel appears and writes the original word Virgin in bright red letters. This "business" is repeated; and in the end the angel appears to Simeon and tells him that he will not taste death before seeing the Redeemer. Mary then enters with the infant Jesus, and at the conclusion of this episode Simeon sings, "Nunc dimittis."

Returning now to David Rogers, we may ask some obvious questions. He says, "these pagiantes or cariage was a highe place made like ahowse with ij rowmes beinge open on the tope the lower rowme they apparrelled & dressed them selues, and in the higher rowme they played." Unless the wagons were built like pyramids, they could not have borne the weight on top required for a tomb above a dressing room — and for appearances and disappearances there simply must be some sort of machinery *above* the stage. Our ancestors did not have at their service actual angels who came fluttering down from Heaven when required. But, so long as there is a roof over the stage, and a bit of thin wire is available, anybody can contrive a satisfactory appearance and disappearance of heavenly creatures. A white costume against a white gauzy background will also very efficiently create an illusion of appearance and disappearance — but even this trick is impossible on a stage open to the heavens. The Coventry records have many references to a "wynd" and windlass, obviously for hoisting angels.[20] But the angels cannot be hoisted and left in the air: they must be hoisted into a disappearance, i.e., into a roof.

Further, what are the acoustics of the open air? A normal speaking voice can be heard at perhaps thirty feet; surely children, women, and angels in the plays did not shriek and bawl their parts so as to be heard by thousands of spectators. Even our crude ancestors would hardly require the Virgin Mary to bark and bellow like a sergeant major on parade. When the Mayor and Aldermen sat in the Pentice to hear the plays, they must have been at least fifty feet from the stage. And though the crowds at the Roodee stood on the hillside up which voices might rise, the actors would still need a sounding board. That sounding board a roofed wagon supplied.

A roof was also necessary to protect the rich vestments borrowed from the Church. The sunniest spot in all England can hardly boast more than fifty days of uninterrupted sunshine in the year; and one light shower would cause expensive damage.

Finally, corroboration of the roofed stage may be found in the expenses of the Coventry Smiths who in 1480 "paid to a carpenter for the pagent rowf vj^d."[21] Similarly, a Norwich pageant described in 1565 had "a square topp to sett over ye sayde Howse."[22]

We should remember that religious plays began within the church before the High Altar, that is to say, on a roofed stage. When they

---

[20] Hardin Craig, *Two Coventry Plays*, pp. 99, 101, etc.
[21] *Ibid.*, p. 89.
[22] O. Waterhouse, *The Non-Cycle Mystery Plays*, Early English Text Society, Extra Series, CIV, xxxii; Chambers, *Med. St.*, II, 388.

moved outside the church, it was simply a matter of placing the chancel, choir and altar and all, first on a platform at the great west door, and later on wheels. How, otherwise, did James Burbage come to think of placing a roof over the stage in the first theatre built in England? He roofed his stage because the stage had always been roofed, even when it was only a wagon blocking the entrance to an inn; and the stage had always been roofed because a sounding board was necessary, to say nothing of machinery and apparatus for ascensions and descents.

Indeed, when Shakespeare in *Cymbeline* has Jove sweeping down from the heavens upon the back of an eagle, hurling thunderbolts as he descends, he is using stage machinery which has been in existence for hundreds of years; and when Sir James Barrie in *Peter Pan* shows the children in flight about their bedroom, he also lies under direct debt to the makers of mystery plays — those crude ancestors of ours — half a thousand years ago.[23]

Let us question the stage requirements of some other plays. In the Ascension of Our Lord, Play XX, after Jesus appears to the Disciples in the upper room and is made known to them in breaking the bread, the stage direction tells us, "Then He will lead the disciples into Bethany, and when He arrives at that place, Jesus, standing in the place where He will ascend, says. . . ." Of course! What else are we to expect? There has to be a *place where He will ascend,* a place where the machinery is ready to draw Him up — and while He speaks, the necessary fittings are unobtrusively arranged. The next stage directions are also interesting: "Then Jesus will ascend, and while ascending He will sing as follows"; and, "Having finished the song, Jesus will stand in the midst as if above the clouds." Hereupon the First Angel will demand:

> Who is this that commeth within
> The blisse of heauen that neuer shall blyn?
> Blody out of the world of synne
> And harrowëd hell hath he.

After further speeches, we are told, "Then He will ascend, and the angels will sing the following hymn while He ascends." Then the

---

[23] Scholarship in general, however, from the time of Thomas Sharpe and his *Dissertation on the Pageants . . . at Coventry,* 1825, down to the present has accepted the open stage of Rogers for all the mysteries of England. Thus, for a sampling, C. F. Tucker Brooke, *Tudor Drama,* p. 10; Katherine Lee Bates, *The English Religious Drama* (New York: Macmillan, 1917, first printed 1893), quotes, p. 41, from the *Breviarye,* and on p. 43 speaks of "the English scaffold presenting but one open stage, with the story below curtained off as a green room." Most surprising of all, Allardyce Nicoll in his *Masks, Mimes and Miracles* (New York: Harcourt Brace, 1931) has many illustrations of stages of all sorts, not one of which is without a roof, yet accepts (p. 203) Rogers' open stage.

angels descend, singing, "Men of Galilee, what do you gaze upon in the heavens?" Then they in turn ascend once more. How can all this ascending and descending be done in "an open place on top of a wagon"? It can be done on a roofed stage, and clouds can be painted on a backdrop or arranged with gauzy hangings — indeed, at Chelmsford in 1562, fifty fathoms of linen were bought to make clouds[24] — and it can be a scene of great beauty and devout reverence, impressive in holiness, if only we get rid of the naïve notion that our ancestors were childish and crude.

A play which must have had similar machinery is the Assumption of Our Lady which was eliminated from the cycle, for obvious reasons, early in the sixteenth century. This play is said to have been performed *solus* at the High Cross in 1488; and, seeing that there were no women actors on Shakespeare's stage, it is interesting to note that the Assumption was produced, and no doubt performed, by the Worshipful Wives of the City. But in other plays also women took their parts as naturally as men.

In the Creation when Cain and Abel prepare sacrifices, that of Cain is left untouched on the altar, for he has tried to cheat God. He says:

> Hit were pittye, by my penne,
> This eared corne for to bren!
> Therefore the diuill hang me than,
> And Thou of this get ought!

> This earles corne grew nye the waye.
> Of this offer I will to daye;
> For cleane corne, by my faye,
> Of me getts Thou noughte!

Then he addresses his sacrifice to the Lord:

> Loe, God, here may Thou see
> Such corne as grew to me;
> Part of it I bring to thee
> Anon, withouten let.

> I hope Thou wilt quite me this
> And sende me more of worldlie blisse;
> Els, forsoth, Thou doest amisse,
> And Thou be in my debte.

Abel sacrifices in better spirit, and the stage direction tells us, "Then a flame of fire will come upon the sacrifice of Abell." How this flame of fire was managed, I do not know; but the trick was an ancient one. In the days of Alexander the Great, one "Kratisthenes could make fire burn spontaneously."[25] And the flame that descends upon the

---

24 Chambers, *Med. St.*, II, 346.   25 Nicoll, *Masks*, p. 35.

sacrifice of Abel is nothing more or less than evidence of the continuity of mime, juggler, and magician down through the Dark and Middle Ages.

We have heard often enough of the Hell-mouth belching fire and smoke in the mystery plays. There is no Hell-mouth in the Chester Judgment Play; but the Demons make a grisly job of carrying off the wicked to Hell. Before passing on, I may stop just a moment with the grave of Antichrist. The speakers refer to laying the body of Antichrist under the earth and gravel. After a time he rises to prove his godly powers. The stage directions refer to his *tumulus*, whereas the Tomb of Christ is called *Sepulchrum*. In other words, there has to be a pit or trap in the floor of the stage — the grave of Ophelia has a somewhat dishonourable ancestry. . . .

If we take money at our former valuation, and say that a penny would buy a day of unskilled labour in the sixteenth century, and $8 or $9 will buy the same today, then we must reckon that in 1554 the Smiths paid about $6000 to produce a play of 336 lines consisting of two short scenes which could certainly be performed in twenty minutes. Of course there were several performances — indeed, four: at the Abbey, at the High Cross, before the Castle, and on the Roodee. The Painters in 1568 spent not £3/4/7, but £4/2/6. It is true a good part of the money went into food, drink, and rejoicing; nevertheless the plays were expensive.

Now in a day when a penny was a fair — or an accepted — wage for a day's labour, what about Old Simeon who received forty times that amount, 3/4? Was he an unskilled actor?[26] It is not the general nature of business men to pay for services more than the services are worth; and the inescapable fact is that the Smiths paid Simeon 3/4 at the same time that they paid the workmen in their shops a penny or less for a day's work. Fees on the same scale may be found in other expense accounts, not only at Chester but everywhere. Surely there can be no escape from the conclusion that the professional

[26] Allardyce Nicoll says in *British Drama*, p. 27, "The actors in these pieces were all amateurs — members of the various companies who for a time put aside their labour to perform in the sacred mysteries." In his *Masks*, pp. 193–4, he seems cautiously and guardedly to favour a view that "the mimes and the *jongleurs* were called in to aid the amateur actors," because "the boasting tyrant [e.g., Herod], the jealous husband [e.g., Joseph], the shrewish wife [e.g., Mrs. Noah], the comic Devil with his canvas club and his warts [not to be found in the Chester Plays, although Nicoll seems to think he can be] — all these have their prototypes in the mimic theatre." In his *Development of the Theatre* (3rd ed., New York: Harcourt Brace, 1946), p. 76, he seems to return to his earlier view; "The gilds, having taken over the management of the cycles, provided the actors from among their own members. Generally these actors were paid a small fee. At Coventry one man received three shillings and fourpence for 'pleayng God,' etc." But 3/4 is not a small fee. Having received it, "God" could go fishin' for a month!

actor had a part in these plays; and if so, he must go much further back into history than we have assumed. Old Simeon had to get 3/4 for his day's work because his working days were few; and it may well be that the "letall God" who took the part of the child Christ before the Doctors, was his apprentice. Those actors who received tenpence or less may have been talented local folk.

That professional actors were abroad in the land long before the sixteenth century, we may be perfectly sure — but I need not again labour that point. Only, when we find on the title-pages of morality plays statements like "foure men may well and easelye playe thys Interlude," or "foure may easely play this playe" (*Impacyente Pouerte*, 1560; *Welth and Helth*, c. 1525), we can be sure there is a reason for such a general recommendation.

Further, when the gilds paid actors forty times what they paid the journeymen in their shops, would they be content with stuttering, inadequate, inaudible performance? We have seen that they held as many as four rehearsals, of plays that average four hundred lines. No doubt, part of the large fee granted the actor is due to the time spent in preparation; but the four rehearsals also indicate anxiety that the plays be acceptable to God and man.

The records show concern also that the actors be properly clothed and made up for their parts. The clothes of Pilate and Herod seem to have been rather special, for both of them had pages to hold up their trains ("Payde for the carynge of pylates clothes vj$^\text{d}$"; "Paied unto pylat and to him that caried arrats clothes & for there gloves vij$^\text{s}$"). The face of the "letall God" was gilded for the day; and Joseph is represented with "beard like a buske of breeres With a pownd of heare about his mouth and more." The accounts of the Painters for 1575 show that they spent 6$^\text{d}$ "for the hayare of the ij bardes and trowes cape." In the same year they spent 3$^\text{d}$ for "ij gat skynes for trow shous" (Trow's shoes; Trow is a comic character in the Painters' Play), and paid "peter of mosten for makynge of trouwes shoues & hys paynes xij$^\text{d}$." Herod's visor, which cost 3$^\text{d}$ to mend, must have been an improvement upon nature. But perhaps the most interesting costume is that of Satan in the Creation play. He says:

> A manner of an Adder is in this place,
> That wynges like a byrd she hase,
> Feete as an Adder, a maydens face.

He proposes to adopt this semblance, and later says, "My adders coat I will put on." Shakespeare's Caliban has no wings. He is, rather, a manner of fish. But the habitat, *par excellence*, of fabulous creatures is the Middle Ages. We may confidently say that Ariel in flight is a manner of an angel, and Caliban is not the son of Sycorax alone.

We look back sometimes with a sort of nostalgia to the Middle Ages when the artistic talent of every individual in every department of life could find expression. There were no assembly lines, then, to destroy the soul of a man; the individual was not an expendable cog in a vast machine; and we treasure today surviving pieces of their handiwork which must have been commonplace to them. If the gilds seized in the mystery plays the opportunity to advertise the handiwork by which they earned their bread, they can hardly be blamed. There is even, in the late Banns of Chester, a suggestion that the Bakers distributed samples to the crowds! They are told to "cast god loaves Abroade with A Cheerfull harte." Nor should we be shocked at the general jollification in which they indulged during the supreme event of their year. The amounts they spent on food and drink seem incredible — but so they are at a modern convention of the Rotarians or Shriners. Of one thing we can be certain: the mystery plays were extremely expensive to produce, and they required the zealous effort of the whole community. If, with all that labour and all that cost, they failed to attract the artistic genius that flowered so abundantly in the Middle Ages, one ought to be astonished. But the question of their intrinsic and artistic value is one which I shall leave to another lecture.

PART THREE

The Renaissance Theatre

I

Stage Production

THE NEW SCENERY

The theatre of Renaissance Europe was infinitely varied. The dramatic impulse in the sixteenth and early seventeenth centuries found expression in a multiplicity of staging forms — ranging in complexity from the rude platforms of wandering English and Italian mountebanks to the elaborate and spectacular perspective settings of Medici court celebrations.

The dramas of this eclectic period shared one characteristic in common, no matter what their country of origin. They were, as one critic has aptly called them, "man-centered dramas" — the antithesis of the God-centered mystery cycles that absorbed the theatrical energies of Europe during the last years of the Middle Ages. In England these man-centered plays were performed in great outdoor theatres, each equipped with a jutting platform stage, similar to the *platea*, or neutral playing space of the medieval theatre. These outdoor theatres, the most celebrated of which was Shakespeare's Globe, were perfectly adapted to fluid, panoramic production style — a style based very closely on medieval precedent.

The Italian theatre of this period followed an entirely different path. The dramas of Cardinal Bibbiena, Machiavelli and their contemporaries were closely based on classical models, particularly the comedies of Plautus and Terence. These comedies were in many ways the antithesis of the medieval drama. Highly concentrated in structure, observing for the most part a unity of place, the classical and pseudo-classical plays called for a single scene of action.

The Renaissance revival of interest in ancient drama can be dated from the discovery by enterprising scholars in 1427 of twelve Plautine plays. This discovery in turn led to attempts to reconstruct the stage for which Plautus had written. Unfortunately at this time no large body of information on the Roman theatre was available to would-be producers and actors. As a result, the first productions of the old plays were performed more or less in an essentially unsuitable medieval style.

In 1486, however, the first important body of information about the classical stage became available to Renaissance producers by virtue of the rediscovery of an important ancient architectural treatise by Marcus Vitruvius Pollio (fl. 70–15 B.C.).

235

Book X of Vitruvius' treatise is concerned with the theatre. Much of the information contained is misleading and inaccurate; nevertheless, the book had a considerable influence on theatre architects, designers and scholars.

Among the hitherto forgotten facts about the Greek and Roman playhouses which Renaissance scholars learned from Vitruvius were the following:

1. The Greek theatre in the time of Aeschylus had at least one designer, Agatharcus, who used the principles of perspective, or perhaps more accurately, foreshortening, to create flat scenery which had the appearance of depth.

2. The Imperial Roman theatre had a semicircular orchestra and auditorium, in addition to a stage backed by a two-and-a-half or three-storied *scenae frons* (permanent scenic façade), elaborately decorated.

3. The scenery of the ancient theatre was divided into three types: tragic scenery (consisting of temples, palaces, and other similar buildings); comic scenery (consisting for the most part of private dwellings, taverns, brothels, and other places of common resort); and satyric scenery (consisting for the most part of trees, rocks, caves, and other rustic objects).

This newly discovered information inspired a number of experiments in stagecraft. In the 1490's, a Roman scholar named Junius Pomponius Laetus collaborated with the actor Inghirami to present two Plautine plays and a Senecan tragedy on improvised stages, each backed by an elaborately decorated Vitruvian *scenae frons*. Shortly after 1500, inspired by Vitruvius' account of Agatharcus, designers like Pellegrino da Undino, Girolamo Genga, Baldassare Peruzzi, and Raffael San Gallo began to apply the principles of perspective painting to scene design. Illusionism, the attempt to create the detailed fiction of a single place on the stage, received a great impetus from these early experiments, and indeed the picture-frame stage of the modern realistic theatre can be traced directly to the work of men like Pellegrino and Peruzzi and through them presumably to Vitruvius.

No Renaissance stage-craftsman, however, was more dependent on Vitruvian precedent than the architect Sebastiano Serlio (1475–1554), whose observations on theatre construction, first published in 1545 as Book II of his *Architettura*, remain today an important primary source of information about the sixteenth-century Italian theatre. Serlio's precepts take the form of a detailed description of a theatre which he had erected in the 1530's for a learned academy in Vicenza. His stated intention in building the theatre was to place in a converted hall "all those parts of an ancient [outdoor] theatre as an . . . [indoor structure] . . . might contain"; to reproduce, in other words, as nearly as conditions would permit, a Vitruvian classic stage. His desire to imitate Vitruvius forced Serlio to arrange his *gradi* (raised tiers of seats) in a semicircular pattern, even though such a pattern was more suitable to an outdoor theatre than to an oblong hall, 80 feet by 60 feet. Vitruvius also was the inspiration for the three kinds of scenery (tragic, comic, and satyric) which Serlio devised for his stage and for Serlio's assumption that all plays in the Italian repertoire could be accommodated by these stock scenes, without resort to special decorations designed for a particular drama.

It is interesting to note that Serlio's stage was divided into two parts — a level forestage on which the actors actually performed and a raked, or slanted, backstage on which the painted scenery was placed. Scenery was not at this time, as it is today, an environment for the actors. It was instead simply an illustration of the place in which the action is supposed to occur and a decoration of the stage. Indeed, an actor had to be careful not to approach too closely the painted scenes. The perspective was sharply forced, and a distant building might in fact be no higher than the hero's waist.

Serlio's system of stage mounting depended on a backdrop or back flats and a series of angle wings. (An angle wing was a double wooden canvas-covered frame with one part of the frame extending off-stage and the other part set on one of two converging lines drawn to the central vanishing point.) There was, incidentally, only one vanishing point in Serlio's theatre, and his designs were free from distortion only in the very center of the auditorium.

Angle wings have the advantage of permitting a greater illusion of depth than simple flat painting, but they have also one major drawback. They are cumbersome, and their use makes efficient scene-shifting difficult. Indeed, Serlio's somewhat academic system is appropriate only for the decoration of the plays which are limited by the classical unity of place. In their commentaries on Aristotle, theorists like Julius Caesar Scaliger (1484-1558) and Lodovico Castelvetro (1506?-1571) had insisted that such a unity was an unalterable law for drama. And the rigid stage of Serlio answered the practical problems of production according to rule.

Although, as we shall see, exciting experiments in a new kind of stage spectacle were taking place elsewhere in Italy, some architects continued to be devoted to Serlio's pseudo-Vitruvian monoscenic stage. Forty years after Serlio's book was published, and also in Vicenza, this tradition reached a glorious climax with the opening of the Teatro Olimpico, designed by Andrea Palladio (1508-1580) and completed after Palladio's death by Vicenzo Scamozzi (1522-1616). Scamozzi finished the building in 1584 and added permanent perspective vistas the following year. The Palladio-Scamozzi theatre, one of the most beautiful ever built, is still in existence and used for performances.

The idea behind the Teatro Olimpico is the same one that animated Serlio's treatise: the attempt to adapt the structure of a giant outdoor Roman theatre to the narrower dimensions of indoor performance. In so doing the architects had to abandon the semi-circular design of the Roman *cavea* (seating area) and settle for a semi-elliptical auditorium with thirteen *gradi*, surrounded by a colonnade and behind the colonnade a balustrade lined with statues. In front of the playing area, as in Serlio's theatre, is an area corresponding to the Roman orchestra.

The stage is rectangular, shallow (22 feet) and wide (82 feet). The narrowness of the platform is another imitation of the Roman pattern.

Behind the playing area was an elaborate *scenae frons* with five openings—behind which are permanent vistas of wood and plaster painted to represent a classical city. Scamozzi used a complex ground plan for these vistas, so that everyone in the auditorium would have some sight of the perspective.

The Teatro Olimpico is a magnificent achievement, but upon its completion it was already outdated. The advanced theatre of the day was not so pure or academic, and changeable scenery was the wave of the future.

Sebastiano Serlio

THE STAGE*

(from *The Second Book of Architecture*, 1545)

A mong all things made by hand of man few in my opinion bring greater contentment to the eye and satisfaction to the spirit than the unveiling to our view of a stage setting. Here the art of perspective gives us in a little space a view of superb palaces, vast temples, and houses of all kinds, and, both near and far, spacious squares surrounded by various ornate buildings. There are long vistas of avenues with intersecting streets, triumphal arches, soaring columns, pyramids, obelisques, and a thousand other marvels, all enriched by innumerable lights (large, medium, small, according to their position), at times so skillfully placed that they seem like so many sparkling jewels — diamonds, rubies, sapphires, emeralds, and other gems.

Here the horned and lucent moon rises slowly — so slowly that the spectators have not been aware of any movement. In other scenes the sun rises, moves on its course, and at the end of the play is made to set with such skill that many spectators remain lost in wonder.[1] With like skill gods are made to descend from the skies and planets to pass through the air. Then there are presented diverse

---

* From Barnard Hewitt, ed., *The Renaissance Stage: Documents of Serlio, Sabbattini and Furttenbach* (Coral Gables, Fla.: University of Miami Press, 1958), pp. 24–33. Copyright 1958 by University of Miami Press. Translated by Allardyce Nicoll; footnotes are the translator's.

1 "That there was a definite relation between the idea of the 'artificial day' which was being advocated at this time as the manifestation of the unity of time and this sun rising at the beginning of the play and going down at its close 'most artificially' seems certain" (L. B. Campbell, *Scenes and Machines*, p. 41, note 4). A moving moon is called for in the production of *La Mélite*, 1630 (*Le Memoire de Mahelot* (ed. Lancaster, Paris, 1920) p. 76 f.). Suns and moons were frequent in England. The inventories of the Admiral's Men in 1598 (*Henslowe Papers* 117) include "the clothe of the Sone and Moone" (Chambers, *Elizabethan Stage*, iii, 77, n. 1). Part II of the *Contention*, scene V, 9, requires that "three sunnes appeare in the aire." *I Troublesome Reign*, Scene xiii, 131, states: "There the five Moones appeare" (Chambers, *Elizabethan Stage*, iii, 76). For elaborate sun and moon effects after the Restoration see Montague Summers, *Restoration Theatre*, p. 194 ff. Cf. the sun at the center of the glory described by Furttenbach in *Mannhaffter Kunstspiegel* . . . Cf. Nicoll, *Stuart Masques*, p. 137.

intermezzi, richly staged, in which performers appear dressed in various sorts of strange costumes both to execute morris dances[2] and play music. Sometimes one sees strange animal costumes worn by men and children who play, leap, and run, to the delighted wonder of the spectators. All these things are so satisfying to the eye and the spirit that nothing made by the art of man could seem more beautiful.

Since we are dealing with the art of perspective, I will proceed with the subject further. The general art of perspective we have hitherto considered was concerned with flat planes parallel to the front, while this second perspective method is concerned with plastic scenes in relief. Obviously the latter must follow different rules. First of all, it is usual to begin the platform at eye level; from front to back this is raised a ninth part, i.e., the depth is divided into nine parts and the stage raised at the back as much as one of these parts. The platform must be made very even and strong to accommodate the dancers.

This slope of the platform I have found from experience to be effective. For in Vicenza, the richest and proudest among cities of Italy, I built an auditorium and stage of wood, perhaps — nay, without doubt — the largest erected in our times, where for the marvellous *intermezzi* which were presented there, introducing chariots, elephants, and diverse morris dances, I built in front of the sloping stage a level floor, the depth of which was 12 feet and the width 60 feet. This I found to be both convenient and effective. As this front platform was level, the floor was marked out with perfect squares (not in perspective), but on the sloping platform the squares diminished as they approached the horizon.

There are some who have placed the vanishing point at the back wall of the scene, in which case it must be placed on the stage itself at the bottom of the wall. This produces a very bad effect, for the houses all seem to run into one. It is my practice to carry the vanishing point further back.[3] This I have found so very successful that I have always held to it and always advise it to others.

The scenes for plays are of three kinds — Comic, Tragic, and Satyric.[4] First I shall deal with the Comic. The houses for this scene

2 Serlio, like some other Renaissance writers, uses morris dance as a general term for theatrical dancing.

3 English ed. 1611, "place the Horizon before the doore."

4 Serlio takes his classification of scenes directly from Vitruvius. The same classification existed, of course, in Aristotle's *Poetics,* but Aristotle had emphasized the two types of Comedy and Tragedy. The Renaissance did not have a satyr drama similar to that of the Greeks, but the plays of the popular pastoral tradition had similar scenes of woodlands and meadows, and characters equally low in social rank. Serlio has in mind the classical concept of rude and free-spoken peasants. But the two concepts were soon confused; Leone di Somi speaks of satyr plays and eclogues in the same breath, as reflecting "that sim-

should be those of private persons. These scenes generally are set up at one end of a hall with rooms behind to accommodate the actors. There one sets up the stage as I have demonstrated in the cross section and the plan.

The part C is the level platform with squares, let us say, of two feet. The sloping floor is marked B with similar squares that diminish in perspective starting from two feet. As I have said above, I do not purpose to place the vanishing point at the back of the scene, but to carry it back from there to a distance equal to the distance from the edge of the sloping platform to the back of the scene. Then all the lines are carried to this back vanishing point. The two lines of points mark the wall at the end of the hall.[5] The houses and other objects will show better in the foreshortening when all the squares approach the same vanishing point and diminish according to their distance. On the squares are erected the houses, both those with faces parallel to the stage front and those in perspective, as indicated by the heavy lines of the plan. Such houses I have always made of frames over which I have stretched cloth,[6] making the openings for doors on either face as occasion required. At times I have heightened the effectiveness of the scene by making some parts of wood, cut in relief, as I will explain in due time.[7] All the space between the setting and the wall, marked A, is the off-stage space for the performers. Care must be taken that the back of the set is at least two feet from the rear wall so that the performers may pass from one side of the stage to the other without being seen. A point is established at L at the edge of the platform B of the same height as the vanishing point, and thence a horizontal line is drawn to the vanishing point. The point at which this line cuts the back wall of the set is the vanishing point for that wall. But this line will not serve as a guide in constructing any other part of the set, except that it is of use for determining the size of the objects depicted on faces parallel to the back wall. The first vanishing point, which is behind the wall of the hall, is to serve for all the perspective faces of the houses. Since in order to use this vanishing point in the making of actual measurements it would be necessary to break through this wall — a thing not possible — I have

---

plicity, purity and joy of the early ages." Serlio's design for satyr plays became a model for pastoral plays.

Later Italian designers and others such as Mahelot and Inigo Jones frequently used the three types of scenes Serlio gives but many other types were added, and the neat distinction of the three according to social class and appropriate setting was broken down in actual practice.

[5] In the elevation drawing the wall is represented by two solid lines.

[6] English ed. 1611, "spars, or rafters or lathes, covered with linnin cloth."

[7] English ed. 1611, "I have also made some things of halfe planks of wood which were great helpe to the Paynters to set out things at life."

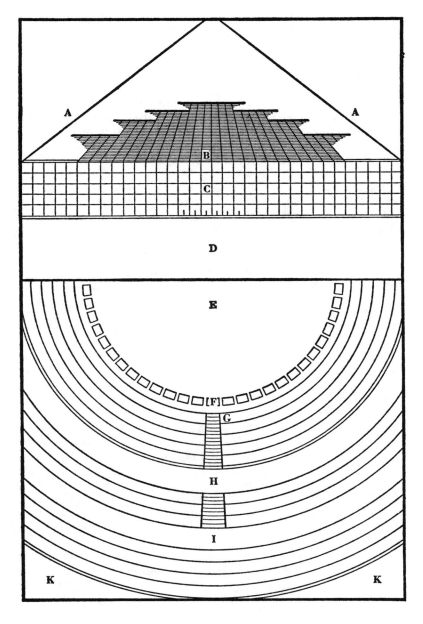

Serlio's Ground Plan of a Theatre

always made a small model of cardboard and wood, carefully executed to scale, from which I could easily and correctly execute each piece separately in the large. Although this procedure may seem difficult to some, nevertheless much time and care may profitably be devoted to the making of such models and in practice, so that by careful application of principles the method may be mastered.

Although halls (however large they may be) could not accommodate theatres such as the ancients had, nevertheless in order to follow the ancients as closely as possible, I have included in my plan such parts of the ancient theatre as a great hall might contain. Thus the part D corresponds to the *proscenio,* the circular part marked E corresponds to the *orchestra,* raised one step from the *proscenio.* Around it are the seats for the most noble persons at F. The first tiers, G, are for the most noble ladies. The parts H and F are a passageway. The other tiers are for the less noble men, with steps for easy access. The large spaces marked K are for the common people, and will be larger or smaller according to the size of the hall. The greater the hall, the more nearly will the theatre assume its perfect form.

This first scene, the Comic scene, has houses appropriate to private persons, as citizens, lawyers, merchants, parasites, and other similar persons. Above all, the scene should have its house of the procuress (*ruffiana*), its tavern, and its church. I have already shown how these houses are placed in position, and I now discuss the details of their construction. In a small print, of course, I can do no more than suggest some details certain to please, such as an open portico with arches in the modern style leading to another house. The balconies, called *pergoli* by some, by others *renghiere,* give an excellent effect on the perspective faces, as do the cornices whose ends, cut on the inside, form projecting corners on the houses. For the same reason those houses which have projections are especially successful — such as the tavern of the moon in this design. Above all else one must select some smaller buildings to be placed in front, so that over their roofs the other buildings may be seen, such as you may see above the house of the procurer (marked by the sign of the hooks, commonly called *hami*). The superior height of the houses further back gives the appearance of grandeur, and better completes the scene in that part, which would not be the case if each house were lower than the one in front.

Although the detail is painted with shadows as from a single light at one side, nevertheless it is better to illuminate the scene from the middle because of the greater power of a light hanging at the center. Those roundels and squares that appear throughout the scene are all transparent artificial lights of various colors; the means for making these I will give at the end of this book. It will be well to put light

Top: The *Teatro Olimpico* in Vicenza, the finest example of the academic Italian adaptations of Classical theatres as described by Vitruvius.

Bottom: Serlio's interpretation of the Comic scene as described by Vitruvius.

Top: Perspective scene with single vanishing point in the early Renaissance style. Designed by Andrea Peruzzi (1481-1537).

Bottom: A later version of the one-point perspective style. A design by Giacomo Torelli for a French production (Act IV of *Andromede* by Corneille, 1651).

behind the windows in the front faces, but an especially good effect will be secured by making these of glass or paper or painted cloth. If, however, I were to make all the suggestions I could concerning these things, I should be considered prolix. Therefore I will leave them to the imagination of those who are interested in such things.

The Tragic scene is for the representation of tragedies. In this setting the houses must be those of great persons, because amorous adventures, sudden accidents, and violent and cruel deaths such as we read of in ancient and modern tragedies alike have always taken place in the houses of lords, dukes, grand princes, and particularly kings. Therefore, as I have said, you must introduce here none but stately houses, such as those indicated in the following figure; you must note, however, that, because of the limitations of space, I have not been able to sketch those grand edifices of kings and lords that I could show in more ample space. The architect concerned with these things needs no more than a suggestion of the general method, which he may adapt according to the setting and subject called for. As I have said in the section on the comic scene, the builder must take care to arrange the parts of his setting in such a way as to give the best impression to the spectators, placing, for instance, a small building in front of a higher one.

I have made all my scenes on flat frames. Since these sometimes fail to appear convincing, it is necessary to avail oneself of wooden relief — as in the building on the left side of the stage, the pillars of which rest on a base with several steps. In this case the base must be made of low relief raised above the floor, and upon it are set two frames, one facing the audience, the other in perspective. They extend upwards only to the top of the parapet which runs above the first arches. Now because the second arches are set back so as to make room for this parapet, the two upper frames also must be set back so as to produce the effect desired. What I say of this building applies also to others which have certain parts set back — especially to the houses near the front of the stage. If the house is set very far to the back, however, one frame will be sufficient, so long as all its parts are skillfully designed and painted.

Concerning artificial lights enough has already been said in the section on the comic scene.

All the superstructures on the roofs, such as chimneys, belfries, and the like, although they are not indicated on the illustration, are to be made of thin board and cut in profile and drawn and colored with skill. Similarly, statues supposed to be of marble or bronze will be made of thick cardboard or even thin wood, cut to size, and shadowed. They are to be so placed in the distance that the spectators cannot see them from the side.

Some artists are in the habit of painting supposedly living characters in these scenes — such as a woman on a balcony or in a doorway,
even a few animals. I do not recommend this practice, however, because although the figures represent living creatures they show no
movement. On the other hand, it is quite appropriate to represent
some person who sleeps, or some dog or other animal that sleeps,
because no movement is expected here. I can recommend painting on
the back shutter statues or similar objects supposedly of marble or of
other material, as well as scenes of history and legend. Concerning
the representation of living things having motion I shall speak at the
end of this book; there I will tell how this is to be accomplished.

The Satyric scene is used for Satyric plays, in which all those who
live licentiously are reproved and even castigated. In ancient satyr
plays lines were spoken which referred, almost without respect to
persons, to certain men known in the community to lead evil and
vicious lives. Such license, however, as one may readily comprehend,
would be conceded only to people who could speak without respect
for rank — namely, rustics. Hence Vitruvius in dealing with scenery
recommends that these scenes be composed of trees, rocks, hills,
mountains, herbs, flowers, and fountains, — together with some rustic
huts, such as those in the illustration. And since in our times these
performances are generally given in the winter when few trees and
bushes have flowers and foliage, these will have to be made artificially
of silk, and will receive more praise than the natural objects themselves. Just as in the comic and tragic scenes houses and other buildings are to be imitated by the art of painting, so in this too, imitation
is to be made of trees and bushes with flowers.

The more costly these things are, the more they are worthy of
praise, because in truth they then express the generosity of rich lords
and their enmity to ugly stinginess. Some time ago my eyes beheld
such scenes carried out by the architect Girolamo Genga at the instance of his lord, Francesco Maria, Duke of Urbino. In these I witnessed as much liberality in the prince as taste and skill in the architect.
Such beauty was there in the setting as I have never seen in any other
similar work. Oh immortal God! what wonder it was to see so many
trees and fruits, so many herbs and diverse flowers, all made from the
finest silk of the most beautiful colors, the cliffs and rocks covered
with diverse sea shells, with snails and other animals, with coral
branches of many colors, with sea crabs among the rocks, with so
great diversity of beauteous things that to write about all of them
would take too long. I will not speak of the costumes of satyrs,
nymphs, and sirens or of the shapes of monsters and strange animals,
skillfully constructed to be worn by men and children according to
their size. The movements of the actors seemed to bring these animals

to life, each according to its own nature. And if it were not that I should prove too prolix, I should tell of the superb costumes of some shepherds made of rich cloth of gold and silk, furred with the finest skins of wild animals. I could speak also of the costumes of some fishermen which were no less rich than the others, whose nets were of thread of fine gold and whose other tackle was all gilded. I could also describe some shepherdesses whose costumes put avarice to shame. But all these things I will leave to the taste and judgement of the architects, who will always be able to make things of this sort when they find similar patrons, generously willing to give them full license to carry out all they desire.

Some years before Scamozzi built his perspective vistas in Vicenza, poets and painters in other parts of Italy had been at work on a new kind of entertainment—one that depended on rapidly changing spectacular scenery. The intermezzo, as the form came to be called, was a short allegorical interlude or pageant, illustrating in song, dance and sometimes mute narration, a mythological, legendary or pastoral story. It was performed before and between the acts of a legitimate play to vary the monotony of the classically-prescribed setting. There were usually six intermezzi in a performance, and each one often had six or seven transformations of scene.

This novel entertainment first appeared at Ferrara in the 1490's. It reached its zenith at the Medici Court in Florence as part of lavish celebrations intended to add splendor to a wedding or other state occasion. Between 1539 and 1589 many great artists contributed to intermezzi, including Bastiano da San Gallo (1481-1551), Giorgio Vasari (1511-74), Baldassare Lanci (1510-71) and Bernardo Buontalenti (1536-1608).

The Florentine intermezzo hada brief but glorious life. Near the end of the century its splendors were borrowed by another Florentine entertainment—the opera.

The modest beginnings of this significant theatre form were some experiments conducted by Count Giovanni Bardi (1534-1614?) and La Camerata, an aristocratic society of young poets and musicians who wished to recreate the vanished art of Greek tragedy. (They had learned from Vitruvius that ancient plays were mostly sung, not declaimed).

The ambition of La Camerata was to give their musical drama

purity and classical simplicity, but the success of intermezzi had created
a hunger for ostentatious display. As a result opera soon became as much
a visual as an aural art. Indeed, if the inventors of this new form had not
interested Claudio Monteverdi (1567-1643) in their fledgling efforts, the
musical part of the new entertainment might have been no more than
incidental.

The first important designers of opera—Buontalenti, his student Guilio
Parigi (d. 1635), Giulio's son Alfonso (d. 1656) and Giambattista Aleotti
(1546-1636)—imbued the new art with the spirit of the older one. And
operas for a time seemed no more than extended intermezzi without any
troublesome legitimate play to interrupt the flow of scenes.

Aleotti was an architect as well as a designer. In 1606 he created an
intimate theatre at Sabbioneta and then was called to Parma where he
designed a large opera house in the Farnese palace. Instead of the five
openings at the Teatro Olimpico, the Teatro Farnese had one large
opening—a picture frame of the sort that was to dominate the European
theatre almost to the present time. Aleotti is also credited with the
invention of flat wings (simple canvas frames in grooves) which were
much easier to shift than Serlio's angle wings and provided more
flexibility than the periaktoi (revolving triangular prisms mentioned by
Vitruvius) which had figured in the experiments of other designers.

It now seems certain that Buontalenti, not Aleotti, invented flat wings,
but Aleotti did equip his new theatre at Parma with machinery which
made shifting quicker and easier.

In Aleotti's day, opera was still an aristocratic toy—produced only on
festival occasions. (Indeed the Teatro Farnese was completed in 1618,
but not used until needed for a wedding ten years later.) But news of
these private displays created a public demand. In 1637 an opera house
opened in Venice, and in the 1640's several others were built. The chief
designer in residence was Giacomo Torelli (1608-78). A clever
machinist, Torelli invented a chariot-counterweight system which greatly
improved the efficiency of *a vista* scene shifts in the new picure-frame
theatres.

It would be hard to exaggerate the importance of the great sixteenth-
century entertainments at the Medici court. The news of these events
spread throughout Europe and established a perspective scenery in the
Italian manner as the style of the future.

Of all the Florintine-based artists, Buontalenti was the most ingenious
and inventive. Here is A.M. Nagler's reconstruction of his finest
achievement—the 1589 intermezzi for *La Pellegina,* a comedy by
Girolamo Bargagli, as performed for the wedding celebration of Grand
Duke Ferdinand and Christine of Ferrara. The show took place in a
theatre in the Uffizi building, one which had been designed by
Buontalenti three years earlier for another ducal entertainment.

A.M. Nagler
INTERMEZZI FOR *LA PELLEGRINA*[*1]

The principal theatrical event of this "Maggio Fiorentino" was the performance of Girolamo Bargagli's comedy *La Pellegrina*, or more accurately, the attendant six intermezzi. As in 1586, Count Giovanni Bardi was commissioned to invent the ideas for the interludes. Warburg's investigations[2] furnish proof that on this occasion the Count succeeded in working out a coherent plan for the content of the six intermezzi, with the influence of music in the lives of the gods and men providing the continuity of theme. Emilio de' Cavaleri was entrusted with organizing the spectacle. Execution of the set designs once again lay in the hands of Bernardo Buontalenti.

[*]A.M. Nagler, *Theatre Festivals of the Medici*, 1539-1637 (New Haven & London: Yale University Press, 1964), pp. 70-92.

[1] Primary sources: [Bastiano de' Rossi] Descrizione / dell' Apparato, / e degl' Inter- / medi. / Fatti per la Commedia rappre- / sentata in Firenze. / Nelle nozze de' Serenissimi Don Ferdinando / Medici, e Madama Cristina di / Loreno, Gran Duchi di / Toscana. / In Firenze. Per Anton Padovani M.D. LXXXIX.

Diario / descritto / da Giuseppe / Pavoni / Delle feste celebrate nelle solennissime Nozze delliSerenissimi Sposi, il. Sig. Don Ferdinando Medici, & Sig. Donna Christina di Loreno Gran Duchi di Toscana. / Nel quale con breuita si esplica il Torneo, la Battaglia nauale, la Comedia con gli Intermedy, & attre feste occorse di giorno per tutto il di 15. di Maggio. MDLXXXIX. Alli molto illustri, & miei Patroni osservandiss. li Signori Giasone, & Pompeo fratelli de' Vizani. / Stampano in Bologna nella Stamperia di Giovanni Rossi, di permissione delli Signori Superiori. 1589.

Raccolta di tutte / le solenissime Feste / nel Sponsalitio / della Serenissima / Gran Duchessa / di Toscana / fatte in Fiorenza il mese di Maggio 1589. / Con brevita raccolte da Simone Cavallino da Viterbo. / All' Illustriss. et Revendiss. sig. Patriarca Alessandrino, Caetano. / In Roma / Appresso Poalo Baldo Stampatore Camerale 1589.

[Anon.] Li / sontuosissimi / apparecchi, / trionfi, e feste, / fatti nelle nozze / della Gran Duchessa / di Fiorenza: / Con il nome, & numoro de Duchi, Prencipi, Marchesi, Baroni, & altri gran Personaggi: postovi il modo del vestire, manirere, & livree. / Et la descrittione de gl'Intermedi rappresentati in una Comedia noblissima, recitata da gl'Intronati Senesi. / Aggiontovi l'ordine, & modo che s'e tenuto nel Coronare l'Altezza della Serenissima Gran Duchessa. / Stampata in Fiorenza, & in Ferrara per Vittoio Baldini. / Et ristampata in Venetia per Lodivico Larduccio. 1589.

A german observer at the performance of *La Pellegrina* was one Barthold von Gadentedt (1560-1631), who travelled throughnItaly in the years 1587-89, and whose manuscript journal has been preserved in the Herzog August Bibliothek in Wolfenbuttel (Cod. Guelf. 67.6 Extrav. fol.).

Warburg, in *Gesammelte Schriften*, I, 259-300, with addenda by the editor, Getrrud Bing, on pp. 394-422, and with excerts from the *Memorie e ricordi* of Girolamo Ser Jacopi (in the Archivio di Stato in Florence).

Angelo Solerti, *Gli Albori del melodramma*, 2 (Milan-Palermo-Napoli, 1904-05), 17-18: excerts from Settimani's Diario (in the Archivio di stato in Florence).

Emil Vogel, *Bibliothek der gedruckten weltlichen Volamusik Italiens 1500-1700*, I (Berlin, 1892), 382-85, with references to the musicians who collaborated in the "stampa musicale" edited by Cristofano Malvezzi: Canot / Intermedii / et Concerti, / Fatti per la Commedia rappresentata in / Fierenze / Nelle Nozze del serenissimo / Don Ferdinando Medici, / e Madama Christina di Loreno, Gran Duchi di Toscana. / in Venetia, / Appreso Giacomo Vincenti. / M.D. XCI

[2] Warburg, in Gesammelte Schriften I, 425.

The performance took place in the Uffizi Theatre.[3] The seating arrangement was the same as three years before, and the auditorium was again surrounded by degrees ("tutta circondata di gradi"), except, of course, for the side along the stage. Situated in the middle of the hall was the dais for princely personages. The dècor of the auditorium, however, differed from that of 1586. Lorenzo Francini and Francesco Rosselli contributed new paintings. Ideas for the new statues, in which the various arts of poetry were given concrete form, were conceived by Giovambattista Strozzi.[4] And when all of the torches in the hall seemed to light up by themselves,[5] the spectators were apparently stunned.

An oval staircase four ells high led up to the raked stage, which, at its highest point in the rear was elevated five ells above the auditorium floor. This time the stage had a depth of twenty-five ells, making it five ells deeper than in 1586. The breadth of the stage could not have exceeded thirty-five ells. A balustrade ran along its edge, with lamps built into the balusters[6] to illuminate the stage floor—in other words, footlights. The stage was closed off on each side by a gigantic statue of a river god: on one side, the Arno with winged heraldic lion and the lily; on the other, the Moselle, which irrigated the homeland of the new Grand Duchess. The latter was surrounded by herons, and a heron motif embellished the sixteen chandeliers (each with eighteen tapers) in the hall.

Before the performance began, the stage was draped across by a red house curtain.[7] Once this hanging had dropped,[8] the spectators viewed a painted prospect which contained the Corinthian architectural elements and gold tones of the auditorium, thus creating an "anfiteatro perfetto." Shortly afterward the second curtain likewise descended, exposing the first decor. We learn from Rossi's description that the audience was presented with a *veduta*[9] of Rome, and that Buontalenti, thanks to the skill of his perspective scene painting, was able to set the stage with the most imposing structures of the ancient and modern city.[10] It is notable that neither Giuseppe Pavoni nor the anonymous chronicler mention the

---

3 The following account is based on Rossi, *Descrizione dell' apparato.*

4 Ibid., pp. 8, 11-14.

5 Ibid., p. 15. Baldinucci, *Notizie*, 8, 53, states in his chapter on Buontalenti that these torches seemed to ignite themselves, and that no trace of "fuoco lavorato" was in evidence, causing no little astonishment among the spectators.

6 Rossi, *Apparato*, p. 35: "ogni balastro nascondea un lume."

7 Ibid., p. 16: "paramento incarnato"; Pavoni, p. 14: "tela rossa."

8 Pavoni, pp. 14-15: "mandate giu."

9 "View."

10 Rossi, *Apparato*, p. 17: "aueua l'Artefice con l'eccellenza dell'arte saputo adombrare il uero, e con lo sfondato allontanarne dagli occhi i piu nobili e piu superbi edifici antichi e moderni della sourana citta."

Roman perspective but refer instead to a "blue curtain"[11] which provided the backdrop for the lowering of a cloud machine.

FIRST INTERMEZZO: HARMONY OF THE SPHERES

The prelude to the first intermezzo evidently made use of the Roman background. In a downstage position stood a Doric temple built of ashlars. A cloud descended from the heavens, and on it sat the Doric Mode (Armonia Doria), accompanying her madrigal on a lute. On a lower level she was flanked on each side by three women who appeared to be attentive to her song. These were the six other Modes, the Phrygian, Lydian, Mixolydian, Hypodorian, Hypophrygian, and Hypolydian. The "Harmonies" were painted with the utmost verisimilitude.[12] Several sunbeams burst forth from behind the cloud, which was altogether "convincing," and the spectators were at a loss to say how it moved as it gradually floated to the earth, headed toward the temple, and then vanished into it, along with Armonia Doria. Immediately afterward, the temple also disappeared, perhaps into a trap, and the scene changed ("spari la scena di Roma") for the second part of the first intermezzo.

After a "cambio di case" the starry heavens appeared, with four clouds rising up. So realistic were these imitations that one might have expected rain at any moment. Sitting on the low-hovering clouds were the eight Platonic sirens, plus two others who belonged to the ninth and tenth spheres.[13] Following their madrigal, the heavens parted in three places, and three clouds issued from these openings. On the central cloud sat Necessity on her throne, holding the spindle of the cosmos between her knees. She was encircled by the three Parcae. Seated on the other two clouds were the seven Planets (Luna, Venus, Mars, Saturn, Mercury, Jupiter and Sol) and Astraea. The celestial background glowed brilliantly through the three apertures, at least toward the zenith; in the lower regions its luminescence was dimmed by the colors of the rainbow. On high were twelve heroes divided into pairs to portray the six virtues: Justice was represented by Numa Pompilius and the Egyptian Queen Isis; Religion by Masinissa and a Vestal Virgin; Piety by Aeneas and a devout young girl, who was noted by Valerius Maximus; Conjugal Love by Tiberius Gracchus and Portia; Magnanimity by Hieron, King of

---

[11] Pavoni, p.15: "tela azurra." Barthold von Gadenstedt alsomfails to mention the Roman decor in his journal (fol 671), but he does refer to the "blaue seidene Decke."

[12] Rossi, *Apparato*, pp. 18-19: "con tal rilieuo dipinte, che elle parnean uiue."

[13] To Gadenstedt (fol. 672) these were all simple "*Engell.*"

Syracuse, and by Busa, the Apulian woman who fed the Roman soldiers who had fled to Canusium after the battle of Cannae; Valor by Lucius Siccius Dentatus and Camilla.

The cloud-borne sirens ascended to the heavens, singing a musical exchange with the Planets. As the clouds rose from the lower part of the stage, sunlight streamed in, while in the upper regions night was swiftly approaching. After a concluding madrigal sung by the sirens, the Planets, and the Parcae, the seven clouds dispersed, the heavens closed, the stars grew pale, sunlight flooded the sky, and, as if by magic, a view of the city of Pisa appeared upon the stage. How did this scenic change take place? Rossi declares[14] that the clouds of the first intermezzo had concealed the Pisa setting and then merely disappeared. Thus the perspective of Pisa would have been built up behind the cloud decor, which had concealed ("coprieno") the veduta until the scene was changed. Pavoni,[15] however, describes the process as follows: "Et in vn tratto si volto la Scena, apperendo in prospettiua la Citta di Pisa."[16] According to the anonymous account: "subito si uolta la Prospettiua tutta e apparisce la Citta di Pisa." The use of the verb *voltarsi* may point to the utilization of a turning mechanism. And the German word, *umwenden*, employed by Barthold von Gadenstedt, tends to confirm this view.

We can trace the idea of the first intermezzo, the musical harmony of the cosmos, to concepts that Plato expounded in the tenth book of his *Republic*: a diamond spindle turns between the knees of Necessity, and on each of its eight whorls stands a siren, giving forth a tone to harmonize with the tones of her sisters, thus creating the harmonious music of the spheres. The Moirai, daughters of Necessity, sit at their mother's feet, accompanying the harmony of the sirens with their song. Lachesis sings of the past, Clotho of the present, and Atropos of the future. Even the celestial heroes were prefigured by Plato, and the invigorating Doric mode was admitted as a prelude to the intermezzo, because in his Utopia Plato gave it preferred status.

Count Bardi put such high demands on his audience that, in fact, only classical philologists could have followed him. As Rossi's erudite commentary did not appear until after the performance, we should not be surprised that Pavoni took no cognizance of the Platonic cosmos, but saw merely "il Paradiso."[17] Nor did he even grasp the Armonia Doria,

---

[14] Apparato, p.35: "sparite uia le nugole, che la [prospettiua[corpieno."
[15] p.25.
[16] "And all of a sudden the scene was turned, the City of Pisa appearing in perspective." (ed.)
[17] p. 15.

but saw only "vna donna" sitting on a cloud and singing "molto soauemente,"[18] a madrigal that ended in adulation of the bridal couple. To be sure, Pavoni recognized the Planets and could identify the sirens as well, probably because they were partly dressed as birds. Of Necessitas and the Parcae, however, he makes no mention. To the anonymous chronicler Armonia Doria was simply an "Idra" [Hydra] "quale canta sola eccellentissamente."[19] Simone Cavallino da Viterbo noticed only "una donna da angiola vestita."[20] and admired the singing of Vittoria Archilei.[21] As Warburg has pointed out,[22] not even the cultivated spectators could grasp the obtrusive symbolism of the costuming. But that would scarcely have perturbed Count Bardi, who may have shared the sentiments of Ben Jonson, as expressed, twenty years later, in his *Masque of Queens*: "A Writer should always trust somewhat to the capacity of the Spectator, especially at these Spectacles; Where Men, beside inquiring eyes, are vnderstood to bring quick eares, and not those sluggish ones of Porters and Mechanicks, that must be bor'd through, at euery act, with Narrations."

As to the costuming, a few examples should suffice here. Bardi envisaged Armonia Doria as a woman of imposing majesty. Thus she wore a dress of dark green velvet with ornaments of solid gold. Her girdle was set with precious stones, and seven jewels adorned her golden crown. For the attributes and the costume of Necessitas, Buontalenti followed the description of Horace, in his Ode to Fortuna (C.1.35): bronze hands holding two stout nails, such as one might use to fasten beams together; wedges (the "cunei" of Horace) and strong but light fetters, similar to the catgut with which criminals were bound; hooks and molten lead painted on her throne; a robe of grey satin with silver embellishments and a cypress crown; between her knees, the diamond spindle. The Parcae were dressed in white and wore headbands, just as Plato had pictured them. In order to heighten the effect,[23] Buontalenti embroidered some additional details. Each of the Planets had his particular "house" and was surrounded by an aureole which formed a

---

[18] "Very sweetly."

[19] "Who sings the aria excellently."

[20] "A woman dressed like an angel."

[21] Cavallino, p. 3. Neither did Barthold von Gadenstedt identify the Doric Mode, but he was transported by the loveliness of her singing.

[22] Warburg, in *Gesammelte Schriften*, I, 281.

[23] Rossi, *Apparato*, p. 25: "perche facesser piu bella vista."

kind of *mandorla*. Mars, for example, had his seat over a scorpion. His gilded armor, adorned with monsters, corresponded to Statius' description in the *Thebais*: a glowing helmet that seemed to be ablaze; a shield that appeared in a blood-red light. Painted on the seat was his chariot, drawn by two of the horses, Fear and Terror, mentioned by Homer. Winged Fama stood on the prow of the car as described by Virgil in the fourth book of the *Aeneid*. Ptolomy, Claudian, and Ovid were cited as authorities for the planet Luna, as were Suda and Pausanias for Jupiter.

It was impossible to grasp the significance of the heroes in the Platonic heavens without commentary. How should the spectators have identified the nobleman armed in African fashion, who wore a crown-shaped helmet and a purple cape over his sky-blue robe? The key to this baffling figure lay in the two elephant tusks in his right hand and the statue of religion in his left: he was Masinissa, a portrayal of the religious man who restored the tusks which had been stolen by one of his captains to their rightful place because sacrilege was abominable to him. With Aeneas, on the other hand, the spectators should have had less difficulty, for he carried an old man on his shoulders, a small child on his arm, and in his free hand held a naked sword.

Pictorial documentation for the first intermezzo is fairly extensive. A pen-and-ink wash drawing, preserved in the Victoria and Albert Museum, conveys an overall impression of the setting in impressionistic form. James Laver[24] is of the opinion that this is an original sketch by Buontalenti. There also exists an engraving by Agostino Caracci which, in contrast to the design, was executed with a strict central perspective. Necessitas and her spindle are identifiable both in the design and the engraving, while the remaining figures, the sirens, Planets, and heroes, are not recognizable as such. Details of the Planets' costumes, however, can be gleaned from two of Buontalenti's drawings in the Florentine National Library in which the attributes of the gods and Astraea are clearly intelligible. Other original sketches by Buontalenti for Necessitas and the Parcae, as well as for individual sirens, the Vestal Virgin of the heroes' heavens, and Armonia Doria, are preserved in Florence. For the first intermezzo forty-five costumes in all were fitted, as indicated in the

[24] "Stage Designs for the Florentine Intermezzi of 1589," *Burlington Magazine*, 60 (1932), 294-300.

Libro di Conte,[25] which has been examined by Warburg. This account book, in the Florentine municipal archives, contains a summary of the fabrics used, daily notations of the tailors' wages, and entries concerning the production of the plays. The two tailors, Oreto Belardi and Niccolo Serlosi, were responsible for sewing the costumes with the help of fifty assistants. The account book yields information only concerning those singers who participated in the first intermezzo.[26] With the exception of Armonia Doria, sung by Vittoria Archelei, all the roles were filled by male singers. The Planets, sirens, Parcae, heroes, and Necessitas were portrayed by members of the court chapel of the Grand Duke or by singers from Bernardo Franciosino's musical academy. A few independent artists also took part. Masks were prepared for all the participants. Moreover, in order to rid the singers of their masculine appearance, paper-mache breasts and chests ("poppo e petti di cartone") were fitted on them.[27] The sirens' costume presented a special problem: as they were birdlike creatures, feathers were required, but real plume would have been too costly. Therefore, the tailors were instructed to fashion them out of canvas and paint them accordingly.[28]

Gertrud Bing has disclosed one of the most important sources of the performance in her supplement to Warburg's essay. This contains excerpts from the *Memorie e ricordi* [*Memoirs and Recollections*] by Girolamo Ser Jacopi, the engineer-commandant of the fortifications, who was entrusted with supervising the technical production of the intermezzi. His notes permit us to take a look behind the wings. Ser Jacopi took Buontalenti's directives and noted the wishes of Emilio de' Cavalieri, functioning as an intermediary between the set designer and stage manager on the one hand, and the craftsmen and stage crew on the other. Buontalenti chose the technicians who were to operate the machines of the first intermezzo. According to Ser Jacopi's entries, some of the crew members were responsible for setting the cloud of Signora Vittoria in motion; others had to man the windlasses ("arghani") by means of which the clouds holding the sirens were lowered; a third detachment stood ready by the grooves in which the shutter was pushed

[25] Warburg, in *Gesammelte Schriften*, I, 275-76.
[26] Cf. the list in Warburg-Bing, in ibid., p. 398.
[27] Warburg, p. 431.
[28] Ibid.

to expose the central opening in the heavens.[29] Other workers were posted expressly for the purpose of lighting and watching over the oil lamps ("lucerne"); they were admonished to exercise the utmost care in trimming the wicks and refilling ("riempiere") the lamps. One of the artisans was commissioned to camouflage the ropes ("canapi") and beams ("travi") of the clouds with felt. One painter had to add another coat of paint to the spindle to give it a more diamond-like appearance. Even the musical instruments were embellished with golden rays. In his notes Ser Jacopi never refers to the right or left sides of the stage but rather to "the side where the rooms of the *zanni* [clowns] are located"— i.e., where the dressing rooms were, or to "the side toward the corridor."[30]

The lyrics of Armonia Doria's madrigal, written by Giovanni Bardi, were set to music by Emilio de' Cavalieri.[31] Vittoria accompanied herself on a *leuto grosso* [large lute] supported by two *chitarroni* [guitars] played backstage by her husband and Antonio Naldi.[32] The texts of the subsequent madrigals were written by Ottavio Rinuccini, with music by Cristofano Malvezzi.[33]

THE SETTING FOR *LA PELLEGRINA*

Pisa supplied the locale for Bargagli's comedy. The spectators saw the cathedral with its leaning tower, the Church of San Giovanni, the noble edifice of the Campo Santo, the palace of the Knights of the Holy Order of St. Stephan and its church, and many other structures designating the quarter known as Lungarno, all of them "maestreuolmente Contrafatte."[34] Concealed illumination ("nascosi lumi") intensified the effect of perspective depth ("la lontanezza che procedeua sfondato"). Everything was calculated to gently deceive ("dolce inganno") the spectators' senses. Buontalenti achieved this through a combination of curved and straight lines ("linee rette"): into the rectangular open space issued curved lanes ("le strade di linea curva"). Rossi assures us that Buontalenti was the first set designer to build a decor using a combination of straight lines and curves. He mentions further "tre fori,"

[29] "Le guide della bucha del mezzo nelle aperature del cielo."
[30] And where the musicians, also, played.
[31] Rossi, *Apparato*, p. 19.
[32] Vogel, *Bibliothek, I*, 383.
[33] For the instrumentation, cf. ibid., pp. 383-84.
[34] "Counterfeited in a masterly manner."

which enable us to posit the existence of a back scene constructed in the form of a tripartite screen. The downstage houses ("le prime case") were twenty ells high. Further upstage the height of the houses was scaled down as demanded by the vanishing point ("sou punto"). The style of architecture was Tuscan, mixed with Doric, Ionic, and Corinthian, or an amalgam of these elements.

During each intermezzo this "great machine" ("così gran macchina") was transformed *à vista*. In this way, the architect displayed seven settings ("prospettiue") with rapidity and ease and without the slightest incident, so that the spectators had the feeling that it was all taking place as in a dream (Rossi). In addition to the lightning-swift ("come baleno") transformations, there was the astonishing effect of flying machines which rose out of the earth and into the heavens, thence to descend earthward again, frequently after soaring over the stage in all directions. These maneuvers were all the more astounding in that the clouds were always loaded with performers. Buontalenti took every precaution to place the costumes designed by him in their proper light. Each flying machine contained an abundance of lamps. The lateral dècor pieces for the intermezzi were illuminated by lamps mounted on the back walls of the houses in the Pisa setting ("appiccati alle case"); these light sources were moveable ("mobili") and could be rotated ("uoltando"). When permanently attached to the main setting, such lamps are hardly compatible with the use of periaktoi, whereas they could be reconciled with an embryonic flat-wing system. We would thus find a fixed Pisa setting, in which the side houses would be covered ("coprire") during the intermezzi by projecting frames of painted canvas. This explains how the lamps, fastened to the rear of the permanent Pisa elements, cast light on the intermezzo wings. Rossi also informs us of the method used to light up the heavens ("Cielo"). For reasons of ventilation, the sky was perforated ("tutto sfondato"). In each of the apertures lamps were concealed, so that the heavens could be made to shine with the brightness of day. I assume that Rossi here uses the expression "Cielo" in the sense of a gridiron. The chimneys of the city smoked ("fumicanti, quasi naturali, cammini"), but it was a perfumed smoke, the aroma of which was wafted out into the audience. The addition of the chimneys to the houses created some difficulties. From Ser Jacopi's notes[35] we discover that during a rehearsal Cavalieri objected that "le case della prospettiva" had been improperly set up, thus marring the view of the

[35] Warburg-Bing, in *Gesammelte Schriften, I*, 402.

clouds. A carpenter was commissioned to install practicable doors in the first two houses, thus enabling the actors ("istrioni") to make their entrances and exits.[36]

SECOND INTERMEZZO:
CONTEST OF THE PIERIDES AND THE MUSES

Now the Pisa veduta transformed itself into a garden "which covered the houses [of Pisa],"[37] so that no part of the city remained in view. Orange and lemon trees grew in the garden landscape, as did cedars, with many trees in blossom and others already laden with fruit. Perfumed water was sprayed in order to sustain the illusion. Vine leaves were entwined in trellises; low hedges ran along the ground; aromatic plants were set in ornamental urns; jasmine was planted between the rose bushes; and flowers sprouted from the lawn. Apart from the luxuriant flora, there were also representatives of the animal kingdom: hares, hedgehogs, tortoises, and, perched on the trees, birds whose song was deceptively imitated. Moreover, a "Sinfonia" was played by "dua [sic] Arpe, due Lire, un Basso di viola, due Leuti, un violino, una Viola bastarda, & un Chitarrone."

The spectators were given time to feast their eyes on Buontalenti's scenery. Then the stage floor opened, and from the trap arose a mountain, overgrown with vegetation, attaining the impressive height of twelve ells. This seemed all the more astounding in that the trap room itself was only about five ells high. On this Mount Helicon sat sixteen hamadryads on stony seats covered with blossoms. Before the machine had risen to its full altitude, a moss-covered grotto opened on each side.[38] In the right grotto sat the nine daughters of Pierus, and in the left, the nine Muses, for this was the intermezzo in which the song contest between the Muses and the Pierides, as well as the eventual metamorphosis of the haughty challengers into magpies, took place. The tree nymphs officiated as judges. After a madrigal by the Pierides came the song of the Muses. The texts for these madrigals were written by Ottavio Rinuccini, to music by Luca Marenzio. The Pierides were

---

[36] Ibid., p. 401.

[37] Rossi, Apparato, p. 37: "che ricoperse in modo le case." Pavoni, p. 15, only has: "si mutta la prospettiua."

[38] The anonymous description mentions 18 "musichi" who sat on the mountain and sang. During the madrigal, "subito si uolta prospettiua da due bande, e ne nasce due antri," with twelve musicians in each one. The "suito si uolta" indicates that Buontalenti was here working with miniature revolving stages, a method which was later adopted by Inigo Jones as *machina versatilis* for his *Masque of Queens* (1609) and by Tommaso Francini for his *Ballet de la delivrance de Renaud* (1617). Barthold von Gadenstedt mentions the fact that at the end the two side grottos closed again: "und die 2 kleinen berge auch weider vmbgewendet."

transformed into magpies in full view of the spectators. Croaking and chattering, they hopped about before taking off for the forest, just as Ovid had related in the fifth book of his *Metamorphoses*. We thus have an *à vista* change of costume such as Buontalenti had already successfully carried out in 1569, when, in the Leto intermezzo, peasants were metamorphosed into frogs. At length the mountain vanished, probably by sinking into the trap room, and the garden "dissolved" ("dileguarsi").

The sixteen hamadryads, musical instruments in their hands, wore satin costumes of a single cut but varying iridescent hues: dark blue, red, purple, white, green, yellow, sky blue, and orange. Their blond locks cascaded over their shoulders, and their headdresses consisted of gold or silver veils. They wore chaplets of oak leaves because, according to Ovid's fable of Erysichthon, they dwelled in oak trees. Buontalenti added embroidery to give their tucked-up costumes a barklike appearance. The pierides wore satin costumes of varying colors richly trimmed with embroidery. To emphasize their vanity, they were laden with gold ornaments and jewelry. Since they wore masks, they could be ranked by age, the youngest being about fifteen years old, the eldest twenty-three. In contrast to the Pierides, the Muses were dressed with simplicity: cloaks of green velvet; inner garments of a pink and white iridescent material, embellished with a beautiful border; and a "simple" headdress, but one which glittered nonetheless with gold and jewels, and, of course, had a veil. Their headpieces were made of colorful sirens' feathers, and they carried musical instruments.

Buontalenti's pen-and-ink wash drawing for the second intermezzo has been preserved in the Victoria and Albert Museum. In the center we see the mount of the hamadryads, with the Pierides on one side and the Muses on the other. The side grottos are not visible. We also possess Buontalenti's detailed design for the hamadryad's mountain. Only twelve of the nymphs are provided for in this sketch, while Rossi mentions sixteen, and the anonymous chronicler eighteen. Further costume designs for a Pieride, a Muse, and a magpie may be found in the Florentine National Library. In 1592 Epifanio d'Alfiano made an engraving which differs essentially from both the original design and Rossi's description. Warburg[39] has pointed out the differences and accounted for them by the fact that the picture was engraved three years after the event. It shows Apollo on the peak of the mountain, with the

[39] In *Gesammelte Schriften, I,* 298-99.

Muses sitting in three rows, and beneath them in a grotto, the Spirit of
the Castalian spring. Nine other deities are situated in two grottos to the
right and left, perhaps the hamadryads, while the Pierides, transformed
into magpies, frolic about.

We learn from Ser Jacopi's entries that the crew stood ready to
uncover the stage ("scoprire il palco")[40] so that the mountain could be
raised. Other workers operated a small winch ("verricellino") in order to
thrust up the "beginning of the mountain ("il principo del monte"). A
much larger windlass was probably required to lift the main bulk of the
mountain; in any case, supports ("puntelli") were used to hold it in place
after its ascent.

THIRD INTERMEZZO:
APOLLO'S SLAYING OF THE PYTHON

After the disappearance of the mountain and the garden, the Pisa
setting returned ("ritorno la scena al primiero modo"), and the second act
of Bargagli's comedy began. At the end of this act "the houses were
again covered ("furono ricoperte le case"), this time with oak, chestnut,
beech, and other trees, and the entire stage was transmuted into a sylvan
glade ("tutta la scena divento bosco").[41] Rossi's wording, "ricoperte le
case," again indicates that painted frames were shoved out in front of the
Pisa scene, for we may not assume that Buontalenti was here following
the method described by Sabbattini in Chapter 5 of the second book of
his *Practica*.[42] In the middle of the boscage was a gloomy, rocky cave,
from which the surrounding vegetation seemed to have been burned off,
in contrast to the trees standing farther away, which were green and
heavy with fruit, and whose tops seemed to touch the sky.[43]

Eighteen Delphic men and women entered in couples from the left, in
pseudo-Greek robes that differed from each other only in color and
ornamentation. In their madrigal they alluded to the dragon that was
devastating the countryside. As they sang, another nine couples appeared
from the opposite side, and in their madrigal they likewise made mention
of the Python. then the beast itself emerged, thrusting its ghastly head

---

[40] Warburg-Bing, in ibid., p. 403.

[41] Pavoni, p. 16, simply states: "si muta la Scena a guisa selua."

[42] Sabbattini recommended this method only when the upper ridges of the house frames
were straight; in any case, no chimneys could be tolerated; Buontalenti's Pisa houses,
however, had chimneys. Neither could this be achieved by Sabbattini's second method of
changing scenes, but it was possible to attain this effect by pushing forward painted flats.

[43] Rossi, *Apparato*, p. 42.

out of the cavern's mouth to sun itself for a while.[44] Perceiving the "drago d'inestimabil grandezza" ["a dragon of tremendous size"] the Delphic couples began to pray for liberation from the monster. With a single thrust, it issued from its lair and spread its wings, which were spangled with mirrors. Its body was a color between green and black. Its gaping jaws were set with three rows of teeth. Catching sight of the humans, the Python began to emit flames, and its tongue glowed. But Apollo, armed with bow and arrow, was already soaring down from above. Now began the Pythian combat as described by Julius Pollux. Five stages could be distinguished. At first, Apollo scanned the terrain to determine whether it was suitable for doing battle. In the second phase he antagonized the dragon. In the third, he fought in iambic rhythm. The fourth part of the struggle was conducted in spondaic rhythm, ending with the triumph of the god and the death of the monster. In the concluding stage Apollo executed a swift victory dance. The spectators marveled at the rapidity with which Apollo descended from the heavens: a ray of light could not have traveled more swiftly; and their astonishment was all the greater in that they were at a loss to discover how the god—a puppet—had been kept aloft. The "Apollo finto" landed behind the stage, and promptly a dancer personifying the god appeared to carry out the combat in pantomime. Apollo wore a golden robe. In order not to impede the dancer, the traditional aureole was omitted. In the recognition sequence he danced with consummate skill about the dragon from a certain distance. He then made his challenge, posing valiantly as the beast hissed, gnashed its teeth, and beat its wings. The actual fight was waged once again through the medium of the dance. Apollo drove his arrows into the dragon's back, and the monster broke them off as inky blood gushed from its wounds. The howling serpent pursued its antagonist until it finally expired. At the end of his dance of victory, Apollo planted his foot on the dragon's head. Four Delphians who had been following the struggle from the edge of the forest now approached the beast, which lay in a pool of black blood. They summoned their companions and sang a hymn to Apollo. Meanwhile, the dragon was removed from the stage, and Apollo began a dance of joy. The intermezzo concluded with a second hymn by the Delphians, composed by Luca Marenzio.

Count Bardi had prescribed Hellenic costumes ("abiti tendenti al greco")[45] for the choral singers, but gave Buontalenti freedom to choose

---

[44] Rossi mentions, p. 43, "lo splendore della cosi bene allumata scena."
[45] Ibid., p. 46.

his colors, leaving them to the "discrezion dell' Artefice."[46] Just as in their own day the theologians had stood guard over the use of symbols in Christian art, prescribing the elements of iconography for medieval artists, so Bardi, the "theologian" of ancient myth, kept strict account of every detail, insisting that the Delphic couples be distinguished by some sort of "cose marine," whether headpieces of coral branches or sea-shell ornamentation. For Bardi was aware that the Pythian combat had taken place in Delos and that certain writers ascribed the founding of Delos or Delphi to Delphus, a son of Neptune, whence the "cose marine."

A pen-and-ink wash drawing by Buontalenti for the third interlude is preserved in the Victoria and Albert Museum in London. The Florentine National Library possesses the artist's drawings for Apollo and the dragon, as well as designs for the costumes of the Delphic couples and for an Apollo costume. Apollo's assault from the air was given permanence in an engraving by Agostino Caracci. While Caracci's monster shows great similarity to Buontalenti's original, the engraver's Delphic couples bear no resemblance to the costume designer's sketches. Thirty-eight costumes were sewn for this third intermezzo.

A few technical details for which we are indebted to Ser Jacopi: stage hands were directed to push the shutter ("sportello") away from the opening through which the dragon emerged;[47] a skeleton ("ossatura") was made for the monster, with head and paws fabricated out of paper-mache, a task assigned to Valerio Cioli, who had acquired a reputation as a restorer of antiques; the dragon's head was 1 3/4 ells long and 1 1/8 high; the paws were 1 1/2 ells high;[48] and the "Apollo finto" was suspended by an iron wire.

FOURTH INTERMEZZO: THE INFERNO

After the third act of the comedy, before the setting changed ("auanti che si muta la prospettiua"),[49] a kind of prelude to the fourth intermezzo took place still within the Pisa veduta. A sorceress in the person of Lucia Caccini appeared on a flying machine.[50] Her golden chariot was set with precious stones. She wore an unbelted robe of green velvet, her tangled hair fell down around her shoulders, and a bright blue veil billowed from her head down to her unshod feet. In her right hand the Maga held a lash,

[46] "Discretion of the craftsmen."
[47] Warburg-Bing, in *Gesammelte Schriften, I*, 403.
[48] Ibid., p. 400.
[49] Rossi, *Apparato*, p. 49.
[50] Pavoni, p. 17: "in aria." Barthold von Gadenstedt mistook the sorceress for the goddess Juno.

and with her left she curbed two (according to Gadenstedt, three) winged dragons which stuck out their tongues, spewing flames. This was intended to give the impression that the monsters were panting with effort. When the car reached the middle of the stage, the sorceress forced the animals to halt. She reached for her lute, which she kept in the chariot, and began to accompany her own song. At the same time, she crossed over the stage to conjure up the fire demons to which Plato alludes in several passages. After her madrigal of conjuration, she climbed back into her car and lashed the dragons, which shook their heads madly, champing their bits.

The car withdrew and a fiery sphere ("un monte di fuoco") appeared in the air, which, having reached the middle of the stage, opened to form a crescent.[51] In it stood the demons whom the Maga had conjured up, singing a madrigal. Their red taffeta wings were spangled with silver and trimmed with blue feathers. Their long crinkly hair seemed to be made of silver and fire. An intense glow was seen on their faces (probably masks). Their silver brocade surcoats reached down to the middle of their thighs, and their undergarments of gold and green silk came to the knees. Their azure foot-coverings were worked in gold. The overall impression was one of angels from paradise. After the madrigal, the cloud closed and withdrew, thus ending the prelude.

In an instant the stage was covered ("la scena in uno stante fu coperta tutta")[52] with fiery rocks, chasms, and caverns, from which flames leapt and smoke billowed up. The stage floor opened ("s'aperse il palco"), disclosing an inferno from which two hosts of demons and Furies emerged. These were melancholy devils who sat on the rocks (which must, therefore, have been three-dimensional), with tormented looks, lamenting their fate in a madrigal. Two of the Furies wore tights of a sooty flesh color, making them appear naked. Their unclean, sagging breasts were entwined with serpents, and their hands and faces were smeared with blood. They shook their snaky locks with wild abandon. Instead of girdles, they wore serpents to cover their pudenda. The winged devils had eagles' claws on their hands and feet, and wore silk tights that gave the appearance of snakeskin. Two horns projected from their unkempt hair. Distinguished from the Furies by the fewer number of serpents coiled on their bodies were two other female *maschere* [masked figures]. The devils and the Furies stood on the right side, while on the left stood a similar group of lemures.

---

[51] According to Pavoni, however, p.18: "facendo la vista sua triangolare."
[52] Rossi, *Apparato*, p.51.

The hell itself was "tutto fuoco e fiamma" ["all flame and fire"]. Souls stood in the crackling flames undergoing torment by devils. Charon was visible in his bark at the mouth of hell, just as Dante described him in the third canto of the *Inferno*: with a white beard and flaming wheels for eyes, he kept striking at recalcitrant souls with his fiery oar. In the midst of the inferno stood Lucifer, with his torso rising out of a circular lake to a height of eight ells—another echo from Dante (*Inferno*, Canto 34, vv.55-60), whose visions guided the designer. Lucifer had three faces, the foremost red as blood, the one over the left shoulder black, and the right one white and yellow. Beneath each of the faces were two bat wings, and over the forehead was a great comb, borrowed from Dante. The Prince of Darkness was sheathed in a furry garment of sooty appearance. While he was busy devouring souls, an activity also alluded to by Dante, two of them, portrayed by agile children ("certi fanciuletti assai destri") slipped out of his maw. They were soon recaptured, however, by two small devils, one of whom impaled one of the fugitives on a kind of pitchfork and stuffed him into Lucifer's jaws, while the other seized the second soul with his claws, and since he could not reach up into those same jaws, clambered onto Lucifer's wooly flanks and climbed until he could cram the soul into one of his other mouths. At Lucifer's right stood Geryon, king of the legendary island of Erythea, who, by his friendliness, lured strangers to his table and then slew them. Dante also includes him in the seventeenth Canto of his *Inferno*. Buontalenti had been advised by Bardi to give that giant a kind-looking face but the tail of a serpent and scorpion (again as envisaged by Dante). Minos, too, was in the Uffizi inferno, wearing a purple robe and a royal crown on his head; his unusually long tail was derived from the fifth Canto of the *Inferno*, in which it figures as a signpost for the damned. Harpies and Centaurs also inhabited this hell, as well as the Minotaur, Cerberus, and their ilk. The souls were held fast in the frozen lake, some of them immersed up to their necks, others up to their breasts; here and there individual limbs projected from the ice. Scarcely had the demonic singers on the rocks finished their mournful song than they plunged howling into the abyss. Lucifer too was swallowed up, and the inferno closed ("si richiuse lo'nferno"). The rocks and chasms "dissolved" ("dileguarono"), and the Pisa setting returned for the fourth act of the comedy.

No original sketches exist for the fourth intermezzo,[53] but, fortunately, we are in possession of an engraving by Epifanio d'Alfiano which brings the hell scene to life for us. Soaring aloft are the demons of the region of

[53] For the Prelude to the fourth intermezzo the Cabinet des Dessins of the Louvre possesses a drawing (pen and ink, with watercolor) ascribed to Buontalenti. The attribution is questionable. If we are to accept the Buontalenti drawings in the Victoria and Albert Museum as genuine, the Louvre montage can hardly be claimed as typical of the artist's style. A reproduction of the Louvre design may be found in Jean Jacquot, ed., *La vie theatrale au temps de la Renaissance* (Paris, 1963), Pl. 8, facing p. 95.

fire. In the middle stands the Maga on her dragon car, and beneath her, three-headed Lucifer, encircled by devils who torment the singers. Here again we have a composite design, with the scenes which unfolded in temporal sequence placed in simultaneous juxtaposition.

A partial record of the tasks allocated to individual stage workers is contained in Ser Jacopi's *Memorie*. The stage had to be uncovered ("scoprire il palco") so that Lucifer, drawn up by means of a winch ("verricello"), could emerge from the trap. However, since the trap was so large that one could see into it, the trap room had to be painted so as to simulate another part of the inferno ("Dipignere l'inferno di dentro cioe sotto il palco"). Some members of the crew were directed to open the mouth of hell ("Per aprire la bocha del Inferno").[54] Others cut figures out of pasteboard ("dintornare").[55] At a rehearsal it was discovered that the Maga's cloud did not stand out boldly enough from the celestial background; hence its outlines had to be accentuated by further painting. The viols and trombones were camouflaged to resemble serpents. Forty-two costumes were fashioned for the fouth intermezzo. Giovambattista Strozzi wrote the texts to the madrigals. The Maga's song was set to music by Giulio Caccini,[56] the subsequent madrigals by Cristofano Malvezzi, and the dirge of the mournful demons by Giovanni Bardi.

FIFTH INTERMEZZO: THE RESCUE OF ARION

Once again "la scena si coperse tutta,"[57] this time with side scenes on which reefs had been painted. The stage floor ("il palco") transformed itself into a surging sea contained by the lateral reefs. Small barks were visible in the distance, tossing on the waves; thus depth of perspective ("lo sfondato") was achieved. A mother-of-pearl shell, five ells wide and three high, emerged from the sea. It was drawn by two dolphins which bounded ahead, squirting perfumed water in the air. In the shell sat Vittoria Archilei as Amphitrite in a seamless flesh-colored sheath, which, for feigned nudity, left nothing to the imagination. She wore a blue-green cape embroidered with snails, shells, and fish, a headdress of coral branches, a mother-of-pearl crown, and shoes that resembled fish with silver scales. Pearls adorned her neck and ear lobes, and coral hung

---

[54] Warburg-Bing, in *Gesammelte Schriften*, I, 405.
[55] Ibid., p. 403.
[56] Rossi, Apparato, p. 50.
[57] "The stage was completely covered."

on her arms.

Fourteen Tritons and an equal number of naiads arose simultaneously with the shell. The Tritons wore garlands of sedge in their blue hair, which dripped as they came up between the waves. Their tails were of turquoise-colored satin, trimmed with silver scales. The nymphs were as "nude" as Amphitrite, but they wore neither crown nor pearls. The sea gods carried instruments on which they began to play. Amphitrite accompanied herself on a lute, alluding in her madrigal to the Medici nuptials. A musical compliment to the newlyweds was also paid by the naiads. Finally, the Tritons amused themselves by splashing each other in the water.

At length the water gods submerged, and a well-fitted galley appeared, its crew plowing through the waves with their oars. The vessel was completely equipped with mast, yards, sails, oars, and anchor. It was fifteen paces ("passi andanti") long, and correspondingly broad and high. With its crew of forty, the ship executed various maneuvers: for example, it pointed its prow toward the princely personages in the auditorium; and all sails were struck in homage to the bridal couple. Arion was aboard the vessel, returning to Corinth. This role was played by Jacopo Peri, who also sang "con mirabil attentione di gli ascoltanti,"[58] an aria which he himself composed. Here Bardi followed the narrative in Plutarch's *Moralia*. The singer stood on the gilded poop with his harp, attired like the ancient poet in red-gold brocade and the customary laurel wreath. When the crew was just about to [pounce on him with their knives, Arion plunged into the sea, and the water sprayed high in the air. He emerged again, riding on the back of a dolphin. But the sailors believed him dead and sang a merry tune, feeling themselves secure in the possession of his treasure. According to Pavoni,[59] the ship executed a few more turns before departing through the "strada" by which it had entered.

We are in possession of Epifanio d'Alfiano's engraving of this décor. Six of Buontalenti's costume designs relating to the intermezzo are preserved in the Florentine National Library; the costume for Arion and one for a sea nymph, as well as four costume sketches for sailors. Ser Jacopi informs us that the dolphin was four ells in length, fabricated of papier-mâché, and covered with silver foil ("Stagnuolare con argento il delfino").[60] Arion-Peri's harp was made of pasteboard. The naiads' musical instruments were fashioned to resemble shells. The ships tossing about in the distance were cut from pasteboard and moved in grooves ("canali in sul palco"). Once again the texts for the madrigals were furnished by Rinuccini, with music by Christofano Malvezzi (except for Arion's solo).

SIXTH INTERMEZZO: ASSEMBLY OF THE GODS

After the last line of the comedy had been spoken, the stage was filled with clouds ("ricoperta tutta la scena"). The heavens opened, revealing a consistory of some twenty pagan deities which shone so radiantly that Rossi was reminded of some verses from Dante's *Paradiso*. Seven clouds appeared through openings, each of them adorned with blossoms, alluding to Dante's "nuvola di fiori." Five clouds descended to earth, and two remained hovering aloft. The cloud in the central aperture was larger than the others and held Apollo, Bacchus, Harmony, and Rhythm. On a second one, next to the first but somewhat lower, stood the three Graces. The Muses were scattered over several. Here the myth as told in Plato's *Laws* was brought to visual realization: taking pity on the harassed human race, Jupiter had given Apollo, Bacchus, and the Muses his mandate to dispatch Harmony and Rhythm to earth, so that men could obtain relief from their burdens in singing and dancing. As the five clouds descended in a slow tempo, a host of winged *amoretti* held fast to their festoons of blossoms, thus giving the impression that they were supporting the clouds. The first madrigal was sung by Apollo; the second by the three Graces and three of the Muses, and the third by the six remaining Muses scattered on the two lower-hanging clouds. Twenty pairs of mortals simultaneously appeared in pastoral dress. Lured by the sweet music issuing from the clouds, they came on stage from four directions. As soon as the clouds touched down upon the stage, the gods alighted and the clouds disappeared "as in a flash" ("come baleno."). A ballet of nymphs and shepherds concluded the evening.

A pen-and-ink wash drawing by Buontalenti is preserved in the Victoria and Albert Museum, and a sketch for an Apollo in the Florentine National Library may have been drawn for this intermezzo. Gertrud Bing discovered a Fortuna design by Buontalenti in the London collection of Henry Oppenheimer.[61] In all events, ninety costumes were prepared for the final intermezzo. Epifanio d'Alfiano has captured the

[61] Ibid., Pl. 53, Ill. 94.

spirit of this scene with an engraving.

The texts for the madrigals were composed by Ricuccini and the music by Malvezzi. For the final dance *canzone*, set to music by Emilio de' Cavalieri, the words were contributed by Laura Lucchesini. One could hear the voices of Vittoria Archelei and Lucia and Margherita Caccini in the *terzetti*. [62]

On the sixth and thirteenth of May the intermezzi were repeated, but no longer in connection with *La Pellegrina*. Since the Comici Gelosi, then the most celebrated of the commedia dell' arte troupes, had arrived in Florence, the Grand Duke proposed that the impromptu comedians perform a comedy "à gusto loro."[63] The choice of a piece presented difficulties, inasmuch as the troupe then had two prima donnas, Isabella Andreini, a permanent member of the Gelosi, and Vittoria Pissimi, who had evidently left the Confidenti troupe temporarily and joined the Gelosi. As was to be expected, the rivalry between the two leading ladies was pronounced, with the result that Vittoria insisted on appearing in her star role in *La Zingara*, while Isabella wished to display her talents in her showpiece, *La Pazzia*. Finally, the problem was solved by permitting Vittoria to appear in *La Zingara* on the sixth of May, while the thirteenth was reserved for Isabella's *La Pazzia*. On both occasions Bardi's intermezzi were repeated.

Pavoni calls Vittoria's portrait of the gypsy woman a "cosa rara & marauigliosa,[64] but the real sensation was Isabella's "madwoman." Pavoni outlines[65] the plot of the *Pazzia* as follows: Isabella, the only daughter of Pantalone de' Bisognosi, and Fileno, a stalwart young man, fall in love. Isabella's maid and Fileno's manservant do the same. Meanwhile, a student by the name of Flavio loses his heart to Isabella, but his love goes unrequited, as she cares only for Fileno. When Fileno sends a confidant to Pantalone to ask him for the hand of his daughter and is informed that he is too young to marry Isabella, the lovers resolve to flee. While they are discussing the means for carrying out the elopement and agree upon a sign of recognition for Fileno, Flavio overhears them. Somewhat before the scheduled rendezvous with Fileno, Flavio appears and gives the stipulated sign. Isabella comes out of her father's house and flees with Flavio, whom she believes to be Fileno. A few moments later, when Fileno appears in front of the house, he finds— instead of his beloved—the maid, vainly searching for her mistress.

---

[62] Vogel, *Bibliothek*, p. 385. ["Trio"]
[63] Pavoni, p. 29. ["To their liking."]
[64] Ibid., p. 30.
[65] Ibid., pp. 44-46.

Fileno grows frenzied, and Isabella likewise loses her reason when she discovers that her abductor is Flavio. In her madness, she begins to soliloquize in various tongues—Spanish, Greek, and French. To the great delight of Christine of Lorraine, Isabella also sang in French. She then imitated her fellow actors by speaking in the accents of Pantalone, Gratiano, the Zanni, and Il Capitano. At length a potion is given to her which restores her sanity. She then proclaims "con elegante & dotto stile" the joys and torments of love. The eloquent art of Isabella Andreini absolutely transported the spectators.

On the eleventh of May, in the Pitti Palace,[66] the tourney and sea battle took place. A red ceiling cloth closed off the cortile above. 600 white tapers and 410 oil lamps provided the illumination. Grandstands for the ladies were set up beneath the loffias. Guests by invitation had to establish their identities upon entering with "segni di Porcellana." In front of the arcades and along the Boboli side a bulkhead was built up to a height of three ells and caulked with pitch ("bittumata"), so that no open joints remained. This was to prepare for the naumachy that followed the tourney. On the garden side, a fortress was constructed which was to be defended by Turks. Just as the tilt was about to start, a thundershower broke out which lasted for an hour and played havoc with the scenery. Worst of all, the downpour prematurely innundated the cortile. Two hundred bags of sawdust were procured to dry it out. After this delay, the tilt could begin. The participants rode in on *carri trionfali* ["triumphal chariots"] which brought them in with an abundance of scenic surprises. On one of the cars a sorcerer appeared, muttering conjurations. Another chariot, in which musicians were concealed, was pulled by a huge dragon. The challenge in front of the Turkish fortress was executed by the Duke of Mantua and Pietro de' Medici. For the next surprise, a mountain conceived as Aetna was shoved into the arena. As it opened to face the bride, two knights descended. After a brief jousting prelude, other cars were drawn into the cortile, decorated with fountains, clouds, shrubbery, animals, ships, boulders, sirens, giant birds, and elephants. One of the vehicles was drawn in by two "lions" and two "bears." Cavallino informs us[67] that for this purpose four donkeys were covered with bearskins and the hides of lions. Don Virginio enjoyed himself in the role of Mars, making his entrance on a vast mountain pulled by a crocodile. But the greatest excitement was caused by a garden which, propelled by invisible forces, moved into the courtyard and unfolded on all sides to the twittering of birds. In the garden were imitations of towers, fortresses, pyramids, ships, horsemen, and animals,

---

[66] For the following, cf. ibid., pp. 35-43.
[67] p. 43.

all made out of greenery ("fatto di verdura"). A cloud of birds swarmed up before the Grand Duchess, and one of the animals landed in the bride's lap, a good omen. Then began the joust with pikes and rapiers, concluded by fireworks that suddenly blazed up from the barriers.

While the spectators retired to the palace to fortify themselves with a repast, the cortile was transformed into a basin. Water gushed into the courtyard from subterranean aqueducts until it reached a level of approximately five feet.[68] An etching by Orazio Scarabelli gives us an impression of the eighteen galleys of various sizes that floated upon this sea.[69] After a round of cannon shots had lured the guests from the buffet back into the courtyard, the sea battle between the Turks and their beseigers could begin (Figure 65). The Christians were victorious and conquered the fortress with the help of rope ladders.

ELIZABETHAN AND JACOBEAN PUBLIC THEATRES

The great outdoor public theatres of Elizabethan England, in sharp contrast to the stages of the Italian Renaissance, were derived from medieval rather than classical precedent. Their structure was based on the plan of the polygonal wooden arenas which had been used since the middle of the sixteenth century for exhibitions of baiting, a cruel Elizabethan sport in which chained animals (bears or bulls) were torn to pieces by a pack of dogs.

The principal outdoor public playhouses in the suburbs of London during the Renaissance were the following: the *Theatre* (built by James Burbage in Shoreditch, 1576); the *Curtain* (from the Latin *cortina*, meaning enclosure, 1577); the *Rose* (opened on the South side of the Thames by Phillip Henslowe [the most affluent theatre owner of the period], 1587); the *Swan* (a large theatre financed by the goldsmith Francis Langley, 1595); the *Globe* (on the South bank, owned by the Burbage family and a number of actors from the Lord Chamberlain's Men, including Shakespeare, 1599); the *Fortune* (built in the north of London by Henslowe and his partners, 1600); the *Red Bull* (a showcase for melodrama and spectacle in Clerkenwell, owned by an illiterate, Aaron Holland, 1606); the *Hope* (equipped with a stage that could be removed to show bearbaitings, 1613); the *second Globe* (built in 1614 on the site of the first *Globe*, which had burned the year

---

[68] "forse cinque piedi" (Pavoni. p. 40.). According to Cavalino, p. 44, the artificial sea had a depth of 4 braccia. But this seems incredible.

[69] According to Cavalino, 22 vessels were involved.

before).

There is not enough evidence to reconstruct any one of these theatres in every detail. However, the gaps in our knowledge have not prevented a whole generation of scholars from trying to do it, their focus being the *Globe*, of course, since it was the scene of the first performance of most of Shakespeare's mature plays.

Recently some important information has been added to our inadequate store of primary evidence. During the course of excavating for some office buildings in what was once the Bankside (south of the Thames), the foundations of the *Rose Theatre* were exposed, and a few months later, a small part of the second *Globe*. These new discoveries answered some important questions, but still left lacunae in our knowledge.

What have we learned that we didn't know before? The *Rose* was apparently an irregular 14-sided polygon, straighter and narrower on its southern edge, which in Elizabethan times abutted an open sewer. The external diameter of this polygon was 72 feet. The playhouse was remodeled by Henslowe in 1592 when a new stage was installed north of the original platform. Architectural remains of both stages have been found. The front of the platform in each case was a solid wall of brick and timber. To everyone's surprise the stage was tapered. The first platform was an elongated hexagon, 16 feet 5 inches in depth, 36 feet 9 inches in width at the back, narrowing to 26 feet 10 inches in front. The second stage had a more rectangular shape but was still slightly tapered. In general the playhouse was smaller and less regular than we expected. There is no evidence of an external stair tower.

What we still lack, of course, is any information about the structure of the *Rose* above its foundation. Was there a "discovery" space? Was the "tiring house" (the area behind the scenes) a part of the frame of the theatre or built separately within it? In the case of the *Rose*, the former seems to have been the case, but it is impossible to say with any certainty.

As I write, only five percent of the *Globe* has been uncovered; the rest lies beneath a block of protected Georgian houses, and it may be some time before more of Shakespeare's playhouse is exposed. X-ray pictures of the covered foundation may give us further clues. On the basis of this very slight evidence, John Orrell, the author of *The Quest for Shakespeare's Globe* (1983), made some guesses which may be hard to authenticate.[1] Orrell assumes the *Globe* was a regular polygon of twenty sides. He reserves judgement about an external stair turret, which he

---

[1] In a paper, "After the Rose: Problems in the Design at the Globe," delivered February 17, 1990 at a conference on the subject, "New Issues in the Reconstruction of Shakespeare's Theatre" at the University of Georgia.

reminds us is not shown in a print of the Bankside by Wenzel Hollar (1644). Clearly the *Globe* was much larger than the *Rose*. It may have had an independent tiring house within the theatre, jutting out onto the area bounded by the stage.

Was the *Globe* a regular polygon with twenty sides? Until more is uncovered, Orrell's surmises cannot be validated. And, of course, we don't know anything from these damaged remains about what the *Globe* looked like above ground level.

Before recent discoveries, the principal sources of primary information about the playhouses were builders' contracts (for the *Fortune* and the *Hope*) and a drawing by a foreign visitor of the Swan from 1596.

The so-called "Swan Drawing" was discovered in a Dutch library in 1888. It is a copy of a sketch by Johannes de Witt, and its value is limited by the inaccuracy of its scale and perspective.[2] It remains, however, our only contemporary picture of the interior of an Elizabethan theatre. It shows a round auditorium framing a tiring house ("mimorum aedes" is the label on the drawing). There are two doors leading to a low platform stage under which supports are visible. Three actors are shown on the stage, but no spectators in the three galleries that are part of the frame of the theatre. However, we can see some people in a small gallery (separate from the frame) above the doors of the tiring house. The stage appears to be rectangular.

In De Witt's Latin commentary on the drawing he speaks of four London theatres, of which the largest is "that whereof the sign is the swan." He tells us that it can hold 3,000 people, that it is "built of a concrete of flint stones . . . and supported by wooden columns, painted in such excellent imitation of marble that it might deceive even the most cunning." He says he was moved to depict the playhouse because of its resemblance to a Roman amphitheater.

We search vainly in De Witt's drawing for anything resembling an "inner stage." In 1941, John C. Adams in *The Globe Playhouse* (London) postulated the presence of such an alcove at the *Globe*, complete with draw curtain and recessed into the tiring house. Thanks to Adams, the inner stage has become one of the persistent myths of Elizabethan scholarship. The absence of such an alcove in the Swan Drawing is considered strong proof of its non-existence.[3]

The "inner stage" is likewise not mentioned anywhere in the Fortune Contract, another important piece of contemporary evidence about the Elizabethan public theatre. The Fortune Contract, like the Swan

---

[2] The copy was made by a friend of de Witt, Arend van Buchel.

[3] Adams' reconstruction of the *Globe* has been generally discredited, especially with respect to his alcove. But then in the face of the Swan drawing, he also insisted that the *Globe* had a tapered stage. And now we know that the *Rose* stage was tapered.

Drawing, has some unfortunate limits to the information it contains. The contract was drawn up between Henslowe and Peter Streete, the carpenter who one year earlier had constructed the *Globe* theatre. When a feature of the *Globe* pleased Henslowe, he simply included in the contract an instruction to Streete to build that feature in the manner of the *Globe*. This circumstance leaves us with some dark areas in our knowledge. Moreover, the *Fortune* had an atypical shape. It was the only one of the major Elizabethan *outdoor* theatres which was square rather than round or a many-sided polygon.

Nonetheless, the contract is extremely valuable. It contains, among other things, the dimensions of the outer building, the inner yard, the stage and the three galleries.

A thorough analysis of the Swan Drawing, the Fortune Contract and other pieces of evidence is contained in A.M. Nagler's *Shakespeare's Stage* (New Haven: Yale, 1958), C. Walter Hodges' *The Globe Restored* (London, 1953), John Orrell's *The Quest for Shakespeare's Globe* (Cambridge, 1985), and Andrew Gurr's *The Shakespearean Stage 1574-1642* (Cambridge, 1970, 1980).

However, students may wish to examine the primary documents themselves first, form an estimate of them and then compare their opinions to the reasoning of the experts, as represented here by an extract from Hodges. One must remember, of course, that this is an open subject and that more evidence may be forthcoming.

THE "SWAN DRAWING"

From a sketch of the Swan theatre
by Johannes de Witt, 1596

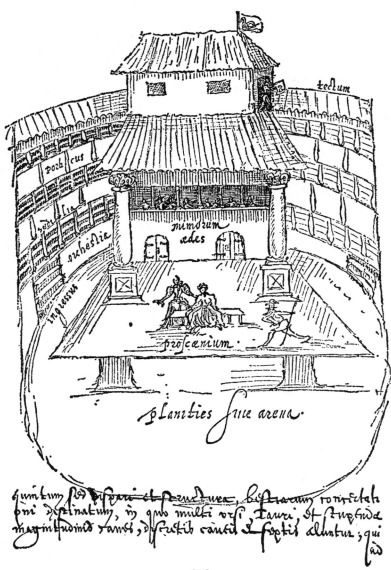

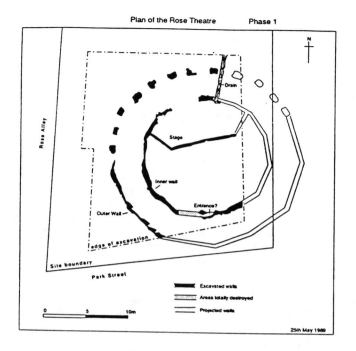

Plan of the Rose Theatre   Phase 1

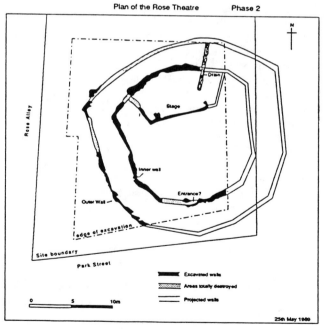

Plan of the Rose Theatre   Phase 2

273   Courtesy of Museum of London.

THE CONTRACT FOR BUILDING THE
FORTUNE THEATRE, 1599*

*T*his Indenture made the Eighte daie of Januarye 1599, and in the Twoe and Fortyth yeare of the Reigne of our sovereigne Ladie Elizabeth, by the grace of god Queene of Englande, Fraunce and Irelande, defender of the Faythe, &c. betwene Phillipp Henslowe and Edwarde Allen of the parishe of Ste Saviours in Southwark in the Countie of Surrey, gentlemen, on thone parte, and Peeter Streete, Cittizen and Carpenter of London, on thother parte witnesseth That whereas the saide Phillipp Henslowe & Edward Allen, the daie of the date hereof, haue bargayned, compounded & agreed with the saide Peter Streete ffor the erectinge, buildinge & settinge upp of a new howse and Stadge for a Plaiehouse in and vppon a certeine plott or parcell of grounde appoynted oute for that purpose, scytuate[1] and beinge nere Goldinge lane in the parishe of Ste Giles withoute Cripplegate of London, to be by him the saide Peeter Streete or somme other sufficyent woorkmen of his provideinge and appoyntemente and att his propper costes & chardges, for the consideracion hereafter in theis presentes expressed, made, erected, builded and sett upp in manner & forme followinge (that is to saie); The frame of the saide howse to be sett square and to conteine ffowerscore foote of lawfull assize everye waie square withoutt and fiftie fiue foote of like assize square everye waie within, with a good suer[2] and stronge foundacion of pyles, brick, lyme and sand bothe without & within, to be wroughte one foote of assize att the leiste aboue the grounde; And the saide fframe to conteine three Stories in heighth, the first or lower Storie to conteine Twelue foote of lawful assize in heighth, the second Storie Eleaven foote of lawfull assize in heighth, and the third or vpper Storie to conteine Nyne foote of lawfull assize in height; All which Stories shall conteine Twelue foote and a halfe of lawfull assize in breadth througheoute, besides a juttey forwardes in either of the saide twoe vpper Stories of Tenne ynches of lawfull assize, with ffower convenient divisions for gentlemens roomes, and other sufficient and convenient divisions for Twoe pennie roomes, with necessarie seates to be placed and sett, aswell in those roomes as througheoute all the rest of the galleries of the saide howse, and with suchelike steares,[3] conveyances & divisions withoute & within, as are made & contryved in and to the late erected Plaiehowse on the Banck in the saide parishe of Ste Saviours called the Globe; With a Stadge and Tyreinge howse to be made, erected &

* From the text given by Dr. W. W. Greg in *Henslowe Papers* (1907).
1 situated.   2 sewer.   3 stairs.

settupp within the saide fframe, with a shadowe or cover over the saide Stadge, which Stadge shalbe placed & sett, as alsoe the steare-cases of the saide fframe, in suche sorte as is prefigured in a plott thereof drawen, and which Stadge shall conteine in length Fortie and Three foote of lawfull assize and in breadth to extende to the middle of the yarde of the saide howse; The same Stadge to be paled in be-lowe with good, stronge and sufficyent newe oken bourdes, and like-wise the lower Storie of the saide fframe withinside, and the same lower storie to be alsoe laide over and fenced with stronge yron pykes; And the saide Stadge to be in all other proporcions contryved and fash-ioned like vnto the Stadge of the saide Plaie howse called the Globe; With convenient windowes and lightes glazed to the saide Tyreinge howse; And the saide fframe, Stadge and Stearecases to be covered with Tyle, and to haue a sufficient gutter of lead to carrie & convey the water frome the coveringe of the saide Stadge to fall backwardes; And also all the saide fframe and the Stairecases thereof to be suffi-cyently enclosed withoute with lathe, lyme & haire, and the gentle-mens roomes and Twoe pennie roomes to be seeled with lathe,[4] lyme & haire, and all the fflowers of the saide Galleries, Stories and Stadge to be bourded with good & sufficyent newe deale bourdes of the whole thicknes, wheare need shalbe; And the saide howse and other thinges beforemencioned to be made & doen to be in all other contrivitions, conveyances, fashions, thinge and thinges effected, finished and doen accordinge to the manner and fashion of the saide howse called the Globe, saveinge only that all the princypall and maine postes of the saide fframe and Stadge forwarde shalbe square and wroughte palaster-wise, with carved proporcions called Satiers to be placed & sett on the topp of every of the same postes, and saveinge alsoe that the said Peeter Streete shall not be chardged with anie manner of pay[ntin]ge in or aboute the saide fframe howse or Stadge or anie parte thereof, nor rendringe the walls within, nor seeling anie more or other roomes then the gentlemens roomes, Twoe pennie roomes and Stadge before remembred. Nowe theiruppon the saide Peeter Streete dothe covenant, promise and graunte ffor himself, his executours and administratours, to and with the saide Phillipp Henslowe and Edward Allen and either of them, and thexecutours and administratours of them and either of them, by their presentes in manner & forme followeinge (that is to saie); That he the saide Peeter Streete, his executours or assignes, shall & will att his or their owne propper costes & chardges well, woorkmanlike & substancyallie make, erect, sett upp and fully finishe in and by all thinges, accordinge to the true meaninge of theis pres-entes, with good, stronge and substancyall newe tymber and other

4 thin narrow strips of wood nailed to rafters to make a groundwork for plas-tering, tiling, etc.

necessarie stuff, all the saide fframe and other woorkes whatsoever in and vppon the saide plott or parcell of grounde (beinge not by anie aucthoretie restrayned, and haveinge ingres, egres & regres to doe the same) before the ffyue & twentith daie of Julie next commeinge after the date hereof; And shall alsoe at his or theire like costes and chardges provide and fine all manner of woorkmen, tymber, joystes,[5] rafters, boordes, dores, boltes, hinges, brick, tyle, lathe, lyme, haire, sande, nailes, lade, iron, glasse, woorkmanshipp and other thinges whatsoever, which shalbe needefull, convenyent & necessarie for the saide fframe & woorkes & euerie parte thereof; And shall alsoe make all the saide fframe in every poynt for Scantlings lardger and bigger in assize then the Scantlinges of the timber of the saide newe erected howse called the Globe; And alsoe that he the saide Peeter Streete shall furthwith, aswell by himself as by suche other and soemanie woorkmen as shalbe convenient & necessarie, enter into and vppon the saide buildinges and woorkes, and shall in reasonable manner proceede therein withoute anie wilfull detraccion vntill the same shalbe fully effected and finished. In consideracion of all which buildinges and of all stuff & woorkemanshipp thereto belonginge, the saide Phillipp Henslowe & Edward Allen and either of them, ffor themselues, theire, and either of theire executours & administratours, doe joynctlie & seuerallie covenante & graunte to & with the saide Peeter Streete, his executours & administratours by theis presentes, that they the saide Phillipp Henslowe & Edward Allen or one of them, or the executours administratours or assignes of them or one of them, shall & will well & truelie paie or cawse to be paide vnto the saide Peeter Streete, his executours or assignes, att the place aforesaid appoynted for the erectinge of the saide fframe, the full somme of Fower hundred & Fortie Poundes of lawfull money of Englande. . . .

C. Walter Hodges in *The Globe Restored* has made a considerable contribution to our knowledge of the Elizabethan public theatres. (It was Hodges who most effectively questioned the idea of the "inner stage.") In the following essay he attacks the popular theory that the theatre of Shakespeare and his contemporaries was intended for the ear only and not for the eye.

[5] small timbers or beams ranged parallelwise from one wall to another to support a floor or to support laths of a ceiling.

C. Walter Hodges

THE STATELY-FURNISHED SCENE*

The criticism by Richard Flecknoe, in Restoration days, about the "plain and simple" methods of Shakespeare's theatre, as having no scenery "nor Decorations of the Stage, but onely old Tapestry and the Stage strewed with Rushes," has been more often quoted and had a much wider effect than the somewhat contradictory statement with which he followed it: "For Scenes and Machines they are no new invention, our Masks and some of our Playes in former times (though not so ordinary) having had as good or rather better than we have now." In Victorian times the "plain and simple" view went unchallenged, though with it there went a puritanical approval of plainness and simplicity. The anonymous author of a popular educational work, *Old England,* published about 1857, may be taken as typical. He writes of the fire which ended the career of the first Globe, a fire which, as is known, was started by some burning material from a theatre cannon which was shot accidentally into the thatched roof. "The clumsy management of the cannons," says the writer, "and the *thatched* theatre, shows how comparatively unfamiliar were those who first witnessed the representation of the most wonderful series of plays the world has seen, with those costly and laboured contrivances to which in our day the soul of the art has been sacrificed. Poetry, wit, passion, humour, wisdom, could be relished by our ancestors without them. . . . One illustration of the stage ceremony of our ancestors is delightful for its almost infantine simplicity. In Greene's *Pinner of Wakefield* two parties are quarrelling: 'Come, Sir,' says one, 'will you come to the town's end, now?' 'Ay, Sir, come,' replies his adversary. And in the next line, having, we may suppose, made as distant a movement as the narrow stage admitted of, he continues, with amusing faith in the imaginative power of the audience, 'Now, we are at the town's end, what shall we say now?' "

We nowadays do not necessarily regard such methods as "infantine," and indeed the imaginative powers of modern audiences have been well schooled in every kind of theatrical style and convention. Yet the writer just quoted was evidently a discerning man, and it is at first hard for us to suppose that he was far wrong about the simplicity of the Globe when one remembers the matter of the thatched roof. The

thatch, the tapestry and the rush-strewn stage: there come into the
mind's eye the unmistakable features of a cottage — can it be Anne
Hathaway's? And below the thatch one imagines the quaint criss-
cross of Old English half-timbering — can it be Shakespeare's birth-
place in Henley Street, Stratford? One recalls the inn-yards where the
players used to act; the rumbustious scene paints itself for us in the
manner of a Christmas card, and persuades us to accept its implied
simplicity of manner because it is so picturesque in effect. But is this,
after all, the right effect? Until quite recently it used to be believed
that Shakespeare's plays were originally acted in the ordinary costume
of his own day. This we now know to be untrue — or at least a very
misleading over-simplification — but it is still widely taught that the
architectural background of the stage in Shakespeare's theatre was
deliberately intended to give the impression of the normal domestic
architecture of the day. Adams, in *The Globe Playhouse*, takes this
for granted. "The façade of the tiring-house," he says, "differed from
its model, *a short row of London houses*, mainly in having . . . curtains suspended in the middle."[1] But there is no reason at all for supposing that any feature of an Elizabethan playhouse was ever based
on any such model. The idea is contrary to the very nature of Elizabethan drama. It is true that there was an important group of Elizabethan plays which dealt with the contemporary scene; but the great
majority of their drama was otherwise. Of Shakespeare's thirty-seven
plays not one was set in the England of his own day: all were evoca-
tions of the romantic past or the romantic distance, or both; and all
very intentionally so. Not even *Twelfth Night*, which one would take
to be very contemporary and English in feeling, was allowed to come
nearer home than Illyria. One may say that this was merely a nod in
the direction of the prevailing Italianate fashion; but, even so, that
fashion was itself the fashion of the splendid and romantic scene, and
was the vein which inspired the greater part of all the work of every
dramatist of the time except Ben Jonson; and even he, the great exemplar of English social satire, produced many works in a heroic or
romantic mode. Temples, palaces and towers were the characteristic
backgrounds of the Elizabethan drama; the theatre was a place for
"Heroick and Majestique recreacions."[2] Therefore, unless it can be
shown that Elizabethan managers and actors were ignorant of any
architecture but that of their own streets, or else had not the means
or the imagination to provide themselves with any other, we ought
surely to suppose that their theatres were furnished in a style at least

---

[1] Adams, *The Globe Playhouse*, p. 135. [Italics Hodges'.]
[2] This phrase is found in the prospectus of an Amphitheatre which was under
consideration in 1620. Cf. Leslie Hotson, *The Projected Amphitheatre*, in
Shakespeare Survey 2.

suggestive of some sort of fantasy and splendour. In fact, we know that the imagination, the means and the style were all at hand. And since a robust and fanciful ostentation has been typical of all popular entertainment from the most ancient times, one would surely expect to find evidence of it on the Elizabethan stage, of all stages.

The evidence is not lacking. "Behold," cries the preacher Thomas White, "behold the sumptuous theatre houses, a continual monument of London's prodigality and folly." He goes on to say that they are schools of vice, dens of thieves and theatres of all lewdness, and if his testimony stood alone one might well brush aside his mention of sumptuousness as the exaggeration of a zealous Puritan who could not tell the difference between a piece of tinsel and an orgiastic carouse. But it does not stand alone. Here is another Puritan, John Stockwood, declaiming in 1578 against "the gorgeous playing place erected in the fields." Sumptuous and gorgeous already; and then a year or two later Stephen Gosson, in a pamphlet written against the theatres, still has to allow "the beauty of the houses and the stages"; while Thomas Nashe in another, defending them, says "Our Scene is more stately furnished than ever it was in the time of Roscius. . . ."

The quotations given above range over a period from 1577, the year after the first theatre was built, until 1592. Since the theatres continued to prosper and were increasingly patronised by people of taste and culture, it is hardly likely that they decreased in splendour as time went on; and when in 1611 Thomas Coryat published, in his *Crudities,* an account of his travels in Europe, he had this to say of a theatre he visited in Venice: "I was at one of their playhouses, where I saw a comedy acted. The house is very beggarly and base in comparison of our stately play-houses in England: neither can their actors compare with us for apparel shews and music."

Defenders and detractors alike, then, agree in this, that the theatres were decked out in some sort of splendour, and Nashe even believed the London theatres to have outrivalled the admired model of Imperial Rome. For in fact the Roman model, so far as there was a model at all, was the one. Johannes de Witt, the Flemish visitor to the Swan whose report originated the famous drawing, was particularly struck, as we have seen, by what he considered a resemblance between that theatre and a Roman original, and the drawing is annotated with the corresponding classical references, expressly to point the fact. Ben Jonson, whose classically minded approach to the theatre was famous, has given us on the title-page of the 1616 edition of his *Works,* a picture of a classical "theatrum" as he supposed it to have appeared. . . . The picture is clearly founded upon information from antiquarian sources, but the English engraver has restored it to what he and/or Ben Jonson must have supposed was its proper original form, by the addition of some huts over the top, after the style of those familiar huts over the theatres on Bankside.

Edmund Spenser, in his *Thalia*, speaks of "the painted theatres." Johannes de Witt speaks also of painting: he says that the Swan was "supported by wooden columns, painted in such excellent imitation of marble that it might deceive even the most prying observer." This is momentous information, but before following it up, let us look at another aspect of theatre painting. We have already noted in Chapter II that the roof called the Heavens, over the stage, is believed to have been ornamentally painted, probably with stars, suns, moons, or with allegorical and zodiacal figures. Adams quotes a fascinating list of references to the painted ceiling above the actors' heads, as for instance this from Dekker's *The Whore of Babylon:*

> 3 *King:*   Can yonder roof, that's nailed so fast with stars
> Cover a head so impious, and not crack?

and from Massinger's *Very Woman:*

> *Almira:*   — But look yonder!
> Amongst a million of glorious lights
> That deck the heavenly canopy, I have
> Discerned his soul, transformed into a star.
> Do you not see it?
> *Leonora:*   Lady!
> *Almira:*   Look with my eyes.
> What splendour circles it! The heavenly archer
> Not far off distant, appears dim with envy,
> Viewing himself outshined.

A similar reference occurs in *The Silent Woman*, III, i. Captain Otter, the henpecked sportsman, is complaining of his wife's unreasonable attitude in the matter of bulls and bears. His friend Clerimont says:

> *Cler.:*   Ay, she must hear argument. Did not Pasiphae, who was
> a queen, love a bull: And was not Calisto . . . turn'd
> into a bear, and made a star, mistress Ursula, in the
> heavens?
> *Otter:*   O lord! that I could have said as much!
> I will have these stories painted in the Bear-garden, *ex
> Ovidii metamorphosi.*

If this is not a reference to a painted Heavens in the Bear-garden it must refer to some other painted decorations there (presumably of classical subjects) which were topical at the time of the play's original production, either because they were just being done or else because they were in some special way a feature of that house; one might suppose them as being painted around the parapet of the middle gallery, very like those scenes that are painted in a primitive and boisterous style upon the fascias of roundabouts and booths at fairgrounds to-day.

Indeed, one should bear this style always in mind when imagining the ornament of the Elizabethan stage. One should be on one's guard against supposing a refinement of taste beyond what a journeyman painter could do out of his copy-book. . . .

The theatres were prosperous, scenic painters and builders were available with their Flemish copy-books at hand; the baroque style was paramount, the audience expected it, and actors everywhere else in Europe flourished in it. Moreover, our particular evidence confirms the detail of marbled and allegorical painting, and of sumptuousness in the Elizabethan theatre. In view of all this it should be difficult to prove, not that this was in fact the style with which the Elizabethan stage was embellished, but rather that any other style was ever likely to have been considered.

Upon stages of this sort, then, arrayed with pillars, pilasters, posts and "carved proportions," painted in marbling and in bright colours, picked out with gilding and hung with arras and curtains, the plays were mounted. We are well informed of the accessories that further enriched them. We know the details of Henslowe's property room at the Rose, from his famous inventory of March 1598. I here reprint the selection given in modern spelling by Dr. G. B. Harrison:[3]

> i rock, i cage, i tomb, i Hell mouth.
> i tomb of Guido, i tomb of Dido, i bedstead.
> viii lances, i pair of stairs for Phaeton.
> ii steeples, & i chime of bells, & i beacon.
> i heifer for the play of Phaeton, the limbs dead.
> l globe, & i golden sceptre; iii clubs.
> ii marchpanes, & the City of Rome.
> i golden fleece; ii rackets; i bay tree.
> i wooden hatchet; i leather hatchet.
> i wooden canopy; old Mahomet's head.
> i lion skin; i bear's skin; & Phaeton's limbs & Phaeton's chariot; & Argus' head.
> Neptune's fork and garland.
> i 'crosers' staff; Kent's wooden leg.
> Iris head, & rainbow; i little altar.
> viii visards; Tamberlain's bridle; i wooden mattock.
> Cupid's bow, & quiver; the cloth of the Sun & Moon.
> i boar's head & Cerberus' iii heads.
> i Caduceus; ii moss banks, & i snake.
> ii fanes of feathers; Bellendon stable; i tree of golden apples; Tantalus' tree; ix iron targets.
> i copper target, & xvii foils.
> iiii wooden targets; i greeve armour.
> i sign for Mother Redcap; i buckler.
> Mercury's wings; Tasso's picture; i helmet with a dragon; i shield, with iii lions; i elm bowl.
> i chain of dragons; i gilt spear.

---

[3] *Introducing Shakespeare*, by G. B. Harrison, p. 85.

ii coffins; i bull's head; and i 'vylter'.
iii timbrels; i dragon in Faustus.
i lion; ii lion heads; i great horse with his legs; i sackbut.
i wheel and frame in the Siege of London.
i pair of wrought gloves.
i Pope's mitre.
iii Imperial crowns; i plain crown.
i ghost's crown; i crown with a sun.
i frame for the heading in Black Joan.
i black dog.
i cauldron for the Jew.

One hesitates to rifle this rich store for items to comment upon, but certain of them may require it. It should be noted that the "Hell mouth" and the "dragon in Faustus," for example, come straight from the medieval stage; that the "City of Rome" and the "cloth of the Sun & Moon," give rise to the idea of a limited use of painted pictorial backgrounds in certain circumstances (Heywood, in the *Iron Age*, made use of a Trojan horse which may also have been painted upon a cloth of this kind). The "cauldron for the Jew," which must have been the cauldron into which Barabas falls at the end of *The Jew of Malta;* and the "frame for the heading" was, as Dr. Harrison explains, a piece of stage machinery to produce the illusion of a beheading. . . .

In this connexion the Elizabethan taste for gory realism should be mentioned. In their frequent scenes of battle, murder and sudden death, the actors used to carry hidden bladders of pig's blood which spouted forth when they were pricked. They staged scenes of execution in which the entrails of animals bought from the slaughterhouses were plucked out from the "victims" and exhibited to the spectators, as was done in earnest at the hanging, drawing and quartering of victims by the executioner at Tyburn. Audiences were well able to reconcile all this with their "heroic and majestic recreations," and liked to see "a Hector all besmeared in blood, trampling upon the bulkes of Kinges; a Troilus returning from the field, in the sight of his father Priam, as if man and horse, even from the steed's rough fetlockes to the plume on the champion's helmet, had bene together plunged into a purple ocean; to see a Pompey ride in triumph, than a Caesar conquer that Pompey; labouring Hannibal alive, hewing his passage through the Alpes. To see as I have seene, Hercules, in his owne shape, hunting the boare, knocking down the bull, taming the hart, fighting with Hydra, murdering Geryon, slaughtering Diomed, wounding the Stymphalides, killing the Centaurs, pashing the lion, squeezing the dragon, dragging Cerberus in chaynes, and lastly, on his high pyramides waiting *Nil ultra,* Oh, these were sights to make an Alexander!" So wrote Thomas Heywood in *An Apology for Actors,* and he was writing not only of what he had seen (as he said) but of what he himself created upon the stage. In his tetralogy of *The Four Ages* there was enacted a long series of the deeds of Jupiter, Hercules, Jason, Meleager and other heroes from the beginnings of Olympus to the burning of Troy and "the deaths of Agamemnon, Menelaus, Clitemnestra, Helena, Orestes, Egistus, Pillades, King Diomed, Pyrhus, Cethus, Synon, Thersites &c." This cycle of more than Wagnerian proportions was very popular at the time when Shakespeare was writing *Cymbeline* and *The Tempest,* and continued to be put on at one theatre or another for many years. These four plays had little literary merit, and one may suppose their popularity lay principally in their abundance of spectacle. Their stage directions show, if nothing else, the stuff the Jacobean theatre was made of. Here, for example, are some taken at random:

> Enter Busyris with his Guard and Priests to sacrifice; to them two strangers, Busyris takes them and kils them upon the Altar; enter Hercules disguis'd, Busyris sends his Guard to apprehend him, Hercules discouering himselfe beates the Guard, kils Busyris, and sacrificeth him upon the Altar, at which there fals a shower of raine, the Priests offer Hercules the Crowne of Aegypt which he refuseth. (*The Brazen Age.*)

> Two fiery Buls are discovered, the Fleece hanging over them, and the Dragon sleeping beneath them: Medea with strange fiery-workes, hangs above in the Aire in the strange habite of a Conjuresse. (*The Brazen Age.*)

> Sounde a dumbe shew. Enter the three fatall sisters, with a rocke, a threed, and a paire of sheeres; bringing in a Gloabe, in which they put three lots. Jupiter drawes heaven; at which Iris descends and presents him with his Eagle, Crowne and Scepter, and his thunderbolt. Jupiter first ascends upon the Eagle, and after him Ganimed. (*The Golden Age.*)

> Sound. Pluto drawes hell: the Fates put upon him a burning Roabe, and present him with a Mace, and burning crowne. (*The Golden Age.*)

> Hercules sinkes himselfe. Flashes of fire; the Divels appeare at every corner of the stage with several fire-workes. The Judges of hell, and the three sisters run over the stage, Hercules after them: fire-workes all over the house. Enter Hercules. (*The Silver Age.*)

> Hercules kils the Sea-Monster, the Trojans on the walles, the Greekes below. (*The Silver Age.*)

The four plays were unusual in the great amount of spectacle which they offered, but there seems to have been nothing unusual in the means used to present it. The chief mechanical aids were the flying throne which brought down the gods from the Heavens, or else the stage trap which let the devils out from Hell. For the latter it is interesting to note how, for all the classical predilections of the age, and the then available knowledge, which was not negligible, of the modes and manners of antiquity, the presumably classical Hades into which Hercules descended in *The Brazen Age* was inhabited by the same snout-faced, horn-and-claw devils, all fizzing with squibs, which Marlowe had used in *Doctor Faustus* and which were the popular stock-in-trade the theatres had inherited from the Middle Ages. Shakespeare called only twice upon this inheritance, in his first play and in his last. In *I Henry VI* there are the Fiends which enter with thunder at the summons of La Pucelle; and in *The Tempest* there is Caliban, the "freckled whelp hag-born — not honoured with a human shape," whose costume we know had fishy scales upon it. He was after all only a development of the old Vice, the comic devil of the Morality Plays, in a Renaissance setting.

Shakespeare was not an innovator, as Ben Jonson was, and he was generally content to use material as he found it within the prevailing fashions of the theatre. But he did not have much use — and may, like Jonson, have had only scorn — for the Heaven and Hell devices of the popular stage. Both he and Jonson did, however, sometimes make use of the Hell trap in the conventional way for bringing in ghosts and apparitions, and there are two instances in Shakespeare of the use of the flying machine — though both of these are almost certainly interpolations by another hand, catering to the popular taste. The first is in *Macbeth,* III, v, where Hecate flies aloft seated in a "foggy cloud"; and the second is in *Cymbeline,* V, iv, where Jupiter descends mounted on an eagle. It is interesting to note that Heywood's use of this effect in *The Brazen Age*, as given in the stage direction above, dates from within one year of the first production of *Cymbeline*, so that, if one production did not influence the other, both must have been availing themselves of a then fashionable invention.[4] Another point in this scene from *Cymbeline* is that in this case the Heavens ceiling through which the machine came down appears not to have been painted like the sky after the usual fashion, but with marbling; for, as Jupiter ascends and disappears through it, one of the characters on the stage below says: "The marble pavement closes, he is entered his radiant roof."[5]

4 There is a design by Inigo Jones showing Jupiter mounted on an eagle in the masque *Tempe Restored*, in 1632.
5 This tallies in an interesting way with a further reference, in *Timon of Athens*, IV, iii, where Timon speaks of Heaven as "the marbled mansion all above." I suppose one must be on one's guard against reading too much into such metaphors, but I am inclined to wonder whether, since both *Cymbeline* and *Timon* are dated at about the time when the King's Men began to play at the "private" Blackfriars theatre, a Heavens there might have been a marbled one.

One has only to visualise for a moment what the spectacular dumb shows in Heywood's *Ages* plays must have looked like in reality, bearing in mind what a lot of them there were to be got through in each play, to realise that they must have been dealt with in a very summary fashion. It was all very much of a pasteboard parade; but it is from studying the constant factors of popular taste at this level, rather than the masterpieces of exceptional men like Shakespeare and Jonson, that we are likely to learn most about the basic character of this theatre. We find that is was violent, ornate, fantastic, abundant in poetic and processional emblems, and very noisy. Some of the effects which the Elizabethans set out to achieve were so far removed from our own tastes that they cannot be judged by our theatrical standards at all. For instance, we should miss altogether the significance of the emblematic imagery which it was an intellectual fad of that time to read and decipher. "Enter Rumour, painted full of tongues," is an image which we understand at once when seen *in words* at the beginning of *2 Henry IV*, but it may be doubted whether we should at once "read" the significance of the costume if it were newly shown to us, without a written explanation, on the stage. Fame with her trumpet, or sometimes for good measure with two . . . , we can easily understand, but Shame with a *black* trumpet, in the early play of *Cambyses*, has a distinction we might miss.

This emblematic method was particularly applicable to the design of costumes, and was developed to a high degree in masques and other courtly shows, so that the details of which a dress was composed might be studied, and its symbols well digested by the spectator. Thus the figure representing Sleep in *The Vision of Twelve Goddesses*, a Court masque given in 1604, was shown wearing "a white thin Vesture cast over a black, to signify both the day and the night, with wings of the same colour, a Garland of Poppy on his head; and instead of his ivory and transparent horn, he was shewed wearing a black wand in his left hand and a white in the other." What nowadays should we make of those white and black wands, with their distant classical reference to the Gates of Horn and Ivory which opened from the House of Dreams?

It is appropriate to bring in some mention of the Court Masques at this point, because although they were in themselves an exceptional and luxurious form of private entertainment, not of the same family or derivation as the public stage, yet their forms and methods were reflected on the public stage, and their poetic references were common to both. The masque which Shakespeare introduced into *The Tempest* was conceived in the same terms as the masques at Whitehall, and indeed the only recorded performance of the play during Shakespeare's lifetime took place at Whitehall before the King. . . .

As for Ariel, we may suppose that as an airy spirit he would have been dressed in pale blue, or perhaps like the "Ayrely Sprites" of Inigo Jones's *Temple of Love* designs, who had "Garments and Caps all of feathers." In the latter case it will be understood that the association of feathers is with birds and lightness, and thus with airiness by way of its emblems, and not by way of an airy or spiritual appearance. In the same way a Spirit of Air in Somerset's masque in 1613 was dressed in "a sky-coloured skin-coat with a mantle painted with Fowle and on his head an Eagle."

The reading of emblems or allegorical "devices" was closely allied to the Elizabethan conception of heraldry as it was presented at the spectacular jousts and "barriers" which were a feature of Court life. In these the knightly champions, each splendidly armed and caparisoned in his chosen lady's colours, was led into the lists by damsels, and accompanied by a page who explained the meaning of the poetic device and motto on his shield. Thus Sir Henry Lee, a famous champion at these shows, when he was growing old, appeared in a caparison

> . . . charged with crowns
> Oershadowed with a withered running vine
> As who would say "My spring of youth is past."

The atmosphere of this chivalric jousting is intentionally represented by Shakespeare in *Henry V*, where the knights compare horses and armour and comment on the devices of their shields before the morning of Agincourt. It is also echoed closely in two other instances: in the procession of the Greek knights returning from battle in *Troilus and Cressida*, I, ii (for it must be remembered that tales of the heroes of ancient Greece were visualised by the Elizabethans as chivalric romances in the manner of Chaucer's *Palamon and Arcite*), and more closely still in *Pericles*, II, ii, where the knights pass over the stage on the way to the jousting, and as each passes, his squire presents his shield to the Princess Thaisa, who explains the device to her father:

> *Simonides:*   What is the fourth?
> *Thaisa:*   A burning torch that's turned upside down
>   The word, *Quod me alit, me extinguit.*
> *Simonides:*   Which shows that beauty hath his power and will
>   Which can as well inflame as it can kill.

At the end of the procession comes Pericles himself clad in rusty armour and carrying his own shield, which shows:

>   a withered branch, that's only green at top
>   The motto, *in hac spe vivo.*
> *Simonides:*   A pretty moral:
>   From the dejected state wherein he is,
>   He hopes by you his fortunes yet may flourish.

This mode of romantic chivalry, which was summed up for the Elizabethans in Spenser's *The Faery Queen,* and which, as has just been
said, was accepted as the model by which the Elizabethans visualised
the heroic Greeks, does not appear to have been similarly accepted
by them for the heroic Romans. The general appearance of Roman
armour was well known to the Elizabethans, and to some extent they
made use of their knowledge on the stage. . . .

Enough has now been said to establish the claim that the Elizabethan theatre, so far from being plain and simple in its appointments,
was accustomed to shows of elaborate spectacle against a background
ornamented, perhaps very elaborately, in the baroque manner. We
may guess, if we will, that much of this was in a garish taste, and
perhaps, after all, much of it was "infantine," as the Victorian writer
quoted early in this chapter said it was. It was a mixed bag, in which
Hamlet was jostled on either hand by Ralph Roister Doister and Old
Hieronimo. It played to the allegorical refinements of courtiers, and
to groundlings who, as Hamlet complained, were "capable of nothing
but inexplicable dumb-shows and noise." Of the dumb-shows we have
seen something, and since noise has once already been mentioned as
a characteristic feature of the public stage, it would be as well to point
out that noise seems to have been enjoyed by the Elizabethan groundling as a pleasure in its own right. The German traveller Paul Hentzner said of Englishmen that they were "vastly fond of great noises
that fill the ear, such as the firing of cannon, drums, and the ringing
of bells, so that in London it is common for a number of them that
have got a glass in their heads, to go up into some belfry, and ring the
bells for hours together for the sake of exercise." Without taking this
report too solemnly it is true that the plays were full, not only of the
noise of trumpets and drums, as indeed one might expect, but also of
the noise of gunfire which they used on every possible occasion.
Shakespeare is full of it. Cannons are shot off not only in battle scenes,
but also to give effect to merriment and carouse, as at the feasting of
King Claudius in *Hamlet;* and it was the firing of cannon at Cardinal
Wolsey's festivities in *Henry VIII* that burned the Globe down in
1613. The acme of all cannonading on the Elizabethan stage was the
sea battle, and when in *Antony and Cleopatra* there "is heard the noise
of a sea-fight," that noise was of gunfire from the cannons just outside
the theatre. There was at one time a fashion for seafaring plays,
largely no doubt because of the rich opportunities for cannonading
which they offered. "The battle at Sea in '88, with England's victory,"
was to have been one of the attractions of *England's Joy.* And, in *The
Silent Woman,* the old curdmudgeon Morose, who could bear no
noise, being distraught at the uproar which his new wife had brought
upon him, named among the noisy penances he would be willing
to endure to be rid of her: "London Bridge, Paris-garden, Billingsgate,

when the noises are at their height and loudest. Nay," he concluded
to crown it all, "Nay, I would sit out a play, that were nothing but
fights at sea, drum, trumpet and target."

COURTLY ENTERTAINMENT: MASQUES

As Hodges correctly observes, the spectacle in the Elizabethan and Jacobean public theatres was emblematic rather than
illusionistic. Perspective scenery in the Italian manner first made
its English appearance not at the Theatre, the Rose, the Globe
or the Fortune, but instead at court in private performances, held
for the most part at Whitehall during the Christmas season.

These performances, called *masques*, were in Shakespeare's
day complex allegorical entertainments combining dance and
spectacle. The participants in the masques were nearly always
amateurs. Frequently the king, the queen, and their most-
favored courtiers had leading parts.

The masque, which had its greatest flowering during the
Jacobean and Caroline periods under the direction of the talented
scene designer and architect Inigo Jones (1573–1652), was actually an outgrowth of a much simpler form of entertainment,
also called *masque*, which had been imported into England from
Italy by Henry VIII. As performed by the Tudor court, this
prototype of Inigo Jones's later triumphs was no more than an
elaborate invitation to the dance. Between the courses of a
banquet, the king and his friends, disguised in fantastic costumes, walked into the hall and asked the ladies to dance. The
only spectacle in the performance was the spectacle of the costumes worn by the masquers.

As the masque developed in complexity, however, it became
more decorative, and soon the masquers no longer walked into
the room, but were wheeled in on a pageant car containing set
pieces executed in the medieval manner.

During the reign of Queen Elizabeth, the pageant car was replaced, first by dispersed mansion-like scenery placed around
the four corners of the banquet room, and then by a series of
mansions juxtaposed on a single raised stage.

But it was Jones, a disciple of Giulio Parigi and the Florentine
school, who first conceived the idea of substituting perspective
illusionistic scenery for the older medieval-type settings. His
greatest innovation occurred on January 6, 1605, in *The Masque
of Blackness*, a spectacular entertainment presented immediately
after Jones' return from eight years of study in Italy. The poet
who supplied the words for this masque was Ben Jonson. Jonson
was to collaborate with Jones on several other similar

entertainments before the two men argued bitterly and parted company in 1631.

The Masque of Blackness had a painted front curtain and a proscenium frame. The single perspective setting was a sea-scape, capped by a great concave shell (painted in imitation of mother-of-pearl) which framed the masquers and which appeared to move on the waves. No scene changes were employed, and it is quite possible that the basic setting was painted on Serlio's angle wings.

Jones's next royal masque (again based on a text by Jonson) was *The Masque of Hymen,* produced in 1606. A turning machine was used in this production, the masquers being hidden by a "great globe," constructed in the form of a hollow hemisphere which rotated during the course of the performance to reveal the dancers.

Further advances in the complexity of "stage motions" were made by Jones in his next two efforts, *The Masque of Beauty* and *The Hue and Cry After Cupid* (both 1608). However, no scene changes in the Italian sense were attempted by him until 1609 when, with Jonson, he produced *The Masque of Queens* on February 2 at Whitehall. Jonson conceived the idea of opening with an anti-masque in this production as a foil to the beauty of the principal part of the entertainment. The anti-masque was a vivid hell scene, decorated with spectacular fire and smoke effects by Jones, who arranged his scenery so that upon the "sound of loud music" the hell instantaneously changed to a "glorious and magnificent building figuring the house of fame." The effect of this transformation must have seemed almost miraculous to an audience unaccustomed to the Italian techniques.

How Jones accomplished the scene shift in *The Masque of Queens* it is impossible to say. Almost certainly he did not use flat wings, a device he seems to have first employed in 1640 in his last and most spectacular masque, *Salmacida Spolia* (based on a text by William Davenant, later one of the most important post-Commonwealth theatrical managers). Perhaps *periaktoi* (three-sided rotating prisms to which painted scenery panels could be attached) or some similar device was used in *The Masque of Queens.* Whatever the method, this elaborate "mumming" introduced a scenic technique which, after the Commonwealth period, and through the agency of theatre men like Davenant and John Webb (Jones's assistant and later designer for the Duke's Company in the Restoration), became standard theatrical fare in the public theatres.

Here then is Jonson's text for *The Masque of Queens,* together with his own footnotes.

Ben Jonson

THE MASQUE OF QUEENS*

*Celebrated from the House of Fame, by the Queen of Great Britain,
with Her Ladies, at Whitehall, Feb. 2, 1609.*

*I*t increasing now to the third time of my being used in these services
to her majesty's personal presentations, with the ladies whom she
pleaseth to honour; it was my first and special regard to see that the
nobility of the invention should be answerable to the dignity of their
persons. For which reason I chose the argument to be *A Celebration
of honourable and true Fame, bred out of Virtue;* observing that rule
of the best artist,[1] to suffer no object of delight to pass without his
mixture of profit and example. And because Her Majesty (best
knowing that a principal part of life in these spectacles lay in their
variety) had commanded me to think on some dance, or shew, that
might precede hers, and have the place of a foil, or false masque: I
was careful to decline, not only from others, but mine own steps in
that kind, since the last year.[2] I had an anti-masque of boys; and
therefore now devised that twelve women, in the habit of hags or
witches, sustaining the persons of Ignorance, Suspicion, Credulity, &c.,
the opposites to good Fame, should fill that part, not as a masque,
but a spectacle of strangeness, producing multiplicity of gesture, and
not unaptly sorting with the current and whole fall of the device.

His majesty then being set, and the whole company in full expectation, the part of the Scene which first presented itself was an ugly
Hell; which flaming beneath, smoked unto the top of the roof. And
in respect all evils are morally said to come from hell; as also from that
observation of Torrentius upon Horace's *Canidia,*[3] *quae tot instructa
veneris, ex Orci faucibus profecta videri possit:* these witches, with a
kind of hollow and infernal music, came forth from thence. First one,
then two, and three, and more, till their number increased to eleven,
all differently attired; some with rats on their heads, some on their
shoulders; others with ointment-pots at their girdles; all with spindles,
timbrels, rattles, or other venefical instruments, making a confused
noise, with strange gestures. The device of their attire was Master
Jones's, with the invention and architecture of the whole scene and

---

* From *The Works of Ben Jonson,* Vol. III (London: Chatto & Windus,
1910), pp. 45–62.

[1] *Hor. in Art. Poetic.*

[2] In the masque at my lord Haddington's wedding.

[3] *Vide Laevin. Tor. comment. in Hor. Epod.* lib. ode 5.

machine. Only I prescribed them their properties of vipers, snakes, bones, herbs, roots, and other ensigns of their magic, out of the authority of ancient and late writers, wherein the faults are mine if there be any found; and for that cause I confess them.

These eleven WITCHES beginning to dance (which is an usual ceremony[4] at their convents or meetings, where sometimes also they are vizarded and masked), on the sudden one of them missed their chief, and interrupted the rest with this speech: —

> *Hag.*   Sisters, stay, we want our Dame;[5]
> Call upon her by her name,
> And the charm we use to say;
> That she quickly anoint,[6] and come away.

1 *Charm.*

> "Dame, dame! the watch is set:
> Quickly come, we all are met. —
> From the lakes, and from the fens,[7]
> From the rocks, and from the dens,
> From the woods, and from the caves,
> From the churchyards, from the graves,
> From the dungeon, from the tree
> That they die on, here are we!"

> Comes she not yet?
> Strike another heat.

2 *Charm.*

> "The weather is fair, the wind is good,
> Up, dame, on your horse of wood:[8]

[4] See the king's majesty's book (our sovereign) of *Demonology, Bodin. Remig. Delrio. Mal. Malefi.* and a world of others in the general: but let us follow particulars.

[5] Amongst our vulgar witches, the honour of dame (for so I translate it) is given with a kind of pre-eminence to some special one at their meetings: which Delrio insinuates, *Disquis. Mag.* lib. ii. quæst. 9, quoting that of *Apuleius, lib. de Asin. aureo. de quadam caupona, regina Sagarum.* And adds, *ut scias etiam tum quasdam ab iis hoc titulo honoratas.* Which title *M. Philipp. Ludwigus Elic. Dæmonomagiae* quæst. 10, doth also remember.

[6] When they are to be transported from place to place, they use to anoint themselves, and sometimes the things they ride on. . . .

[7] These places, in their own nature dire and dismal, are reckoned up as the fittest from whence such persons should come, and were notably observed by that excellent Lucan in the description of his *Erichtho,* lib. vi.

[8] *Delrio, Disq. Mag.* lib. ii, has a story out of Triezius of this horse of wood: but that which our witches call so, is sometimes a broom-staff, sometimes a reed, sometimes a distaff. See *Remig. Dæmonol.* lib. i. cap. 14. *Bodin,* lib. ii. cap. 4, &c.

Or else tuck up your grey frock,
And saddle your goat,[9] or your green cock,[10]
And make his bridle a bottom of thrid,
To roll up how many miles you have rid.
Quickly come away;
For we all stay."

Nor yet! nay then,
We'll try her agen.

3 *Charm.*

"The owl is abroad, the bat, and the toad,
    And so is the cat-a-mountain,
The ant and the mole sit both in a hole,
    And the frog peeps out o' the fountain;
The dogs they do bay, and the timbrels play,
    The spindle is now a turning;[11]
        The moon is red, and the stars are fled,
        But all the sky is a burning:
The ditch is made,[12] and our nails the spade,
    With pictures full of wax and of wool;
Their livers I stick, with needles quick;
There lacks but the blood, to make up the flood.

---

9 The goat is the Devil himself, upon whom they ride often to their solemnity, as appears by their confessions in Rem. and Bodin. *ibid.* His majesty also remembers the story of the devil's appearance to those of *Calicut,* in that form, *Dæmonol.* lib. ii. cap. 3.

10 Of the green cock we have no other ground (to confess ingenuously) than a vulgar fable of a witch, that with a cock of that colour, and a bottom of blue thread, would transport herself through the air; and so escaped (at the time of her being brought to execution) from the hand of justice. It was a tale when I went to school; and somewhat there is like it in *Mart. Delr. Disqu. Mag.* lib. ii. quæst. 6. . . . .

11 All this is but a periphrasis of the night, in their charm, and their applying themselves to it with their instruments, whereof the spindle in antiquity was the chief: and beside the testimony of Theocritus, in *Pharmaceutria* (who only used it in amorous affairs) was of special act to the troubling of the moon. . . .

12 This rite also of making a ditch with their nails is frequent with our witches, whereof see *Bodin. Remig. Delr. Malleus Mal. Godelman.* lib. ii. *de Lamiis,* as also the antiquity of it most vively exprest by *Hor. Satyr.* 8, lib. i. where he mentions the pictures, and the blood of a black lamb. All which are yet in use with our modern witchcraft. . . . *Bodin. Dæmon,* lib. ii. cap. 8, hath (beside the known story of king Duffe out of Hector Boetius) much of the witches' later practice in that kind, and reports a relation of a French ambassador's, out of England, of certain pictures of wax, found in a dunghill near Islington, of our late queen's: which rumour I myself (being then very young) can yet remember to have been current.

Quickly, dame, then bring your part in,
Spur, spur upon little Martin,[13]
Merrily, merrily, make him sail,
A worm in his mouth, and a thorn in's tail,
Fire above and fire below,
With a whip i' your hand to make him go."

O, now she's come!
Let all be dumb.

At this the Dame[14] *entered to them, naked-armed, barefooted, her frock tucked, her hair knotted, and folded with vipers; in her hand a torch made of a dead man's arm, lighted, girded with a snake. To whom they all did reverence, and she spake, uttering, by way of question, the end wherefore they came.*[15]

Dame.   Well done, my Hags! And come we fraught with spite,
To overthrow the glory of this night?
Holds our great purpose?

Hag.   Yes.

Dame.   But wants there none
Of our just number?

Hags.   Call us one by one,
And then our dame shall see.

Dame.   First then advance,[16]

---

13 Their little Martin is he that calls them to their conventicles, which is done in a human voice, but coming forth, they find him in the shape of a great buck goat, upon whom they ride to their meetings, *Delr. Disq. Mag.* quæst. 16, lib. ii. . . .

14 This Dame I make to bear the person of Ate, or Mischief (for so I interpret it) out of Homer's description of her, *Il.* A, where he makes her swift to hurt mankind, strong, and sound of her feet; and *Iliad.* T, walking upon men's heads. . . . I present her barefooted, and her frock tucked, to make her seem more expedite, by Horace's authority, *Sat.* 8. lib. i. . . .

15 Which if it had been done either before, or otherwise, had not been so natural. For to have made themselves their own decipherers, and each one to have told upon their entrance *what they were, and whither they would,* had been a piteous hearing, and utterly unworthy any quality of a poem: wherein a writer should always trust somewhat to the capacity of the spectator, especially at these spectacles; where men, beside inquiring eyes, are understood to bring quick ears, and not those sluggish ones of porters and mechanics, that must be bored through at every act with narrations.

16 In the chaining of these vices, I make as if one link produced another, and the Same were born out of them all. . . . Nor will it appear much violenced.

My drowsy servant, stupid Ignorance,
Known by thy scaly vesture; and bring on
Thy fearful sister, wild Suspicion,
As she names them they come forward.
Whose eyes do never sleep; let her knit hands
With quick Credulity, that next her stands,
Who hath but one ear, and that always ope;
Two-faced Falsehood follow in the rope;
And lead on Murmur, with the cheeks deep hung;
She, Malice, whetting of her forked tongue;
And Malice, Impudence, whose forehead's lost;
Let Impudence lead Slander on, to boast
Her oblique look; and to her subtle side,
Thou, black-mouthed Execration, stand applied;
Draw to thee Bitterness, whose pores sweat gall;
She, flame-eyed Rage; Rage, Mischief.

Hags.   Here we are all.

Dame.   Join now our hearts, we faithful opposites[17]

To Fame and Glory. Let not these bright nights
Of honour blaze, thus to offend our eyes;
Shew ourselves truly envious, and let rise
Our wonted rages: do what may beseem
Such names and natures; Virtue else will deem
Our powers decreased, and think us banished earth,
No less than heaven. All her antique birth,
As Justice, Faith, she will restore; and, bold
Upon our sloth, retrieve her Age of gold.
We must not let our native manners thus
Corrupt with ease. Ill lives not but in us.

---

if their series be considered, when the opposition to all virtue begins out of
Ignorance, that Ignorance begets Suspicion, (for Knowledge is ever open and
charitable) that Suspicion, Credulity, as it is a vice; for being a virtue, and
free, it is opposite to it: but such as are jealous of themselves, do easily credit
any thing of others whom they hate. Out of this Credulity springs Falsehood,
which begets Murmur: and that of Murmur presently grows Malice, which
begets Impudence: and that Impudence, Slander: that Slander, Execration: Execration, Bitterness: Bitterness, Fury: and Fury, Mischief. Now for the personal
presentation of them, the authority in poetry is universal. . . .

17 Here again by way of irritation, I make the dame pursue the purpose
of their coming, and discover their natures more largely: which had been nothing, if not done as doing another thing, but *moratio circa vilem patulumque
orbem;* than which, the poet cannot know a greater vice; he being that kind of
artificer, to whose work is required so much exactness, as indifferency is not
tolerable.

I hate to see these fruits of a soft peace,
And curse the piety gives it such increase.
Let us disturb it then,[18] and blast the light;
Mix hell with heaven, and make nature fight
Within herself; loose the whole hinge of things;
And cause the ends run back into their springs.

Hags. What our Dame bids us do,
We are ready for.

Dame. Then fall to.
But first relate me[19] what you have sought,
Where you have been, and what you have brought.

1 *Hag.* I have been all day looking after[20]
A raven feeding upon a quarter;
And soon as she turned her beak to the south,
I snatched this morsel out of her mouth.

2 *Hag.* I have been gathering wolves' hairs,
The mad dog's foam, and the adder's ears;
The spurging of a dead-man's eyes,
And all since the evening star did rise.[21]

3 *Hag.* I last night lay all alone
On the ground, to hear the mandrake groan;

18 These powers of troubling nature, frequently ascribed to witches, and challenged by themselves wherever they are induced, by Homer, Ovid, Tibullus, Pet. Arbiter, Seneca, Lucan, Claudian. . . .

19 This is also solemn in their witchcraft, to be examined, either by the devil or their dame, at their meetings, of what mischief they have done: and what they can confer to a future hurt. . . . And this doth exceedingly solicit them all, at such times, lest they should come unprepared. But we apply this examination of ours to the particular use; whereby, also, we take occasion, not only to express the things (as vapours, liquors, herbs, bones, flesh, blood, fat, and such like, which are called *Media magica*) but the rites of gathering them, and from what places, reconciling as near as we can, the practice of antiquity to the neoteric, and making it familiar with our popular witchcraft.

20 For the gathering pieces of dead flesh, *Cornel. Agrip. de occult. Philosoph.* lib. iii. cap. 42, and lib. iv. cap. ult. observes, that the use was to call up ghosts and spirits, with a fumigation made of that (and bones of carcasses) which I make my witch here, not to cut herself, but to watch the raven. . . . As if that piece were sweeter which the wolf had bitten, or the raven had pick'd, and more effectuous: and to do it, at her turning to the south, as with the prediction of a storm. Which, though they be but minutes in ceremony, being observed, make the act more dark and full of horror.

21 *Spuma canum, lupi crines, nodus hyenae, oculi draconum, serpentis membrana, aspidis aures,* are all mentioned by the ancients in witchcraft. . . .

And plucked him up, though he grew full low;
And as I had done the Cock did crow.[22]

4 *Hag.*   And I ha' been choosing out this skull
From charnel-houses that were full;
From private grots and public pits;
And frighted a sexton out of his wits.

5 *Hag.*   Under a cradle I did creep
By day; and when the child was asleep
At night I sucked the breath; and rose,
And plucked the nodding nurse by the nose.

6 *Hag.*   I had a dagger: what did I with that?
Killed an infant to have his fat.
A piper it got, at a church-ale,
I bade him again blow wind i' the tail.[23]

7 *Hag.*   A murderer yonder was hung in chains,
The sun and the wind had shrunk his veins;
I bit off a sinew; I clipped his hair,
I brought off his rags that danced i' the air.

8 *Hag.*   The scrich-owl's eggs and the feathers black,
The blood of the frog and the bone in his back,
I have been getting; and made of his skin
A purset to keep Sir Cranion in.

9 *Hag.*   And I ha' been plucking plants among,
Hemlock, henbane, adder's-tongue,
Night-shade, moon-wort, libbard's-bane;
And twice by the dogs was like to be ta'en.

22 Pliny writing of the mandrake, *Nat. Hist.* lib. xxv. cap. 13, and of the
digging it up, hath this ceremony, *Cavent effossuri contrarium ventum, et tribus
circulis ante gladio circumscribunt, postea fodiunt ad occasum spectantes.* But
we have later tradition, that the forcing of it up is so fatally dangerous, as the
groan kills, and therefore they do it with dogs, which I think but borrowed
from Josephus's report of the root Baæras, lib. vii. *de Bel. Judaic.* Howsoever, it being so principal an ingredient in their magic, it was fit she should
boast, to be the plucker up of it herself. And, that the cock did crow, alludes
to a prime circumstance in their work: for they all confess, that nothing is so
cross, or baleful to them in their nights, as that the cock should crow before
they have done. Which makes that their little masters or martinets, whom I
have mentioned before, use this form in dismissing their conventions. . . .
23 Their killing of infants is common, both for confection of their ointment
. . . as also out of a lust to do murder. *Sprenger in Mal. Malefic.* reports that a
witch, a midwife in the diocese of Basil, confessed to have killed above forty
infants (ever as they were new born, with pricking them in the brain with a
needle) which she had offered to the devil. . . .

10 *Hag.* I from the jaws of a gardener's bitch
Did snatch these bones, and then leaped the ditch:
Yet went I back to the house again,
Killed the black cat, and here's the brain.

11 *Hag.* I went to the toad breeds under the wall,
I charmed him out, and he came at my call;
I scratched out the eyes o' the owl before,
I tore the bat's wing: what would you have more?

Dame. Yes, I have brought, to help our vows,
Horned poppy, cypress boughs,
The fig-tree wild that grows on tombs,
And juice that from the larch-tree comes,
The basilisk's blood and the viper's skin:
And now our orgies let's begin.[24]

Here the dame *put herself in the midst of them, and began her following Invocation:*[25]

You fiends and furies (if yet any be
Worse than ourselves), you that have quaked to see
These knots untied and shrunk, when we have charmed.
You that to arm us have yourselves disarmed,
And to our powers resigned your whips and brands
When we went forth, the scourge of men and lands.
You that have seen me ride when Hecate
Durst not take chariot; when the boisterous sea,
Without a breath of wind, hath knocked the sky;
And that hath thundered, Jove not knowing why:
When we have set the elements at wars,
Made midnight see the sun, and day the stars;
When the winged lightning in the course hath stayed;
And swiftest rivers have run back, afraid,
To see the corn remove, the groves to range,
Whole places alter, and the seasons change;
When the pale moon, at the first voice down fell
Poisoned, and durst not stay the second spell.
You, that have oft been conscious of these sights;
And thou,[26] three-formed star, that on these nights

24 After all their boasted labours, and plenty of materials, as they imagine, I make the dame not only to add more, but stranger. . . .
25 Wherein she took occasion to boast all the power attributed to witches by the ancients, of which every poet (or the most) do give some. . . .
26 Hecate, who is called Trivia, and Triformis. . . . She was believed to govern in witchcraft; and is remembered in all their invocations. . . .

Art only powerful, to whose triple name
Thus we incline, once, twice, and thrice the same;
If now with rites profane and foul enough
We do invoke thee; darken all this roof
With present fogs: exhale earth's rot'nest vapours,
And strike a blindness through these blazing tapers.
        Come, let a murmuring Charm resound,
        The whilst we bury all i' the ground.
        But first, see every foot be bare;
        And every knee.

Hag.   Yes, Dame, they are.

4 *Charm.*
        "Deep,[27] O deep we lay thee to sleep;
We leave thee drink by, if thou chance to be dry;
Both milk and blood, the dew and the flood.
We breathe in thy bed, at the foot and the head;
We cover thee warm, that thou take no harm:
And when thou dost wake,
        Dame Earth shall quake,
        And the houses shake,
        And her belly shall ake,
        As her back were brake,
        Such a birth to make,
        As is the blue drake:
        Whose form thou shalt take."

Dame.   Never a star yet shot!
        Where be the ashes?

Hag.   Here in the pot.

Dame.   Cast them up; and the flint-stone
        Over the left shoulder bone;
        Into the west.[28]

27 Here they speak, as if they were creating some new feature, which the
devil persuades them to be able to do often, by the pronouncing of words and
pouring out of liquors on the earth. . . . All which are mere arts of Satan,
when either himself will delude them with a false form, or troubling a dead
body, makes them imagine these vanities the means: as, in the ridiculous circumstances that follow, he doth daily.

28 This throwing of ashes and sand, with the flint-stone, cross-sticks, and
burying of sage, &c., are all used (and believed by them) to the raising of
storm and tempest. . . . And when they see the success, they are more confirmed, as if the event followed their working. The like illusion is of their
phantasie, in sailing in egg-shells, creeping through augur-holes, and such like,
so vulgar in their confessions.

Hag.   It will be best.

5 *Charm.*

> "The sticks are across, there can be no loss,
> The sage is rotten, the sulphur is gotten
> Up to the sky, that was in the ground.
> Follow it then, with our rattles, round;
> Under the bramble, over the brier,
> A little more heat will set it on fire:
> Put it in mind to do it kind,
> Flow water and blow wind.
> Rouncy is over, Robble is under,
> A flash of light, and a clap of thunder,
> A storm of rain, another of hail.
> We all must home in the eggshell sail;
> The mast is made of a great pin,
> The tackle of cobweb, the sail as thin,
> And if we go through and not fall in —"

Dame.   Stay[29] all our charms do nothing win
             Upon the night; our labour dies,
             Our magic feature will not rise —
             Nor yet the storm! we must repeat
             More direful voices far, and beat
             The ground with vipers till it sweat.

6 *Charm.*

> "Bark dogs, wolves howl,
> Seas roar, woods roule,
> Clouds crack, all be black,
> But the light our charms do make."

Dame.   Not yet, my rage begins to swell;
             Darkness, Devils, Night, and Hell
             Do not thus delay my spell.
             I call you once, and I call you twice;
             I beat you again, if you stay me thrice:
             Through these crannies where I peep,
             I'll let in the light to see your sleep.[30]

---

29 This stop, or interruption, shewed the better, by causing that general silence, which made all the following noises, inforced in the next charm, more direful, first imitating that of Lucan. . . .

30 This is one of their common menaces, when their magic receives the least stop. . . .

And all the secrets of your sway
Shall lie as open to the day
As unto me. Still are you deaf!
Reach me a bough[31] that ne'er bare leaf,
To strike the air; and Aconite,[32]
To hurl upon this glaring light;
A rusty knife,[33] to wound mine arm;
And as it drops I'll speak a charm,
Shall cleave the ground, as low as lies
Old shrunk-up Chaos, and let rise
Once more his dark and reeking head,
To strike the world and nature dead,
Until my magic birth be bred.

7 *Charm.*

"Black go in, and blacker come out;
At thy going down, we give thee a shout.
                    Hoo!
At thy rising again thou shalt have two,
And if thou dost what we would have thee do,
Thou shalt have three, thou shalt have four,
Thou shalt have ten, thou shalt have a score."
                    Hoo! Har! Har! Hoo!

8 *Charm.*

"A cloud of pitch, a spur and a switch,
To haste him away, and a whirlwind play,
Before and after, with thunder for laughter,
And storms for joy, of the roaring boy;
His head of a drake, his tail of a snake."

9 *Charm.*

"About, about, and about,
Till the mist arise, and the lights fly out,
The images neither be seen nor felt;
The woollen burn and the waxen melt:

31 That wither'd straight, as it shot out, which is called *ramus feralis,* by
some, and *tristis* by *Senec. Trag. Med.*
32 A deadly poisonous herb, feigned by *Ovid. Metam.* lib. vii. to spring out of
Cerberus's foam. Pliny gives it another beginning of name. *Nat. Hist.* lib.
xxvii. cap. 3. . . . Howsoever the juice of it is like that liquor which the devil
gives witches to sprinkle abroad, and do hurt, in the opinion of all the magic
masters.
33 A rusty knife I rather give her, than any other, as fittest for such a devilish
ceremony, which Seneca might mean by *sacro cultro* in the tragedy, where he
arms Medea to the like rite. . . .

> Sprinkle your liquors upon the ground,
> And into the air; around, around.
>> Around, around,
>> Around, around,
>> Till a music sound,[34]
>> And the pace be found,
>> To which we may dance,
>> And our charms advance."

At which, with a strange and sudden music, they fell into a magical dance, full of preposterous change and gesticulation.[35]

In the heat of their dance, on the sudden was heard a sound of loud music, as if many instruments had made one blast; with which not only the Hags themselves, but the hell into which they ran, quite vanished, and the whole face of the Scene altered, scarce suffering the memory of such a thing; but in the place of it appeared a glorious and magnificent building, figuring the House of Fame, *in the top of which were discovered the twelve Masquers, sitting upon a throne triumphal, erected in form of a pyramid, and circled with all store of light. From whom a person by this time descended, in the furniture of* Perseus, *and expressing heroic and masculine* Virtue, *began to speak.*

Heroic Virtue

> So should at Fame's loud sound and Virtue's sight,
> All dark and envious witchcraft fly the light.
> I[36] did not borrow Hermes' wings, nor ask
> His crooked sword, nor put on Pluto's casque,
> Nor on mine arm advanced wise Pallas' shield,
> (By which, my face aversed, in open field
> I slew the Gorgon) for an empty name:

[34] Nor do they want music, and in a strange manner given them by the devil, if we credit their confessions in *Remig. Dæm.* lib. i. cap. 19. Such as the *Syrbenaean Quires* were, which Athenaeus remembers out of *Clearchus, Deipnos.* lib. xv. where every one sung what he would, without hearkening to his fellow; like the noise of divers oars, falling in the water. . . .

[35] But most applying to their property: who at their meetings do all things contrary to the custom of men, dancing back to back, and hip to hip, their hands joined, and making their circles backward, to the left-hand, with strange phantastic motions of their heads and bodies. All which were excellently imitated by the maker of the dance, M. Hierome Herne, whose right it is here to be named.

[36] The ancients expressed a brave and masculine virtue in three figures (of Hercules, Perseus, and Bellerophon.) Of which we choose that of Perseus, armed as we have described him out of *Hesiod. Scut. Herc.* See Apollodor. the grammarian, lib. ii. *de Perseo.*

When Virtue cut off Terror, he gat Fame.
And if, when Fame was gotten, Terror died,
What black Erynnis, or more hellish Pride,
Durst arm these hags, now she is grown and great,
To think they could her glories once defeat?
I was her parent, and I am her strength.
Heroic Virtue sinks not under length
Of years or ages; but is still the same,
While he preserves, as when he got good fame.
My daughter then, whose glorious house you see
Built all of sounding brass, whose columns be
Men-making poets, and those well-made men,
Whose strife it was to have the happiest pen
Renown them to an after-life, and not
With pride to scorn the Muse, and die forgot;
She, that enquireth into all the world,
And hath about her vaulted palace hurled
All rumours and reports, or true, or vain,
What utmost lands, or deepest seas contain,
But only hangs great actions on her file;
She, to this lesser world, and greatest isle,
To-night sounds honour, which she would have seen
In yond' bright bevy, each of them a queen.
Eleven of them are of times long gone.[37]
PENTHESILEA, the brave Amazon,[38]
Swift-foot CAMILLA, Queen of Volscia,[39]
Victorious THOMYRIS of Scythia,[40]

[37] And here we cannot but take the opportunity to make some more particular description of their scene, as also of the persons they presented; which, though they were disposed rather by chance, than election, yet it is my part to justify them all: and then the lady that will own her presentation, may.

[38] To follow, therefore, the rule of chronology, which I have observed in my verse, the most upward in time was PENTHESILEA. She was queen of the Amazons, and succeeded Otrera, or (as some will) Orithya; she lived and was present at the siege of Troy, on their part, against the Greeks. . . . She is no where named but with the preface of honour and virtue; and is always advanced in the head of the worthiest women. Diodorus Siculus makes her the daughter of Mars. She was honoured in her death to have it the act of Achilles. . . .

[39] Next follows CAMILLA, queen of the Volscians, celebrated by Virgil, than whose verses nothing can be imagined more exquisite, or more honouring the person they describe. . . .

[40] The third lived in the age of Cyrus, the great Persian monarch, and made him leave to live, THOMYRIS, queen of the Scythians, or Massagets. A heroine of a most invincible and unbroken fortitude: who, when Cyrus had invaded her, and taking her only son, (rather by treachery than war, as she objected), had slain him; not touched with the grief of so great a loss, in the juster comfort she took of a great revenge, pursued not only the occasion and honour of conquering so potent an enemy, with whom fell two hundred thousand soldiers: but (what was right memorable in her victory) left not a messenger surviving of his side to report the massacre. . . .

Chaste ARTEMISIA, the Carian dame,[41]
And fair-haired BERONICE, Aegypt's fame,[42]
HYPSICRATEA, glory of Asia,[43]
CANDACE, pride of Aethiopia,[44]
The Britain honour, VOADICEA,[45]

[41] The fourth was honoured to life in time of Xerxes, and was present at his great expedition into Greece; ARTEMISIA, the queen of Caria: whose virtue Herodotus, not without some wonder, records. That a woman, a queen, without a husband, her son a ward, and she administering the government, occasioned by no necessity, but a mere excellence of spirit, should embark herself for such a war; and there so to behave her, as Xerxes, beholding her fight, should say: *Viri quidem extiterunt mihi feminae, feminae autem viri.* She is no less renowned for her chastity, and love to her husband Mausolus, whose bones (after he was dead) she preserved in ashes, and drank in wine, making herself his tomb; and yet built to his memory a monument, deserving a place among the seven wonders of the world, which could not be done by less than a wonder of women.

[42] The fifth was the fair-haired daughter of Ptolomaeus Philadelphus, by the elder Arsinoë; who, married to her brother Ptolomaeus, surnamed Evergetes, was after queen of Egypt. I find her written both BERONICE and BERENICE. This lady, upon an expedition of her new-wedded lord into Assyria, vowed to Venus, if he returned safe, and conqueror, the offering of her hair: which vow of hers (exacted by the success) she afterward performed. But her father missing it, and therewith displeased, Conon, a mathematician, who was then in household with Ptolemy, and knew well to flatter him, persuaded the king that it was taken up to heaven, and made a constellation; shewing him those seven stars, *ad caudam Leonis*, which are since called *Coma Berenices*. Which story then presently celebrated by Callimachus, in a most elegant poem, Catullus more elegantly converted: wherein they call her the magnanimous even from a virgin: Alluding (as Hyginus says) to a rescue she made of her father in his flight, and restoring the courage and honour of his army, even to a victory. . . .

[43] The sixth, the famous wife of Mithridates, and queen of Pontus, HYPSICRATEA, no less an example of virtue than the rest; who so loved her husband, as she was assistant to him in all labours and hazard of the war, in a masculine habit. For which cause (as Valerius Maximus observes) she departed with the chief ornament of her beauty. . . . And afterward, in his flight from Pompey, accompanied his misfortune, with a mind and body equally unwearied. She is so solemnly registered by that grave author, as a notable precedent of marriage loyalty and love: virtues that might raise a mean person to equality with a queen; but a queen to the state and honour of a deity.

[44] The seventh, that renown of Ethiopia, CANDACE: from whose excellency the succeeding queens of that nation were ambitious to be called so. A woman of a most haughty spirit against enemies, and a singular affection to her subjects. I find her celebrated by Dion, and Pliny, invading Egypt in the time of Augustus: who, though she were enforced to a peace by his lieutenant Petronius, doth not the less worthily hold her place here. . . .

[45] The eighth, our own honour, VOADICEA, or BOADICEA; by some Bunduica, and Bunduca, queen of the Iceni, a people that inhabited that part of our island which was called East-Anglia, and comprehended Suffolk, Norfolk, Cambridge, and Huntingdon shires. Since she was born here at home, we will first honour her with a home-born testimony; from the grave and diligent Spenser:
——— Bunduca Britoness,
Bunduca, that victorius conqueress,
That lifting up her brave heroic thought
'Bove woman's weakness, with the Romans fought;
Fought, and in field against them thrice prevail'd, &c.
To which see her orations in story, made by Tacitus and Dion: wherein is expressed all magnitude of a spirit, breathing to the liberty and redemption of her country. . . . All of which doth weigh the more to her true praise, in

The virtuous Palmyrene, ZENOBIA,[46]
The wise and warlike Goth, AMALASUNTA,[47]
The bold VALASCA, of Bohemia;[48]
These, in their lives, as fortunes, crowned the choice
Of womankind, and 'gainst all opposite voice
Made good to time, had, after death, the claim
To live eternized in the House of Fame.
Where hourly hearing (as, what there is old?)
The glories of BEL-ANNA so well told,[49]

---

coming from the mouths of Romans, and enemies. She lived in the time of
Nero.

46 The ninth, in time, but equal in fame, and (the cause of it) virtue, was
the chaste ZENOBIA, queen of the Palmyrenes, who, after the death of her husband Odenatus, had the name to be reckoned among the thirty that usurped the
Roman empire from Galienus. She continued a long and brave war against
several chiefs; and was at length triumphed on by Aurelian. . . . She lived in a
most royal manner, and was adored to the custom of the Persians. When she
made orations to her soldiers, she had always her casque on. A woman of a
most divine spirit, and incredible beauty. In Trebellius Pollio read the most
notable description of a queen and her, that can be uttered with the dignity of
an historian.

47 The tenth, succeeding, was that learned and heroic AMALASUNTA, queen
of the Ostrogoths, daughter to Theodoric, that obtained the principality of
Ravenna and almost all Italy. She drave the Burgundians and Almaines out of
Liguria, and appeared in her government rather an example than a second. She
was the most eloquent of her age, and cunning in all languages of any nation
that had commerce with the Roman empire. . . .

48 The eleventh was that brave Bohemian queen, VALASCA, who, for her
courage, had the surname of Bold: that to redeem herself and her sex from the
tyranny of men, which they lived in, under Primislaus, on a night, and at an
hour appointed, led on the women to the slaughter of their barbarous husbands
and lords. And possessing themselves of their horses, arms, treasure, and
places of strength, not only ruled the rest, but lived many years after with the
liberty and fortitude of Amazons. . . .

49 The twelfth, and worthy sovereign of all, I make BEL-ANNA, royal queen
of the ocean; of whose dignity and person, the whole scope of the invention
doth speak throughout: which, to offer you again here, might but prove offence
to that sacred modesty, which hears any testimony of others iterated with more
delight than her own praise. She being placed above the need of such ceremony,
and safe in her princely virtue, against the good or ill of any witness. The
name of Bel-anna I devised, to honour hers proper by; as adding to it the at-
tribute of Fair: and is kept by me in all my poems, wherein I mention her
majesty with any shadow or figure. Of which, some may come forth with a
longer destiny than this age commonly gives to the best births, if but helped
to light by her gracious and ripening favour.

But here I discern a possible objection, arising against me; to which I must
turn: as, *How I can bring persons of so different ages, to appear properly together? or why (which is more unnatural) with Virgil's Mezentius, I join the
living with the dead?* I answer to both these at once. Nothing is more proper;
nothing more natural. For these all live, and together, in their fame: and so I
present them. Besides, if I would fly to the all-daring power of poetry, where
could I not take sanctury? or in whose poem? For other objections, let the
looks and noses of judges hover thick; so they bring the brains: or if they do
not, I care not. When I suffer it to go abroad, I departed with my right:

Queen of the Ocean; how that she alone
Possest all virtues, for which one by one
They were so famed: and wanting then a head
To form that sweet and gracious pyramid
Wherein they sit, it being the sovereign place
Of all that palace, and reserved to grace
The worthiest queen: these, without envy on her,
In life, desired that honour to confer,
Which, with their death, no other should enjoy.
She this embracing with a virtuous joy,
Far from self-love, as humbling all her worth
To him that gave it, hath again brought forth
Their names to memory; and means this night
To make them once more visible to light:
And to that light from whence her truth of spirit,
Confesseth all the lustre of her merit.
To you, most royal and most happy king,
Of whom Fame's house in every part doth ring
For every virtue, but can give no increase:
Not though her loudest trumpet blaze your peace.
To you, that cherish every great example
Contracted in yourself; and being so ample
A field of honour cannot but embrace
A spectacle so full of love and grace
Unto your court: where every princely dame

---

and now, so secure an interpreter I am of my chance, that neither praise nor dispraise shall affect me.

There rests only that we give the description we promised of the scene, which was the house of Fame. The structure and ornament of which (as is profest before) was entirely master Jones's invention and design. First, for the lower columns, he chose the statues of the most excellent poets, as Homer, Virgil, Lucan, &c., as being the substantial supporters of Fame. For the upper, Achilles, Æneas, Caesar, and those great heroes, which these poets had celebrated. All which stood as in massy gold. Between the pillars, underneath, were figured land-battles, sea-fights, triumphs, loves, sacrifices, and all magnificent subjects of honour, in brass, and heightened with silver. In which he profest to follow that noble description made by Chaucer of the place. Above were sited the masquers, over whose heads he devised two eminent figures of Honour and Virtue for the arch. The friezes, both below and above, were filled with several-coloured lights, like emeralds, rubies, sapphires, carbuncles, &c., the reflex of which, with our lights, placed in the concave, upon the masquers' habits, was full of glory. These habits had in them the excellency of all device and riches; and were worthily varied by his invention, to the nations whereof they were queens. Nor are these alone his due; but divers other accessions to the strangeness and beauty of the spectacle: as the hell, the going about of the chariots, and binding the witches, the turning machine, with the presentation of Fame. All which I willingly acknowledge for him: since it is a virtue planted in good natures, that what respects they wish to obtain fruitfully from others, they will give ingenuously themselves.

Contends to be as bounteous of her fame
To others, as her life was good to her.
For by their lives they only did confer
Good on themselves; but by their fame to yours,
And every age the benefit endures.

Here the throne wherein they sat, being machina versatilis, *suddenly changed; and in the place of it appeared* Fama bona, *as she is de-described (in* Iconolog. di Cesare Ripa) *attired in white, with white wings, having a collar of gold about her neck, and a heart hanging at it: which* Orus Apollo, *in his hierogl. interprets the note of a good* Fame. *In her right-hand she bore a trumpet, in her left an olive-branch: and for her state, it was as Virgil describes her, at the full, her feet on the ground, and her head in the clouds. She, after the music had done, which waited on the turning of the machine, called from thence to Virtue, and spake this following speech.*

FAME

Virtue, my father and my honour; thou
That mad'st me good as great; and dar'st avow
No fame for thine but what is perfect: aid
To-night the triumphs of thy white-winged maid.
Do those renowned queens all utmost rites
Their states can ask. This is a night of nights.
In mine own chariots let them crowned ride;
And mine own birds and beasts, in geers applied
To draw them forth. Unto the first car tie
Far-sighted eagles, to note Fame's sharp eye,
Unto the second, griffons, that design
Swiftness and strength, two other gifts of mine.
Unto the last, our lions, that imply
The top of graces, state, and majesty.
And let those Hags be led as captives, bound
Before their wheels, whilst I my trumpet sound.

At which the loud music sounded as before, to give the Masquers *time of descending.*

By this time imagine the masquers descended, and again mounted into three triumphant chariots, ready to come forth. The first four were drawn with eagles (whereof I gave the reason, as of the rest, in Fames's speech), their four torch-bearers attending on the chariot's sides, and four of the Hags bound before them. Then followed the second, drawn by griffons, with their torch-bearers, and four other

Hags. Then the last, which was drawn by lions, and more eminent (wherein her Majesty was), and had six torch-bearers more, peculiar to her, with the like number of Hags. After which a full triumphant music, singing this SONG, while they rode in state about the stage: –

> Help, help, all tongues, to celebrate this wonder:
> The voice of Fame should be as loud as thunder.
> Her house is all of echo made,
> Where never dies the sound:
> And as her brows the clouds invade,
> Her feet do strike the ground.
> Sing then, good Fame, that's out of Virtue born:
> For who doth Fame neglect, doth Virtue scorn.

Here they alighted from their chariots, and danced forth their first dance: then a second immediately following it: both right curious, and full of subtle and excellent changes, and seemed performed with no less spirits than of those they personated. The first was to the cornets, the second to the violins. After which they took out the men, and danced the measures; entertaining the time, almost to the space of an hour, with singular variety: when, to give them rest, from the music which attended the chariots, by that most excellent tenor voice, and exact singer (her Majesty's servant, Master Jo. Allin) this ditty was sung: —

> When all the ages of the earth
> Were crowned but in this famous birth:
> And that when the would boast their store
> Of worthy queens, they knew no more:
> How happier is that age can give
> A Queen in whom all they do live!

After it succeeded their third dance; than which a more numerous composition could not be seen: graphically disposed into letters, and honouring the name of the most sweet and ingenious Prince, CHARLES Duke of York. Wherein, beside that principal grace of perspicuity, the motions were so even and apt, and their expression so just, as, if mathematicians had lost proportion, they might there have found it. The author was Master Thomas Giles. After this they danced galliards and corantos. And then their last dance, no less elegant in the place than the rest, with which they took their chariots again, and triumphing about the stage, had their return to the House of Fame celebrated with this last SONG; whose notes (as the former)

were the work and honour of my excellent friend Alfonso Ferra-
bosco:

> Who, Virtue, can thy power forget,
> That sees these live, and triumph yet?
> Th' Assyrian pomp, the Persian pride,
> Greeks' glory, and the Romans dyed:
>   And who yet imitate
> Their noises tarry the same fate.
> Force greatness all the glorious ways
>   You can, it soon decays;
> But so good Fame shall never:
> Her triumphs, as their causes, are for ever.

. . . .

I I

The Popular Theatre

COMMEDIA DELL' ARTE

The most vital movement in the theatre of the Italian Renaissance was not the written drama, which for the most part consisted of pallid imitations of Seneca, Terence, and Plautus. Instead, it was a tradition of non-literary performance called *commedia all' improviso,* improvised comedy, or alternatively, *commedia dell' arte,* professional comedy as distinguished from the amateur comedy performed by court gentlemen.

Commedia dell' arte was a unique style of theatre that began in Italy some time before 1550, reached its climax early in the seventeenth century, and for the most part passed out of existence during the eighteenth century, although its influence on theatrical tradition continues until this day. The origins of the *commedia* have been disputed. Some scholars trace its roots to the Atellan farces, a type of indecent pantomime, popular in the Roman world during the second century A.D. Others point to the influence of Plautine plots and character types, and still others insist that the *commedia* owes much to the performances of wandering minstrels and mimes during the Middle Ages.

Whatever its origins, however, the mature *commedia* style contained a number of decidedly original characteristics. A troupe of *commedia* actors performed without playscripts. They were provided instead with a *sogetto,* that is to say, a bare outline of the plot, including brief descriptions of each scene to be performed. It was then their task to fill in this outline with appropriate dialogue and action. Much of the dialogue was improvised, but not all of it. Each actor memorized a number of stock speeches, or *concetti,* suitable to his character, which could be inserted into the action at appropriate moments. A man who played a lover's part either composed or plagiarized a number of declarations of devotion, which could be used in play after play. An actor playing an old man needed to learn stock pieces of fatherly advice and so forth.

In addition to the *concetti,* most *commedia* actors had at their disposal a number of amusing comic actions called *lazzi,* which had no connection with the plot and which could therefore be used over and over again. These traditional pieces of comic business were handed down from one generation of actors to the next, and most of them had descriptive names, like "the *lazzo* of tearing the wings from a fly" or "the *lazzo* of fear during a storm."

The *lazzi*, for the most part, were the property of the low comedians of the company, the *zanni*, usually functioning as the servants of the other principal persons in the plot. The *zanni* are among the most important of the *commedia* characters. Arlecchino (Harlequin) was one such, as were Pulcinella (Punch) and Scaramouche. An actor usually chose a character and a costume at the beginning of his career and continued to play that character and wear that costume until he retired, adding to the traditional figure his own eccentricities of delivery and gesture. Arlecchino, for example, was originally the invention of the great *commedia* actor, Tristano Martinelli, who played the part in Italy between 1588 and 1599 and then moved to Paris where his clever pantomime immediately captured the imagination of the French audience. As Martinelli performed the role, Arlecchino was one of the stupid *zanni*, and the humor of the part depended on his coarse and clumsy blunders in language and action. After Martinelli's death, the next important actor to assume the role was Guiseppe-Domenico Biancolelli (1640–88), who spent most of his professional life in France and performed under the name Dominique. Biancolelli was an athlete and dancer who had a raspy voice. He took the traditional personality of Arlecchino (as Martinelli had performed it) and adapted it to his own remarkable acrobatic talents. The whole tone of the character changed, and Arlecchino was transformed into a kind of boyish innocent, whose skilful, athletic, and for the most part silent escapes from danger were an unending source of amusement.

The other stock characters of the *commedia* were similarly modified by the personality and special abilities of each performer. The principal character-types, or masks (as they were called), included the following: two *zanni* (at least one clever and one stupid servant); Il Dottore, the Bolognese scholar (a caricature of a learned man); Pantalone, the Venetian merchant (usually a henpecked husband and foolish aging lover); Il Capitano, the Spanish soldier (a bragging warrior of the Plautine type); and finally, the Amoroso and Amorosa (the only unmasked figures in the drama), serious characters who provide the love interest.

Around these recurring types a great number of highly conventional intrigues were woven. The style of performance was boisterous; the humor frequently grotesque and brutal. In the eighteenth century the stories were softened and the comic tone became increasingly sentimental. But the Renaissance *commedia* was a hard and savage drama. The savagery can be detected by glancing at pictures of the traditional costumes worn by the characters. Who can ever forget the mean, pig-eyed mask of the early Arlecchino; the hunched back of the sixteenth-century Pulchinella; the thin, sapless, bird-like profile of Pantalone; the long nose and pointed chin that distinguished the mask of the seventeenth-century Capitano. The humor of the *commedia dell' arte* was based to a large extent on physical and moral deformity, a cynical but at the same time very striking mixture of bitter irony and wild farce.

The *commedia dell' arte* flourished in a great variety of guises. Straggling troupes of four and five actors performed rough farces on improvised platforms that were carried in carts from town to town. The most successful and accomplished companies performed in spectacular court settings created by the most advanced scene designers of the day. The most famous of the elite troupes was the *Gelosi* company, sponsored by the Ferrara court and led by the celebrated Francesco Andreini (1548–1624), whose performance as a braggart captain won him a reputation as the wittiest actor of his day. The Amorosa of the *Gelosi* was Francesco's wife, Isabella, without peer as an actress in her own time and unquestionably one of the most charming, intelligent, and beautiful women ever to appear on a stage. She joined the *Gelosi* in 1578 and soon became the company's leading attraction. For twenty-six years she captivated audiences in Italy and France, and her death in 1604 caused her husband to dismiss his troupe.

Associated also with the *Gelosi* during this period was the actor and author, Flaminio Scala (died c. 1622). Scala in 1611 published a series of forty-eight *sogetti*, presumably used by the *Gelosi* and by the *Confidenti*, another troupe with whom he was associated.

Of these forty-eight *sogetti*, forty are comedies. The *sogetto* for *The Portrait* (c. 1590), one of the forty, is reproduced below. We have reason to believe that it was first performed by the *Gelosi*, with Andreini creating his traditional part of Captain Spavente and Scala playing the less important role of Flavio.

The Portrait is representative of the kind of conventional plot to which the *commedia* actors attached their frequently inspired improvisations, the improvisations which later were to exert a considerable influence on the literary drama through the efforts of writers like Molière and Carlo Goldoni.

Flaminio Scala

THE PORTRAIT*

(A Scenario)

A troupe of actors were playing in Parma. As was the custom, the principal actress was visited by many callers. ORATIO, a cavalier of the city, while calling on her, took from his neck a locket in which was concealed the portrait of a very beautiful woman, who had herself given the locket to him.

Always catty, the actress whose name was VITTORIA, slyly extracted the portrait from the locket before returning it to the cavalier at the end of his visit.

A few days afterwards, the husband of the said lady, coming to see VITTORIA, who did not know him, was by chance shown the portrait of his wife.

The husband, whose name was PANTALONE, was greatly surprised. He made urgent entreaties to the actress to tell him the name of the man who had given her the portrait.

She answered him courteously. PANTALONE dissimulated the reason for his interest in the affair and returned home in a fury with the intention of inflicting an exemplary chastisement on his culpable better half. However, on his arrival, his wife exculpated herself with such good excuses that she succeeded in appeasing his wrath.

The persons are, besides the actress VITTORIA and her comrade PIOMBINO: the two old men, PANTALONE and GRATIANO; their wives ISABELLA and FLAMINIA, and the lovers of these last, ORATIO and FLAVIO. PEDROLINO is valet to PANTALONE; HARLEQUIN is valet to CAPTAIN SPAVENTE. A young Milanese woman, SILVIA, disguised as a page, comes under the name of LESBINO to offer her services to the CAPTAIN, whom she loves.

ACT I

SCENE I

Following the quarrel which had occurred at their home between ISABELLA and her husband, upon the subject of the portrait which was last seen in the hands of the actress VITTORIA, ISABELLA becomes sus-

* Translated by Ethel van der Meer. *From World Drama*, Volume 2, by Barrett H. Clark; copyright 1933 by Barrett H. Clark; published by Dover Publications, Inc., and reprinted by permission of the publisher.

picious. She thereupon orders PEDROLINO to go to ORATIO and demand of him the portrait which she, ISABELLA, had given him some time before.

SCENE II

CAPTAIN SPAVENTE tells HARLEQUIN how, obliged to assist in the theater, he has fallen in love with the SIGNORA VITTORIA. HARLEQUIN tells him he is wasting his time.

SCENE III

Later, after asking a number of foolish questions as to LESBINO's bravery and military talents, the CAPTAIN consents to take him on as page.

SCENE IV

FLAMINIA, at her window, calls HARLEQUIN and asks him to convey a letter to a cavalier named FLAVIO, whom he will encounter in the place where she gives rendezvous to gentlemen. HARLEQUIN takes the letter and promises to deliver it to him to whom it is addressed. FLAMINIA gives him some money and withdraws. HARLEQUIN attentively regards FLAMINIA's window.

SCENE V

DOCTOR GRATIANO, husband of FLAMINIA, seeing HARLEQUIN gazing, letter in hand, at his wife's window, becomes suspicious. He demands what he wants and from whom the letter has come. HARLEQUIN replies that a certain FLAVIO gave it him to deliver to a lady. The doctor takes the letter and raps HARLEQUIN with his cane.

SCENES VI TO X

PANTALONE interposes between the doctor and HARLEQUIN. FLAVIO presents himself. GRATIANO, exceedingly angry, returns the letter to him. FLAVIO receives it with deep humility. Alone, FLAVIO reads the letter, in which FLAMINIA begs him no longer to frequent the theater.

SCENE XI

ORATIO, of whom PEDROLINO asks the return of the portrait to ISABELLA, explains that this is impossible at this time. He makes the excuse that the locket is being repaired at the jeweler's. PEDROLINO smiles and asks him how long it has been since he has visited the theater, questions him about all the actors and lastly about the SIGNORA VITTORIA.

SCENE XII

ISABELLA comes in at this moment. She dissembles at first and requests the return of her portrait. ORATIO repeats what he had told

PEDROLINO. She calls him a traitor and tells him that she is not ignorant of his love for the actress, to whom he has given her portrait.
Vexed, and unwilling to listen to ORATIO, she goes back, ordering
PEDROLINO to follow her. ORATIO complains of his ill-fortune and
curses the presence of the players, whose coming brought all the
trouble. He expresses himself in abusive terms regarding VITTORIA
who had played him such a mischievous trick.

SCENE XIII

The CAPTAIN, hearing what ORATIO says of the players and of VIT-
TORIA in particular, takes up her defense. He maintains that the
theater is a noble diversion and that the SIGNORA VITTORIA is an honorable lady. ORATIO, furious, replies that he is a liar. He puts his
hand to his sword, whereupon the CAPTAIN asks ORATIO if he will
fight a duel with him. ORATIO replies that he is ready. The CAPTAIN
then says he goes to write a letter exculpating him from responsibility
in the event that he is killed, and which he will give to him in case the
police should misunderstand and seek his adversary. He suggests that
ORATIO do the same for him, and leaves. HARLEQUIN comments that
his master has all the appearances of wishing to sidestep the affair
gracefully. Thus ends the first act.

ACT II

SCENE I

VITTORIA, richly clad, with golden necklaces, pearl bracelets, diamonds and rubies on her fingers, rents herself, through PIOMBINO, to
the DUKE and all his entourage, recalling the infinite courtesies she
has received every day from the nobility of the city of Parma.

SCENES II TO V

PEDROLINO boasts of his master PANTALONE to VITTORIA. PANTALONE
unexpectedly appears, but seeing his wife at the window, dares not
approach VITTORIA. PEDROLINO persuades PANTALONE that the actress
is in love with him. PANTALONE, flattered, expresses the intention of
making her a present.

SCENE VI

While ORATIO recounts the unhappy history of the portrait to his
friend FLAVIO, HARLEQUIN offers the letter of release from the CAP-
TAIN. ORATIO receives him with a blow of the fist and dashes off to the
theater.

Scenes VII to XII

Flavio and Pedrolino, and then Flaminia, attempt to reconcile Isabella with Oratio. Isabella softens, but declares he will have nothing from her, so long as he does not return the portrait; and she forbids him, moreover, to go himself to negotiate for its restoration. Pedrolino divulges to them the fact that the two old men, Pantalone and Gratiano, are attentive to the actress.

Scene XIII

Now arrives the doctor. Pedrolino pretends to be arguing with Flaminia and says: "How should I know whether your husband goes to the theater or not?" Flaminia, entering into the deception, pretends to be jealous of her husband.

Scene XIV

Piombino presents his compliments to the doctor on behalf of the Signora Vittoria. He requests him to provide the actress with a silver pitcher and basin of which she has need in a piece she is going to present. The doctor replies that he will send these by Pedrolino. Piombino assures him that the actress is smitten with him, and that on his account she scorns all the gentlemen who pay court to her at the theater. The doctor is vastly pleased, and promises a reward to Piombino.

Scene XV

The Captain converses with his page regarding the passion inspired in him by the actress. Lesbino endeavors to turn him away from this passion which he cannnot make honorable. The page asks him if he has ever before been in love. The Captain says that, in Milan, he had been in love with a very beautiful young girl named Silvia.

Scene XVI

Harlequin interrupts his master to inform him that Vittoria is waiting near by, at the jeweler's. Lesbino, despairing, seeks to persuade Harlequin that he must kill him, Lesbino, because he has conceived the intention of assassinating his master. Harlequin abuses and maltreats the page. Flaminia and Isabella intervene.

Scene XVII

Having divined a woman under the attire of Lesbino, they remove him to the residence of Flaminia. Thus ends the second act.

ACT III

SCENE I

VITTORIA and PIOMBINO go to dine at the house of a rich gentleman who gives them magnificent presents. They rejoice between
themselves over the custom of making gifts to the players, a custom
prevalent throughout the cities of Italy, and which is seldom neglected
by persons of distinguishing rank. VITTORIA confesses that she laughs
at all the lovers who are not generous with her. PIOMBINO promises to
provide well for her old age.

SCENES II AND III

PANTALONE comes to call. VITTORIA thanks him for the gifts he
has brought and invites him to come to the theater at the première.
PANTALONE promises to be present. Afterwards FLAVIO arrives, and
the actress detains him with a diverting conversation.

SCENE IV

But FLAMINIA has observed them from her window. She goes out
angrily and boxes FLAVIO's ears, then returns into the house without
uttering a word. VITTORIA bursts into laughter.

SCENE V

PANTALONE, who has witnessed this striking event, blames the ef-
frontery of FLAMINIA. He felicitates himself upon the modesty and
good breeding of his wife. After these reflections he exchanges compliments with the actress. But ISABELLA appears.

SCENE VI

She reproaches her husband for seeking other women and neglect-
ing her. She recites all the facts, with embellishments, and adds that
he does not deserve a wife like her. She flies into a mounting rage,
exciting herself over him until he flees. Turning to VITTORIA she tells
her that if his sense of honor does not keep him from compromising
himself with an actress, she will teach him manners, and returns to
her dwelling. VITTORIA laughs softly, remarking that wherever one
finds a troupe of actors playing, there also one will find married women
with a sour mouth.

SCENE VII

GRATIANO arrives in his turn. "Behold the other pigeon waiting to
be plucked," says PIOMBINO. The actress does, in fact, coquette with

on chez saDame en mulle veut aller·
ment defens qui la tourmentes? pieque

Dont Pantalon se plant mais Zani luy replique
Iuistre un zut demare une mulle parler

Masked actors in the *commedia dell'arte*.
Top: Il Capitano, Pantalone and Zani, early seventeenth century (1608-20).

Bottom: Inamorata and Pantalone, late seventeenth century.

Three of hundreds of costume designs by Bernardo Buontalenti for the Intermezzi of 1589.

the doctor. PIOMBINO reminds her of the silver pitcher and basin he has promised her. GRATIANO joyfully takes PEDROLINO with him in order to bring back the presents. The players jeer at his stupidity.

SCENE VIII

ORATIO, greeting VITTORIA, demands the portrait of ISABELLA. She laughingly replies that she doesn't know what he is talking about, and takes herself off with PIOMBINO.

SCENE IX

ISABELLA has seen ORATIO talking with the actress. She reproaches him for not keeping his promise. HARLEQUIN tells ORATIO that ISABELLA and FLAMINIA have taken away his master's page and are keeping him there with them. ISABELLA, seizing the occasion to spite ORATIO, calls FLAMINIA and tells her to bring her new lover to the window. LESBINO appears and says to ISABELLA: "What do you require of me, Signora?" ORATIO, at sight of this unknown person, becomes enraged and goes off cursing ISABELLA.

SCENE X

PANTALONE demands the cause of all this noise. ISABELLA says that ORATIO wished to take the page away from her. "And what do you want with this page?" inquires PANTALONE angrily. ISABELLA then recounts the adventure of SILVIA, the Milanese. She urges PANTALONE to go in search of the CAPTAIN and bring him there if possible. For PANTALONE, this is precisely the opportunity he himself needed to go to the theater.

SCENES XI TO XVII

The lovers start another quarrel. PEDROLINO suggests that as the husbands are at the play, which lasts just six hours in the evening, they might employ their time to better advantage. The lovers see the reasonableness of this and become reconciled. The valets take counsel as to the best means of restoring SILVIA to the CAPTAIN's favor. The latter appears.

SCENE XVIII

PEDROLINO tells the CAPTAIN that he will find VITTORIA at the residence of PANTALONE. He enters by way of the basement and there discovers SILVIA divested of her masculine costume.

SCENE XIX

The two valets, PEDROLINO and HARLEQUIN, are alone in the theater. They seat themselves on the floor, agreeing between them what they would say if the two old men were suddenly to return. At this time some amusing pantomime takes place. A knave, bearing a lantern, sees the two valets. He weeps and laments because he has lost a great deal of money at cards, and has left not more than a dozen half-crowns. The valets invite him to play with them. They play. The swindler wins the money and finally the clothing of PEDROLINO and HARLEQUIN, and they suffer themselves to be left in their shirts. The valets are chagrined.

SCENE XX

There is great excitement in the theater. PANTALONE, GRATIANO and PIOMBINO rush in bringing VITTORIA, whom they beg to sustain herself amidst the dangers which threaten her, a brawl having taken place on her account. The gentlemen, the *bravi*, their swords bared, pour in and perceiving VITTORIA, seize her and hastily carry her off. PIOMBINO follows with a gesture of despair.

SCENE XXI

PANTALONE and GRATIANO, finding themselves face to face with their valets who are attired only in their shirts, demand of them what has happened. The valets cleverly explain that it is the men just going out of the theater who have robbed them. They add philosophically that while the theater brings pleasurable distraction, it is also the source of a number of scandals. While they are giving themselves up to these sage reflections, ISABELLA and FLAMINIA descend upon them and demand of their husbands to know if the comedy is already ended.

SCENE XXII

PANTALONE replies that a brawl interrupted it and that he has not seen the CAPTAIN. ISABELLA recounts how they had told the CAPTAIN that he would find VITTORIA awaiting him in the basement where SIL-VIA, in lieu of the actress, is waiting. Fearing that the CAPTAIN, thus misled, might commit some kind of violence, they had urged the SIGNOR ORATIO and the SIGNOR FLAVIO to remain. PANTALONE and GRATIANO approve.

SCENE XXIII

The CAPTAIN goes out of the house swearing he has been betrayed. ORATIO and FLAVIO seek to calm him. PANTALONE and all the others intercede in SILVIA's behalf. He recognizes that SILVIA is of honorable lineage, that she is the daughter of a wealthy Milanese merchant and that he loves her. Bewitched by this diabolical actress, he had for a time forgotten poor SILVIA, but now returns to her and consents to marry her.

SCENE XXIV

They fetch SILVIA, who realizes that her lover reciprocates her tenderness.

ISABELLA and FLAMINIA exhort their husbands to keep away from the playhouse and watch over their households and the behavior of their wives. Everybody goes to PANTALONE's to celebrate the nuptials of SILVIA and the CAPTAIN, and it is thus that the comedy of *The Portrait* is ended.

Clever actors in the *commedia dell'arte* composed their own concetti and invented their own lazzi, but less spontaneous performers could consult manuscript collections of these materials which were passed from hand to hand. Some of the most accomplished performers—Frencesco Andreini, Tristano Martinelli, Isabella Andreini, among them—published their best speeches and jests.

However acquired, each actor of a mask needed instantly to have available memorized pieces appropriate to his part in the sogetti. A lover needed sentimental addresses to his beloved; Pantalone, stock pieces of advice for his children and curses; Il dottore, strings of dates, names and foolish scholarly citations.

Examples of this material follow, collected by Giacomo Oreglio.

LAZZI FOR THE ZANNI*

LAZZO *of the goodness of Pulcinella*

The lazzo of the goodness of Pulcinella is that he, having heard from the Captain or from others that they want to kill him, and not being known to them, freely praises himself with the words: 'Pulcinella ia a man of infinite wit, a humble man, a good man.'

LAZZO *of the fly*

Pulcinella, having been left by his master to guard the house, on being asked if there is anyone inside, replies that there isn't even a fly. The master discovers three men there and reproaches Pulcinella, who replies: 'You didn't find any flies, you only found men.'

LAZZO *shut up*

While his master is talking Pulcinella is continually interrupting. Three times his master tells him to shut up. Then when he calls for Pulcinella, the latter pays him back in the same coin and says 'Shut up!'

LAZZO *of the O*

Coviello asks Pulcinella what is the name of his beloved; Pulcinella says that it begins with O and that he must guess it. Coviello says: 'Orsola, Olimpia, Orcana.' Then Pulcinella says that her name is Rosetta. Coviello protests that this name begins with an R and not with an O. Pulcinella replies: 'And if I want to begin it with an O what business is that of yours?'

---

* In *The Commedia dell'Arte*, tr. Lovett F. Edwards (N.Y.: Hill & Wang, 1968), pp.14-16, 82-3, 107-111.

LAZZO *of the three hunters*
Pulcinella tells a story. 'There were once three hunters; the first was
armless, the second eyeless and the third legless. The armless one says:
"I will carry the gun"; the eyeless one says: "I will shoot as soon as I see
it" and the legless one says: "I will run and pick it up". They go hunting.
The armless one says:"There is the hare"; the eyeless one shoots at it and
the legless one runs to pick it up. Then, wanting to cook it, they go to a
house without a floor, without doors or windows and without a roof; the
one wtihout hands knocks at the door and the man who is not at home
appears and says: "What do you want?" They ask for the loan of a pot of
water. The man who is not at home brings a pot, without a bottom, full
of water, when all of a sudden a man who isn't there, without eyes,
wtihout hands and without feet, carries off the hare.'

LAZZO *'at iam gravi'*
This *lazzo* is that either the Doctor or the Pedant says: 'At *Regina gravi
iamdudum saucia cura*' (but the Queen long wounded by this grievous
worry) and Pulcinella explains: 'The Queen being pregnant, twice ate
raw sausage.' (*La Regina essendo gravida mangio due volte la salsiccia
cruda.*)

LAZZO *of the shoes*
When they are about to take Pulcinella to prison he says he must first tie
his shoe laces. Then he bends down, grabs the legs of his two guards,
throws them down and runs away.

A CONCETTO FOR PANTALONE

(The original is in broad Venetian dialect.)

Oh son (I almost said of a randy old goat) how have you repaid all that I
have done for you, the sleepless nights you have caused me, the bezants
I have paid for you, the labours I have undertaken for you? With what
ingratitude you repay a father who has done so much for you!...

But since you want to live like a beast, may all the beasts of the world be
against you; may the cocks disturb your sleep, the dogs gnaw your
bones, the cats scratch your hands, the crows peck out your eyes, the lice
eat your flesh and shame you in your clothes; may the fleas, the bugs, the
horseflies, give you no rest with their pricks, their bites, their stink and
their puncturings. When you go out into the country may the snakes bite
you, the wasps sting you, the oxen lacerate you, the bulls gore you; when

you are in the city may the donkeys jostle you and the horses trample on you; should you travel by sea may the dog-fishes poison you, may the dolphins signal tempest for you; if you travel by land may the litters and the carriages break your collar-bone and, finally, may all the animals created for the service of man become for you toads, serpents, dragons, panthers, basilisks, hydras and Spanish flies.

(From Andrea Perrucci, *Dell' arte rappresentativa, premeditata e all' improvviso*, 1699.)

DIALOGUE FOR IL CAPITANO
CAPTAIN SPAVENTO AND TRAPPOLA[1]

TRAPPOLA. Captain Spavento, my lord and master, you have many times told me that you are not like other folk and that you were not born, nursed, reared and educated like other people. I am extremely curious to know what sort of birth you had and what bearing is has on the other things you have told me. I therefore beg, implore and entreat you, as a mark of favour to me, to tell me the full story of your life and career. In return for this favour I vow that for your sake I shall expose my miserable self to whatever danger may arise.

CAPTAIN. The man who serves me cannot live in danger for I am crowned with honour and laden with trophies. Nor need that man expose his life to risks and dangers, for wherever I appear all risks, dangers and awful accidents disappear.

TRAPPOLA. To live in peace and quiet is the best thing I know. Now begin your story. I want to hear every detail. I desire nothing more than to listen.

CAPTAIN. My coming to this great stage of the world was not like the comings of the rest of God's creatures. Other children are born naked and crying; but I — I came clad in breastplate and coat of mail; I roared like a mad lion and hissed like a raging serpent.

TRAPPOLA. I can see that it must have taken a long time before your mother's womb was clean again after such an extraordinary delivery.

CAPTAIN. When other children are born, they are immediately washed with warm water, swaddled in linen, and fed milk and pap. But at the moment I came into the world I was washed in melted lead, swathed in red-hot bands of steel, and fed upon deadly poisons and gunpowder.

---

[1] As Andreini played the part with the *Gelosi,* his captain always had an impudent servant to act as his scourge and straightman.

TRAPPOLA. Well, that fixes the charlatans once and for all. You know the ones who prepare their hands before they wash them in boiling fat to impress the spectators.

CAPTAIN. When other boys grow up, they are sent to school to learn reading, writing, and 'rithmetic, and then to study grammar, logic, philosophy, law and medicine. But as soon as I had finished the business of being born, nursed and reared, I was sent while still in my boyhood to go to a school of murderers to learn how to wound, kill, and cut people into small pieces; and therefore scarcely a day goes by without my wounding, killing, or cutting somebody into small pieces.

TRAPPOLA. Ah, that's why there are so many spoils of war and so many trophies hanging outside the city gate! It's all your work! Master, you are unique! And I can see that you are full of pity and compassion; for you are a master of your profession and you kill quickly. It is a common saying that to kill quickly is a sign of great sympathy, and that only amateur, bungling slayers let their victims suffer.

CAPTAIN. But that's nothing compared to what awaits them afterwards!

TRAPPOLA. Let that be a warning to you, you poor devils and wretches! Don't fall into the hands of my master! In my mind's eye I can see you broken on the wheel and nailed to the posts!

CAPTAIN. And since I am not like mortal man in any respect, I even keep different company.

TRAPPOLA. What can that mean? What sort of company?

CAPTAIN. Heroes, gods, demigods. Mark, and mark well, the truth of what I say, for in so doing you will quickly learn to comprehend and understand. To comply with the rules of courtly etiquette and not to show myself unworthy of my position I invited to dine with me one day my friends Death and the Devil.

TRAPPOLA. Oh, good. Then things will be quiet for us both in life and death, since both Death and the Devil are friends of yours.

CAPTAIN. When the sumptuous banquet was over, the Devil bade us farewell and returned to the gloomy shores of Acheron. But Death wanted to stay behind to have a midnight supper and then go to bed with me.

TRAPPOLA. Death must have been in love with you. Oh. my lord, you have such a beautiful and charming beloved and you haven't said a word about it! I assure you you can put aside all suspicions and jealousies, for every man will run to avoid seeing her.

CAPTAIN. Death stayed to sup with me. The supper was prepared and served, and the bed was made ready for love's battles. That night we ate, and laughed, and drank, and then went to lie together in one and the same bed, Death and I.

TRAPPOLA. You might say as Petrarch said: "The bed is a cruel battlefield."

CAPTAIN. And since we had been drinking in good earnest from morning to night, and since I was on fire from the wines of Bacchus and the seductions of Venus, I enjoyed the whole of that happy night the ecstasies of love with Death.

TRAPPOLA. God save me from such company and such ecstasies!

CAPTAIN. And our satisfaction was so complete that Death became pregnant by me.

TRAPPOLA. How the devil could you be satisfied? And how is it possible to make her with child? She's nothing but skin and bones.

CAPTAIN. Death is a magnificent woman to the man who understands these things. And a woman whom one should not by any means despise. She's a woman who knows what it is all about and doesn't tire one out like other women who don't know their business and never come to the point. When Death noticed that she was pregnant and was about to give birth, she sent for Erebus and Night, her parents, that they might assist her during labour. Death gave birth under terrible pains and horrible cries and brought into the world the Guelphs and the Ghibellines. Now that was a bit of business worthy of a brave soldier.

TRAPPOLA. And what happened afterwards to your beloved Death?

CAPTAIN. She said goodbye and returned with her father and mother to the underworld.

TRAPPOLA. My lord and master, if the philosopher Simonides was twice saved from death for burying a body he found on the shore and was warned by the dead man, how much more do you not deserve as a reward for having made Death with child? Certainly, much, much, more, and I am sure that she will never come to claim you.

CAPTAIN. Living is nothing more than a continuous dying, as the philosopher says, since life slips away from us day by day, but still I have been born to escape from the tyranny of time and death.

TRAPPOLA. That is true, my lord and master, but those who have not been granted the same privileges as you must accommodate themselves to fate and death. Our life is like a snowdrift in the sunshine or like a stone tossed into the whirlpool to spin around a few times before it sinks.

CAPTAIN. I regret that the laws of fate condemn humankind to death; but I shall try to make up for this in some way, and if I cannot help everyone, I shall at least help those men of worth and honour who deserve to live. All I have to do is say a few words to my good friend Fate, and the matter is settled. Then each and every one can live as long as he likes.

TRAPPOLA. If you were to succeed in this endeavour, which I for my part very much doubt, I should wish that we might take advantage of our time on earth and enjoy ourselves, provided we were allowed to. If we were to live forever, one could fear the worst. Men would become so insolent and women so abandoned that life would not be bearable, and everything would fall to pieces. The courts would not be able to function, thieves and murderers would rule everywhere, no one would be safe in his own house, women would become common property, and the world would collapse into the primordial chaos. I think it might be best if you let matters remain as at present, for all created things must have their end in time. Life is given one on loan, and has to be returned on demand.

CAPTAIN. Trappola, the road to death is never blocked. If you wish to die, you won't lack for the means of it. And if you want your life to have an honourable and brilliant end, let me tell you how to accomplish it. This sword of mine can in one stroke separate your head from your trunk; you will thus die an honourable death at my hands, and your wish will be realized.

TRAPPOLA. Indeed, it is said that only two days are truly one's own: the day one is born and the day one dies; but still I want to try to live as long as I can. I thank you humbly for your offer, and offer you in return my most respectful farewell.

(From Francesco Andreini: *Le Bravure del Capitano Spavento*, 1607.)

THE ELIZABETHAN JIG

The closest English equivalent to the Italian *zanni* were the clowns of the Elizabethan public theatres. These clowns were frequently noted for their extemporal wit, a quality which occasionally angered the playwrights, as a famous passage in *Hamlet* indicates. "And let those that play your clowns," Hamlet tells the visiting players, "speak no more than is set down for them. For there be of them that will themselves laugh to set on some quantity of barren spectators to laugh too, though in the meantime some necessary question of the play be then to be considered. That's villainous and shows a most pitiful ambition in the fool that uses it."

It is generally acknowledged that the fool to whom Hamlet refers was Will Kempe (d. 1603), who had departed from the King's Men in 1599 after a stormy association of three years. Kempe, who created Dogberry in *Much Ado About Nothing*, Peter in *Romeo and Juliet,* and other early Shakespearean clown parts, was a boisterous low comedian and a lively dancer, who by no means confined his fooling to the legitimate drama. Kempe was a specialist in the performance of *jigs:* short, rhymed afterpieces sung and danced after the final act of a tragedy. Kempe undoubtedly learned his jigmaking from his tutor, the greatest of all Elizabethan clowns, Richard Tarleton (d. 1588), who specialized in rustic fools and whose dancing was greatly admired by Queen Elizabeth.

Both Tarleton and Kempe undoubtedly appeared in hundreds of farcical pieces like *Singing Simpkin* (c. 1600), a typical Elizabethan jig, set, as was the custom, to current popular tunes.

Singing Simpkin*

The Names of the Persons.

Simpkin, a Clown.
Bluster, a Roarer.
An old Man.
His Wife.
A Servant.

Enter the wife, Simpkin following

Wife. Blind *Cupid* hath made my heart for to bleed,
 Fa la, la, la, la, la, la, la, la.
Simp. But I know a man can help you at need,
 With a fa la, la, la, la, fa, la, la, la, la, la.

Wife. My husband he often a hunting goes out,
 Fa la, la, la, &c.
Simp. And brings home a great pair of horns there's no doubt;
 with a fa la, la, la, &c.

VVife. How is't Monsieur *Simkin,* why are you so sad?
 Fa la, la, la, &c.
Simp. I am up to the ears in love, and it makes me stark mad,
 with a fa la, la, la, &c.

I am vext, I am tortur'd, and troubled at heart,
 Fa la, la, &c.
VVife. But Ile try my skill to take off your smart,
 with a fa la, la & c.

And on that condition I give you a kiss.
 Fa la, la, &c.
Simp. But what says your husband when he hears of this?
 with a fa la, la, &c.

VVife. You know my affection, & no one knows more,
 with a fa la, la, &c.   *Knock within.*
Simp. 'Uds niggers noggers who knocks at the door?
 with a fa la, la, &c.

---

* Reprinted from *The Elizabethan Jig,* ed. Charles R. Baskervill, by permission of The University of Chicago Press. Copyright 1929 by The University of Chicago.

Enter Servant. The tune alters.

Serv. There is a Royster at the door,
  he seems a Fellow stout.
Simp. I beseech you worthy friend,
  which is the back way out?
Serv. He swears and tears he will come in,
  And nothing shal him hinder.   *Exit Servant.*
Simp. I fear hee'l strip me out my skin.
  And burn it into tinder.

VVife. I have consider'd of a way,
  and twill be sure the best.
Simp. What may it be my dearest Dear?
  VVife. Creep into this same Chest.   *A chest set out.*
And though he roar, speak you no word,
  If you'l preserve my favour.
Simp. Shut to the chest, I pray, with speed,
  For something has some savour.

                                                  Enter Bluster.

Blust. I never shal be quiet
  if she use me in this fashion.
Wife. I am here to bid you welcom;
  what mean you by this passion?
Blust. With some sweet-fac'd fellow
  I thought gone out you were.
Simp. in the chest. No sooth, the sweet fac'd fellow
  is kept a prisoner here.

Blust. Where is the foole thy husband?
  Say, whither is he gone?
Wife. The Wittall[1] is a hunting.
  Blust. Then we two are alone:
But should he come And find me here,
  what might the Cuckold think?
Perhaps hee'd call the neighbours in,
  Simp. And beat you till you stink.

Blust. Yet in the bloody war full oft,
  My courage I did try.
Wife. I know you have kild many a man.
  Simp. You lie, you slut, you lie.

1 Wittol: man who is aware of wife's infidelity and submits to it.

Blust. I never came before a foe,
  By night nor yet by day.
But that I stoutly rouz'd my self,
  Simp. And nimbly ran away.

Blust. Within this chest Ile hide my self,
  If it chance he should come.
Wife. O no my love, that cannot be,
  Simp. I have bespoke the room.
Wife. I have a place behind here,
  Which yet is known to no man.
Simp. She has a place before too,
  But that is all to common.

                                              Old man within.

Old man. Wife, wherefore is the door thus bar'd?
  what mean you pray by this?
Wife. Alas! it is my husband.
  Simp. I laugh now till I piss.
Blust. Open the chest, Ile into it,
  My life else it may cost.
Wife. Alas I cannot open it.
  Simp. I beleeve the key is lost.

Wife. I have bethought my self
  upon a dainty trick.
Blust. What may it be my dearest love?
  I prethee now be quick.
Wife. You must say that your enemy
  Into this house is fled,
And that your heart can take no rest,
  Untill that he be dead.

Draw quickly out your furious blade,
  And seem to make a strife.
Swear all th' excuses can be made,
  Shall not preserve his life.
Say that the Rogue is fled in here,
  That stole away your coin,
And if Ile not deliver him,
  You'l have as much of mine.

Blust. Here's no man but my self,
  On whom shall I complain?

Wife. This great fool does not understand,
 This thing you must but faign.
My husband thus must be deceiv'd,
 and afterwards wee'l laugh.   *Enter old man.*
Old man. Wife, since you will not ope the door,
 Ile break't ope with my staff.

Blust. Good woman shew me to the slave,
 His limbs I strait wil tear.
Wife. By all the honesty I have,
 Theres no man came in here.
Blust. When I have fought to purchase wealth,
 And with my blood did win it,
This Rogue has got my purse by stealth.
 Simp. But never a peny in it.

Old man. She's big with child, therefore take heed
 you do not fright my wife.
Blust. But know you who the Father is?
 Simp. The Roarer on my life.
Old man. She knows not of your enemy,
 then get you gone you were best.
Wife. Peace husband, peace, I tell you true,
 I have hid him in the chest.

Old man. I am glad on't at my heart,
 but doe not tell him so.
VVife. I would not for a thousand pound
 the Roarer should it know.
Blust. When next we meet his life is gone,
 no other must he hope;
Ile kill him whatsoere comes on't,
 Simp. Pray think upon a rope.

Old man. What kind of person is it
 that in the chest does lie?
VVife. A goodly hansome sweet young man,
 as ere was seen with eye.
Old man. Then let us both entreat of him —
 Pray put us not in fear:
we do beseech you go from hence.
 Blust. But to morrow Ile be here.   *Exit Blust.*

Old man. Wife, run with all the speed you can,
 and quickly shut the dore,

I would not that the roaring man
   should come in any more.
Mean time I will release the youth,
   and tell him how we have sped. —
Be comforted my honest friend.   *Simpkin comes forth.*
   Simp. Alas, I am almost dead.

my heart is tortur'd in my breast
   with sorrow, fear and pain.
Old man. Ile fetch some *Aqua vitae,*
   to comfort you again.
Simp. And cause I will requite you,
   Whose love doth so excell,
Ile graft a pair of horns on your head,
   That may defend it well.

VVife. Good husband, let the man stay here,
   'Tis dang'rous in the street.
Old man. I would not for a crown of gold,
   The Roarer should him meet.
For should he come by any harm,
   They'd say the fault were mine.
VVife to Simpkin. There's half a crown, pray send him out
   to fetch a quart of wine.

Simp. There's money for you Sir, —
   Pray fetch a quart of Sack.[2]
Old man. 'Tis well, 'tis well, my honest friend,
   Ile see you shall not lack.
VVife. But if he should dishonest me,
   For there are such slipp'ry men.
Old man. Then he gets not of his half crown
   One peny back agen.   *Exit.*

Simp. Thy husband being gone my love,
   Wee'l sing, wee'l dance, and laugh,
I am sure he is a good fellow,
   And takes delight to quaff.
VVife. I'le fold thee in my arms my love,
   No matter for his listning.
         The Old man and his servant listen.
Simp. Gentlemen, some forty weeks hence
   You may come to a Christning.
  [2] A strong white wine from Southern Europe.

Old man. O sirrah, have I caught you,
   Now do the best you can,
Your Schoolmaster nere taught you
   To wrong an honest man.
Simp. Good sir, I never went to Schole,
   Then why am I abused?
The truth is, I am but a foole,
   And like a fool am used.

Old man. Yet sirrah you had wit enough
   to think to Cuckold me.
VVife. I jested with him, husband,
   his knavery to see.
Simp. But now you talk of knaverie,
   I pray where is my Sack?
Old man. You shall want it in your belly, Sir,
   And have it on your back.

                                 They beat him off. Exeunt.

THE ELIZABETHAN ·AUDIENCE

◈ The theatre, unlike fiction or poetry, is not a private but a public art. Plays are intended not for silent contemplation by a reader in a study, but for performance before an audience, and the form and content of a drama is to a great extent determined by the nature of that audience. In attempting to come to terms with a play from another era, it is frequently helpful to learn something about the spectators who first paid money to witness that play.

When we read in the prologues of Terence about the boisterous crowds that attended performances at the *Ludi Romani*, we can place the rough humor of his *Eunuchus* in its proper context. We can make a similar connection between the idle, courtly spectators of the theatres of the English Restoration and the elegance and essentially amoral wit of Wycherley and Congreve.

But what about the spectators who first came to see the plays of Shakespeare and his great contemporaries? What features of Elizabethan and Jacobean drama can be illuminated for us by a knowledge of the structure and character of a typical audience at the Globe, the Fortune, or the Rose?

Scholars like Muriel St. Clare Byrne and Alfred Harbage have attempted to answer that question for us. Professor Harbage's study, part of which is reproduced in this chapter, is a painstaking examination of hundreds of references to Elizabethan playgoing, and it seriously challenges a great many over-simple, but popular generalizations about the crowd whom it was Shakespeare's business to please.

Harbage very correctly implies that these generalizations are derived mainly from satirical portraits of certain classes of playgoers, and he cautions us to remember that "audiences never are assemblies of caricatures." The groundlings who paid a penny to stand in the yard of the Globe were probably not nearly so noisy, undisciplined, and illiterate as we might imagine from the satirical thrusts aimed at them by Shakespeare and his colleagues. Nor in all likelihood were the gallants, satirized by the playwright Thomas Dekker (1571?–1632) in his pamphlet *The Gull's Hornbook* (1609), nearly as vain and rude as his exaggerated account of their behavior would indicate.

We must, however, be careful not to err in the other direction. We must not dismiss the angry and amusing observations of men like Dekker as unjust or unfounded. Purposely exaggerated *The Gull's Hornbook* may be, but the exaggeration is based firmly on what must have been disagreeable fact.

Dekker's pamphlet was not concerned exclusively with playgoing; it was instead a general indictment of gallant manners.

The section on the theatre (Chapter VI of the original text, reproduced here with modernized spelling) must have been particularly heartfelt. Dekker, as a practicing professional playwright, had good reason to fear and despise the idlers who thrust
themselves "on the very rushes where the comedy is to dance."

Thomas Dekker

from THE GULL'S HORNBOOK[1]

How a Gallant Should Behave Himself
in a Playhouse

*T*he theater is your poet's royal exchange, upon which their muses
(that are now turned to merchants) meeting, barter away that light
commodity of words for a lighter ware than words, plaudities,[2] and
the breath of the great beast;[3] which, like the threatenings of two
cowards, vanish all into air. Players and their factors, who put away
the stuff, and make the best of it they possibly can (as indeed 'tis
their parts so to do), your gallant, your courtier, and your captain
had wont to be the soundest paymasters; and I think are still the
surest chapmen;[4] and these, by means that their heads are well
stocked, deal upon this comical freight by the gross; when your
groundling[5] and gallery-commoner[6] buys his sport by the penny and,
like a haggler, is glad to utter it again by retailing.

Sithence then the place is so free in entertainment, allowing a stool
as well to the farmer's son as to your templar;[7] that your stinkard[8] has
the selfsame liberty to be there in his tobacco fumes, which your
sweet Courtier hath; and that your carman and tinker claim as strong
a voice in their suffrage, and sit to give judgment on the play's life
and death, as well as the proudest momus[9] among the tribes of critic;
it is fit that he, whom the most tailors' bills do make room for, when he
comes, should not be basely (like a viol) cased up in a corner.

Whether therefore the gatherers[10] of the public or private playhouse
stand to receive the afternoon's rent, let our gallant (having paid it)
presently advance himself up to the throne of the stage. I mean
not into the lord's room,[11] which is now but the stage's suburbs; no,

1 i.e. "The Simpleton's Primer."   2 applause.
3 the multitude, or the audience.
4 merchants or tradesmen.   5 person standing in the pit.
6 playgoer who purchases a seat in the gallery.
7 member of one of the Inns of Court where one studied law.
8 common fellow.   9 hostile critic.
10 those who collected the admission fee at the theatres.
11 box located close to the stage.

those boxes, by the iniquity of custom, conspiracy of waiting women and gentlemen ushers, that there sweat together, and the covetousness of sharers,[12] are contemptibly thrust into the rear, and much new satin is there damned by being smothered to death in darkness. But on the very rushes[13] where the comedy is to dance, yea, and under the state[14] of Cambyses[15] himself, must our feathered estridge,[16] like a piece of ordnance, be planted, valiantly (because impudently) beating down the mews and hisses of the opposed rascality.[17]

For do but cast up a reckoning, what large comings-in are pursed up by sitting on the stage. First a conspicuous eminence is gotten; by which means the best and most essential parts of a gallant (good clothes, a proportionable leg, white hand, the Persian lock,[18] and a tolerable beard) are perfectly revealed.

By sitting on the stage you have a signed patent to engross[19] the whole commodity of censure; may lawfully presume to be a girder;[20] and stand at the helm to steer the passage of scenes; yet no man shall once offer to hinder you from obtaining the title of an insolent, overweening coxcomb.

By sitting on the stage, you may, without traveling for it, at the very next door ask whose play it is; and, by the quest of inquiry, the law warrants you to avoid much mistaking; if you know not the author, you may rail against him; and peradventure so behave yourself that you may enforce the author to know you.

By sitting on the stage, if you be a knight you may happily get you a mistress; if a mere Fleet-street gentleman, a wife; but assure yourself, by continual residence, you are the first and principal man in election to begin the number of We Three.[21]

By spreading your body on the stage, and by being a justice in examining of plays, you shall put yourself into such true scenical authority that some poet shall not dare to present his muse rudely upon your eyes, without having first unmasked her, rifled her, and discovered all her bare and most mystical parts before you at a tavern, when you most knightly shall, for his pains, pay for both their suppers.

By sitting on the stage, you may (with small cost) purchase the dear acquaintance of the boys; have a good stool[22] for sixpence; at any time know what particular part any of the infants[23] present; get your match lighted, examine the play-suits' lace, and perhaps win wagers

---

12 shareholders in a theatrical company.
13 floor covering.
15 hero of an Elizabethan tragedy.
17 the public in the pit.   18 hair style.
20 one who sneers.
21 a popular joke about three asses.
23 boy-actors.

14 throne.
16 ostrich.
19 buy the whole of.
22 i.e., seat on the stage.

upon laying[24] 'tis copper, etc. And to conclude, whether you be a fool
or a justice of peace, a cuckold or a captain, a lord-mayor's son or a
dawcock, a knave or an under-sheriff; of what stamp soever you be,
current or counterfeit, the stage, like time, will bring you to most
perfect light and lay you open; neither are you to be hunted from
thence, though the scarecrows in the yard[25] hoot at you, hiss at you,
spit at you, yea, throw dirt even in your teeth; 'tis most gentleman-
like patience to endure all this and to laugh at the silly animals; but if
the rabble, with a full throat, cry, "Away with the fool," you were
worse than a madman to tarry by it; for the gentleman and the fool
should never sit on the stage together.

Marry, let this observation go hand in hand with the rest; or rather,
like a country servingman, some five yards before them. Present not
yourself on the stage (especially at a new play) until the quaking
prologue hath (by rubbing) got color into his cheeks, and is ready to
give the trumpets[26] their cue that he's upon point to enter; for then
it is time, as though you were one of the properties or that you
dropped out of the hangings, to creep from behind the arras, with
your tripos or three-footed stool in one hand and a teston[27] mounted
between a forefinger and a thumb in the other; for if you should
bestow your person upon the vulgar when the belly of the house is
but half full, your apparel is quite eaten up, the fashion lost, and the
proportion of your body in more danger to be devoured than if it
were served up in the counter amongst the poultry; avoid that as
you would the bastome.[28] It shall crown you with rich commendation
to laugh aloud in the midst of the most serious and saddest scene of
the terriblest tragedy; and to let that clapper, your tongue, be tossed
so high that all the house may ring of it. Your lords use it; your
knights are apes to the lords, and do so too; your Inn-a-Court-man[29]
is zany to the knights, and (marry, very scurvily) comes likewise
limping after it; be thou a beagle to them all, and never lin[30] snuffing,
till you have scented them; for by talking and laughing (like a plowman in a morris[31]) you heap Pelion upon Ossa,[32] glory upon glory;
as first, all the eyes in the galleries will leave walking after the players
and only follow you; the simplest dolt in the house snatches up your
name, and when he meets you in the streets, or that you fall into his
hands in the middle of a watch,[33] his word shall be taken for you;

---

[24] betting.   [25] the pit.
[26] the trumpets blown for announcing the play is about to begin.
[27] a coin worth sixpence.   [28] cudgel.   [29] law-student.
[30] cease.   [31] morris dance.
[32] two mountains; the Titans tried to climb Olympus by piling Ossa on top of
Pelion.
[33] when the night watchmen are on duty.

he'll cry "He's such a gallant," and you pass. Secondly, you publish your temperance to the world, in that you seem not to resort thither to taste vain pleasures with a hungry appetite; but only as a gentleman to spend a foolish hour or two, because you can do nothing else; thirdly, you mightily disrelish the audience and disgrace the author; marry, you take up (though it be at the worst hand) a strong opinion of your own judgment, and enforce the poet to take pity of your weakness and, by some dedicated sonnet, to bring you into a better paradise only to stop your mouth.

If you can, either for love or money, provide yourself a lodging by the water side;[34] for, above the convenience it brings to shun shoulder-clapping and to ship away your cockatrice[35] betimes in the morning, it adds a kind of state unto you to be carried from thence to the stairs of your playhouse; hate a sculler[36] (remember that) worse than to be acquainted with one o' the scullery. No, your oars are your only sea-crabs, board them, and take heed you never go twice together with one pair; often shifting is a great credit to gentlemen; and that dividing of your fare will make the poor water-snakes be ready to pull you in pieces to enjoy your custom; no matter whether upon landing you have money or no; you may swim in twenty of their boats over the river upon ticket;[37] marry, when silver comes in, remember to pay treble their fare, and it will make your flounder-catchers to send more thanks after you when you do not draw than when you do; for they know it will be their own another day.

Before the play begins, fall to cards; you may win or lose (as fencers do in a prize) and beat one another by confederacy, yet share the money when you meet at supper; notwithstanding, to gull the ragamuffins that stand aloof gaping at you, throw the cards (having first torn four or five of them) round about the stage, just upon the third sound,[38] as though you had lost; it skills not if the four knaves[39] lie on their backs, and outface the audience; there's none such fools as dare take exceptions at them, because, ere the play go off, better knaves than they will fall into the company.

Now, sir, if the writer be a fellow that hath either epigrammed you, or hath had a flirt at your mistress, or hath brought[40] either your feather, or your red beard, or your little legs, etc., on the stage, you shall disgrace him worse than by tossing him in a blanket or giving

---

[34] i.e., near the Thames River.
[35] prostitute.   [36] oarsman on a Thames ferry.
[37] on credit.   [38] the third sound of the trumpets (see note 26, above).
[39] the fellows with a strong hand in the card game.
[40] mimicked (for the purpose of satirizing).

him the bastinado in a tavern, if, in the middle of his play (be it pastoral or comedy, moral or tragedy), you rise with a screwed and discontented face from your stool to be gone; no matter whether the scenes be good or no; the better they are the worse do you distaste them; and, being on your feet, sneak not away like a coward, but salute all your gentle acquaintance that are spread either on the rushes or on stools about you, and draw what troop you can from the stage after you. The mimics[41] are beholden to you for allowing them elbowroom; their poet cries, perhaps, "A pox go with you," but care not for that, there's no music without frets.

Marry, if either the company or indisposition of the weather bind you to sit it out, my counsel is then that you turn plain ape, take up a rush, and tickle the earnest ears of your fellow gallants, to make other fools fall a-laughing; mew at passionate speeches, blare at merry, find fault with the music, whew at the children's action, whistle at the songs; and above all, curse the sharers, that whereas the same day you had bestowed forty shillings on an embroidered felt and feather (Scotch-fashion) for your mistress in the court or your punk[42] in the city, within two hours after you encounter with the very same block[43] on the stage, when the haberdasher swore to you the impression was extant[44] but that morning.

To conclude, hoard up the finest play-scraps you can get, upon which your lean wit may most savorly feed, for want of other stuff, when the Arcadian and Euphuized[45] gentlewomen have their tongues sharpened to set upon you; that quality (next to your shuttlecock) is the only furniture to a courtier that's but a new beginner, and is but in his A B C of compliment. The next places that are filled, after the playhouses be emptied, are (or ought to be) taverns. Into a tavern then let us next march, where the brains of one hogshead must be beaten out to make up another.

41 actors.   42 prostitute.
43 fashion.   44 in vogue.   45 pretentiously artificial.

⟩ Professor Harbage's account in Shakespeare's audience, referred to earlier in this section, was first published in 1941, but as an example of exhaustive scrutiny to which historians of the theatre must continually subject popular generalizations, it can serve as an excellent model for beginning researchers. One chapter of it is reproduced here, together with Harbage's own footnotes citing his sources.

Alfred Harbage

SHAKESPEARE'S AUDIENCE: WHAT KIND OF PEOPLE?*

Some future age may take the satirical portraits which our journalism has produced — of traveling salesman, social butterfly, collegiate youth, and the like — and attempt to recreate our audiences. The results will be peculiar. Audiences never are assemblies of caricatures. We are obviously in error if we people the Globe with multiples of Davies' Inns-of-Courtier, Dekker's Gull, Beaumont's Apprentice, and Fitzgeffrey's Bobadil.[1] Only one alternative is open to us: we must think of the many thousands of Londoners and the many factors governing their selection of pastimes — such factors as purchasing power, available time, religious scruples, age, sex, and personal tastes. Thus we may obtain some idea of the several thousand representatives sent forth from the city to gather about *Hamlet* one weekday afternoon a long time ago.

The theatres, I have estimated, were within walking distance of 160,000 people in 1605, of slightly fewer in 1601. These thousands were divided into various classes. Lamenting in 1616 that the weakness of men and the "pride of women" drew many people from the country "because the new fashion is to bee had no where but in London," King James made a summary pronouncement: "And now out of my owne mouth I declare unto you . . . that the Courtiers, Citizens, and Lawyers, and those that belong unto them, and others as haue Pleas in Terme time, are onely necessary persons to remaine about this Citie; others must get them into the Countrey."[2] Had the

---

* From Alfred Harbage, *Shakespeare's Audience* (New York: Columbia University Press, 1941). Copyright 1941 Columbia University Press; reprinted by permission of the publishers.

[1] The "types" are pleasantly assembled by Byrne, "Shakespeare's Audience," in Shakespeare Association, *A Series of Papers on Shakespeare and the Theatre*, pp. 186–216.

[2] "A Speach in the Starre-Chamber," June 20, in *Political Works*, ed. McIlwain, p. 344.

order been obeyed, the term "Citizens" read literally, the London area would have been largely depopulated. A more useful idea of the major divisions of urban population is provided by a muster roll of 1608,[3] classifying the men between twenty and sixty years of age in the towns of Gloucester, Tewkesbury, and Cirencester. The following is a simplified analysis showing the percentage of each classification:

Gentry, professional men, and officials	6.3
Dealers and retailers	19.3
Craftsmen	52.0
Laborers, carriers, etc.	c.15.0
Servants and miscellaneous	c.7.4

The classification is only suggestive, even as applied to the towns of Gloucester county, and has no authority for London; nevertheless, it gives us a starting point. In the London area, the presence of the court with all its administrative offices — particularly the law courts with their appendages, the Inns of Court and Chancery — and the standing of the city in the world of fashion would have raised the proportion of "Gentry, professional men, and officials" perhaps to as high as 10 percent. At the other end of the scale there is a category wholly unaccounted for in the muster roll — what Gregory King was later to call "Transitory People" — cashiered soldiers and seamen ashore, as well as vagrants, paupers, thieves, and peddlers. Shakespeare's London probably succeeded in submerging more than the traditional tenth.

But when all adjustments are made, the group remaining by all odds the largest, although not so large as 52 percent of the whole, will be the "Craftsmen" — the carpenters, masons, bookbinders, and button makers, with their helpers, the whole contingent of artisans, or "handicraft men," and those who were dependent upon them. It is with this group that we had better begin.

In 1601 the average weekly wage for artisans in England, master workmen and helpers together, was about 5s. 3½d. per man; a bricklayer or mason received 1s. a day, his helper 10d.[4] Artisans in London, however, were paid above the average. Between 1593 and 1602 the masons working on London Bridge received between 14d. and 16d. a day[5] as compared with the national average of 12d. Since the building crafts paid somewhat more poorly than the newer industries,[6] we may take the higher figure, or 16d., as representing the average

---

[3] Tawney and Tawney, "An Occupational Census of the Seventeenth Century," *Economic History Review*, V (1934–35), 36.

[4] Rogers, *History of Agriculture and Prices in England*, V, 664–65, 826.

[5] Knoop and Jones, *Mediaeval Mason*, p. 236.

[6] Nef, "Prices and Industrial Capitalism in France and England, 1540–1640," *Economic History Review*, VII (1936–37), 164.

daily wage of master workmen in London. This is 33⅓ percent more than the national average; hence the weekly wage of London workmen generally may be put at 33⅓ percent more than the national average of 5s. 3½d. Exactitude in the matter is scarcely possible, but we shall err by very little, and probably on the side of generosity, if we place the average weekly wage of London workmen at 7s. in the year of *Hamlet*.

Fortunately, my task is not to explain how workmen lived and reared their children. That prices had terribly outdistanced wages by 1601 is common knowledge. For Dekker, despite the breadth of his sympathies, workmen were "Stinkards": herrings and onions, alas, were among the few foods they could afford to buy; bread was an expensive luxury. As we review the cost of other pleasures as compared with that of theatregoing, it will be helpful to keep in mind the earnings of workmen today as a relative gauge. Skilled craftsmen, such as earned 16d. a day in Shakespeare's London, no longer form a large percentage of wage earners; they are now, deservedly, a highly paid aristocracy. The most appropriate figure to use for equation is the average weekly wage of the millions of contemporary industrial workers. In America, in the month of the present investigation, that wage is $25.46 or 98.2 percent of the 1923–25 norm.[7] The norm appears to be $25.93 as the average weekly wage of modern American industrial workers, as compared with the 7s. average weekly wage of workmen in Shakespeare's London. Considered as a proportion of income, each penny spent by a workman then was equivalent to each 31 cents spent by a workman now. The wage earner of that time, therefore, could go to the theatre almost as cheaply as his modern counterpart can go to the movies. We shall see that he could purchase no other pleasures at modern rates. I am speaking, of course, of commercialized pleasures: fortunately, the Elizabethan could walk into the country and "drink the waters of the crisped spring."

Nashe gives the following alternatives for spending a vacant afternoon in London: "that pleasure they deuide (howe vertuously it skils not) either into gameing, following of harlots, drinking, or seeing a Playe."[8] An earlier pamphleteer lists as "the places of expense" the taverns, the alehouses, The Theatre and Curtain, and Paris Garden.[9] With the following of harlots we need not linger, except to remark

[7] U. S. Bureau of Labor Statistics, *Monthly Labor Review*, LI (1940), 474. [Harbage's figures should of course be revised upward if the current year is to be used as a yardstick. — Eds.]

[8] *Pierce Penilesse, His Supplication to the Divell* (1592), in McKerrow, ed., *Works*, I, 212.

[9] T. F., *Newes from the North* (1585), quoted in Graves, "Some References to Elizabethan Theaters," *Studies in Philology*, XIX (1922), 317.

that the terms "sixe-penny whoredome" and "six-pennie damnation"[10] give an idea of the minimum rate. Paris Garden was the center of bearbaiting; and bearbaiting, like cockfighting and even bowling, tennis, and archery, attracted spectators chiefly interested in gambling. The cost of passing the time at such activities, as at dice and cards themselves, must remain problematical. No doubt it was high. Expense accounts of the time, recording gains and losses, yield familiar information: in the long run the amateur always lost.

When it comes to taverns and alehouses, we are on surer ground. In his *Survey* of 1603, Stow wrote, "quaffing . . . is mightily encreased, though greatly qualified among the poorer sort, not of any holy abstinencie, but of meer necessitie, Ale and Beere being small, and Wines in price aboue their reach."[11] An afternoon in a tavern over a quart of sack — assuming that Falstaff's two gallons were not the normal requirement — would have cost our workman at least 8*d*. If he believed that a quart of ale was "a dish for a king," he could have had it at a minimum rate of 4*d*.; or if alehouse company would have compensated him for base drink, he could have had painfully small beer at 1*d*. a quart. A reckless bachelor, anxious to ape the gentry, might have smoked tobacco — at the rate of 3*d*. for each small pipe-load.[12]

Dining in public might have appealed to some workman (or his wife) as an anniversary luxury. The threepenny ordinary is the cheapest I have encountered — for "your London Usurer, your stale Bachilor, and your thrifty Atturney . . . the roomes as full of company as a Iaile."[13] Observe that artisans were not looked for even in these niggardly surroundings. Sixpenny ordinaries were not lavish. Eight-

---

10 Nashe, *Christs Teares over Ierusalem* (1593) and *Pierce Penilesse, His Supplication to the Divell* (1592), in McKerrow, ed., *Works*, II, 148, and I, 217. Dekker also, as I recall, uses the phrase. Nashe (*Christs Teares over Ierusalem* [1593], in *ibid.*, II, 149) says that about a half crown is the "sette pryce of a strumpets soule" (i.e., first offense?).

11 *Survey of London*, ed. Kingsford, I, 83.

12 Sack cost 8*d*. a quart in London in 1595 (Rogers, *History of Agriculture and Prices in England*, VI, 415). Falstaff, paying 5*s*. 8*d*. for his two gallons, was not cheated, Shakespeare's prices being anachronistic. Sack at Eton in 1608 cost 11*d*. per quart (Beveridge, *Prices and Wages in England*, p. 113). In 1584, in spite of the injunction that ale or strong beer was to be sold at 1*d*. a quart, small beer at 1*d*. a pottle (2 quarts) in sealed measures, the actual selling price in Castle Baynard Ward was 3 farthings for a short pint ("Aleconners Complaint," in Stow, *Survey of London*, ed. Kingsford, I, lxiv–lxv). In 1614 Dame Ursla (Jonson's *Bartholomew Fair*, Act II, Scene ii) gets 6*d*. for a bottle of frothed ale, between 2*d*. and 3*d*. a quart for beer, and 3*d*. a pipeload for adulterated tobacco. She was a profiteer, but, except that her tobacco was mixed with coltsfoot, her charge for this item was not above average.

13 Dekker, *Guls Horne-Booke* (1609), in Grosart, ed., *Non-Dramatic Works*, II, 244–45.

penny ordinaries were, in 1631, for your country attorneys willing to "endure the Vnwholesome ayre."[14] Twelvepenny ordinaries were fashionable, and eighteenpenny ordinaries were, in 1592, for "Cauaⁱ liers and braue courtiers."[15]

I shall add at random the cost of a few other nonessentials. Two printed broadsides, usually containing ballads, cost 1*d.*, a prose romance of about 180 pages octavo 1*s.*,[16] a ride in a wherry from Paul's Wharf to Westminster 3*d.*,[17] more or less, depending on the waterman's powers in debate. The cheapest place in the private playhouse in Blackfriars could be had for 6*d.* We may now tabulate these prices, indicating the modern equivalents:

	Cost to Elizabethan workman (pence)	Cost to modern workman at Elizabethan rates (dollars)		Actual cost of modern equivalent (dollars)
Low price, public theatre	1	.31		(average
Middle price, public theatre	2	.62	.29	movie
High, but not highest, price, public theatre	3	.93		ticket)
Low price, private theatre	6	1.86	.55	(theatre)
Quart of sack	8	2.48	1.25	(gin)
Quart of ale	4	1.24	.20	(beer)
Quart of small beer	1	.31		(no sale)
Pipeload of tobacco	3	.93	.01	
Cheapest dinner, table d'hôte	3	.93	.40	
Transportation fare	3	.93	.075	
Two printed sheets	1	.31	.03	(newspaper)
Small book	12	3.72	.05	(magazine)

That a penny was a considerable sum of money and that theatregoing was one of the few commercialized pleasures within the workman's means may readily be seen. In fact, the Elizabethan artisan paid so much more proportionately for necessities — food, clothing, fuel — that a penny for pleasure must have been more thoughtfully laid out than even its thirty-one cent equivalent need be at the present time. It is possible, however, that the high cost of living worked in

[14] Thomas Powell, *Tom of All Trades* (1631), ed. Furnivall, New Shakspere Society Publications, Ser. VI, No. II, p. 141.

[15] Nashe, *Pierce Penilesse, His Supplication to the Divell* (1592), in McKerrow, ed., *Works*, I, 170.

[16] Plant, *English Book Trade*, p. 220.

[17] This was the official rate, and it seems to have been roughly adhered to: see "for Gibson . . . his boate hier four times between Lambeth and Ivy Bridge xiid." in Historical Manuscripts Commission, *Rutland MSS*, IV, 419–20.

favor of the theatres in one way: if the penny spent on food meant
only an additional cucumber or two, one might as well squander it
on a play. "Sights" in general were cheaper than material commodi-
ties in an age of scarcity. A penny fee would admit one to a puppet
show,[18] a conducted tour of the monuments in Westminster Abbey, a
view from the roof of St. Paul's Cathedral, a glimpse of a six-legged
calf, or other "monster," or of the lions in the tower; by 1641, at least,
it would purchase a stroll in a private garden where a nosegay was
given as a souvenir.[19] But these were evanescent joys, to be tasted
now and then, whereas beer, ballads, plays, and animal fights were
staples. A play meant over two hours' entertainment in impressive
surroundings — entertainment of a quality not to be found in the
beer and ballads. Craftsmen, then, with their families, journeymen,
and apprentices, must have composed the vast majority of "groundlings." Many were highly skilled, performing functions now alloted
to the chemist, architect, and engineer. Let us not be too much influenced by contemptuous allusions to how the "barmy Jacket of a
Beer-brewer"[20] contaminated the public theatres. London craftsmen
were the best in the country. Those at the Globe had chosen playgoing in preference to boozing and animalbaiting.

After the "Craftsmen" the next largest group in the London area
was composed of the "Dealers and retailers." A few of these were
merchants, wealthy and powerful, importing great cargoes and
manipulating great sums. They would have been able to order without extravagance £10 dramatic performances in their homes. The
greater number were, however, simply shopkeepers. In 1688 Gregory
King reckoned the income of tradesmen as a class at only 12.5 percent higher than that of craftsmen. If the proportion held in 1601,
the average shopkeeper earned 7s. 11d. weekly to the craftsman's 7s.
and should have been grateful for penny admissions. Of course,
many shopkeepers, and craftsmen too, could have afforded seats in
the galleries and would have been pleased with the added penny's
worth of comfort and dignity — especially when they brought their
wives.

Among the "Gentry, professional men, and officials" the range of
income was wide. In the professional group, teachers made least[21]
(somewhat less than artisans), lawyers most. The witnesses are
unanimous that in litigious London the lawyer prospered. Authors

18 *Bartholomew Fair,* Act V, Scene i. Twopence were asked of "gentlefolk."
19 Peacham, *Worth of a Penny* [1647 for 1641], in Arber, ed., *English
Garner,* VI, 245–88.
20 Marston, *Jack Drum's Entertainment* (1600), Act V, Scene i, in Wood,
ed., *Plays.*
21 Plant, *English Book Trade,* p. 42.

could make a living if they wrote for the stage. In 1599 about £35 passed into the hands of Thomas Dekker,[22] as compared with £18 4s. for the average artisan, but Dekker wrote in that year all of three plays and parts of six more. "Gentry," of course, is scarcely an occupational term. Those who were not professional men, officials, or heads of their own households were usually "serving men" — attendants at court or in the households of nobles or other gentlemen. Since living was provided, stipends in most cases may be considered as spending money. Dekker speaks of "bare forty shillings a yeere (seruing-mens wages),[23] and when we consider that a groom of the chamber for Queen Elizabeth received £2 13s. 4d., the rate seems not improbable. On the other hand, Elizabeth's gentlemen of the privy chamber received £50 and perquisites.[24] Forty shillings a year meant nine pence and a farthing in weekly spending money. The twopenny gallery, for all its bourgeois flavor, might well have been considered expensive enough by the younger or lesser gentry. Money was scarce among the majority of all classes. I am not speaking, to be sure, of the income of elder sons who had come into their estates. I am not speaking, either, of knights, baronets, and temporal lords. But of these no more than a sprinkling could be looked for in any audience: there weren't enough in all England to fill the Globe.

A great lord was expected to pay more for all things than lesser men. There follows a few illustrative items from the personal expense account of the Earl of Rutland in 1598–99:

> Item for Sir Ph. Sidneys *Arcadia* [3d ed.?], ixs.
> Item for my Lorde's supper at Courte, 28 *Octoberis*, ixs. iid. . . . the cooke in the pryvy kitchen, xs. . . . tobacco pipes, viiid.
> Item, 28 September, my Lorde's boatehier to Lambeth and back againe, xviiid. . . . boatehire 1 October, for his Lordship and his men, and the play, and James his going to Lambeth to see Capten Whitlock, viiis.
> Item the foteman's boatehire to Lambeth and to the play howse sondry tymes, iis. iiiid.
> Item, 28 *Julii*, an oz. of ball tobacco, vs.; boatehier for his Lordship that day, xiid.; to the buttery at Nonesuch, vs.
> Item, 18 November, for an oz of tobacco, iis. vid. . . . boatehier and a play, vis.[25]

Playhouse prices were not designed for earls. Although his lordship seems to have paid above the highest rate, plays were still the least of his

22 *Henslowe's Diary*, ed. Greg, I, 100–117. Some payments may not be recorded.
23 *Worke for Armourours* (1609), in Grosart, ed., *Non-Dramatic Works*, IV, 130.
24 Chambers, *Elizabethan Stage*, I, 50.
25 Historical Manuscripts Commission, *Rutland MSS*, IV, 419–20.

extravagances. It appears that on one occasion a regular theatre party for himself and an unspecified number of retainers, besides boat hire and miscellaneous expenses, cost Rutland only 8*s.*, or 3*s.* more than he later paid for one ounce of tobacco, 2*s.* less than he had previously tipped the queen's cook.

Descending now to the opposite end of the scale, to those below the rank of artisan — to the carman, the peddler, the ditcher, and the household drudge — most of these could have found a holiday penny not urgently needed to keep body and soul together:

> Nay many poore pincht, needie creatures, that liue of almes, and that haue scarce neither cloath to their backe, nor foode for the belley, yet wil make hard shift but they will see a Play, let wife & children begge, languish in penurie, and all they can rappe and rend, is little enough to lay vpon such vanitie.[26]

But their numbers at any one performance would have been limited indeed.

Any amusement over the admission prices to Shakespeare's theatre is apt to disappear upon a scrutiny of the facts. Actually the 1*d.*, 2*d.*, and 3*d.* range, with a few removed places at 6*d.* and 12*d.*, was designed to fit the purses of London. These prices were truly popular. The only improvement one might have suggested would have been additional places at a farthing. Cheap labor and high prices insure great profits and stimulate commercial enterprise; periods of "price inflation" have been accredited with various triumphs, including, whimsically one supposes, the plays of Shakespeare. It is true that the theatres were built in the midst of that period of expansion marked by high prices and low wages, but the theatrical industry, before the advent of the "private" theatres, may be pointed out as an exception to, as well as exemplification of, the inflationary tendencies of the period. Admission prices were calculated, as prices in general were not, to what workmen could afford to pay. We must conclude, first, that audiences were composed largely of shopkeepers and craftsmen, people of low income taking advantage of the almost unique opportunity to get their money's worth; and, second, that those who limited their expenditure to 1*d.* and remained "groundlings" must not be thought of as a rabble. Another thing is certain. When the "private" theatres opened and placed the minimum charge at 6*d.*, no more effective means could have been devised for excluding utterly the great majority of the former audience. This was price inflation with a vengeance. The thrifty citizen who has blundered into Salisbury Court Theatre in 1629 is made to say:

[26] Crosse, *Vertues Common-Wealth; or, The High-Way to Honour* (1603), signature Q^{v}.

I will hasten to the money Box
And take my shilling out again, for now
I have considered that it is too much;
I'll go to th' Bull, or Fortune, and there see
A Play for two pense, with a Jig to boot.[27]

He is portrayed as ridiculous, but he was completely right: a shilling was indeed too much. And the price inflation at the private theatres begat no second Shakespeare.

Factors others than expense affect theatrical attendance. That only two in fifteen Elizabethan Londoners went to the theatre weekly, as compared with the ten in fifteen modern Americans who go to the movies, was partly due to the scarcity of pennies. It was partly due also to the scarcity of leisure. Plays were performed, not two or three times a day, at the public's convenience, but usually only once, and then during working hours. Drama competed with labor in the use of daylight, and opportunity for playgoing was accordingly limited. In our day, many housewives and young people during the afternoon, and workers generally during the evening, are free agents. Shakespeare's actors had to look forward to holidays, and theatres were built huge to accommodate holiday crowds. The analogy between the modern movie and the Elizabethan theatre is in many ways a poor one. Mechanical reproduction now makes possible a constantly varied bill. In any city and in most towns one may go to the movies every day in the week without seeing the same picture twice. In "Middletown" with a population of between thirty-five and forty thousand, nine movies were offering twenty-two programs and three hundred performances each week in 1923.[28] Our eighty-five million weekly spectators are made up largely of those who go from two to four times a week.[29] In Shakespeare's time, one visit a week would more than have exhausted the possibilities of the theatres so far as mere novelty was concerned. We live in an age of expert salesmanship, and, whereas Elizabethans had to go to the theatres, the movies come to us. There are seventeen thousand movie theatres in the United States — roofed, comfortably heated (sometimes even cooled), and usually "palatial." This means about one theatre for every 7,647 inhabitants. To equal these facilities, London of the year of *Hamlet* would have needed over twenty "neighborhood" theatres dotting every locality from Lambeth to Mile End.[30] Actually there were four in operation, rigidly

27 Praeludium, *The Careless Shepherdess.*
28 Lynd and Lynd, *Middletown*, p. 263.
29 Although eighty-five million attend the movies weekly, only forty million, about 30 percent of our population, are said to "really have the movie habit." See Thorp, *America at the Movies*, p. 3.
30 They were larger, of course, than the average movie theatre. A seat is said to be available for every twelve Americans. In the theatres operating in 1601, I should say that there was a space available for every twenty-three Londoners.

restricted to particular districts. London was small in area; nevertheless, the average citizen had to walk more than a mile to reach the
Rose or the Globe. The distance from St. Paul's Cathedral was about
a mile and a half; from Wapping, two miles; from St. James Clerken-
well, over two miles; from Westminster, three miles and a half. Of
course, one might ride the Thames, but that meant additional expense.

Standards of convenience are, however, relative. Official London
considered the theatres damnably convenient, and unofficial London
considered them commodious and magnificent. "Commedies," lamented Gosson, "are neither chargable to ye beholders purse, nor
painful to his body; partly, because he may sit out of the raine to
viewe the same, when many other pastimes are hindred by wether."[31]
Under harder conditions of life, mere shelter may seem a luxury. The
conflict of playtime with working hours was the more serious obstacle.
Nashe speaks of "the after-noone beeing the idlest time of the day;
wherein men that are their owne masters (as Gentlemen of the Court,
the Innes of the Courte, and the number of Captaines and Souldiers
about London) do wholy bestow themselues vpon pleasure."[32] The vast
majority did not belong to this select company. Shopkeepers to a
degree were their own masters, workmen less so, although not so completely regimented by time clocks as now. The workday varied in
length from about eight hours in midwinter to about twelve hours in
midsummer, consisting of the period of clear daylight with dinner-
time and drinking time off.[33] Possibly one could pool his time off and
use it to go to the theatre. The leathersellers agreed that work was to
cease early on Saturdays, vigils, and festivals.[34] Vigils and festivals
were many, and they varied for various crafts; the various crafts imitated the practice if not the precept of the leathersellers. Individual
workmen had their private holidays, and there were intermissions
between one job and the next. Beyond a certain point restraint upon
human conduct becomes impossible. That they drew workmen from
their work was one of the chief of the official counts against plays.
Schoolboys and apprentices must have been given, or must have taken,
their times of recreation. We may assume that the idler classes formed
a higher percentage of audiences than of the population generally but
never that they composed more than a minority.

Personal and religious scruples kept some Londoners away from the
theatres but fewer than we are apt to suppose. If the theatres were
respectable enough to be frequented by the Earl of Rutland and his

[31] *Playes Confuted in Fiue Actions* (1582), in Hazlitt, ed., *English Drama and Stage*, p. 202.
[32] *Pierce Penilesse, His Supplication to the Divell* (1592), in McKerrow, ed., *Works*, I, 212.
[33] Knoop and Jones, *Mediaeval Mason*, p. 236.
[34] Dunlop, *English Apprenticeship and Child Labour*, p. 45.

class, we might assume that the average citizen would not shrink from them; however, it may be best to make no assumptions about the sense of propriety of the English middle classes. Actually there has been much misunderstanding about the association of the playhouses with brothels and about their location in the sinister suburbs. If there were playhouses in the suburbs, there were also numerous churches; certainly the wardens of St. Saviour's did not think the neighborhood of Southwark a blight upon the drama.[35] If there were brothels in Shoreditch and Southwark, there were brothels also elsewhere. The royal suburb of Westminster was notorious for them. The slums were in the suburbs, but the suburbs were not the slums. Many substantial households were established there. A dweller in the intramural city who refused to go into them would have been a virtual prisoner, cut off from the innocent pleasures of the open fields and from much of his everyday business. The intramural city itself was not uniformly a place for the fastidious.

Religious scruples require a more extended consideration. It is certain that an increasing number of Londoners stayed away from plays on moral and religious grounds and that this number by 1642 had become formidable. The strict Calvinist William Perkins had more delicate consciences in his keeping than any other Elizabethan, and Perkins had decided that plays were not permissible.[36] This particular venality, I should say however, drew fire only from his lighter artillery. So far as I can discover, nothing ever came of the attempt, partly inspired by pressure from the pulpits, to force masters and wardens of the London companies to forbid their apprentices, servants, and journeymen to go to plays;[37] nor have I ever heard of articles of apprenticeship outlawing playgoing, although cardplaying and tavern-haunting were invariably forbidden. The very strict regulations of the Merchant Adventurers of Bristol forbidding apprentices to "daunce dice carde mum or use any musick eyther by night or day in the streetes"[38] are silent about the mere witnessing of amusements. The very shrillness of the pulpit attacks upon playgoing suggests frustration. The people found the ministers "sumwhat too sour in preaching awey theyr pastime." We can hear them argue back:

> they wil saie, you are a man of the Sabboth you are verie precise; you wil allowe vs nothing; you wil haue nothing but the worde of God:

---

[35] For their protest against the presence of the theatres, see Chambers, *Elizabethan Stage*, IV, 325.

[36] "Cases of Conscience," *The Workes of that Famous and Worthy Minister of Christ in the University of Cambridge, Mr. William Perkins* (1613), II, 140.

[37] "Dramatic Records of the City of London: the Repertories, Journals, and Letter Books," in *Malone Society Collections*, II, Part III, 313.

[38] Dunlop, *English Apprenticeship and Child Labour*, p. 189.

you wil permit vs no recreation, but haue men like Asses, who neuer rest but when they are eating.

Seeke to withdrawe these felowes from the Theater vnto the sermon, they wil saie, By the preacher they mai be edified, but by the plaier both edified and delighted.[39]

Comparison of plays with sermons as edification the preachers found especially infuriating. The people must have found equally so the preachers' tendency to define recreation as the fifteen-minute rest periods allowed to harvesters.

The preachers themselves, individual pietists, and small congregations of sectaries — small, that is, in Shakespeare's time and in London — would have stayed away from plays on religious grounds, but not the rank and file of otherwise faithful parishioners. An analogy may be found in the habits of the eight million American Methodists who, until it was recently amended, honored their "Discipline" (forbidding dancing and cardplaying) chiefly in the breach. We must concede, of course, that Puritanism is no longer a rising tide. Milton had no objection to the well-trod stage, to Jonson's learned sock, and to Shakespeare's wood-notes wild. The attitude of John Chamberlain toward worldly vanities was stiff, and, when he saw Tobie Matthew on his way to a play, he thought that "playeng and Fridayes fasting agree not so well together as prayeing in a man of so much profession."[40] Yet he himself was not "so sowre nor severe" but that he would unbend occasionally: in 1597, when the new "play of humors" was "in very great request," he "was drawn alonge to yt by the common applause";[41] and, in 1614, hearing that the rebuilt Globe playhouse was the "fayrest that ever was in England," he planned to look in at it.[42]

Tobie Matthew was a Roman Catholic convert, his conduct an object of general interest. Like their fellow nonconformists, the extreme Puritans, the Catholics were expected to adhere to the strict way of life. Amusing evidence of their attitude toward the theatres exists in manuscript.[43] On March 9, 1617 [1618?], William Harrison, Archpriest, "Forasmuch as there haue been seueral complaincts made, & aduertisement giuen, that not a few are scanalised, and more disedified by the goeing of certain Priests to playes, acted by common plaiers upon common stages" prohibited "all & euery" of the priests under his direction from going to the theatres on penalty of the loss of "his

---

[39] Second and Third Blast of Retrait from Plaies and Theaters (1580), in Hazlitt, ed., English Drama and Stage, pp. 139–40.
[40] February 7, 1618. Letters of John Chamberlain, ed. McClure, II, 137.
[41] Ibid., I, 32.   [42] Ibid., p. 544.
[43] Manuscript in the Folger Shakespeare Library: Prohibition of William Harison, Archpriest, wherein English secular priests are forbidden to attend the theatres, March 9, 1617, with Thomas Leke's protest against the prohibition, April 25, 1618, and Harison's (?) answer to Leke.

or theyr faculties." On April 25, 1618, one Thomas Leke protested, raising the issue of "Ecclesiastical libertie" and objecting that the prohibition ran "generallie against all plaies, & not rather with a limitation against scurril playes, or wherein religion is disgraced." This drew forth a rejoinder, presumably from Harrison. It is lengthy and partly *ad hominem*. He says that the prohibition was put in general terms only to save the face of Leke himself, with two other chief offenders, Mr. Thules and Mr. Canon. He explains that the prohibition was against "going to theatres," not against "seeing plays," and that attendance at performances at court, the universities, the Inns of Court, and gentlemen's houses was not forbidden. Of public performances he is more than distrustful:

> For such playes are made to sport, and delight the auditorie, which consisting most of young gallants, and Protestants (for no true Puritanes will endure to bee present at playes) how unlikely is it, but that there are, and must bee, at least some passages in the playes, which may relish, and tickle the humor of such persons, or else good night to the players.[44]

Harrison was obviously a practical thinker. Leke had observed that the Jesuits and Benedictines made no objection to plays and that: "Wee knowe, that most of the principal Catholicks about London doe goe to plays, and all for ye most part of my ghostly children do knowe that I sometimes goe, and are not scandalised." To which Harrison rejoined: "the Catholicks that use to playes are the young of both sexes, and neither matrons, nor graue, or sage man is there seen." On this note of conflict in the testimony we must leave the matter, recognizing, however, that Father Leke had a more intimate knowledge of audiences than had Father Harrison. We know of one "ghostly child" who went to the playhouse and was there subjected to the amorous attentions of no less a person than the Venetian ambassador.[45] She must have been young, but Tobie Matthew was past fifty and an ordained priest on that fasting day when Chamberlain met him on his way to the theatre.

On moral grounds the theatres were defended as well as attacked — as well they might have been in view of the general character of the plays and of the freedom of the premises from gambling, the national vice. Taverns and alehouses were afflicted with dicing and cardplaying; sporting events, even bowling and tennis matches, with betting. Drunkenness was already a common vice. We learn from the Overburian characters that only the playhouses can keep the water-

44 Folio 13.
45 Public Record Office, *Calendar of State Papers, Venice and Northern Italy, 1615–1617*, XIV, 593.

man sober;[46] from Nashe, that only the playhouses can heal the de-
bauchee:

> Faith, when Dice, Lust, and Drunkennesse, and all haue dealt vpon
> him, if there be neuer a Playe for him to goe too for his pennie, he
> sits melancholie in his Chamber, deuising vpon felonie or treason, and
> howe he may best exalt himselfe by mischiefe.[47]

Heywood's *Apology for Actors* bases its defence partly upon the
grounds of public morality, and each of the writers of commendatory
verses for the volume comes forth with his personal testimonial:

> Have I not knowne a man, that to be hyr'd
> Would not for any treasure see a play,
> Reele from a taverne?

asks Robert Pallant.

> Thou that do'st raile at me for seeing a play,
> How wouldst thou have me spend my idle houres?
> Wouldst have me in a taverne drinke all day? . . .
> To drabbe, to game, to drinke, all these I hate,

says Richard Perkins, who affirms moreover that he is proud to sit
"even in the stages front" where all may see him. Arthur Pallant is
even more emphatic:

> To call to church Campanus bels did make;
> Playes, dice and drink invite men to forsake.[48]

The professional moralists were unwilling to make concessions; one of
them, nevertheless, after showing scant regard for theatres, is forced
to conclude: "notwithstanding, if we marke how young men spend
the latter end of the day in gaming, drinking, whoring, it were better
to tollerate Playes."[49] We must be careful not to assume that the
theatres were the particular haunt of the irreligious or the debased.

Neither cost, nor inconvenience, nor a belief that the playhouses
were contaminative would have kept large sectors of the populace
from plays. What of delicacy or shyness, such as might be supposed to
influence the habits of women? It is surprising, in view of the evidence to the contrary, how many authoritative works convey the impression that few women went to the Elizabethan public theatres.
We read in A. W. Ward that "no respectable woman might appear at
a playhouse except with her face concealed under a mask."[50] Now it
is certain that women generally did not wear masks at the plays. In

46 Overbury, *Overburian Characters*, Percy Reprints, No. XIII, p. 68.
47 *Pierce Penilesse, His Supplication to the Divell* (1592), in McKerrow,
ed., *Works*, I, 214.
48 Heywood, *Apology for Actors* (1612), Shakespeare Society Publications,
No. III, pp. 8–11.
49 Joseph Wyburne, *New Age of Old Names* (1609), p. 53.
50 *History of English Dramatic Literature*, I, 477.

Restoration times wearing masks became common and allusions to them legion. In Elizabethan times allusions are hard to find — an unlikely concomitant of so conspicuous and vulnerable a custom — and such few as exist do not associate masks with respectability.[51] We read in Ashley H. Thorndike that at Shakespeare's first play "the galleries contained a fair proportion of women" (the galleries only?) and that "in the early days . . . there were few women and no young girls."[52] I do not know to what early days the statement can apply. Even before the regular theatres were built, the audiences in London innyards were said to offer occasion for "inveglynge and alleurynge of maides speciallye orphanes, and good Cityzens Children vnder Age, to previe and vnmete Contractes,"[53] and in 1579 Gosson *Schoole of Abuse* contained a special epistle "To the Gentlewomen Citizens of London" beseeching them to withdraw their patronage from plays. We read in Sir Edmund Chambers that: "The galleries were full of light women who found them a profitable haunt, but whose presence did not altogether prevent that of ladies of position, probably in the private rooms, and possibly masked."[54] Wholly disregarded here is a feminine category, large in any age we trust, composed of neither "ladies of position" nor "light women." Either there is a lode of information uncited and unknown to me, or the authorities have decided that Shakespeare's theatre was no place for a lady and are imposing their own sense of decorum upon the Elizabethans.

The "light women" will concern us in the next chapter. At the moment we shall consider those who merit a presumption of innocence, who came from all classes of society, and who sometimes may have stood in the pit, side by side with their menfolk although all naturally would prefer the galleries. That there were women in the pit is suggested by one of Robert Greene's anecdotes of 1592. A young "nip" is in a packed theatre observing the technique of a master cutpurse. The youth, the expert, and a young woman are pressed close among "a company of seemly men":

> In short time the deed [stealing the purse] was performed, but how, the young nip could not easily discern, only he felt him shift his hand toward his trug, to convey the purse to her, but she, being somewhat mindful of the play, because a merriment was then on the stage, gave no regard.[55]

51 It is "the light-taylde huswiues," the sirens and Circes, who wear masks at the "Bank-sides round-house" in John Lane's *Tom Tell-Troths Message, and His Pens Complaint* (1600), ed. Furnivall, New Shakespeare Society Publications, Ser. VI, No. II, p. 133.

52 *Shakespeare's Theater*, pp. 404, 409.

53 "Dramatic Records from the Lansdowne Manuscripts," in *Malone Society Collections*, I, Part II, 175.

54 *Elizabethan Stage*, II, 549.

55 *Thirde and Last Parte of Connycatching* (1592), in Judges, ed., *Elizabethan Underworld*, p. 195.

The "nip," less susceptible to the appeal of drama, substituted his own hand and edged off with the purse. Now, unless there had been other women among the throng, the value of the "trug" as receiver would have been nil. My representative of female groundlings is none too respectable, but I am thinking of those who covered her presence.

In London the women outnumbered men thirteen to ten, although more than the reverse would have been true in the upper crust.[56] There were fewer than thirty women among Queen Elizabeth's fifteen hundred courtiers,[57] and in the Inns of Court and among fashionable sojourners males of course predominated. Some of the male courtiers, to be sure, had families established in Westminster or London; the women of fashion were numerous enough, and their numbers rapidly increasing. English women, high and low, were great "gadders abroad." On this point natives and foreigners agreed. Chamberlain writes dryly to Alice Carleton that he has tried to see her married sister twice, but the first time she was away at a neighbor's house playing cards, the second time at the Globe.[58] England, said the foreigners, was "a woman's paradise." Platter describes how "they have more liberty than in other lands, and know how to make good use of it," going constantly abroad while "the men must put up with such ways, and may not punish them for it."[59] It is hard to believe his statement that "what is particularly curious is that the women as well as the men, in fact more often than they, will frequent the taverns or alehouses for enjoyment."[60]

Whatever their attitude toward taverns, the women of London displayed little shyness about going to theatres. It is for the wives and daughters of ordinary citizens that Stephen Gosson was especially concerned in 1579. When he says finally, "I have seene many of you whiche were wont to sporte your selues, at Theatres, when you perceiued the abuse of those places, schoole your selues, and of your owne accorde abhorre Playes,"[61] he is resorting to cajolery. Female attendance did not fall off, and in 1617 Robert Anton wrote bitterly of the theatres' attracting "Swarmes of Wiues."[62] The most objective

---

[56] I assume that the proportion at the end of the century (see Gregory King, "Natural and Political Observations," in Barnett, ed., *Two Tracts by Gregory King*, p. 22) held good for the beginning. King refines his analysis further: husbands and wives, 37 percent; widows and widowers (mostly widows then as now), 9 percent; children, 33 percent; servants, 13 percent; sojourners, etc., 8 percent.

[57] Cheyney, *History of England*, I, 18–19, 47.

[58] June 30, 1614. *Letters of John Chamberlain*, ed. McClure, I, 544.

[59] *Thomas Platter's Travels in England, 1599*, pp. 181–82.

[60] *Ibid.*, p. 170.

[61] *Schoole of Abuse* (1579), ed. Arber, English Reprints, No. III, p. 58.

[62] *Vices Anotimie Scourged and Corrected*, cited in Graves, "Notes on Puritanism and the Stage," *Studies in Philology*, XVIII (1921), 146.

descriptions of Elizabethan theatres have come to us from foreign visitors, and on one subject these visitors were agreed. Said Platter in 1599:

> With these and many more amusements the English pass their time, learning at the play what is happening abroad; *indeed men and womenfolk visit such places without scruple,* since the English for the most part do not travel much, but prefer to learn foreign matters and take their pleasures at home.[63]

And Philip Julius in 1602:

> there are always a good many people present, *including many respectable women* [*auch viele ehrbare Frauens*] because useful arguementa, and many good doctrines, as we were told, are brought forward there.[64]

And Father Busino in 1614:

> *These theatres are frequented by a number of respectable and handsome ladies, who come freely and seat themselves among the men without the slightest hesitation.*[65]

The second statement applies to the public as well as the private theatres, the first and third specifically to public theatres. Together they seem to me conclusive. The proportion of men and women is now irrecoverable, but it is worth noting that the only contemporary "sampling" of an audience which has survived — a casualty list after the collapse of Paris Garden in 1583 — yields five men, four women, and one child.[66] They were assembled at a bearbaiting.

Young men and maids, husbands and wives, went to the theatres together, sometimes in family parties. The ground lease for the earliest of the theatres stipulated that, provided "Gyles [Alleyn] hys wyfe and familie doe com and take ther places before they shalbe taken vpp by any others,"[67] they might see any play free of charge. Jonson's *Every Man out of His Humor* (1599) offers a sop, uncommon with the writer, to the "graue, wise citizen, or modest matron"[68] lest they take offense at the portrait of Deliro and his wife. Examples might be multiplied. No one need be reminded of George the Grocer, Goodwife Nell, and Ralph the Apprentice in *The Knight of the Burning Pestle.*

---

[63] *Thomas Platter's Travels in England, 1599,* p. 170 (italics mine).
[64] "Diary of the Journey of Philip Julius, Duke of Stettin-Pomerania, through England in the Year 1602," eds. G. von Bülow and W. Powell, in *Royal Historical Society Transactions,* New Series, VI, 29 (italics mine).
[65] "Diaries and Despatches of the Venetian Embassy at the Court of King James I, in the Years 1617, 1618," *Quarterly Review,* CII (1857), 416 (italics mine).
[66] The list is given on p. 263.
[67] Chambers, *Elizabethan Stage,* II, 387.
[68] Grex, Act II.

About 20 percent of the metropolitan population was under ten years of age, about 30 percent under sixteen years of age.[69] A few children would have been taken to the theatres by their parents, but it is doubtful if many could have commanded both the freedom and the penny that would make them independent playgoers until they were sixteen — the age at which girls were marriageable and boys ready to enter their apprenticeship. If we let the age at which Londoners began going to plays hover between ten and sixteen we eliminate 25 percent of the population and come upon the first major restriction upon a concept of the audience as a mere cross section of London's humanity. The restriction does not lessen the probability that Shakespeare's audience was youthful. It was about as true in 1601 as in 1696 that "the Males & Females in the Kingdome in General are Aged one with another 27½ years."[70] Mean ages are, however, deceptive at best and especially so in those earlier times when such large numbers failed to survive childhood. There are better reasons for speaking of the youthfulness of Shakespeare's audience.

Standing for several hours or bustling for a place in the galleries would have diminished in appeal as a man grew older. At a popular play one could obtain a good place only by coming early and enduring a long wait. The arduousness of playgoing rather than the frivolity seems to have acted as a restraint upon the elderly John Chamberlain. The drama, in any case, has always made its first call to youth. Two groups are mentioned again and again in contemporary allusions to the theatres — the students of the Inns of Court and the apprentices of London.

London was the third university city of the kingdom. About 1595 we hear that

> the clamorous frie of Innes of Court
> Filles vp the priuate roomes of greater prise:[71]

Before and after 1595, we come upon constant reminders that the plays were a magnet for the students. The number of these was not great. In 1574 there were 593 students in the four Inns, in addition to the 51 benchers and 125 utter barristers.[72] In the reign of James the number had risen to about 720 students, in addition to about 80 benchers and 240 utter barristers.[73] But it was not unusual for the

---

[69] I base this percentage on the figures of King, "Natural and Political Observations," in Barnett, ed., *Two Tracts by Gregory King*, pp. 22–23. The child population in London was smaller per capita than in the rest of the kingdom. . . .

[70] "Natural and Political Observations," in Barnett, ed., *Two Tracts by Gregory King*, p. 23.

[71] Sir John Davies, "In Sillam," Epigram No. 28, in Grosart, ed., *Complete Poems*, II, 27–28.

[72] *Calendar of Inner Temple Records*, ed. Inderwick, I, 468–69.

[73] Wheatley, *London, Past and Present*, II, 261.

students to have young friends and relatives lodging with them, and what the group lacked in total numbers was counterbalanced by the large proportion of those numbers possessing the money, leisure, and inclination for playgoing. A student at the Inns of Court was a well-born, affluent, university-educated young man in his earlier twenties. He lived in a society devoted to intellectual pursuits and well disposed towards belles-lettres. He must have made a good spectator. We cannot generalize too far, of course, and an epigram by Davies will serve to shade our portrait:

> Publius student at the Common-law
> Oft leaves his Bookes, and for his recreation,
> To Paris-garden doth himselfe withdrawe,
> Where he is rauisht with such delectation,
> As downe among the beares and dogges he goes;
> Where, whilst he skipping cries "to head to head,"
> His satten doublet and his veluet hose
> Are all with spittle from aboue be-spread.[74]

Turning now from gown to town, we must recognize that the apprentices of London would have outnumbered the students ten to one. They had no income except what spending money was allowed them by parents or masters, and theoretically they had no weekday leisure, but by hook or crook they flocked to the theatres. Their tastes are often supposed to be reflected in Jonson's familiar lines:

> He rather prayes, you will be pleas'd to see
> One such, to day, as other playes should be.
> Where neither Chorus wafts you ore the seas,
> Nor creaking throne comes downe the boyes to please;[75]

and their habits in accounts like the following:

> The little devils are the apprentices, alias shopboys, who, on two days of the year, which prove fatal to them, Shrove Tuesday and the first of May, are so riotous and outrageous, that in a body, three or four thousand strong, they go committing excesses in every direction, killing human beings and demolishing houses.[76]

This portrait has too much shade. The Shrove Tuesday riot of 1617, for which the apprentice saturnalia furnished only a pretext, explains the horrified tone of the writer. Normally apprentices were well behaved: they had to be.

Apprentices were not all "boyes." They were compelled by statute

---

[74] "In Publium," Epigram No. 43, in Grosart, ed., *Complete Poems*, II, 40–41.
[75] Prologue, *Every Man in His Humor* (1598), in Herford and Simpson, eds., *Ben Jonson.*
[76] "Diaries and Despatches of the Venetian Embassy at the Court of King James I, in the Years 1617, 1618," *Quarterly Review*, CII (1857), 413–14.

to be twenty-four years of age before coming out of their apprenticeship — single, native-born, and mentally and physically fit. They
formed, indeed, a superior class. The sons of unskilled laborers and
husbandmen were generally barred from apprenticeship and certain
guilds insisted upon property qualifications in the parents and educational qualifications in the boy. Gentle birth was not uncommon.
The apprentices were lodged with householders; they were soberly
dressed (with cropped hair) and compelled to walk a chalk line.[77]
But in London they walked with the pride of possession: some of them
would become lord mayors, dining magnificently foreign noblemen
and receiving visits in state by the Archbishop of Canterbury. Many
of them, perhaps the majority, had about as much formal education
as Shakespeare himself. They, like the students, should have made
pretty good spectators. One of the bourgeois traits of Beaumont's apprentice, Ralph, is that he recites at length from Shakespeare — with
somewhat fewer errors than would be made by a modern college
student. The term "apprentice," of course, is loosely used to designate
all the boys of London, among whom no doubt there were plenty of
ragamuffins.

We have now glanced at all of the major factors controlling theatrical attendance — save one. None of these factors except that of age
can be said conclusively to have kept from the theatres more than a
fraction of the available public. Together they help to explain why
only two in fifteen Londoners went to the theatres weekly, but they
fail to explain why from sixty to seventy thousand "adult" Londoners
never went to the theatres at all.[78] The explanation of that phenomenon lies in the one factor not hitherto examined. It is obvious enough.
Many people stayed away from the theatres because they did not care
for plays. A dramatic and poetic age confers no universal taste for
poetry and drama. Elizabethans could be Philistines, and thousands
of them were.

Purely external considerations argue for the heterogeneity of the
audience, for little selection on the basis of class, occupation, sex,
respectability (or its opposite), and the like. The argument is sustained by the cataloguing descriptions of the audiences which the age
produced. I shall set these down without comment, asking the
reader to take each with reserve, in view of the angry or satirical mood
of the speakers, but to let all together form the synthesis:

[77] Dunlop, *English Apprenticeship and Child Labour*, pp. 52, 55–56.
[78] Taking the estimated population of 160,000 in 1605 and subtracting 25
percent for the underage group leaves 120,000. Subtracting the probable
number of playgoers, no greater in 1605 than 50,000 to 60,000 . . . we have
60,000 to 70,000 left.

Anno 1582

the common people which resorte to Theatres being but an assemblie of Tailers, Tinkers, Cordwayners, Saylers, olde Men, yong Men, Women, Boyes, Girles, and such like.[79]

Anno 1583

Mentioned as killed, injured, or miraculously saved when Paris Garden collapsed while a thousand people were watching a bear-baiting on Sunday:

Adam Spencer, a felmonger of Southwark.
William Cockram, a baker of Shoreditch.
John Burton, a clerk of St. Marie Wolmers in Lombard St.
Mathew Mason, a servant with Master Garland of Southwark.
Thomas Peace, a servant with Rob. Tasker of Clerkenwell.
Alice White, a servant to a pursemaker without Cripplegate.
Marie Harrison, daughter to John, a water-bearer of Lombard St.
Mrs. Webb, wife of a pewterer of Limestreet.
An unidentified woman and her small child.[80]

Anno 1595

For, as we see at all the play-house doores,
When ended is the play, the dance, and song,
A thousand Townesmen, gentlemen, and whores,
Porters and serving-men together throng.[81]

Anno 1597

They are the ordinary places for vagrant persons, Maisterles men, thieves, horse stealers, whoremongers, Coozeners, Conycatchers, contrivers of treason and other idele and daungerous persons to meet together. . . . They maintaine idlenes in such persons as haue no vocation & draw apprentices and other seruants from their ordinary workes and all sorts of people from the resort vnto sermons and other Christian exercises to the great hinderance of traides & pphanation of religion.[82]

Anno 1608

The wise, and many headed Bench, that sits
Upon the Life and Death of playes, and Wits,
Compos'd of Gamester, Captain, Knight, Knight's man,
Lady or Pusill that wears mask or fan,
Velvet, or Taffata cap, rank'd in the dark
With the shops Foreman, or some such brave spark.[83]

---

[79] Gosson, *Playes Confuted in Fiue Actions,* in Hazlitt, ed., *English Drama and Stage,* p. 184.

[80] John Field, *A Godly Exhortation,* quoted in Chambers, *Elizabethan Stage,* IV, 220.

[81] Sir John Davies, "In Cosmun," Epigram No. 17, in Grosart, ed., *Complete Poems,* II, 18.

[82] "Dramatic Records of the City of London: The Remembrancia," in *Malone Society Collections,* I, Part I, 80.

[83] Jonson's commendatory verses to *The Faithful Shepherdess.*

Anno 1609
[Dramatic cakes]
fit for ladies: some for lords, knights, squires,
Some for your waiting wench, and city-wires,
Some for your men, and daughters of white-Friars.[84]

Anno 1624

I doubt not but you have heard of our famous play of Gondomar, which hath been followed with extraordinarie concourse, and frequented by all sorts of people old and younge, rich and poore, masters and servants, papists and puritans, wise men et ct., churchmen and statesmen as Sir Henry Wotton, Sir Albert Morton, Sir Benjamin Ruddier, Sir Thomas Lake, and a world besides; the Lady Smith wold have gon yf she could have persuaded me to go with her. I am not so sowre nor severe but that I wold willingly have attended her, but I could not sit so long, for we must have ben there before one a clocke at farthest to find any roome.[85]

Anno 1641

[Plays are] First for strangers, who can desire no better recreation than to come and see a play: then for Citizens to feast their wits: then for Gallants who otherwise perhaps would spend their money in drunkennesse and lasciviousnesse, [and] doe find a great delight and delectation to see a Play: then for the learned it does increase and adde wit constructively to wit: then for Gentlewomen, it teacheth them how to deceive idlenesse: then for the ignorant it does augment their knowledge.[86]

The descriptions fused into one composite portrait give us, I believe, the truth about the kind of people in Shakespeare's audience. If the descriptions seem to make the type of spectators appear more genteel as time passes, it is partly because of the accident that some of the later writers were thinking primarily about that portion of the general theatrical public patronizing "private" theatres after 1599, more of which in a moment. The last description mentions a category of playgoers numerically few but of considerable interest: the "strangers." London was renowned through Europe for its theatres, and foreign visitors always saw a play or two, even when they could not understand the language. "Playing," said Heywood, "is an ornament to the city, which strangers of all nations repairing hither report of in their countries, beholding them here with some admiration."[87] Fortunately some of the reports survive, and to travelers like Kiechel of Ulm,

84 Prologue, Epicoene (1609), in Herford and Simpson, eds., Ben Jonson.
85 Chamberlain to Carleton, August 21. See Letters of John Chamberlain, ed. McClure, II, 577–78.
86 Stage-Players Complaint (1641), in Hazlitt, ed., English Drama and Stage, pp. 256–57.
87 Apology for Actors (1612), Shakespeare Society Publications, No. III, p. 52.

De Witt of Utrecht, Platter of Basle, Busino of Venice, and Paul Hentzner we owe our most revealing descriptions of the English theatres.[88] Some were men of consequence: Prince Lewis of Anhalt-Cöthen, Prince Lewis Frederick of Württemberg, and Duke Philip Julius of Stettin-Pomerania, who visited the playhouses three times during a week's stay in London in 1602. The foreign embassies also provided playhouse patrons. We hear of the French ambassador and his wife going to the Globe to see *Pericles*,[89] of the Spanish ambassador with all his train going to the Fortune and then banqueting with the players,[90] of the Venetian ambassador going to the Curtain and there behaving so much like the rude multitude that in Florentine eyes at least he was "pantalonissima."[91] The foreigners show no particular preference for the private as opposed to the public playhouses; probably the public playhouses had the more pronounced color that would interest visitors from abroad.

Thus far I have said little about the audiences of the private playhouses as such — and for good reason: Shakespeare had little experience with them. His audience was that of the Rose, The Theatre, the Curtain, and the Globe. The King's Men began using Blackfriars as a winter house only after 1608, and even from that late date until he left London, the recorded performances of Shakespeare's plays were all at the Globe. His last play, *Henry VIII*, was certainly first brought out there. Some misapprehension must lie behind a statement like the following: "While Shakespeare, unconsciously writing for all time, kept in his mind's eye the approval of lordly patrons of Blackfriars, Thomas Heywood and his kind catered to apprentices and shopkeepers who haunted the Red Bull."[92] We cannot have the thing both ways. If Heywood wrote for apprentices and shopkeepers, so also did Shakespeare; or if Shakespeare wrote for "lordly patrons," so also did Heywood. A source of confusion exists in the different types of audience vaguely perceived to have existed in or about Shakespeare's time. The matter requires clarification, and a preliminary word must be said about the "private" audiences.

As soon as the playhouses at Paul's and Blackfriars began to rival the Globe and Fortune, we hear that a man need no longer "be choakte with the stench of Garlicke" for at Paul's "Tis a good gentle

---

88 See Rye, *England as Seen by Foreigners, passim;* Chambers, *Elizabethan Stage, passim;* and citations in the present study.
89 Chambers, *Elizabethan Stage,* II, 549.
90 July 21; 1621. See *Letters of John Chamberlain,* ed. McClure, II, 391.
91 Chambers, "Elizabethan Stage Gleanings," *Review of English Studies,* I (1925), 186. I have mentioned earlier the playhouse adventures of Ambassador Foscarini.
92 Wright, *Middle-Class Culture in Elizabethan England,* p. 18.

Audience,"[93] while at Blackfriars there are "Select, and most respected
Auditours,"[94] and plays can count on

> gentle presence, and the Sceans suckt up
> By calme attention of choyce audience.[95]

The playwrights later discovered that the attention was neither uniformly, nor choice; however, at the rates charged, it continued
"gentle." In the reign of James, multitudes of coaches were causing
traffic congestions outside Blackfriars; and in that of Charles, traffic
regulations were discommoding "diverse persons of great quality, especially Ladies and Gentlewomen"[96] on their way to the theatre. In
1636 the Duke of Lenox and the Lord Chamberlain were disputing
over possession of a Blackfriars box. Between 1631 and 1641, Sir
Humphrey Mildmay, during his sojourns in London, records fifty-seven
visits to the theatres, usually Blackfriars, with his wife or in polite
theatrical parties "with good Company." On one occasion, at least,
"good Company" palled: "To dynner came Sr Chr: Abdy & wente
to the Newe playe with my wife. J wente abroade by my selfe to
worse places alone."[97] After the theatres were closed in 1642, a
spokesman for the Phoenix, Salisbury Court, and Blackfriars affirmed
that at these houses "none use to come but the best of the Nobility
and Gentry" and disclaims with high disdain "boystrous Butchers,
cutting Coblers, hardhanded Masons, and the like."[98] The gentility
of the private playhouse audiences we dare not question.

But the private playhouses between 1599 and 1642 did not create
this audience. They merely segregated and perhaps augmented it.
It had been segregated once before in some slight degree, as evidenced
by Lyly's allusions in the eighties to the advantages of "presenting
our studies before Gentlemen" at Paul's,[99] and to the "woonted cour-
tisies" of the spectators at Blackfriars.[100] It existed during the nineties
but was then merged with other elements from the population to form
the universal audience of the public theatres. We should distinguish
among three Elizabethan audiences, recognizing that various occasions

93 Marston, *Jack Drum's Entertainment* (1600), Act V, Scene ii, in Wood,
ed., *Plays.*
94 Marston, Prologue, *Antonio and Mellida* (1599–1600).
95 Marston, *Antonio's Revenge* (1599–1601), Act V, Scene vi, ed. Greg,
Malone Society Reprints.
96 Adams, *Shakespearean Playhouses*, p. 231.
97 December 13, 1635. The dramatic extracts from Mildmay's journal (Harl.
MS 454) appear in Bentley, "The Diary of a Caroline Theatregoer," *Modern
Philology*, XXXV (1937–38), 61–72.
98 *Actors Remonstrance or Complaint* (1643), in Hazlitt, ed., *English Drama
and Stage*, p. 261.
99 Prologue, *Midas* (c. 1589), in Bond, ed., *Complete Works.*
100 Prologue, *Campaspe* (c. 1584), in *ibid.* See also the Prologue to *Sapho
and Phao* (c. 1584), in *ibid.*

and various theatres would obscure our distinction: there was the
genteel audience of the private theatres; there was the plebeian audience of such theatres as the Red Bull and perhaps the Fortune after
the private houses had filched the gentry away; and then there was
that audience both genteel and plebeian, or neither, of the nineties
and, because of its peculiar prestige, of the Globe in the early decades
of the seventeenth century. It was the audience for which nearly all
great Elizabethan plays were written. It was Shakespeare's audience.

All that we can say of the composition of Shakespeare's audience,
other than that it was a cross section of the London population of his
day, is that youth may have predominated somewhat over age, male
over female, the worldly over the pious, and, of course without the
"perhaps," the receptive over the unreceptive. Although the more
leisured classes would have been better represented than by their pro
rata of the population, it was predominately a working-class audience
because of the greater numerical superiority of the working classes in
the London area and because theatrical tariffs had been designed
largely for them. It was not much different from the assemblage
which gathered to hear the sermons at Paul's Cross. Stephen Gosson,
the one really likable antagonist of the Elizabethan stage, says with a
kind of weary resignation: "Indeede I must confesse there comes to
Playes of all sortes, old and young; it is hard to say that all offend"
— then his higher nature triumphs — "yet I promise you, I wil sweare
for none."[101]

[101] *Schoole of Abuse* (1579), ed. Arber, *Eng. Reprints,* No. III, p. 60.

PURITAN ATTACKS, AND AN
ACTOR'S DEFENSE

𝒴 Throughout the Elizabethan, Jacobean, and Caroline periods, the Puritans waged a relentless war against the theatrical
profession, a war which ended in 1642 with the temporary closing of the theatres. To the Puritans the playhouses were "monuments of vice and folly," which must be suppressed at all cost.
Countless pamphlets were issued and sermons preached attacking the immorality of theatres and the impiety of the plays they
presented.

Occasionally the actors struck back. In 1612 Thomas Heywood (1574?–1641), performer and journeyman playwright for
the Lord Admiral's Men, wrote a spirited defense of his profession entitled *An Apology for Actors*. Three years later the
pseudonymous Puritan pamphleteer, I. G., wrote a point-by-
point refutation of Heywood's arguments. The exchange of views,
while frequently naïve, is nevertheless lively and informative.
The important question of the "usefulness" of drama, a question
which had concerned critics since the days of Horace, is examined in Book III of Heywood's work. Excerpts from his observations and from I. G.'s reply to them are reproduced below.

Thomas Heywood

OF ACTORS AND THE TRUE USE OF THEIR QUALITY*

*T*ragedies and Comedies, saith *Donatus,*[1] had their beginning *arebus
divinis,* from divine sacrifices, they differ thus: in Comedies, *turbu-
lenta prima, tranquilla ultima,* in Tragedies, *tranquilla prima, turbu-
lenta ultima,* Comedies begin in trouble, and end in peace; Tragedies
begin in calms, and end in tempest. Of Comedies there be three kinds,
moving Comedies, called *Motoriae,* standing Comedies, called *Statariae,*
or mixed betwixt both, called *Mistae:* they are distributed into four
parts, the Prologue, that is, the preface; the *Protasis,* that is, the proposition, which includes the first Act, and presents the Actors; the
Epitasis, which is the business and body of the Comedy; the last the
Catastrophe, and conclusion: the definition of the Comedy, according

---

* From Thomas Heywood, *An Apology for Actors* (New York: Scholars' Facsimiles & Reprints, 1941); reprinted in excerpt, with modernized spelling.

1 Aelius Donatus, Latin grammarian and commentator on Vergil and Terence
(*fl.* 333). Heywood took the material of this paragraph from prefatory comment on Terence, *De fabula* of Euanthius, and the *Excerpta de comoedia.*

to the *Latins:* a discourse consisting of diverse institutions, comprehending civil and domestic things, in which is taught, what in our lives and manner is to be followed, what to be avoided. . . . *Cicero* saith, a Comedy is the imitation of life, the glass of custom, and the image of truth,[2] in *Athens* they had their first original. The ancient Comedians used to attire their actors thus: the old men in white, as the most ancient of all, the young men in parti-colored garments, to note their diversity of thoughts, their slaves and servants in thin and bare vesture, either to note their poverty, or that they might run the more lighter about their affairs: their Parasites wore robes that were turned in, and intricately wrapped about them; the fortunate in white, the discontented in decayed vesture, or garments, grown out of fashion; the rich in purple, the poor in crimson, soldiers wore purple jackets, hand-maids the habits of strange virgins, bawds, pied coats, and Courtesans, garments of the color of mud, to denote their covetousness: the stages were hung with rich Arras, which was first brought from King *Attalus* into *Rome:* his state-hangings were so costly, that from him all Tapestries, and rich Arras were called *Attalia.*

. . . .

This [acting] being a thing ancient as I have proved it, next of dignity, as many arguments have confirmed it, and now even in these days by the best, without exception, favorably tolerated, why should I yield my censure, grounded on such firm and established sufficiency, to any Tower, founded on sand, any castle built in the air, or any trivial upstart, and mere imaginary opinion. . . .

I hope there is no man of so unsensible a spirit, that can inveigh against the true and direct use of this quality: Oh but say they, the *Romans* in their time, and some in these days have abused it, and therefore we volley out our exclamations against the use. Oh shallow! Because such a man had his house burnt, we shall quite condemn the use of fire, because one man quaffed poison, we must so bear to drink, because some have been shipwrecked, no man shall hereafter traffic by sea. Then I may as well argue thus: he cut his finger, therefore must I wear no knife, yond man fell from his horse, therefore must I travel afoot; that man surfeited, therefore dare not I eat. What can appear more absurd than such a gross and senseless assertion? I could turn this unpointed weapon against his breast that aims it at mine, and reason thus: *Roscius*[3] had a large pension allowed him by the Senate of *Rome,* why should not an actor of the like dessert, have the

---

2 This is reported by Donatus. Jonson quotes it in *Every Man Out of His Humour,* III, vi, 206–207.

3 Quintus Roscius (d. 62 B.C.), the most famous Roman comic actor of his day. Pliny tells us his yearly earnings amounted to 50 million sesterces.

like allowance now? or this, the most famous City and Nation in the world held plays in great admiration. . . . These are not the Bases we must build upon, nor the columns that must support our architecture. . . .

To proceed to the matter: First, playing is an ornament to the City, which strangers of all Nations, repairing hither, report of in their Countries, beholding them here with some admiration: for what variety of entertainment can there be in any City of Christendom, more than in *London?* But some will say, this dish might be very well spared out of the banquet: to him I answer, *Diogenes,* that used to feed on roots, cannot relish a Marchpane.[4] Secondly, our *English* tongue, which hath been the most harsh, uneven, and broken language of the world, part *Dutch,* part *Irish, Saxon, Scotch, Welsh,* and indeed a gallimaufry of many, but perfect in none, is now by this secondary means of playing, continually refined, every writer striving in himself to add a new flourish unto it; so that in process, from the most rude and unpolished tongue, it is grown to a most perfect and composed language, and many excellent works, and elaborate Poems writ in the same, that many Nations grow inamored of our Tongue (before despised). . . . Thus you see to what excellency our refined *English* is brought, that in these days we are ashamed of that *Euphony* & eloquence which within these 60 years, the best tongues in the land were proud to pronounce. Thirdly, plays have made the ignorant more apprehensive, taught the unlearned the knowledge of many famous histories, instructed such as cannot read in the discovery of all our *English* Chronicles: & what man have you now of that weak capacity, that cannot discourse of any notable thing recorded even from *William* the *Conqueror,* nay from the landing of *Brute,* until this day, being possessed of their true use. For, or because Plays are writ with this aim, and carried with this method, to teach the subjects obedience to their King, to show the people the untimely ends of such as have moved tumults, commotions, and insurrections, to present this with the flourishing estate of such as live in obedience, exhorting them to allegiance, dehorting them from all traitorous and felonious stratagems. . . .

Use of Tragedies. If we present a Tragedy, we include the fatal and abortive ends of such as commit notorious murders, which is aggravated and acted with all the Art that may be, to terrify men from the like abhorred practices. If we present a *Uses of Historical Plays.* foreign History, the subject is so intended, that in the lives of *Romans, Grecians,* or others, either the virtues of our Countrymen are extolled, or their vices reproved, as thus, by the example of *Caesar* to stir soldiers to valor, & magnani-

4 Diogenes was a Greek Cynic philosopher (c. 412–323 B.C.). Marchpane is a sweetmeat made of a paste of pounded almonds, sugar, etc.

mity: by the fall of *Pompey,* that no man trust in his own strength: we present *Alexander,* killing his friend in his rage, to reprove rashness: *Midas,* choked with his gold, to tax covetousness: *Nero* against tyranny: *Sardanapalus,*[5] against luxury: *Ninus,*[6] against ambition, with

Use of Morals.

infinite others, by sundry instances, either animating men to noble attempts, or attaching the consciences of the spectators, finding themselves touched in presenting the vices of others. If a moral, it is to persuade men to humanity and good life, to instruct them in civility and good manners, showing them the fruits of honesty, and the end of villainy. . . .

If a Comedy, it is pleasantly contrived with merry accidents, and in-

Use of Comedies.

termixed with apt and witty jests, to present before the Prince at certain times of solemnity, or else merely fitted to the stage. And what is then the subject of this harmless mirth? either in the shape of a Clown, to show others their slovenly and unhandsome behavior, that they may reform that simplicity in themselves, which others make their sport, lest they happen to become the like subject of general scorn to an auditory, else it entreats of love, deriding foolish inamorates, who spend their ages, their spirits, nay themselves, in the servile and ridiculous employments of their Mistresses: and these are mingled with sportful accidents, to recreate such as of themselves are wholly devoted to Melancholy, which corrupts the blood: or to refresh such weary spirits as are tired with labor, or study, to moderate the cares and heaviness of the mind, that they may return to their trades and faculties with more zeal and earnestness, after some small soft and pleasant retirement. Sometimes they discourse of Pantaloons, Usurers that have unthrifty sons, which both the fathers and sons may behold to their instructions: sometimes of Courtesans, to divulge their

Use of Pastorals.

subleties and snares, in which young men may be entangled, showing them the means to avoid them. If we present a Pastoral, we show the harmless love of Shepherds diversely moralized, distinguishing betwixt the craft of the City, and the innocence of the sheep-coat. Briefly, there is neither Tragedy, History, Comedy, Moral or Pastoral, from which an infinite use cannot be gathered. I speak not in the defense of any lascivious shows, scurrilous jests, or scandalous invectives: If there be any such, I banish them quite from my patronage. . . .

Eupolis, Cratinus, Aristophanes,[7] and other Comic Poets in the time of *Horace,* with large scope, and unbridled liberty boldly and plainly

---

[5] Last Assyrian king, noted (according to legend) for his luxury and effeminacy.

[6] King of Assyria, reputed founder of Nineveh.

[7] Eupolis (c. 446–c. 411 b.c.), Old Comedy writer, as was Cratinus (c. 520–c. 423). Aristophanes (c. 448–c. 380) was the greatest poet of Old Comedy.

scourged all such abuses as in their ages were generally practised, to
the staining and blemishing of a fair and beautiful Commonweal. . . .
But I should tire my self to reckon the names of all *French, Roman,
German, Spanish, Italian,* and *English* Poets, being in number infinite,
and their labors extant to approve their worthiness.

Is thy mind Noble? and wouldst thou be further stir'd up to magnanimity? Behold, upon the stage thou mayest see *Hercules, Achilles,
Alexander, Caesar* . . . with infinite others in their own persons qualities, & shapes, animating thee with courage, deterring thee from cowardice. Hast thou of thy Country well deserved? and art thou of thy
labor evil requited? to associate[8] thee thou mayest see the valiant
Roman Marcellus[9] pursue *Hannibal* at *Nola,* conquering *Syracusa,*
vanquishing the *Gauls,* all *Padua,* and presently (for his reward) banished his Country into *Greece.* There thou mayest see *Scipio Africanus,*[10] now triumphing for the conquest of all *Africa,* and immediately exil'd the confines of *Romania.* Art thou inclined to lust? behold the falls of the *Tarquins,* in the rape of *Lucrece:*[11] the guerdon
of luxury in the death of *Sardanapalus.* . . . Art thou proud? our Scene
presents thee with the fall of *Phaeton,*[12] *Narcissus*[13] pining in the love
of his shadow. . . . We present men with the ugliness of their vices,
to make them the more to abhor them, as the *Persians* use, who above
all sins, loathing drunkenness, accustomed in their solemn feasts, to
make their servants and captives extremely overcome with wine, and
then call their children to view their nasty and loathsome behavior,
making them hate that sin in themselves, which showed so gross and
abominable in others. The like use may be gathered of the drunkards
so naturally imitated in our plays, to the applause of the Actor, content of the auditory, and reproving of the vice. . . .

To end in a word. Art thou addicted to prodigality? envy? cruelty?
perjury? flattery? or rage? our Scenes afford thee store of men to shape
your lives by, who be frugal, loving, gentle, trusty, without soothing,

---

8 Accompany.

9 Marcus Claudius Marcellus (c. 268–208 B.C.), Roman consul, besieged
Syracuse and captured it in 212 B.C.

10 Scipio Africanus Major (234?–183 B.C.), the conqueror of Hannibal. He
had many jealous enemies and ordered at his death that his body should not be
buried in Rome.

11 Tarquinius Superbus, seventh legendary king of Rome, and his son
Sextus were banished from Rome after the latter had ravished the virtuous
Lucretia, forcing her to commit suicide.

12 Proud son of Phoebus, who begged his father to allow him to drive the
chariot of the sun. However, he was incapable of the task and threatened the
earth with a conflagration. Zeus hurled a thunderbolt which struck him, and he
fell into the river Eridanus.

13 A beautiful young man who saw his image in a fountain and fell in love
with it. His fruitless attempts to approach this object drove him to death. He
was changed into the flower which bears his name.

and in all things temperate. Wouldst thou be honorable? just, friendly, moderate, devout, merciful, and loving concord? thou mayest see many of their fates and ruins, who have been dishonorable, unjust, false, gluttonous, sacrilegious, bloody-minded, and broachers of dissention. Women likewise that are chaste, are by us extolled, and encouraged in their virtues. . . . What can sooner print modesty in the souls of the wanton, than by discovering unto them the monstrousness of their sin? It follows that we prove these exercises to have been the discoverers of many notorious murders, long concealed from the eyes of the world. To omit all far-fetched instances, we will prove it by a domestic, and home-borne truth, which within these few years happened. At *Lin* in *Norfolk*, the then Earl of Suffolk players acting the old History of Friar *Francis*,[14] & presenting a woman,

A strange accident happening at a play.

who insatiately doting on a young gentleman, had (the more securely to enjoy his affection) mischievously and secretly murdered her husband, whose ghost haunted her, and at diverse times in her most solitary and private contemplations, in most horrid and fearful shapes, appeared, and stood before her. As this was acted, a townswoman (till then of good estimation and report) finding her conscience (at this presentment) extremely troubled, suddenly screeched and cried out Oh my husband, my husband! I see the ghost of my husband fiercely threatening and menacing me. At which shrill and unexpected outcry, the people about her, moved to a strange amazement, inquired the reason of her clamor, when presently un-urged, she told them, that seven years ago, she, to be possessed of such a Gentleman (meaning him) had poisoned her husband, whose fearful image personated itself in the shape of that ghost: whereupon the murderess was apprehended, before the Justices further examined, & by her voluntary confession after condemned. That this is true, as well by the report of the Actors as the records of the Town, there are many eyewitnesses of this accident yet living, vocally to confirm it.

As strange an accident happened to a company of the same quality some 12 years ago, or not so much, who playing late in

A strange accident happening at a play.

the night at a place called *Perin* in *Cornwall*, certain *Spaniards* were landed the same night unsuspected, and undiscovered, with intent to take in the town, spoil and burn it, when suddenly, even upon their entrance, the players (ignorant as the townsmen of any such attempt) presenting a battle on the stage with their drum and trumpets struck up a loud alarm: which the enemy hearing, and fearing they were discovered, amazedly retired, made some few idle shot in a bravado, and so in a hurly-burly fled disorderly to their boats. At the report of this

14 Lost play.

tumult, the townsmen were immediately armed, and pursued them to the sea, praising God for their happy deliverance from so great a danger, who by His providence made these strangers the instrument and secondary means of their escape from such imminent mischief, and the tyranny of so remorseless an enemy.

Another of the like wonder happened at *Amsterdam* in *Holland,* a company of our *English* Comedians (well known) traveling those Countries, as they were before the Burgers and other the chief inhabitants, acting the last part of the 4 sons of *Aymon,*[15] towards the last act of the history, where penitent *Renaldo,* like a common laborer, lived in disguise, vowing as his last penance, to labor & carry burdens to the structure of a goodly Church there to be erected: whose dilegence the laborers envying, since by reason of his stature and strength, he did usually perfect more work in a day, than a dozen of the best (he working for his conscience, they for their lucres). Whereupon by reason his industry had so much disparaged their living, conspired amongst themselves to kill him, waiting some opportunity to find him asleep, which they might easily do, since the sorest laborers are the soundest sleepers, and industry is the best preparative to rest. Having spied their opportunity, they drave a nail into his temples, of which wound immediately he died. As the Actors handled this, the audience might on a sudden understand an outcry, and loud shriek in a remote gallery, and pressing about the place, they might perceive a woman of great gravity, strangely amazed, who with a distracted & troubled brain oft sighed out these words: Oh my husband, my husband! The play, without further interruption proceeded; the woman was to her own house conducted, without any apparent suspicion, every one conjecturing as their fancies led them. In this agony she some few days languished, and on a time, as certain of her well disposed neighbors came to comfort her, one amongst the rest being Church-warden, to him the Sexton posts, to tell him of a strange thing happening him in the ripping up of a grave: see here (quoth he) what I have found, and shows them a fair skull, with a great nail pierced quite through the brain-pan, but we cannot conjecture to whom it should belong, nor how long it hath lain in the earth, the grave being confused, and the flesh consumed. At the report of this accident, the woman, out of the trouble of her afflicted conscience, discovered a former murder. For 12 years ago, by driving that nail into that skull, being the head of her husband, she had treacherously slain him. This being publicly confessed, she was arraigned, condemned, adjudged, and burned. But I draw my subject to greater length than I purposed: these therefore out of other infinites, I have collected, both for their familiarness and lateness of memory.

A strange accident happening at a play.

15 Another lost play.

Thus our Antiquity we have brought from the *Grecians* in the time of *Hercules:* from the *Macedonians* in the age of *Alexander:* from the *Romans* long before *Julius Caesar,* and since him, through the reigns of 23 Emperors succeeding, even to *Marcus Aurelius:* after him they were supported by the *Mantuans, Venetians, Valencians, Neopolitans,* the *Florentines,* and others: since, by the *German* Princes, the *Palsgrave,* the *Landsgrave,* the Dukes of *Saxony,* of *Brunswick,* &c. The

Cardinal Alfonsus.

Cardinal at *Brussels,* hath at this time in pay, a company of our *English* Comedians. The *French* King allows certain companies in *Paris, Orleans,* besides other Cities: so doth the King of Spain, in *Seville, Madrid,* and other provinces. But in no Country they are of that eminence that ours are: so our most royal, and ever renowned sovereign, hath licensed us in London: so did his predecessor, the thrice virtuous virgin, Queen *Elizabeth,* and before her, her sister, Queen *Mary, Edward* the sixth, and their father, *Henry* the eighth: and before these in the tenth year of the reign of *Edward* the fourth, Anno 1490. *John Stowe,*[16] an ancient and grave Chronicler, records (amongst other varieties tending to the like effect) that a play was acted at a place called Skinners well, fast by Clerken-well, which continued eight days, and was of matter from *Adam* and *Eve* (the first creation of the world). The spectators were no worse than the Royalty of England. And amongst other commendable exercises in this place, the Company of the Skinners of *London* held certain yearly solemn plays. In place whereof, now in these late days, the wrestling, and such other pastimes have been kept, and is still held about *Bartholmew-tide.* Also in the year 1390, the 14 year of the reign of *Richard* the second, the 18 of July, were the like *Interludes* recorded of at the same place, which continued 3 days together, the King and Queen, and Nobility being there present. Moreover, to this day, in diverse places of *England,* there be towns that hold the privilege of their Fairs, and other Charters by yearly stage-plays, as at *Manningtree* in *Suffolk, Kendall* in the *North,* & others. To let these pass, as things familiarly known to all men. Now to speak of some abuse lately crept into the quality, as an inveighing against the State, the Court, the Law, the City, and their governments; with the particularizing of private men's humors (yet alive) Noblemen, & others. I know it distastes many; neither do I any way approve it, nor dare I by any means excuse it. The liberty which some arrogate to themselves, committing their bitterness, and liberal invectives against all estates, to the mouths of Children, supposing their juniority to be a privilege for any railing, be it never so violent. I could advise all such to curb

16 John Stow (1525?–1605), chronicler and antiquary. He wrote a number of books, among which are: *The Workes of Geffrey Chaucer, The Chronicles of England, A Survey of London.*

and limit this presumed liberty within the bands of discretion and government. But wise and judicial Censurers, before whom such complaints shall at any time hereafter come, will not (I hope) impute these abuses to any transgression in us, who have ever been careful and provident to shun the like. I surcease to prosecute this any further, lest my good meaning be (by some) misconstrued: and fearing likewise, lest with tediousness I tire the patience of the favorable Reader, here (though abruptly) I conclude my third and last TREATISE.

I. G.

from A REFUTATION OF THE APOLOGY FOR ACTORS[*]

*H*itherto have I proceeded in Refutation and opposition of Master *Actors Apology:* Omitting nothing worthy of notice, which I have not touched, or shall not touch in this my last treatise. And now that I have declared the abominable original with Ancient and present indignity of Players; I come lastly to handle the use of their quality: wherein according to my former method, after I have convinced M. *Actors* Arguments and affirmations, with Reasons and negations: I will set down the most abominable abuse, and impious quality of them.

Tragedies and Comedies saith he, out of *Donatus,* had their beginning *a Rebus Divinis,* from Divine sacrifices. It's true; they were first instituted of Devils and for Devils, and therefore as things first consecrated to Devils, ought to be abandoned.

Next M. *Actor* sets down his definition of a Comedy: for which he should have alleged his Author, because he saith it is according to the Latins. But suppose it were of his own brain gathered from *Cicero's* saying (I know not where) which he afterward allegeth thus: A Comedy is the Image of truth. Well then; to disprove his definition I must confute *Cicero:* And that thus.

Whatsoever is the Image of truth, is like unto truth. For Images are said to be like unto what they represent.

But a Comedy is not like unto truth:

Ergo: It is not the Image of Truth.

My Assumption I confirm thus. A Comedy is not like unto truth, because it is wholly composed of Fables and Vanities: and Fables and Vanities, are lies and deceits: and lies and deceits are clean contrary to truth, and altogether unlike it, even as virtue is unlike to

---

[*] From *A Refutation of the Apology for Actors* (New York: Scholars' Facsimiles & Reprints, 1941). Spelling partly modernized.

vice. Wherefore my Assumption being true my conclusion is also firm. But beside this refutation of his Definition, I will lay down another in opposition of it, gathered out of the works of *Atheneus:* Thus

Definition of plays. Plays are the fruit of vintage and drunkenness, consisting of sundry impieties, comprehending evil and damnable things, wherein is taught how in our lives and manners we may follow all kind of vice with Art. For they are full of filthy words and gestures, such as would not become very lackeys and Courtesans: and have sundry inventions which

The riches of plays. infect the spirit, and replenish it with unchaste, whorish, cozening, deceitful, wanton and mischievous passions: besides which inconveniences Stage-Players do oftentimes envy, and gnaw at the honor of an other, and to please the vulgar people, set before them lies, and teach much dissolution and deceitfulness: by this means turning upside down all discipline and good manners. Hereupon *Tully*[1] complaineth in all vain, who being to speak of Comedians and Poets, when he came to them saith: *The clamor and approbation of the people, when it is joined with these Poetical fictions, as the testimony of some great and learned matter, oh what darkness doth it involve a man in? what fears it inflicts, what lust it inflames?* . . .

After this he will seem to answer an objection, which because it is but a piece of an objection, extorted, both it and his answer I will omit. The objection is, that the Romans in their time, and some in these days have abused Plays: but they have not only abused them, for they are abuse itself (as I shall instance further hereafter) and ever were.

After this again he saith.

> *Plays are in use as they are understood:*
> *Spectators eyes may make them bad or good.*

O right excellently well said! In what a doubtful case would the use of plays then stand, if none but fools (as commonly they all are) or none but blindmen were their auditors? the one kind could not understand, the other could not see, and consequently neither give right judgment of them: For the one could not understand what vice to avoid, the other could not see acted to the life what magnanimous virtue for to follow.

But to leave this forked argument, and with more plain reasons to touch his meaning. I deny his maxim. For although this Axiom . . . be true, every thing is received according to the capacity of that which receiveth: yet it extendeth itself not so far as M. *Actors* inten-

1 Cicero is often referred to as Tully in English literature.

tion. For then according to the discretion of fools and blind men, if Plays were evil (as they are not to be thought otherwise) by their good accepting of them they were good; which how absurd a reason it is let all men judge. Besides which if there were any good in Plays, yet for the evil, which is greater, they are not tolerable. And we are taught not to do good if any evil may ensue thereby. For good when it is the occasion of evil, ceaseth any longer to be good, but is turned into sin: For evil, and the occasion of evil are under the same predicament of sin.

Next M. *Actor* inferreth many vocations and institutions of life wherein men live, amongst which there hath been some bad: and thereupon demandeth, whether the general shall be condemned for the particulars sake. I answer no; But the *Genus* of plays comes not under the protection of this reason, because they are wholly evil, as more at large I will shew towards the end of my discourse. Next M. *Actor* proceeds in the use of Plays, and shows first that they are an Ornament to the City. But I think the saying of *Valerius Maximus*[2] of more authority than this: who saith, Plays were never brought up . . . without shame to the Kingdom. Secondly, he sheweth (and to the disgrace of his mother tongue) that our English was the rudest language in the world, a Gallymafry of Dutch, French, Irish, Saxon, Scotch, and Welsh, but by Play-Poets it hath been refined. But doth he not forget that whiles they add Greek, Latin, and Italian, they make a great mingle-mangle. Nay, before the Conquest by Bastard *William* that the French came in, our English tongue was most perfect, able to express any Hebruism, which is the trial of perfection in Languages, and now it will very hardly expound a Greek Lecture. For after that the French had once corrupted it it was but of late years that it could recover a common Dialect again. . . . But what refinedness is in our language, it's not from Poets, but from other learned men's writings, from whom they borrow all the refined words they have.

Thirdly, he affirms that Plays have taught the ignorant knowledge of many famous Histories. They have indeed made many to know of those Histories they never did, by reason they would never take the pains to read them. But these that know the Histories before they see them acted, are ever ashamed, when they have heard what lies the Players insert amongst them, and how greatly they deprave them. If they be too long for a Play, they make them curtails; if too short, they enlarge them with many Fables, and whether too long or too short, they corrupt them with a Fool and his Babbles: whereby they make them like Leaden rules, which men will fit to their work, and not

---

2 Valerius Maximus (1st century B.C.–1st century A.D.), Roman compiler of anecdotes.

frame their work to them. So that the ignorant instead of true History shall bear away nothing but fabulous lies. . . .

Now have I opposed and confuted the grand Arguments of M. *Actors* third book, such as concerns some, though not the more particular use of Plays, which now I come generally to handle. . . .

But now to examine plays according to the four general causes, the *Efficient, Material, Formal,* and *Final* cause of all things, all men shall see the goodness that they contain in them: or much rather the great evil wherewith they abound.

The *Efficient* cause of Plays I have already shewed in sundry places of this work to be the Devil, chiefly by his own command, and secondarily heretofore by his heathenish agents, first the Idolatrous *Greeks,* and after the pagan *Romans,* and at present by his Ministers, the almost-heathenish Poets. Wherefore I will insist no longer herein.

The *Material* cause or matter of Plays is their Subject whereupon they speak and entreat, and that is two fold, either *Divine* or *Profane.* If Plays be of *Divine* matter, then are they most intolerable, or rather Sacriligeous: for that the sacred word of God is to be handled reverently, gravely, and sagely, with veneration to the glorious majesty of God: and not with scoffs and jibes, or with the jests of a Fool, as it is in interludes without any worship or reverence to the same. The word of our salvation, the price of Christ's blood, the merits of his life and passion, the holy Scriptures, were not given to be abusively acted on a Stage, but to be Preached by his Godly Ministers; it was not given to be mixed and interlaced with scurrilous and uncomely gestures, laughters, and vain locutions, but to be gravely handled, and with veneration expounded in God's assembly. . . . Wherefore whosoever abuseth the word of God on Stages in Plays and Interludes, abuseth the Majesty of God which shineth in the same, and maketh a mocking stock of him, and thereby purchaseth judgment to himself. And no marvel, for the sacred word of God & God himself, is never to be thought on, or once named, but in Fear and Reverence to the same. All the whole company of Heaven, Angels, Archangels, Cherubim, Seraphim, Thrones, Dominations, Virtues, Principalities, Potentates, and all powers whatsoever, yea the Devils themselves do tremble and quake at the naming of God, and at his presence: And do these mockers and flouters of his Majesty, these dissembling *Hypocrites,* think to escape unpunished. Beware therefore you Players, *Hypocrites,* and like good comptists cast up your accounts beforehand, what will be your reward in the end. Abuse God no more, corrupt his people no longer with your dregs, and intermingle not his blessed Word with your profane vanities. . . .

On the other side, if the matter of plays be profane, then tend they to the dishonor of God, and nourishing of vice, both which are damnable. So that whether they be divine or profane, they are quite contrary to the word of grace, and sucked out of the Devil's teats to nourish us in Idolatry, heathenry, and sin. To describe the matter of profane plays, we are to consider the general kinds of Plays, which is the *Tragedy*, and the *Comedy*. The matter of *Tragedies* is haughtiness, arrogancy, ambition, pride, injury, anger, wrath, envy, hatred, contention, war, murder, cruelty, rapine, incest, rovings, depredations, piracies, spoils, robberies, rebellions, treasons, killing, hewing, stabbing, dagger-drawing, fighting, butchery, treachery, villainy &c. and all kind of heroic evils whatsoever. Of *Comedies* the matter is love, lust, lechery, bawdry, scortation, adultery, uncleanness, pollution, wantonness, chambering, courting, jesting, mocking, flouting, foolery, venery, drabbery, knavery, cozenage, cheating, hypocrisy, flattery, and the like. And as complements and appendants to both kinds of plays is swearing, cursing, oathes, and blasphemies, &c.

Hence ariseth the formal cause, or form of plays, which consisteth in the action, and in the Actors. The action is two-fold, in word, and in deed. The action in word is lascivious speeches, idle and vain scoffing, jesting, and foolery, and cozenage, knavery, flattery, and whatsoever else, set forth in their colors, phrases, and terms, and with the grace, elegancy, and lustre of the tongue. The action in deed is the setting forth of all enormities, and exorbitances, with the personating of the doers of them; with false representations, lying shows, killing, stabbing, hanging, and fighting; active demonstration of cozenage, whorish enticing, all kind of villainy, and hypocrisy; with embracing, clipping, culling, dandling, kissing; all manner wanton gestures, and the like. The form that consists in the Actors, is the parts they play: And these are jointly both in Tragedies and Comedies. Tyrannous Kings and Queens; ambitious Potentates, Nobles, Peers; unjust Judges, Magistrates, Officers, covetous Citizens, spend-all Gentlemen . . . and finally contemners of God, his laws, and the Kings, and blasphemers of his holy name; with such like of infinite variety. That if there were nothing else but this, it were sufficient to withdraw a good Christian from beholding of them. For as often as they go to Theaters to see Plays, they enter into *Venus Palace* and *Satan's Synagogue*, to betray and ensnare their own souls. And therefore these Players, through the parts they act carrying the note and brand of all kind of cursed people on their backs, wheresoever they go, are to be hissed out of all Christian kingdoms, if they will have truth and not vanity, *Christ* and not the Devil to dwell among them. The final cause or end of Plays particularly toucheth their use and qualities, wherein I am to answer three main objections.

The first objection is, that they instruct men what vices to avoid, what ordinances to observe, what enormities to abandon & what virtues to embrace. Which M. *Actor* pretendeth to be the final cause why the Greeks admitted Plays in their common-wealth, and which I promised in my first Book particularly to answer and refute. Therefore let him know that God only gave authority of public instruction and correction but to two sorts of men: to his Ecclesiastical Ministers, and temporal Magistrates: he never instituted a third authority of Players, or ordained that they should serve in his Ministry: and therefore are they to be rejected with their use and quality. . . .

And so to conclude Players assume an unlawful office to themselves of instruction and correction: and therefore it becometh sin unto them, because God never ordained them unto it, which is the reason that never any profited in goodness but in wickedness by them. This is sufficient to refute the first objection. But because this opinion of the use of plays was but the supposition of the heathen Greeks I will further convince it with the authority & reasons of an heathen man, speaking of the licentious liberty of Poets and Players tongues, saith thus: *Whom did not the Poet touch, nay whom did he not vex, whom spared he? Perhaps* saith one, *he quipped a sort of wicked, vulgar, seditious fellows . . . but it were fitter for such faults to be taxed by the Censor, than by the Poet.* . . .

The second objection is the vulgar opinion of *Actors*, and the most part of their profane auditors, some whereof I have even heard with mine own ears to pronounce and affirm: Plays to be as good, or may do as much good, as Sermons are, or may do. Oh blasphemy intolerable! Are obscene Plays, and filthy Interludes comparable to the word of God, the food of life, and life itself? It is all one as if they had said, Bawdry, Heathenry Paganism, Scurrility, and Deviltry, itself is equal with God's Word: or that *Satan* is equipollent with the Lord. . . .

The third objection is, that many good examples may be learned out of them. And truly so there may: For if you will learn to do any evil, skilfully, cunningly, covertly, or artificially, you need go no other where than to the Theater: If you will learn falsehood, if you will learn cozenage, if you will learn indirect dealing, if you will learn to deceive. . . . And therefore let all Players and founders of Plays, as they tender the salvation of their own souls, and others, leave off that cursed kind of life, and betake themselves to such honest exercises and godly mysteries, as God hath commanded in his word to get their living withall. For who will call him a wise man that playeth the fool and the vice? Who can call him a good Christian that playeth the part of a Devil the sworn enemy of Christ? who can call him a just man that playeth the dissembling hypocrite? who can call him a straight dealing man, that playeth a cozener's trick: and so of all the rest. The wise man is ashamed to play the fool, but Players will seem to be such in the public view to all the world: a good Christian hateth the Devil; but Players will become artificial Devils excellently well: a just man cannot endure hypocrisy; but all the acts of Players is dissimulation, and the proper name of Player (witness the *Apology* itself) is *hypocrite:* a true dealing man cannot endure deceit, but Players get their living by craft and cozenage. For what greater cheating can there be than for money to render that which is not money's worth. Then seeing they are fools, artificial Devils, hypocrites and cozeners; most evident it is that their Art is not for Christians to exercise, as being diabolical, and themselves infamous: such indeed as the *Lacedemonians* had, and we also have great reason to extrude out of our commonwealth, for they are Idle, vicious, dishonest, malicious, prejudicial and unprofitable to the same. . . . But among any others that go to the Theaters, when shall you see an ancient citizen, a chaste matron, a modest maid, a grave Senator, a wise Magistrate, a just Judge, a godly Preacher, a religious man not blinded in ignorance, but making conscience of his ways? you shall never see any of these men at Plays, for they count it shameful and ignominious, even an act of reproach that may redound unto them.

Then to conclude all, seeing Plays are the institution of the Devil himself, and the practise of Heathen people nuzzled in ignorance: seeing they took original from Paganism, and were dedicated to their Idol-Gods, as now also they are the house, stage and apparel to *Venus,* the music to *Apollo,* the penning to *Minerva,* the songs to the *Muses,* the action and pronunciation to *Mercury:* seeing they are enriched with fables, lies, dishonesties and all kind of knaveries: seeing the actors of them have been counted ignominious, and in all ages by the best men branded with infamy: seeing by the wisest men they have been expelled out of their commonwealth, and esteemed as vagabonds, corrupters of good manners, subverters of religion in people's hearts, and seducers of men to destruction: seeing by some they have not been admitted to the Lord's table: seeing their action both in word and deed is to be abhorred: seeing they carry the note & brand of all kind of cursed people on their backs: seeing they were never ordained of God to give instruction, but by the Devil to teach lewdness and dissolution: seeing they are idle drones, and prejudicial to the commonwealth: seeing none of the best sort will frequent their theaters for very shame: seeing the theater is Satan's Synagogue and the devil's own house: seeing Plays have been condemned by Pagans and Christians, by Synods and Counsels, by ancient Fathers and late Writers, by both the old and the new Testament: seeing their subject and matter is nothing but filthiness and villainy: seeing they are full of abuses, against which sundry places of Scripture do testify: seeing from them can be learned no good, but any evil that wickedness can desire. Then do I earnestly entreat every one, as they love their own souls, to detest and abandon them. . . .

III

Playwrights and Their Sources

CRITICISM IN RENAISSANCE ENGLAND

§ The paragraphs reproduced below from *The Defense of Poesy*, by a gifted young courtier, Sir Philip Sidney (1554–86), refer to the tendencies of the Elizabethan theatre to embrace freedom of style and dramatic form, a freedom that culminated in the plays of Marlowe, Shakespeare, and their successors. Sidney was prompted to write his famous essay as a reply to an attack on poetry and the stage, *The School of Abuse* (1579), which its Puritan author, Stephen Gosson, had dedicated to him. Although he refuted Gosson's charge, that poetry is inimical to morality, Sidney was critical of the extravagantly romantic, diffuse plays of the popular stage, plays that freely combined comedy and tragedy, "Kings and Clowns." Like other humanists of the Renaissance, who revered and tried to imitate the Greek and Roman classics, Sidney preferred a "regular" type of tragedy which observed the rule of the unities (of time, place, and action) according to Aristotle as misinterpreted by Renaissance scholars such as Castelvetro and the Scaligers. For this reason Sidney reserved his praise for the early blank-verse tragedy, *Gorboduc* (1565), by the young scholars Sackville and Norton, a drama which telescoped its multifarious events and which suppressed violence on the stage by means of long-winded reports by messengers. In comparing *Gorboduc* favorably with Seneca, Sidney intended high praise, for Seneca was the tragedian of the Renaissance. Sidney's enthusiasm for Gorboduc was not shared by the Elizabethan public, and the popular drama to which Sidney objected continued its dynamic "rule-breaking" course.

379

Sir Philip Sidney
from The Defense of Poesy

*O*ur tragedies and comedies (not without cause, cried out against) observing rules neither of honest civility nor of skilful poetry, excepting *Gorboduc*[1] (again I say of those that I have seen), which notwithstanding, as it is full of stately speeches and well-sounding phrases, climbing to the height of Seneca's style, and as full of notable morality, which it does most delightfully teach, and so obtain the very end of poesy; yet, in truth, it is very defectious in the circumstances, which grieves me because it might not remain as an exact model of all tragedies. For it is faulty both in place and time, the two necessary companions of all corporal actions. For where the stage should always represent but one place, and the uttermost time presupposed in it should be, both by Aristotle's precept,[2] and common reason, but one day, there is both many days and many places inartificially imagined.

But if it be so in *Gorboduc*, how much more in all the rest? where you shall have Asia of the one side, and Afric of the other, and so many other under kingdoms, that the player, when he comes in, must ever begin with telling where he is, or else the tale will not be conceived. Now you shall have three ladies walk to gather flowers, and then we must believe the stage to be a garden. By and by, we hear news of shipwreck in the same place, and then we are to blame if we accept it not for a rock. Upon the back of that comes out a hideous monster, with fire and smoke, and then the miserable beholders are bound to take it for a cave; while, in the meantime, two armies fly in, represented with four swords and bucklers, and then, what hard heart will not receive it for a pitched field?

Now, of time they are much more liberal; for ordinary it is, that two young princes fall in love; after many traverses she is got with child; delivered of a fair boy; he is lost, groweth a man, falls in love, and is ready to get another child; and all this in two hours' space; which, how absurd it is in sense, even sense may imagine; and art hath taught and all ancient examples justified, and at this day the ordinary players in Italy will not err in. Yet will some bring in an example of the *Eunuch* in Terence, that containeth matter of two days, yet far

---

1 By Thomas Sackville (Lord Buckhurst, 1536–1608) and Thomas Norton (1532–84), published in 1565.
2 Sidney, like other Renaissance scholars, makes an unwarranted extension of Aristotle's remarks in his *Poetics* about unity of time and place in tragedy.

short of twenty years. True it is, and so was it to be played in two days, and so fitted to the time it set forth. And though Plautus have in one place done amiss, let us hit it with him, and not miss with him.

But they will say, How then shall we set forth a story which contains both many places and many times? And do they not know that a tragedy is tied to the laws of poesy, and not of history; not bound to follow the story, but having liberty either to feign a quite new matter, or to frame the history to the most tragical conveniency? Again, many things may be told, which cannot be showed: if they know the difference betwixt reporting and representing. As, for example, I may speak, though I am here, of Peru, and in speech digress from that to the description of Calicut; but in action I cannot represent it without Pacolet's horse.[3] And so was the manner the ancients took, by some *Nuntius*[4] to recount things done in former time, or other place.

Lastly, if they will represent an history, they must not, as Horace saith, begin *ab ovo*,[5] but they must come to the principal point of that one action which they will represent. By example this will be best expressed. I have a story of young Polydorus,[6] delivered, for safety's sake, with great riches, by his father Priamus to Polymnestor, King of Thrace, in the Trojan war time. He, after some years, hearing the overthrow of Priamus, for to make the treasure his own, murdereth the child; the body of the child is taken up by Hecuba; she, the same day, findeth a sleight to be revenged most cruelly of the tyrant. Where, now, would one of our tragedy-writers begin, but with the delivery of the child? Then should he sail over into Thrace, and so spend I know not how many years, and travel numbers of places. But where doth Euripides? Even with the finding of the body; leaving the rest to be told by the spirit of Polydorus. This needs no further to be enlarged; the dullest wit may conceive it.

But, besides these gross absurdities, how all their plays be neither right tragedies nor right comedies, mingling kings and clowns, not because the matter so carrieth it, but thrust in clowns by head and shoulders to play a part in majestical matters, with neither decency nor discretion; so as neither the admiration and commiseration, nor the right sportfulness, is by their mongrel tragi-comedy obtained. I know Apuleius[7] did somewhat so, but that is a thing recounted with space of time, not represented in one moment: and I know the ancients have one or two examples of tragi-comedies, as Plautus hath

---

3 The magic horse in a romance, *Valentine and Orson.*
4 A messenger.   5 From the egg, that is, from the first.
6 Character in Euripides' *Hecuba.*
7 Roman writer (born about A.D. 125), famous for his prose romance, *Metamorphoses* or *Golden Ass.*

Amphitruo. But, if we mark them well, we shall find that they never, or very daintily, match hornpipes and funerals. So falleth it out, that, having, indeed, no right comedy in that comical part of our tragedy, we have nothing but scurrility, unworthy of any chaste ears; or some extreme show of doltishness, indeed fit to lift up a loud laughter, and nothing else; where the whole tract of a comedy should be full of delight as the tragedy should be still maintained in a well-raised admiration.

But our comedians think there is no delight without laughter, which is very wrong; for though laughter may come with delight, yet cometh it not of delight, as though delight should be the cause of laughter; but well may one thing breed both together. Nay, in themselves, they have, as it were, a kind of contrariety. For delight we scarcely do, but in things that have a conveniency to ourselves, or to the general nature. Laughter almost ever cometh of things most disproportioned to ourselves and nature: delight hath a joy in it, either permanent or present; laughter hath only a scornful tickling. . . .

The only Elizabethan or Jacobean playwright who showed any interest in formal canons of criticism was Ben Jonson (1572–1637), many of whose ideas were derived from Sidney, and who was therefore much more classical in his approach to drama than most of his less pedantic colleagues. Jonson's major critical treatise, a translation of the *Ars Poetica* of Horace with appended notes, unfortunately has been lost; but scattered observations remain, from which his literary attitudes can be deduced.

In Jonson's induction to his play, *Every Man Out of His Humour* (1600), he gives us some insight into his theories of comedy. The savagery of Asper's remarks in this passage underlines Jonson's conception of the comic playwright as a kind of moral gadfly whose purpose is corrective. This is certainly a classical interpretation of comic art and contrasts sharply with the practice if not the theory of the romantic and sentimental playwrights who were Jonson's principal comic rivals. Included in this famous induction is Jonson's explanation of the term *humour*, a term he borrows from medieval physiology, then redefines to suit his purposes. The idea of the "humourous" man is the basis of most of Jonson's satirical characterizations.

Jonson's ideas of tragedy are briefly set forth in his remarks to the readers of *Sejanus* (1605). Here again Jonson's ideas are more classical than those of most of his rivals. He insists, for example, on "truth of argument," that is, on fidelity to historical fact; and indeed he takes great pains to cite his source material in footnotes to the published edition, both of this play and of his other tragedy *Cataline* (1611). While Jonson in his address to the reader stresses the fact that he is not pedantically attempting to "observe the old state and splendor of dramatic poems," nevertheless he clearly favors a greater degree of regularity in tragic drama than most of his colleagues. Unfortunately, in Jonson's case, "regularity" produced a certain coldness of tone which made *Sejanus* and *Cataline* unpopular with the Jacobean audience, while the less accurate tragedies of Shakespeare flourished.

Two passages about Shakespeare conclude this selection of Jonson's criticism. The first, from *Timber; or Discoveries Made upon Men and Matter*, a miscellany published in 1641, shows Jonson's distaste for the careless freedom of Shakespeare's workmanship; the second, a poem attached to Shakespeare's first Folio (1623), reflects Jonson's ability to recognize and praise a genius which differed radically from his own.

Ben Jonson

THE INDUCTION

from *Every Man Out of His Humour*

Enter Cordatus, Asper, and Mitis.

Cordatus. Nay, my dear Asper, —
Mitis.   Stay your mind.
Asper.   Away!
Who is so patient of this impious world
That he can check his spirit, or rein his tongue?
Or who hath such a dead, unfeeling sense,
That Heaven's horrid thunders cannot wake?
To see the earth, cracked with the weight of sin,
Hell gaping under us, and o'er our heads
Black, ravenous ruin, with her sail-stretched wings,
Ready to sink us down, and cover us.
Who can behold such prodigies as these,
And have his lips sealed up? not I: my soul
Was never ground into such oily colours,
To flatter vice, and daub iniquity:
But, with an armed and resolved hand,
I'll strip the ragged follies of the time,
Naked, as at their birth —
   Cordatus.   Be not too bold.

Asper. You trouble me — and with a whip of steel,
Print wounding lashes in their iron ribs.
I fear no mood stamped in a private brow,
When I am pleased t'unmask a public vice.
I fear no strumpet's drugs nor ruffian's stab,
Should I detect their hateful luxuries;
No broker's, usurer's, or lawyer's gripe,
Were I disposed to say they're all corrupt.
I fear no courtier's frown, should I applaud
The easy flexure of his supple hams.
Tut, these are so innate and popular,
That drunken custom would not shame to laugh
In scorn, at him that should but dare to tax 'em.
And yet, not one of these, but knows his works,
Knows what damnation is, the devil, and Hell;
Yet hourly they persist, grow rank in sin,
Puffing their souls away in perj'rous air,
To cherish their extortion, pride, or lusts.
   Mitis. Forbear, good Asper, be not like your name.
   Asper. O, but to such, whose faces are all zeal,
And with the words of Hercules invade
Such crimes as these! that will not smell of sin,
But seem as they were made of sanctity!
Religion in their garments, and their hair
Cut shorter than their eyebrows! when the conscience
Is vaster than the ocean, and devours
More wretches than the Counters.
   Mitis.   Gentle Asper,
Contain your spirit in more stricter bounds,
And be not thus transported with the violence
Of your strong thoughts.
   Cordatus.   Unless your breath had power
To melt the world, and mould it new again,
It is in vain to spend it in these moods.
   Asper.   I not observed this thronged round till now.
                              His address to the people.
Gracious and kind spectators, you are welcome;
Apollo and the Muses feast your eyes
With graceful objects, and may our Minerva
Answer your hopes, unto their largest strain!
Yet here mistake me not, judicious friends.
I do not this to beg your patience,
Or servilely to fawn on your applause,
Like some dry brain, despairing in his merit.

Let me be censured by th' austerest brow,
Where I want art or judgment, tax me freely.
Let envious censors, with their broadest eyes,
Look through and through me; I pursue no favour.
Only vouchsafe me your attentions,
And I will give you music worth your ears.
O, how I hate the monstrousness of time,
Where every servile, imitating spirit,
Plagued with an itching leprosy of wit,
In a mere halting fury, strives to fling
His ulc'rous body in the Thespian spring,
And straight leaps forth a poet! but as lame
As Vulcan, or the founder of Cripplegate.[1]

   Mitis. In faith, this humour will come ill to some;
You will be thought to be too peremptory.

   Asper. This humour? good! And why this humour, Mitis?
Nay, do not turn, but answer.

   Mitis.   Answer, what?

   Asper. I will not stir your patience, pardon me,
I urged it for some reasons, and the rather
To give these ignorant, well-spoken days
Some taste of their abuse of this word "humour."[2]

   Cordatus. O, do not let your purpose fall, good Asper,
It cannot but arrive most acceptable,
Chiefly to such as have the happiness
Daily to see how the poor, innocent word
Is racked and tortured.

   Mitis.   Ay, I pray you proceed.

   Asper. Ha, what? what is't?

   Cordatus.   For the abuse of "humour."

   Asper. O, I crave pardon, I had lost my thoughts.
Why, humour, as 'tis "ens," we thus define it
To be a quality of air or water,
And in itself holds these two properties,
Moisture and fluxure; as for demonstration,

---

[1] A narrow gate to the city of London. The historian John Stow, in his A *Survey of London* (1598), tells us that the gate was so named because it was the gathering place for the lame and the halt.

[2] The four "humours," according to medieval physiology, were fluids in the body which had considerable influence on personality and character. A proper balance of these four humours produced a balanced personality. An excess of one of them produced an eccentric personality. Too much blood, for example, would make a person "sanguine"; too much bile would make him choleric; too much black bile would make him melancholy; too much phlegm would make him phlegmatic. Jonson's application of the term, however, is, as he indicates, not so much technical as metaphorical.

Pour water on this floor, 'twill wet and run.
Likewise the air, forced through a horn or trumpet,
Flows instantly away, and leaves behind
A kind of dew; and hence we do conclude
That whatsoe'er hath fluxure and humidity,
As wanting power to contain itself,
Is humour. So in every human body,
The choler, melancholy, phlegm, and blood,
By reason that they flow continually
In some one part, and are not continent,
Receive the name of humours. Now thus far
It may, by metaphor, apply itself
Unto the general disposition:
As when some one peculiar quality
Doth so possess a man, that it doth draw
All his affects, his spirits, and his powers,
In their confluxions, all to run one way,
This may be truly said to be a humour.
But that a rook, in wearing a pied feather,
The cable hat-band, or the three-piled ruff,
A yard of shoe-tie, or the Switzer's knot
On his French garters, should affect a humour —
O, it is more than most ridiculous!
    Cordatus. He speaks pure truth. Now, if an idiot
Have but an apish or fantastic strain,
It is his humour!
    Asper.   Well, I will scourge those apes;
And to these courteous eyes oppose a mirror,
As large as is the stage whereon we act,
Where they shall see the time's deformity
Anatomized in every nerve and sinew,
With constant courage and contempt of fear.
    Mitis. Asper, I urge it as your friend, take heed.
The days are dangerous, full of exception,
And men are grown impatient of reproof.
    Asper.   Ha, ha!
You might as well have told me, yond' is heaven;
This, earth; these, men; and all had moved alike.
Do not I know the time's condition?
Yes, Mitis, and their souls, and who they be,
That either will or can except against me:
None but a sort of fools, so sick in taste,
That they contemn all physic of the mind,
And, like galled camels, kick at every touch.

Good men and virtuous spirits, that loathe their vices,
Will cherish my free labours, love my lines,
And, with the fervour of their shining grace,
Make my brain fruitful to bring forth more objects,
Worthy their serious and intentive eyes.
But why enforce I this? as fainting? No.
If any here chance to behold himself,
Let him not dare to challenge me of wrong;
For, if he shame to have his follies known,
First he should shame to act 'em. My strict hand
Was made to seize on vice, and with a gripe,
Squeeze out the humour of such spongy natures
As lick up every idle vanity.
    Cordatus. Why, this is right Furor Poeticus!
Kind gentlemen, we hope your patience
Will yet conceive the best, or entertain
This supposition: that a madman speaks.
    Asper. What! are you ready there? — Mitis, sit down,
And my Cordatus. — Sound ho! and begin. —
I leave you two, as censors, to sit here.
Observe what I present, and liberally
Speak your opinions upon every scene,
As it shall pass the view of these spectators.
Nay, now you're tedious, sirs, for shame, begin.
And, Mitis, note me, if, in all this front,
You can espy a gallant of this mark:
Who, to be thought one of the judicious,
Sits with his arms thus wreathed, his hat pulled here;
Cries mew, and nods, then shakes his empty head;
Will show more several motions in his face
Than the new London, Rome, or Nineveh;
And, now and then, breaks a dry biscuit jest,
Which, that it may more easily be chewed,
He steeps in his own laughter.
    Cordatus.   Why? will that
Make it be sooner swallowed?
    Asper.   O, assure you.
Or if it did not, yet as Horace sings,
"Jejunus raro stomachus vulgaria temnit,"
Mean cates[3] are welcome still to hungry guests.
    Cordatus. 'Tis true, but why should we observe 'em, Asper?
    Asper. O, I would know 'em, for in such assemblies
They're more infectious than the pestilence:

    3 Dainties or provisions.

And therefore I would give them pills to purge,
And make 'em fit for fair societies.
How monstrous and detested is't to see
A fellow that has neither art nor brain
Sit like an Aristarchus,[4] or stark ass,
Taking men's lines with a tobacco face,
In snuff, still spitting, using his wryed looks,
In nature of a vice, to wrest and turn
The good aspect of those that shall sit near him,
From what they do behold! O, 'tis most vile.

 Mitis. Nay, Asper.

 Asper.   Peace, Mitis, I do know your thought;
You'll say your guests here will except at this.
Pish! you are too timorous, and full of doubt.
Then he, a patient, shall reject all physic,
'Cause the physician tells him, "You are sick."
Or, if I say that he is vicious,
You will not hear of virtue. Come, you're fond.
Shall I be so extravagant to think
That happy judgments and composed spirits
Will challenge me for taxing such as these?
I am ashamed.

 Cordatus. Nay, but good pardon us,
We must not bear this peremptory sail,
But use our best endeavours how to please.

 Asper. Why, therein I commend your careful thoughts,
And I will mix with you in industry
To please — but whom? attentive auditors,
Such as will join their profit with their pleasure,
And come to feed their understanding parts.
For these I'll prodigally spend myself,
And speak away my spirit into air;
For these I'll melt my brain into invention,
Coin new conceits, and hang my richest words
As polished jewels in their bounteous ears.
But stay, I lose myself, and wrong their patience;
If I dwell here, they'll not begin, I see.
Friends, sit you still, and entertain this troop
With some familiar and by-conference;
I'll haste them sound. — Now, gentlemen, I go
To turn an actor, and a humourist;
Where, ere I do resume my present person,

 [4] A celebrated ancient critic who was in charge of the library at Alexandria
from 180–143 B.C.

We hope to make the circles of your eyes
Flow with distilled laughter. If we fail,
We must impute it to this only chance:
Art hath an enemy called Ignorance.   *Exit.*

    Cordatus. How do you like his spirit, Mitis?

    Mitis. I should like it much better, if he were less confident.

    Cordatus. Why, do you suspect his merit?

    Mitis. No, but I fear this will procure him much envy.

    Cordatus. O, that sets the stronger seal on his desert. If he had no enemies, I should esteem his fortunes most wretched at this instant.

    Mitis. You have seen his play, Cordatus? Pray you, how is't?

    Cordatus. Faith, sir, I must refrain to judge. Only this I can say of it: 'tis strange, and of a particular kind by itself, somewhat like *Vetus Comoedia,*[5] a work that hath bounteously pleased me; how it will answer the general expectation I know not.

    Mitis. Does he observe all the laws of comedy in it?

    Cordatus. What laws mean you?

    Mitis. Why, the equal division of it into acts, and scenes, according to the Terentian manner; his true number of actors; the furnishing of the scene with Grex, or chorus; and that the whole argument fall within compass of a day's business.

    Cordatus. O no, these are too nice observations.

    Mitis. They are such as must be received, by your favour, or it cannot be authentic.

    Cordatus. Troth, I can discern no such necessity.

    Mitis. No?

    Cordatus. No, I assure you, signior. If those laws you speak of had been delivered us, *ab initio,* and in their present virtue and perfection, there had been some reason of obeying their powers. But 'tis extant that that which we call *Comoedia* was at first nothing but a simple and continued song, sung by one only person, till Susario invented a second; after him, Epicharmus a third; Phormus and Chionides devised to have four actors, with a prologue and chorus; to which Cratinus, long after, added a fifth and sixth; Eupolis, more; Aristophanes, more than they; every man, in the dignity of his spirit and judgment, supplied something. And though that in him this kind of poem appeared absolute and fully perfected, yet how is the face of it changed since, in Menander, Philemon, Cecilius, Plautus, and the rest; who have utterly excluded the chorus, altered the property of the persons, their names and natures, and augmented it with all liberty, according to the elegancy and disposition of those times

    [5] Literally "Old Comedy," a technical term for the fifth-century Athenian comedies of Aristophanes and his colleagues.

wherein they wrote. I see not, then, but we should enjoy the same licence, or free power, to illustrate and heighten our invention as they did; and not be tied to those strict and regular forms, which the niceness of a few — who are nothing but form — would thrust upon us.

Mitis. Well, we will not dispute of this now. But what's his scene?

Cordatus. Marry, Insula Fortunata, sir.

Mitis. O, the Fortunate Island! Mass, he has bound himself to a strict law there.

Cordatus. Why so?

Mitis. He cannot lightly alter the scene, without crossing the seas.

Cordatus. He needs not, having a whole island to run through, I think.

Mitis. No? how comes it, then, that in some one play we see so many seas, countries, and kingdoms passed over with such admirable dexterity?

Cordatus. O, that but shows how well the authors can travail in their vocation, and outrun the apprehension of their auditory. But, leaving this, I would they would begin once; this protraction is able to sour the best settled patience in the theatre.

Mitis. They have answered your wish, sir, they sound.[6]

Cordatus. O, here comes the Prologue.

Ben Jonson

To the Readers

from *Sejanus, His Fall*

The following and voluntary labours of my friends,[1] prefixed to my book, have relieved me in much whereat, without them, I should necessarily have touched. Now I will only use three or four short and needful notes, and so rest.

First, if it be objected, that what I publish is no true poem, in the strict laws of time, I confess it: as also in the want of a proper chorus; whose habit and moods are such and so difficult, as not any, whom I have seen, since the ancients, no, not they who have most presently

---

6 A reference to the trumpet which in Elizabethan theatres signaled the beginning of a play.

1 George Chapman, William Strachey, and others prefixed commendatory verses to the quarto of this play.

affected laws, have yet come in the way of. Nor is it needful, or almost possible in these our times, and to such auditors as commonly things are presented, to observe the old state and splendour of dramatic poems, with preservation of any popular delight. But of this I shall take more seasonable cause to speak, in my observations upon Horace his *Art of Poetry*, which (with the text translated), I intend shortly to publish.[2] In the meantime, if in truth of argument, dignity of persons, gravity and height of elocution, fulness and frequency of sentence, I have discharged the other offices of a tragic writer, let not the absence of these forms be imputed to me, wherein I shall give you occasion hereafter (and without my boast) to think I could better prescribe, than omit the due use for want of a convenient knowledge.

The next is, lest in some nice nostril the quotations might savour affected, I do let you know, that I abhor nothing more; and I have only done it to show my integrity in the story, and save myself in those common torturers that bring all wit to the rack; whose noses are ever like swine spoiling and rooting up the Muses' gardens; and their whole bodies like moles, as blindly working under earth, to cast any, the least, hills upon virtue.

Whereas they are in Latin, and the work in English, it was presupposed none but the learned would take the pains to confer them; the authors themselves being all in the learned tongues, save one,[3] with whose English side I have had little to do. To which it may be required, since I have quoted the page, to name what editions I followed: *Tacit. Lips. in quarto, Antwerp, edit.* 1600. *Dio. folio, Hen. Steph.* 1592. For the rest, as *Sueton. Seneca,* &c., the chapter doth sufficiently direct, or the edition is not varied.

Lastly, I would inform you, that this book, in all numbers, is not the same with that which was acted on the public stage; wherein a second pen[4] had good share: in place of which, I have rather chosen to put weaker, and, no doubt, less pleasing, of mine own, than to defraud so happy a genius of his right by my loathed usurpation.

Fare you well, and if you read farther of me, and like, I shall not be afraid of it, though you praise me out.

Neque enim mihi cornea fibra est.[5]

But that I should plant my felicity in your general saying, *good*, or *well*, &c., were a weakness which the better sort of you might worthily contemn, if not absolutely hate me for.

[2] These were lost in the burning of his study in 1623.
[3] Tacitus, translated by Greenaway.
[4] Unidentified. Beaumont, Fletcher, and Middleton have been suggested, but they seem unlikely. Chapman is the favorite choice, but the fact that Shakespeare is known to have acted in the play makes his collaboration seem possible.
[5] "For I do not have horny fibers." — PERSEUS.

Ben Jonson

DE SHAKESPEARE NOSTRAT[I][1]

(from *Timber; or Discoveries Made upon Men and Matter*)

I remember the players have often mentioned it as an honor to Shakespeare, that in his writing, whatsoever he penned, he never blotted out a line. My answer hath been, Would he had blotted a thousand, which they thought a malevolent speech. I had not told posterity this but for their ignorance, who chose that circumstance to command their friend by wherein he most faulted; and to justify mine own candor, for I loved the man, and do honor his memory on this side idolatry as much as any. He was, indeed, honest, and of an open and free nature; had an excellent fancy, brave notions, and gentle expressions, wherein he flowed with that facility that sometime it was necessary he should be stopped. "*Sufflaminandus erat*,"[2] as Augustus said of Haterius. His wit was in his own power; would the rule of it had been so too. Many times he fell into those things [which] could not escape laughter, as when he said in the person of Caesar, one speaking to him: "Caesar, thou dost me wrong." He replied: "Caesar did never wrong but with just cause;"[3] and such like, which were ridiculous. But he redeemed his vices with his virtues. There was ever more in him to be praised than to be pardoned.

Ben Jonson

TO THE MEMORY OF MY BELOVED MASTER WILLIAM SHAKESPEARE

And What He Hath Left Us

*T*o draw no envy, Shakespeare, on thy name,
Am I thus ample to thy book and fame;
While I confess thy writings to be such,
As neither man, nor Muse, can praise too much.
'Tis true, and all men's suffrage. But these ways

---

1 "Of our countryman, Shakespeare."
2 "He should have been hindered."
3 This speech is not found in the version we have of *Julius Caesar*. Instead the following lines appear: "Know, Caesar doth not wrong, nor without cause/Will he be satisfied." (III, 1, 47–48) Perhaps Shakespeare altered the offending line because of criticism like Jonson's.

Were not the paths I meant unto thy praise;
For silliest ignorance on these may light,
Which, when it sounds at best, but echoes right;
Or blind affection, which doth ne'er advance
The truth, but gropes, and urgeth all by chance;
Or crafty malice might pretend this praise,
And think to ruin, where it seem'd to raise.
These are, as some infamous bawd, or whore,
Should praise a matron; what could hurt her more?
But thou art proof against them, and indeed,
Above the ill fortune of them, or the need.
I therefore will begin. Soul of the age!
The applause! delight! the wonder of our stage!
My Shakespeare, rise! I will not lodge thee by
Chaucer, or Spenser, or bid Beaumont lie
A little further to make thee a room:
Thou art a monument without a tomb,
And art alive still, while thy book doth live,
And we have wits to read, and praise to give.
That I not mix thee so, my brain excuses,
I mean with great, but disproportion'd Muses:
For if I thought my judgement were of years,
I should commit thee surely with thy peers,
And tell how far thou didst our Lyly outshine,
Or sporting Kyd, or Marlowe's mighty line.
And though thou hadst small Latin and less Greek,
From thence to honour thee, I will not seek
For names: but call forth thund'ring Aeschylus,
Euripides, and Sophocles to us,
Pacuvius,[1] Accius,[2] him of Cordova dead,[3]
To life again, to hear thy buskin tread,
And shake a stage: or when thy socks were on,
Leave thee alone for the comparison
Of all, that insolent Greece, or haughty Rome
Sent forth, or since did from their ashes come.
Triumph, my Britain, thou hast one to show,
To whom all scenes of Europe homage owe.
He was not of an age, but for all time!
And all the Muses still were in their prime,
When, like Apollo, he came forth to warm

---

[1] Roman tragic poet, born about 220 B.C. Only fragments of his work survive.
[2] Last important writer of tragedy for the Roman stage.
[3] Marcus Lucanus (Lucan), great epic poet, was born in Cordova, A.D. 39.
The tragedian Seneca was also a native of this city.

Our ears, or like a Mercury to charm!
Nature herself was proud of his designs,
And joy'd to wear the dressing of his lines!
Which were so richly spun; and woven so fit,
As, since, she will vouchsafe no other wit.
The merry Greek, tart Aristophanes,
Neat Terence, witty Plautus, now not please;
But antiquated and deserted lie,
As they were not of nature's family.
Yet must I not give nature all; thy art,
My gentle Shakespeare, must enjoy a part.
For though the poet's matter nature be,
His art doth give the fashion: and, that he
Who casts to write a living line, must sweat,
(Such as thine are) and strike the second heat
Upon the Muses' anvil; turn the same,
And himself with it, that he thinks to frame;
Or for the laurel, he may gain a scorn;
For a good poet's made, as well as born.
And such wert thou! Look how the father's face
Lives in his issue, even so the race
Of Shakespeare's mind and manners brightly shines
In his well turned and true filed lines:
In each of which he seems to shake a lance,
As brandish'd at the eyes of ignorance.
Sweet Swan of Avon! what a sight it were
To see thee in our waters yet appear,
And make those flights upon the banks of Thames,
That so did take Eliza, and our James!
But stay! I see thee in the hemisphere
Advanced, and made a constellation there!
Shine forth, thou Star of poets, and with rage,
Or influence, chide, or cheer the drooping stage,
Which, since thy flight from hence, hath mourn'd like night,
And despairs day, but for thy volume's light.

THEORY AND PRACTICE IN THE SPANISH THEATRE

Elizabethan England produced no great theorist of the romantic or panoramic theatre. As a result we must turn to Spain for a Renaissance defense of the sprawling, lusty, tragi-comic drama, humanistic in spirit but medieval in structure, which dominated the stages of Madrid and London during the sixteenth and seventeenth centuries.

The drama of what has been called the Golden Age of Spain was produced in outdoor theatres, *corrales,* which demanded a production style not very different from that employed by Shakespeare's company at the Globe. The central place of action was a non-localized performing area (similar to the *platea* of the fifteenth-century stage), dotted with the emblematic scenery painted in the medieval style. The audience that attended this theatre was an authentic cross section of Spanish life. It was a noisy audience that included not only the rowdy *mosqueteros* (laborers and artisans who stood at the rear of the theatre) and the raucous working-class women who sat in the *cazuela* (or stew-pan, a gallery located over the main entrance), but also a fair sprinkling of aristocrats who peered at the play from window-like boxes on the second story of the building.

The audience was voracious in its hunger for drama, and the Spanish playwrights worked feverishly to keep their public supplied with lusty entertainment. Chief among the popular dramatists was Lope Félix de Vega Carpio (1562-1635), an adventurer, poet and backsliding churchman who found time in a life crammed with other activities to write 1500 plays (by his own count), of which about 400 survive. Clearly the most prolific playwright of all time, Lope was accurately described by Cervantes as "a monster prodigy of nature."

Many of Lope's plays were *comedias*, three-act dramas in verse, not comedies in the classical sense, but lively tragi-comedies in which melodramatic action, high seriousness and wild farce existed side by side. These *comedias* embraced a great many subjects—royal intrigues, pastoral romances, peasant folk-plays, biblical adventure stories and martyr tragedies about the lives of the saints. There was no unity of time, place or action in these high-spirited dramas, nor for that matter was there even a unity of tone or impression. Historical subjects were translated into lively images of seventeenth-century Spanish life, and plots drawn from contemporary incidents were related in a fluid verse which was at the same time colloquial, fanciful and romantic.

It says something about the provincialism of the English-speaking theatre, that the most fluent and many-faceted playwright the world has ever known, is chiefly remembered in our country for one drama, *Fuente Ovejuna* (*The Sheep Well*), the story of a peasant revolt against a cruel overlord. As good as this piece may be, it hardly by itself gives any impression of the facility and variety of Lope's art. As one might expect, some of the four hundred surviving plays show the effects of carelessness and haste, but there are many masterpieces among them.

Punishment Without Revenge is a grim tragedy from the annals of the court of Ferrara, a study of jealousy (with a certain resemblance to the *Hippolytus* of Euripides). It is frequently compared to *Othello*. Among Lope's most admired light comedies are *Wiser Than She Looks* (*La Dama Boba*), and *The Waters of Madrid*, both of which provided Molière with source material. The former figures in *The Learned Ladies*, and the latter in *The Physician in Spite of Himself*. In *The Gardener's Dog*, sometimes called *The Dog in the Manger*, Lope created one of the greatest of all romantic comedies. Tristan, the *gracioso* (or comic servant) of the play is a rogue to be compared with Autolycus of Shakespeare and with all those servants in Molière, male and female, who are wittier and wiser than their masters.

Surprisingly in a society that suppressed women, Lope's plays contain many greatly imagined and sympathetic female parts. But then Lope was a practical playwright, and unlike Shakespeare, whose Cleopatra was a boy, he had actresses for which to write. In fact, women appeared on the professional stages of Madrid as early as 1590, thus anticipating the English theatre by seventy years.

In 1609, Lope, stung by neoclassical criticism of his unfettered dramas, defended himself and his technique in a verse essay entitled *The New Art of Writing Plays in This Age*. In this treatise he attempts to show that he is not unfamiliar with classical precepts, but that he has been forced in practice to "banish Terence and Plautus from...[his] study" in order to gratify the taste of his audience. A number of practical suggestions follow for playwrights who wish to pursue Lope's lead, and the treatise, as a whole, affords us excellent insight into the theories and techniques of the panoramic drama.

Lope de Vega

THE NEW ART OF WRITING PLAYS IN THIS AGE*

*Y*ou command me, noble spirits, flower of Spain, — who in this congress and renowned academy will in short space of time surpass not only the assemblies of Italy which Cicero, envious of Greece, made famous with his own name, hard by the Lake of Avernus,[1] but also Athens, where in the Lyceum of Plato was seen high conclave of philosophers, — to write you an art of the play which is to-day acceptable to the taste of the crowd.

2. Easy seems this subject, and easy it would be for any one of you who had written very few comedies, and who knows more about the writing of them and of all these things; for what condemns me in this task is that I have written them without art.

3. Not because I was ignorant of the precepts; thank God, even while I was a tyro in grammar, I went through the books which treated the subject, before I had seen the sun run its course ten times from the Ram to the Fishes;

4. But because, in fine, I found that comedies were not at that time, in Spain, as their first devisers in the world thought that they should be written; but rather as many rude fellows managed them, who confirmed the crowd in its crudeness; and so they were introduced in such wise that he who now writes them artistically dies without fame and guerdon; for custom can do more among those who lack light of art than reason and force.

5. True it is that I have sometimes written in accordance with the art which few know; but, no sooner do I see coming from some other source the monstrosities full of painted scenes where the crowd congregates and the women who canonize this sad business, than I return to that same barbarous habit, and when I have to write a comedy I lock in the precepts with six keys, I banish Terence and Plautus from my study, that they may not cry out at me; for truth, even in dumb books, is wont to call aloud; and I write in accordance with that art which they devised who aspired to the applause of the crowd; for, since the crowd pays for the comedies, it is fitting to talk foolishly to it to satisfy its taste.

---

* Translated by William T. Brewster, in *Papers on Play-Making* (New York: Hill and Wang, 1957; Dramabooks edition), pp. 12–19. Reprinted by permission of Mr. Henry W. Wells, Curator of the Brander Matthews Dramatic Museum, Columbia University.
1 Alludes to Cicero's *Puteolanum*, where he wrote his *Academic Questions*.

6. Yet the comedy has its end established like every kind of poem or poetic art, and that has always been to imitate the actions of men and to paint the customs of their age. Furthermore, all poetic imitation whatsoever is composed of three things, which are discourse, agreeable verse, harmony, that is to say music, which so far was common also to tragedy; comedy being different from tragedy in that it treats of lowly and plebeian actions, and tragedy of royal and great ones. Look whether there be in our comedies few failings.

7. *Auto* was the name given to them, for they imitate the actions and the doings of the crowd. Lope de Rueda[2] was an example in Spain of these principles, and to-day are to be seen in print prose comedies of his so lowly that he introduces into them the doings of mechanics and the love of the daughter of a smith; whence there has remained the custom of calling the old comedies *entremeses,*[3] where the art persists in all its force, there being one action and that between plebeian people; for an *entremes* with a king has never been seen. And thus it is shown how the art, for very lowness of style, came to be held in great disrepute, and the king in the comedy to be introduced for the ignorant.

8. Aristotle depicts in his *Poetics,* — although obscurely, — the beginning of comedy; the strife between Athens and Megara as to which of them was the first inventor; they of Megara say that it was Epicharmus,[4] while Athens would have it that Maynetes was the man. Ælius Donatus says it had its origin in ancient sacrifices. He names Thespis as the author of tragedy, — following Horace, who affirms the same, — as of comedies, Aristophanes. Homer composed the *Odyssey* in imitation of comedy, but the *Iliad* was a famous example of tragedy, in imitation of what I called my *Jerusalem* an epic, and added the term *tragic;* and in the same manner all people commonly term the *Inferno,* the *Purgatorio,* and the *Paradiso* of the celebrated poet, Dante Alighieri, a comedy. . . .

9. Now, everybody knows that comedy, as if under suspicion, was silenced for a certain time, and that hence also satire was born, which being more cruel, more quickly came to an end, and gave place to the New Comedy. The choruses were the first things; then the fixed number of the characters was introduced; but Menander, whom Terence followed, held the choruses in despite, as offensive. Terence was more circumspect as to the principles; since he never elevated the style of comedy to the greatness of tragedy, which many have con-

---

[2] Lope de Rueda (1510–65), a playwright and actor, often considered the founder of Spanish Renaissance drama.

[3] One-act farcial entertainments.

[4] Epicharmus (c. 550–460 B.C.) of Syracuse. Greek comic poet, most important poet in Sicilian-Greek comedy which influenced Old Comedy.

demned as vicious in Plautus; for in this respect Terence was more wary.

10. Tragedy has as its argument history, and comedy fiction; for this reason it was called flat-footed, of humble argument, since the actor performed without buskin or stage. . . .

11. With Attic elegance the men of Athens chided vice and evil custom in their comedies, and they gave their prizes both to the writers of verse and to the devisers of action. For this Cicero called comedies "the mirror of custom and a living image of the truth,"[5] — a very high tribute, in that comedy ran even with history. Look whether it be worthy of this crown and glory!

12. But now I perceive that you are saying that this is merely translating books and wearying with painting this mixed-up affair. Believe me, there has been a reason why you should be reminded of some of these things; for you see that you ask me to describe the art of writing plays in Spain, where whatever is written is in defiance of art; and to tell how they are now written contrary to the ancient rule and to what is founded on reason, is to ask me to draw on my experience, not on art, for art speaks truth which the ignorant crowd gainsays.

13. If, then, you desire art, I beseech you, men of genius, to read the very learned Robortello of Udine[6] and you will see in what he says concerning Aristotle and especially in what he writes about comedy, as much as is scattered among many books; for everything of to-day is in a state of confusion.

14. If you wish to have my opinion of the comedies which now have the upper hand and to know why it is necessary that the crowd with its laws should maintain the vile chimera of this comic monster, I will tell you what I hold, and do you pardon me, since I must obey whoever has power to command me, — that, gilding the error of the crowd, I desire to tell you of what sort I would have them; for there is no recourse but to follow art, observing a mean between the two extremes.

15. Let the subject be chosen and do not be amused, — may you excuse these precepts! — if it happens to deal with kings; though, for that matter, I understand that Philip the Prudent, King of Spain and our lord, was offended at seeing a king in them; either because the matter was hostile to art or because the royal authority ought not to be represented among the lowly and the vulgar.

16. This is merely turning back to the ancient Comedy, where we see that Plautus introduced gods, as in his *Amphitryon* he represents

---

5 Cicero's remark is quoted here from Donatus. The same quotation appears in Heywood's *Apology for Actors*.
6 Robortello was a sixteenth-century scholar and critic who wrote an important commentary on Aristotle.

Jupiter. God knows that I have difficulty in giving this my approbation, since Plutarch, speaking of Menander, does not highly esteem ancient Comedy. But since we are so far away from art and in Spain do it a thousand wrongs, let the learned this once close their lips.

17. Tragedy mixed with comedy and Terence with Seneca, though it be like another minotaur of Pasiphae, will render one part grave, the other ridiculous; for this variety causes much delight. Nature gives us good example, for through such variety it is beautiful.

18. Bear in mind that this subject should contain one action only, seeing to it that the story in no manner be episodic; I mean the introduction of other things which are beside the main purpose; nor that any member be omitted which might ruin the whole of the context. There is no use in advising that it should take place in the period of one sun, though this is the view of Aristotle; but we lose our respect for him when we mingle tragic style with the humbleness of mean comedy. Let it take place in as little time as possible, except when the poet is writing history in which some years have to pass; these he can relegate to the space between the acts, wherein, if necessary, he can have a character go on some journey; a thing that greatly offends whoever perceives it. But let not him who is offended go to see them.

19. Oh! how lost in admiration are many at this very time at seeing that years are passed in an affair to which an artificial day sets a limit; though for this they would not allow the mathematical day! But, considering that the wrath of a seated Spaniard is immoderate, when in two hours there is not presented to him everything from Genesis to the Last Judgment, I deem it most fitting if it be for us here to please him, for us to adjust everything so that it succeeds.

20. The subject once chosen, write in prose, and divide the matter into three acts of time, seeing to it, if possible, that in each one the space of the day be not broken. Captain Virués, a worthy wit, divided comedy into three acts, which before had gone on all fours, as on baby's feet, for comedies were then infants.[7] I wrote them myself, when eleven or twelve years of age, of four acts and of four sheets of paper, for a sheet contained each act; and then it was the fashion that for the three intermissions were made three little *entremeses,* but to-day scarce one, and then a dance, for the dancing is so important in comedy that Aristotle approves of it, and Athenaeus, Plato and Xenophon treat of it, though this last disapproves of indecorous dancing; . . . The matter divided into two acts,[8] see to the connection from the beginning until the action runs down; but do not permit the untying

[7] Cristobal de Virués (born c. 1550) erroneously claimed in the prologue to one of his plays that he had first invented the technique of dividing a play into three acts.

[8] An apparent contradiction of Lope's earlier suggestion that a play should have three acts. In practice most of Lope's own dramas were composed in three acts.

of the plot until reaching the last scene; for the crowd, knowing what the end is, will turn its face to the door and its shoulder to what it has awaited three hours face to face; for in what appears, nothing more is to be known.

21. Very seldom should the stage remain without some one speaking, because the crowd becomes restless in these intervals and the story spins itself out at great length; for, besides its being a great defect, the avoidance of it increases grace and artifice.

22. Begin then, and, with simple language, do not spend sententious thoughts and witty sayings on family trifles, which is all that the familiar talk of two or three people is representing. But when the character who is introduced persuades, counsels or dissuades, then there should be gravity and wit; for then doubtless is truth observed, since a man speaks in a different style from what is common when he gives counsel, or persuades, or argues against anything. Aristides, the rhetorician, gave us warrant for this; for he wishes the language of comedy to be pure, clear, and flexible, and he adds also that it should be taken from the usage of the people, this being different from that of polite society; for in the latter case the diction will be elegant, sonorous, and adorned. Do not drag in quotations, nor let your language offend because of exquisite words; for, if one is to imitate those who speak, it should not be by the language of Panchaia,[9] of the Metaurus, of hippogriffs, demi-gods and centaurs.

23. If the king should speak, imitate as much as possible the gravity of a king; if the sage speak, observe a sententious modesty; describe lovers with those passions which greatly move whomever listens to them; manage soliloquies in such a manner that the recitant is quite transformed, and in changing himself, changes the listener. Let him ask questions and reply to himself, and if he shall make plaints, let him observe the respect due to women. Let not ladies disregard their character, and if they change costumes, let it be in such wise that it may be excused; for male disguise usually is very pleasing. Let him be on his guard against impossible things, for it is of the chiefest importance that only the likeness of truth should be represented. The lackey should not discourse of lofty affairs, not express the conceits which we have seen in certain foreign plays; and in no wise let the character contradict himself in what he has said; I mean to say, forget, — as in Sophocles one blames Oedipus for not remembering that he has killed Laius with his own hand. Let the scenes end with epigram, with wit, and with elegant verse, in such wise that, at his exit, he who spouts leave not the audience disgusted. In the first act set for the case. In the second weave together the events, in such wise that until the middle of the third act one may

9 An imaginary island famous for its perfumes, mentioned by Virgil.

hardly guess the outcome. Always trick expectancy; and hence it may come to pass that something quite far from what is promised may be left to the understanding. Tactfully suit your verse to the subjects being treated. . . . Let rhetorical figure be brought in, as repetition or anadiplosis, and in the beginning of these same verses the various forms of anaphora; and also irony, questions, apostrophes, and exclamations.

24. To deceive the audience with the truth is a thing that has seemed well. . . . Equivoke and the uncertainty arising from ambiguity have always held a large place among the crowd, for it thinks that it alone understands what the other one is saying. Better still are the subjects in which honor has a part, since they deeply stir everybody; along with them go virtuous deeds, for virtue is everywhere loved; hence we see, if an actor chance to represent a traitor, he is so hateful to every one that what he wishes to buy is not sold him, and the crowd flees when it meets him; but if he is loyal, they lend to him and invite him, and even the chief men honor him, love him, seek him out, entertain him, and acclaim him.

25. Let each act have but four sheets, for twelve are well suited to the time and the patience of him who is listening. In satirical parts, be not clear or open, since it is known that for this very reason comedies were forbidden by law in Greece and Italy; wound without hate, for if, perchance, slander be done, expect not applause, nor aspire to fame.

26. These things you may regard as aphorisms which you get not from the ancient art, which the present occasion allows no further space for treating; since whatever has to do with the three kinds of stage properties which Vitruvius speaks of, concerns the impresario. . . .

27. Of costume Julius Pollux[10] would tell us if it were necessary, for in Spain it is the case that the comedy of to-day is replete with barbarous things: a Turk wearing the neck-gear of a Christian, and a Roman in tight breeches.

28. But of all, nobody can I call more barbarous than myself, since in defiance of art I dare to lay down precepts, and I allow myself to be borne along in the vulgar current, wherefore Italy and France call me ignorant. But what can I do if I have written four hundred and eighty-three comedies, along with one which I have finished this week? For all of these, except six, gravely sin against art. Yet, in fine, I defend what I have written, and I know that, though they might have been better in another manner, they would

---

10 Julius Pollux, an encyclopedist of the second century of the Christian era, included in his *Onomastikon* some information on the Greek theatre, including a famous list of tragic and comic masks.

not have had the vogue which they have had; for sometimes that which is contrary to what is just, for that very reason, pleases the taste.

> How comedy reflects this life of man,
>   How true her portraiture of young and old;
> How subtle wit, polished in narrow span,
>   And purest speech, and more too you behold;
> What grave consideration mixed with smiles,
>   What seriousness, along with pleasant jest;
> Deceit of slaves; how woman oft beguiles
>   How full of slyness is her treacherous breast;
> How silly, awkward swains to sadness run.
>   How rare success, though all seems well begun.

Let everyone hear with attention, and dispute not of the art; for in comedy everything will be found of such a sort that in listening to it everything becomes evident.

In the seventeenth century, the drama of Catholic Spain and that of Protestant England shared many features in common—an exuberant disregard of rules, a cast of characters chosen from all degrees of society, a tendency to juxtapose tragedy and farce, a free uncluttered production style that was not dependent on verisimilitude.

But the pressures of the Counter-Reformation insured that certain themes from medieval drama would continue to flourish in Spain long after they had been suppressed in England. Lope—in addition to his cape-and-sword plays, his heroic historical dramas, his peasant comedies—wrote sacred *comedias* about the lives of saints and several hundred (twelve surviving) *autos sacramentales*, one-act plays in verse intended for performance on Corpus Christi day and designed to illustrate some religious truth, often the doctrine of the Real presence in the Eucharist. These *autos* might be described as the equivalent in Spanish of the English morality plays.

Pedro Calderón de la Barca (1600-81), the successor to Lope and leading playwright of the next generation, wrote more than seventy of these *auto sacramentales* and considered the Corpus Christi plays his most important work. A nobleman by birth who was educated by Jesuits, Calderón took Holy Orders. In fact, many of the Golden Age playwrights, including Lope himself, became priests, although Calderón seems to have had the most sincere religious vocation.

Like Lope, Calderón wrote both for the popular public theatre and also for court performances, where he played Ben Jonson to the Inigo Jones of Cosme Lotti (d. 1650), a Florentine designer and machinist, who, at the invitation of Philip IV, introduced perspective scenery in the Italian manner to performances at the Buen Retiro palace.

But Calderón's best plays were intended for the exuberant, non-illusionistic stages of the *corrales*. He was not as prolific as Lope de Vega (who was?), but in addition to his *autos*, he has left us with 108 *comedias*, more polished in their language and construction than those of his great predecessor and just as varied in tone, style and subject matter.

Many of his plays revolve around questions of honor and the cruel code, partly Moorish in origin, that governed family life. Under the provisions of this code, domestic honor was enforced by domestic authority. A husband had the power of life and death over a wife who was even suspected of infidelity, a rumor of offense being as punishable as a verified act. In the case of an unmarried woman, the same power belonged to her brother or her fiance. A stain upon the family honor required payment in blood, and the revenge must be secret lest the stain should spread and a husband's reputation suffer.

This aristocratic code has created a barrier between Calderón and non-Spanish modern audiences. Some of Calderón's "honor" plays with his female victims seem parochial, even barbaric—especially his tragedies, *Secret Vengeance for Secret Insult, The Physician of His Own Honor* and *The Painter of His Own Dishonor*. But Calderón was also capable of taking the same code and using it as the basis for light-hearted romantic comedies of intrigue, like *A House With Two Doors Is Difficult to Guard* and *The Phantom Lady*. By general consensus Calderón's best and most enduring play is his philosophical romance, *Life Is a Dream*. Long before Strindberg and Pirandello discovered the theme, Calderón was writing of the ephemeral nature of life and posing questions about reality and illusion.

Of Calderón's sacred *comedias, Devotion to the Cross* is at the same time one of his most popular and most problematic. Its story, judged by realistic standards, is a tissue of absurdities, but the play contains some of Calderón's most inspired verse. Despite its ridiculous intrigue plot and its arcane theology, it is still revived, especially in France, where Albert Camus' inspired version is popular.

Edward Honig, an admirer of the play and its English translator, offers a cogent defense of *Devotion to the Cross* by seeing Calderón as an allegorist, and this piece as a mature example of a complex, essentially abstract art.

Edward Honig

CALDERON'S STRANGE MERCY PLAY*

*T*he Spanish reputation for pride—fierce, glorious, and absurd—goes back at least as far as the Cid. Starting as an obscure soldier-squire, the epic hero is tricked and banished by powerful enemies among the nobility, vengefully returns, becomes a rich conqueror, sees his enemies punished, and his daughters married to kings. This type of Christian warrior, whose ideals are rooted in a mixed heritage of Visigothic and Moorish honor, later conquers the New World, spreading his peculiarly anachronistic version of militant Catholicism, at once zealously mystical and egregiously imperialistic. When we come upon him again in Don Quixote, with all his ideals chastened by defeat, his persistent absurdity wrings a momentous Pyrrhic victory from his misadventures. Paradoxically in this way he revives the standard of Spanish pride so successfully that he becomes a sort of secular saint — the counterpart to the only other Spanish saint whose order endures, Ignatius Loyola.

In Spanish Golden Age drama something else happens to heroic pride. Methodized and internalized, it becomes the conscientious resource of heroes who feel themselves estranged from society yet act strictly according to its unwritten, vengeful code of honor. The honor code lends itself to the intolerably burdened conscience, the embattled condition of outraged pride, a state of personal fear mirroring society's fear of contamination and the assault against its autocratic rule. The burdened conscience resorts to a desperate ultrarational dialectic, a kind of Holy Inquisition (viz. the stocktaking soliloquies and dialogues in the honor plays), a legalistic tourney justifying the precise foul means involved in regaining lost personal honor. The medicine of hypocrisy is often used to bring about the catharsis, the shedding of the burden in murder, whereby the social law is preserved and the individual is sacrificed. Even where an alternative is offered in a series of frenzied aggressive acts justified by religious devotion and supernatural mercy, the redeeming action seems almost as hypocritical, self-defensive, and criminally directed as the vengeance principle it is meant to combat. The hero engaged in either cause is similarly induced by disguised sexual passion to perform acts of violence and sadism as grim as the traditional auto da fe.

[The honor play became a convention before Calderón, mainly

*From *Massachusetts Review*, 3 (1961), pp. 80-107. Reprinted by permission.

because it gave the dramatist a sure-fire formula to capture popular audiences. In a dramatic handbook of the period, Lope de Vega wrote, "Incidents concerning honor are preferable because they move all people forcefully." When as a new playwright in the 1620s Calderón picked up the formula, he made it serve unexpected ends. In his plays honor is more than a thematic convenience or an exemplification of a code; it becomes the chief implement of design, shaping, infusing with life and dramatic necessity the very substance of his plays.]

The reason for this is that Calderón, more than any other dramatist of his time, is temperamentally disposed to view the world and his art allegorically. His secular plays show a more and more symbolic orientation in their typological use of character and situation, leading toward the form of the auto, the sacramental morality, with which he was almost exclusively concerned in the last thirty years of his career.

To the allegorist the world is a permanent battleground for the strategic maneuvers of body and soul, best typified in the *Psychomachia* of Prudentius, the Early Spanish-Latin poet. The literary allegorist gives first importance to this theme, exploiting it with the whole armory of his artistic contrivances until it becomes inextricable from the work itself. Calderón turned the honor code into a complex dramaturgical machine entirely directed to serving as an allegorical purveyor of his theme. To anyone aware of the multiple effects, the condensations of meaning, and the urgent tone of anxiety which such a form produces, the language and craftsmanship of Calderón's plays immediately appear to be full of allegorical devices. One cannot in any case disregard the devices, for they are used with uncommon persistence. And when such uses are probed they reveal something wholly different from the chilling artifices, monstrous rhetoric, and casuistic apology they are often taken for. They point to a triumph of sensibility over severely limited materials and the effects of a relentless, largely forbidding, ideology. It is only when these matters are mistakenly viewed by realistic criteria that Calderón's work collapses into absurdity.

In Calderón's definitive honor play, *Secret Vengeance for Secret Insult* (1635), honor's surrogate is the king and its instrument is Don Lope, "membered to the body" of the state. For the most part, the dramatic action is significantly internalized through Lope's soliloquies. The legalistic development of the theme is worked out appropriately in secret, through definitions of his state of mind, implemented by his conscientious strategy. Symbolic counterparts to this action appear in the critically realistic speeches of his servant Manrique, in the recurrent elemental symbolism throughout the play, and through the various inset actions and witnessings which the other characters introduce. Dramatically we are aware of a constant balancing and symmetry of processes; the play's highly schematized structure, based on the allegorical treatment of theme, makes for sharp but discrete doubling effects, like sounds counterposed to echoes and images counterposed to mirrored reflections.

In *Devotion to the Cross* (1633),[1] where the honor theme is eclipsed by an incest situation and transcended by supernatural mercy, there is a blurring of dramatic action, an impression of structural imbalance and of a thematic resolution which shocks belief. One reason for this difference between the plays is that the action of thought in *Devotion* is largely externalized; there is no nice thematic complimentariness set up between auxilliary characters and the principal agents. And because the allegory is revealed through what the main characters do, the course of action must be taken as a continuous analogue to the archetypal situation of man's fall and redemption. Though the play is structurally ragged and aesthetically less satisfying than *Secret Vengeance,* it is more moving. Like *Hamlet* or *Doctor Faustus* the play's dramaturgic failure is somehow overcome by its resonant tone of outrage and the depths of implication at its center. The gross melodrama enforces a pathetic, and strategically delayed, action of self-realization, and this is achieved by a flouting of the very credibility the play insists upon in order to make its point.

For us the play is problematic; for Calderón's contemporaries it was little more than a religious thriller, a lesson in heavenly clemency steeped in blood and spiced with incest. But our problem with it is not how to swallow the melodrama with its religious message in one gulp, which is what troubled nineteenth-century critics of the play. For Albert Camus, who adapted *Devotion* in French, neither the dramatic tenor nor the morality was anachronistic when he remarked:

> Grace transfiguring the worst of criminals, goodness wakened by excessive evil are for us, believers and non-believers alike, familiar themes. But it was three centuries before Bernanos that Calderón in the Devotion provocatively illustrated the statement that "Grace is everything," which still tempts the modern conscience in answer to the non-believer's "Nothing is just."

---

[1] All translations from *Devotion to the Cross* are from *Calderón: Four Plays* (New York: Hill and Wang, Inc., 1961), edited, with an introduction, by Edward Honig. Reprinted by permission of the publisher.

To go further: the larger problem of belief depends upon how we understand the implications of honor and incest in the play. What, we may ask, has honor to do with incest and, if there is a real connection, does this account for the resonances we feel in the play as well as the shock of poetic justice underlying the thurmaturgic actions at the end? Unless we frame the problem this way we must stop with a literal reading of the play, and a literal reading of *Devotion* leads to a tangle of absurdities.

Lisardo has challenged his friend Eusebio to a duel for daring to court Julia, Lisardo's sister, without asking permission of Curcio, their father. Eusebio, as Lisardo tells him, would not qualify as her suitor anyway since he is presumably not of noble blood. So Lisardo must now redress the blight on the family honor brought about by Eusebio's rash suit, and Julia must be made to end her days in a convent. Eusebio tells Lisardo the story of his strange birth at the foot of a cross and the charmed life he has led; then, vowing to have Julia at any price, he mortally wounds his antagonist. But in answer to the dying Lisardo's plea to be shriven, Eusebio carries him off to a monastery. Following this, Eusebio enters Curcio's house secretly, speaks with Julia, hides when her father appears and, after the body of Lisardo is brought in and Curcio leaves, Eusebio emerges and carries on an impassioned dialogue with her over Lisardo's corpse; then at Julia's bidding he escapes, promising never to see her again.

In Act Two Eusebio is a refugee from justice and the leader of a band of highwaymen, notorious for their crimes in the mountain passages and nearby villages. Eusebio spares the life of a traveling priest, Alberto, and exacts a promise from him to be shriven before dying. Next, he breaks into Julia's convent, where he is about to rape her when he discovers she bears the same sign of the cross on her breast which he bears on his. He will have nothing to do with her now, and escapes. She leaves the convent to search for him, although he does not know this. Meanwhile Curcio, directed by the law to capture Eusebio dead or alive, leads a group of peasants an soldiers through the mountains. There he reveals the story, partly hinted at in the first act, of his mistrust and jealousy of his wife Rosmira. We learn of a ruse by which he brought her to the mountains when she was pregnant, and of his attempt to kill her there. We also learn that he had left Rosmira for dead at the foot of a cross, where she had given birth to twins; on returning home he found her, miraculously transported there, with the infant Julia, the other child having been lost.

In Act Three Julia, disguised as a man, is captured and brought before Eusebio. Left alone with him, she first attempts to kill him, then is persuaded to tell her story, which turns out to be a fantastic tale of multiple murders she has committed since leaving the convent. She is interrupted by the report of Curcio's arrival. When Eusebio and Curcio meet both are momentarily immobilized by a feeling of mutual sympathy. They fight briefly without swords and are interrupted by Curcio's men, who chase Eusebio; they slash at him until he topples from the cliff and falls dying at the foot of the same cross where he was born. Discovered there by Curcio, he is acknowledged as a long-lost son, Julia's twin, and dies. Meanwhile the approach of Alberto, the priest, causes the dead Eusebio to revive and call out. The priest confesses him and Eusebio gives up the ghost in a scene witnessed by Curcio and his group, as well as the disguised Julia and the highwaymen. Revealing herself now, Julia publicly confesses her crimes, but when her father advances to strike her, she reaches for the cross, which ascends heavenward and bears her away with the dead Eusebio.

Most critics have been annoyed by the play's hypocrisy, its crude religious propaganda, its perverse morality which pardons the devout but unsympathetic criminal. Among the few contrary opinions are William Entwhistle's view of the play as "a representable idea" and A.A. Parker's insistence that it be read in terms of the unity of its theme. Actually, only when the play is read allegorically does it become intelligible despite its strange immorality.

Through Eusebio, its chief character, *Devotion* represents the figurative fall and redemption of mankind. As a figure for the fallen Adam, Eusebio is redeemed by the Cross ("tree divine"), which bears him heavenward, and thus fulfills his "secret cause"—a prefiguration, as Adam in the Bible prefigures Christ. At infancy he is abandoned (assumed to be "lost") at the foot of the cross where, we learn later, his mother fell under the hand of his jealous father. Having no identity, Eusebio takes the cross as a totemic object which corresponds to the talisman etched on his breast like a birthmark. This makes him a candidate for salvation, as it does Julia his twin, who is similarly marked. As Eve may be said to have been Adam's twin, and as both victims of the tree of the knowledge of good and evil, so Eusebio and Julia share a common destiny, part of which is to be restored through grace by the Cross, the tree of eternal life. The implication of incest, which underlies the act of original sin in Genesis, is here metaphysically, if not sacramentally, material to Calderón's allegory. The reason for this is that Eusebio must learn who he is, which he can do only by discovering and rejoining Julia, his other half. But to do so he must relive symbolically the primal scene in the garden, whose analogue in the play is the convent where Julia, as "the bride of Christ," is immured.

Another analogue suggested here is that of the body and soul, the twin or complimentary entities. The soul (Eusebio) seeks to be restored to the body (Julia) from which it has been separated. When Eusebio finds Julia in the convent and is about to re-enact the primal deed, he dimly senses in her talismanic sign some heavenly purpose linking her to his secret cause. This foreboding makes him reject her, much as a figure of the new Adam, forewarned of his cause, would reject the old sexual crime —incest, original sin. Yet he must suffer Adam's fall literally as well as symbolically; and this occurs when Eusebio falls from the ladder by the convent wall. In her turn Julia, the fallen body and rejected spouse, is separated by means of the same wall and ladder from re-entering the garden-convent. In ignorance of her destiny, she follows Eusebio and tries to destroy him. The crimes she commits on the way are, like Eusebio's earlier crimes, committed in blind outrage at having been separated from the other half.

In the worldly terms represented by the shepherds, Eusebio's and Julia's cause is criminally absurd. But since at the play's end, worldly discretion and justice are both foiled by the twin's heavenly ascension, it seems clear that it is the spiritual significance of the action, symbolically represented, which interested Calderón.

A Christian hero, Eusebio, like the heroes of all myths, is at the start unaware of his origin, though supremely conscious of some unrevealed fate he has been designated to fulfill. While still ignorant of when and how his fate will be revealed, and because he cannot know if his duel with Lisardo will end disastrously, he tells the story of his life, ticking off each miraculous episode as if to indicate his triumphs over merely earthbound, mortal forces. To Lisardo's grim reminder of Eusebio's inferior blood, Eusebio retorts, "Inherited nobility / is not superior to / nobility that's been acquired." He can say this because he knows he has a patent to act in ways that transcend a nobleman's prerogatives; his "escutcheon" is "inherited from this Cross." He has been tested and has triumphed before; he will triumph again: in the wilderness of the mountain, in the garden-convent, and finally—to his eternal reward when he dies—at the foot of the same cross where he was born. To that cross he is to speak later as Adam might have spoken to God, remembering the paradise tree: "Forgive me for the injury / of that first crime against you." And again like Adam with foreknowledge of his sin, he will say, "I do not blame / my father for denying me / a cradle. He must have sensed / the evil that was in me." Eusebio's invocation to the cross at the end is shot through with transfigured consciousness:

> Oh Tree, where Heaven chose to hang
> the one fruit to ransome man
> for his first forbidden mouthful!
> Oh flower of paradise regained!
> Rainbow light that spanned the Flood
> and thus pledged peace to all mankind!
> Oh faithful vine; the harp of yet
> another David; and the tablets
> of another Moses:
> Here I am, a sinner seeking grace.

Eusebio has been transformed from the human agent of his crimes into a symbolic force voicing the redemptive hope of all mankind. In this way he defeats the exactions of earthly penalties, and incidentally overcomes the harsh, tyrannical laws of honor represented by Curcio, the father who survives his wife and all his children.

Indeed, what about the honor theme which is so abruptly transcended at the end of the play by divine law? The question of honor not only bulks large throughout the play but is also curiously altered in the light of Eusebio's cause. Further inquiry tells us something about the unconscious motivations supporting the honor code as shown in the implicit incest-relationship lividly darting forth from the root situation of the play. For as they affect human motives, the impulsions and repulsions of the characters, the conventions of honor relate to certain basic though unspecified taboos concerning the sexual assault of male against female in the same family. But we must begin with the first recorded sexual relationship, in Genesis, and then go on to the society represented in Calderón's plays.

In effect the Genesis story demonstrates an archetypal incest situation inherent in man's disobedience, his fall from God's grace, and his knowledge of good and evil. Taken as a paradigm for man's earthly condition, the sexual crime called original sin derives from a transgression against divine command, a transgression that brings with it the knowledge of guilt. Instigated by Eve, man rebels against a paternal authority, Jehovah, who punishes her accordingly: "I will greatly multiply thy sorrow and thy conception; in sorrow thou shalt bring forth children; and thy desire shall be to thy husband, and he shall rule over thee." Later in Genesis (V, 2), one finds, "Male and female created he them; and blessed them, and called their name Adam, in the day when they were created." The creation of man and woman out of one body, the division of interests indicated between male and female, the transgression against authority, the sorrow of sex and childbearing, and the dominance of Adam over Eve are set down as almost simultaneous events and become an archetypal situation.[2]

It may be assumed, then, that Eve's transgression is congenital and innate: as woman, she will always rebel against the authoritarian principles. Eve, "the mother of all living," will be a divisive force in fallen society, just as she was in paradise. One way to counteract her innate rebelliousness is to idealize her, as the Middle Ages did: first, symbolically, by elevating the Virgin Mary as an object of worship; secondly, by lodging the image of woman as a venerated but scarcely attainable love object in the tradition of courtly love. Another way is to bind her, as the prize and victim of transgression, to a code of honor — a role descending from the courtly tradition and modified by the needs of an authoritarian society, typical of seventeenth-century Spain.

The peculiarly tight, claustrophobic condition of the honor code appears to derive from an already tense, anxiety-ridden view, featured in myth and religion, of woman's unreconciled position between transgressor and idol. In addition, this view is overlaid by the historical and social exigencies of an imperial Spain warring against Protestantism as it had for centuries warred against Islam. In this struggle the impossible myth of Spanish Christian purity and pure-blooded (castizo)

---

[2] I have summarized elsewhere J.J. Bachofen's view of such a situation: "Archetypal situations of this sort apparently involve the dynamic interplay of two broad, antagonistic principles. One might say the conflict between these two principles is nearly persuasive enough to affect every emotion and every move a person makes or thinks of making. Together these principles engender the dichotomies of art evolving out of authoritarian religion, and relate to the biases of artistic expression we call classical or romantic, rational or enthusiastic. One principle is the dominance of woman and the natural virtues imputed to her, which are culturally shaped into the matriarchal ideals of love, equality, peace, mercy, fecundity, the reassuring periodicity of nature, human freedom, brotherhood, and the world as an earthly paradise. In opposition is the powerful and now triumphant principle of male authority, which encompasses all the virtues of civilized life: law, conscience, justice, military heroism; the concepts of hierarchy, primogeniture, and individualism; and the material conquest over nature." (*Dark Conceit: the Making of Allegory* [Evanston: Northwestern University Press, 1959], p. 35.)

descent would have been sustained against the millennial evidence of intermarriage with Berbers, Moslems, and Jews, not to mention cultural assimilation with other peoples of Western and Mediterranean Europe, going back to the early Phoenicians. The avowal that one is an "old Christian Catholic," repeated so often in Renaissance Spanish literature, becomes a self-destructive cry; vainglorious and perversely aggressive, it reminds one of Nazi Germany's self-conscious aryanism. And so where the invasion of one's honor code is sexually directed, an attack on one's personal pure-bloodedness, with social and religious implications, is also immediately assumed.

In the autocratic society of Calderón's plays, every family seems to be a Spain-in-little seeking to preserve itself against the real or imagined, but always chronic, invasions of lawless forces from the outside. That the laws of honor are inhuman and tyrannical—a protest constantly being voiced by Calderón's heroes—does not interfere with their being fulfilled. And as they are being fulfilled, often in the strictest secrecy, we are struck by the incredible, tragic strength of will involved in acting upon an impossible ideal according to an impossible sense of justice.

The fear of incest and the fear of sexual assault become one and the same thing; particularly notable in *Devotion to the Cross,* the same fear is evident in most of Calderón's honor plays. In addition, the incest barrier is complemented by the religious barrier between different faiths as well as by the social barrier between classes; and behind such barriers lurks the constant fear of contamination. Life under these circumstances is seen as warfare, catastrophe, and fatality, in which the vaguest hint of misdemeanor is as culpable as any number of overt murders. Where authoritarian justice rules, whether theocratic or monarchic, to think or be tempted as a human being (the hero in *Secret Vengeance* exclaims, "How is it one thinks or speaks at all?") is as dangerous as to put one's thoughts and temptations into action. What makes the honor code so strange to us is that it is a reduction (often to absurdity) of an imperialistic legal structure, from its embodiment in ecclesiastical and state authority to an individual psychological problem, without any mitigation of its impersonal emphasis. What would justify legal punishment by state or church—the impersonal need to preserve the community against assaults by criminal or heretic—becomes bizarre when voiced as a rationale by human beings following the letter of the honor code. They act as though they had set some gigantic, superhuman machine in motion, which is just what they have done. What makes for further bizarreness is the unconscious irony with which they speak in rationalizing their human pride as the cause of justice while being ignorant that they themselves are part of the machine and that their voice is actually the voice of the machine. The pride they boast of concerns the acts and strategies of will—their skill, their cunning; what they do not know is that such pride is simply the fuel that makes the honor machine run. Human pride, then, frequently becomes a sign not of personal satisfaction but of the personal glorification of the legal structure; and the act which the human agents engineer in its name becomes a personal auto da fe, a self-punishing sacrifice in the name of a super-personal faith.

That this makes for dramatic irony in Calderón's plays may be seen in the various views, ranging from satiric to sacramental, with which the central character's situation is regarded by other characters as well as the opposing views he has of it himself. The dramatic irony is further evident in the rapid glimpse we get of the hero's fate at the end of the play, where he appears at best a Pyrrhic victor, exhausted, wrung out by the machine, and hardly distinguishable from his victim. Dramatic irony is highly schematized in Calderón's plays, being part of, if not indeed the instrument for creating, a larger moral irony. It is interesting to see how the ironic form shapes the honor-bound figure of Curcio in *Devotion*.

An aspect of the moral irony made explicit here is that the avenger complains against the tyrannical laws of honor, though they are the only laws he can follow in exacting his revenge. But an even more pronounced irony is that the object of Curcio's revenge, Eusebio, is redeemed at the end by a higher law than that of honor, so that the matter is literally taken out of Curcio's hands. Since the action of the play is allegorical, we can no more read this final turn of events realistically than we can any other part of the play. The literal meaning is apparent: Curcio is not avenged, and in not being avenged, the course of honor which he has pursued throughout is defeated. How then are we to take his defeat and, by clear analogy, since he is its implement, the defeat of honor? The obvious answer is that honor has been suspended by a miracle; the intervention of divine powers indicates that Eusebio is not to be punished, but having entered into a state of grace is, on the contrary, given his heavenly reward along with Julia. Curcio's last speech—his final remarks to the audience are simply conventional and do not count —is clearly a revenger's furious threat addressed to Julia, an intended victim: "I shall kill you with my own two hands, / and have you die as violently / as you have lived." She pleads to the Cross, and as Curcio "is about to strike her," she embraces it and so is lifted heavenward with

Eusebio. Curcio could not have been more plainly foiled, and to say that his vengeance, including his authority for seeking it, has been superceded by divine intervention, does not seem a full or satisfactory answer. For apparently Curcio was mistaken—just as badly mistaken here, when about to kill his daughter, as he was earlier when striking at his innocent wife, who was similarly rescued by the Cross. The deeper moral irony, then, is that the laws of honor, so assiduously upheld by Curcio, are indeed defeated and their justification, as enacted by their avenger here, is shown to be reprehensible on the highest possible authority.

Is honor here defeated or merely suspended? To seek a fuller answer to the question, one must rephrase it to accord with Curcio's allegorical role in the play. In what way is Curcio, the surrogate of honor and an omnipotent figure in the community, responsible for the fate which his family suffers? First, and most generally, it is evident that by accusing his wife of infidelity and seeking to kill her on admittedly groundless evidence, Curcio touches off a series of actions which ends with the death of his three children and his wife. Secondly, it is made clear that Curcio is temperamentally handicapped: he is prodigal, rash, desperate, and overweeningly proud. Some of these attributes are inherited and reinforced to his own detriment by his own children, in a way suggestive of King Lear. Lisardo's brief appearance before he is killed by Eusebio seems at least partly intended to characterize his father:

> My father
> was a profligate who rapidly
> consumed the great estate
> his family had left him.
> In so doing, he was heedless
> of the straitened circumstances
> to which his children were reduced.
> And yet, although necessity
> may beggar one's nobility,
> it does not lessen in the least
> the obligations one is born with.

Following his inherited obligation, Lisardo must challenge Eusebio for lacking the noble qualifications to court his sister Julia. Lisardo's pronouncement concerning his sister, considering it is addressed to her lover who is also his friend, seems precipitous and mechanical, as though echoing a catechism learnt from his father:

> An impoverished gentleman
> who finds his fortune does not meet
> the requirements of his rank
> must see to it his maiden daughter,
> rather than pollute his blood
> by marriage, is taken off
> in safety to a convent.
> In all this, poverty's the culprit.
> Accordingly, tomorrow, my sister
> Julia will quickly take the veil,
> whether she wishes to or not.

Julia's subsequent report confirms the fact of her brother's anxious nature. Lisardo's face pales, drained of suspicion; he prevaricates— "snatched the key / impulsively, and angrily / unlocked the drawer," to discover the evidence of Eusebio's courtship; then, "without a single word, oh God? / he rushed out to find my father. / Then inside his room behind locked doors, / the two of them spoke loud and long—/ to seal my fate..." Lisardo is hardly distinguished from his father, whose purpose he is serving before he is killed. Later, when Julia questions Curcio's decision to put her into a convent, his voice seems simply a magnification of Lisardo's catechism. "Right or wrong, my will / is all you need to know." "My decision will suffice, and that / has been resolved. The matter's closed." "Rebel, hold your tongue! Are you mad? / I'll twist your braids around your neck, / or else I'll rip that tongue of yours / out of your mouth with my own hands / before it cuts me to the quick again." Curcio immediately identifies Julia's rebellion with her dead mother's, now impulsively finding "proof" where later he admits no evidence existed.

> So at last I have the proof
> of what I long suspected:
> that your mother was dishonorable,
> a woman who deceived me.
> So you attack your father's honor,
> whose luster, birth, nobility
> the sun itself can never equal
> with all its radiance and light.

It is apparent from this moment on that Curcio, hiding his defects behind the shield of honor, is steering a course which must victimize

Julia as surely as he has victimized his elder son Lisardo and wife
Rosmira. Though victimized as well, Eusebio listens to a higher law in
his worship of the Cross. It would be possible to show similarly that
Curcio's defects of despair, pride, and simple-minded credulity also
influence the course of events. And though the exemplification of such
personal defects would suffice to support the action in realistic terms,
this is not what we get in *Devotion to the Cross*. What we get instead is
allegorical action, action by analogy, by symbolic counterpart. By such
action Curcio figures dominantly as a type of vengeful Jahveh, the
thunder god in Genesis, the creator and punisher of the incestuous pair
who exceeded the commandment and attained to a knowledge of good
and evil—as in their separate ways Eusebio and Julia do. In the Bible the
vengeful god is superceded by a sacrificed human God, who comes as
Christ and redeems the Adamic sin. The code of honor, one might say, is
similarly transcended in *Devotion*. It is superceded and defeated as a
partial truth, but without being destroyed or removed—as the Old
Testament is superceded by the New.

The attraction and repulsion which lead Eusebio towards and away
from Julia, and which induce her to act in complementary movements,
have been discussed in terms of the Adam and Eve analogy and the
body-soul analogy. Similarly, a movement from repulsion to attraction is
evident in the relationship between Curcio and Eusebio, and the effect is
concentrated wholly in Act Three. Two of Curcio's speeches summarize
this shift: "his chilling blood cries out / to me so timidly. And if / his
blood were not my own in part, / it would not beckon me, / nor would I
hear it cry." "How I hated him / alive; now how I grieve his death!" As
soon as father and son confront one another, there is a mutual affinity
between them, though they do not know they are related. It is so intense
that Eusebio refuses to use his sword to fight Curcio. When they struggle
barehanded, the sense of their combat is dreamlike—a scene reminiscent
of a more famous father-son contention in Calderón's *Life Is a Dream*,
who is unwilling to surrender to the law, will nevertheless give himself
up to Curcio, out of "respect." And Curcio, though he has long hunted
Eusebio, suddenly offers to let him escape. Eusebio refuses, and when
Curcio's men arrive, the father intervenes; to his men's astonishment he
suggests the alternative of a legal trial: "I'll be / your advocate before the
law." But it is too late; the honor machine has already moved closer to
its inexorable goal: Eusebio is mortally wounded by Curcio's men at the
foot of the Cross.

In his despair Curcio recognizes the inefficacy of the honor machine and admits a guilt he can no longer hide from himself. The mystery of the twin birth at the cross is a mystery which he, as the surrogate of honor and fallen pride, is not prepared to contend with. Mercy is not a principle which autocratic honor accepts. We witness Curcio's gradually increasing helplessness, a condition which the avenging thunder god of Genesis might experience in confronting the imminent redemption of his "son," Adam, gradually transfigured into Christ. Overwhelmed by the clemency of the Cross, Curcio further astonishes his men by telling them to "Take up this broken body / of Eusebio's, and lay it / mournfully aside till there is time / to build an honorable / sepulcher from which his ashen gaze / may contemplate my tears." To this request they reply with the outraged belief of men who have similarly become cogs in the honor machine.

Tirso: What? How can you think of burying a man in holy ground who died beyond the pale of Church and God?

Blas: For anyone like that, a grave here in the wilderness is good enough!

Curcio: Oh, villainous revenge! Are you still so outraged you must strike at him beyond the grave?

　　　　　　　　　　　　　　　[Exit Curcio, weeping.]

But there is still the final and clinching irony to account for. If Curcio admits the defeat of honor before the miracle of heavenly clemency, how can he suddenly revert to the vengeance principle at the end when he tries to destroy Julia? Curcio unwittingly instigates this turn and countermovement by recognizing the mercy principle; his recognition calls forth Julia's confession.

Curcio: My dearest son! you were not so wretched or forsaken after all, when in your tragic death you merit so much glory. Now if only Julia would recognize her crime.

Julia: God help me! What is this I hear, what ominous revelation? Can it be that I who was Eusebio's lover was his sister too? Then let my father and the whole wide world, let everybody know about my crimes. My perversions hound and overwhelm me, but I shall be the first to shout them out. Let every man alive be told that I am Julia, Julia the criminal, and of all the infamous women ever born, the worst. Henceforth my penances will be as public as the sins I have confessed. I go now to beg forgiveness of the world for the vile example I have given it, and pray that God forgive the crime of all my life.

Here Curcio erupts and attempts to kill her, at which she pledges her word to the Cross to "atone beneath your sign / and be born again to a new life," and the Cross bears her away to heaven. If we momentarily overlook this heavy melodramatic turn, Calderón's serious allegorical purpose will emerge. Desperate and defeated though he is, Curcio still incarnates the vengeance principle—a principle which survives him, even after he has been chastened by the higher law. In this he is like Eusebio, who represents the mercy principle and must survive his own death and revive in order to be shriven. Because he embodies the honor code, Curcio must strike out as he does, spontaneously, against Julia's offense and dishonor. And her offense in this instance is precisely her public confession of guilt instigated by Curcio's wishful remark. For according to the code, the public admission that one's honor has been wronged compounds the wrong that has already been committed against it. And so Julia's public declaration not only constitutes the last blow against her father's crumbling defenses but also makes explicit the cruel inoperativeness of the honor code when faced with any personal human cry for clemency. Julia's assertion that she will make her penances public is intolerable to honor and inadmissable to a code which categorically denies forgiveness. By implication there is no forgiveness on earth but only in heaven.

If as an honor figure Curcio cannot extend mercy, he is likewise incapable, as a figure for the Genesis thunder god, of offering reconciliation to Julia. And in the final exchange between the two, we are also reminded that Julia's "crime of all my life" like Eve's "crime" is not forgivable in terms of the old dispensation in Genesis, where the sexual act is incestuous and the original crime of the creation underlies the discovery of good and evil. Significantly, it is when she learns of the incestuous relationship with Eusebio that Julia makes her public declaration. As a type of Eve, Julia is the quintessential criminal ("of all / the infamous women ever born, / the worst"), universally damned by authoritarian law. Only the figure of a sacrificed god, according to the new dispensation, can redeem her, as Eusebio does at the end. We see then that honor is a form of the old, merciless, unregenerated, earthbound, dehumanized, patriarchal law, which is ultimately self-defeating. It prevails to the end, and presumably will continue to exist on earth opposing the merciful, regenerative, humane, and matriarchal law of heaven, symbolized in the Cross which has vanquished it.

At the conclusion of the play, where the Cross triumphs so resolutely, so providentially, and so patently as a *deus ex machina,* we are inclined to minimize its connection with the rest of the drama. Yet its function throughout is not only essential to the theme but also integral to the action. One might say that the final appearance of the Cross culminates many symbolic manifestations, from the beginning, of an extraordinarily complex role. And that role, in fact, is to serve dramatically as a complementary mechanism, a machine working in countermotion to the honor machine.

We first hear of the Cross early in the first act in Eusebio's lengthy recital of the events of his life, while holding off Lisardo. Eusebio's story is eager, rapt, proud, enthusiastic. He has been the subject of strange, benevolent miracles; he rapidly imparts his sense of wonder and mystery at these happenings — and is never so confident again. The effect of the speech, more notable for the feeling it releases than for its literal sense, is to introduce a sensation of power and authority into a tense situation. The tension leading to an impasse is exemplified in the opening scene of the play by the peasants Gil and Menga, vainly trying to drag their stalled donkey out of the mud. When Lisardo and Eusebio arrive, the impasse is augured in their pale, silent, distraught appearance. Gil describes them: "My, how pale / they look, and in open fields / so early in the morning! / I'm sure they must have eaten mud / to look so constipated." Whenever the Cross is introduced subsequently, the effect is similarly to dispel an impasse, initiate a contrary action, or metaphorically to lend a new dimension to the scene. Eusebio's Cross "that towered over me at birth, / and whose imprint is now pressed / upon my breast" is a talisman object which he serves and which actively serves him, symbolic of his paternity, a charismatic "symbol of some secret cause / unrevealed as yet." And its "secret cause" gradually begins to emerge in a series of significant actions.

Lisardo's dying plea "by the Cross Christ died on" deflects Eusebio's sword and makes him carry the fallen man away to be shriven, an action which later aids in Eusebio's own redemption. When Lisardo's corpse lies between the divided lovers, Julia and Eusebio, there is a curious dramatic effect which the theatricality of the scene emphasizes. Curcio's two living children seem here to form the horizontal appendages of a cruciform figure whose vertical stalk is the dead Lisardo. As the pair speak across the corpse we realize that it is the only time when the three children are joined together in the play. Joined, but also divided by the visible presence of the dead brother. That one power of the Cross is to join and another is to separate will appear significantly again.

At the beginning of Act Two, Alberto, the priest, is saved when Eusebio's bullet is stopped by the holy book the priest carries in his tunic. The metaphor Eusebio uses underlies the merciful power of the Cross to deflect the course of violence: "How well that flaming shot / obeyed your text by turning / stubborn lead softer than wax!" By this token Eusebio releases the priest who will reappear only once, in the third act, to confess him. The next reference to the Cross occurs in Curcio's soliloquy describing the miracle which saved his wife after she protested her innocence at the foot of the Cross, where he thought he had killed her. There the twins Eusebio and Julia were born, though, as we learn later, Eusebio was left behind when Rosmira was rescued by divine intervention and brought home with Julia. Subsequently, when Eusebio forces his way into the convent to violate Julia, he discovers that she too bears the imprint of the Cross on her breast, and fearfully withdraws. Here the Cross serves to prevent the incestuous act, and in doing so separates the Adamic from the Christ figure in Eusebio. Julia and Eusebio are not meant to repeat the paradisiacal crime under the Eden tree; they must now be separated from one another. They are only destined to be joined in an act of heavenly redemption at the Cross where they were born.

As we observed, when Eusebio falls from the ladder leaning against the convent wall, he symbolically enacts Adam's fall. Of this fact he seems dimly aware on rising: "Oh Cross Divine, this I promise you / and take this solemn vow / with strict attention to each word: / wherever I may find you, / I shall fall upon my knees / and pray devoutly, with all my heart." Julia, too, vaguely senses that her destiny is to follow Eusebio's "fall" by way of the ladder, though she is not impelled by heavenly signs nor aware, as he is, of the Cross's "secret cause." At this point she may simply be following the Genesis prescription — "and thy desire shall be to thy husband, and he shall rule over thee" — when she says, "This is where he fell; then I / must fall there too and follow him." Or perhaps she is feeding her desire with a later rationalization: "Does not my creed tell me / that once I give assent in thought / I thereby commit the crime?" Yet when she continues in this vein, we see that she has clearly identified her destiny with Eusebio's though she may not know what that destiny is.

> Did not Eusebio scale
> these convent walls for me?
> And did I not feel pleased

> to see him run such risks
> for my sake? Then why am I afraid?
> What scruple holds me back?
> If I leave now I do the very thing
> Eusebio did when he entered;
> and just as I was pleased with him,
> he'll be pleased to see me too,
> considering the risks I've taken
> for his sake. Now I have assented,
> I must take the blame. And if
> the sin itself be so tremendous,
> will enjoying it be any
> less so? Since I have assented
> and am fallen from the hand of God...

In modern terms the covert incest motive may be fused here with the affinity science has noted between closely related persons, particularly twins, causing similar behavior patterns because of similarities between their neuro-electrical activities. But in Christian terms it is clear that once Julia "falls" (i.e. descends the ladder), she is seized by the chilling evil of the symbolic act: "I find that my esteem for mankind, / honor, and my God is nothing / but an arid waste. Like an angel / flung from heaven in my demonic / fall I feel no stirring of / repentance."

With this admission she becomes Eve, the transgressor in Eden and cohort of the fallen angel, the eternal rebel against the patriarchal order of society. Her rebellion is an assault against man's contempt, the authoritarian abuse of her fruitful power to love and to heal the divisive prohibitions which sacrifice individual men to its order:

> I am alone, in my confusion
> and perplexity. Ingrate, are these
> your promises to me? Is this
> the sum of what you called your love's mad
> passion, or is it my love's madness?
> How you persisted in your suit—
> now by threats, now by promises,
> now as lover, now as tyrant,
> till I at last submitted to you.
> But no sooner had you become
> master of your pleasure

and my sorrow than you fled
before you had possessed me.
Now in escaping you have
vanquished me entirely.
Merciful Heaven, I am lost
and dead! Why does nature provide
the world with poisons when the venom
of contempt can kill so swiftly?
So his contempt will kill me,
since to make the torment worse
I must follow him who scorns me.
When has love been so perverse before?...
Such is woman's nature that
against her inclination
she withholds that pleasure
which she most delights to give.

The capacity to sin is no different from the capacity to hurt and be hurt,
perversely, against one's inclination. But to tell one's hurt, confess one's
sin and be forgiven is to triumph over the corruptions of evil enforced by
social law. As Julia says, this forgiveness can be extended by the
restorative power of providence:

faith teaches
there is nothing which the clemency
of Heaven cannot touch or reach:
all the sparkling constellations,
all the sands of all the oceans,
every atom, every mote upon
the air, and all these joined together,
are as nothing to the sins
which the good Lord God can pardon.

Contempt, scorn, division, separation, hopelessness, despair—these are
the goads to crime and destructiveness. And this is what Julia recognizes
when the ladder leading back to the convent is withdrawn:

Ah, but I begin to understand
the depths of my misfortune.
This is a sign my way is barred,
and thus when I would strive

> to creep back, a penitent,
> I am shown my cause is hopeless.
> Mercy is refused me.
> Now a woman doubly scorned,
> I shall perpetrate such
> desperate deeds even Heaven
> will be astounded, and the world
> will shudder at them till
> my perfidy outrages all time
> to come, and the deepest pits
> of hell shall stand agape
> with horror at my crimes.

Understood symbolically, according to the dialectic of fall and redemption, male and female principles, the subversion of humanity by the authoritarian necessity of honor, Julia's intentions and subsequent crimes are not the ludicrous things they appear to be when viewed according to the cause-and-effect realism. They are dramatic epiphanies proceeding from closely related lines of thought, feeling, and action rising from the implications of the thematic "devotion to the cross." It is only the misuse of symbolic meaning which is ludicrous. Calderón makes this clear immediately following Julia's speech, at the start of Act Three.

Gil enters "covered with crosses; a very large one is sewn on his breast." The situation is reversed: a man is now following a woman's "bidding," as Gil says with regard to Menga, adding,

> I go . . .
> scouring the mountainside for firewood,
> and for my own protection
> I've concocted this strategem.
> They say Eusebio loves crosses.
> Well, here I am, armed from head to foot
> with them.

But Gil's cross is not charismatic. He sees Eusebio, hides in a bush and is immediately stuck with thorns. Eusebio at this point is brooding over the meaning of the Cross inscribed on Julia's breast: "I was driven, by the impulse of a higher power / whose cause prevailed against my will, / forbidding me to trespass on / the Cross—the Cross that I respect.../ Oh Julia, the two of us were born / subject to that sign, and thus I fear / the

portents of a mystery / which only God can understand." And the scene
where he discovers Gil is oddly discordant, mixing serious and comic
elements to such effect that Eusebio's cause appears ludicrous.

Gil [aside]:	I can't stand it any longer; I'm stung all over!
Eusebio:	There is
	someone in the bushes. Who's there?
Gil [aside]:	Well, here's where I get tangled in my snare.
Eusebio [aside]:	A man tied to a tree,
	and wearing a cross on his breast!
	I must be true to my word and kneel.
Gil:	Why do you kneel, Eusebio?
	Are you saying prayers, or what?
	First you tie me up, then you pray
	to me. I don't understand.
Eusebio:	Who are you?
Gil:	Gil. Don't you remember?
	Ever since you tied me up here
	with that message, I've been yelling out
	my lungs but, just my luck,
	nobody's yet come by to free me.
Eusebio:	But this is not the place I left you.
Gil:	That's true, sir.
	The fact is, when I realized that
	no one was passing by, I moved on,
	still tied, from one tree to the next,
	until I reached this spot.
	And that's the only reason
	why it seems so strange to you.
	[Eusebio frees him.]
Eusebio [aside]:	This simpleton may be of use
	to me in my misfortune.
	—Gil, I took a liking to you
	when we met the other time.
	So now let us be friends.
Gil:	Fair enough,
	and since we're friends I'll never
	go back home but follow you instead.
	And we'll be highwaymen together.
	They say the life's ideal—not a stitch
	of work from one year to the next.

Gil's mention of "the other time" refers to the occasion in Act Two when Eusebio found Gil and Menga in the mountains, had them tied to tree-trunks, and left them with a crucial message for Curcio—a message Gil fails to deliver. The message has to do with something Curcio does not yet know, and by its means Eusebio would attempt to reconcile himself with Lisardo's father and absolve himself from the charge of murder. Eusebio does not know that Gil did not deliver the message, nor is it certain that if Gil had done so the effect would be to alter the course of events up to this point. But Gil's appearance immediately after Julia's speech at the end of Act Two, the absurd story he tells Eusebio about progressing "still tied, from one tree to the next," and Eusebio's own curiously quixotic reaction to Gil's cross are all, at first glance, puzzling and disconcerting details. For Gil's antics are bathetic to the same degree that Eusebio's devoutness is ludicrous, so that both seem to be defects of taste and dramatic emphasis.

Considered symbolically, however, the scene is anything but bathetic or implausible; on the contrary, it comes as a sharp, immediate reminder of the opposing claims of honor and mercy, of vengeance and devotion, the very theme developed in the play's movements and countermovements we have been tracing. In effect Calderón is reminding us that Eusebio's devotion is a cause squarely opposed to Curcio's vengeance, and that the one has its provenance in a heavenly mystery symbolized by the Cross as the other has in the code of honor. Troubled by the symbol on Julia's breast, Eusebio is caught off-guard when Gil's presence interrupts his thoughts. He does not know it is Gil; all he sees is the cross on Gil's breast, to which he automatically responds by kneeling respectfully, according to his vow. It is the symbol and not the man he responds to. The act immediately makes him out to be a fool—not the crazy fool Gil takes him for, but the "fool in Christ," the devoted servant of the Cross. Gil, of course, has correctly guessed that wearing the cross will protect him from Eusebio, just as it saved Alberto, the priest, at the beginning of Act Two. What Gil does not understand is the objective power and principle of the cross; and we may see in his being entangled in briars until Eusebio frees him an exemplum of this mistaken view. The absurd story he tells about moving "still tied, from one tree to the next" is an extension of his mistaken view because it supposes that Eusebio, though dangerous, is merely simple-minded. But the effect of Gil's story is to identify him and to bring Eusebio's attention away from the symbol in order to recognize "the simpleton" who is wearing it. Eusebio awakes to his own situation, his self-

defensive strife against Curcio's pursuit of vengeance, in which Gil
"may be of use" to him as one who knows the mountainous terrain. On
the other hand, all Gil can conclude about Eusebio's offer of friendship
is that the other's addiction to crosses somehow involves the charmed
life of brigandry—"not a stitch / of work from one year to the next." The
fact is, however, that Eusebio's situation is narrowing and, as later
events show, he is ridden by anxiety and the burden of his course. He is
fast approaching his own end, which will entail the complete revelation
of heaven's secret symbolized by the Cross. But while waiting for the
mystery to unfold, he must contend with Curcio's vengeance. As a
result, he acts feverishly, half terrified, half audacious, as a man aware of
some impending catastrophe would act.

This is notable in his response to Julia, who has reappeared dressed as
a man, and who after attempting to kill him has told the story of her
crimes. He says:

> I listen to you fascinated,
> enchanted by your voice,
> bewitched by everything you say
> although the sight of you
> fills me with dread...
>   I fear Heaven's
> retribution looming over me...
> I live in such horror of that Cross,
> I must avoid you.

His anxiety is also apparent in the orders he gives his men, and later in
his hand-to-hand encounter with his father.

> I do not know what reverence
> the sight of you instills in me.
> But I know your suffering awes me
> more than your sword . . .
> and the truth to tell, the only
> victory I seek is to fall
> upon my knees and beg you
> to forgive me.

And so it is almost with relief that he receives the mortal wound at the
hands of Curcio's men. He can at last yield to his father and die; but
also—and this he does not know —he is to be resurrected in order to

receive absolution at the foot of the cross where he was born. In this way his destiny is fulfilled, his secret cause revealed, his life career run full cycle. But there is also the posthumous miracle of his heavenly ascension which includes the sanction of Julia. Besides proving Julia's earlier declaration that "there is nothing which the clemency / of Heaven cannot touch or reach," this last miracle reclaims her from the perversely male-dominated role of revenger ("The symbol / of terrifying vengeance") in which the honor machine had cast her. There is perhaps a conclusive irony in this last turn: that the monolithic, all-pervasive engine of the honor machine on earth can only be transcended by the more powerful, absolutist machine of heavenly mercy.

SOURCE MATERIAL FOR TRAGEDY

☙ Elizabethan playwrights drew plot inspiration from many sources. Anything which might provide an impressive tragic theme or a diverting comic incident was considered fair game for literary plunder. Ancient chronicles, Roman histories, contemporary Italian *novelle*—these were raw materials with which the dramatist worked, reshaping the structure of the story into an entertaining and theatrical action.

We conclude our examination of the Renaissance theatre with a brief anthology of source material for four of the great tragic dramas of the Elizabethan and Jacobean periods: Christopher Marlowe's *Doctor Faustus* and Shakespeare's *Julius Caesar, Hamlet,* and *Macbeth.*

Doctor Faustus was first produced in 1588 or 1589 when its author (born the same year as Shakespeare) was no more than twenty-five. Marlowe based his powerful and very subtle dramatization of man's attempt to escape human limitations on a crude German version of a medieval legend, the *Faustbuch,* published in 1587. An English translation of this *Faustbuch* was not printed until 1592, although it may have been available to Marlowe in manuscript before that time.

One thing is certain. Whatever version Marlowe used—German or English—he far transcended the source. Nowhere in the crude moralizing of the older tale do we have even a suggestion of the complex figure that Marlowe paints for us—a man who is both hero and sinner and whose quest for freedom is at the same time godlike and depraved.

(Source for Marlowe's *Doctor Faustus*)

from THE ENGLISH FAUST-BOOK OF 1592*

How Doctor Faustus bewayled to thinke on Hell, and of the miserable paynes therein provided from him.

Chapter 61

*N*ow thou FAUSTUS, damned wretch, howe happy wert thou if as an unreasonable beast thou mightest die without soule, so shouldest thou not feele any more doubts. But nowe the divell will take thee away both body and soule, and set thee in an unspeakable place of darknesse: for although others soules have rest and peace, yet I poore damned wretch must suffer all manner of filthy stench, paines, colde, hunger, thirst, heate, freezing, burning, hissing, gnashing, and all the wrath and curse of God, yea all the creatures that God hath created are enemies to mee. And now too late I remember that my Spirit MEPHOSTOPHILES did once tell mee, there was a great difference amongst the damned; for the greater the sinne, the greater the torment: for as the twigges of the tree make greater flame than the trunke therof, and yet the trunke continueth longer in burning; even so the more that a man is rooted in sinne, the greater is his punishment. Ah thou perpetuall damned wretch, now art thou throwne into the everlasting fiery lake that never shall be quenched, there must I dwell in all manner of wayling, sorrow, misery, payne, torment, griefe, howling, sighing, sobbing, blubbering, running of eyes, stinking at nose, gnashing of teeth feare to the eares, horror to the conscience, and shaking both of hand and foote. Ah that I could carry the heavens on my shoulders, so that there were time at last to quit me of this everlasting damnation! Oh who can deliver me out of these fearful tormenting flames, *the* which I see prepared for me. Oh there is no helpe, nor any man that can deliver me, nor any wayling of sins can help me, neither is there rest to be found for me day nor night. Ah wo is me, for there is no help for me, no shield, no defence no comfort. Where is my hold? knowledge dare I not trust: and for a soule to God wards that have I not, for I shame to speak unto him: if I doo, no answere shall be made me, but hee will hide his face from me, to the end that I should not beholde the joyes of the chosen. What meane I then to complaine where no help is. No, I know no hope resteth in my gronings. I have desired that it should bee so,

* *The English Faust-Book of 1592*, ed. Logeman, Université de Gand, 1900.

and God hath sayd AMEN to my misdoings: for now I must have
shame to comfort me in my calamities. . . .

An Oration of Faustus to the Students

Chapter 63

My trusty and welbeloved friends, the cause why I have invited
you into this place is this: Forasmuch as you have knowne me this
many yeares, in what maner of life I have lived, practising all manner
of conjurations and wicked exercises, the which I have obtayned
through the helpe of the divel, into whose divelish fellowship they
have brought me, the which use the like Arte and practise, urged by
the detestable provocation of my flesh, my stiffe necked and rebellious
will, with my filthy infernall thoughts, the which were ever before me,
pricking mee forward so earnestly, that I must perforce have the consent of the divell to ayde me in my devises. And to the end I might
the better bring my purpose to passe, to have the Divel's ayd and
furtherance, which I never have wanted in mine actions, I have
promised unto him at the ende and accomplishing of 24. yeares, both
body and soule, to doe therewith at his pleasure: and this day, this
dismall day those 24. yeares are fully expired, for night beginning my
houre-glasse is at an end, the direfull finishing whereof I carefully
expect: for out of all doubt this night hee will fetch mee, to whom
I have given my selfe in recompence of his service, both body and
soule, and twice confirmed writings with my proper blood. Now
have I called you my welbeloved Lords, friends, brethren, and fel-
lowes, before that fatall houre to take my friendly farewell, to the end
that my departing may not hereafter be hidden from you, beseeching
you herewith courteous, and loving Lords and brethren, not to take
in evil part any thing done by mee, but with friendly commendations
to salute all my friends and companions wheresoever: desiring both
you and them, if ever I have trespassed against your minds in any
thing, that you would all heartily forgive me: and as for those lewd
practises the which this full 24. yeares I have followed, you shall
hereafter finde them in writing: and I beseech you let this my lamentable ende to the residue of your lives bee a sufficient warning,
that you have God always before your eyes, praying unto him that
he would ever defend you from the temptation of the divell, and all
his false deceits, not falling altogether from God, as I wretched and
ungodly damned creature have done, having denied and defied
Baptisme, the Sacraments of Christ's body, God himselfe, all heavenly
powers, and earthly men, yea, I have denied such a God, that desireth

not to have one lost. Neither let the evill fellowship of wicked companions misselead you as it hath done me: visit earnestly and oft the
Church, warre and strive continually agaynst the Divell with a good
and stedfast beliefe on God, and Jesus Christ, and use your vocation in
holines. Lastly, to knitte up my troubled Oration, this is my friendly
request, that you would to rest, *and* let nothing trouble you: also if
you chance to heare any noise, or rumbling about the house, be not
therwith afrayd, for there shall no evil happen unto you: also I pray
you arise not out of your beds. But above all things I intreate you,
if you hereafter finde my dead carkasse, convay it unto the earth, for
I dye both a good and bad Christian; a good Christian for that I am
heartely sorry, and in my heart alwayes praye for mercy, that my soule
may be delivered: a bad Christian, for that I know the Divell will have
my bodie, and that would I willingly give him so that he would leave
my soule in quiet: wherefore I pray you that you would depart to
bed, and so I wish you a quiet night, which unto me notwithstanding
will be horrible and fearefull.

This Oration or declaration was made by Doctor FAUSTUS, *and* that
with a hearty and resolute minde, to the ende hee might not discomfort them: but the Students wondered greatly thereat, that he was
so blinded, for knavery, conjuration, and such like foolish things, to
give his body and soule unto the divell: for they loved him entirely,
and never suspected any such thing before he had opened his mind
to them: wherefore one of them sayd unto him; ah, friend FAUSTUS,
what have you done to conceale this matter so long from us, we
would by the help of good Divines, and the grace of God, have
brought you out of this net, and have torne you out of the bondage
and chaynes of Sathan, whereas nowe we feare it is too late, to the
utter ruine of your body and soule? Doctor FAUSTUS answered, I
durst never doo it, although I often minded, to settle my selfe unto
godly people, to desire counsell and helpe, as once mine olde neighbour counsailed mee, that I shoulde follow his learning, and leave all
my conjurations, yet when I was minded to amend, and to followe that
good man's counsell, then came the Divell and would have had me
away, as this night he is like to doe, and sayd so soone as I turned
againe to God, hee would dispatch mee altogether. Thus, even thus,
(good Gentlemen, and my dear friends) was I inthralled in that
Satanicall band, all good desires drowned, all pietie banished, all
purpose of amendment utterly exiled, by the tyranous threatnings of
my deadly enemy. But when the Students heard his words, they gave
him counsaile to doo naught else but call upon God, desiring him for
the love of his sweete Sonne Jesus Christ's sake, to have mercy upon
him, teaching him this forme of prayers. O God bee mercifull unto
me, poore and miserable sinner, and enter not into judgement with

me, for no flesh is able to stand before thee. Although, O Lord, I must leave my sinfull body unto the Divell, being by him deluded, yet thou in mercy mayest preserve my soule.

This they repeated unto him, yet it could take no holde, but even as CAINE he also said his sinnes were greater than God was able to forgive; for all his thought was on his writing, he meant he had made it too filthy in writing it with his owne blood. The Students *and* the other that were there, when they had prayed for him, they wept, and so went foorth, but FAUSTUS taryed in the hall: and when the Gentlemen were laid in bed, none of them could sleepe, for that they attended to heare if they might be privy of his ende. It happened between twelve and one a clock at midnight, there blewe a mighty storme of winde against the house, as though it would have blowne the foundation therof out of his place. Hereupon the Students began to feare, and got out of their beds, comforting one another, but they would not stirre out of the chamber: and the Host of the house ran out of doores, thinking the house would fall. The Students lay neere unto that hall wherein Doctor FAUSTUS lay, and they heard a mighty noyse and hissing, as if the hall had beene full of Snakes and Adders: with that the hall doore flew open wherein Doctor FAUSTUS was, then he began to crie for helpe, saying: murther, murther, but it came foorth with halfe a voyce hollowly: shortly after they heard him no more. But when it was day, the Students that had taken no rest that night, arose and went into the hall in the which they left Doctor FAUSTUS, where notwithstanding they found no FAUSTUS, but all the hall lay besprinckled with blood, his braines cleaving to the wall: for the Divel had beaten him from one wall against another, in one corner lay his eyes, in another his teeth, a pitifull and fearefull sight to beholde. Then began the Students to bewayle and weepe for him, and sought for his body in many places: lastly they came into the yarde where they found his bodie lying on the horse dung, most monstrously torne, and fearefull to beholde, for his head and all his joynts were dasht in peeces.

The forenamed Students and Masters that were at his death, have obtayned so much, that they buried him in the Village where he was so grievously tormented. After the which, they returned to WITTENBERG, and comming into the house of FAUSTUS, they found *the* servant of FAUSTUS very sad, unto whom they opened all the matter, who tooke it exceeding heavilie. There found they also this history of Doctor FAUSTUS noted, and of him written as is before declared, all save onely his ende, the which was after by the students thereto annexed: further, what his servant had noted thereof, was made in another booke. . . .

⤷ Plutarch's *Lives* in the superb Elizabethan translations of Sir Thomas North (1535–1601?) provided Shakespeare with some of the material for four of his plays: *Julius Caesar, Antony and Cleopatra, Timon of Athens,* and *Coriolanus.* The first-named of these was based to a great extent on the lives of Julius Caesar and Marcus Brutus. Many of the details of Shakespeare's plot were elaborations of incidents briefly described in North. An insight into Shakespeare's genius for dramatic invention can be gained by a comparison of the murder of Caesar as it appears in the narrative and in the drama; or by noting how Plutarch's brief description of the content of Antony's oration is given dramatic life by Shakespeare in a breath-taking display of cynical but effective rhetoric.

(Source for Shakespeare's *Julius Caesar*)

Plutarch

LIVES*

I

From the *Life of Julius Caesar*

*C*aesar also had Cassius in great jealously and suspected him much: whereupon he said on a time to his friends, "What will Cassius do, think ye? I like not his pale looks." Another time, when Caesar's friends complained unto him of Antonius and Dolabella, that they pretended some mischief towards him: he answered them again, "As for those fat men and smooth-combed heads," quoth he, "I never reckon of them: but these pale-visaged and carrion lean people, I fear them most": meaning Brutus and Cassius. Certainly, destiny may easier be foreseen than avoided: considering the strange and wonderful signs that were said to be seen before Caesar's death. For, touching the fires in the element and spirits running up and down in the night, and also the solitary birds to be seen at noon-days sitting in the great market place: are not all these signs perhaps worth the noting in such a wonderful chance as happened? But Strabo the Philosopher writeth that divers men were seen going up and down in fire: and furthermore, that there was a slave of the soldiers, that

---

* From the translation by Sir Thomas North, 1579.

did cast a marvellous burning flame out of his hand, insomuch as
they that saw it thought he had been burnt, but when the fire was out,
it was found he had no hurt. Caesar self also, doing sacrifice unto the
gods, found that one of the beasts which was sacrificed had no heart:
and that was a strange thing in nature, how a beast could live without a heart. Furthermore, there was a certain Soothsayer that had
given Caesar warning long time afore, to take heed of the day of the
Ides of March (which is the fifteenth of the month), for on that
day he should be in great danger. That day being come, Caesar going unto the Senate-house, and speaking merrily to the Soothsayer,
told him, "The Ides of March be come": "So be they," softly answered
the Soothsayer, "but yet are they not past." And the very day before, Caesar, supping with Marcus Lepidus, sealed certain letters,
as he was wont to do, at the board: so, talk falling out amongst them,
reasoning what death was best, he preventing their opinions cried out
aloud, "Death unlooked for." . . . The Senate having set upon the
top of Caesar's house, for an ornament and setting forth of the same, a
certain pinnacle, Calpurnia dreamed that she saw it broken down,
and that she thought she lamented and wept for it. Insomuch that,
Caesar rising in the morning, she prayed him if it were possible not
to go out of the doors that day, but to adjourn the session of the
Senate until another day. And if that he made no reckoning of her
dream, yet that he would search further of the Soothsayers by their
sacrifices, to know what should happen him that day. Thereby it
seemed that Caesar likewise did fear and suspect somewhat, because
his wife Calpurnia until that time was never given to any fear or
superstition: and then, for that he saw her so troubled in mind with
this dream she had. But much more afterwards, when the Soothsayers, having sacrificed many beasts one after another, told him that
none did like them: then he determined to send Antonius to adjourn
the session of the Senate. But in the meantime came Decius Brutus,
surnamed Albinus, in whom Caesar put such confidence, that in his
last will and testament he had appointed him to be his next heir, and
yet was of the conspiracy with Cassius and Brutus: he, fearing that if
Caesar did adjourn the session that day the conspiracy would out,
laughed the Soothsayers to scorn, and reproved Caesar, saying: that
he gave the Senate occasion to mislike with him, and that they might
think he mocked them, considering that by his commandment they
were assembled, and that they were ready willingly to grant him all
things, and to proclaim him king of all the provinces of the Empire of
Rome out of Italy, and that he should wear his Diadem in all other
places both by sea and land. And furthermore, that if any man should
tell them from him they should depart for the present time, and return again when Calpurnia should have better dreams: what would

his enemies and illwillers say, and how could they like of his friends' words? And who could persuade them otherwise, but that they would think his dominion a slavery unto them, and tyrannical in himself? "And yet, if it be so," said he, "that you utterly mislike of this day, it is better that you go yourself in person, and saluting the Senate to dismiss them till another time." Therewithal he took Caesar by the hand, and brought him out of his house. Caesar was not gone far from his house, but a bondman, a stranger, did what he could to speak with him: and, when he saw he was put back by the great press and multitude of people that followed him, he went straight unto his house, and put himself into Calpurnia's hands to be kept till Caesar came back again, telling her that he had great matters to impart unto him. And one Artemidorus also, born in the Isle of Gnidos, a Doctor of Rhetoric in the Greek tongue, who by means of his profession was very familiar with certain of Brutus' confederates, and therefore knew the most part of all their practices against Caesar, came and brought him a little bill written with his own hand, of all that he meant to tell him. He, marking how Caesar received all the supplications that were offered him, and that he gave them straight to his men that were about him, pressed nearer to him, and said: "Caesar, read this memorial to yourself, and that quickly, for they be matters of great weight, and touch you nearly." Caesar took it of him, but could never read it, though he many times attempted it, for the number of people that did salute him: but holding it still in his hand, keeping it to himself, went on withal into the Senate-house. . . . Now Antonius, that was a faithful friend to Caesar, and a valiant man besides of his hands, him Decius Brutus Albinus entertained out of the Senate house, having begun a long tale of set purpose. So, Caesar coming into the house, all the Senate stood up on their feet to do him honour. Then part of Brutus' company and confederates stood round about Caesar's chair, and part of them also came towards him, as though they made suit with Metellus Cimber, to call home his brother again from banishment: and thus, prosecuting still their suit, they followed Caesar, till he was set in his chair. Who denying their petitions, and being offended with them one after another, because the more they were denied, the more they pressed upon him, and were the earnester with him: Metellus at length, taking his gown with both his hands, pulled it over his neck, which was the sign given the confederates to set upon him. Then Casca behind him strake him in the neck with his sword: howbeit the wound was not great nor mortal, because, it seemed, the fear of such a devilish attempt did amaze him, and take his strength from him, that he killed him not at the first blow. But Caesar, turning straight unto him, caught hold of his sword, and held it hard: and they both cried out, Caesar in

Latin: "O vile traitor Casca, what doest thou?" And Casca in Greek
to his brother, "Brother, help me." At the beginning of this stir, they
that were present, not knowing of the conspiracy, were so amazed
with the horrible sight they saw, that they had no power to fly,
neither to help him, not so much as once to make any outcry. They
on th' other side that had conspired his death compassed him in on
every side with their swords drawn in their hands, that Caesar turned
him nowhere but he was stricken at by some, and still had naked
swords in his face, and was hacked and mangled among them, as a
wild beast taken of hunters. For it was agreed among them that
every man should give him a wound, because all their parts should
be in this murther: and then Brutus himself gave him one wound
about his privities. Men report also that Caesar did still defend himself against the rest, running every way with his body: but when he
saw Brutus with his sword drawn in his hand, then he pulled his
gown over his head, and made no more resistance, and was driven
either casually or purposedly by the counsel of the conspirators against
the base whereupon Pompey's image stood, which ran all of a gore-
blood till he was slain. Thus it seemed that the image took just
revenge of Pompey's enemy, being thrown down on the ground at his
feet, and yielding up his ghost there for the number of wounds he
had upon him. For it is reported that he had three-and-twenty wounds
upon his body. . . .

II

From the *Life of Marcus Brutus*

. . . When this was done, they came to talk of Caesar's will and
testament, and of his funerals and tomb. Then Antonius thinking good
his testament should be read openly, and also that his body should be
honourably buried, and not in hugger mugger, lest the people might
thereby take occasion to be worse offended if they did otherwise:
Cassius stoutly spake against it. But Brutus went with the motion,
and agreed unto it: wherein it seemeth he committed a second fault.
For the first fault he did was when he would not consent to his
fellow-conspirators, that Antonius should be slain: and therefore he
was justly accused, that thereby he had saved and strengthened a
strong and grievous enemy of their conspiracy. The second fault was
when he agreed that Caesar's funerals should be as Antonius would
have them: the which indeed marred all. For first of all, when Caesar's
testament was openly read among them, whereby it appeared that
he bequeathed unto every Citizen of Rome 75 Drachmas a man, and
that he left his gardens and arbours unto the people, which he had
on this side of the river of Tiber, in the place where now the temple

of Fortune is built: the people then loved him, and were marvellous sorry for him. Afterwards, when Caesar's body was brought into the market place, Antonius making his funeral oration in praise of the dead, according to the ancient custom of Rome, and perceiving that his words moved the common people to compassion: he framed his eloquence to make their hearts yearn the more, and, taking Caesar's gown all bloody in his hand, he laid it open to the sight of them all, shewing what a number of cuts and holes it had upon it. Therewithal the people fell presently into such a rage and mutiny, that there was no more order kept amongst the common people. For some of them cried out, "Kill the murtherers": others plucked up forms, tables, and stalls about the market place, as they had done before at the funerals of Clodius, and having laid them all on a heap together they set them on fire, and thereupon did put the body of Caesar, and burnt it in the midst of the most holy places. And furthermore, when the fire was thoroughly kindled, some here, some there, took burning fire-brands, and ran with them to the murtherers' houses that had killed him, to set them afire. Howbeit the conspirators, foreseeing the danger before, had wisely provided for themselves, and fled.

The ultimate source of Shakespeare's *Hamlet* is a fairly primitive medieval chronicle, the *Historica Danica,* written in Latin about 1210 by the Danish historian Saxo Grammaticus. The story of Hamlet (called Amleth in the original history) was first published in 1514 and was adapted into a French novella by François de Belleforest, who included his version in a book called *Histoire tragiques,* printed in 1576. Belleforest's story was in turn the subject of an English play, perhaps by Thomas Kyd, written some time before 1589. The play is lost, but we have every indication that it was a typical revenge play: bombastic, bloody, and in every way Senecan in tone.

Despite the fact that two other versions of the legend stand between Saxo Grammaticus and Shakespeare's subtle melodrama, the old Danish chronicle is of more than passing interest to us, if only because it is the crudest and earliest attempt to tell the story that was later to serve as the action for what many critics call the most fascinating play ever written.

(Source for Shakespeare's *Hamlet*)

Saxo Grammaticus

from the HISTORICA DANICA*

*H*e [Horwendil] had now passed three years in valiant deeds of war; and, in order to win higher rank in Rorik's favour, he assigned to him the best trophies and the pick of the plunder. His friendship with Rorik enabled him to woo and win in marriage his daughter Gerutha, who bore him a son Amleth.

Such great good fortune stung Feng with jealousy, so that he resolved treacherously to waylay his brother, thus showing that goodness is not safe even from those of a man's own house. And behold, when a chance came to murder him, his bloody hand sated the deadly passion of his soul. Then he took the wife of the brother he had butchered, capping unnatural murder with incest. For whoso yields to one iniquity, speedily falls an easier victim to the next, the first being an incentive to the second. Also the man veiled the monstrosity of his deed with such hardihood of cunning, that he made up a mock pretence of goodwill to excuse his crime, and glossed over fratricide with a show of righteousness. Gerutha, said he, though so gentle that she would do no man the slightest hurt, had been visited with her husband's extremest hate; and it was all to save her that he had slain his brother; for he thought it shameful that a lady so meek and unrancorous should suffer the heavy disdain of her husband. Nor did his smooth words fail in their intent; for at courts, where fools are sometimes favoured and backbiters preferred, a lie lacks not credit. Nor did Feng keep from shameful embraces the hands that had slain a brother; pursuing with equal guilt both of his wicked and impious deeds.

Amleth beheld all this, but feared lest too shrewd a behaviour might

* From *The Sources of Hamlet*; with an essay on the legend, by Sir Israel Gollancz (Humphrey Milford, Oxford University Press, 1926), pp. 101–103, 113–117; translated by Oliver Elton.

make his uncle suspect him. So he chose to feign dulness, and pretend an utter lack of wits. This cunning course not only concealed his intelligence but ensured his safety. Every day he remained in his mother's house utterly listless and unclean, flinging himself on the ground, and bespattering his person with foul and filthy dirt. His discoloured face and visage smutched with slime denoted foolish and grotesque madness. All he said was of a piece with these follies; all he did savoured of utter lethargy. In a word, you would not have thought him a man at all, but some absurd abortion due to a mad fit of destiny.

. . . .

. . . Feng was purposely to absent himself, pretending affairs of great import. Amleth should be closeted alone with his mother in her chamber; but a man should first be commissioned to place himself in a concealed part of the room and listen heedfully to what they talked about. For if the son had any wits at all he would not hesitate to speak out in the hearing of his mother, or fear to trust himself to the fidelity of her who bore him. The speaker, loth to seem readier to devise than to carry out the plot, zealously proffered himself as the agent of the eavesdropping. Feng rejoiced at the scheme, and departed on pretence of a long journey. Now he who had given this counsel repaired privily to the room where Amleth was shut up with his mother, and lay down skulking in the straw. But Amleth had his antidote for the treachery. Afraid of being overheard by some eavesdropper, he at first resorted to his usual imbecile ways, and crowed like a noisy cock, beating his arms together to mimic the flapping of wings. Then he mounted the straw and began to swing his body and jump again and again, wishing to try if aught lurked there in hiding. Feeling a lump beneath his feet, he drove his sword into the spot, and impaled him who lay hid. Then he dragged him from his concealment and slew him. Then, cutting his body into morsels, he seethed it in boiling water, and flung it through the mouth of an open sewer for the swine to eat, bestrewing the stinking mire with his hapless limbs. Having in this wise eluded the snare, he went back to the room. Then his mother set up a great wailing, and began to lament her son's folly to his face; but he said: "Most infamous of women! dost thou seek with such lying lamentations to hide thy most heavy guilt? Wantoning like a harlot, thou hast entered a wicked and abominable state of wedlock, embracing with incestuous bosom thy husband's slayer, and wheedling with filthy lures of blandishment him who had slain the father of thy son. This, forsooth, is the way that the mares couple with the vanquishers of their mates; for brute beasts are naturally incited to pair indiscriminately; and it would seem that thou, like them, hast clean forgot thy first husband. As for me, not idly do I wear the mask of folly; for I doubt not that he who destroyed his brother will riot as ruthlessly in the blood of his kindred. Therefore it is better to choose the garb of dulness than that of sense, and to borrow some protection from a show of utter frenzy. Yet the passion to avenge my father still burns in my heart; but I am watching the chances, I await the fitting hour. There is a place for all things; against so merciless and dark a spirit must be used the deeper devices of the mind. And thou, who hadst been better employed in lamenting thine own disgrace, know it is superfluity to bewail my witlessness; thou shouldst weep for the blemish in thine own mind, not for that in another's. On the rest see thou keep silence." With such reproaches he rent the heart of his mother and redeemed her to walk in the ways of virtue; teaching her to set the fires of the past above the seductions of the present. . . .

There is no question that Shakespeare's most useful source of plot incident was the second edition of the *Chronicles* of Raphael Holinshed (d. 1581?), revised and edited by John Hooker and published in 1587. Shakespeare went to Holinshed's extensive history of Britain for material which he used in at least twelve plays, including all the "historical" dramas, except perhaps *King John;* one comedy, *Cymbeline;* and two of his major tragedies, *Macbeth* and *King Lear.*

In the history plays, Shakespeare attempted, with some notable exceptions, to stay fairly close to the stories as Holinshed had recorded them. ·In preparing *Macbeth,* however, and working with materials which even in Holinshed are based largely on legend, he felt free to deviate from his source whenever he could make the plot more stageworthy. Events are freely telescoped and characters combined. Indeed, many of the details of Duncan's murder are drawn, not from Holinshed's story of Macbeth, but from his account of King Duff and Donwald, two other shadowy figures from Scotland's remote past.

By comparing relevant passages from the *Chronicles* with Shakespeare's finished tragedy, one can gain considerable insight into the methods of England's greatest dramatic genius.

(Source for Shakespeare's *Macbeth*)

Raphael Holinshed
from CHRONICLES*

I

From the account of Macbeth

After Malcolm succeeded his nephew Duncan the son of his daughter Beatrice: for Malcolm had two daughters, the one which was this Beatrice, being given in marriage unto one Abbanath Crinen, a man of great nobility, and thane of the Iles and west parts of Scotland, bare of that marriage the foresaid Duncan; the other called Doada, was married unto Sinell the thane of Glammis, by whom she had issue one Macbeth a valiant gentleman, and one that if he had not been somewhat cruel of nature, might have been thought most worthy the government of a realm. On the other part, Duncan was so soft and gentle of nature, that the people wished the inclinations and manners of these two cousins to have been so tempered and interchangeably bestowed betwixt them, that where the one had too much of clemency, and the other of cruelty, the mean virtue betwixt these two extremities might have reigned by indifferent partition in them both, so should Duncan have proved a worthy king, and Macbeth an excellent captain. The beginning of Duncan's reign was very quiet and peaceable, without any notable trouble; but after it was perceived how negligent he was in punishing offenders, many misruled persons took occasion thereof to trouble the peace and quiet state of the commonwealth, by seditious commotions which first had their beginnings in this wise.

Banquho the thane of Lochquhaber, of whom the house of the Stewards [*sic*] is descended, the which by order of linage hath now for a long time enjoyed the crown of Scotland, even till these our days . . . gathered the finances due to the king. . . .

Then doubting not but for such contemptuous demeanor against the king's regal authority, they should be invaded with all the power the king could make, Macdonwald one of great estimation among them, making first a confederacy with his nearest friends and kinsmen, took

---

* From *Holinshed's Chronicles* edited by Allardyce and Josephine Nicoll. Everyman's Library Edition. Reprinted by permission of E .P. Dutton & Co., Inc., and J. M. Dent & Sons Ltd.

upon him to be chief captain of all such rebels as would stand against
the king. . . . He used also such subtle persuasions and forged allure-
ments, that in a small time he had gotten together a mighty power of
men. . . .

At length Macbeth speaking much against the king's softness, and
overmuch slackness in punishing offenders, . . . he promised notwithstanding, if the charge were committed unto him and unto Banquho,
so to order the matter, that the rebels should be shortly vanquished &
quite put down, and that not so much as one of them should be found
to make resistance within the country.

And even so it came to pass: for being sent forth with a new power,
at his entering into Lochquhaber, the fame of his coming put the
enemies in such fear, that a great number of them stole secretly away
from their captain Macdonwald, who nevertheless enforced thereto,
gave battle unto Macbeth, with the residue which remained with
him: but being overcome, and fleeing for refuge into a castle (within
the which his wife & children were enclosed) at length when he saw
how he could neither defend the hold any longer against his enemies,
nor yet upon surrender be suffered to depart with life saved, he first
slew his wife and children, and lastly himself, lest if he had yielded
simply, he should have been executed in most cruel wise for an example to others. . . . Thus was justice and law restored again to the
old accustomed course, by the diligent means of Macbeth. . . .

Shortly after happened a strange and uncouth wonder, which afterward was the cause of much trouble in the realm of Scotland, as ye
shall after hear. It fortuned as Macbeth and Banquho journeyed
towards Fores, where the king then lay, they went sporting by the
way together without other company, save only themselves, passing
through the woods and fields, when suddenly in the midst of a land,
there met them three women in strange and wild apparel, resembling
creatures of elder world, whom when they attentively beheld, won-
dering much at the sight, the first of them spoke and said: "All hail,
Macbeth, thane of Glammis!" (for he had lately entered into that
dignity and office by the death of his father Sinell). The second of
them said: "Hail, Macbeth, thane of Cawdor!" But the third said,
"All hail, Macbeth, that hereafter shalt be king of Scotland!"

Then Banquho: "What manner of women" (saith he) "are you,
that seem so little favorable unto me, whereas to my fellow here,
besides high offices, ye assign also the kingdom, appointing forth
nothing for me at all?" "Yes" (saith the first of them), "we promise
greater benefits unto thee, than unto him, for he shall reign in deed,
but with an unlucky end: neither shall he leave any issue behind
him to succeed in his place, where contrarily thou in deed shalt not
reign at all, but of thee those shall be born which shall govern the

Scottish kingdoms by long order of continual descent." Herewith the foresaid women vanished immediately out of their sight. This was reputed at the first but some vain fantastical illusion by Macbeth and Banquho, insomuch that Banquho would call Macbeth in jest, king of Scotland; and Macbeth again would call him in sport likewise, the father of many kings. But afterwards the common opinion was, that these women were either the weird sisters, that is (as ye would say) the goddesses of destiny, or else some nymphs or fairies, indued with knowledge of prophesy by their necromantical science, because every thing came to pass as they had spoken. For shortly after, the thane of Cawdor being condemned at Fores of treason against the king committed; his lands, livings, and offices were given of the king's liberality to Macbeth.

The same night after, at supper, Banquho jested with him and said: "Now Macbeth thou hast obtained those things which the two former sisters prophesied, there remaineth only for thee to purchase that which the third said should come to pass." Whereupon Macbeth revolving the thing in his mind, began even then to devise how he might attain to the kingdom: but yet he thought with himself that he must tarry a time, which should advance him thereto (by the divine providence) as it had come to pass in his former preferment. But shortly after it chanced that king Duncan, having two sons by his wife which was the daughter of Siward earl of Northumberland, he made the elder of them, called Malcolm, prince of Cumberland, as it were thereby to appoint him his successor in the kingdom, immediately after his decease. Macbeth sore troubled herewith, for that he saw by this means his hope sore hindered (where, by the old laws of the realm, the ordinance was, that if he that should succeed were not of able age to take the charge upon himself, he that was next of blood unto him should be admitted) he began to take counsel how he might usurp the kingdom by force, having a just quarrel so to do (as he took the matter) for that Duncan did what in him lay to defraud him of all manner of title and claim, which he might in time to come, pretend unto the crown.

The words of the three sisters also (of whom before ye have heard) greatly encouraged him hereunto, but specially his wife lay sore upon him to attempt the thing, as she that was very ambitious, burning in unquenchable desire to bear the name of a queen. At length therefore, communicating his purposed intent with his trusty friends, amongst whom Banquho was the chiefest, upon confidence of their promised aid, he slew the king at Enuerns, or (as some say) at Botgosuane, in the sixth year of his reign. Then having a company about him of such as he had made privy to his enterprise, he caused himself to be proclaimed king, and forthwith went unto Scone, where

(by common consent) he received the investure of the kingdom
according to the accustomed manner. The body of Duncan was first
conveyed unto Elgin, & there buried in kingly wise; but afterwards
it was removed and conveyed unto Colmekill. . . .

II

From the account of Donwald

[Donwald] conceived such an inward malice towards the king
(though he showed it not outwardly at the first) that the same continued still boiling in his stomach, and ceased not, till through setting
on of his wife, and in revenge of such unthankfulness, he found
means to murder the king within the foresaid castle of Fores where
he used to sojourn. For the king being in that country, was accustomed to lie most commonly within the same castle having a special
trust in Donwald, as a man whom he never suspected.

But Donwald, not forgetting the reproach which his linage had
sustained by the execution of those his kinsmen, whom the king for a
spectacle to the people had caused to be hanged, could not but show
manifest tokens of great grief at home amongst his family: which his
wife perceiving, ceased not to travel with him, till she understood
what the cause was of his displeasure. Which at length when she
had learned by his own relation, she as one that bare no less malice in
her heart towards the king, for the like cause on her behalf, than her
husband did for his friends, counselled him (since the king oftentimes
used to lodge in his house without any guard about him, other than
the garrison of the castle, which was wholly at his commandment) to
make him away, and showed him the means whereby he might
soonest accomplish it.

Donwald thus being the more kindled in wrath by the words of
his wife, determined to follow her advice in the execution of so
heinous an act. Whereupon devising with himself for a while, which
way he might best accomplish his cursed intent, at length got opportunity, and sped his purpose as followeth. It chanced that the king
upon the day before he purposed to depart forth of the castle, was
long in his oratory at his prayers, and there continued till it was late
in the night. At the last, coming forth, he called such afore him as
had faithfully served him in pursuit and apprehension of the rebels,
and giving them hearty thanks, he bestowed sundry honorable gifts
amongst them, of the which number Donwald was one, as he that had
been ever accounted a most faithful servant to the king.

At length, having talked with them a long time, he got him into
his privy chamber, only with two of his chamberlains, who having

brought him to bed, came forth again, and then fell to banqueting with Donwald and his wife, who had prepared diverse delicate dishes, and sundry sorts of drinks for their rear supper or collation, whereat they sat up so long, till they had charged their stomachs with such full gorges, that their heads were no sooner got to the pillow, but asleep they were so fast, that a man might have removed the chamber over them, sooner than to have awaked them out of their drunken sleep.

Then Donwald, tho he abhorred the act greatly in heart, yet through instigation of his wife he called four of his servants unto him (whom he had made privy to his wicked intent before, and framed to his purpose with large gifts) and now declaring unto them, after what sort they should work the feat, they gladly obeyed his instructions, & speedily going about the murder, they enter the chamber (in which the king lay) a little before the cocks crow, where they secretly cut his throat as he lay sleeping, without any buskling at all. . . .

Donwald, about the time that the murder was in doing, got him amongst them that kept the watch, and so continued in company with them all the residue of the night. But in the morning when the noise was raised in the king's chamber how the king was slain, his body conveyed away, and the bed all berayed with blood; he with the watch ran thither, as though he had known nothing of the matter, and breaking into the chamber, and finding cakes of blood in the bed, and on the floor about the sides of it, he forthwith slew the chamberlains, as guilty of that heinous murder, and then like a mad man running to and fro, he ransacked every corner within the castle, as though it had been to have seen if he might have found either the body, or any of the murderers hid in any privy place: but at length coming to the postern gate, and finding it open, he burdened the chamberlains, whom he had slain, with all the fault, they having the keys of the gates committed to their keeping all the night, and therefore it could not be otherwise (said he) but that they were of counsel in committing of that most detestable murder. . . .

III

More from the account of Macbeth

Malcolm Cammore and Donalbain the sons of king Duncan, for fear of their lives (which they might well know that Macbeth would seek to bring to end for his more sure confirmation in the estate) fled into Cumberland, where Malcolm remained, till time that saint Edward the son of Ethelred recovered the dominion of England from the Danish power, the which Edward received Malcolm by way of most friendly entertainment: but Donald passed over into Ireland, where he was tenderly cherished by the king of that land. . . .

The prick of conscience (as it chanceth ever in tyrants, and such as attain to any estate by unrighteous means) caused him ever to fear, lest he should be served to the same cup, as he had ministered to his predecessor. The words also of the three weird sisters would not out of his mind, which as they promised him the kingdom, so likewise did they promise it at the same time unto the posterity of Banquho. He willed therefore the same Banquho, with his son named Fleance, to come to a supper that he had prepared for them; which was indeed, as he had devised, present death at the hands of certain murderers, whom he hired to execute that deed; appointing them to meet with the same Banquho and his son without the palace, as they returned to their lodgings, and there to slay them, so that he would not have his house slandered, but that in time to come he might clear himself, if anything were laid to his charge upon any suspicion that might arise.

It chanced yet, by the benefit of the dark night, that, though the father were slain, the son yet, by the help of almighty God reserving him to better fortune, escaped that danger; and afterwards having some inkling (by the admonition of some friends which he had in the court) how his life was sought no less than his father's, who was slain not by chance medley (as by the handling of the matter Macbeth would have had it to appear) but even upon a prepensed device: whereupon to avoid further peril he fled into Wales. . . .

But to return unto Macbeth, in continuing the history, and to begin where I left, ye shall understand that, after the contrived slaughter of Banquho, nothing prospered with the foresaid Macbeth: for in manner every man began to doubt his own life, and durst not appear in the king's presence; and even as there were many that stood in fear of him, so likewise stood he in fear of many, in such sort that he began to make those away by one surmised cavilation or other, whom he thought most able to work him any displeasure.

At length he found such sweetness by putting his nobles thus to death, that his earnest thirst after blood in this behalf might in no wise be satisfied: for ye must consider he won double profit (as he thought) hereby: for first they were rid out of the way whom he feared, and then again his coffers were enriched by their goods which were forfeited to his use, whereby he might better maintain a guard of armed men about him to defend his person for injury of them whom he had in any suspicion. Further, to the end he might the more cruelly oppress his subjects with all tyrantlike wrongs, he builded a strong castle on the top of a high hill called Dunsinane, situated in Gowrie, ten miles from Perth, on such a proud height, that, standing there aloft, a man might behold well near all the countries of Angus, Fife, Stermond, and Ernedale, as it were lying underneath him. This castle, then, being founded on the top of that high hill, put the realm to great charges before it was finished, for all the stuff necessary to the building could not be brought up without much toil and business. But Macbeth, being once determined to have the work go forward, caused the thanes of each shire within the realm, to come and help towards that building, each man his course about.

At the last, when the turn fell unto Macduff, thane of Fife, to build his part, he sent workmen with all needful provision, and commanded them to show such diligence in every behalf, that no occasion might be given for the king to find fault with him, in that he came not himself as other had done, which he refused to do, for doubt lest the king, bearing him (as he partly understood) no great good will, would lay violent hands upon him, as he had done upon diverse other. Shortly after, Macbeth coming to behold how the work went forward, and because he found not Macduff there, he was sore offended, and said: "I perceive this man will never obey my commandments, till he be ridden with a snaffle; but I shall provide well enough for him."

Neither could he afterwards abide to look upon the said Macduff, either for that he though his puissance over great; either else for that he had learned of certain wizards, in whose words he put great confidence (for that the prophecy had happened so right, which the three fairies or weird sisters had declared unto him), how that he ought to take heed of Macduff, who in time to come should seek to destroy him.

And surely hereupon had he put Macduff to death, but that a certain witch, whom he had in great trust, had told that he should never be slain with man born of any woman, nor vanquished till the wood of Birnam came to the castle of Dunsinane. By this prophecy Macbeth put all fear out of his heart, supposing he might do what he would, without any fear to be punished for the same, for by the one prophecy he believed it was impossible for any man to vanquish him, and by the other impossible to slay him. This vain hope caused him to do many outrageous things, to the grievous oppression of his subjects. At length Macduff, to avoid peril of life, purposed with himself to pass into England, to procure Malcolm Cammore to claim the crown of Scotland. But this was not so secretly devised by Macduff, but that Macbeth had knowledge given him thereof: for kings (as is said) have sharp sight like unto Lynx, and long ears like unto Midas. For Macbeth had, in every nobleman's house, one sly fellow or other in fee with him, to reveal all that was said or done within the same, by which slight he oppressed the most part of the nobles of his realm.

Immediately then, being advertised whereabout Macduff went, he came hastily with a great power into Fife, and forwith besieged the castle where Macduff dwelled, trusting to have found him therein. They that kept the house, without any resistance opened the gates, and suffered him to enter, mistrusting none evil. But nevertheless Macbeth most cruelly caused the wife and children of Macduff, with all other whom he found in that castle, to be slain. Also he confiscated the goods of Macduff, proclaimed him traitor, and confined him out of all the parts of his realm; but Macduff was already escaped out of danger, and gotten into England unto Malcolm Cammore, to try what purchase he might make by means of his support, to revenge the slaughter so cruelly executed on his wife, his children, and other friends.

At his coming unto Malcolm, he declared into what great misery the estate of Scotland was brought, by the detestable cruelties exercised by the tyrant Macbeth, having committed many horrible slaughters and murders, both as well of the nobles as commons; for the which he was hated right mortally of all his liege people, desiring nothing more than to be delivered of that intolerable and most heavy yoke of thralldom, which they sustained at such a caitiff's hands.

Malcolm, hearing Macduff's words, which he uttered in very lamentable sort, for mere compassion and very ruth that pierced his sorrowful heart, bewailing the miserable state of his country, he fetched a deep sigh; which Macduff perceiving, began to fall most earnestly in hand with him, to enterprise the delivering of the Scottish people out of the hands of so cruel and bloody a tyrant, as Macbeth by too many plain experiments did show himself to be: which was an easy matter for him to bring to pass, considering not only the· good title he had, but also the earnest desire of the people to have some occasion ministered, whereby they might be revenged of those notable injuries, which they daily sustained by the outrageous cruelty of Macbeth's misgovernance. Though Malcolm was very sorrowful for the oppression of his countrymen the Scots, in manner as Macduff had declared; yet doubting whether he were come as one that meant unfeignedly as he spoke, or else as sent from Macbeth to betray him, he thought to have some further trial, and thereupon, dissembling his mind at the first, he answered as followeth:

"I am truly sorry for the misery chanced to my country of Scotland, but though I have never so great affection to relieve the same, yet, by reason of certain incurable vices, which reign in me, I am nothing meet thereto. First, such immoderate lust and voluptuous sensuality (the abominable fountain of all vices) followeth me, that, if I were made king of Scots, I should seek to deflower your maids and matrons, in such wise that mine intemperancy should be more importable unto you, than the bloody tyranny of Macbeth now is." Hereunto Macduff answered: "This surely is a very evil fault, for many noble princes and kings have lost both lives and kingdoms for the same; nevertheless there are women enough in Scotland, and therefore follow my counsel. Make thyself king, and I shall convey the matter so wisely, that thou shalt be so satisfied at thy pleasure, in such secret wise that no man shall be aware thereof."

Then said Malcolm, "I am also the most avaricious creature on the earth, so that, if I were king, I should seek so many ways to get lands and goods, that I would slay the most part of all the nobles of Scotland by surmised accusations, to the end I might enjoy their lands, goods, and possession. . . . Therefore" saith Malcolm, "suffer me to remain where I am, lest, if I attain to the regiment of your realm, mine unquenchable avarice may prove such that ye would think the displeasures, which now grieve you, should seem easy in respect of the unmeasurable outrage, which might ensue through my coming amongst you."

Macduff to this made answer, how it was a far worse fault than the other: "for avarice is the root of all mischief, and for that crime the most part of our kings have been slain and brought to their final end. Yet notwithstanding follow my counsel, and take upon thee the crown. There is gold and riches enough in Scotland to satisfy thy greedy desire." Then said Malcolm again, "I am furthermore inclined to dissimilation, telling of leasings, and all other kinds of deceit, so that I naturally rejoice in nothing so much, as to betray and deceive such as put any trust or confidence in my words. Then since there is nothing that more becometh a prince than constancy, verity, truth, and justice, with the other laudable fellowship of those fair and noble virtues which are comprehended only in soothfastness, and that lying utterly overthroweth the same; you see how unable I am to govern any province or region: and therefore, since you have remedies to cloak and hide all the rest of my other vices, I pray you find shift to cloak this vice amongst the residue."

Then said Macduff: "This yet is the worst of all, and there I leave thee, and therefore say: Oh ye unhappy and miserable Scotsmen, which are thus scourged with so many and sundry calamities, each one above other! Ye have one cursed and wicked tyrant that now reigneth over you, without any right or title, oppressing you with his most bloody cruelty. This other, that hath the right to the crown, is so replete with the inconstant behavior and manifest vices of Englishmen, that he is nothing worthy to enjoy it; for by his own confession he is not only avaricious, and given to unsatiable lust, but so false a traitor withal, that no trust is to be had unto any word he speaketh. Adieu, Scotland, for now I account myself a banished man forever, without comfort or consolation": and with those words the brackish tears trickled down his cheeks very abundantly.

At the last when he was ready to depart, Malcolm took him by the sleeve, and said: "Be of good comfort, Macduff, for I have none of these vices before remembered, but have jested with thee in this manner, only to prove thy mind; for diverse times heretofore hath Macbeth sought by this manner of means to bring me into his hands, but the more slow I have showed myself to condescend to thy motion and request, the more diligence shall I use in accomplishing the same." Incontinently hereupon they embraced each other, and, promising to be faithful the one to the other, they fell in consultation how they might provide for all their business, to bring the same to good effect.

Soon after, Macduff, repairing to the borders of Scotland, addressed his letters with secret dispatch unto the nobles of the realm, declaring how Malcolm was confederate with him, to come hastily into Scotland to claim the crown, and therefore he required them, since he was right inheritor thereto, to assist him with their powers to recover the same out of the hands of the wrongful usurper.

In the meantime, Malcolm purchased such favor at King Edward's hands, that *old Siward* earl of Northumberland was appointed *with ten thousand men* to go with him into Scotland, to support him in this enterprise, for recovery of his right. After these news were spread abroad in Scotland, the nobles drew into two several factions, the one taking part with Macbeth, and the other with Malcolm. Hereupon ensued oftentimes sundry bickerings, & diverse light skirmishes; for those that were of Malcolm's side would not jeopard to join with their enemies in a pight field, till his coming out of England to their support. But after that Macbeth perceived his enemies' power to increase, by such aid as came to them forth of England with his adversary Malcolm, he recoiled back into Fife, there purposing to abide in camp fortified, at the castle of Dunsinane, and to fight with his enemies, if they meant to pursue him; howbeit some of his friends advised him, that it should be best for him, either to make some agreement with Malcolm, or else to flee with all speed into the Iles, and to take his treasure with him, to the end he might wage sundry great princes of the realm to take his part, & retain strangers, in whom he might better trust than in his own subjects, which stole daily from him; but he had such confidence in his prophecies, that he believed he should never be vanquished, till Birnam wood were brought to Dunsinane; nor yet to be slain with any man, that should be or was born of any woman.

Malcolm, following hastily after Macbeth, came the night before the battle unto Birnam wood; and, when his army had rested a while there to refresh them, he commanded every man to get a bough of some tree or other of that wood in his hand, as big as he might bear, and to march forth therewith in such wise, that on the next morrow they might come closely and without sight in this manner within view of his enemies. On the morrow when Macbeth beheld them coming in this sort, he first marveled what the matter meant, but in the end remembered himself that the prophecy which he had heard long before that time, of the coming of Birnam wood to Dunsinane castle, was likely to be now fulfilled. Nevertheless, he brought his men in order of battle, and exhorted them to do valiantly; howbeit his enemies had scarcely cast from them their boughs, when Macbeth perceiving their numbers, betook him straight to flight; whom Macduff with great hatred even till he came unto Lunfannaine where Macbeth perceiving that Macduff was hard at his back, leapt beside his horse, saying: "Thou traitor, what meaneth it that thou shouldst thus in vain follow me that am not appointed to be slain by any creature that is born of a woman? come on therefore, and receive thy reward which thou hast deserved for thy pains," and therewithal he lifted up his sword, thinking to have slain him.

But Macduff, quickly avoiding from his horse, there he came at him, answered (with his naked sword in his hand) saying: "It is true, Macbeth, and now shall thine insatiable cruelty have an end, for I am even he that thy wizards have told thee of; who was never born of my mother, but ripped out of her womb:" therewithal he stepped unto him, and slew him in the place. Then cutting his head from his shoulders, he set it upon a pole, and brought it unto Malcolm. This was the end of Macbeth, after he had reigned 17 years over the Scotsmen. . . .

Selective Bibliography

A N D

Topics for Investigation

SELECTIVE BIBLIOGRAPHY
and
TOPICS FOR INVESTIGATION

The bibliographies, as noted, are "selective" rather than comprehensive. For a more extensive bibliography, the student is referred to *The Oxford Companion to the Theatre*, the *Enciclopedia della Spettacolo*, John Gassner's *Masters of the Drama* (pages 805–840 in the revised third edition, 1954), and Blanche Baker's *Dramatic Bibliography*. It will also be useful to consult some of the many general histories of the theatre and drama: for example, Allardyce Nicoll's *World Drama* and *The Development of the Theatre* and John Gassner's *Masters of the Drama*. Karl Mantzius' pioneer work, *A History of Theatrical Art in Ancient and Modern Times,* is available in translation and, although unreliable in many particulars, remains for the most part a useful source of information. The literature of the theatre has, of course, been extensively anthologized. John Gassner's *A Treasury of the Theatre*, Haskell Block and Robert Shedd's *Masters of Modern Drama,* and Barrett Clark's *World Drama* are representative of those collections which are parallel in scope to *Theatre and Drama in the Making* in whole or in substantial part. For materials on stage production, Professor Alois M. Nagler's *Source Book in Theatrical History* (N.Y., 1952) is a thoughtful and scholarly book which has become an important item in the library of every serious student of the theatre. Likewise valuable are three recent collections of source material: *Actors on Acting, Directors on Directing,* and *Playwrights on Playwriting*, edited by Toby Cole (the first two in collaboration with Helen Krich Chinoy). Among the many useful anthologies of dramatic criticism, Barrett H. Clark's *European Theories of the Drama* (the amplified Crown Publishers edition, which contains an American supplement) is the most comprehensive. For students with a particular interest in the American theatre, an excellent source book is Barnard Hewitt's *Theatre U.S.A.: 1668–1957* (N.Y., 1959). A comprehensive summary of stage history in English which covers developments in the Orient as well as the Occident is *A History of the Theatre* by George Freedley and John A. Reeves ("Newly Revised with a Supplementary Section by George Freedley," N.Y., 1955).

Classic Theatre: Greece and Rome

SELECTIVE BIBLIOGRAPHY

Allen, James Turney. *Stage Antiquities of the Greeks and Romans and Their Influence*. N.Y., 1927.

Alton, J.F.D. *Horace and His Age*. London, 1917.

Arnott, Peter. *The Ancient Greek and Roman Theatre*. N.Y., 1971.

Barnett, L.D. *Greek Drama*. London, 1900.

Beare, William. *The Roman Stage*. London, 1972.

Bieber, Margarete. *The History of the Greek and Roman Theatre*. Princeton, 1961.

Bowra, C.M. *Sophoclean Tragedy*. Oxford, 1944.

Butcher, S.H. *Aristotle's Theory of Poetry and Fine Art*. London, 1895; 4th ed., 1911.

Capps, E. *Vitruvius and the Greek Stage*. Chicago, 1893.

Coleman-Norton, P.R. "Review of Old Age in Roman Drama," *Classical Bulletin*, XXIII (1947), 33-40.

Cooper, Lane. *Aristotle on the Art of Poetry*. N.Y., 1913.

Cornford, Francis Macdonald. *The Origin of Attic Comedy*. London, 1914.

Cunliffe, John W. *The Influence of Seneca on Elizabethan Tragedy*. London & N.Y., 1893.

Dover, K.J. *Aristophanic Comedy*. London, 1972.

Duckworth, George E. *The Nature of Roman Comedy*. Princeton & London, 1952.

_____."The Unnamed Characters in the Plays of Plautus," *Classical Philology*, XXXIII (1938), 267-82.

Duff, J. Wright. *A Literary History of Rome*. London, 1928.

Edmonds, John Maxwell. *The Fragments of Attic Comedy after Meineke, Bergk and Kock*. Leiden, 1957.

Eliot, T.S. "Seneca in Elizabethan Translation," (1927) in *Selected Essays 1917-1932*. N.Y., 1932.

Else, Gerald. *Aristotle's Poetics: The Argument*. Cambridge, Mass., 1957.

Forehand, Walter. *Terence*. Boston, 1985.

Fowler, W.W. *The Roman Festivals of the Period of the Republic*. London, 1899.

Gilbert, Allan H. "Aristotle's Four Species of Tragedy (Poetics 18) and Their Importance for Dramatic Criticism," *American Journal of Philology*, LXVIII (October 1947), 363-81.

Godolphin, F.R.B. *The Chronology of Greek Middle Comedy*. Ann Arbor, 1939.

Greenwood, L.H.G. *Aspects of Euripidean Tragedy*. London, 1953.

Grube, G.M.A. *The Drama of Euripides*. London, 1941.

Haigh, Arthur Elam. *The Attic Theatre: A Description of the Stage and Theatre of the Athenians, and of the Dramatic Performances at Athens.* Oxford, 1889.
_____. *The Tragic Drama of the Greeks.* Oxford, 1896.
Hamilton, Edith. *The Greek Way.* N.Y., 1930.
_____. *The Roman Way.* N.Y., 1930.
Kitto, H.D.F. *Greek Tragedy, a Literary Study.* London, 1961.
Korfmacher, W.C. "Some Comical Scenes from Plautus and Terence," *The Classical Journal,* XLVI (January 1951), 165-70.
Lever, Katharine. *The Art of Greek Comedy.* London, 1956.
Lord, Louis E. *Aristophanes: His Plays and His Influence.* Boston, 1925.
Mahr, August C. *The Origin of the Greek Tragic Form, a Study in the Early Theatre in Attica.* N.Y., 1938.
Murray, Gilbert. *Aeschylus, the Creator of Tragedy.* Oxford, 1940.
_____. *Aristophanes, a Study.* Oxford, 1938.
_____. *Euripides and His Age.* N.Y., 1913.
Norwood, Gilbert. *The Art of Terence.* Oxford, 1923.
_____. *Greek Comedy.* N.Y. & London, 1931.
_____. *Greek Tragedy.* London & N.Y., 1920.
Pack, Roger O. "On Guilt and Error in Senecan Tragedy," *Transactions of the American Philological Association,* LXXI (1940), 360-71.
Pickard-Cambridge, A.W. *Dithyramb, Tragedy and Comedy.* Oxford, 1927.
_____. *The Dramatic Festivals of Athens.* Oxford, 1968.
_____. *The Theatre of Dionysus in Athens.* Oxford, 1946.
Post, Levi Arnold. *From Homer to Menander. Forces in Greek Poetic Fiction.* Berkeley, 1951.
Pratt, N.T. *Dramatic Suspense in Seneca and His Greek Precursors.* Princeton, 1939.
Segal, Erich. *Roman Laughter: The Comedy of Plautus.* Harvard, 1968.
Shisler, Famee Lorene. "The Use of Stage Business to Portray Emotion in Greek Tragedy," *American Journal of Philology,* LXVI, 4 (1945), 377-97.
Sutton, Dana Ferrin. *Seneca on the Stage.* Leiden, 1986.
Symonds, John Addington. *Studies of the Greek Poets.* 2 vols. London, 1893; new ed., 1920.
Trendall, A.D. & T.B.L. Webster. *Illustrations of Greek Drama.* London, 1971.
Vitruvius. *Ten Books of Architecture.* Cambridge, Mass., 1914.
Webster, T.B.L. *Greek Theatre Production.* London, 1956.

TOPICS FOR INVESTIGATION
1.   The Function of the Chorus in Greek Tragedy.
2.   The Function of the Chorus in Greek Comedy—"Old

Comedy"—"New Comedy" and Satyr Drama.
3. The Development of the Scene Building (the *skene*) from Aeschylus to Menander.
4. Costuming Conventions and Their Effect on the Classic Drama.
5. The Development of Acting Styles in the Classic Theatre.
6. The Use of Music in the Classic Theatre.
7. The Organization of Classic Greek and Roman Festivals.
8. The Use of Theatre Machinery in the Classic Age.
9. Theories of the Origins of Greek Drama.
10. The Influence of Greek Comedy on Roman Comedy (Plautus and Terence).
11. Senecan Treatment of Classic Themes.
12. Roman Stage Conventions.

Medieval Theatre

SELECTIVE BIBLIOGRAPHY

Adams, J.Q. *Chief Pre-Shakespearean Dramas*. Boston, 1924.
Axton, Richard. *European Drama of the Early Middle Ages*. London, 1974.
Bates, Katharine Lee. *The English Religious Drama*. London & N.Y., 1893.
Bolton, Brenda. *The Medieval Reformation*. London, 1983.
Brody, Alan. *The English Mummers and Their Play*. London, 1970.
Chambers, Sir E.K. *The Medieval Stage*. 2 vols. Oxford, 1903.
Clarke, Stanley W. *The Miracle Play in London, an Account of the Early Religious Drama*. London, 1897.
Coffman, George R. "The Miracle Play: Notes and Queries," *Renaissance Studies in Honor of Hardin Craig, Philological Quarterly*, XX (1941), 205-11.
_____. "A New Approach to Medieval Latin Drama," *Modern Philology*, XXII (1925) , 3.
Cohen, G. *Histoire de la mise en scène dans le théâtre religieux français du moyen âge*. Paris, 1951.
Craig, Hardin. *English Religious Drama of the Middle Ages*. Oxford, 1955.
Cunliffe, J.W. *Early English Classical Tragedies*. Oxford, 1912.
Evans, M. Blackmore. *The Passion Play of Lucerne*. N.Y. & London, 1943.
Frank, G. *The Medieval French Drama*. Oxford, 1954.
Harbage, Alfred. *Annals of English Drama, 975-1700*. London & Phila., 1940.
Hardison, O.B. *Christian Rite and Christian Drama in the Middle Ages: Essays in the Origin and Early History of Modern Drama*. Baltimore, 1965.

Kahl, Stanley J. *Traditions of Medieval Drama.* London, 1974.

Kernodle, George R. and Portia. "Dramatic Aspects of the Medieval Tournament," *Speech Monographs,* IX (1942), 161-72.

Leach, A.F. "Some English Plays and Players, 1220-1548," in *An English Miscellany Presented to Dr. F.J. Furnivall,* 1901.

Loomis, Roger S. "Some Evidence for Secular Theatres in the Twelfth and Thirteenth Centuries," *Theatre Annual,* 1945 , 33-46.

Manly, J.M. *Specimens of the Pre-Shakespearean Drama.* Boston, 1897.

Marshall, Mary. "The Dramatic Tradition Established by the Liturgical Plays," *Publications of the Modern Language Association,* LVI, 962-91.

Nagler, A.M. *The Medieval Religious Stage, Shapes and Phantoms.* N.Y. & London, 1976.

Norris, Edwin. *The Ancient Cornish Drama.* 2 vols. N.Y., 1859.

Penn, D. *The Staging of the "Miracles de Notre Dame."* Oxford, 1927.

Pollard, Alfred. *English Miracle Plays, Moralities, and Interludes.* Oxford, 1927.

Potter, R. *The English Morality Play.* London, 1975.

Reed, A.W. *Early Tudor Drama — Medwall, the Rastells, Weywood and the More Circle.* London, 1926.

Rossiter, A.P. *English Drama from Early Times to the Elizabethans.* London, 1950.

Salter, F.M. *Medieval Drama in Chester.* Toronto, 1955.

Southern, Richard. *The Mediaeval Theatre in the Round.* London, 1957.

Sticca, Sandro, ed. *The Medieval Drama.* N.Y., 1972.

Wallace, C.W. *The Evolution of the English Drama up to Shakespeare.* London, 1912.

Wickham, Glynne. *Early English Stages, 1300 to 1600.* Vol. I. London & N.Y., 1959.

_____. *The Medieval Theatre.* London & N.Y., 1974.

Young, Karl. *The Drama of the Mediaeval Church.* 2 vols. Oxford, 1933.

TOPICS FOR INVESTIGATION

1. The Development of Liturgical Drama from the *Quem Quaeritis* and Other Tropes.
2. Medieval Staging Conventions: The *Platea* and the *Loca.*
3. The Development of the Continental Mystery Cycles.
4. The Use of the Pageant Wagon in England and Spain.
5. The Association of Craft Guilds with the Production of Mystery Cycles.
6. Medieval Costuming and Its Relationship to Religious Drama.
7. The Fainctes: Medieval Stage Technology.

8.   Hrotsvitha's Imitations of Terence.
9.   Itinerant Mimes and Minstrels in the Middle Ages.
10.   The Evolution of the Morality Play.

Renaissance Italy

SELECTIVE BIBLIOGRAPHY

1. Commedia dell' Arte

Burckhardt, Jacob. *The Civilization of the Renaissance in Italy.* Oxford, 1981.

Croce, Benedetto. "*Commedia dell' Arte,*" tr. Phyllis deKay Bury, *Theatre Arts,* XVI (December 1933), 929.

Duchartre, Pierre Louis. *The Italian Comedy, the Improvisation, Scenarios, Lives, Attributes, Portraits and Masks of the Illustrious Characters of the* Commedia dell' Arte, tr. Randolph T. Weaver. London & N.Y., 1929, reprinted 1966.

Firth, Felicity. "Comedy in Italy," in *Comic Drama: The European Heritage,* ed. W.D. Howarth. London, 1978.

Kennard, J. *The Italian Theatre.* 2 vols. N.Y., 1932.

Lea, K.M. *Italian Popular Comedy, a Study in the* Commedia dell' Arte, *1500-1620.* 2 vols. Oxford, 1934.

McDowell, John H. "*Commedia dell' Arte* Acting," *Dramatic Magazine,* XIX (November 1941), 3-4.

_____. "Some Pictorial Aspects of Early *Commedia dell' Arte* Acting," *Studies in Philology,* XXXIX (January 1942), 47-64.

Mastropaqua, F. and Molinari, C. *Ruzante e Arlecchino.* Parma, 1970.

Nicoll, Allardyce. *The World of Harlequin.* Cambridge, 1963.

Niklaus, Thelma. *Harlequin Phoenix, or the Rise and Fall of a Bergamask Rogue.* London, 1956.

Oreglia, Giacomo. *The Commedia dell' Arte.* London, 1971.

Pandolfi, V. *La commedia dell' arte.* 5 vols. Florence, 1957-60.

_____. *Il teatro del rinoscimento e la commedia dell' arte.* Rome, 1969.

The Roguish Tricks of Coviello, a Scenario, tr. Cesare Levi, *The Mask,* VI (1913-14), 353-36.

Sand, Maurice. *The History of the Harlequinade.* 2 vols. London, 1915.

Schwartz, Isadore A. *The* Commedia dell' Arte *and Its Influence on French Comedy in the Seventeenth Century.* Paris, 1933.

Smith, Winifred. *The* Commedia dell' Arte, *a Study in Italian Popular Comedy.* N.Y., 1912.

_____. *Italian Actors of the Renaissance.* N.Y., 1930.

2. Stage Spectacle and Theatre Architecture

Barbaro, Daniele. *La practica della perspettiva.* Venice, 1569.

Bjurstrom, P. *Giacomo Torelli and Baroque Scene Design.* Stockholm, 1962.

Campbell, Lily Bess. *Scenes and Machines on the English Stage during the Renaissance.* Cambridge, 1923.

Chiaramonti, Scipione. *Della scene e teatri.* 1675.

Ferrari, Guglio. *La Scenographia.* Milan, 1902.

Hewitt, Barnard, ed. *The Renaissance Stage: Documents of Serlio, Sabbattini, and Furttenbach.* tr. Allardyce Nicoll. Coral Gables, Fla. 1958.

Kernodle, George R. *From Art to Theatre. Form and Convention in the Renaissance.* Chicago, 1943.

Mariani, Valerio. *Storia della scenographia italiana.* Florence, 1930.

Nagler, A.M. *Theatre Festivals of the Medici, 1539-1637.* New Haven, 1964.

Nicoll, Allardyce. *The Development of the Theatre. A Study of Theatrical Art from the Beginnings to the Present Day.* London, 3rd ed., 1948.

_____. *Masks, Mimes and Miracles, Studies in the Popular Theatre.* London & N.Y., 1931.

Oenslager, Donald. *Scenery Then and Now.* N.Y., 1936.

Pozzo, Andrea. *Rules and Examples of Perspective Proper for Painters and Architects.* London, 1707.

Simonson, Lee. *The Stage Is Set.* N.Y., 1932.

Theatrical Designs. *From the Baroque through Neoclassicism.* 3 vols. N.Y., 1940.

TOPICS FOR INVESTIGATION

1. *Commedia dell' Arte*

1. Theories Concerning the Sources of the *commedia dell' arte.*
2. The Characteristics of a Typical *commedia soggetto.*
3. A History of the Principal Masks of the *commedia dell' arte:* Their Nationality, Their Costume, Their Plot Function.
4. The Use of *concetti* and *lazzi* in a *commedia* Performance.
5. The Influence of the *commedia dell' arte* on French and English Comedy of the Seventeenth and Eighteenth Centuries.
6. Three Zanni: Arlecchino, Brighella and Pulcinello in the *commedia sogetti* and in Subsequent Dramatic Literature.
7. A History of the Gelosi and Fideli Troupes.
8. Types of Improvised Humor from Andreini to Goldoni.

2. *Stage Spectacle and Theatre Architecture*

1. The Rediscovery of Roman Drama during the Fifteenth Century and Consequent Attempts to Reconstruct the

Classical Stage.
2. The Influence of Vitruvius' *De Architectura* on Early
    Renaissance Scene Design.
3. The *Intermezzo:* Allegory and Spectacle.
4. Early Attempts to Apply the Rules of Perspective to Scene
    Design (Pellegrino da Undino, Genga, Peruzzi).
5. Serlio's Static Stage.
6. Renaissance Theatres Based on Classical Prescription: *Teatro
    Olimpico* and *Teatro Farnese.*
7. The Stagecraft of Sabbattini.
8. Periaktoi on the Renaissance Stage from Lanci to Furttenbach.
9. Stage Spectacles at the Medici court: Buontalenti and Parigi.
10. The Chariot-Counterweight System of Giacomo Torelli.

Tudor and Jacobean England

SELECTIVE BIBLIOGRAPHY

Adams, John Q. *The Globe Playhouse.* Cambridge, Mass., 1942.
Bakeless, John. *Christopher Marlowe, the Man in his Time.* London
    & N.Y., 1938.
Bald, R.C. "The Chronology of Middleton's Plays," *Modern
    Language Review,* XXXII (January 1937), 33-44.
Bamborough, J.B. *Ben Jonson.* London, 1970
Bentley, Gerald E. *Jacobean and Caroline Stage.* 7 vols. Oxford,
    1941-68.
Boas, Frederick S. *An Introduction to Tudor Drama.* N.Y., 1933.
_____. *Marlowe and His Circle, a Biographical Survey.*
    London, 1929.
Bowers, Fredson T. *Elizabethan Revenge Tragedy, 1587-1642.*
    Princeton, 1940.
Bradbrook, Muriel C. *Growth and Structure of Elizabethan Comedy.*
    London, 1955.
_____. *The Rise of the Common Player.* London, 1962.
Brooke, C.F. Tucker. *The Tudor Drama.* Boston, 1911.
Campbell, Lily Bess. *Scenes and Machines on the English Stage
    During the Renaissance.* Cambridge, 1923.
Cawley, R.R. *The Voyagers in Elizabethan Drama.* Oxford, 1938.
Chambers, E.K. *The Elizabethan Stage.* 4 vols. Oxford, 1923.
Creizenach, William. *The English Drama in the Age of Shakespeare.*
    tr. Cecile Hugon. London, 1916.
Eich, Louis M. "Ned Alleyn versus Dick Burbage," *Speech
    Monographs,* VI (1939), 110-26.
Ellis-Fermor, Una. *Christopher Marlowe.* London. 1927.
Evans, H.A. *English Masques.* London, 1900.
Feuillerat, A. *Documents Relating to the Office of the Revels in the
    Time of Queen Elizabeth.* Louvain, Leipzig & London, 1908.

Gotch, J. Alfred. *Inigo Jones*. London, 1928.

Graves, T.S. *The Court and the London Theatres during the Reign of Elizabeth*. London, 1913.

Gregg, W.W. *Dramatic Documents from the Elizabethan Playhouses*. 2 vols. Oxford, 1931, reprinted 1969.

_____. *Henslowe's Diary*. 2 vols. London, 1904-08.

_____. *Henslowe Papers*. London, 1907.

Gurr, Andrew. "Who Strutted and Bellowed?" *Shakespeare Survey*, 16 (1963).

Harbage, Alfred. "Elizabethan Acting," *Publications of the Modern Language Association*, LIV (September 1939), 685-708.

Harrison, G.B. *Elizabethan Plays and Players*. London, 1940.

Hodges, C. Walter. *The Globe Restored*. London, 1953.

Hosking, G.L. *The Life and Times of Edward Alleyn*. London, 1951.

Jones, Inigo. *Designs for Masques and Plays at Court*. Oxford, 1924.

Joseph, Bertram L. *Elizabethan Acting*. London, 1951.

Kirschbaum, Leo. "Marlowe's Faustus: A Reconsideration," *Review of English Studies*. XIX (July 1943), 225-41.

Klein, David. *Literary Criticism from the Elizabethan Dramatists, Repertory and Synthesis*. N.Y., 1910.

Knights, L.C. *Drama and Society in the Age of Jonson*. London, 1937.

Langbaine, Gerald. *An Account of the English Dramatick Poets*. Oxford, 1691.

Lawrence, W.J. *The Elizabethan Playhouse and Other Studies*. Philadelphia, 1912.

Levin, Harry. *The Overreacher. A Study of Christopher Marlowe*. Cambridge, Mass., 1952.

McDowell, John H. "The Tudor Court Staging: A Study in Perspective," *Journal of English and Germanic Philology*, XLIV (April 1945), 194-207.

Maxwell, Baldwin. *Studies in Beaumont, Fletcher and Massinger*. Chapel Hill, 1939.

Mitchell, Lee. "The Advent of Scenic Design in England," *Quarterly Journal of Speech*, XXIII (April 1937), 189-97.

Murray, J.T. *English Dramatic Companies, 1558-1642*. 1910.

Nicoll, Allardyce. *Stuart Masques and the Renaissance Stage*. N.Y., 1938.

Nungezer, Edwin. *A Dictionary of Actors and of Other Persons Associated with the Public Representation of Plays in England before 1642*. New Haven & Oxford, 1929.

Orrell, John. *The Theatres of Inigo Jones and John Webb*. Cambridge, 1985.

Palmer, John. *Ben Jonson*. London, & N.Y., 1934.

Parrott, T.M. "Comedy in the Court Masque," *Philological Quarterly*, XX (1941), 428-41.

Putt, S. Gorky. *The Golden Age of English Drama*. Woodbridge, 1981.

Reed, A.W. *Early Tudor Drama*. London, 1926.

Reynolds, George F. "Aims of a Popular Elizabethan Dramatist," *Philological Quarterly*, XX (July 1941), 148-52.

_____. *The Staging of Elizabethan Plays at the Red Bull Theatre, 1605-1625*. N.Y., 1940.

Ribner, Irving. *Patterns in Shakespearian Tragedy*. London, 1960.

_____. *Jacobean Tragedy: The Quest for Moral Order*. N.Y., 1940.

Schelling, Felix E. *Elizabethan Drama, 1558-1642*. 2 vols. N.Y., 1908.

_____. *Elizabethan Playwrights*. N.Y., 1925.

Sensabaugh, George F. *The Tragic Muse of John Ford*. Stanford, 1944.

Sharpe, Robert B. "Jonson's 'Execration' and Chapman's 'Invective': Their Place in Their Authors' Rivalry," in *Studies in Language and Literature*, ed. G.R. Coffman. Chapel Hill, 1945, pp. 177-85.

Simpson, Percy. *Studies in Elizabethan Drama*. Oxford, 1955.

Sullivan, Mary. *The Court Masques of James I*. N.Y., 1913.

Symons, Arthur. *Studies in the Elizabethan Drama*. London & N.Y., 1920.

Welsford, Enid. *The Court Masque*. Cambridge, 1927.

Wickham, Glynne. *Early English Stages, 1500-1650*. 3 vols. London, 1959-72.

Shakespeare

Adams, Joseph Quincy. *A Life of William Shakespeare*. London & N.Y., 1923.

Andrews, John F., ed. *William Shakespeare: His World, His Work, His Influence*. 3 vols. N.Y., 1985.

Babcock, R.W. "Historical Criticism of Shakespeare," *Modern Language Quarterly*, XIII (March 1952), 6-20.

Baker, George Pierce. *The Development of Shakespeare as a Dramatist*. N.Y., 1907.

Baldwin, Thomas. *The Organization and Personnel of the Shakespearean Company*. Princeton, 1927.

_____. *Shakespeare's Five-Act Structure*. Urbana, 1947.

Beckerman, Bernard. *Shakespeare at the Globe, 1599-1609*. N.Y., 1962.

Bentley, G.E. "Shakespeare and the Blackfriars Theatre," *Shakespeare Survey*, I (1948), 38-50.

Bethell, Samuel L. "Shakespeare's Actors," *Review of English Studies*, n.s., I (July 1950), 193-205.

_____. *Shakespeare and the Popular Dramatic Tradition*. London, 1944.

Boas, F.S. *Shakespeare and His Predecessors*. London, 1896.

Boughner, Daniel C. "Traditional Elements in Falstaff," *Journal of English and Germanic Philology*, XLIII (1944), 417-28.

Brandes, Georg. *William Shakespeare*. London, 1904.

Brown, Ivor. *Shakespeare*. 1949.

Chambers, E.K. *William Shakespeare, a Study of Facts and Problems*. 2 vols. Oxford, 1930.

Charlton, H.B. *Shakespearian Comedy*. London & N.Y., 1938.

Chute, Marchette. *Shakespeare of London*. N.Y. & London, 1951.

Clemen, W.H. *The Development of Shakespeare's Imagery*. London, 1951.

Davis, Michael Justin. *The England of William Shakespeare*. N.Y., 1987.

Dowden, Edward. *Shakespeare, His Mind and Art*. N.Y., 1918.

Fergusson, Francis. "Hamlet: The Analogy of Action," *Hudson Review*, II (Summer 1949), 165-210.

Fiedler, Leslie. *The Stranger in Shakespeare*. N.Y., 1972.

Fox, Levi, ed. *The Shakespeare Handbook*. Boston, 1987.

French, Marilyn. *Shakespeare's Division of Experience*. N.Y., 1980

Frye, Roland M. *Shakespeare: The Art of the Dramatist*. London, 1982.

Granville-Barker, H. *Prefaces to Shakespeare*. London, 1933.

Grebanier, Bernard D. *Then Came Each Actor: Shakespearean Actors*. N.Y., 1975.

Gurr, Andrew. *Playgoing in Shakespeare's London*. Cambridge, 1987.

_____. *The Shakespearean Stage 1574-1642*. Cambridge, (1970, 1980).

Halliday, F.E. *Shakespeare and His Critics*. London, 1949.

Hamilton, Charles. *In Search of Shakespeare: A Reconnaissance into the Poet's Life and Handwriting*. San Diego, 1985.

Harbage, Alfred. *Shakespeare's Audience*. N.Y., 1941.

_____. *A Theatre for Shakespeare*. Toronto & London, 1955.

Harrison, G.B. *A Companion to Shakespeare Studies*. Cambridge, 1934.

Hazlitt, William. *Characters of Shakespeare's Plays*. London, 1817.

Hill, Errol. *Shakespeare in Sable: A History of Black Shakespearean Actors*. Amherst, 1984.

Holinshed, R. *Chronicles of England*. London, 1586.

Hooker, Ward. "Shakespeare's Apprenticeship in the Portrayal of Villainy," *Bucknell Review*, II (October 1950), 80-89.

Isaacs, J. *Shakespeare in the Theatre*. Oxford, 1927.

Jones, Emrys. *The Origins of Shakespeare*. Oxford, 1977.

Jorgensen, Paul A. *William Shakespeare: The Tragedies*. Boston, 1985.

Kernan, Alvin E. *The Playwright as Magician*. New Haven, 1979.

Lee, Sidney. *Life of Shakespeare*. N.Y., 1929.

_____. *Shakespeare's England*. Oxford, 1932.

Lenz, Carolyn, Gayle Green & Carol Thomas Neely. *The Woman's Part: Feminist Criticism of Shakespeare*. Urbana, 1980.

Lewis, Roland B. *The Shakespeare Documents*. Stanford, 1940.

Matthews, Brander. *Shakespeare as a Playwright*. N.Y., 1913.

Myrick, Kenneth O. "The Theme of Damnation in Shakespeare Tragedy," *Studies in Philology*, April 1941.

Nagler, A.M. *Shakespeare's Stage*. New Haven, 1958.

Ogburn, Charlton. *The Mysterious William Shakespeare: the Myth and the Reality*. N.Y., 1984.

Ornstein, Henry. *Shakespeare's Comedies: From Roman Farce to Romantic Mystery*. Newark, Del. 1986.

Orrell, John. *The Quest for Shakespeare's Globe*. 1983.

Palmer, John. *Comic Characters of Shakespeare*. London, 1946.

_____. *Political Characters of Shakespeare*. London, 1945.

Saccio, Peter. *Shakespeare's English Kings*. N.Y., 1977.

Spencer, Theodore. "Appearance and Reality in Shakespeare's Last Plays," *Modern Philology*, XXXIX (1942), 265-74.

Sprague, A.C. *Shakespeare and the Audience, a Study in Exposition*. Cambridge, Mass., 1935.

Stoll, E. *Shakespeare and Other Masters*. Cambridge, Mass., 1940.

Taylor, Gary. *Reinventing Shakespeare: A Cultural History*. N.Y., 1989.

Taylor, George. "Shakespeare's Use of the Idea of the Beast in Man," *Studies in Philology*. XLII (1945), 530-43.

Thorndike, Ashley H. *Shakespeare's Theatre*. N.Y., 1916.

Watkins, Ronald. *On Producing Shakespeare*. N.Y., 1950.

Wilson, J. Dover. *The Essential Shakespeare*. Dambridge, 1935.

TOPICS FOR INVESTIGATION

1. The Development of the Secular Interlude from the Morality Tradition: John Rastell and John Heywood.
2. Plautine and Senecan Influences on Tudor Drama.
3. Academic Stage Productions in the Sixteenth Century: The Universities and the Public Schools.
4. Drama in the Tudor Law Societies: Seneca and *Gorboduc*.
5. A History of Stage Production at the Principal Tudor and Jacobean Choir Schools.
6. A history of the Principal Elizabethan and Jacobean Public Theatres: The Theatre, The Curtain, The Rose, The Swan, The Globe, The Fortune, The Red Bull and The Hope.
7. The Structure of the Blackfriars Theatre and Other "Private" Playhouses.
8. The Structure of a Typical Elizabethan Playhouse as Revealed by the Fortune Contract, The Swan Drawing and Other Contemporary Documents.
9. The Character and Composition of the Elizabethan Audience.

Note: To list with any thoroughness suitable subjects for investigation in the dramatic literature of the English Renaissance would require many more pages than the editors have at their disposal. Appropriate and rewarding research topics might cluster around some or all of the plays of the following important dramatists: John Lyly, George Peele, Thomas Kyd, Christopher Marlowe, Ben Jonson, Thomas Heywood, John Webster, Cyril Tourneur, Francis Beaumont, John Fletcher, Philip Massinger, Thomas Middleton, Thomas Dekker and John Ford. The plays of Shakespeare, both singly and collectively, are of course an inexhaustible source of research topics. A perusal of any one of the books listed in the admittedly truncated Shakespearean bibliography compiled by the editors will immediately suggest many worthwhile subjects to the reader.

The Golden Age of Spain

SELECTIVE BIBLIOGRAPHY

Allen, John J. *The Reconstruction of a Spanish Golden Age Playhouse*. Gainesville, 1983.

Buchanan, M.A. "Cervantes as a Dramatist," *Modern Language Notes*, XXXIII (1908).

Chaytor, H.J. *Dramatic Theory in Spain. Extracts from Literature before and during the Golden Age*. Cambridge, 1925.

Crawford, J.P.W. *Spanish Drama before Lope de Vega*. London & Phila., 1922; rev. ed. 1937.

Holland, Henry Richard, Lord. *Some Account of the Life and Writings of Lope de Vega Carpio*. London, 1806.

Kelly, James Fitzmaurice. *Lope de Vega and the Spanish Drama.* London, 1902.

_____. *A New History of Spanish Literature.* Oxford, 1926.

Kennedy, Ruth Lee. "Certain Phases of the Sumptuary Decrees of 1623 and their Relations to Tirso's Theatre," *Hispanic Review,* April 1942, 91-115.

Lewes, George Henry. *The Spanish Drama, Lope de Vega and Calderón.* London, 1846.

McClelland, I.L. *Tirso de Molina: Studies in Dramatic Realism.* Liverpool, 1948.

Parker, Alexander A. *The Allegorical Drama of Calderón, an Introduction to the autos sacramentales.* Oxford, 1943.

_____. "The Approach to the Spanish Drama of the Golden Age," *Diamante VI,* published by Hispanic & Luso-Brazillian Councils, London, 1957.

Rennert, Hugo Albert. *The Life of Lope de Vega.* Phila., 1904.

_____. *The Spanish Stage in the Time of Lope de Vega* (1582-1635). N.Y., 1909, reprinted 1963.

Schevill, Rudolph. *The Dramatic Art of Lope de Vega.* Berkeley, 1918.

Shergold, N.D. *A History of the Spanish Stage from Medieval Times until the End of the Seventeenth Century.* Oxford, 1967.

Shoemaker, William Hutchinson. *The Multiple Stage in Spain during the 15th and 16th Centuries.* Princeton, 1955.

Sloman, A.E. *The Dramatic Craftsmanship of Calderón: His Use of Early Plays.* Oxford, 1969.

Surtz, Ronald E. *The Birth of a Theatre: Dramatic Convention from Juan del Encina to Lope de Vega.* Princeton, 1979.

Williams, Ronald Boal. *The Staging of Plays in the Spanish Peninsula prior to 1555* (Univ. of Iowa Studies, Spanish, No.5), 1934.

TOPICS FOR INVESTIGATION

1. The *auto sacramentales:* Religious Drama on the Sixteenth and Seventeenth Century Spanish Stage.
2. The Staging of Religious Plays at Seville and Madrid during the Early Renaissance.
3. Lope de Rueda (1510-65): His Plays, His Staging Techniques and the Organization of His Acting Company.
4. A History of the Origin and Development of Public Theatres in Madrid, with Particular Attention to the Role Played by *Cofradia de la Sagrada Pasión.*
5. The Structure of a Typical *Corral* or Courtyard theatre during the Spanish Renaissance.
6. The Development of Stage Spectacle in the Spanish theatre form the Age of Lope de Rueda to the Age of Calderón.

7. Artistic dictatorship by *Los Mosqueteros:* The Influence of the Audience on the Style and Content of Seventeenth Century Spanish Drama.
8. The Structure and Organization of Spanish Acting companies of the Sixteenth and Seventeenth Centuries.
9. Dramatic Theory in the Golden Age: The Scope and Influence of Lope's *Arte Nuevo*.

Note: The works of the extremely prolific playwrights of Spain's Golden Age, particularly Lope de Vega, Tirso de Molina and Pedro Calderón de la Barca, can furnish many subjects for literary and dramatic investigation.

CLASSICAL COMEDY
GREEK AND ROMAN: Six Plays
Edited by Robert W. Corrigan

The only book of its kind: for the first time Greek and
Roman masters of comedy meet in this extraordinary
new forum devised and edited by a master scholar of
comedy himself, Robert Corrigan. Corrigan has enlisted
six superb translations to create an unmatched Olympi-
ad of classical comedy.

ARISTOPHANES	**LYSISTRATA** translated by Donald Sutherland **THE BIRDS** translated by Walter Kerr
MENANDER	**THE GROUCH** translated by Sheila D'Atri
PLAUTUS	**THE MENAECHMI** translated by Palmer Bovie **THE HAUNTED HOUSE** translated by Palmer Bovie
TERENCE	**THE SELF-TORMENTOR** translated by Palmer Bovie

paper • ISBN: 0-936839-85-6

CLASSICAL TRAGEDY: GREEK & ROMAN

edited byRobert W. Corrigan

"Essential plays in highly readable translations ... useful in any course whose goal is to acquaint students with the masterpieces of Greece and Rome."
Harold Nichols
Author, *The Status of Theatre Research*
Kansas State University

"Outstanding essays ... with the right plays ... I am recommending them for our own Freshman Studies Program."
E. Peter Sargent
Associate Dean, Webster University

"Each play is preceded by an insightful introduction ... carefully compiled anthologies."
Jed H. Davis
Editor, *Theatre Education: Mandate for Tomorrow*
Dean, College of Fellows of the American Theater

"Compelling ... offers a rich variety of translation-voices. ... The essays are unerringly chosen for their variety of critical approaches, accessibility, and potential to stimulate discussion and further reflection."
Felicia Londré
Author, *Tennessee Williams*
University of Missouri

"Corrigan remains one of our most visionary critics of dramatic literature ... [He] demonstrates his genius ... for finding the right critical commentaries to encourage students to discover the true classic nature of these plays."
Douglas C. Sprigg
Chair of Theatre & Film Dept.
Middlebury College

Paper • ISBN: 1-55783-046-0

MEDIEVAL AND TUDOR DRAMA

Twenty-four Plays
Edited and with introductions by John Gassner

The rich tapestry of medieval belief, morality and manners shines through this comprehensive anthology of the twenty-four major plays that bridge the dramatic worlds of medieval and Tudor England. Here are the plays that paved the way to the Renaissance and Shakespeare. In John Gassner's extensively annotated collection, the plays regain their timeless appeal and display their truly international character and influence.

Medieval and Tudor Drama remains the indispensable chronicle of a dramatic heritage — the classical plays of Hrotsvitha, folk and ritual drama, the passion play, the great morality play *Everyman*, the Interlude, Tudor comedies *Ralph Roister Doister* and *Gammer Gurton's Needle*, and the most famous of Tudor tragedies *Gorboduc*. The texts have been modernized for today's readers and those composed in Latin have been translated into English.

paper • ISBN: 0-936839-84-8

ELIZABETHAN DRAMA
Eight Plays
Edited and with Introductions by
John Gassner and William Green

Boisterous and unrestrained like the age itself, the Elizabethan theatre has long defended its place at the apex of English dramatic history. Shakespeare was but the brightest star in this extraordinary galaxy of playwrights. Led by a group of young playwrights dubbed "the university wits," the Elizabethan popular stage was imbued with a dynamic force never since equalled. The stage boasted a rich and varied repertoire from courtly and romantic comedy to domestic and high tragedy, melodrama, farce, and histories. The Gassner-Green anthology revives the whole range of this universal stage, offering us the unbounded theatrical inventiveness of the age.

Arden of Feversham, **Anonymous**

The Spanish Tragedy, by **Thomas Kyd**

Friar Bacon and Friar Bungay, by **Robert Greene**

Doctor Faustus, by **Christopher Marlowe**

Edward II, by **Christopher Marlowe**

Everyman in His Humour, by **Ben Jonson**

The Shoemaker's Holiday, by **Thomas Dekker**

A Woman Killed with Kindness, by **Thomas Heywood**

paper • ISBN: 1-55783-028-2

SOLILOQUY!
The Shakespeare Monologues
Edited by Michael Earley and Philippa Keil

At last, over 175 of Shakespeare's finest and most performable monologues taken from all 37 plays are here in two easy-to-use volumes (MEN and WOMEN). Selections travel the entire spectrum of the great dramatist's vision, from comedies and romances to tragedies, pathos and histories.

"Soliloquy is an excellent and comprehensive collection of Shakespeare's speeches. Not only are the monologues wide-ranging and varied, but they are superbly annotated. Each volume is prefaced by an informative and reassuring introduction, which explains the signals and signposts by which Shakespeare helps an actor on his journey through the text. It includes a very good explanation of blank verse, with excellent examples of irregularities which are specifically related to character and acting intentions. These two books are a must for any actor in search of a 'classical' audition piece."

ELIZABETH SMITH
Head of Voice & Speech
The Juilliard School

paper-MEN: ISBN 0-936839-78-3 • WOMEN: ISBN 0936839-79-1

APPLAUSE

LIFE IS A DREAM
and Other SPANISH Classics
Edited by Eric Bentley
Translated by Roy Campbell

LIFE IS A DREAM
by Calderon de la Barca

FUENTE OVEJUNA
by Lope de Vega

THE TRICKSTER OF SEVILLE
by Tirso de Molina

THE SIEGE OF NUMANTIA
by Miguel de Cervantes

paper • ISBN: 1-55783-006-1

ACTING IN RESTORATION COMEDY

Based on the BBC Master Class Series
By Simon Callow

The art of acting in Restoration Comedy, the buoyant, often bawdy romps which celebrated the reopening of the English theatres after Cromwell's dour reign, is the subject of Simon Callow's bold new investigation. There is cause again to celebrate as Callow, one of Britain's foremost actors, aims to restore the form to all its original voluptuous vigor. Callow shows the way to attain clarity and hilarity in some of the most delightful roles ever conceived for the theatre.

Simon Callow is the author of *Being an Actor* and *Charles Laughton: A Difficult Actor.* He has won critical acclaim for his performances in numerous productions including *Faust, The Relapse,* and *Titus Andronicus.*

paper • ISBN: 1-55783-119-X

THE THEATRE OF BLACK AMERICANS
Edited by Errol Hill

From the origins of the Negro spiritual and the birth of the Harlem Renaissance to the emergence of a national black theater movement, THE THEATRE OF BLACK AMERICANS offers a penetrating look at the black art form that has exploded into an American cultural institution. Among the essays:

Some African Influences on the Afro-American Theatre
James Hatch

Notes on Ritual in the New Black Theatre
Shelby Steele

The Lafayette Players
Sister M. Francesca Thompson, O.S.F.

The Role of Blacks in the Federal Theatre, 1935-1939
Ronald Ross

paper • ISBN: 0-936839-27-9

PLAYS BY AMERICAN WOMEN: 1900-1930

Edited by
Judith E. Barlow

These important dramatists did more than write significant new plays; they introduced to the American stage a new and vital character— the modern American woman in her quest for a forceful role in a changing American scene. It will be hard to remember that these women playwrights were ever forgotten.

A MAN'S WORLD
Rachel Crothers

TRIFLES
Susan Glaspell

PLUMES
Georgia Douglas Johnson

MACHINAL
Sophie Treadwell

MISS LULU BETT
Zona Gale

paper • ISBN: 1-55783-008-8   cloth • ISBN: 1-55783-007-X

BLACK HEROES

SEVEN PLAYS

Edited, with an Introduction, by Errol Hill

Some of America's most outstanding playwrights of the last two centuries have catapulted the lives of legendary black men and women out of the history books and onto the stage. Errol Hill has collected the most resonant of these powerful examples in *Black Heroes* where we meet Nat Turner, Frederick Douglass, Harriet Tubman, Martin Luther King, Paul Robeson, Marcus Garvey and Jean Jacques Dessaline.

EMPEROR OF HAITI
Langston Hughes

NAT TURNER
Randolph Edmonds

HARRIET TUBMAN
May Miller

IN SPLENDID ERROR
William Branch

I, MARCUS GARVEY
Edgar White

PAUL ROBESON
Phillip Hayes Dean

ROADS OF THE MOUNTAIN TOP
Ron Milner

paper • ISBN: 1-55783-027-4

THE LIFE OF THE DRAMA
by Eric Bentley

" ... Eric Bentley's radical new look at the grammar of theater ... is a work of exceptional virtue, and readers who find more in it to disagree with than I do will still, I think, want to call it central, indispensable. ... The book justifies its title by being precisely about the ways in which life manifests itself in the theater. If you see any crucial interest in such topics as the death of Cordelia, Godot's non-arrival ... This is a book to be read and read again."

— **Frank Kermode**
THE NEW YORK REVIEW OF BOOKS

paper • ISBN: 1-55783-110-6

THE MISANTHROPE
AND OTHER FRENCH CLASSICS
Edited by Eric Bentley

"I would recommend Eric Bentley's collection to all who really care for theatre."

—Harold Clurman

THE MISANTHROPE
by Mollère
English version by Richard Wilbur

PHAEDRA
by Racine
English version by Robert Lowell

THE CID
by Corneille
English version by James Schevill

FIGARO'S MARRIAGE
by Beaumarchais
English version by Jacques Barzun

paper • ISBN: 0-936839-19-8

ONE–ACT COMEDIES OF MOLIÈRE

Translated by Albert Bermel

- *THE JEALOUS HUSBAND* •
- *THE FLYING DOCTOR* •
- *TWO PRECIOUS MAIDENS RIDICULED* •
- *THE IMAGINARY CUCKOLD* •
- *THE REHEARSAL AT VERSAILLES* •
- *THE FORCED MARRIAGE* •
- *THE SEDUCTIVE MISTRESS* •

These are the best of Molière's masterful one-acts, blending broad farce and pointed wit to express his never-ending delight in human foibles.

But Molière is more than just the "master of the laugh," as Albert Bermel writes in the introduction. For behind the comic words and gestures of these matchless rogues, tightfisted masters, possessive lovers and elegant ladies lurk fears and insecurities and their consequences. In Molière, yes, in truth, there are many kinds of laughter.

"Bermel's Molière translations are, with those of Richard Wilbur, by far the most amusing we have." —Eric Bentley

paper • ISBN: 1-55783-109-2

THE ACTOR'S MOLIÈRE

A New Series of Translations for the Stage by

Albert Bermel

THE MISER and GEORGE DANDIN

ISBN: 0-936839-75-9

THE DOCTOR IN SPITE OF HIMSELF and THE BOURGEOIS GENTLEMAN

ISBN: 0-936839-77-5

SCAPIN and DON JUAN

ISBN: 0-936839-80-5

SHAKESPEARE'S PLAYS IN PERFORMANCE
by John Russell Brown

In this volume, John Russell Brown snatches Shakespeare from the clutches of dusty academics and thrusts him centerstage where he belongs—in performance.

Brown's thorough analysis of the theatrical experience of Shakespeare forcibly demonstrates how the text is brought to life: awakened, colored, emphasized, and extended by actors and audiences, designers and directors.

"A knowledge of what precisely can and should happen when a play is performed is, for me, the essential first step towards an understanding of Shakespeare."
—*from the Introduction by John Russell Brown*

paper•ISBN 1-55783-136-X•

SHAKESCENES: SHAKESPEARE FOR TWO

The Shakespeare Scenebook

EDITED AND WITH AN INTRODUCTION
BY JOHN RUSSELL BROWN

Thirty-five scenes are presented in newly edited
texts, with notes which clarify meanings, topical
references, puns, ambiguities, etc. Each scene has
been chosen for its independent life requiring only
the simplest of stage properties and the barest of
spaces. A brief description of characters and situation
prefaces each scene and is followed by a commentary
which discusses its major acting challenges and
opportunities.

paper ∎ ISBN 1-55783-049-5

Michael Caine • John Cleese
Eric Bentley • John Houseman
Michael Chekhov • John Patrick Shanley
Cicely Berry • John Russell Brown
Jerry Sterner • Steve Tesich
Harold Clurman • Sonia Moore
Bruce Joel Rubin • Jonathan Miller
Josef Svoboda • Terry Jones
Stephen Sondheim • Larry Gelbart

These Applause authors have their work available
in discerning bookshops across the country.

If you're having trouble tracking down an Applause title in your area,
we'll ship it to you direct! Write or call toll-free for our free catalog of
cinema and theatre titles.

When ordering an Applause title, i
book, $2.95 for the first book and $1.90
(New York and Tennessו
please include applicabl
Check/Mastercard/ν

Send your orders to: **Applause**
211 West 7
New York, ℕ

Fax: 212-7

Or order toll-free: 1-8(

APPLAUSE
❦ B O O K S ❦